Numerical Methods in Economics

Numerical Methods in Economics

Kenneth L. Judd

The MIT Press
Cambridge, Massachusetts
London, England

This book was set in Times New Roman on the Monotype "Prism Plus" PostScript Imagesetter by Asco Trade Typesetting Ltd., Hong Kong.

Printed and bound in the United States of America.

Library of Congress Cataloging-in-Publication Data

Judd, Kenneth L.
  Numerical methods in economics / Kenneth L. Judd.
     p.   cm.
  Includes bibliographical references (p.   ) and index.
  ISBN 0-262-10071-1 (hc)
  1. Economic—Statistical methods.   I. Title
HB137.J83   1998
330′.01′5195—dc21   98-13591
                                              CIP

10 9 8 7 6 5 4 3

Dedicated to the memory of Joyce Lewis Judd

Contents

Preface

Computers are increasingly important in human activities. In order to harness the full power of this technology, economists will need to learn a broad range of techniques from the numerical mathematics literature. This book presents these techniques and shows how they can be useful in economic analysis.

This book is the result of my studying, teaching, and using numerical methods in economics. I have used drafts of this book in courses at the Stanford Graduate School of Business, and the Departments of Economics at Stanford University, the University of California at Berkeley, and Tel Aviv University. I thank them for letting me use their students as test subjects in this endeavor.

This book is intended to be suitable for second-year doctorate student in economics. It is assumed that the reader is familiar with just the basics of linear algebra, multivariate calculus, probability, econometrics, optimization, competitive general equilibrium theory, Nash equilibrium, optimal control, and dynamic programming. I draw on this material for examples, and I limit them to be relatively simple.

Many graduate student research assistants have assisted me in this book and the research behind it. I first thank Antonio Bernardo, Clark Burdick, Pamela Chang, Kwang-Soo Cheong, Jess Gaspar, Sy-Ming Guu, Felix Kubler, Michael Lee, Bo Li, Karl Schmedders, Andrew Solnick, and Sevin Yeltekin. I must single out Ben Wang for his exceptionally careful reading of the manuscript and numerous suggestions. I have also benefited from discussions with many others. I must mention William Brock, Larry Christiano, John Geweke, Wouter den Haan, Mordecai Kurz, Michael Magill, Steve Matthews, John Rust, Ariel Pakes, Harry Paarsch, Stan Reiter, Tom Sargent, Chris Sims, and Joseph Traub and apologize to the others who are not listed here.

I thank the Hoover Institution for providing me with the resources and time needed for a long-term project such as this. I also thank the National Science Foundation for its generous support. Most of all, I am indebted to the taxpayers of the state of Wisconsin, whose support of higher education made it possible for me to pursue a life of study and research.

Finally, I am grateful for the understanding and patience of Teresa Terry Judd, who married me despite my absorption in writing this book.

I INTRODUCTION

1 Introduction

Computers are changing economic science, offering economists the opportunity to examine economic issues with far greater generality and precision. Some changes are evolutionary, such as more sophisticated empirical analysis and improvements in applied general equilibrium. More important and radical are the new ways economists are using computation to explore economic theories in far greater detail than pure theory alone can, to determine which problems are important and which are not, and to examine new models of agent behavior and social interactions.

If economists are to make full use of the power of computational technology, they must have a firm grasp of the key mathematical techniques used in computational analyses. This book presents many techniques from numerical analysis and applied mathematics that have been or are likely to be useful in computational analyses of economic problems. The purpose of this text is to teach the reader the basic methods so that he can effectively apply the computer to substantive problems in economics. Along the way the reader will hopefully learn some economics as well.

This chapter describes the book's goals, discusses the many roles of computation in economics, and gives an overview of the topics covered in this book. Computation is not new in economics. However, in recent years economists have expanded the range of problems they can analyze computationally and the roles for computation in economic analysis. We first discuss what economists now know how to compute and how they are applying computational methods. We then present some examples of computational successes in other sciences that illustrate how important computation has become. We next argue that the computational power available today is negligible compared to what will soon be available, and that the advantages of computational approaches will grow rapidly. We conclude this chapter with some basic mathematical notation and theorems we will rely on.

1.1 What Economists Can Compute

Many economic models can now be computed in reliable and efficient fashions. Some methods are well known, but the recent upsurge in interest in computational methods has generated a large amount of new work, allowing us to solve models previously considered intractable. We review this literature to indicate the substantial potential of computational methods.

The computational general equilibrium (CGE) literature is the most mature computational literature in economics. This literature took off in the 1960s; see Shoven and Whalley (1992) and Dixon and Parmenter (1996) for surveys. Recent work has studied variational inequalities, a more general class of problems; see the book by

Nagurney (1993) for recent work in this area and economic applications. The recent work of Brown et al. (1994) and Schmedders (1996) now makes it possible to compute general equilibrium with incomplete asset markets.

Some economists have made use of linear-quadratic models of dynamic equilibrium in both competitive and game-theoretic contexts, with and without perfect information. Even today progress is being made in improving the solution methods for the Ricatti equations that arise in linear-quadratic control problems. Hansen and Sargent (1995) and Anderson et al. (1997) presents many of these techniques. The linear-quadratic approach to approximating nonlinear stochastic models, formulated in Magill (1977), has been extensively used in the real business cycle (RBC) literature. Using computational methods, Kydland and Prescott (1982) argued that fairly simple dynamic general equilibrium models can display the type of economic fluctuations we observe in the macroeconomy. Prior to that many argued that macroeconomic data were inconsistent with the standard competitive model, arguing instead for Keynesian alternatives. While the full RBC research program remains controversial and unfinished, it is a major contender in current intellectual battles and is an example of research which relies heavily on computation.

The limitations of the linear-quadratic framework has spurred work on nonlinear dynamic models. Dynamic programming is an integral part of dynamic economic theory. In the economics literature the most common approach to numerical solutions is to discretize a problem and apply methods developed in the 1950s. Recent work has produced far faster methods; see the review in Rust (1996).

Perfect foresight models have been developed to study deterministic dynamic economic equilibrium. These models typically reduce to two-point boundary value problems, mathematical problems for which there are numerous solution methods. The work of Auerbach and Kotlikoff (1985), Fair and Taylor (1983), Bovenburg and Goulder (1991), Boucekkine (1995), Gilli and Pauletto (1998), Juilliard et al. (1998), and Hughes Hallet and Piscatelli (1998) are typical examples of such models.

Many economists have developed computational methods for nonlinear stochastic rational expectations models. Gustafson (1958) began the literature with a study of equilibrium grain storage; Wright and Williams (1982, 1984) and Miranda and Helmburger (1988) developed efficient methods to compute rational expectations equilibrium even in the presence of frequently binding constraints. Tauchen (1986) applied Fredholm integral equation methods to solve asset pricing models. Judd (1992) used projection methods from the numerical analysis literature to develop efficient schemes for solving rational expectations models. Laitner (1984, 1987), Srikant and Basar (1991), Budd et al. (1993), Bensoussan (1988), Fleming (1971), Fleming and Souganides (1986), Judd (1996), and Judd and Guu (1996) have computed high-order Taylor expansions of rational expectations models, including dynamic games. Dixit (1991), Samuelson (1970), and Judd and Guu (1996) derived approximation methods for asset problems. Ausubel (1990), Bernardo and Judd (1995), and Bernardo (1994) have solved models of asymmetric information much more general than the special exponential-Gaussian example.

There has also been success in developing algorithms for computing Nash equilibria of games. Lemke and Howson (1964) computed Nash equilibria of two-person games, and Wilson (1971) extended this to general n-person games. Wilson (1992) also developed an algorithm to compute stable equilibria. Despite the large body of work on this topic, there have been few applications of these methods to specific problems. Dynamic games with linear-quadratic structures are easily solved, but outside of few exceptions (Judd 1985; Reynolds 1987; Fershtman and Kamien 1987), this approach is almost never taken in theoretical industrial organization. In contrast, these methods are used in the international policy competition literature and monetary policy games, as in Canzoneri and Henderson (1991). More recently Maguire and Pakes (1994) applied numerical methods to dynamic games of entry and exit, and Miranda and Rui (1997) applied orthogonal polynomial approximation methods for computing Nash equilibria of general nonlinear dynamic games. Judd and Conklin (1995, 1996) have developed methods for finding all subgame perfect equilibria in infinite-horizon games, including problems with state variables.

There has also been an increasing use of Monte Carlo simulation schemes to study dynamic economic systems with nontraditional models of behavior. Standard dynamic general equilibrium analysis makes strong assumptions concerning agents' ability to analyze information and make forecasts. Some have argued that real people are far less capable than the rational agents that populate these models. Some of this work is called *agent-based computational economics, artificial life,* or *evolutionary models.* This work focuses on modeling the decision rules used by economic agents and investigates the aggregate implications of these rules. The Santa Fe web page on artificial life at http://alife.santafe.edu/ and Leigh Tesfatsion's web page on agent-based economics at http://www.econ.iastate.edu/tesfatsi/abe.htm are excellent resources.

This quick, and very limited, review shows that we now have numerical methods for solving a wide variety of basic problems. In fact it is difficult to think of a problem in economic theory for which there does not now exist a reasonable algorithm to use. However, after reviewing the array of available methods, I am disappointed with the limited role any of them, even the well-known "golden oldies," plays in economic analysis. I suspect one reason is that many economists are unaware of these methods. This book endeavors to make the basic methods of numerical analysis and applied mathematics accessible to the typical economist and help him to exploit them in economic analyses.

1.2   Roles of Computation in Economic Analysis

Advances in computation will affect economic analysis in two ways. Of course, standard applications will be made more efficient. More interesting, however, are the possible novel roles computation may have in economic analysis and where it fits in methodologically. The power of modern computing makes it possible to analyze both the qualitative and quantitative dimensions of models far more complex and realistic than those usually employed in economic theory. In this section we discuss the roles computation can play in economic analysis.

Quantitative versus Qualitative Analysis

An important weakness of standard theoretical analysis is that the results are only qualitative. Consider general equilibrium theory, arguably the best example of an economic theory. Existence of equilibrium is an important question, but existence does not tell us much about equilibrium. Efficiency results are also important, but they usually come at the cost of many unrealistic assumptions such as zero transaction costs and perfect information. When we relax some assumptions, we may end up with equilibrium being generically inefficient, but the stark judgment—efficient or inefficient—is of little practical value. It may be that equilibrium is inefficient, but if the amount of inefficiency is small or if there are no practical corrective policies, then equilibrium is essentially efficient.

Computation can help identify what is important and what is not. Theory can identify qualitative features of an equilibrium but cannot easily indicate the quantitative significance of any feature. Since theory is so general, its results do not always have much quantitative significance. For example, general equilibrium theory assumes arbitrary concave utility functions, permitting any mixture of curvature and substitutability consistent with concavity. Only when we make some specific assumptions motivated by observations and compute their implications can we reach quantitatively substantive conclusions.

However, we often need only a little empirical information in order to find strong results. For example, consider the theoretical monetary analysis in Fischer (1979). He investigated a Sidrauski model of money demand and rational expectations and asked whether it displayed the Tobin effect, that is, whether inflation affected growth by encouraging agents to save through real investment instead of monetary assets. He showed that a Tobin effect existed in that model. However, Balcer and Judd (1985) computed the Tobin effect in his model for a large range of empirically reasonable values for the critical parameters in a generalization of Fischer's model and found that increasing annual inflation from zero to one hundred percent would increase net investment by at most *one-tenth of a percent*. An effect that small would not seem worth studying and would be undetectable in the data. Furthermore, if we did find a significant relation between inflation and growth in real-world data, these quantitative results tell us that the explanation does not lie in the elements of Fischer's model. Balcer and Judd did not use just a few parameter estimates; instead, their computations included any parameter values even remotely consistent with the data. Therefore the Fischer analysis does show that the Tobin effect is consistent with rational expectations but surely not in a quantitatively significant fashion in actual economies.

The theory literature is full of qualitative analyses that never consider the quantitative importance of their results. These analyses are valuable in providing basic insight and illustrating new concepts. However, many of these papers also claim real-world relevance, proclaim success when their model produces the desired *qualitative* correlation only, and totally ignore the question of whether the analysis is *quantitatively* plausible. Rather little of the theoretical literature is subjected to any such quantitative testing.

Theoretical analyses also often make simplifying assumptions that lead to non-robust conclusions. An excellent example of this occurs in the executive compensation literature. Jensen and Murphy (1990) found that the management of a typical corporation earns, at the margin, only three dollars per thousand dollars of firm profits. They argued that this was too small to create the proper incentives for managers and that this low level of performance incentives could not be explained by managerial risk aversion. This view seems reasonable initially, since we know that marginal compensation should be one dollar per dollar of profits if managers were risk neutral and should be zero if managers were infinitely risk averse. Since managers are more likely to be closer to zero risk aversion than infinite risk aversion, one might guess that managerial incentives should exceed three dollars per thousand. Risk neutrality assumptions are common in the incentives literature because they eliminate the complexities that come with nonlinear utility functions and are presumed to be reasonable approximations to finitely risk averse managers. In response, Haubrich (1994) actually computed some optimal contracts with plausible estimates of risk aversion and showed that optimal contracts would give managers small marginal incentives; he showed that for many reasonable cases, the marginal incentive would be in fact *three dollars per thousand*!

Conventional theoretical analysis is very good at telling us what is possible and at exploring the qualitative nature of various economic phenomena. However, only after we add quantitative elements to a theory can we determine the actual importance of an analysis. That step requires computation.

Deductive versus Computational Analyses of A Theory

Conventional theory can answer many important questions, but generally it cannot answer *all* important questions. Computation can pick up where the usual theoretical approaches end. To see how that can be, we must have a broad view of what constitutes theoretical analysis.

A theory is a collection of definitions and assumptions. After specifying a theory, one wants to determine its implications. In economics this is typically done by proving theorems; call this *deductive theory*. Some questions are best answered with theorems. Existence theory and efficiency analysis are important because they teach us how to approach many critical issues. Only deductive methods can prove the existence of equilibrium. More generally, only deductive methods can determine the qualitative structure of a theory. For example, deductive methods tell us if equilibrium depends on parameters in a continuous fashion, or if an agent's equilibrium decision rule is increasing, continuous, and/or concave in the agent's state variable.

Some questions can be addressed in general, but many other questions cannot. We are often unable to prove general results and instead turn to tractable special cases. These special cases are just examples of the general theory and are likely unrepresentative of the general theory. Their appeal often lies more in their tractability and in the theorems that follow than in their reasonableness. It is at this point that computation has much to offer, for it can provide approximate solutions to a much broader range of examples of a general theory than can special cases with tractable solutions.

One problem with computation is that the solutions are approximate, whereas theorems are exactly true. Many approach economic theory in the same way we approach a mathematical theory. However, economics and mathematics have very different logical architectures. Pure mathematics is a cumulative activity where the result of one theorem is used in proving many others. The path from definitions and assumptions to final proof is very long for most of mathematics. When the structure of a theory is so deep, it is imperative that the foundations and intermediate development be completely justified. It is understandable why theorem-proving is and will remain the dominant mode of analysis in mathematics.

This is not the case is economics. All economic theories consist of a shallow layer of economic modeling lying on top of a deep mathematical foundation. The usual proof of an economic theorem relies little on previous economic theorems and draws instead on mathematical theorems.

It is therefore natural to use a computational approach to study an economic theory. By this I mean describing a theory in terms of its definitions and assumptions, focus on a representative set of examples, solve them computationally, and look for patterns in the computational results. A computational approach will have to focus on computationally tractable cases, but those cases will be far more general than cases that are analytically tractable and amenable to theorem-proving. In the past this approach would not have been too useful because one could only solve a few instances of a theory, far too few to rely on. Current technologies allow us to compute a thousand times as many instances as we could twenty years ago, and we will be able to increase that by another factor of a thousand in the near future. While one may not want to rely on apparent patterns in 10 examples, it is harder to ignore a robust pattern across 10,000 examples, and difficult to ignore 10,000,000 confirming cases of a hypothesis.

While most agree that theoretical models are generally too simple, they may feel that computational analysis is not a good alternative. Many argue that the results of a computational study are unintuitive and incomprehensible because the computer program that generates the result is essentially an impenetrable black box.

The black box criticism should give us pause, but it is not damning. First, this is often more a comment on the poor fashion most computational work is exposited. When a computation gives an answer, we do want to know which economic forces and considerations determined the answer. One way to address this demand is to conduct several alternative computations. Many numerical papers offer little in the way of sensitivity analysis.

Second, we need to recall Einstein's recommendation—a model should be "as simple as possible, but not simpler." Economists study complex questions, a fact that is true if we are macroeconomists or tax economists studying national economies and their policies, microeconomists studying firms, or labor economists studying decision-making in a family. This consideration is often ignored in applied economic theory where unicausal analyses dominate. For example, the industrial organization literature is filled[1] with models that explore one interesting feature of economic interaction in isolation. A typical model may study moral hazard *or* adverse selection, *or* entry *or* investment *or* learning *or* R&D, *or* asymmetric information about cost *or* demand, *or* sharing information about cost, *or* sharing information about demand, and so on. To see how limiting this is, suppose that meteorologists took this approach to studying the weather; they would ignore complex models and their "black box" computer implementations and instead study evaporation, *or* convection, *or* solar heating, *or*

---

1. See, for example, Judd (1985).

the effects of the earth's rotation. Both the weather and the economy are phenomena greater than the sum of their parts, and any analysis that does not recognize that is inviting failure. Simple, focused theoretical studies give us much insight, but they can only serve as a step in any substantive analysis, not the final statement.

Necessity of Approximation

When we face up to the complexities of economic analysis, we see that the issue is not *whether* we use approximations but *where* in our analysis we make those approximations, what kind of approximation errors we tolerate, and how we interpret the inevitable approximation errors. Simple, unicausal models make approximation errors by ignoring all but one feature of the real world. They are at best instructive parables. While we may be able to prove theorems about those one-dimensional models, the results have only approximate, if any, validity concerning the real world. Computational methods can be much more realistic, but they bring with them approximation errors of a numerical kind. We are generally presented with a trade-off: Achieve logical purity while sacrificing realism and inviting specification error, or bring many elements of reality to the analysis and accept numerical error. The proper choice will depend on the context. As computational costs fall and algorithms improve, computational methods will more often be that choice.

Partners in Analysis

Our purpose in these last sections was to argue that neither the purely deductive nor the purely computational approach to analyzing a theory is adequate. Both have much to offer, and both have weaknesses. We next discuss some of the synergistic ways in which computational methods and conventional economic theory can interact.

The goal of deductive theory in economics is to describe the nature of economic interaction. A complete characterization of even simple theories is often impossible using deductive methods. However, deductive analyses can often provide a partial characterization, which can then be used by computational methods to produce efficient numerical approaches which yield economically substantive results.

A particularly good example of this kind of partnership is in the literature on dynamic contracts. Spear and Srivastava (1987) studied a general model of dynamic principal-agent contracting under repeated moral hazard. Initially the problem appears to be infinite-dimensional, intractable from both a theoretical and computational view. Spear and Srivastava came up with an insight that reduced the problem to a one-dimensional dynamic programming problem. This reduction did not make pure theory much easier, but it drastically simplified the computational problem.

Later Phelan and Townsend (1991) computed examples that illustrated many properties of those contracts.

Deductive theory can be very useful in reducing extremely complex problems to equivalent problems with a much simpler structure. When we combine these results with other qualitative properties established by deductive theory, such as differentiability and monotonicity, we can develop efficient computational approaches. These technical complementarities will become increasingly important as economists examine ever more complex economic models.

Theory without Theorems

In some cases there may be no comprehensible theorem. A problem may have a very complicated pattern of results that defies summarization in a tidy theorem. What are we to do then? The following is a good example of what is probably not an unusual situation and how a computational approach to analyzing an economic theory can succeed where deductive theory will fail.

Quirmbach (1993) asked a basic and important question in the economics of innovation and antitrust policy. Suppose that several firms pursue a research and development project that has a probability of success equal to τ independent across firms. The successful firms then all produce the new product (patenting is presumed unavailable). The issue is how the market structure and conduct of the output market affects the ex ante R&D effort and net expected social welfare. Some argue that excessive ex post competition will reduce profits among the successful innovators, and discourage ex ante R&D effort. This suggests that antitrust policy should be lax when it comes to high-tech industries. Quirmbach asked what form of ex post oligopolistic interaction and regulation would lead to the greatest social welfare.

In the typical paper one would make enough specific assumptions for the demand function, the cost function, and the specification of imperfect competition in order to prove theorems. Few attempts are made to generalize the results for general tastes, technology, or mode of competition. Instead of attempting to prove a theorem ranking the ex post market structures, Quirmbach computed the social welfare for hundreds of examples. Figure 1.1 displays a typical plot of social welfare W against τ found by Quirmbach, which illustrates many critical facts. First, Quirmbach found no "theorems," if by "theorem" we mean a precise, compact, and understandable statement summarizing the results. Each market structure dominates the others at some parameters. It is not even possible to describe the dependence on τ, since Bertrand and Cournot ranks switch due to discontinuities in the Bertrand performance. Any "theorem" that tries to summarize Quirmbach's results would be long, twisted, and incomprehensible.

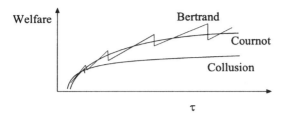

Figure 1.1
Quirmbach's results for social welfare and market structure

Second, despite the absence of simple theorems, Quirmbach's computations produced important and robust findings. Even though he could not rank the market structures absolutely, perfect collusion is usually much worse. When collusion does outperform Bertrand and Cournot, the difference is insignificant. Even though no simple theorem can summarize these facts, Quirmbach's computations contain much economic content and clearly reject the argument that collusion should be tolerated because of innovation considerations.

I suspect that robust analyses of many important questions in economics would resemble the situation in figure 1.1. The normal approach of finding a model simple enough to come up with clean results can easily lead us away from the real truth. Using efficient computational methods to produce solutions to numerous cases can avoid these problems.

An Economic Theory of Computational Economic Theory

Even if there are some theorems, it is unclear if they dominate the kind of computationally intense analysis displayed in Quirmbach. The most controversial use of computers in economic theory would be the use of computations instead of proofs to establish general propositions. One example is not a proof of a proposition; neither do a million examples constitute a proof of any proposition. While the latter is far more convincing than one example, a theorem about a continuum of special tractable cases does not prove anything general. Furthermore, what is the marginal value of a proof once we have a million confirming examples? In some cases that marginal value is small, and may not be worth the effort. In fact in some cases computation alone can provide a proof.

As economists, we believe that the allocation of scarce resources in economic research will follow the laws of economics. The objective of economic science is understanding economic systems. Theories and their models will continue to be used to summarize our understanding of such systems and to form the basis of empirical studies. We have argued that the implications of these theories can be analyzed by deductive theorem-proving, or they can be determined by intensive computations. The inputs of these activities include the time of individuals of various skills and the use of computers, either as word processors or number crunchers. Theorem-proving intensively uses the time of highly trained and skilled individuals, a resource in short supply, whereas computation uses varying amounts of time of individuals of various skill levels plus computer time.

Decision-makers sometimes use economic research. Many of these end-users care little about the particular mode of analysis. If a million instances covering the space of reasonably parameterized models of a smooth theory follow a pattern, most decision-makers will act on that information and not wait for the decisive theorem. In the absence of a proof, most will agree that the computational examples are better than having nothing. Most end-users will agree that the patterns produced by such computations are likely to represent general truths and tendencies, and so form a reasonable guide until a conclusive theorem comes along.

The picture drawn here is one where the alternative technologies of deductive analysis and intensive computation can produce similar services for many consumers. Economic theory tells us what will likely happen in such a circumstance. In the recent past the theorem-proving mode of theoretical analysis was the only efficient method, but now the cost of computation is dropping rapidly relative to the human cost of theorem-proving. I anticipate that by the end of the next decade, it will be typical for an individual to outline a theory to a computer which, after a modest delay, will deliver the results of a computationally intensive analysis.

The clear implication of economic theory is that the computational modes of theoretical analysis will become more common. In some cases computational modes will dominate theorem-proving. In other cases increased computing power will increase the value of theoretical analysis. In either outcome it is increasingly valuable for economists to become familiar with computational methods. This text aims to help economists in that task.[2]

1.3 Computation in Science

Computer solutions of complex problems in physics give us examples of how numerical methods can make substantial contributions to scientific analysis. One of

---

2. This section owes much to and freely borrows from a George Stigler talk on the mathematization of economics. While less dramatic, the computerization of economics may be similar in terms of how it affects the style, emphasis, and allocation of effort in economic research.

my favorite examples is the work on Jupiter's Red Spot. Astronomers generally believed that there must be some peculiar feature of Jupiter causing this long-lived hurricane in the Jovian atmosphere. A computer simulation showed that the Red Spot is really not unexpected once we analyze a sufficiently sophisticated model of Jupiter's atmosphere. Assuming only the basic gravitational properties of Jupiter and the thermal and fluid properties of its atmosphere, computer simulations showed that such disturbances occur naturally and are stable on Jupiter even though they are not stable on Earth. Therefore the Red Spot could be explained from basic principles, a conclusion possible only through intensive computation.

Closer to home is the question of why Earth has a magnetic field, a problem that Einstein called one of the five most important questions in science. Numerical work predicted that the magnetic field is caused by Earth's molten iron core rotating faster than the rest of the planet by about one day per 400. This prediction was recently borne out by seismic evidence.

Astronomical and meterological examples of computational modeling are appropriate for economists. Since astronomy, meterology, and economics are all primarily observational sciences,[3] they all have to take what they observe and infer the causes without the benefit of controlled experiments. Computer modeling operates as a substitute for experimentation in screening possible explanations for plausibility and consistency.

These examples are academic problems where computation was successful. However, computation is important for real problems and limits on computational capabilities can have real consequences. Consider, for example, the development of nuclear weaponry. Both Allied and German scientists worked hard to design fission devices at the beginning of the Second World War. A key scientific problem was estimating critical mass, the amount of U-235 necessary for a self-sustaining reaction. All agreed that the question could be analyzed using the theory of quantum mechanics. The challenge they faced was computing solutions to the key equations. They were severely limited by their computational "equipment"—primarily fingers, pencil, paper, and adding machines. This forced them to make extensive approximations in their analysis to reduce the mathematics to something simple enough for their computational capabilities. Historians have often wondered why the German bomb effort failed, only recently discovering that Heisenberg and his colleagues failed in their critical mass calculations. They had used a poor approximation strategy,

---

3. The parallel is not exact. The nonexperimental nature of most economics research is a political fact, not a necessary feature of economic science. If economic research were given a budget equal to that given to the search for the Higgs boson, top quark, and other exotic particles, economics could also be an experimental science.

estimated that any bomb would require tons of U-235, and concluded that it was not feasible for any combatant to build and deliver one. Allied scientists used better methods and estimated that 25 pounds would suffice. With this estimate in hand, the Manhattan Project was authorized. It turned out that 25 pounds was more than adequate. Computational technology continues to play a major role in nuclear matters. The testing of nuclear weapons may soon be banned by international treaty. A necessary ingredient for any such agreement is that all nuclear powers be confident that their computer simulations can reliably predict the performance of nuclear devices, making testing unnecessary.

Note that these examples are all cases where scientists and engineers have an accepted theory—fluid dynamics, electrodynamics, quantum mechanics—for their problem, and they want to know what that theory implies. They do not aim for closed-from solutions of the underlying equations, nor do they focus on proving theorems. Instead, they used numerical methods to explore the implications of their theory. These examples illustrate not only the usefulness of computational strategies but also the importance of using state-of-the-art computational methods that allow one to examine the theory in a robust and realistic manner.

1.4 Future of Computing

Economists are discussing computation today more than in the past mostly because of the substantial advances in computational tools. Advances on the hardware and algorithm fronts indicate that we will be able to solve an increasingly large collection of economic problems. To appreciate the potential of computational methods, we need to be familiar with the basic reasons for these advances and their likely trends.

First, the raw speed of computer components is increasing exponentially. Progress in semiconductor technology has been roughly following *Moore's law*: a doubling of component density (and speed) every eighteen months for silicon chips. This feature of standard semiconductor technology will hit limits in the future, but not for another decade. Furthermore there is no reason to think that we are close to fundamental physical limits for computation (see Bennett and Landauer 1985). Even when we have reached the limit with silicon, there are many other technologies that may allow us to continue this pace. Beyond that, quantum computing promises to solve in minutes problems that would take current computers millions of years to do.

Figure 1.2 displays the recent progress in computer technology. We measure raw computational speed in terms of floating point operations per second (flops). There is substantial variation in computational power across computers, but the basic trends are clear. The first computers of the 1940s could perform a few thousand flops. The

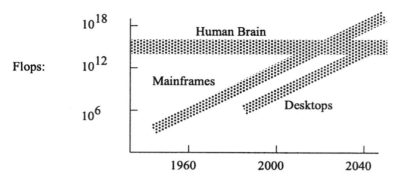

Figure 1.2
Trends in computing speeds

leading supercomputer today has *teraflop* power (one trillion flops). Over this period the computational power of the leading machines (denoted as "mainframes" in figure 1.2) has increased (roughly) by a factor of 1,000 every twenty years. Smaller and cheaper machines (denoted "desktops" in figure 1.2) were introduced in the 1970s and lag the leading computers by about twenty years. For example, today's desktops are more powerful than the first supercomputers of the 1970s.

By comparison, the human brain with its "wet" hardware is a far more powerful computer, with estimated performance at up to a quadrillion (10^{15}) flops—a *petaflop* machine. It is not surprising that it can perform many tasks, such as hand-eye coordination, which computers based on "dry" technologies cannot currently do well. Unfortunately, there is no discernible positive trend in the capabilities of the human brain.

Figure 1.2 shows that at current trends the raw power of many computers will reach that of the human brain in a few decades. Extrapolation of trends is risky, but most experts agree that current trends will continue for at least twenty years. Furthermore the most important index is the real cost of computing power. Economies of scale in production combined with the economies of scale promised by parallel processing will improve this index even in the absence of hardware progress. Barring many unexpected technical problems, affordable petaflop computers will be here in the next few decades.

Second, there also is progress in algorithm development. In fact advances in numerical analysis have improved algorithm speed as much as hardware advances for many important problems. Rice (1983) discusses this for algorithms solving two- and three-dimensional elliptic partial differential equations, a class of numerical problems that arise naturally in continuous-time stochastic economic modeling. He argues that we were able to solve these problems 4 million to 50 billion times faster in 1978 than

in 1945, of which a factor of 2,000 to 25 million can be attributed to software improvements, as much if not more than can be attributed to hardware improvements.

Even if we have petaflop machines, it may be difficult to write programs that
harness that power. On this front, genetic algorithms and genetic programming pro-
pose methods for describing a problem to the computer and then letting a computer
find programs for solving it.

There are clear synergies in this process. When faster computers become available,
algorithmic research focuses on developing methods that become useful only when
applied to large problems. New hardware architecture, such as parallel processing,
stimulates algorithmic research that can exploit it. Furthermore, as one uses better
algorithms on faster machines, it becomes easier to design even faster machines and
even better algorithms. Even if the genetic programming approach is costly, writing a
program is a fixed cost that is easier to justify the more that program is used.

Progress in speed combined with algorithmic advances will allow us to accurately
solve increasingly complex problems. This means that we will analyze larger data sets
with more powerful estimation techniques and solve larger CGE models. It also will
allow economists to change how they approach economic analysis in the directions
discussed in section 1.2.

1.5   Objectives and Nature of This Book

I now make clearer what this book is and what it is not. The book is primarily an
attempt to introduce economists to numerical methods and other computational
procedures that are of proven or potential value in solving economic problems. The
choice of topics and the depth of their development reflects this focus.

This book is *not* a formal, theorem-proving presentation of numerical analysis. The
objective is to familiarize the reader with the basic algorithms, show which algorithms are suitable for which problems, and provide intuition and experience to guide
the readers in their applications of numerical methods to economic problems. References are provided for the readers who want to become more familiar with the formal
development of the subject. This text is mostly a user's manual for those who want to
use methods from numerical analysis and applied mathematics.

Another reason why this book presents few theorems is that numerical analysis is
as much an art as a precise science. The so-called theorems in numerical analysis have
limited direct applicability, and their assumptions are often impossible to verify. For
example, there are many theorems that state that an algorithm converges *if one
begins with a good initial guess*, leaving one with the problem of finding good initial
guesses. We will also often want to use algorithms for which we have no good theory.

The "truths" of numerical analysis are not black and white but come in many shades of gray. One can appreciate this only after direct experience with a wide variety of problems and algorithms.

This book differs substantially from standard numerical analysis texts in its choice of material and in the detail with which it is developed. For example, standard numerical analysis texts give far greater detail on numerical linear algebra algorithms than does chapter 3. My objective is to have the reader become familiar with the basic problems and concepts of numerical linear algebra, but since there are many good numerical packages available, there is no need for the reader to write the code to solve linear algebra problems. In fact the reader is encouraged to use standard packages to solve numerical problems.

In contrast, integration theory in chapters 7, 8, and 9 is developed well beyond what is typical in introductory numerical analysis texts. Many economics problems involve multidimensional integration, leading us to include advanced methods for multidimensional integration. Since there do not exist efficient general multidimensional integration algorithms, the economic analyst will generally need to choose the method appropriate for the particular problem and write an integration code using the most appropriate techniques. Given the importance of integration in many economic models, economists will often develop their own, specialized integration methods (this is already the case in Bayesian econometrics); such work requires more than a shallow grasp of numerical integration. Chapter 9 on quasi–Monte Carlo methods may appear particularly advanced, obscure, and excessively mathematical; however, its topic is one of the few numerical methods ever discussed in the *Wall Street Journal.*

In between the chapters on linear equations and integration are discussed the basics of optimization, nonlinear equations, and approximation theory. Much of the optimization material will be familiar, but the book covers optimization more completely than is usual in an econometrics course. Chapter 5 discusses the range of methods available to solve nonlinear equations, laying the foundation not only for solving Arrow-Debreu general equilibrium models but also for solving a variety of dynamic, stochastic models. Chapter 6 on approximation theory discusses techniques for approximating functions ranging from regression-style methods familiar to economists to multidimensional neural networks.

While these methods are all very powerful, few problems in economics can be solved solely through an application of nonlinear equations, optimization, or approximation theory. This is obvious once we think about the typical economics problem—individual agents maximize utility (an optimization problem), supply equals demand (a nonlinear equation problem), individuals follow a decision rule (an approximation problem), and agents form expectations (an integration problem).

Combining these methods to solve interesting economic problems appears at first to be daunting, but the numerical functional analysis approach called projection methods (a.k.a. method of weighted residuals, finite element, Galerkin, etc.) provides us with a framework in which we can solve a vast range of economic problems; projection methods are introduced in chapter 11, and applied frequently thereafter.

This book is *not* a comprehensive description of computational practice in economics. Many "innovations" in computational economics are straightforward applications of standard numerical methods, inferior reinventions of earlier work, or ad hoc procedures with little mathematical foundation. This book instead endeavors to show how *formal, standard,* and *proven* concepts and methods from numerical analysis are or *can be* used in economics. If a technique has been used in the economics literature, it may be used as an example. If the economics literature uses a different ad hoc procedure, we may compare it with the standard method from numerical analysis, particularly if this is necessary to avoid confusion.

Some economists have made substantial contributions to the development of efficient numerical procedures. I suspect that in the future economists will make contributions in areas of special interest to economists, just as econometricians have made contributions to statistical practice. However, we must first learn the basics of numerical and computational mathematics. Much of what is presented in this book has never been used before in economics. This is not a backward-looking textbook describing the numerical methods that have been used in economics, nor an intellectual history of computation in economics, but instead the book attempts to focus on methods that will be of value.

This book is idiosyncratic, reflecting very much the author's experience, interests, training, and point of view. I do not attempt to present every contribution to computational economics. Instead, my priority is to give a unified treatment of important topics, and base it on standard mathematical practice.

This book is not intended to be a statement of what is and is not "computational economics." There are many computational topics that are not included here because of lack of space. Accordingly the title of this book is not *Computational Economics*.

The book minimizes overlap with the highly developed areas of computational economics. Little space is given to CGE, except as an example of nonlinear equation solving. This was done for two reasons. First, I do not want to spend too much effort on a specific application of computation, and second, excellent books are available that extensively cover this topic. A course that emphasizes CGE could easily supplement this book with a text on CGE methods. This book instead introduces a wide variety of applications although not all the possible interesting applications. The problems at the end of each chapter and in the book's web site introduce other applications.

[handwritten: neural networks]
[handwritten: simulation methods   genetic algorithms]

The other factor determining the book's coverage is the aim that it serve as a text for a second-year graduate course in numerical methods in economics. This book contains enough material for a year-long course. I know of no graduate program that offers such a course. An important objective of this text is thus to show what such a course might look like.

For all these reasons the coverage of recent work is very limited. For example, I do not discuss the artificial life, agent-based computational economics, and similar learning and evolution literature. However, I do describe some of the basic tools used in those literatures such as neural networks and genetic algorithms. Furthermore the Monte Carlo and quasi–Monte Carlo chapters are relevant to anyone who uses simulation methods.

This book presents the basic tools of numerical analysis and related computational methods; how they are put together to analyze economic issues is up to the user. It can serve only as an introduction; hence this book also aims to be a guide to the numerical literature for those who want to learn about methods particularly useful for economic analysis. Advanced topics and further developments are quickly discussed at the end of each chapter to help the reader continue his study.

1.6 Basic Mathematics, Notation, and Terminology

There is a large amount of notation and terminology in this book. At this point, along with a list of some basic notation, I want to discuss the approach I take to terminology, and then review some basic mathematical results that arise frequently.

Scientific Notation

This book will use a modification of scientific notation to represent many numbers. In general, $a(m)$ represents $a \times 10^m$. This is done to eliminate needless zeros. For example, 0.0000012 becomes $1.2(-6)$.

Vectors and Matrices

Unless indicated otherwise, a vector $x \in R^n$ will be a column vector,

$$\begin{pmatrix} x_1 \\ x_2 \\ \vdots \\ x_n \end{pmatrix}.$$

The *transpose* of x is the row vector $(x_1, x_2, \ldots, x_n)$ and is denoted by $x^\top$. The symbol x_i will denote component i of the vector x. Superscripts will generally denote distinct vectors; for example, x^l is the lth vector is a sequence of vectors, $x^1, x^2, \ldots$. The special vector $e^j \in R^n$ will denote the vector where all components are zero except for component j which is unity; that is, e^j is the unit vector in dimension j. There will also be other special vectors and matrices: 0_n and $0_{n \times n}$ denote the vector and matrix of zeros, $1_n \in R^n$ is the vector of ones, and I_n is the $n \times n$ identity matrix.

If $f: R^n \to R$ is a scalar-valued function of R^n, its *gradient* is the row vector function $\nabla f: R^n \to R^n$ defined by

$$\nabla f(x) = \left(\frac{\partial f}{\partial x_1}(x), \frac{\partial f}{\partial x_2}(x), \ldots, \frac{\partial f}{\partial x_n}(x) \right)$$

and is denoted f_x. the *Hessian* of f is the matrix-valued function $f_{xx}: R^n \to R^{n \times n}$ defined by

$$f_{xx}(x) = \begin{pmatrix} \frac{\partial^2 f}{\partial x_1 \partial x_1}(x) & \frac{\partial^2 f}{\partial x_2 \partial x_1}(x) & \cdots & \frac{\partial^2 f}{\partial x_n \partial x_1}(x) \\ \frac{\partial^2 f}{\partial x_1 \partial x_2}(x) & \frac{\partial^2 f}{\partial x_2 \partial x_2}(x) & \cdots & \frac{\partial^2 f}{\partial x_n \partial x_2}(x) \\ \vdots & \vdots & \cdots & \vdots \\ \frac{\partial^2 f}{\partial x_1 \partial x_n}(x) & \frac{\partial^2 f}{\partial x_2 \partial x_n}(x) & \cdots & \frac{\partial^2 f}{\partial x_n \partial x_n}(x) \end{pmatrix}.$$

The system of m functions in n variables $f : R^n \to R^m$ is a column vector of scaler functions,

$$\begin{pmatrix} f^1 \\ f^2 \\ \vdots \\ f^m \end{pmatrix},$$

and its Jacobian is the matrix-valued function $f_x: R^n \to R^{m \times n}$,

$$f_x(x) = \begin{pmatrix} \frac{\partial f^1}{\partial x^1}(x) & \frac{\partial f^1}{\partial x^2}(x) & \cdots & \frac{\partial f^1}{\partial x^n}(x) \\ \frac{\partial f^2}{\partial x^1}(x) & \frac{\partial f^2}{\partial x^2}(x) & \cdots & \frac{\partial f^2}{\partial x^n}(x) \\ \frac{\partial f^m}{\partial x^1}(x) & \frac{\partial f^m}{\partial x^2}(x) & \cdots & \frac{\partial f^m}{\partial x^n}(x) \end{pmatrix}.$$

Table 1.1
Mathematical notation

R	Real numbers
R^n	n-dimensional Euclidean space
$|x|$	Absolute value of x for $x \in R$
$\lceil x \rceil$	Smallest integer greater than or equal to $x \in R$, or the ceiling of x
$\lfloor x \rfloor$	Largest integer smaller than or equal to $x \in R$, or the floor of x
$\|x\|$	Euclidean norm of $x \in R^n$
∂D	Boundary of the set $D \subset R^n$
$X \times Y$	Tensor product of the sets X and Y: $\{(x,y)|x \in X, y \in Y\}$
X^k	k-wise tensor product of the set X
$C^k(X)$	Space of k-times differentiable functions f, $f : X \subset R^n \to R$; we often drop X when it is clear from context
$L^p(X)$	Space of functions $f : X \to R$ such that $\int_X |f|^p \, d\mu < \infty$
$L^2(X)$	Space of square integrable functions $f : X \to R$
$L^\infty(X)$	Space of essentially bounded integrable functions $f : X \to R$
$\|f\|_p$	L^p norm of $f \in L^p(X)$
$N(\mu, \Sigma)$	Normal distribution with mean μ and variance-covariance matrix Σ
$U[a,b]$	Uniform distribution on $[a,b]$

Algorithms

Most chapters contain descriptions of algorithms. I use an informal style of presentation which is hopefully self-explanatory. One could write programs based on these algorithms. However, these should be treated as expositional devices since far better implementations are available from software archives, including that of this book.

Notation

Table 1.1 lists other standard notation.

Linear Algebra

Let A be a square matrix, $A \in R^{n \times n}$. Many of the important properties of a matrix are summarized by its eigenvalues and eigenvectors.

DEFINITION   Let C denote the complex plane. $\lambda \in C$ is an *eigenvalue* of A if and only if there is some $x \in C^n$, $x \neq 0$, such that $Ax = \lambda x$. Let $\sigma(A)$ denote the set of eigenvalues of A; we refer to it as the *spectrum* of A. If $Ax = \lambda x$ for a nonzero x, then x is an *eigenvector* corresponding to $\lambda \in \sigma(A)$. The *spectral radius* of A is $\rho(A) \equiv \max\{|\lambda| : \lambda \in \sigma(A)\}$.

If x is an eigenvector, then so is any scalar multiple of x; hence eigenvectors are defined only up to a proportionality constant. Also $\lambda \in \sigma(A)$ if and only if $\det(A - \lambda I) = 0$, the *characteristic equation* of A, implying that $\lambda \in \sigma(A)$ if and only if $A - \lambda I$ is singular. It is often useful to decompose a matrix into the product of other matrices. A particularly useful decomposition is the *Jordan decomposition*. Suppose that A is a $n \times n$ nonsingular square matrix and has n distinct eigenvalues. Then $A = NDN^{-1}$ where D is a diagonal matrix with the distinct eigenvalues on the diagonal, and the columns of N are right eigenvectors of A. Equivalently we can express $A = N^{-1}DN$, where the diagonal elements of D are the left eigenvalues of A and the rows of N are left eigenvectors of A.

Order of Convergence Notation

Our convergence concepts are compactly expressed in the "Oh" notation. We say that $f: R^k \to R^l$ is $\mathcal{O}(\|x\|^n)$ if $\lim_{x \to 0} \|f(x)\|/\|x\|^n < \infty$, and that $f: R^k \to R^l$ is $o(\|x\|^n)$ if $\lim_{x \to 0} \|f(x)\|/\|x\|^n = 0$.

Taylor's Theorem

The most frequently used theorem in numerical analysis is **Taylor's theorem**. Given its central role, we first state the R version:

THEOREM 1.6.1 (**Taylor's theorem for** R) If $f \in C^{n+1}[a,b]$ and $x, x_0 \in [a,b]$, then

$$f(x) = f(x_0) + (x - x_0)f'(x_0) + \frac{(x - x_0)^2}{2}f''(x_0)$$

$$+ \cdots + \frac{(x - x_0)^n}{n!}f^{(n)}(x_0) + R_{n+1}(x), \qquad (1.6.1)$$

where

$$R_{n+1}(x) = \frac{1}{n!} \int_{x_0}^x (x - t)^n f^{(n+1)}(t)\, dt$$

$$= \frac{(x - x_0)^{(n+1)}}{(n+1)!} f^{(n+1)}(\xi)$$

for some ξ between x and x_0.

Taylor's theorem essentially says that one can use derivative information at a single point to construct a polynomial approximation of a function at a point. We next state the R^n version:

THEOREM 1.6.2 (Taylor's theorem for R^n) Suppose that $f: R^n \to R$ and is C^{k+1}. Then for $x^0 \in R^n$,

$$f(x) = f(x^0) + \sum_{i=1}^{n} \frac{\partial f}{\partial x_i}(x^0)(x_i - x_i^0)$$

$$+ \frac{1}{2} \sum_{i=1}^{n} \sum_{j=1}^{n} \frac{\partial^2 f}{\partial x_i \partial x_j}(x^0)(x_i - x_i^0)(x_j - x_j^0)$$

$$\vdots$$

$$+ \frac{1}{k!} \sum_{i_1=1}^{n} \cdots \sum_{i_k=1}^{n} \frac{\partial^k f}{\partial x_{i_1} \cdots \partial x_{i_k}}(x^0)(x_{i_1} - x_{i_1}^0) \cdots (x_{i_k} - x_{i_k}^0)$$

$$+ \mathcal{O}(\|x - x_0\|^{k+1}). \tag{1.6.2}$$

Functions and Functional Operators

A function involving Euclidean spaces is denoted $f: R^n \to R^m$. We will often want to express the distinction between an argument of a function and a parameter. The notation $f(\cdot\,; a): R^n \to R^m$ denotes a function with domain R^n corresponding to a specific value for the parameter vector $a \in R^l$. If both $x \in R^n$ and $a \in R^l$ are viewed as variables, then we can also view $f(x; a)$ as $f: R^n \times R^l \to R^m$.

We will work with functions on function spaces. For example, suppose that X and Y are both spaces of functions from $Z \subset R^n$ to $W \subset R^m$. Then $\mathscr{F}: X \to Y$ will denote a function that maps functions in X to functions in Y. Sometimes we will write $g = \mathscr{F}(f)$ to state that g is the image of f under $\mathscr{F}$. Sometimes we will write the expression $g(z) = \mathscr{F}(f)(z)$ which says that when we evaluate the function $\mathscr{F}(f) \in Y$ at $z \in Z$ the image is $g(z)$. Of course $g = \mathscr{F}(f)$ if and only if $g(z) = \mathscr{F}(f)(z)$ for all $z \in Z$. Note that the slightly different expression $\mathscr{F}(f(z))$ is not defined because $f(z) \in W \subset R^m$, whereas the domain of $\mathscr{F}$ is X, a space of functions.

One of the more famous functionals is the *Laplace transform*. In general, if $f(t): R \to R$, then the Laplace transform of $f(t)$ is $L\{f\}: R \to R$, where $L\{f\}(s) \equiv \int_0^\infty e^{-st} f(t)\, dt$. The key property used in linear differential equations is that $L\{f'\}(s) = sL\{f\}(s) - f(0)$, transforming the derivative of f to algebraic operations on the Laplace transform of f.

Terminology

This book follows standard terminology from the numerical analysis literature. The larger problem facing anyone writing in this area is that there are many places in the economic literature where idiosyncratic terms have been created and used. It is important that economists adopt terminology consistent with the numerical analysis literature; otherwise, an economist who wants to use the existing numerical literature will find it difficult to locate and understand desired material. Therefore the book often ignores terminology used in the economic literature and uses appropriate terms from the numerical analysis literature; where there is possible confusion, it provides the map between the terms that economists have used and the mathematical terms.

However, the book does use precise terminology to the extent reasonable. Some economists have used vague, overly broad terms to describe numerical procedures, making it difficult to distinguish varieties that are substantially different from a numerical perspective. Proper and precise terminology is essential to communicating the method used in a numerical study. The mathematical literature takes great pains to distinguish even slightly different methods. For example, Newton's method for optimization is different from the quasi-Newton *family*, which includes the Davidon-Fletcher-Powell and Broyden-Fletcher-Goldfarb-Shanno algorithms. In this book I similarly use and, where necessary, invent terminology describing various techniques used in economics. The terminological choices made here are governed by the desire for precision and consistency with the mathematical literature.

1.7 Software and Supplemental Material

This book focuses on the main ideas behind numerical methods. For that reason I do not spend time on discussing particular programs, for that would involve coding details and force me to choose some language. Given the variety of techniques discussed, the book would have to teach and use several languages.

Nevertheless, numerical mathematics without software is not useful. To address these needs, I have created an archive of supplemental material for this book. To find it, the reader should consult the author's web page at http://www-hoover.stanford. edu/bios/judd.html. This web site includes code in various languages that helps solve the problems at the end of each chapter and the examples in each chapter. This archive also includes a variety of additional material, including supplemental text, bibliography, examples, problems, and solutions. This collection of supplementary material will grow over time to respond to readers' questions and requests, and thus will provide material that was left out of the text. The reader should also consult the web site for up-to-date information on typos.

To gain any real expertise in numerical analysis, the reader must know some basic computing language and do the exercises. The reader will need to find a computer to replicate the examples and do the exercises in this book, and should get acquainted with software that can implement basic linear algebra operations, solve systems of nonlinear equations, and solve constrained optimization problems. None of the exercises require large programs, so Fortran, Gauss, Matlab, C, or almost any other language can be used in completing them. Because of the availability of NAG, IMSL, LAPACK, MINPACK, NPSOL, MINOS, and other software, Fortran is still the dominant language for serious numerical analysis. It is possible that C will catch up in the future, but Fortran90 is more flexible than Fortran77 and has adopted many features of C, possibly slowing down the drift to C. Packages such as Gauss and Matlab are very flexible, excellent for solving linear problems, and most likely adequate for anything done in this book. However, they are slower than Fortran or C in executing nonlinear problems.

There is a substantial amount of high-quality commercial software. IMSL and NAG are the two most complete collections of software and available at any serious computing facility. The advantages of such libraries is that they have been extensively tested and improved over time. The disadvantage is their cost.

There are also many programs freely available and not included in IMSL or NAG. Of particular usefulness is the NETLIB facility run by Argonne Labs; consult its web page at http://www.netlib.org/. One very useful collection of advanced programs in netlib is called "toms," a collection of algorithms on a wide variety of problems published originally in the ACM Transactions on Mathematical Software.

I use public domain software wherever possible to solve examples, since this will facilitate the dissemination of programs. The disadvantage is that such software is not as reliable, nor as sophisticated as the commercial packages. Any serious programming should use the most recent versions of IMSL or NAG or a similar collection.

All of the public domain programs I use are available at the book's web site. Readers are free to take any or all programs. These programs are not copyrighted. As always, you use them at your risk. The programs are free; I accept no responsibility for their use nor offer any guarantee of their quality.

There is much free material available on the web. Bill Goffe's web site "Resources for Economists on the Internet" at http://econwpa.wustl.edu/EconFAQ/ is an excellent source.

1.8 Further Reading

Several methodological issues are discussed at greater length in the author's "Computational Economics and Economic Theory: Complements or Substitutes?" In particular, that paper lays out more completely the way in which computational methods can be used to analyze economic theories. See also Kendrick's "The Wishes" essay on computational economics. Kendrick (1993) is a NSF report on a research agenda for computational economics.

Exercises

These exercises do not presume too much familiarity with economic theory and applications, though they make frequent use of some basic economics problems, savings-consumption and portfolio problems in particular, that are familiar to most readers. A growing list of more interesting exercises are available at the book's web site.

These first exercises are warmup problems; readers having any difficulty should stop and learn a computing language.

1. Write a subroutine (procedure, etc.), called ADDXY, that takes as input two scalars, x and y, and produces $x + y$ as output. Similarly write a routine MXY that takes x and y and produces $x\,y$, and a routine DXY that takes x and y and produces x/y. Write a program that reads two scalars, x and y, applies each of MXY, DXY, and ADDXY to x and y, and prints the answers in a readable fashion. For example, the printout should consist of statements like "THE SUM OF —— AND —— IS —— ", "THE PRODUCT OF —— ...," and so on.

2. Write a routine FEVAL that takes as input a function of two variables F and two scalars x and y and produces as output the value of $F(x, y)$. Write a program that reads two scalars x and y, applies FEVAL to each of MXY, DXY, and ADDXY together with the scalars x and y, and prints the answers in a readable fashion. For example, the printout should consist of statements like "THE SUM OF —— AND —— IS —— ", "THE PRODUCT OF ——," and so on.

3. Write a routine that declares a one-dimensional array A of length 10, reads in the values of the components of A from an imput file, computes the sum of the components of A, and outputs the sum.

4. Write a routine that declares a two-dimensional array A with 5 rows and 3 columns, reads in the values of the components of A from an input file, computes the sum of the components of each row of A, and outputs these sums.

5. Write a routine that declares a two-dimensional array A with 5 rows and 3 columns, a row vector b of length 5, a column vector c of length 3, reads in the values of the components of A, b, and c from an input file, computes Ac and bA, and outputs the resulting vectors.

6. Write a program to determine the relative speeds of addition, multiplication, division, exponentiation, and the sine function and the arc tangent function on your computer. Do so in various languages and computers, and compare the results across languages and computers.

2 Elementary Concepts in Computation

The study of mathematical algorithms to solve problems arising in real analysis and functional analysis is called *numerical analysis*. Other methods from applied mathematics used to approximate solutions to such problems include *perturbation methods* and *asymptotic analysis*. This chapter gives the basic facts on computers and the elementary ideas used in numerical methods and approximation procedures. Impatient readers may feel that the material in this chapter is too elementary for them. That would be a mistake. While this material is basic, a firm grasp of it and the associated terminology is essential to understanding the later chapters.

Because it is concerned with actual computation on actual computers, numerical analysis begins with some simple ideas. However, there are important differences between pure mathematics and numerical methods. In pure mathematics we deal with pure, abstract objects, many of which have only impure realizations on a computer. In particular, any computer can represent only a finite number of integers and is capable of only finite precision arithmetic. In contrast, in numerical problems we must keep in mind not only the abstract mathematical problems which we are trying to solve but the impure fashion which these problems are represented and solved on the computer.

Further, and more fundamentally, time is a critical constraint on calculation. To paraphrase a renowned pigskin philosopher, speed is not everything, it is the only thing. In pure mathematics, we frequently use processes of infinite length, whereas in real-life computations we have no such luxury. Space limits also constrain us, but in practice it is the time constraint that binds. If it were not for the constraints of time and space, there would be no errors in computation, and numerical and pure mathematics would be identical. Our finite endowment of time makes pure mathematical objects unattainable and forces us to accept the impure, error-prone approximations of real-life computing.

We will consider later in this chapter some ways to economize on the time constraint, and also the errors, their sources in the imperfect computer representations, their propagation, strategies to minimize their impact on the final results, and ways to give economic meaning to the inevitable errors.

2.1 Computer Arithmetic

To understand the limitations of computational methods, let us begin by looking at the way numbers are represented in a computer. Integers are stored in binary form, but only a finite number of integers can be represented. Rational numbers are stored in the form $\pm m2^{\pm n}$ where m, the *mantissa*, and n, the *exponent*, are integers; of course m and n are limited by the fact that the combination of m and n must fit into the space that the computer allocates for a real number. Individual calculations can be more precise as the permissible range for m is increased, and we can represent a greater range of magnitudes on the computer as the permissible range for n is increased. Even though we pretend to store real numbers, the only numbers explicitly stored in a computer are rational numbers of this form.

The range of numbers that are machine-representable varies greatly across machines; one should always have a good idea of their value when working on a computer. *Machine epsilon* is the smallest *relative* quantity that is machine representable. Formally this is the smallest ε such that the machine knows that $1 + \varepsilon > 1 > 1 - \varepsilon$. It is also important to know *machine infinity*, that is, the largest number such that both it and its negative are representable. *Overflow* occurs when an operation takes machine representable numbers but wants to produce a number which exceeds machine infinity in magnitude. A *machine zero* is any quantity that is equivalent to zero on the machine. *Underflow* occurs when an operation takes nonzero quantities but tries to produce a nonzero magnitude less than machine zero. The analyst must either know these important constants for his machine or make conservative guesses. Much of the software in the public domain contains a section where the user must specify these arithmetic constants.

The other important distinction is between *single precision* and *double precision*. Single precision usually has 6 to 8 decimal digits of accuracy while double precision has 12 to 16 digits. This distinction arose in the early days when machine words were small and the hardware could execute only single precision arithmetic. Today's arithmetic processing units make this distinction of little use; accordingly, modern standards strongly suggest that all work be done in at least double precision.

There are ways to work with even higher precision, but they are generally costly. Some machines have *quadruple precision*; in fact double precision on CRAY supercomputers is really quadruple precision. These distinctions concern the numbers that can be handled by the arithmetic part of the CPU. One can represent more precise numbers as strings of low-precision numbers and then write software that interprets these strings as high-precision numbers. This approach substantially slows down computation and is not discussed in this text. I know of no case related to the topics in this book where double precision on a personal computer is not adequate *if one is using the appropriate algorithms*.

The second important aspect of computer arithmetic are the operations. Inside the CPU is an arithmetic unit that performs at least the basic arithmetic operations of addition, subtraction, multiplication, and division and possibly also performs exponentiation, logarithmic, and trigonometric operations. In older machines, the more advanced operations were performed by software. Today's machines perform these operations in the arithmetic unit at much greater speed. However, the only operations that are actually executed are the four basic operations; all other operations are approximated using methods discussed in chapter 6. On most computers addition is faster than multiplication which is a bit faster than division. Computing transcendental functions is generally slower; in particular, exponentiation is up to ten times slower than multiplication. The exact relative speeds of the basic mathematical operations vary across machines.

We must always keep in mind the limitations of the computer. In reality, all it can understand are integers, and it can do only simple arithmetic. Everything else is approximated.

2.2   Computer Processing and Algorithms

During a numerical computation, the computer is constantly taking numbers from input, swapping them between storage, internal registers, and the arithmetic units, and ultimately outputting them. There are several processing modes that computers can use. Since it is becoming increasingly important in serious computing to understand these, let us consider the various processing modes in use today.

The simplest operating mode for a computer is the *serial processing mode*. Strictly speaking, a serial processor is one that performs one operation at a time, executing one instruction only when all earlier instructions are finished. This is the mode we usually assume when we write programs.

Most modern computers are not strictly serial machines. It is common for a computer to have separate processors for fetching from or writing to memory, and for reading from or writing to an I/O device, where these devices perform their jobs at the same time that the arithmetic unit is working. In general, such a structure is called *multiprocessing*. Simple forms of multiprocessing are important even in desktop personal computers. Current processors even "look ahead," making guesses about what the next steps will be and preparing for these future steps while still working on the current step. This preparation can greatly speed execution when the guesses are correct.

A particularly powerful form of multiprocessing is used in *vector processors*. Vector processors, such as those in CRAY supercomputers, have several arithmetic units that can independently and simultaneously perform arithmetic operations. The term vector processing is appropriate because vector processors are particularly good at performing vector and matrix operations. To see this, consider computing the inner product of the vectors (a, b) and (c, d), which equals $ac + bd$. A vector processor is able to compute the products ac and bd nearly simultaneously, with the results being reported to the CPU which then assigns an arithmetic unit to compute their sum. The long inner products that are common in linear operations can make good use of the potential power in vector processors.

However, while vector processing was the leading supercomputer design, it did not performed as well as hoped. First, many problems do not have a structure that is amenable to vector processing. Second, even when a problem is "vectorizable," many programmers do not make the effort to write the code in the special fashion necessary to exploit the vector processor.

The idea of multiple simultaneous processes has been taken to its logical limit in *parallel processing* where more than one CPU is used simultaneously. In *massively parallel processing* we literally have hundreds of fully functional CPUs executing instructions at the same time. Parallel processing is thought to be the way (or at least part of the way) in which we will increase computing power; the human brain is a parallel processor with billions of CPUs. *Distributed computing* connects individual computers to work together to solve problems. Networks of desktop computers communicating via e-mail have been used to solve difficult problems. Since most computers spend most of their time turned off or waiting for people to do something, distributed computing has the potential of creating virtual supercomputers at low cost.

The key task in using parallel processing is organizing the communication among the individual CPUs. The simplest way to organize parallel processing and distributed computing is by a master-slave model. In this model there is one processor, the master, which manages all communication. The master issues commands to its slave processors, where the commands can be single arithmetic operations or complex programs. When a slave processor finishes one command, it tells the master processor the results and waits for the next command. The master processor keeps track of the results of all the slave processors, coordinating their operations and using their results appropriately.

The critical aspect of writing a program for parallel processing is the choice of synchronization. An algorithm is *synchronous* if the master gives out a set of commands to the slaves and waits for all the slaves to report before issuing the next set of commands. An algorithm is *asynchronous* if a slave can be given a new task independent of the progress the other slaves have made with their old tasks. Sometimes it is not known how much time a slave processor needs to perform its assignment. Synchronous algorithms can be held up by one slow processor, thereby being only as fast as the slowest subprocess. Asynchronous algorithms keep all the slave processors working all the time but may not take advantage of all information in the most efficient fashion because of their imperfect coordination. Few algorithms are purely synchronous or asynchronous, but these terms are useful in describing the coordination problems present in an algorithm. The choice of algorithm will often depend on the extent to which the hardware and software can exploit multiprocessing possibilities.

2.3 Economics of Computation

Discussing efficient computational methods is natural for economists. Numerical analysis is the enterprise of devising algorithms that not only solve problems but do so in a fashion that economizes on scarce resources. In computational work the scarce resources are human programming time, computer runtime, and computer storage space. The basic objective of a numerical approach is to compute approximate solutions with minimal error in minimal computer time, using minimal computer storage and minimal programmer time. This multiple objective forces us to consider many trade-offs, just as any consumer must consider trade-offs among the various uses of his endowment. Numerical analysis and related applied mathematics methods provide us with a large variety of methods that comprises the *production possibility set*. When we attack any particular problem, we must be aware of the relative value of these objectives; that is, we must know our *indifference curves* in order to make an efficient choice of technique. One objective of this book is to describe a large variety of techniques so that readers can find combinations that are efficient for their problems and situations.

Say, as is sometimes true, we want to compute just a few examples of a model to illustrate the quantitative importance of some phenomenon. The greatest cost would likely be the programmer time rather than the computer runtime. If we further want an accurate result, we would choose an algorithm that is easy to implement and will reliably give an accurate answer. There would be little effort made to minimize computer time.

Say we want to solve several examples in order to find patterns that suggest theorems. In this case we do not need the highest accuracy, but we do care about runtime, since a faster program will produce more examples. Also we do not want to spend a large amount of programmer time on the computational project if the ultimate objective is to prove theorems.

If we rather want to demonstrate a general proposition by purely numerical means, then we will need a large number of accurately computed examples. Limitations on available computer time will likely bind, so it is desirable to have methods that maximize execution speed, even if it is at the cost of extra programmer time. Accuracy is an important factor in this case because we do not want the results to depend on errors, which may be systematic instead of random.

The basic lesson is that the choice of algorithm depends on the goal of the computation and the costs of inputs. For any set of objectives and costs, it is useful to have a variety of methods available. Essentially there is a production possibility frontier that expresses the trade-offs among programmer time, space, accuracy, and runtime. Such a production set approach is useful in thinking about algorithm evaluation. Since the marginal rate of substitution across those objectives can change depending on available resources and opportunity costs, the availability of a variety of methods allows an analyst to find one that suits each situation.

2.4 Efficient Polynomial Evaluation

The importance of speed in calculation is what separates numerical mathematics from pure mathematics. We present an example of a simple computation where some insight allows us to economize on computational costs relative to the "natural" algorithm.

Consider the computational cost of evaluating the polynomial,

$$\sum_{k=0}^{n} a_k x^k. \tag{2.4.1}$$

We want to know how many additions, multiplications, and exponentiations are needed to evaluate the typical polynomial. The obvious direct method for evaluating a polynomial is to compute the various powers of x, x^2, x^3, and so on, then multiply each a_k by x^k, and finally add the terms. This procedure (we call this direct method 1) results in $n - 1$ exponentiations, n multiplications, and n additions. Such a method is obviously expensive because of the exponentiations. Since the powers are all integers, we could replace the expensive exponentiations with multiplications; to do so, we compute x^2 by computing $x x$, then compute $x^3 = (x^2) x$, and so on, replacing the $n - 1$ exponentiations with $n - 1$ multiplications. This is some improvement, yielding direct method 2 and using $2n - 1$ multiplications and n additions.

We can do even better by being clever. The most efficient way to evaluate polynomials is by *Horner's method*. The idea is illustrated by the following identity for a generic third-degree polynomial:

$$a_0 + a_1 x + a_2 x^2 + a_3 x^3 = a_0 + x(a_1 + x(a_2 + x \cdot a_3)). \tag{2.4.2}$$

This factorization makes the most use out of each multiplication, bringing us down to three multiplications and three additions for the cubic polynomials.

Table 2.1
Polynomial evaluation costs

	Additions	Multiplications	Exponentiations
Direct method 1	n	n	$n - 1$
Direct method 2	n	$2n - 1$	0
Horner's method	n	n	0

Horner's method can be simply implemented for an arbitrary polynomial. First, we need to determine how a polynomial is represented in the computer. To do this, we define a one-dimensional array $A(\cdot)$ that stores the a_k coefficients. More precisely let $A(k + 1) = a_k$ for $k = 0, 1, \ldots, N$; the $+1$ shift is needed because some languages do not permit $A(0)$. Second, we compute the polynomial in accordance with the factorization in (2.4.2). Algorithm 2.1 is a Fortran program (and similar to corresponding BASIC, Gauss, and Matlab programs) which implements Horner's method for computing (2.4.1) at X, and Table 2.1 presents the relative operation counts of three methods for evaluating a degree n polynomial.

Algorithm 2.1   Horner's Method

```
SUM=A(N+1)
DO I=N,1,-1
  SUM=A(I)+SUM*X
ENDDO
```

This example shows us how to solve an important computational problem. It also illustrates the lesson that slight reformulations of a problem, reformulations of no consequence from a theoretical perspective, can result in a dramatic speedup. Even for the simplest problem, ingenuity has a large return.

2.5   Efficient Computation of Derivatives

The computation of derivatives is an important feature of many algorithms. In many problems, particularly in optimization and nonlinear equations, most of the computing time is devoted to obtaining first-order derivatives, such as gradients and Jacobians, and second-order derivatives, such as Hessians. Since derivative computations play an important role in so many problems, we will take up the topic here to teach some important numerical formulas, and investigate the economies of scale which arise in analytical calculations of derivatives.

Finite Differences

The most common ways to compute derivatives are *finite difference* methods. Specifically, if $f : R \to R$, then one way to approximate $f'(x)$ is the *one-sided finite difference* formula

$$f'(x) \doteq \frac{f(x+h) - f(x)}{h}, \tag{2.5.1}$$

where $h = \max\{\varepsilon|x|, |x|\}$ is the step size and ε is chosen appropriately,[1] usually on the order of 10^{-6}. The relation between ε and h is motivated by two contrary factors; first, we want h to be small relative to x, but second, we want h to stay away from zero to keep the division and differencing in (2.5.1) well-behaved. More generally, if $f : R^n \to R$, then the one-sided formula for $\partial f / \partial x_i$ is

$$\frac{\partial f}{\partial x_i} \doteq \frac{f(x_1, \ldots, x_i + h_i, \ldots, x_n) - f(x_1, \ldots, x_i, \ldots, x_n)}{h_i} \tag{2.5.2}$$

with $h_i = \max\{\varepsilon|x_i|, |x_i|\}$. Note that the marginal cost of computing a derivative of $f(x, y, z)$ at (x_0, y_0, z_0) equals one evaluation of f, since it is assumed that one computes $f(x_0, y_0, z_0)$ no matter how the derivative is computed. Hence the marginal cost of a finite difference derivative equals its average cost. The problem of computing the Jacobian of a multivariate function $f : R^n \to R^m$ reduces to the first-order derivative formula (2.5.2), since each element in the Jacobian of f is the first derivative of one of the component functions of f. Elements of the Hessian of $f : R^n \to R$ are of two types. Cross partials are approximated by

$$\frac{\partial^2 f}{\partial x_i \partial x_j} \doteq \frac{1}{h_j} \left(\frac{f(\ldots, x_i + h_i, \ldots, x_j + h_j, \ldots) - f(\ldots, x_i, \ldots, x_j + h_j, \ldots)}{h_i} \right.$$
$$\left. - \frac{f(\ldots, x_i + h_i, \ldots, x_j, \ldots) - f(\ldots, x_i, \ldots, x_j, \ldots)}{h_i} \right), \tag{2.5.3}$$

and the second partials are approximated by

$$\frac{\partial^2 f}{\partial x_i^2} \doteq \frac{f(\ldots, x_i + h_i, \ldots) - 2f(\ldots, x_i, \ldots) + f(\ldots, x_i - h_i, \ldots)}{h_i^2}. \tag{2.5.4}$$

1. The proper choice of ε is discussed in chapter 7.

Analytic Derivatives

Finite difference methods require multiple evaluations of f and thus can produce excessively large errors. For most functions that arise in economics, we can use algebra and calculus to compute derivatives faster and with more accuracy.

We illustrate this with a function familiar to economists. Suppose that we want to compute both the value of $f(x, y, z) = (x^\alpha + y^\alpha + z^\alpha)^\gamma$ and its gradient $\nabla f \equiv (f_x, f_y, f_z)$. One way is to just analytically derive the derivatives and evaluate them separately. This is typically called *symbolic differentiation*. In this case we would evaluate the three functions $\gamma \alpha x^{\alpha-1}(x^\alpha + y^\alpha + z^\alpha)^{\gamma-1}$, $\gamma \alpha y^{\alpha-1}(x^\alpha + y^\alpha + z^\alpha)^{\gamma-1}$, and $\gamma \alpha z^{\alpha-1}(x^\alpha + y^\alpha + z^\alpha)^{\gamma-1}$, each of which is more costly to compute than the original function. The advantage of symbolic differentiation is the greater accuracy.

If we instead compute the analytic gradient efficiently, the cost will be much lower. The key insight is that by using the chain rule of differentiation, the analytic computation of gradients and Hessians can take advantage of algebraic relations among individual terms. We now compute ∇f using automatic differentiation. First, we compute the original function, $f(x, y, z) = (x^\alpha + y^\alpha + z^\alpha)^\gamma$. Note that this computation produces values for the individual terms x^α, y^α, z^α, $x^\alpha + y^\alpha + z^\alpha$, as well as $(x^\alpha + y^\alpha + z^\alpha)^\gamma$. As we compute $f(x, y, z)$, we store these values for later use. With these values in hand, the computation of $f_x = (x^\alpha + y^\alpha + z^\alpha)^{\gamma-1}\gamma \alpha x^{\alpha-1}$, needs only 2 divisions and 3 multiplications. This is because x^α, $x^\alpha + y^\alpha + z^\alpha$, and $(x^\alpha + y^\alpha + z^\alpha)^\gamma$ are known from the $f(x, y, z)$ computation, and $f_x = (x^\alpha + y^\alpha + z^\alpha)^\gamma / (x^\alpha + y^\alpha + z^\alpha) \cdot \gamma \cdot \alpha \cdot x^\alpha / x$ just involves 3 extra multiplications and 2 extra divisions. Note also how we have used division to compute the necessary exponentiations. In general, if one knows f, f', and f^a, then $(f^a)' = a * f^a * f'/f$. This has the extra advantage of using division to compute an exponentiation, a replacement producing considerable time savings on many computers.

When we move to the other derivatives, we are able to realize even more economies of scale. Since $(x^\alpha + y^\alpha + z^\alpha)^{\gamma-1}\gamma \alpha$ is a common factor among the partial derivatives, we only need one more multiplication and one more division to compute f_y, and similarly for f_z. Hence ∇f can be computed at a marginal cost of 4 divisions and 5 multiplications. In contrast, the finite difference method uses 12 exponentiations, 3 divisions, and 9 addition/subtractions. The savings increase as we move to higher dimensions, since the marginal cost of computing a derivative is one multiplication and one division. The study of methods to exploit these relations and create efficient differentiation code is called *automatic differentiation*. Algorithm 2.2 is Fortran code which efficiently computes f and ∇f.

Algorithm 2.2   Program to Compute Gradient of $(x^{\alpha} + y^{\alpha} + z^{\alpha})^{\gamma}$

```
XALP=X**ALPHA;YALP=Y**ALPHA;ZALP=Z**ALPHA
SUM=XALP+YALP+ZALP
F=SUM**GAMMA
COM=GAMMA*ALPHA*F/SUM
FX=COM*XALP/X;FY=COM*YALP/Y;FZ=COM*ZALP/Z
```

This is just one example of how careful attention to the form of a function can improve the efficiency of derivative computation. Another example would be the exploitation of separability in any $f(x, y, z)$ of the form $f_1(x) + f_2(y) + f_3(z)$. The savings are even greater when we consider computing the Hessian, which can make use of the computations already performed for the gradient as well as the many algebraic relations among the second derivatives. It is also clear that the savings relative to finite difference methods increase as we examine larger problems.

Arguing against using symbolic and automatic differentiation are the considerable algebraic costs. Many functions are difficult to differentiate. Finite difference methods avoid any errors that may arise from human differentiation of the objective. Even if one could reliably compute derivatives, much of the savings of automatic differentiation comes from recognizing common terms across derivatives, another process that challenges human algebraic abilities. Fortunately we can now take out much of the human error. Derivative computations can be done by symbolic software; in fact much of that software was created to do just this sort of computation. Some symbolic software, such as Maple and Macsyma, can form Fortran and C code which computes the function, its gradient, and Hessian and, furthermore, recognizes common terms. This makes it easy to exploit the economies of computation which are available through the analytical computation of gradients and Hessians.

The extensive literature on automatic differentiation formalizes these ideas and their application to real problems. While these methods are potentially very useful, we will not develop them in this text. Kalaba et al. (1983) and Tesfatsion (1992) are early examples of these methods. These ideas have been systematized in the automatic differentiation literature, which is reviewed in Griewank and Corliss (1991) and Berz et al. (1996). Currently the software for implementing these ideas is not as simple as desired; fortunately there is much work on this front and we should soon have seamless software integrating symbolic and numerical methods. Until then the readers should be aware that this approach is available, and that they can implement these ideas themselves if necessary.

Despite the advantages of analytic derivatives, we will stick with finite differences for the exercises in this text. Finite differences are also adequate for most problems in

economics, and they are easier to implement. It is also advisable to use finite difference methods in the early stages of a project; one does not want to work hard to
compute all the derivatives with a Cobb-Douglas production function and then
decide to use the constant elasticity of substitution (CES) specification. In general,
analytic methods are better considered only when needed for accuracy reasons, or as
a final stage of speeding up an otherwise complete program.

2.6   Direct versus Iterative Methods

Methods for solving numerical problems are divided into two basic types. *Direct
methods* are algorithms which, in the absence of round-off error, give the exact
answer in a predetermined finite number of steps. For example, the solution of
$ax = b$ can be computed directly as $x = b/a$. The precision of the answer is as great
as the precision with which the machine expresses a and b, and the algorithm consists
of one division. In general, direct methods take a fixed amount of time and produce
answers of fixed precision. Unfortunately, many problems fail to have direct methods
of solution. For example, a fundamental theorem in algebra says that there is
no direct method for computing the roots of a polynomial of degree 5 or greater.
Even when they exist, direct methods may require too much space or time to be
practical.

When direct methods are absent or too time-consuming, we turn to *iterative
methods*. These methods have the form $x^{k+1} = g^{k+1}(x^k, x^{k-1}, \cdots) \in R^n$. Let x^*
denote the desired solution to the underlying problem. The basic questions for an
iterative method are whether the sequence x^k converges to x^*, and if convergent how
fast it converges. Convergence may depend on the initial guess, x^0. No matter how
fast an algorithm converges or how precise the calculations, we will almost never
reach x^*. We must terminate the sequence at some finite point.

Iterative schemes are flexible in that we can control the quality of the result. We
may need only a rough approximation obtained in a few iterations and little time, or
we may want the greater accuracy obtained by using more iterates. Iterative procedures will generally ask the user for the desired accuracy; no such flexibility is available with direct methods.

2.7   Error: The Central Problem of Numerical Mathematics

The unfortunate fact about computer mathematics is that it is usually approximate.
We saw above how the computer representation of numbers necessarily produces

approximation errors. To keep the final error of a computation to a minimum, we need to understand how errors may arise and how they propagate.

Sources of Error

Most errors arise from two basic aspects of numerical operations. First, a computer must round off the results of many arithmetic results; for example, even 1/10 is not represented exactly on a binary computer. Second, algorithms that implement infinite processes must be stopped before the true solution is reached.

The first source, *rounding*, arises from the fact that the only thing computers can do correctly is integer arithmetic. When we want to represent a number other than an integer or an integral multiple of a (possibly negative) power of two, we must round it. Rounding replaces a number with its nearest machine representable number. This source of error is inherent in the machine representation of real numbers. Increasing the number of bits used to represent a number is the only way to reduce rounding errors.

The second source of error is called *mathematical truncation*. Many mathematical objects and procedures are defined as infinite sums or, more generally, the limit of an infinite process, such as an iterative algorithm. To approximate the limit of an infinite process, we must end it at some finite point. For example, the exponential function is defined as

$$e^x = \sum_{n=0}^{\infty} \frac{x^n}{n!}, \tag{2.7.1}$$

but on some computers it is at best $\sum_{n=0}^{N} x^n/n!$ for some finite N. Mathematical truncation errors are inherent in the desire to compute infinite limits in finite time. One object of numerical analysis is to develop algorithms that have small truncation errors when dealing with infinitistic objects.

Not only do rounding and truncation create errors, they can also turn a continuous function into a discontinuous function. For example, rounding turns the identity function, $f(x) = x$, into a step function. In the case of the exponential function approximated by $\sum_{n=0}^{N} x^n/n!$, a further discontinuity arises because the choice of N usually differs for different x, and changes in x that cause N to change will generally cause a discontinuity in the computed value of e^x. Many computations involve both kinds of errors. For example, if we want to compute $e^{1/3}$, we must first replace $\frac{1}{3}$ with a computer representable rational number, and then we must use an algorithm which approximates (2.7.1).

Error Propagation

Once errors arise in a calculation, they can interact to reduce the accuracy of the final result even further. Let us take a simple example of this problem to see how to solve it.

Consider the quadratic equation $x^2 - 26x + 1 = 0$. The quadratic formula tells us that $x^* = 13 - \sqrt{168} = .0385186\cdots$ is a solution. Suppose that we want to compute this number with a five-digit machine. On such a machine, rounding makes us accept 12.961 as $\sqrt{168}$. If we proceed in the way indicated by the quadratic formula, the result is

$$x^* = 13 - \sqrt{168} \doteq 13.000 - 12.961 = 0.039 \equiv \hat{x}_1.$$

The relative error of the approximation $\hat{x}_1$, $|x^* - \hat{x}_1|/x^*$, is more than 1 percent. The problem here is clear; by subtracting two numbers of similar magnitude, the initial significant digits are zeroed out, and we are left with few significant digits.

A better approach is to rewrite the quadratic formula and produce a second approximation, $\hat{x}_2$:

$$13 - \sqrt{168} = \frac{1}{13 + \sqrt{168}} \doteq \frac{1}{25.961} \doteq 0.038519 \equiv \hat{x}_2,$$

which is correct to five significant digits and a relative error of 10^{-5}. Here we have replaced a subtraction between similar quantities with an addition of the same numbers and obtained a much better answer.

The problem in this case arises from the subtraction of two numbers. In general, the following rules help to reduce the propagation of errors when several additions and subtractions are necessary: First, avoid unnecessary subtractions of numbers of similar magnitude, and second, when adding a long list of numbers, first add the small numbers and then add the result to the larger numbers.

This is just one example of how to deal with error propagation. Again we see that considerations and distinctions that are irrelevant for pure mathematics can be important in numerical procedures.

2.8 Making Infinite Sequences Finite

The desired result of any iterative procedure is the limit of an infinite sequence, not any particular member of the sequence. However, we must choose some element of a sequence as an approximation of its limit, since we do not have an infinite amount of time. This problem arises frequently in numerical methods because most algorithms are iterative. It is, in some sense, an insurmountable problem; since the limit of a sequence does not depend on any initial segment of a sequence, there cannot be any valid general rule based on a finite number of elements for finding the limit. To deal with this problem, and minimize the errors that arise from truncating an infinite sequence, we must use the properties of infinite sequences to develop useful heuristics for approximating their limits.

Rates of Convergence

A key property of a convergent sequence is the rate it converges to its limit. Suppose that the sequence $x^k \in R^n$ satisfies $\lim_{k \to \infty} x^k = x^*$. We say that x^k *converges at rate q to x^** if

$$\lim_{k \to \infty} \frac{\|x^{k+1} - x^*\|}{\|x^k - x^*\|^q} < \infty. \tag{2.8.1}$$

If (2.8.1) is true for $q = 2$, we say that x^k *converges quadratically*. If

$$\lim_{k \to \infty} \frac{\|x^{k+1} - x^*\|}{\|x^k - x^*\|} \le \beta < 1, \tag{2.8.2}$$

we say that x^k *converges linearly*; we also say that it converges *linearly at rate β*. If $\beta = 0$, x^k is said to converge *superlinearly*. Clearly, convergence at rate $q > 1$ implies superlinear and linear convergence.

Stopping Rules

Since we can only examine an initial portion of a sequence, we need good rules for truncating an infinite sequence. Ideally we will want to stop the sequence only when we are close to the limit. Unfortunately, there is no foolproof, general method of accomplishing this. That is inherent in the nature of a sequence: the limit depends on only the asymptotic behavior of the sequence, whereas any particular point on a sequence illustrates only the initial behavior of the sequence. For example, consider the scalar sequence

$$x_k = \sum_{j=1}^{k} \frac{1}{j}. \tag{2.8.3}$$

The limit of x_k is infinite, but any particular x_k is finite; in fact the sequence x_k goes to infinity so slowly that even $x_{1000} = 7.485\ldots$, giving little hint that the limit is infinite.

We must rely on heuristic methods, *stopping rules*, to determine when to end a sequence. In general, one part of any stopping rule is to stop when the sequence is not "changing much." Formally this is often expressed as $|x_k - x_{k+1}|/|x_k| \leq \varepsilon$ for some small ε. As long as x_k is large relative to ε, this says that we stop when the change in the sequence $|x_{k+1} - x_k|$ is small relative to $|x_k|$. This kind of rule may never allow us to stop if x_k converges to zero. To account for this, we stop the sequence if it appears that the changes are small or if the limit appears to be close to zero. The rule that combines these considerations is

Stop and accept x_{k+1} if $\dfrac{|x_k - x_{k+1}|}{1 + |x_k|} \leq \varepsilon.$ $\hspace{2cm}$ (2.8.4)

Therefore criterion (2.8.4) says to stop if changes are small relative to $1 + |x_k|$. The kind of stopping rule in (2.8.4) is not very good but is about as good as one can do in general. For example, it would fail in (2.8.3), since for any ε the test (2.8.4) will cause us to end (2.8.3) at some finite point whereas the true limit is infinite. For example, $\varepsilon = 0.001$ would end (2.8.3) at $k = 9330$ where $x_k = 9.71827$.

Fortunately we often have information about the sequence that will help us. In particular, if we know the rate of convergence, we can develop a more reliable stopping rule. If we know that a sequence that converges quadratically, a simple rule such as (2.8.4) will probably be adequate if $\varepsilon << 1$.

If we know that a sequence is linearly convergent at rate $\beta < 1$, we need a more careful rule than (2.8.4). Knowing β allows us to estimate $\|x^* - x^k\|$. In some cases we can strengthen (2.8.2) to the inequality

$$\|x^{k+1} - x^*\| \leq \beta \|x^k - x^*\| \hspace{2cm} (2.8.5)$$

for all k, not just for sufficiently large k. In this case we know that $\|x^k - x^*\| \leq \|x^k - x^{k+1}\|/(1 - \beta)$. Therefore, if we use the rule

Stop and accept x_{k+1} if $\|x^k - x^{k+1}\| \leq \varepsilon(1 - \beta),$ $\hspace{1.5cm}$ (2.8.6)

the error in accepting x^{k+1} is bounded by $\|x^k - x^*\| \leq \varepsilon$.

For problems where we know (2.8.5), the rule (2.8.6) provides us with a completely reliable stopping rule. For other problems we can use this approach by assuming that we have reached a point where the sequence's terms obey the asymptotic behavior of the sequence and construct a useful heuristic. Suppose that we know that x^k converges linearly and want to conclude that x^n is within ε of x^*. We first compute $\|x^{n-l} - x^n\|/\|x^{n-l-1} - x^n\|$ for $l = 1, 2, \ldots$ to estimate the linear rate of convergence; we let the maximum of these ratios be $\hat{\beta}$. If $\hat{\beta}$ is the true convergence rate and

$\|x^n - x^*\| \leq \varepsilon$, then we should also have $\|x^n - x^{n-1}\| \leq (1 - \hat{\beta})\varepsilon$; if this is not true, we should not stop at x^n. More precisely, for small ε and convergence rate β, $\|x^n - x^{n-1}\| \leq \varepsilon(1 - \beta)$ does imply that $\|x^n - x^*\| \leq \varepsilon$; our heuristic turns this into a general stopping rule when we substitute β with an estimate $\hat{\beta}$. Since most useful algorithms are at least linearly convergent, this approach is generally applicable. However, it is important to make some attempt to determine the rate of convergence and estimate the error. To see that the rule in (2.8.6) is better than (2.8.4), apply it to (2.8.3). If we were to apply (2.8.6) to (2.8.3), we would never conclude that the sequence (2.8.3) converges.

Unfortunately, we can never be sure that the part of the sequence we are looking at really displays the limiting behavior of the sequence. For this reason we should never accept an iterate as the solution to a problem solely because of some convergence test. We should always go back to the original problem and ask how well our estimate of a sequence's limit satisfies the original problem.

Changes in the initial point x^0 or other parametric aspects of the problem will create discontinuities in the final result, just as rounding produces discontinuities. The looser the stopping rule, the more pronounced is the discontinuity. This discontinuity is important because we often approximate continuous functions with truncations of infinite sequences and create discontinuities that can affect numerical performance.

The problems listed in the previous paragraphs may lead the reader to conclude that we should never try to judge when a sequence is near its limit. Fortunately, these heuristic rules do quite well for many problems. As long as we use them carefully and remain mindful of their limitations, they are useful guides.

2.9   Methods of Approximation

There are two basic approaches for generating approximate solutions to problems. The following rough discussion makes some imprecise distinctions between them.

The first approach includes standard numerical analysis methods. A numerical method takes a problem (a set of nonlinear equations, a differential equation, etc.) and computes a candidate solution (a vector or a function) that nearly solves the problem. Numerical methods produce solutions of an arbitrarily large number of examples. From this collection of examples can be observed patterns from which we can infer general results. While this set of approximate solutions may be informative, they will not have the compelling logical force of theorems.

Symbolic methods constitute a second approach to approximating solutions of problems. *Perturbation methods* are the best example of these methods, and they rely on Taylor's theorem, implicit function theorems, and related results. Perturbation methods take a problem that has a known solution for some parameter choice and then derive solutions for similar problems with nearby parameter choices. The results often produce excellent approximations of high-order accuracy. Comparative statics and linearizing around a steady state are perturbation procedures familiar to economists, but they are only the simplest such methods. We will apply a wide variety of perturbation, and related *bifurcation* and *asymptotic* methods, to several economic problems. In many cases perturbation methods can be used to prove theorems for an open set of problems near the initial known case. In this way a theory can be obtained for a nontrivial collection of cases of a model. Perturbation methods can also be used to generate solutions that compete with standard numerical procedures.

Since symbolic methods often proceed by algebraic manipulations of equations, they can be implemented on the computer using symbolic algebra manipulation software, such as Macsyma, Reduce, Maple, and Mathematica. Perturbation methods sometimes combine both algebraic manipulation with standard numerical methods. Another class of symbolic methods is explored in Adomian (1986) and several papers referenced there.

The mathematics literature distinguishes between these methods. In fact, generally, perturbation methods are not discussed in numerical analysis texts. We include both approaches in this book because both are useful in economics, and there is growing interest in merging numerical and symbolic methods to create hybrid methods. We will see an example of the possible synergies between numerical and symbolic methods in chapter 15.

2.10 Evaluating the Error in the Final Result

When we have completed a computation using either numerical or symbolic methods, we want to know how good our answer is. There are two ways to approach this problem. We would really like to know the *magnitude* of the error of the final approximation, but this is often not possible. Alternatively, we take the approximation we have computed and quantify the *importance* of the error to determine whether the approximation is acceptable. The second approach is more generally available.

Error Bounds

When possible, we would always like to put a bound on the actual error, that is, the difference between the true answer, say x^*, and our approximation, say $\hat{x}$. This is the focus of most mathematical analysis of errors of numerical methods. In some cases we can compute a bound on the size of the error, $\|x^* - \hat{x}\|$. This approach is called *forward error analysis*. In the special cases where such bounds can be computed, they can be quite useful; this is the case, for example, in dynamic programming.

Unfortunately, it is usually difficult to determine $\|x^* - \hat{x}\|$ with useful precision. The error bounds that we do have tend to be very conservative, producing, at best, information about the order of magnitude of the error. Many of the error bounds that are available need information about the true solution, which is not available, and must thus be approximated.

The forward approach to error analysis has some general value. For almost any general type of problem, there are special cases where we can determine the true solution with high precision either by using another algorithm that produces an error bound or by deriving a closed-form solution. To gain information about an algorithm's ability to solve the general case, we test it out on the special cases where we can then determine the error. However, error bounds are generally not available for most problems.

Error Evaluation: Compute and Verify

Since we generally cannot bound the error of an answer, we must develop another way to check it. The second, and much more applicable, concept of error evaluation is to measure the extent to which the result of some computation violates some condition satisfied by the true solution. Consider, for example, finding the solution to $f(x) = 0$ for some function f. A numerical solution, $\hat{x}$, will generally not satisfy $f(x) = 0$ exactly. The value $f(\hat{x})$ is a measure of the deviation of $f(x)$ from the target value 0. This deviation may, if properly formulated, provide an economically meaningful measure of the importance of the error implied by the accepting $\hat{x}$ as an approximation of x. I will refer to this procedure as *compute and verify*, since we first *compute* an approximation and then *verify* that it is an *acceptable* approximation according to some economically meaningful criteria. In general, these computation and verification steps are two distinct procedures. Also the verification step involves some additional computation, but this extra cost is generally worth the effort.

To illustrate these ideas, consider the problem $f(x) = x^2 - 2 = 0$. A three-digit machine would produce the answer 1.41. The compute and verify method takes the approximation $\hat{x} = 1.41$ and computes (on the three-digit machine) $f(1.41) = -0.01$. While this computation tells us that 1.41 is not the true answer, the value -0.01 for $f(1.41)$ may help us decide if 1.41 is an acceptable approximation for the zero of $f(x)$.

The value $f(\hat{x})$ can be a useful index of acceptability in our economic problems, *but only if it is formulated correctly*. Suppose that we want to compute the equilibrium price of a single market, where $E(p) = D(p) - S(p)$ is an excess demand function defined in terms of the demand and supply functions. Suppose that our numerical algorithm produces an approximation $\hat{p}$ such that $E(\hat{p}) = 10.0$. Is that an acceptable error? That depends on $D(\hat{p})$ and $S(\hat{p})$. If $D(\hat{p}) = 10^5$, then the approximation $\hat{p}$ implies an excess demand which equals only one ten-thousandth of the volume of trade. In this case most would consider this error economically unimportant and conclude that our computed answer was fine given all the other noise in our analysis and data. However, if $D(\hat{p}) = 2$, we would not want to accept any $\hat{p}$ that implies $E(\hat{p}) > 2$.

While this example is trivial, it does illustrate our general approach. In general, we first use a numerical or approximation procedure to *compute* a candidate solution $\hat{x}$ to $f(x) = 0$. We then *verify* that $\hat{x}$ is an acceptable solution by showing that $g(\hat{x})$ is small where g is a function (perhaps f itself) or a list of functions that have the same zeros as f. In our excess demand example we would solve $E(p) = 0$ but then compute $g(\hat{p}) \equiv S(\hat{p})/D(\hat{p}) - 1$ to check $\hat{p}$.

It is fortunate for economists that in many problems the numerical error of a calculation can be evaluated by some verification calculation. One natural approach is to choose g so that $g(\hat{x})$ can be interpreted as measures of optimization errors on the part of agents, or as "leakage" between demand and supply implied by the approximation $\hat{x}$. If our approximation $\hat{x}$ implies that the agents are making "nearly" optimal decisions and that the difference between demand and supply is "trivial" according to some measure, then we have verified that the approximation $\hat{x}$ is an economically reasonable approximation to the economic problem behind the mathematical equation $f(x) = 0$. We argue that $\hat{x}$ is as plausible a prediction of real-world economic behavior as the true zero of $f(x)$ because we know that real economic agents are not perfect optimizers and that market frictions will keep demand and supply from being exactly equal. Once we have agreed as to what "trivial" and "nearly" mean quantitatively, these interpretations help us evaluate the acceptability of the numerical solutions.

This is one way in which economics differs from physics and the other hard sciences. God may or may not throw dice, but the premise of physics is that he does not make mathematical errors, and therefore there is only one right answer to any physical problem. In contrast, economists do not assign such perfection to the "invisible hand," economists' *deus ex machina*, nor to the individuals who participate in a market. These differences affect how economists interpret the errors arising in computations.

In general, the attitude expressed here is that any model is at best an approximation of reality, and a good approximation of the model's solutions may be as useful an answer as the exact solution. The advantage of numerical methods is that we can analyze more realistic models, reducing the approximation errors arising from using an excessively simple model. The cost of using numerical methods is the inevitable numerical error, but the gain from model realism is often well worth the cost.

A related approach to error analysis, called *backward error analysis,* is to ask if there are similar problems for which the approximate solution would be an exact solution. For example, to see if $x = 1.41$ is an acceptable solution to $x^2 - 2 = 0$, we ask if there are similar equations for which $x = 1.41$ is the true solution. One such equation is $x^2 - 1.9881 = 0$. If we thought that the equation $x^2 - 1.9881 = 0$ was as good a model of our economic problem as the equation $x^2 - 2 = 0$, then we would accept $x = 1.41$ as the solution to our problem. In general, if we have an approximate solution, $\hat{x}$, to $f(x) = 0$, and there is another problem $\hat{f}(x) = 0$ for which $\hat{f}(\hat{x}) = 0$ is exactly true, and the differences between f and $\hat{f}$ are economically insignificant, then we accept $\hat{x}$ as an approximate solution.

Both the compute and verify approach and the backward approach to error analysis have some drawbacks; in particular, they both allow for multiple acceptable, "verifiable," solutions. However, that is already a feature of numerical methods. The existence of multiple acceptable equilibria makes it more difficult for us to make precise statements, such as comparative statics, concerning the nature of equilibrium. However, we could usually run some diagnostics to estimate the size of the set of acceptable solutions. One such diagnostic would be random sampling of x near $\hat{x}$ to see how many other nearby points also satisfy the acceptance criterion.

No matter what approach is taken, it is important that error analysis be implemented to the extent feasible. Many authors make no effort to discuss the methods, if any, they use to check the error in their computational results. While that may be acceptable for analyses applying well-known and previously validated methods in familiar problems, it is not acceptable when introducing a novel method or applying old methods to a substantially different problem. Since easy and cheap diagnostics are generally available, there is no good reason for not performing them. In our discussion of numerical methods, we will frequently discuss checks that can be used. Only by making economically relevant checks on our approximate numerical solutions can computational economists and their work attain and maintain credibility.

2.11   Computational Complexity

Numerical analysts spend much effort on evaluating the computational cost of algorithms, making formal the intuitive economic ideas of the previous section. This work has lead to a literature on optimal algorithms.

This literature focuses on the asymptotic relation between accuracy and computational effort. Specifically, we let ε denote the error and N the computational effort (measured in number of arithmetic operations, number of iterations, or some other appropriate measure of effort). The literature focuses on the limit behavior of $N(\varepsilon)$, the function expressing the computational effort necessary to reduce the error to ε or less, or on the limit behavior of its inverse, $\varepsilon(N)$. For example, if an iterative method converges linearly at rate β and N is the number of iterations, then $\varepsilon(N) \sim \beta^N$ and $N(\varepsilon) \sim (\log \varepsilon)(\log \beta)^{-1}$.

While the results from this literature are interesting, we must be aware of their limitations and understand why, in practice, we often ignore the implications of the asymptotically optimal algorithm theory. If a scheme obeys the convergence rule

$$\lim_{\varepsilon \to 0} \frac{N(\varepsilon)}{\varepsilon^{-p}} = a < \infty$$

then the number of operations necessary to bring the error down to ε is $a\varepsilon^{-p}$ asymptotically. When discussing the asymptotic rankings of algorithms, only the coefficient p matters, since any differences in p across algorithms will dominate any differences in a. Therefore the asymptotically optimal algorithm is the one with the smallest p.

However, we will not always choose the algorithm with the smallest p. This asymptotic analysis assumes that we have access to infinite-precision arithmetic, whereas we have to live with far less. Suppose that we have one convergent scheme using $a\varepsilon^{-p}$ operations and another asymptotically requiring $b\varepsilon^{-q}$ operations, where $q > p > 0$. Asymptotically the $a\varepsilon^{-p}$ scheme is more efficient, independent of the values of a and b, but this asymptotic superiority may hold only for very small ε. Two such algorithms use equal effort for $\varepsilon^* = (b/a)^{1/(q-p)}$, which is less than one if $a > b$ and $q > p$. Therefore the asymptotically superior method is inferior if our accuracy target is less than ε^*. For example, if $q = 2$, $p = 1$, $b = 1$, and $a = 1,000$, then the critical ε is 0.001; that is, if we need to and can make the error to be less than 0.001, we choose the asymptotically superior algorithm, but otherwise we should choose the "nonoptimal" algorithm.

The asymptotically superior scheme is not always best when we consider the desired level of accuracy and the limits of computer arithmetic. Since our target level of accuracy will vary from problem to problem, it is useful to maintain a collection of algorithms that allows us to make an efficient choice relative to our target level of accuracy.

2.12 Further Reading and Summary

In this chapter we have laid out the basic themes of numerical methods. First, computers do only approximate mathematics, and almost every mathematical object is imperfectly represented on a computer. Second, the errors that arise from these considerations must be controlled to keep them from growing during a calculation. Third, time is the scarce factor here; differences that are unimportant in pure mathematics often take on great importance in numerical mathematics. And fourth, a computation produces only an approximation to the true solution and must be evaluated to see if it is adequate for our purposes.

The topics discussed here are presented in far greater detail in many numerical analysis texts. Acton (1996) examines the nature of error in numerical analysis. See Chaitin-Chatelin and Frayssé (1996) for an extensive analysis of forward and backward error analysis and for strategies to limit error. Paskov (1995) develops a theory of optimal stopping criteria. Traub and Wozniakowski (1980) and Traub et al. (1988) discuss a formal treatment of algorithmic complexity.

Automatic differentiation is a topic of increasing interest. Rall (1981) is one of the original treatments of the problem, and the Griewank and Corliss (1991) and Berz et al. (1996) books are useful compilations of recent work. There are many links to automatic differentiation papers and software at http://www.mcs.anl.gov/autodiff/AD_Tools/.

Exercises

The expressions in exercises 1–5 are taken from Kulisch and Miranker (1986), and they have terms added, subtracted, and multiplied in a particular order. Experiment with equivalent but different orderings. Also compare single-precision and double-precision results, and do these exercises on various computers and software.

1. Compute $(1682\,xy^4 + 3x^3 + 29\,xy^2 - 2x^5 + 832)/107751$ for $x = 192119201$ and $y = 35675640$.

2. Compute $8118\,x^4 - 11482\,x^3 + x^2 + 5741\,x - 2030$ for $x = 0.707107$. Use both Horner's method and the straightforward approach.

3. Solve the linear equations $64919121\,x - 159018721\,y = 1$ and $41869520.5\,x - 102558961\,y = 0$

4. Let

$$f(x) = \frac{4970\,x - 4923}{4970\,x^2 - 9799\,x + 4830}.$$

   Use a finite difference approach from section 2.5 to compute $f''(1)$ for $h = 10^{-4}$, 10^{-5}, and 10^{-8}.

5. Compute $83521\,y^8 + 578\,x^2y^4 - 2x^4 + 2x^6 - x^8$ for $x = 9478657$ and $y = 2298912$.

6. Write programs to analytically compute the gradients and Hessian of $(\sum_{i=1}^{n} x_i^5)^2$ for $n = 3$, $4, \ldots, 10$. Compare running times and accuracy to finite difference methods with $\varepsilon = 10^{-2}$, 10^{-3}, 10^{-4}, and 10^{-5}.

7. Write programs to determine the relative speeds of addition, multiplication, division, exponentiation, and the sine function on your computer.

8. Write a program that takes coefficients $a_0, \ldots, a_n$, and compute the polynomial $\sum_0^n a_i x^i$ by Horner's method. Repeat the exercise for computing $\sum_{i=0}^n \sum_{j=0}^n a_{ij} x^i y^j$ and $\sum_{i=0}^n \sum_{j=0}^n \sum_{l=0}^n a_{ijl} x^i y^j z^l$ using the multivariate generalization (which you must figure out) of Horner's method. Compare the efficiency of Horner's method relative to direct methods 1 and 2.

9. Use the program in exercise 8 to evaluate the polynomial

$$f(x, y, z) = \sum_{i=0}^{10} \sum_{j=0}^{10} \sum_{l=0}^{10} x^i y^j z^l$$

for $x, y, z \in \{0, \pm 0.1, \pm 0.2, \pm 0.3, \pm 0.4, \pm 0.5\}$, and put the results in a three-dimensional table. Write a program that allows you to compare the cost of evaluating $f(x, y, z)$ for the values on this grid, and the cost of looking up a typical value.

10. Write a program that determines your machine ε.

11. Apply the stopping rules (2.8.4) and (2.8.6) to the following sequences: (a) $x_k = \sum_{n=1}^{k} 3^n/n!$; (b) $x_k = \sum_{n=1}^{k} n^{-2}$; (c) $x_k = \sum_{n=1}^{k} n^{-1.001}$; (d) $x_k = \sum_{n=1}^{k} n^{-0.5}$. Use $\varepsilon = 10^{-2}$, 10^{-3}, and 10^{-4}. For each ε, determine the number of terms computed before the stopping rule makes a choice and compute the error of the answer.

II BASICS FROM NUMERICAL ANALYSIS ON R^n

3 Linear Equations and Iterative Methods

The most basic task in numerical analysis is solving the linear system of equations

$$Ax = b,$$

where $b \in R^n$ and $A \in R^{n \times n}$. This chapter examines techniques for solving linear equations for three reasons. First, they are important problems in themselves. Second, linear equations are almost the only problem we know how to solve directly. Solution methods for linear problems are basic building blocks for much of numerical analysis, since nonlinear problems are often solved by decomposing them into a sequence of linear problems. Understanding how linear problems are solved and the associated difficulties is important for much of numerical analysis. Third, many of the ideas used in this chapter to solve linear problems are applicable to general problems. In particular, introduced are the basic iterative methods. The presentation of iterative schemes for linear equations will give readers the intuition needed to guide them in developing nonlinear iterative methods.

Linear problems are divided into two basic types depending on the entries of A. We say that A is *dense* if $a_{ij} \neq 0$ for most i, j. On the other hand, we say that A is *sparse* if $a_{ij} = 0$ for most i, j. This terminology is obviously imprecise. In practice, however, matrices that arise in numerical problems tend to either be clearly dense or clearly sparse.

This chapter first describes the basic direct methods for solving linear equations. Then it discusses condition numbers for linear systems and the error bounds they imply. The concept of conditioning is one of the most important ones in numerical analysis and appears in almost all numerical problems. The chapter includes the general principles of iterative methods for solving systems of equations and how these iterative methods are fine-tuned. It ends with discussions of sparse matrix methods, applications to Markov chain theory, and solving overidentified systems.

3.1 Gaussian Elimination, LU Decomposition

Gaussian elimination is a common direct method for solving a general linear system. We will first consider the solution for a simple class of problems, and then we will see how to reduce the general problem to the simple case.

The simple case is that of *triangular* matrices. A is *lower triangular* if all nonzero elements lie on or below the diagonal; that is, A has the form

$$A = \begin{pmatrix} a_{11} & 0 & \cdots & 0 \\ a_{21} & a_{22} & \cdots & 0 \\ \vdots & \vdots & \ddots & \vdots \\ a_{n1} & a_{n2} & \cdots & a_{nn} \end{pmatrix}.$$

Upper triangular matrices have all nonzero entries on or above the diagonal. *A* is a *triangular matrix* if it is either upper or lower triangular. A *diagonal* matrix has nonzero elements only on the diagonal. Some important facts to remember are that a triangular matrix is nonsingular if and only if all the diagonal elements are nonzero, and that lower (upper) triangular matrices are closed under multiplication and inversion.

Linear systems in which *A* is triangular can be solved by *back-substitution*. Suppose that *A* is lower triangular and nonsingular. Since all nondiagonal elements in the first row of *A* are zero, the first row's contribution to the system $Ax = b$ reduces to $a_{11}x_1 = b_1$, which has the solution $x_1 = b_1/a_{11}$. With this solution for x_1 in hand, we next solve for x_2. Row 2 implies the equation $a_{22}x_2 + a_{21}x_1 = b_2$, in which only x_2 is not known. Proceeding down the matrix, we can solve for each component of *x* in sequence. More formally, back-substitution for a lower triangular matrix is the following procedure:

$$x_1 = \frac{b_1}{a_{11}}, \tag{3.1.1}$$

$$x_k = \frac{b_k - \sum_{j=1}^{k-1} a_{kj} x_j}{a_{kk}}, \qquad k = 2, 3, \ldots, n, \tag{3.1.2}$$

which is always well-defined for nonsingular, lower triangular matrices. If *A* is upper triangular, we can similarly solve $Ax = b$ beginning with $x_n = b_n/a_{nn}$.

To measure the speed of this solution procedure, we make an operation count. There are *n* divisions, $n(n-1)/2$ multiplications, and $n(n-1)/2$ additions/subtractions. Ignoring additions/subtractions and dropping terms of order less than n^2, we have an operation count of $n^2/2$. Therefore solving a triangular system can be done in quadratic time.

We will now use the special method for triangular matrices as a basis for solving general nonsingular matrices. To solve $Ax = b$ for general *A*, we first factor *A* into the product of two triangular matrices, $A = LU$ where *L* is lower triangular and *U* is upper triangular. This is called a *LU decomposition* of *A*. We then replace the problem $Ax = b$ with the equivalent problem $LUx = b$, which in turn reduces to two triangular systems, $Lz = b$ and $Ux = z$. Therefore, to find *x*, we first solve for *z* in $Lz = b$ and then solve for *x* in $Ux = z$.

Gaussian elimination produces such an *LU* decomposition for any nonsingular *A*, proceeding row by row, transforming *A* into an upper triangular matrix by means of a sequence of lower triangular transformations. The first step focuses on getting the first column into upper triangular form, replacing a_{i1} with a zero for $i = 2, \ldots, n$.

Suppose that $a_{11} \neq 0$. If we define $l_{i1}^1 = a_{i1}/a_{11}$, $i = 2, \ldots, n$, and $a_{ij}^2 = a_{ij} - l_{i1}^1 a_{1j}$, $j = 1, \ldots, n$, then a_{i1}^2 is zero for $i = 2, \ldots, n$. Let $A^{(1)} = A$. If we define a new matrix $A^{(2)}$ to have the same first row as A, $A_{ij}^{(2)} = a_{ij}^2$ for $i, j = 2, \ldots, n$, and $A_{i1}^{(2)} = 0$, $i = 2, \ldots, n$, then

$$\left[I - \begin{pmatrix} 0 & 0 & \cdots & 0 \\ l_{21}^1 & 0 & \cdots & 0 \\ \vdots & \vdots & \ddots & \vdots \\ l_{n1}^1 & 0 & \cdots & 0 \end{pmatrix} \right] A = \begin{pmatrix} a_{11}^1 & a_{12}^1 & \cdots & a_{1n}^1 \\ 0 & a_{22}^2 & \cdots & a_{2n}^2 \\ \vdots & \vdots & \ddots & \vdots \\ 0 & a_{n2}^2 & \cdots & a_{nn}^2 \end{pmatrix} \equiv A^{(2)}.$$

Note that we have premultiplied A by a lower triangular matrix to get $A^{(2)}$. Proceeding column by column in similar fashion, we can construct a series of lower triangular matrices that replaces the elements below the diagonal with zeros. If $a_{kk}^k \neq 0$, we define

$$l_{ij}^k = \begin{cases} \dfrac{a_{ik}^k}{a_{kk}^k}, & j = k, \; i = k+1, \ldots, n, \\[2mm] 0, & \text{otherwise}, \end{cases} \tag{3.1.3}$$

$$a_{ij}^{k+1} = \begin{cases} a_{ij}^k - l_{ik}^k a_{kj}^k, & i = k+1, \ldots, n, \; j = k, \ldots, n, \\[2mm] a_{ij}^k, & \text{otherwise}, \end{cases} \tag{3.1.4}$$

then we have defined a sequence of matrices such that

$$A^{(k+1)} = \left[I - \underbrace{\begin{pmatrix} 0 & \cdots & 0 & 0 & \cdots & 0 \\ \vdots & \ddots & \vdots & \vdots & & \vdots \\ 0 & \cdots & 0 & l_{k+1,k}^k & \cdots & 0 \\ \vdots & & \vdots & \vdots & \ddots & \vdots \\ 0 & \cdots & 0 & l_{n,k}^k & \cdots & 0 \end{pmatrix}}_{L^{(k)}} \right] A^{(k)}.$$

The result is that $A^{(n)}$ is upper triangular, where the factorization

$$L^{(n-1)} L^{(n-2)} \cdots L^{(2)} L^{(1)} A = A^{(n)} \equiv U$$

implies that $A = LU$ where $L \equiv (L^{(n-1)} \cdots L^{(1)})^{-1}$ is also lower triangular. Algorithm 3.1 summarizes Gaussian elimination.

Algorithm 3.1   Gaussian Elimination

Objective: Solve $Ax = b$.

Step 1. Compute the LU decomposition of A.

Step 2. Solve $Lz = b$ for z by back-substitution.

Step 3. Solve $Ux = z$ for x by back-substitution.

There are two difficulties with Gaussian elimination. First is the possibility that a_{kk}^k is zero, making (3.1.3) ill-defined. However, as long as A is nonsingular, some element of $A^{(k)}$ below a_{kk}^k will be nonzero and a rearrangement of rows will bring a nonzero element to the kth diagonal position, allowing us to proceed; this is called *pivoting*. Even if a_{kk}^k is not zero, a small value will magnify any numerical error from an earlier step. Therefore a good pivoting scheme will use a rearrangement that minimizes this potential problem. See Golub and van Loan (1983) for details about pivoting. Since good pivoting schemes are complex, readers should not write their own LU codes but use the refined codes, such as the programs in LAPACK, which are available. Anderson et al. (1992) describes this package. Second, round-off error can accumulate because of the mixture of additions and subtractions that occur in Gaussian elimination.

To measure the speed of this procedure, we again perform an operation count. The factorization step involves roughly $n^3/3$ multiplications and divisions. Solving the two triangular systems implicit in $LUx = b$ uses a total of n^2 multiplications and divisions. The cost of solving a linear problem depends on the context. Since the factorization cost is borne *once* for any matrix A, if you want to solve the linear problem with m different choices of b, the total cost is $n^3/3 + mn^2$. Therefore the fixed cost is cubic in the matrix dimension n, but the marginal cost is quadratic.

3.2   Alternative Methods

LU decomposition is the most common approach to solving linear equations, but there are other useful methods. This section discusses some of the alternatives and indicates their advantages.

QR factorization

We say that A is *orthogonal* if $A^\top A$ is a diagonal matrix. A *QR factorization* for an arbitrary real nonsingular square matrix A is $A = QR$ where Q is orthogonal and R is upper triangular. Once in this form, we solve $Ax = b$ by noting that $Ax = b$ iff $Q^\top Ax = Q^\top b$ iff $Q^\top QRx = Q^\top b$ iff $DRx = Q^\top b$ where $D = Q^\top Q$ is a diagonal matrix. Therefore DR is upper triangular, and x can be computed by applying back-substitution to $DRx = Q^\top b$. The main task in this procedure is computing Q and R. See Golub and van Loan for the details; in particular, they show that this can be done for arbitrary matrices $A \in R^{n \times m}$.

Cholesky Factorization

The LU and QR decompositions can be applied to any nonsingular matrix. Alternative factorizations are available for special matrices. *Cholesky factorization* can be used for symmetric positive definite matrices. Cholesky factorization is used frequently in optimization problems where symmetric positive-definite matrices arise naturally.

A Cholesky decomposition of A has the form $A = LL^\top$ where L is a lower triangular matrix. L is a Cholesky factor, or "square root" of A. This is just a special case of LU decomposition since $L^\top$ is upper triangular; hence, after computing the Cholesky decomposition of A, one proceeds as in the LU decomposition procedure to solve a system $Ax = b$.

Clearly, A is symmetric positive definite if it has a Cholesky decomposition. One can show by construction that if A is a symmetric positive definite matrix, then A has a Cholesky decomposition. The equation defining a_{11} in $A = LL^\top$ implies that $a_{11} = l_{11}^2$. Hence $l_{11} = \sqrt{a_{11}}$; to pin down any element of L, we will always take positive square roots. In general, the first column of $A = LL^\top$ implies that $a_{i1} = l_{i1}l_{11}$, $i = 2, \ldots, n$, yielding

$$l_{i1} = \frac{a_{i1}}{l_{11}}, \qquad i = 2, \ldots, n. \tag{3.2.1}$$

When we move to the second column of A, we first find that $A = LL^\top$ implies the equation $a_{12} = l_{11}l_{21}$ which fixes l_{21}. Since l_{11} and l_{21} have been fixed, and $l_{11}l_{21} = a_{21}$, this demands that $a_{12} = a_{21}$, which is true when A is symmetric.

The second condition implied by the second column of $A = LL^\top$ is $a_{22} = l_{21}^2 + l_{22}^2$, which implies that $l_{22} = \sqrt{a_{22} - l_{21}^2}$. The difficulty here is that $a_{22} - l_{21}^2$ must be positive if l_{22} is to be real. Fortunately that is true given our solution for l_{21} and the assumption that A is positive definite. The other elements of the second column in $A = LL^\top$ imply that $a_{i2} = l_{i1}l_{21} + l_{i2}l_{22}$, $i = 3, \ldots, n$, which implies, since l_{i1} is known, $i = 1, \ldots, n$, that

$$l_{i2} = \frac{a_{i2} - l_{i1}l_{21}}{l_{22}}, \qquad i = 3, \ldots, n. \tag{3.2.2}$$

Proceeding sequentially in column j, we arrive at the conditions

$$a_{jj} = \sum_{k=1}^{j} l_{jk}^2,$$

$$a_{ij} = \sum_{k=1}^{j} l_{ik} l_{jk}, \qquad i = j+1, \ldots, n. \tag{3.2.3}$$

If A is symmetric positive definite, we can use these conditions sequentially to solve for the elements of L and arrive at the Cholesky decomposition of A.

The advantages of the Cholesky decomposition is that it involves only $n^3/6$ multiplications and n square roots, which is about half the cost of Gaussian elimination for large n. It is also more stable than LU decomposition, particularly since there is no need for pivots. Therefore, if A is known to be symmetric positive definite, Cholesky decomposition is preferred to LU decomposition.

An important application of Cholesky decomposition occurs in probability theory. If $Y \sim N(\mu, \Sigma)$ is a multivariate normal random variable with mean μ and variance-covariance matrix Σ, then Σ is positive definite. If $\Sigma = \Omega \Omega^\top$ is a Cholesky decomposition of Σ, then $Y = \mu + \Omega X$ where $X \sim N(0, I)$ is a vector of i.i.d. unit normals. This tells us that any multivariate normal is really a linear sum of i.i.d. unit normals, a very useful transformation.

Cramer's Rule

Cramer's rule solves for x in $Ax = b$ by applying a direct formula to the elements of A and b. We first need to compute $\det(A)$. The (i,j) *cofactor* of the a_{ij} element of a $n \times n$ matrix A is the $(n-1) \times (n-1)$ matrix C formed from A by eliminating row i and column j of A. The determinant is computed recursively by

$$\det(A) = \begin{cases} A, & A \text{ a scalar,} \\ \sum_i (-1)^{i+1} a_{ij} \det(C_{ij}), & C_{ij} \text{ the } (i,j) \text{ cofactor of } A. \end{cases} \tag{3.2.4}$$

Let A_k be equal to A except that its k'th column is b, and let D_k be the determinant of A_k. Then Cramer's rule says that the solution to $Ax = b$ is

$$x_k = \frac{D_k}{D}, \qquad k = 1, \ldots, n.$$

Cramer's method is very slow, having an operation count of $\mathcal{O}(n!)$. In symbolic computations, however, Cramer's method is used since it is a closed-form expression for the solution x.

3.3   Banded Sparse Matrix Methods

Decomposition methods can be used for any matrix, but for large matrices they will consume much time and space. In many applications we find ourselves working with matrices that have mostly zero entries. When we have a sparse matrix, we can exploit its special structure to construct fast algorithms that use relatively little space. In this section we introduce some special examples of sparse matrices.

Near-Diagonal Methods

The most trivial example of a sparse matrix is a diagonal matrix, D. If we know that a matrix is diagonal, we need only to store the n diagonal elements in a vector, d, where $d_i = D_{ii}$. This reduces storage needs from n^2 to n. Such matrices are denoted $\mathrm{diag}\{d_1, d_2, \ldots, d_n\}$. The inverse of such a matrix is the diagonal matrix formed by inverting the diagonal elements; that is, $D^{-1} = \mathrm{diag}\{d_i^{-1}\}$. Solving a diagonal system of equations is therefore trivial, with $Dx = b$ having the solution $x = D^{-1}b$.

It is also easy to solve sparse matrices where all the nonzero elements are on or close to the diagonal. Consider the case of a *tridiagonal* matrix:

$$A = \begin{pmatrix}
a_{11} & a_{12} & 0 & 0 & 0 & \cdots & 0 \\
a_{21} & a_{22} & a_{23} & 0 & 0 & \cdots & 0 \\
0 & a_{32} & a_{33} & a_{34} & 0 & \cdots & 0 \\
\vdots & \vdots & \vdots & \ddots & \vdots & \vdots & \vdots \\
0 & \cdots & \cdots & a_{n-2,n-3} & a_{n-2,n-2} & a_{n-2,n-1} & 0 \\
0 & \cdots & \cdots & 0 & a_{n-1,n-2} & a_{n-1,n-1} & a_{n-1,n} \\
0 & \cdots & \cdots & 0 & 0 & a_{n,n-1} & a_{nn}
\end{pmatrix}.$$

We will solve the equation $Ax = b$ in a direct fashion. First, note that if $a_{j,j+1} = 0$ for some j, then A decomposes into the block form

$$A = \begin{pmatrix} A_{11} & 0 \\ A_{21} & A_{22} \end{pmatrix},$$

where A_{11} is the $j \times j$ upper left corner of A and A_{22} is the $(n-j) \times (n-j)$ lower right corner, and solving $Ax = b$ reduces to solving smaller tridiagonal systems. Therefore we assume that $a_{j,j+1} \neq 0$ for $j = 1, \ldots, n$.

Consider the variable x_1. The first equation in $Ax = b$, corresponding to the first row in A, tells us that $x_2 = (b_1 - a_{11} x_1)/a_{12}$; if $c_2 = b_1/a_{12}$ and $d_2 = -a_{11}/a_{12}$, then

$$x_2 = c_2 + d_2 x_1 \tag{3.3.1}$$

expresses the solution for x_2 in terms of x_1. The second equation in $Ax = b$ involves x_1, x_2, and x_3, but (3.3.1) expresses x_2 in terms of x_1. Substituting (3.3.1) into $a_{21}x_1 + a_{22}x_2 + a_{23}x_3 = b_2$ implies that $x_3 = (b_2 - a_{21}x_1 - a_{22}x_2)/a_{23}$; this expresses of x_3 in terms of x_1, a relation we denote $x_3 = c_3 + d_3 x_1$. Moving through rows 3 through $n - 1$, we can sequentially solve for x_k, $k = 4, \ldots, n$, in terms of x_1; let $x_k = c_k + d_k x_1$ denote these solutions. As we move through these equations, we compute and store the c_k and d_k coefficients. We next substitute the $x_n = c_n + d_n x_1$ and $x_{n-1} = c_{n-1} + d_{n-1}x_1$ expressions into the nth equation, corresponding to the last row of A, finding

$$b_n = a_{n,n-1} x_{n-1} + a_{nn} x_n$$
$$= a_{n,n-1} (c_{n-1} + d_{n-1}x_1) + a_{nn} (c_n + d_n x_1),$$

which is a single equation in the single unknown x_1. From this we can compute the solution for x_1 and then compute $x_k = c_k + d_k x_1$ to get the solutions for x_k for $k = 2, \ldots, n$.

These ideas can be adapted to solve sparse matrices with particular *banding* properties. A matrix is said to have *bandwidth* $2l + 1$ if all nonzero elements are within l rows of the diagonal. Tridiagonal matrices have bandwidth 3; to solve them, the method above reduces the system to one equation in one unknown, x_1. In general, a matrix with bandwidth $2l + 1$ can be reduced to a system of l equations in $x_1, \ldots, x_l$, in the same fashion as used above for tridiagonal matrices.

Banded matrices can also be stored efficiently. An $n \times n$ matrix, A, with bandwidth $2l + 1$ can be stored in a smaller, $n \times (2l + 1)$, matrix, B. Specifically, $B_{ij} = A_{i, j-l+i-1}$ when $1 \leq j - l + i - 1 \leq n$, and $1 \leq j \leq 2l + 1$, and zero otherwise. This can greatly economize on storage if n is large and l small.

3.4 General Sparse Matrix Methods

Many sparse matrices do not have a special structure such as banding. In this section we present basic ideas for creating and using general sparse matrices.

Storage Scheme for General Sparse Matrices

There are two different ways to approach sparse problems. One way is to find a particular pattern for the nonzero elements and exploit it to develop efficient storage methods and write algorithms specific to that pattern. Banded matrices are one such pattern. Sometimes the nonzero elements in a sparse matrix do not fall into a useful pattern; this forces the use of more general approaches. In this section we will discuss a simple way to store, construct, and use an arbitrary sparse matrix.

We first need to have a way to store all the information in a sparse matrix in a reasonable amount of space. Suppose that we know that $A \in R^{n \times n}$ contains at most N nonzero elements. If a matrix is sparse, we only need to store information about the location and value of nonzero entries. To that end, construct the arrays $B \in R^{N \times 5}$, $ROW \in R^n$, and $COL \in R^n$. Each row of B contains the necessary information about one of the nonzero elements of A. In particular, row l in B contains information about some nonzero a_{ij}. The first three entries in row l give location and value; specifically if $B(l, 1) = i$, $B(l, 2) = j$, then $B(l, 3) = a_{ij}$. If $a_{ij} \neq 0$, then, for some l, the first and second entries of row l of B are i and j, and the third entry is the value a_{ij}.

If we know a_{ij}, we often need to know the next nonzero entries in row i and column j of A. Given that row l in B represents the information about element a_{ij}, the fourth entry of row l in B tells one which row of B contains the next nonzero entry in row i of A; that is, if $i = B(l, 1)$, and $l^R = B(l, 4)$, then $a_{i,k} = 0$ for $j < k < B(l^R, 2)$. Finally, the fifth entry tells us which row of B contains the next nonzero entry in column j of A; that is, if $j = B(l, 2)$, and $l^C = B(l, 5)$, then $a_{k,j} = 0$ for $i < k < B(l^C, 1)$. We interpret nonsense entries (something not between 1 and N; we use zero for this purpose) in the fourth (fifth) entry of a row in B as telling us that we have reached the end of that row (column). To help us get started, ROW_i tells us what row in B contains the first nonzero element in row i of A; if there is no such entry, let $ROW_i = 0$. Similarly COL_j tells us what row in B represents the first nonzero element in column j of A; if there is no such entry, let $COL_j = 0$. Figure 3.1 displays row l of B and related rows.

Essentially B, ROW, and COL give us a map for tracing through the nonzero elements of A. For example, if we want to know the value of $a_{i,j}$, ROW_i would tell us

$\vdots$

row l of B: i j a_{ij} l^R l^C

$\vdots$

row l^R of B: i j' $a_{ij'}$ l^{RR} l^{RC}

$\vdots$

row l^C of B: i' j $a_{i'j}$ l^{CR} l^{CC}

$\vdots$

Figure 3.1
Sparse matrix storage

the column that contained the first nonzero element in row i. From that point we start tracing through row i and continue until we find a_{ij} represented in B, or find that we have passed the (i,j) element, and conclude that $a_{ij} = 0$. Algorithm 3.2 describes how to find the value of a_{ij}.

Algorithm 3.2   Sparse Matrix Lookup

Objective: Given i, j, find the value of $a_{i,j}$ in a sparse matrix stored in the general form in $B \in R^{N \times 5}$.

Step 1. $l = ROW_i$; if $l = 0$, then $a_{i,j} = 0$, and STOP.

Step 2. $j' = B(l, 2)$

Step 3. If $j' < j$, then $l = B(l, 5)$ and go to step 2;
elseif $j' = j$ $a_{ij} = B(l, 3)$ and STOP;
else $a_{ij} = 0$ and STOP;
endif

Creating a Sparse Markov Transition Matrix

Now that we know how to store a sparse matrix, we need to know how to construct one. Suppose that we have a method for determining the elements of a π_{ij} Markov transition matrix Π with a large number of states. This generally takes the form of a function or subroutine which takes (i, j) as input. If Π is sparse, we will want to put it into sparse form use it to compute its stationary distribution. We now present a method for constructing a sparse matrix representation for Π.

Specifically, if there are N nonzero elements of Π we need to form a $N \times 5$ matrix B of the form displayed in figure 3.1. Actually, to compute the stationary distribution, we only need to do left multiplications, $x\Pi$; hence we have no need for column four of B nor the vector ROW. We will construct the remaining elements of B and the vector COL in the following fashion:

First, we initialize COL to be a vector of -1; a -1 value for COL_j will indicate that we have yet to find a nonzero element in column j. We will also use another vector $LAST$. $LAST_j$ will indicate the row in B that contains the last nonzero entry we have found in column j; $LAST$ will also be initialized to -1. The variable l will tell us the next row in B to be filled; l is initialized to 1.

We will traverse Π one row at a time. That is, we begin with row one and find the first column, say j, that contains a nonzero element. This will be our first entry in B; hence $B(1, 1) = 1$, $B(1, 2) = j$, $B(1, 3) = \pi_{1,j}$, $COL_j = 1$, and $LAST_j = 1$. We increment l, making it 2, and then proceed to the next nonzero element in row one of Π.

In general, if the most recent element we have found lies in row i of Π and is coded in row l of B, then we proceed as indicated in steps 1 through 6 of algorithm 3.3:

Algorithm 3.3   Constructing a Sparse Markov Matrix

Objective: Given a procedure to compute Π_{ij} for any i and j, construct a sparse matrix that represents Π_{ij}.

Initialization. Set elements in $COL, LAST \in R^n$ to be -1. Let j be the column containing the first nonzero element in row $i = 1$. Set $B(1,1) = 1$, $B(1,2) = j$, and $B(1,3) = \pi_{i,j}$, $COL_j = 1$, and $LAST_j = 1$. Set $l = 2$.

Step 1. Find the next nonzero element in row i, and go to step 2. If there are no more nonzero elemets in row i, then increment i, and go to step 1; if we have no more rows, go to step 6.

Step 2. Let j equal to the column of the new nonzero element of row i in Π. Set $B(l,1) = i$, $B(l,2) = j$, and $B(l,3) = \pi_{i,j}$.

Step 3. If $COL_j = -1$, then set $COL_j = i$

Step 4. Set $l = l + 1$.

Step 5. Set $B(LAST_j, 5) = l$ and $LAST_j = l$, and go to step 1.

Step 6. Finishing: For $j = 1, \ldots, n$, set $B(LAST_j, 5) = -1$, indicating that the end of a column has been reached. STOP.

This procedure is straightforward. Step 2 deposits the basic information about π_{ij} in row l of B. Step 3 determines if π_{ij} is the first nonzero element in its column and records that fact in COL if true. Step 4 tells us that we move to the next row in B by incrementing l step 5 finds, through the $LAST$ vector, the row in B which contains the element in column j immediately above π_{ij} and records there the fact that π_{ij} is the next nonzero element below it. Step 5 also records the fact that row l now contains the most recently found nonzero element of column j. After we have deposited the critical information in row l of B and the appropriate entry in $LAST$, we go back to start again with the next nonzero element of Π. Step 6 finishes up by filling out the empty column 5 entries in B.

Operations with Sparse Matrices

With our sparse matrix representation, we can easily multiply a row vector, x, by A to produce the row vector, $y = xA$. A similar procedure computes Ax for a column vector x. To compute y_j, we first let $l_1 = COL_j$; then $B(l_1, 1)$ is the row in A that contains the first nonzero element in column j of A. Hence we begin with the assignment $y_j = x_{B(l_1,1)} B(l_1, 3)$. Next let $l_2 = B(l_1, 5)$, since $B(l_1, 5)$ is the row of B

containing information about the next nonzero element of A below the current one. If $l_2 = 0$, we know that there are no more nonzero elements, and we are finished. If $l_2 \neq 0$, we update our computation of y_j with $y_j \leftarrow y_j + x_{B(l_2, 1)} B(l_2, 3)$. In general, we proceed with the iteration,

$$l_k = B(l_{k-1}, 5)$$

if $l_k = 0$,   STOP,

else $y_j \leftarrow y_j + x_{B(l_k, 1)} B(l_k, 3)$

for $k = 2, 3, \ldots$, continuing until we hit some k where $B(l_k, 5) = 0$, which indicates that we have exhausted column j of A. At this point we conclude that y_j has been computed, and we move onto column $j + 1$ and the computation of y_{j+1}.

We have shown how to represent a sparse matrix, and how to multiply a matrix and a vector. One can also multiply sparse matrices, but this is a more complex operation. Multiplication of sparse matrices leads to *fill-in problems*, that is, the result of the operation is less sparse than the inputs. Fill-in problems are severe for LU and QR decompositions and matrix inversion. Sparse methods are most useful when a single sparse matrix is used repeatedly in matrix-vector operations.

3.5   Error Analysis

After solving $Ax = b$, we will want to know how sensitive our solution is to errors. Since linear systems arise in nonlinear problems, the error analysis for linear systems is the basis for error analysis in other problems. Before proceeding, we need to review some basic concepts in matrix analysis.

Matrix Analysis

In our work below, we will need a measure of the "size" of a matrix. We can base a concept of matrix size on any notion of vector length. If $\| \cdot \|$ is a norm on R^n, then the induced norm of A is

$$\|A\| \equiv \max_{x \neq 0} \frac{\|Ax\|}{\|x\|} = \max_{\|x\|=1} \|Ax\|$$

The following theorem ties together the notions of matrix norm and spectral radius:

THEOREM 3.5.1   For any norm $\| \cdot \|$, $\rho(A) \leq \|A\|$.

Error Bounds

We now turn to the analysis of errors that arise in solving $Ax = b$. Specifically, suppose that b is perturbed by errors, such as rounding errors, but there are no errors in A nor any that arise in solving $Ax = b$. Let r be the error in b and $\tilde{x}$ be the solution of the perturbed system; therefore $A\tilde{x} = b + r$. If we define the error $e \equiv \tilde{x} - x$, then by linearity of $A, e = A^{-1} r$.

Suppose that we have chosen a vector norm, $\| \cdot \|$. The sensitivity of the solution of $Ax = b$ to errors will be measured by the *condition number*, and it is defined to be the ratio

$$\frac{\|e\|}{\|x\|} \div \frac{\|r\|}{\|b\|},$$

which is the percentage error in x relative to the percentage error in b. The smallest possible condition number for a linear system of equations is 1. If $A = aI$, then $x = b/a$, and any percentage error in b leads to an identical percentage error in x. This is the best possible case.

The condition number is essentially the elasticity of the solution to a problem with respect to the data, and it can be computed for any problem once an appropriate norm has been chosen. A small condition number is desirable because it indicates that the problem is less sensitive to rounding errors in inputs. While we will here only analyze the condition number of linear problems, it is clear from the definition that the concept can be applied to any problem in general.

Note that $Ae = r$ implies that $\|A\| \, \|e\| \ge \|r\|$ and that $e = A^{-1}r$ implies that $\|A^{-1}\| \, \|r\| \ge \|e\|$. Together with $Ax = b$ this implies that

$$\frac{\|r\|}{\|A\| \, \|A^{-1}\| \, \|b\|} \le \frac{\|e\|}{\|x\|} \le \frac{\|A^{-1}\| \, \|A\| \, \|r\|}{\|b\|}.$$

If we define the *condition number of A* to be

$$\text{cond}(A) \equiv \|A\| \, \|A^{-1}\|,$$

then we have upper and lower bounds

$$\frac{1}{\text{cond}(A)} \frac{\|r\|}{\|b\|} \le \frac{\|e\|}{\|x\|} \le \frac{\|r\|}{\|b\|} \text{cond}(A). \tag{3.5.1}$$

These constructions indicate that the condition number is a useful measure of a matrix being nearly singular; it appears to be the only way to do so. It is clear that the determinant is not a measure of singularity. Even though a zero determinant is a definition of being singular, having a small determinant is not a useful measure of being nearly singular. For example, if $A = \varepsilon I_n$, then $\text{cond}(A) = 1$ and A is a well-behaved matrix, but $\det(A) = \varepsilon^n$ can be arbitrarily small.

What constitutes "small" and "large" condition numbers depends on the machine. Since we are concerned with the number of significant decimal digits, a condition number of 100 indicates that an input error of 10^{-10} results in an output error of up to 10^{-8}, that is, a possible loss of two significant decimal digits. The rough rule of thumb is that as $\text{cond}(A)$ increases by a factor of 10, you lose one significant digit in the solution of $Ax = b$. Normal computers carry about 12 to 16 significant decimal digits. On those machines the condition number is "small" if its base 10 logarithm is about two or three. Any condition number over 10^{10} is considered "large" and unacceptable. Some machines (e.g., double precision on a Cray and quadruple precision on a VAX) carry almost 30 significant decimal digits. On those machines one would not start to worry about poor conditioning unless the condition number exceeds 10^{15}.

Even though the error bound expressions above are natural, they depend on the norm used. It would be more convenient to have norm-independent error bounds. Since $\|A\| \geq \rho(A)$, $\text{cond}(A) \geq \rho(A)\rho(A^{-1})$. A property of eigenvalues is that $\lambda \in \sigma(A)$ if and only if $\lambda^{-1} \in \sigma(A^{-1})$. Hence, for any norm,

$$\text{cond}(A) \geq \frac{\max_{\lambda \in \sigma(A)} |\lambda|}{\min_{\lambda \in \sigma(A)} |\lambda|} \equiv \text{cond}_*(A),$$

where $\text{cond}_*(A)$ is the *spectral condition number* of A.

We would like to replace cond (A) in (3.5.1) with $\text{cond}_*(A)$, since the result would be useful bounds on the errors. Unfortunately, we cannot make that substitution on the right-hand side of (3.5.1) because $\text{cond}_*(A)$ is only a lower bound for $\text{cond}(A)$. However, there are norms that have condition functions arbitrarily close to $\text{cond}_*(A)$; hence we can find norms that nearly allow us to make this substitution.

Therefore we use $\text{cond}_*(A)$ as a norm-independent lower bound to the true condition number, making $\|r\| / \text{cond}_*(A)\|b\|$ a lower bound of the maximum error. Numerical procedures typically use $\text{cond}_*(A)$ as an estimate of the condition number. While this substitution results in some error, we are generally not concerned because we really want only a rough approximation of the condition number corresponding to the norm of interest. Another commonly used condition number is the L^∞ condition number, $\text{cond}_\infty(A) \equiv \|A\|_\infty \|A^{-1}\|_\infty$, where $\|A\|_\infty \equiv \max_{i,j} |a_{i,j}|$.

Table 3.1
Condition numbers of Hilbert matrices

n	3	4	5	6	7	8	9	10
$\text{cond}_*(H_n)$	55	6,000	4.8(5)	1.5(7)	4.8(8)	1.5(10)	4.9(11)	1.6(13)
$\text{cond}_\infty(H_n)$	192	6,480	1.8(5)	4.4(6)	1.3(8)	4.2(9)	1.2(11)	3.5(12)

To illustrate the possible values of the spectral condition number, we now consider a simple example. Consider the Hilbert matrix:

$$H_n \equiv \begin{pmatrix} 1 & \dfrac{1}{2} & \dfrac{1}{3} & \cdots & \dfrac{1}{n} \\[2mm] \dfrac{1}{2} & \dfrac{1}{3} & \dfrac{1}{4} & \cdots & \dfrac{1}{n+1} \\[2mm] \vdots & \vdots & \vdots & \ddots & \vdots \\[2mm] \dfrac{1}{n} & \cdots & \cdots & \cdots & \dfrac{1}{2n-1} \end{pmatrix}.$$

Table 3.1 displays the spectral and L^∞ condition numbers for some small Hilbert matrices.

Note the similar magnitudes of $\text{cond}_* H_n$ and $\text{cond}_\infty H_n$. Even though the norms underlying these condition numbers are substantially different, the condition numbers are "close" in terms of their orders of magnitude, which is really all that matters for our purposes. The condition numbers for these Hilbert matrices rise rapidly as n increases. Anyone using a machine with 12 significant digits cannot be confident about any digit in a solution of $H_n x = b$ if n exceeds 9. This is not a rare example. While in some sense "most" matrices have low to moderate condition numbers, many intuitive procedures, such as least squares approximation procedures, lead to poorly conditioned problems with disastrously high condition numbers.

The error bounds we computed were approximate upper bounds, but that was under the assumption that we could exactly solve the perturbed system. Any solution method will introduce further round-off error. This can be particularly true with Gaussian elimination where subtraction plays a critical role in the LU decomposition. A complete analysis of the errors for any particular solution technique is beyond the scope of this text, but it suffices to say that conditioning considerations apply to all methods and provide us with a useful guide for estimating errors. In the case of Gaussian elimination, $\text{cond}_*(A)$ is still a good summary index for the total error in solving $Ax = b$ including round-off errors in the LU and back-substitution steps.

We should finish with one word on terminology. We have defined the condition number in the usual fashion, but the base ten logarithm of this condition number is also referred to as the "condition number" of a matrix. This is sensible because the base ten logarithm indicates the loss in decimal precision. One can usually tell from the context which definition is being used because the numbers differ by orders of magnitude. In this text we will use the phrase "log condition number" to refer to the logarithmic version.

Ill-conditioned Problems and Preconditioning

The condition number is essentially the elasticity of the solution to a problem with respect to the data. Furthermore it can be computed for any problem, linear or nonlinear, once an appropriate norm has been chosen. In general, the conditioning of the equation $f(x) = 0$ is the condition number of the Jacobian of f at a zero of $f(x) = 0$. A problem is called *well-conditioned* if this elasticity is small and *poorly conditioned* if it is large. The condition number indicates how sensitive the result of an algorithm is to changes in the data and is a property of the mathematical problem, not just a numerical difficulty. We are concerned about it in numerical analysis because errors in the early steps of an algorithm affect the input to later steps. If the later steps are poorly conditioned problems, then the early errors are magnified.

In general, if a problem is poorly conditioned, the hope is that a (possibly nonlinear) transformation will convert it into an equivalent problem which is better conditioned. In the linear case we would consider some simple linear transformations when trying to solve a poorly conditioned system. Suppose that $Ax = b$ is poorly conditioned. *Preconditioning* chooses another nonsingular matrix D and solves the equivalent system $DAx = Db$. If D is chosen well, the new system is better conditioned. See Golub and van Loan (1983) for some examples.

3.6   Iterative Methods

Decomposition methods for linear equations are direct methods of solution. Direct methods can be very costly for large systems, since the time requirements are order n^3 and the space requirements are order n^2. If A is dense, there is no way to avoid a space requirement of order n^2. Even if A is sparse, decomposition methods may not be practical because the LU and QR factors will generally not be sparse.

Fortunately iterative methods are available that economize on space and often provide good answers in reasonable time. In this section we discuss some basic iterative ideas. Studying iteration methods is valuable also because the basic ideas generalize naturally to nonlinear problems.

Fixed-Point Iteration

The simplest iterative approach is *fixed-point iteration* where we rewrite the problem as a fixed-point problem and repeatedly iterate the fixed-point mapping. For the problem $Ax = b$, we define $G(x) \equiv Ax - b + x$ and compute the sequence

$$x^{k+1} = G(x^k) = (A + I)x^k - b. \tag{3.6.1}$$

Clearly x is a fixed point of $G(x)$ if and only if x solves $Ax = b$. Unfortunately, (3.6.1) will converge only if all the eigenvalues of $A + I$ have modulus less than one. Since this is rare, direct application of fixed-point iteration is seldom used.

Gauss-Jacobi Algorithm

One of the simplest iterative methods for solving linear equations is the *Gauss-Jacobi* method. It begins with the observation that each equation is a single linear equation, a type of equation wherein we can solve for one variable in terms of the others. Consider the equation from the first row of $Ax = b$:

$$a_{11}x_1 + a_{12}x_2 + \cdots + a_{1n}x_n = b_1.$$

We can solve for x_1 in terms of $(x_2, \ldots, x_n)$ if $a_{11} \neq 0$, yielding

$$x_1 = a_{11}^{-1}(b_1 - a_{12}x_2 - \cdots - a_{1n}x_n).$$

In general, if $a_{ii} \neq 0$, we can use the ith row of A to solve for x_i, finding

$$x_i = \frac{1}{a_{ii}} \left\{ b_i - \sum_{j \neq i} a_{ij} x_j \right\}.$$

Initially this appears to be just a different way to express the linear system. We now turn this into an iterative process. We start with a guess for x and use the single-equation solutions to compute a new guess for x. This can be compactly expressed (assuming $a_{ii} \neq 0$) as the iteration

$$x_i^{k+1} = \frac{1}{a_{ii}} \left\{ b_i - \sum_{j \neq i} a_{ij} x_j^k \right\}, \qquad i = 1, \ldots, n. \tag{3.6.2}$$

The result is the Gauss-Jacobi method, and it reduces the problem of solving for n unknowns simultaneously in n equations to that of repeatedly solving n equations with one unknown. This only defines a sequence of guesses; the hope is that (3.6.2) will converge to the true solution, a problem to which we return below.

Gauss-Seidel Algorithm

In the Gauss-Jacobi method we use a new guess for x_i, x_i^{k+1}, only after we have computed the entire vector of new values, x^{k+1}. This delay in using the new information may not be sensible. Suppose that x^* is the solution to $Ax = b$. If, as we hope, x_i^{k+1} is a better estimate of x_i^* than x_i^k, using x_i^{k+1} to compute x_{i+1}^{k+1} in (3.6.2) would seem to be better than using x_i^k. The intuitive argument is that new information about x_i^* should be used as soon as possible.

The basic idea of the *Gauss-Seidel method* is to use a new approximation of x_i^* as soon as it is available. More specifically, if our current guess for x^* is x^k, then we compute the next guess for x_1 as in (3.6.2),

$$x_1^{k+1} = a_{11}^{-1}(b_1 - a_{12}x_2^k - \cdots - a_{1n}x_n^k),$$

but use this new guess for x_1^* immediately when computing the other new components of x^{k+1}. In particular, our equation for x_2^{k+1} derived from the second row of A becomes

$$x_2^{k+1} = a_{22}^{-1}(b_2 - a_{21}x_1^{k+1} - a_{23}x_3^k - \cdots - a_{2n}x_n^k).$$

In general, to solve $Ax = b$ by the Gauss-Seidel method, define the sequence $\{x^k\}_{k=1}^{\infty}$ by the iteration

$$x_i^{k+1} = \frac{1}{a_{ii}} \left\{ b_i - \sum_{j=1}^{i-1} a_{ij} x_j^{k+1} - \sum_{j=i+1}^{n} a_{ij} x_j^k \right\}, \qquad i = 1, \ldots, n. \tag{3.6.3}$$

Here we clearly see how the new components of x^{k+1} are used immediately after they are computed, since x_i^{k+1} is used to compute x_j^{k+1} for $j > i$.

Note that in the Gauss-Seidel case, the order in which we solve for the successive components of x matters, whereas the order did not matter for Gauss-Jacobi. This gives the Gauss-Seidel method more flexibility. In particular, if one ordering does not converge, then we could try a different ordering.

Block Gaussian Algorithms

The Gauss-Jacobi and Gauss-Seidel iterative algorithms break a large problem into a large sequence of easy univariate problems. The *block iteration* idea is to break down the large problem into a sequence of smaller, but multivariate, problems. We choose the subproblems so that they are easy to solve exactly but then proceed as in the Gauss-Jacobi or Gauss-Seidel algorithms.

Suppose that we decompose $x \in R^{nm}$ into a list of n subvectors

$$x \equiv \begin{pmatrix} x^1 \\ \vdots \\ x^n \end{pmatrix},$$

where each x^i is in R^m. Decompose b similarly. Next decompose A:

$$A \equiv \begin{pmatrix} A^{1,1} & \cdots & A^{1,n} \\ \vdots & \ddots & \vdots \\ A^{n,1} & \cdots & A^{n,n} \end{pmatrix},$$

where each $A^{k,j} \in R^{m \times m}$. To solve $Ax = b$, the *block Gauss-Jacobi* method executes the iteration

$$A^{i,i} x^{i,k+1} = b^i - \sum_{j \neq i} A^{i,j} x^{j,k}, \qquad i = 1, \ldots, n, \tag{3.6.4}$$

where $x^{i,k}$ is the ith piece of the kth iterate of x. We express each step in (3.6.4) as a linear equation to emphasize the fact that each $x^{i,k}$ is found by solving a linear equation, whereas the alternative form $x^{i,k+1} = (A^{i,i})^{-1}(b^i - \sum_{j \neq i} A^{i,j} x^{j,k})$ might be interpreted as requiring the inversion of each $A^{i,i}$ matrix. Instead, one should think in terms of solving the separate equations in (3.6.4) by some linear equation solution method, such as LU, QR, or Cholesky decomposition. Note that any such decomposition used for the first iterate, $k = 1$, can be reused in each later iteration. Therefore the marginal cost of each iteration k in (3.6.4) is quite small if one can store the decompositions of the $A^{i,i}$ blocks.

The block Gauss-Jacobi method does not update any component of x until one has all of the new components. The *block Gauss-Seidel* method uses new components immediately, executing the iteration

$$A^{i,i} x^{i,k+1} = b^i - \sum_{j=1}^{i-1} A^{i,j} x^{i,k+1} - \sum_{j=i+1}^{n} A^{i,j} x^{i,k}, \qquad i = 1, \ldots, n. \tag{3.6.5}$$

The iteration in (3.6.5) combines the advantages of block constructions and immediate replacement.

Tatonnement and Iterative Schemes

We now give an example of both Gauss-Jacobi and Gauss-Seidel iteration in a familiar economic context. Suppose that we have the inverse demand equation

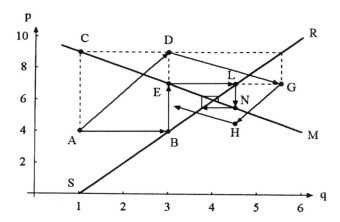

Figure 3.2
Gauss-Jacobi and Gauss-Seidel iteration

$p = 10 - q$ and the supply curve $q = p/2 + 1$, where p is the price and q is quantity. Equilibrium is where supply equals demand and solves the linear system

$$p + q = 10, \tag{3.6.6a}$$

$$p - 2q = -2. \tag{3.6.6b}$$

In figure 3.2 the demand curve is the line CM and is represented by (3.6.6a), and the supply curve is the line SR represented by (3.6.6b).

In Gauss-Jacobi we make an initial guess $p = 4$ and $q = 1$ represented by point A in figure 3.2. To get a new guess, we solve the demand equation for p holding q fixed by moving up to C on the demand equation from A. Similarly we move to the right from A to the B on the supply equation to solve for q holding p fixed. The new guess encompassing these calculations is point D. This process corresponds to the following auctioneer process: An auctioneer starts with $(p_0, q_0) = (4, 1)$. He then asks demanders what the price will be if supply is q_0; their response, $p_1 = 9$, is the new price. He also asks suppliers how much they will produce if price is p_0; the producers' response is the new quantity, $q_1 = 3$. The general iteration is

$$q_{n+1} = 1 + \tfrac{1}{2}p_n,$$
$$\tag{3.6.7}$$
$$p_{n+1} = 10 - q_n.$$

Repeating this procedure from point D, we next move to G, then H, and so on. This iteration process converges, but slowly as indicated by the list of Gauss-Jacobi

Table 3.2
Gaussian methods for (3.6.6)

Iteration	Gauss-Jacobi		Gauss-Seidel	
n	p_n	q_n	p_n	q_n
0	4	1	4	1
1	9	3	7	3
2	7	5.5	5.5	4.5
3	4.5	4.5	6.25	3.75
4	5.5	3.25	5.875	4.125
5	6.75	3.75	6.0625	3.9375
7	5.625	4.125	6.0156	3.9844
10	6.0625	4.0938	5.9980	4.0020
15	5.9766	4.0078	6.0001	3.9999
20	5.9980	3.9971	6.0000	4.0000

iterates in table 3.2. Figure 3.2 also indicates that it spirals into the final equilibrium at $p = 6$ and $q = 4$.

On the other hand, Gauss-Seidel corresponds to a more conventional economic dynamic story. Figure 3.2 also displays the Gauss-Seidel iteration. Start again from A. We first use the supply equation to get a new guess for q, q_1 at B, but then use the new quantity, q_1, at B to get a new guess for price, p_1, from the demand equation. That new point is E. This corresponds to an auctioneer starting from $A = (p_0, q_0) = (4, 1)$, learning from suppliers that supply will be $q_1 = 3$ if price is $p_0 = 4$; and then learning from demanders that the price will be $p_1 = 7$ if quantity is $q_1 = 3$. This iteration continues to L, then N, and so on. This is often referred to as the hog cycle—firms expect p_0, produce q_1, which causes prices to rise to p_1, causing production to be q_2, and so on. The general iteration is

$$q_{n+1} = 1 + \tfrac{1}{2}p_n,$$
$$p_{n+1} = 10 - q_{n+1}.$$

(3.6.8)

The Gauss-Seidel iterates are listed in table 3.2. Note that the Gauss-Seidel method converges more rapidly but that both methods do converge.

3.7 Operator Splitting Approach

While the direct application of fixed-point iteration is not generally useful, it does lead to a powerful approach. The general strategy involves transforming the given problem into *another* problem with the *same* solution where fixed-point iteration *does* work. We next examine how to generate iterative schemes abstractly. In doing so, we will see that the Gauss-Jacobi and Gauss-Seidel methods are both applications of this generalized fixed-point iteration method.

Suppose that we want to solve $Ax = b$. We first express A as the difference of two operators

$$A = N - P, \tag{3.7.1}$$

thereby "splitting" A into two components. Note that $Ax = b$ if and only if $Nx = b + Px$. Next define the iteration

$$Nx^{m+1} = b + Px^m, \tag{3.7.2}$$

which, if N is invertible, can also be written

$$x^{m+1} = N^{-1}(b + Px^m). \tag{3.7.3}$$

If we choose N so that $Nx^{m+1} = b + Px^m$ is quickly solved, then computing the iterates will also be easy. This simplicity condition on N is critical for any iteration scheme, since there is little point to using an iterative scheme if each iteration itself is a difficult problem.

Iterative schemes fit into this framework. The Gauss-Jacobi method corresponds to the splitting

$$N = \begin{pmatrix} a_{11} & 0 & \cdots & 0 \\ 0 & a_{22} & \cdots & 0 \\ \vdots & \vdots & \ddots & \vdots \\ 0 & 0 & \cdots & a_{nn} \end{pmatrix}, \quad P = - \begin{pmatrix} 0 & a_{12} & \cdots & a_{1n} \\ a_{21} & 0 & \cdots & a_{2n} \\ \vdots & \vdots & \ddots & \vdots \\ a_{n1} & a_{n2} & \cdots & 0 \end{pmatrix}.$$

Since N is a diagonal matrix, solving (3.7.2) for x^{m+1} is easy. The Gauss-Seidel method corresponds to the splitting

$$N = \begin{pmatrix} a_{11} & 0 & 0 & \cdots & 0 \\ a_{21} & a_{22} & 0 & \cdots & 0 \\ \vdots & \vdots & \vdots & \ddots & \vdots \\ a_{n1} & a_{n2} & a_{n3} & \cdots & a_{nn} \end{pmatrix}, \quad P = - \begin{pmatrix} 0 & a_{12} & a_{13} & \cdots & a_{1n} \\ 0 & 0 & a_{23} & \cdots & a_{2n} \\ \vdots & \vdots & \vdots & \ddots & \vdots \\ 0 & 0 & \cdots & 0 & 0 \end{pmatrix}.$$

In this case, solving for x^{m+1} in (3.7.2) is quickly accomplished by back-substitution.

It is clear, however, that these are not the only possible splittings of A. The key requirement is that solving (3.7.2) is easy.

General Iterative Scheme

Notice that our discussion of operator splitting did not really depend on linearity. The application of this approach to nonlinear problems can be expressed in a common abstract fashion. Algorithm 3.4 outlines a general iterative scheme for solving a general operator equation $Ax = 0$. Note that all we need is a split into a "nice" N, which leads to a convergent scheme.

Algorithm 3.4   General Iterative Schema for $Ax = b$

Step 1. Find an N with an easily computed N^{-1}, and split the operator $A \equiv N - P$.

Step 2. Construct the iterative scheme $x^{m+1} = N^{-1}(b + Px^m)$.

Step 3. Find acceleration scheme to ensure and/or speed up convergence.

Step 4. Find adaptive scheme to learn acceleration parameters.

3.8   Convergence of Iterative Schemes

Iterative schemes are worthless unless the iterates converge to the solution. Suppose that we have split the linear operator $A = N - P$, where both N and P are linear, and that $Ax^* = b$. Then the linear iterative scheme $Nx^{m+1} = b + Px^m$ implies that the error $e^m \equiv x^* - x^m$ obeys the linear iteration $e^m = (N^{-1}P)^m e^0$. Therefore $e^m \to 0$ if and only if $(N^{-1}P)^m e^0 \to 0$. This holds for any e^0 if and only if $\rho(N^{-1}P) < 1$. The fact that the convergence problem reduces to computing $\rho(N^{-1}P)$ may not be comforting since spectral radii are not easy to compute. On the other hand, all we need for an iterative scheme is to find some splitting which is convergent.

In some important cases we can demonstrate convergence. Consider, for example, the case of a diagonal A. If we apply Gauss-Jacobi or Gauss-Seidel to a diagonal matrix, we will converge after only one iteration. This suggests that if a matrix is "close to being diagonal," these methods will converge. The key concept is *diagonal dominance*. A is diagonally dominant if each diagonal element is greater than the sum of the magnitudes of the nondiagonal elements in its row, that is,

$$\sum_{j \neq i} |a_{ij}| < |a_{ii}|, \qquad i = 1, \ldots, n.$$

In the case of Gauss-Jacobi and Gauss-Seidel, diagonal dominance is a sufficient condition for convergence.

THEOREM 3.8.1   If A is diagonally dominant, both Gauss-Jacobi and Gauss-Seidel iteration schemes are convergent for all initial guesses.

Proof For Gauss-Jacobi, N is the matrix of diagonal elements of A, and P is the matrix of nondiagonal elements of A. The matrix $N^{-1}P$ takes the nondiagonal elements of A and divides each element in a row by the corresponding diagonal element. By the diagonal dominance of A, each element of $N^{-1}P$ is less than unity and the row sum of magnitudes in each row cannot exceed unity. Hence

$$\sum_j |(N^{-1}P)_{ij}| < 1, \qquad i = 1, \ldots, n,$$

which in turn implies that $(N^{-1}P)^m \to 0$ as $m \to \infty$. See Stoer and Bulirsch (1990) for a proof of the Gauss-Seidel case.

The relevance of diagonal dominance is economically intuitive. For example, if $p \in R^n$ is a vector of prices and $(Ap)_i$ is the excess demand for good i, then diagonal dominance implies that the sensitivity of the excess demand for good i to its own price exceeds the sum of its sensitivities to all other prices. This is also known as *gross substitutability*. There are also several other contexts in which diagonal dominance naturally arises, making Gauss-Seidel and Gauss-Jacobi methods useful. While theorem 3.8.1 applies strictly only to linear equations, it gives an indication of what is important for convergence in both linear and nonlinear applications of the ideas behind the Gauss-Jacobi and Gauss-Seidel methods.

A key feature to note about Gauss-Jacobi and Gauss-Seidel methods is that they are at best linearly convergent and that the rate of convergence is given by the spectral radius of $N^{-1}P$. While we cannot affect the linearity of convergence, we next investigate methods that increase the linear rate of convergence.

3.9   Acceleration and Stabilization Methods

Many iterative schemes diverge or converge slowly. We often resort to acceleration and stabilization schemes. Again we should remember that the procedures below can be tried in any context, linear, and nonlinear, which fits the notation of the operator splitting approach.

Extrapolation and Dampening

We next examine a simple scheme that can stabilize unstable iteration schemes and accelerate slow ones. Suppose that we want to solve the linear problem $Ax = b$. Define $G = I - A$. Consider the iteration

$$x^{k+1} = Gx^k + b. \tag{3.9.1}$$

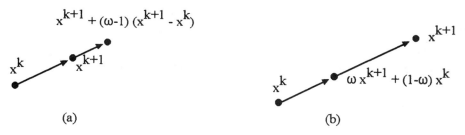

Figure 3.3
Extrapolation (a) and dampening (b)

The scheme (3.9.1) will converge to the solution of $Ax = b$ only if $\rho(G) < 1$, but if $\rho(G)$ is close to 1, convergence will be slow.

Consider next the iteration

$$x^{k+1} = \omega G x^k + \omega b + (1 - \omega)x^k$$

$$\equiv G_{[\omega]}x^k + \omega b \tag{3.9.2}$$

for scalar ω. When $\omega > 1$, the altered iterative scheme in (3.9.2) is called *extrapolation*. Figure 3.3a illustrates the effect of extrapolation when $\omega > 1$. The iteration in (3.9.1) will take us from x^k to $Gx^k + b$ traversing the vector $Gx^k + b - x^k$; extrapolation sets x^{k+1} equal to $Gx^k + b + (\omega - 1)(Gx^k + b - x^k)$, which stretches x^{k+1} beyond $Gx^k + b$. The idea is that if (3.9.1) converges, then $Gx^k + b - x^k$ is a good direction to move, and perhaps it would be even better to move to a point in this direction beyond $Gx^k + b$ and converge even faster.

When $\omega < 1$, (3.9.2) is called *dampening*. Figure 3.3b illustrates the effect of dampening. The iteration in (3.9.1) will take us from x^k to $Gx^k + b$ traversing the vector $Gx^k + b - x^k$; dampening sets x^{k+1} equal to $(1 - \omega)x^k + \omega(Gx^k + b)$, which is a convex combination of the initial point x^k and the iterate in (3.9.1). The idea here is that if (3.9.1) is unstable, it could be that the direction $Gx^k + b - x^k$ is a good one, but that the point $Gx^k + b$ overshoots the solution and results in oscillation and divergence. Setting $\omega < 1$ and using (3.9.2) results in a dampened sequence and hopefully results in convergence.

These ideas are suggestive but will not always work. However, if all of the eigenvalues of G are real, we can surely improve upon (3.9.1) with (3.9.2) for some ω. The stability of $G_{[\omega]}$ depends on its spectrum and spectral radius. If G is nonsingular and has distinct eigenvalues,[1] there is a nonsingular matrix P such that $G = P^{-1}DP$

---

1. The Jordan canonical form can be used to show this for other matrices G.

where D is the diagonal matrix of eigenvalues of G, implying that $\omega G + (1 - \omega)I$ can be written as $P^{-1}(\omega D + (1 - \omega)I)P$ and that $\sigma(\omega G + (1 - \omega)I) = \omega\sigma(G) + 1 - \omega$. From this we see that in the definition of $G_{[\omega]}$, the scalar ω first stretches or shrinks the spectrum of G depending on the magnitude of ω, flips it around 0 if ω is negative, and finally shifts it by $1 - \omega$.

We want to choose ω so as to minimize $\rho(G_{[\omega]})$. When all eigenvalues of G are real, this reduces to

$$\min_{\omega} \quad \max_{\lambda \in \sigma(\omega G + (1-\omega)I)} |\lambda|. \tag{3.9.3}$$

If m is the minimum element of $\sigma(G)$ and M the maximum, then the optimal ω will force the minimal and maximal eigenvalues of $G_{[\omega]}$ to be centered around zero and equal in magnitude; hence $-(\omega m + (1 - \omega)) = \omega M + 1 - \omega$, which implies that the solution to (3.9.3) is

$$\omega^* = \frac{2}{2 - m - M} \tag{3.9.4}$$

and that the new spectral radius is

$$\rho(G_{[\omega^*]}) = \left| \frac{M - m}{2 - M - m} \right|. \tag{3.9.5}$$

Note that if $M < 1$, then $\rho(G_{[\omega^*]}) < 1$, no matter what m is. Therefore, as long as no eigenvalues exceed 1 algebraically, we can find an ω^* that produces a stable iteration. Even if G converges, that is, $-1 < m < M < 1$, we can accelerate convergence by shifting the spectrum so that it is symmetric about 0. Only when $M > 1$ and $m < -1$, that is, when G has both kinds of unstable roots, does (3.9.5) fail.

Successive Overrelaxation

Associated with Gauss-Seidel method is an extrapolation procedure called *successive overrelaxation* (SOR) method. For scalar ω, define

$$x_i^{k+1} = \omega\left(\frac{1}{a_{ii}}\right)\left[b_i - \sum_{j=1}^{i-1} a_{ij} x_j^{k+1} - \sum_{j=i+1}^{n} a_{ij} x_j^k \right] + (1 - \omega) x_i^k. \tag{3.9.6}$$

This makes the ith component of the $k + 1$ iterate a linear combination, parameterized by ω, of the Gauss-Seidel value and the kth iterate.

Note that if the matrix A is decomposed into its diagonal, D, elements below the diagonal, L, and elements above the diagonal, U, then $A = D + L + U$ and SOR has the convenient matrix representation

$(D + \omega L) x^{k+1} = ((1 - \omega) D - \omega U) x^k + \omega b.$

If we define $M_\omega \equiv D + \omega L$ and $N_\omega \equiv (1 - \omega) D - \omega U$, then

$$x^{k+1} = M_\omega^{-1} N_\omega x^k + \omega M_\omega^{-1} b. \tag{3.9.7}$$

To enhance convergence, the best choice for ω is the solution to $\min_\omega \rho(M_\omega^{-1} N_\omega)$. The benefit from acceleration can be large, since the optimal ω, ω^*, can greatly increase the convergence rate. The problem is that ω^* is costly to compute. To address that problem, algorithms have been developed that initially set ω equal to some safe value and then adaptively adjust ω, using information about A generated as the iterations proceed. These *adaptive SOR* methods test several values for ω and try to move toward the best choice. See Hageman and Young (1981) for details.

We have discussed the ideas of stabilization and acceleration only for linear Gauss-Jacobi and Gauss-Seidel schemes. These ideas can also be used to stabilize and accelerate nonlinear methods, as indicated in algorithm 3.4.

Stabilizing an Unstable "Hog Cycle"

Figure 3.2 displayed a stable application of Gauss-Seidel to a tatonnement process. A different example is illustrated in figure 3.4. Here the inverse demand equation is $p = 21 - 3q$, line BD in figure 3.4, and the supply curve is $q = p/2 - 3$, line EC in

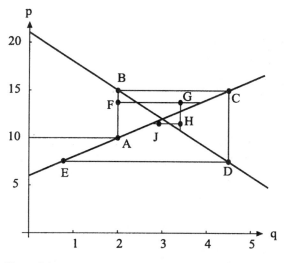

Figure 3.4
Dampening an unstable hog cycle

figure 3.4. The equilibrium system is

$$p + 3q = 21,$$
$$p - 2q = 6. \tag{3.9.8}$$

The system (3.9.8) is not diagonally dominant, indicating that convergence may be problematic. In fact figure 3.4 shows that Gauss-Seidel applied to (3.9.8) produces the iterative scheme

$$p_{n+1} = 21 - 3q_n, \tag{3.9.9a}$$
$$q_{n+1} = \tfrac{1}{2}p_{n+1} - 3, \tag{3.9.9b}$$

which is unstable. If we begin (3.9.9) at point A, where $(p, q) = (10, 2)$, the first iteration moves us first to B then C, and the second iteration moves us to D and then E. Since E is farther from the equilibrium than A, the iteration is diverging.

We will apply (3.9.6) to stabilize (3.9.9). If we choose $\omega = 0.75$, we arrive at the iteration

$$p_{n+1} = 0.75(21 - 3q_n) + 0.25p_n, \tag{3.9.10a}$$
$$q_{n+1} = 0.75(p_{n+1} - 3) + 0.25q_n. \tag{3.9.10b}$$

The difference between (3.9.9) and (3.9.10) is displayed in figure 3.4. In (3.9.9a) we move from the point A on the supply curve up to the point B on the demand curve, whereas in (3.9.10a) we move only 75 percent of the way, stopping at F. Equation (3.9.10b) then moves us from F to a point G that is 75 percent of the way to the supply curve. The impact of $\omega = 0.75$ is to dampen any change we make. The second iteration of (3.9.10) sends us to J, a point much closer to the equilibrium than our starting point of A. This tells us that the dampened Gauss-Seidel process will converge to the equilibrium.

Accelerating Convergence in a Game

Figure 3.4 displayed an application of extrapolation which stabilized an unstable simple iteration. A different example is illustrated in figure 3.5. Here we have the reaction curves of two price-setting duopolists, where firm 2's reaction curve is $p_2 = 2 + 0.80p_1 \equiv R_2(p_1)$ and firm one's reaction curve is $p_1 = 1 + 0.75p_2 \equiv R_1(p_2)$. The equilibrium system is

$$p_1 - 0.75p_2 = 1,$$
$$-0.80p_1 + p_2 = 2. \tag{3.9.11}$$

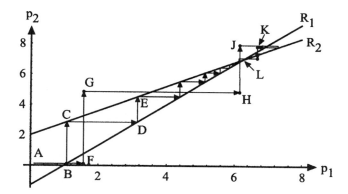

Figure 3.5
Accelerating a Nash equilibrium computation

The system (3.9.11) is diagonally dominant, indicating that both Gauss-Seidel and Gauss-Jacobi will converge. In fact figure 3.5 shows the iterates of Gauss-Seidel applied to (3.9.11), which is the iterative scheme

$$p_1^{n+1} = 1 + 0.75p_2^n, \tag{3.9.12a}$$

$$p_2^{n+1} = 2 + 0.80p_1^{n+1}. \tag{3.9.12b}$$

If we begin (3.9.12) at point A, where $(p_1, p_2) = (0.1, 0.1)$, the first iteration moves us first to B then C, and the second iteration moves us to D and then E, clearly converging to the equilibrium at $(6.25, 7.0)$.

We will apply (3.9.6) to accelerate (3.9.12). If we choose $\omega = 1.5$, we arrive at the iteration

$$p_1^{n+1} = 1.5(1 + 0.75p_2^n) - 0.5p_1^n, \tag{3.9.13a}$$

$$p_2^{n+1} = 1.5(2 + 0.80p_1^{n+1}) - 0.5p_2^n. \tag{3.9.13b}$$

The difference between (3.9.12) and (3.9.13) is displayed in figure 3.5. In (3.9.12a) we move from the point A right to the point B on player one's reaction curve, whereas in (3.9.13a) we move 50 percent further, continuing on to F. Equation (3.9.13b) then moves us from F to a point G which is 50 percent beyond player two's reaction curve. The impact of $\omega = 1.5$ is to exaggerate any change we make. The second iteration of (3.9.13) sends us to J, a point much closer to the equilibrium than point E which is the outcome of two unaccelerated Gauss-Seidel iterations.

However, as we approach the solution, the extrapolated iteration overshoots the solution and must work its way back to the solution. This is illustrated by the fact that from J the accelerated algorithm moves to K which is northeast of the solution. From K the algorithm moves to L, moving back toward the solution. This over-shooting occurs because of the exaggeration inherent in $\omega > 1$. Such an extrapolation gets us in the neighborhood of the true solution more quickly, but it may lead to extraneous oscillation. Even with this overshooting, L is a better approximation to the true solution the unaccelerated Gauss-Seidel iterate after four iterations.

Gauss-Jacobi and Gauss-Seidel schemes and their accelerations are at best linearly convergent; this comment remains true also for the accelerated methods. Acceleration changes the linear rate of convergence but does not change linear convergence to, say, quadratic of convergence. We have not explicitly discussed stopping rules for these iteratives schemes. One can implement the rules discussed in Section 2.8. The key fact is that these schemes, unaccelerated and accelerated, are linearly convergent, and therefore we should use rules like (2.8.6) with estimated rates of convergence.

3.10   Calculating A^{-1}

Computing the inverse of a matrix is a costly problem and is therefore avoided whenever possible. For most purposes in numerical methods, we only need $A^{-1}b$ for a few choices of b, in which case it is better to compute $x = A^{-1}b$ by solving the linear system $Ax = b$. This is an important rule: Whenever you see $x = A^{-1}b$, think $Ax = b$ and use a linear equation solution method.

We will sometimes want to compute A^{-1}. This will be true if we need to compute $A^{-1}b$ for more than n choices of b. Repeated use of the LU method is an efficient way to compute A^{-1}. If e^i is the ith column vector of the identity matrix, then the solution to $Ax = e^i$ is the ith column of A^{-1}. Therefore to compute A^{-1}, one factors A into its LU decomposition which is then used to solve n linear equations, a total of $\mathcal{O}(n^3)$ operations.

Decomposition methods will compute A^{-1} to the precision of the machine. Sometimes we are satisfied with a less precise estimate of A^{-1}. In that case there are some iterative schemes that can be used. It is also possible that an iterative scheme converges rapidly and actually dominates LU decomposition. One iterative scheme to calculate matrix inverses is given by Neuman's lemma and follows the idea of operator splitting and iteration.

LEMMA 3.10.1 (Neuman)   Let B be a $n \times n$ matrix. If $\rho(B) < 1$, then $(I - B)^{-1}$ exists, and

$$(I - B)^{-1} = \sum_{k=0}^{\infty} B^k.$$

Proof Since $\rho(B) < 1$, all of the eigenvalues of B, λ_i, differ from unity, and the eigenvalues of $I - B$, $1 - \lambda_i$, must be nonzero. Therefore $I - B$ is nonsingular. The identity

$$(I - B)(I + B + B^2 + \cdots + B^k) = I - B^{k+1}$$

implies that

$$I + B + \cdots + B^k = (I - B)^{-1} - (I - B)^{-1} B^{k+1}.$$

Since the modulus of each of the eigenvalues of B is less than unity, B^{k+1} goes to zero as k increases, proving the lemma. ■

Neuman's lemma will be important in understanding some dynamic programming methods. Furthermore it is really much more general. The only property of B that we used in the proof was that it was a linear operator all of whose eigenvalues were less than unity in modulus. If the spectral radius is small, then the convergence is rapid, and good approximations to A^{-1} can be quickly computed.

3.11   Computing Ergodic Distributions

A common step in the numerical analysis of stochastic economic models is the computation of an ergodic distribution and its moments. In this section we discuss methods for approximating ergodic distributions.

Finite Markov Chains

Let $\Pi = (\pi_{ij})$ be an n-state Markov transition matrix. If x is the ergodic distribution,[2] then $x\Pi = x$, which can also be expressed as the linear system $x(\Pi - I) = 0$. However, this equation is a homogeneous linear equation; therefore, if x is a solution, so is αx for any $\alpha \in R$. The ergodic distribution is fixed by imposing the additional

---

2. In this section x will be a row vector in order to remain consistent with the notation from probability theory. We then have a problem of the form $xA = b$. This creates no essential problem because it can be transformed into the equivalent problem $A^\top x^\top = b^\top$.

condition $\sum x_i = 1$ which makes x a probability measure. Therefore a direct way to compute the ergodic distribution is to replace the last column of $\Pi - I$ with a vector of ones and solve the resulting linear system:

$$x \begin{pmatrix} \pi_{11} - 1 & \pi_{12} & \cdots & \pi_{1,n-1} & 1 \\ \pi_{21} & \pi_{22} - 1 & \cdots & \pi_{2,n-1} & 1 \\ \vdots & \vdots & \ddots & \vdots & \vdots \\ \pi_{n-1,1} & \pi_{n-1,2} & \cdots & \pi_{n-1,n-1} - 1 & 1 \\ \pi_{n,1} & \pi_{n,2} & \cdots & \pi_{n,n-1} & 1 \end{pmatrix} = (0, \ldots, 0, 1). \tag{3.12.1}$$

We see here that the altered last column forces $\sum x_i = 1$, while the other columns enforce the ergodicity conditions.

An alternative procedure is suggested by a basic theorem of Markov chains:

THEOREM 3.11.1   If Π is a Markov transition matrix, then $x = \lim_{k \to \infty} x^0 \Pi^k$ is an ergodic distribution for any $x^0 \in R^n$. If Π is *irreducible*, that is, for each pair of states (i, j) there is positive probability of going from state i to state j in a finite number of transitions, then x is the unique ergodic distribution.

This suggests that one way to compute an ergodic distribution is to compute the sequence $x^{k+1} = x^k \Pi$ for a large k. The choice between the direct method in (3.12.1), and this iterative method depends on the number of states and how many iterations are necessary for a good approximation. The direct linear equation approach takes $n^3/2$ multiplications. If we start with x^0, it takes mn^2 operations to compute $x^0 \Pi^m$. Therefore, if the number of iterations necessary to approximate the ergodic distribution is small relative to the number of states, one should iteratively calculate $x^0 \Pi^m$; otherwise, use the direct linear equation approach in (3.12.1).

The following example illustrates the principles. Suppose that an individual earns 0, 1, or 2 per period with equal probability. Suppose that he consumes a quarter of his wealth each period. We will approximate the problem with a Markov chain that takes on 12 wealth values, 1 through 12, inclusive. The transition law is approximated by assuming that consumption is rounded to the nearest integer. To compute the ergodic distribution of wealth, we choose an initial vector, v^1, and compute the sequence $v^{k+1} = v^k \Pi$. The columns in table 3.3 indicates the probability of being in state i at periods $k = 4, 8, 16, 32$ if initial wealth is 1, an initial condition represented by the probability vector v with $v_1 = 1$ and all other components equaling zero. Note the rapid convergence. In only 16 iterations we have computed a six-digit approximation of the ergodic distribution.

Table 3.3
Successive distributions of a Markov process

State	$k = 4$	$k = 8$	$k = 16$	$k = 32$
1	0.003906	0	0	0
2	0.082031	0.010117	0.008929	0.008929
3	0.140625	0.029119	0.026786	0.026786
4	0.199219	0.074844	0.071429	0.071429
5	0.242187	0.181837	0.178571	0.178571
6	0.167969	0.215218	0.214286	0.214286
7	0.109375	0.212991	0.214286	0.214286
8	0.050781	0.175156	0.178571	0.178571
9	0.003906	0.068163	0.071429	0.071429
10	0	0.024665	0.026786	0.026786
11	0	0.007890	0.008929	0.008929
12	0	0	0	0

Discrete Approximations of Continuous Chains

We will often want to analyze Markov processes on continuous spaces. One way to do that is to discretize a continuous chain. Suppose that a continuous process on a compact interval, $[a, b]$, is described by $F(x|y)$, that is, the probability of jumping to a point in $[a, x)$ from y equals $F(x|y)$.

We will construct an N-state approximation to the continuous process and compute the approximation's ergodic distribution. To do this, divide $[a, b]$ into N equal-sized intervals, with interval i being

$$I_i = [a + (i - 1)h, a + ih], \qquad i = 1, \dots, N,$$

where $h = (b - a)/N$. To construct the transition matrix, Π, we could focus on the midpoint of each interval and define

$$\pi_{i,j} = F(a + jh|a + (i - \tfrac{1}{2})h) - F(a + (j - 1)h|a + (i - \tfrac{1}{2})h). \qquad (3.12.2)$$

In words, the probability of going to state j from state i in the discrete approximation equals the probability of going to interval j from the center of interval i in the continuous chain.

Alternatively, we could focus on the "average" probability; this approximation is defined by

$$\pi_{i,j} = (b - a)^{-1} \int_{I_i} \int_{I_j} dF(x|y) \, dx \, dy.$$

Here the probability of going to state j from state i in the approximation equals the probability of going to interval j from the "average" point in interval i in the continuous chain.

3.12 Overidentified Systems

We began the chapter discussing the problem $Ax = b$ where A is square. Sometimes we will want to solve the system $Ax = b$ where A has more rows than columns, implying more linear equations than unknowns; this is an *overidentified* problem. Since there may be no solution to overidentified problems, we need first to redefine the concept of solution.

One common way is to define the solution to be the x that minimizes the Euclidean norm of the residual, $(Ax - b)^\top (Ax - b)$; this is called the *least squares solution*. This approach replaces a system of equations with an optimization problem and is equivalent if A is square. The least squares problem has a unique solution $(A^\top A)^{-1} A^\top b$ if $(A^\top A)^{-1}$ is nonsingular.

3.13 Software

There is much software available for linear algebra. The standard library of programs performing the basic linear operations is called BLAS (basic linear algebra subroutines). Double precision versions are often called DBLAS. LAPACK is a library combining linear algebra and eigenvalue routines. It can be downloaded from netlib, but your local mainframe or network is the most appropriate source, since it may have versions tuned to the hardware. To do the exercises in future chapters, one needs programs for matrix and vector arithmetic, matrix inversion, LU and Cholesky decomposition, computing determinants, solving linear systems, and computing eigenvalues and eigenvectors of general matrices. There are several ways to represent sparse matrices. The scheme described in the text is a simple and direct method, but not the most efficient approach. Some of the more popular approaches are the Yale Sparse Matrix Package and PCGPACK.

Software like Matlab and Gauss are very good at doing linear algebra and are easy to use. Matlab offers easy-to-use sparse matrix capabilities. If one is doing only linear algebra, these are as good as Fortran or C and easier to use. However, such languages are not as competitive if one also needs to do nonlinear procedures that cannot be vectorized.

3.14 Summary and Further Reading

This chapter has discussed basic solution methods for linear equations and introduced several basic ideas which are used in many numerical analysis. The basic linear
solution methods, such as LU and Cholesky decomposition, are used in many
numerical procedures. The performance of linear and nonlinear numerical procedures
depends on the condition number of the critical matrices; therefore the conditioning
of a matrix is one of the most important concepts in numerical mathematics.

We introduced iteration ideas and applied them to linear problems. The key features are the construction of iterative schemes applying Gauss-Jacobi or Gauss-Seidel
substitution schemes, and developing stabilization and acceleration ideas. Young
(1971) and Hageman and Young (1981) discuss iterative procedures for linear equations. Many of these ideas are intuitive for economists, since they correspond to basic
ideas in economic dynamics, such as hog cycles and strategic stability. The iteration
ideas introduced here for linear problems are applicable to nonlinear problems as
well.

There are several excellent monographs on numerical linear algebra, including
Golub and van Loan (1983). Most basic numerical analysis texts contain extensive
formal developments of the topics covered in this chapter; in particular, see Stoer and
Burlisch (1980).

Exercises

1. Write programs for LU decomposition (without pivoting) and Cholesky decomposition. Using
    these programs, compute the following:

    a. The LU decomposition of

    $$A = \begin{pmatrix} 54 & 14 & -11 & 2 \\ 14 & 50 & -4 & 29 \\ -11 & -4 & 55 & 22 \\ 2 & 29 & 22 & 95 \end{pmatrix}.$$

    b. The LU decomposition of

    $$B = \begin{pmatrix} 54 & -9 & 18 & 9 \\ 6 & 23 & -2 & 9 \\ -12 & 14 & 34 & -3 \\ -6 & 13 & 20 & 49 \end{pmatrix}.$$

    c. The Cholesky decomposition of A.

2.   Solve $Ax = b$ for

$$A = \begin{pmatrix} 54 & 14 & -11 & 2 \\ 14 & 50 & -4 & 29 \\ -11 & -4 & 55 & 22 \\ 2 & 29 & 22 & 95 \end{pmatrix}, \quad b = \begin{pmatrix} 1 \\ 1 \\ 1 \\ 1 \end{pmatrix},$$

by (a) *LU* decomposition, (b) Cholesky decomposition, (c) Gauss-Jacobi, (d) Gauss-Siedel, (e) successive overrelaxation, (f) block Gauss-Jacobi (two blocks of 2×2 systems), (g) block Gauss-Siedel (two blocks of 2×2 systems), and (h) Cramer's rule.

3.   Define A_n to be the $n \times n$ matrix

$$A_n = \begin{pmatrix} 2 & 1 & 0 & \cdots & 0 \\ 1 & 2 & 1 & \cdots & 0 \\ \vdots & \vdots & \vdots & \ddots & \vdots \\ 0 & \cdots & \cdots & \cdots & 2 \end{pmatrix}.$$

The unique solution to $A_n x = 0$ is $x = 0_n$.

a. Solve $A_n x = 0$ for $n = 5, 10, 20$, and 50 using Gauss-Jacobi, Gauss-Seidel, and successive overrelaxation with $\omega = (0.1)l$, $l = 1, \ldots, 20$, and initial guess $x_i^0 = 1$, $i = 1, \ldots, n$.

b. How many iterations are required for each method to get the error (defined to be the maximum error among the n components of x) under 0.01? under 0.001? under 0.0001?

c. Plot the spectral radius of the $M_\omega^{-1} N_\omega$ matrix in successive overrelaxation (see 3.9.7) as a function of ω.

d. Which value of ω was best? How much better was the best ω relative to $\omega = 1$?

4.   Assume that $x \in R$ follows the process $x_{t+1} = \rho x_t + \varepsilon_{t+1}$ where $\rho < 1$ and that the ε_t are i.i.d. and uniformly distributed on $[-1, 1]$. Write a n-state approximation for the Markov transition matrix for this process, $n = 5, 10, 25, 100$, and compute the ergodic distribution for $\rho = 0.8, 0.5$, 0.2. Compare the two methods discussed in the text for discretizing a continuous-state Markov chain.

5.   Use sparse matrix methods to model the ergodic distribution of wealth where an individual's wealth fluctuates because of i.i.d. wage shocks and expenditures. Assume that there are N possible wealth states and that π is the transition matrix where

$$\pi_{ij} = \text{Prob}\{\text{tomorrow's wealth is } w_j \mid \text{current wealth is } w_i.\}$$

Assume there are $N = 1,001$ wealth states. Assume that in each state there is a small probability, 0.01, of losing all wealth and that wealth stays constant or goes up or down by 10 states. Specifically, if $i < 10$, then $\pi_{i,0} = 0.34$, and $\pi_{i,i} = \pi_{i,i+10} = 0.33$; if $10 \leq i \leq 990$, wealth is equally likely to move to w_{i-10}, w_i, and w_{i+10}; and if $i > 990$, then $\pi_{i,i-10} = \pi_{i,i} = 0.33$, and $\pi_{i,N} = 0.33$. In this case each row of π has three or four nonzero elements.

a. Compute the ergodic distribution of wealth.

b. Compute the mean, variance, and skewness of the ergodic distribution.

c. Repeat this exercise for the $N = 10^2$, 10^3, and 10^4 discretizations of the continuous process $w_{t+1} = 1.03w_t - 0.001w_t^2 + \varepsilon_t$ where the $\varepsilon \sim U[0, 1]$.

6. Suppose that demand for good i is

$$d_i(p) = a_i \sum_{j \neq i} p_j - b_i p_i + c_i, \qquad i = 1, \ldots n,$$

where $a_i > b_i > 0$, and that supply is

$$s_i(p) = A_i + B_i p_i, \quad i = 1, \ldots, n,$$

where $B_i > 0$. Write a program to solve for equilibrium with sensible choices of a_i, b_i, A_i, and B_i. That means read in the parameters, check that they are consistent with commonsense economics (downward sloping demand curves, increasing supply curves, and concave utility), and output the equilibrium prices and outputs.

7. Suppose that three Cournot duopolists have the reaction curves

$$q_1 = 5 - 0.5q_2 - 0.3q_3,$$

$$q_2 = 7 - 0.6q_1 - 0.1q_3,$$

$$q_3 = 4 - 0.2q_1 - 0.4q_2.$$

Compute equilibrium using fixed-point iteration and extrapolation. What is the optimal extrapolation factor?

8. Let A be a matrix of zeros except that $a_{ii} = 2$ for odd i, $a_{ii} = 3$ for even i, and $a_{i,i-1} = a_{i,i+1} = 1$ for $i = 1, 2, \ldots, 1000$. Let $b_i = 1001 - i$, $i = 1, 2, \ldots, 1000$. Solve $Ax = b$.

4 Optimization

The chief behavioral assumption in economics is that agents optimize. Economists assume that firms minimize costs and maximize profits, consumers maximize utility, players maximize payoffs, and social planners maximize social welfare. Econometricians also use optimization methods in least squares, method of moments, and maximum likelihood estimation procedures. These considerations make optimization methods a central numerical technique in economic analysis.

The most general optimization problem minimizes[1] an objective function subject to equality and inequality constraints:

$$\min_x \ f(x)$$

$$\text{s.t.} \quad g(x) = 0,$$

$$\quad\quad h(x) \leq 0,$$

where $f \colon R^n \to R$ is the *objective function*, $g \colon R^n \to R^m$ is the vector of m *equality constraints*, and $h \colon R^n \to R^l$ is the vector of l *inequality constraints*. Examples of such problems include relatively simple problems such as the maximization of consumer utility subject to a linear budget constraint, as well as the more complex problems from principal-agent theory. We generally assume that f, g, and h are continuous, although that will not always be necessary.

All numerical optimization methods search through the space of feasible choices, generating a sequence of guesses that should converge to the true solution. Methods differ in the kind of information they use. The simplest methods compute the objective and constraint functions at several points and pick the feasible point yielding the largest value. These *comparison methods* need no derivative information. A second class of methods uses the gradients of the objective and constraints in their search for better points. A third class of methods uses both gradient and curvature information about the objective and constraints.

This chapter will examine algorithms of all types, since they have different strengths and all have uses in economic problems. Comparison methods require no smoothness conditions on the objective of constraints, but they are generally slow to converge. Comparison methods are suitable for problems with kinks and some kinds of discontinuities. Gradient methods require differentiability of the objective and constraints. They also use little space, an important consideration when the number of variables is large. Methods that use curvature information require even more

---

1. We examine minimization problems, since maximizing f is the same as minimizing $-f$. Also most optimization software is geared for minimization, so we need to get used to transforming maximization problems into minimization problems.

smoothness of the objective and constraints, but they may converge more rapidly to the solution. However, curvature-based methods are generally confined to problems with only a moderate number of variables because of the high cost of computing and storing Hessians.

The chapter first examines one-dimensional unconstrained optimization problems, then multidimensional unconstrained optimization problems, and finally general multidimensional constrained problems. Nonlinear least squares problems are common in economics and have special algorithms which are discussed here. The chapter finishes with applications of optimization to the computation of Nash equilibria, portfolio problems, dynamic life-cycle consumption profiles, and allocation problems affected by incentive compatibility constraints.

4.1   One-Dimensional Minimization

The simplest optimization problem is the scalar unconstrained problem:

$$\min_{x \in R} f(x),$$

where $f: R \to R$. We first focus on one-dimensional problems for two reasons. First, they illustrate basic techniques in a clear fashion. Second, one-dimensional methods are particularly important since many multivariate methods reduce to solving a sequence of one-dimensional problems. Efficient and reliable methods for one-dimensional problems are essential ingredients of efficient multivariate algorithms.

Bracketing Method

The simplest one-dimensional optimization scheme is a comparison method called the *bracketing algorithm*. Suppose that we have found points a, b, and c such that

$$a < b < c,$$
$$f(a), \ f(c) > f(b).$$

$$(4.1.1)$$

Figure 4.1 illustrates such a case, and algorithm 4.1 outlines the bracketing method. These conditions imply that a local minimum exists somewhere in $[a, c]$; that is, we have bracketed a minimum. We now need to find a smaller interval that brackets some minimum in $[a, c]$. To do this, we pick a fourth point $d \in (a, c)$. Suppose that $d \in (a, b]$. Then, if $f(d) > f(b)$, we know that there is some minimum in $[d, c]$. If $f(d) < f(b)$, as in figure 4.1, then there is some minimum in $[a, b]$. If $d \in [b, c)$, we similarly would find a smaller interval that brackets a minimum. In any case we have

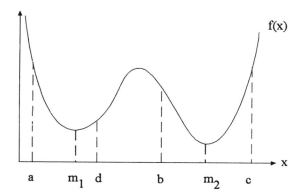

Figure 4.1
Bracketing method

bracketed a minima with a smaller interval. With the new triple, we can repeat this step again, and bracket a minimum with an even smaller interval.

Algorithm 4.1   Bracketing Algorithm

Initialization. Find $a < b < c$ such that $f(a)$, $f(c) > f(b)$. Choose a stopping criterion ε.

Step 1. Choose d: If $b - a < c - b$, then set $d = (b + c)/2$; otherwise, $d = (a + b)/2$.

Step 2. Compute $f(d)$.

Step 3. Choose new (a, b, c) triple: If $d < b$ and $f(d) > f(b)$, then replace (a, b, c) with (d, b, c). If $d < b$ and $f(d) < f(b)$, then replace (a, b, c) with (a, d, b). If $d > b$ and $f(d) < f(b)$, then replace (a, b, c) with (b, d, c). Otherwise, replace (a, b, c) with (a, b, d).

Step 4. Stopping criterion: If $c - a < \varepsilon$, STOP. Otherwise, go to step 1.

Before we begin a comparison procedure, we must find points a, b, and c that satisfy the conditions in (4.1.1). This is generally done by picking some point x_0, constant $\alpha > 1$, and step Δ, computing $f(x_0)$, $f(x_0 \pm \alpha\Delta)$, $f(x_0 \pm \alpha^2\Delta)$, ..., until we get a triple satisfying (4.1.1).

The stopping criterion for the comparison method is quite simple. Since the bracketing interval is (a, c) at each iteration, we just compare $c - a$ to some maximum permissible value ε. We want to choose ε so that bracketing the minimum in (a, c) is "practically" the same as knowing the true minimum, but given the slow speed of the method, ε should not be smaller than necessary.

The comparison method will be slow, but it makes few requirements of the objective function. In particular, it will work for any continuous, bounded function on a finite interval, no matter how jagged it may be. One must keep in mind, however, that the only guarantee is that the comparison method will find a local minimum. In figure 4.1 the comparison method starting with $f(x)$ at a, b, and c will converge to the local minimum at m_1 instead of the global minimum at m_2. This problem of converging to local extrema instead of global extrema will arise with any optimization method. If we know that the problem has only one solution, say, because the objective is convex, then this problem will not arise.

Newton's Method

For C^2 functions $f(x)$, Newton's method is often used. The idea behind Newton's method is to start at a point a and find the quadratic polynomial, $p(x)$, that approximates $f(x)$ at a to the second degree, implying that

$$p(x) \equiv f(a) + f'(a)(x-a) + \frac{f''(a)}{2}(x-a)^2.$$

If $f''(a) > 0$, then p is convex. We next approximately minimize f by finding the point x_m which minimizes $p(x)$. The minimizing value is $x_m = a - f'(a)/f''(a)$. If $p(x)$ is a good global approximation to $f(x)$, then x_m is close to the minimum of $f(x)$. In any case the hope is that x_m is closer than a to the minimum. Furthermore we hope that if we repeat this step, we will get even closer.

These considerations motivate *Newton's method*:[2]

$$x_{n+1} = x_n - \frac{f'(x_n)}{f''(x_n)}. \tag{4.1.2}$$

Note that Newton's method does not care if f is concave or convex. Newton's method is really trying to find critical points, that is, solutions to $f'(x) = 0$. If Newton's method converges to x^*, we must check $f''(x^*)$ to determine if x^* is a local minimum or a local maximum.

The problems with Newton's method are several. First, it may not converge. Second, $f''(x)$ may be difficult to calculate. The good news is that Newton's method converges rapidly if we have a good initial guess.

THEOREM 4.1.1   Suppose that $f(x)$ is minimized at x^*, C^3 in a neighborhood of x^*, and that $f''(x^*) \neq 0$. Then there is some $\varepsilon > 0$ such that if $|x_0 - x^*| < \varepsilon$, then the x_n

2. Actually a more proper name is the Newton-Raphson-Simpson method, but this text uses the term Newton's method. See Ypma (1995) and Kollerstrom (1992) for intellectual histories of Newton's method.

sequence defined in (4.1.2) converges quadratically to x^*; in particular,

$$\lim_{n \to \infty} \frac{|x_{n+1} - x^*|}{|x_n - x^*|^2} = \frac{1}{2} \left| \frac{f'''(x^*)}{f''(x^*)} \right| \tag{4.1.3}$$

is the quadratic rate of convergence.

Proof Since f is C^3, $f'(x^*) = 0 \neq f''(x^*)$ and f' is C^2. Taylor's theorem says that

$$f'(x) = f'(x_n) + f''(x_n)(x - x_n) + \tfrac{1}{2}f'''(\eta_n(x))(x - x_n)^2 \tag{4.1.4}$$

for some function $\eta_n(x) \in [x_n, x] \cup [x, x_n]$. Given (4.1.2) and $f'(x^*) = 0$, the Taylor expansion (4.1.4) at $x = x^*$ implies that

$$|x_{n+1} - x^*| = \frac{1}{2} \left| \frac{f'''(\eta_n(x^*))(x^* - x_n)^2}{f''(x_n)} \right|. \tag{4.1.5}$$

For any $\beta \in (0, 1)$, if $|x_m - x^*|$ is sufficiently small, (4.1.5) shows that $|x_{n+1} - x^*| < \beta |x_n - x^*|$ for $n > m$, which implies $x_n \to x^*$. Furthermore, along a convergent sequence, (4.1.5) implies (4.1.3), which is finite if $f''(x^*) \neq 0$. ∎

This rapid quadratic convergence makes Newton's method particularly powerful. The weaknesses are also significant but often manageable in practice, as we will see later.

Stopping Rule

Even if Newton's method would converge to the true minimum, that is only an asymptotic property. We still need to decide when to stop the iteration. We will want to stop the iteration when $x_k - x^*$ is "unimportant." Even after choosing an acceptable error, ε, it is unclear how to be sure that some x_k is within ε of x^*. Unlike the comparison method the iterates of Newton's method do not bracket a minimum.

In the case of a one-dimensional problem, we could switch to a comparison method once we think Newton's method is close to a solution. That is, once $|x_k - x_{k+1}| < \varepsilon$, then we could begin the comparison method with some interval $[a, b]$ containing $[x_k, x_{k+1}]$ satisfying conditions (4.1.1), thereby bracketing a minimum.

Since $f'(x^*) = 0$, we are inclined to stop whenever $f'(x_k)$ is small; however, the curvature $f''(x^*)$ indicates the wisdom of this. If $f''(x^*)$ is close to zero, there are many points where $f'(x)$ is nearly zero, some not near x^*; hence it is not sufficient to stop when $f'(x_k)$ is nearly zero. Therefore the standard stopping condition requires that $f'(x_k)$ is nearly zero, and that the last two iterates are very close.

When we combine the Newton iteration (4.1.2) with these stopping tests, we arrive at Newton's method:

Algorithm 4.2   Newton's Method in R^1

Initialization. Choose initial guess x_0 and stopping parameters $\delta, \varepsilon > 0$.

Step 1. $x_{k+1} = x_k - f'(x_k)/f''(x_k)$.

Step 2. If $|x_k - x_{k+1}| < \varepsilon(1 + |x_k|)$ and $|f'(x_k)| < \delta$, STOP and report success; else go to step 1.

Since Newton's method is quadratically convergent, the stopping rule in step 2 will produce a solution that has an error of order ε unless f is nearly flat and/or has rapidly changing curvature in a large neighborhood of the solution. We can even test for these problems by computing f'' at some points near the candidate solution.

Consumer Budget Example

To illustrate these three methods, we will consider a utility maximization problem. Suppose that a consumer has \$1 to spend on goods x and y, the price of x is \$2, the price of y is \$3, and his utility function is $x^{1/2} + 2y^{1/2}$. Let θ be the amount spent on x with the remainder, $1 - \theta$, spent on y. The consumer choice problem then reduces to

$$\max_{\theta} \left(\frac{\theta}{2}\right)^{1/2} + 2\left(\frac{1-\theta}{3}\right)^{1/2} \tag{4.1.6}$$

which has the solution $\theta^* = 3/11 = 0.272727\ldots$.

To apply the comparison method, we need to bracket the optimal θ. From the form of the utility function, it is clear that the optimal θ lies between 0 and 1. Therefore we let $a = 0$, $b = 0.5$, and $c = 1.0$ initially, and generate a sequence of (a, b, c) triples, where at each iterate b is the minimal value of θ thus far tested. The new minimum points form the sequence

0.5, 0.5, 0.25, 0.25, 0.25, 0.25, 0.281, 0.281, 0.266, 0.2737.

The apparent rate of convergence is slow as predicted.

We next examine Newton's method. If $\theta_0 = \frac{1}{2}$ is the initial guess, then the Newton iteration applied to (4.1.6) yields the sequence

0.2595917942, 0.2724249335, 0.2727271048, 0.2727272727,

which we see is rapidly converging to the solution. The first iterate has only one correct digit, the second has three, the third has six, and the fourth ten (at least). The convergence is clearly quadratic.

We see here that each method will converge to the true solution. However, the Newton method is far faster once we get close.

Importance of Scaling

We will use the consumer example to illustrate what can happen if we use excessively small or large numbers; the resulting difficulties are called *scaling* problems. We repeat the consumer problem except this time we use the utility function $-e^{-x} - e^{-y}$ and with income \$10,000. In terms of θ, the objective becomes $-e^{-10,000\theta/2} - e^{-10,000(1-\theta)/3}$. On most machines this problem leads to severe difficulties and cannot be solved. The problem is that for any value of θ either $e^{-10,000\theta/2}$ or $e^{-10,000(1-\theta)/3}$ (or both) will cause underflow, leading to the computer stopping or, even worse, continuing by assigning a value of zero to the term.

What is to be done in cases such as this? In this case we must use a different approach. The first-order conditions imply the budget constraint $2x + 3y = 10000$ and the marginal rate of substitution condition $y - x = \log(\frac{2}{3})$, a pair of equations that is easy to solve numerically. In general, we must choose units and/or formulate the problem to minimize the likelihood of overflow and underflow.

Global Optimization

Our optimization methods are designed to find a local minimum of a function; there is no assurance that they will find the global minimum. If one starts a Newton iteration from a point sufficiently close to the global minimum, then theorem 4.1.1 says that Newton's method will converge to the global minimum, but any of these methods may stop at a local minimum different from the global minimum.

There are no good ways to find the global optimum. If we know that a function is convex (concave), then any local minimum (maximum) is also the unique global minimum (maximum). Outside of such special cases, it is difficult to be sure that one has a global minimum. These difficulties arise frequently in economics. Likelihood functions, for example, often have multiple local maxima, making life difficult for econometricians using maximum likelihood estimation. In practice, one deals with this problem by restarting the optimization method with several different initial guesses, taking the best of the resulting local optima as the global optimum. It is easy to be lazy and try just, say, ten restarts. Experience indicates that one should do as many restarts as is feasible. In any case, global optimization problems are difficult outside of special cases, and one must develop careful heuristics to reduce the chance of gross error.

4.2 Multidimensional Optimization: Comparison Methods

Most interesting optimization problems in economics involves several variables. The generic unconstrained problem is

$$\min_x f(x) \tag{4.2.1}$$

for $f: R^n \to R^n$. For convenience, we assume that f is continuous although some of the methods we discuss will work more generally. To solve (4.2.1), we must develop methods more sophisticated than the one-dimensional case. This section discusses the most basic methods applicable to all problems.

Grid Search

The most primitive procedure to minimize a function is to specify a grid of points, say, between 100 and 1000 points, evaluate $f(x)$ at these points, and pick the minimum. We are often impatient and want to immediately use more sophisticated methods, but many practical considerations argue for first doing a grid search.

Even though we would seldom stop at this point, the results of this preliminary search will often be very useful. For example, if we are trying to maximize a likelihood function, the result of these calculations may indicate the general curvature of the likelihood function. If the grid search indicates that the function is flat over a wide range, there is little reason to proceed with more sophisticated methods. If the grid search indicates that there are multiple local optima, then we will need to work hard to find the global optimum. Also, if the Hessian at the best point on the grid is poorly conditioned, then it is unlikely that the more sophisticated methods discussed below can be effective. The grid search should produce good initial guesses for better methods.

If we know that the objective is smooth with well-conditioned curvature and unique local optimum, this preliminary step is less useful. However, outside of such special cases, we need the information provided by a grid search. Even for well-behaved cases, a grid search will at least provide a test of whether we have correctly coded the objective function. Despite the natural inclination to try supposedly better methods first, it is always a good idea to begin with a grid search for any problem.

Polytope Methods

We first examine *polytope* methods, which take a simple but robust approach to multivariate optimization. Polytope methods are multidimensional comparison methods. They require no smoothness conditions on the objective. They are easy to program and are reliable, but slow.

The general idea is to think of someone going down a hill. The method first constructs a simplex in R^n, which we will denote by its set of vertices, $\{x^1, \ldots, x^{n+1}\}$. The simplex should have full dimension, that is, the $n + 1$ vertices should not lie on a

$(n-1)$-dimensional hyperplane. One simple initial choice for this set is $(0, 0, \ldots, 0)$ plus all n points of the form $(0, \ldots, 0, 1, 0, \ldots, 0)$. In each iteration we throw out a vertex with a high objective value and replace it with one of lower value, converging ultimately to a minimum.

Specifically, we begin by numbering the simplex's vertices so that

$$f(x^i) \geq f(x^{i+1}), \qquad i = 1, \ldots, n. \tag{4.2.2}$$

We want to replace the current simplex with another resting on lower points. Since f is greatest at x^1, we try to find some point x to replace x^1 in the simplex. Since f is large at x^1, there is a good chance that f declines along the ray from x^1 to the opposing face. Hence our first guess, y^1, will be the reflection of x^1 through the opposing face. If $f(y^1) < f(x^1)$, then we have succeeded in finding a suitable replacement for x^1, whereupon we drop x^1 from our simplex, add y^1, reorder according to (4.2.2), and again try to find a replacement for the vertex at which f is greatest.

If $f(y^1) \geq f(x^1)$, we then need to check other points. The simple polytope method turns to x^2 and attempts to replace x^2 with its reflection, y^2. We continue this until we find some x^i and its reflection y^i such that $f(y^i) < f(x^i)$. If we succeed in finding such a x^i, we make the replacement, renumber the vertices so that (4.2.2) holds, and begin again trying to replace one of the vertices with its reflection. Sometimes we may not find any such reflection. This will happen when the simplex is too large for the reflection process to work. In this case we shrink (say by half) the simplex toward x^{n+1}, the vertex where f is smallest. We renumber the resulting simplex, and begin again the replacement process.

Algorithm 4.3 Polytope Algorithm

Initialization. Choose the stopping rule parameter ε. Choose an initial simplex $\{x^1, x^2, \ldots, x^{n+1}\}$.

Step 1. Reorder the simplex vertices so that $f(x^i) \geq f(x^{i+1})$, $i = 1, \ldots, n$.

Step 2. Find the least i such that $f(x^i) > f(y^i)$ where y^i is the reflection of x^i. If such an i exists, set $x^i = y^i$, and go to step 1. Otherwise, go to step 3.

Step 3. Stopping rule: If the width of the current simplex is less than ε, STOP. Otherwise, go to step 4.

Step 4. Shrink simplex: For $i = 1, 2, \ldots, n$ set $x^i = \frac{1}{2}(x^i + x^{n+1})$, and go to step 1.

Figure 4.2 gives a typical example of such a simplex in R^2, and illustrates a typical iteration. Suppose that the initial simplex is ABC with $f(A) > f(B) > f(C)$. In this

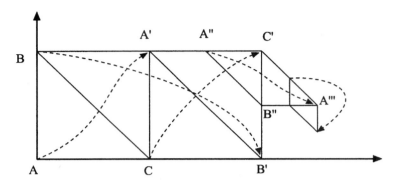

Figure 4.2
Polytope method

example, let $f(A') < f(A)$ where A' is the reflection of A with respect to the simplex ABC; then the first step replaces A with A' to produce the simplex $BA'C$. Suppose that simple comparisons of points with their reflections next replaces B with its reflection relative to $BA'C$, B', to produce $A'B'C$, and then replaces C with C' to arrive at $A'B'C'$. These simple comparisons will generally produce some progress.

However, simple reflection comparisons will eventually come to a halt. Suppose that there is no suitable reflection for $A'B'C'$ but that the lowest value is at C'. The polytope algorithm then replaces $A'B'C'$ with $A''B''C'$ by shrinking A' and B' toward C'. We then attempt the reflection step with $A''B''C'$, arriving at, say $A'''B''C'$, and continue from there with simple reflection comparisons. We continue to alternate between reflection replacements and shrinking steps.

Polytope methods will find a minimum of a continuous function because they have an important property: They always move downhill by a nontrivial amount. They also can handle discontinuous objectives. However, they are slow. For smooth objectives, far faster methods are available.

If we let the polytope algorithm proceed forever, the simplex would converge to a local minima for any continous function $f(x)$. In real life we must derive a criterion that causes the iterations to end in finite time and produce a good approximation to a minimum. We stop when we come to a point where all reflections produce higher values of f and the simplex is smaller than some critical size. However, we must realize that there is no guarantee that a minimum is inside the final simplex, or even near it. This is a major difference between one-dimensional and multidimensional problems; we can bracket minima in one dimension but not in many dimensions.

4.3 Newton's Method for Multivariate Problems

While comparison algorithms for (4.2.1) are generally useful because they rely on little information about the objective, they do not take advantage of extra information when it is available. Objective functions, such as utility functions and profit functions, are often smooth with many derivatives. We can construct superior algorithms by taking advantage of derivatives when they are available. We denote

$$\nabla f(x) = \left(\frac{\partial f}{\partial x_1}(x), \ldots, \frac{\partial f}{\partial x_n}(x) \right), \quad H(x) = \left(\frac{\partial^2 f}{\partial x_i \, \partial x_j}(x) \right)_{i,j=1}^n$$

to be the gradient and Hessian of f at x. Note that x is a column vector and that the gradient is a row vector.

Newton's method is a simple approach that often yields rapid solutions to C^2 problems. Consider the special case of quadratic minimization. If $f(x) = \frac{1}{2}x^\top A x + b^\top x$ where A is symmetric positive definite, the minimum is at $x^* = -A^{-1}b$. If A is not positive definite, x^* is still a critical point of $f(x)$.

If f is convex but not quadratic, we generally cannot directly solve for its minimum. However, we can replace f locally with a quadratic approximation and solve for the minimum of the approximation. In Newton's method we examine a sequence of points, x^k, where at each iteration we replace $f(x)$ with a quadratic approximation of f based at x^k and choose x^{k+1} to be the critical point of the local approximation. At x^k that quadratic approximation is $f(x) \doteq f(x^k) + \nabla f(x^k)(x - x^k) + \frac{1}{2}(x - x^k)^\top H(x^k)(x - x^k)$. If f is convex, then $H(x^k)$ is positive definite, and the approximation has a minimum at $x^k - H(x^k)^{-1} \nabla (f(x^k))^\top$. Newton's method is the iterative scheme

$$x^{k+1} = x^k - H(x^k)^{-1}(\nabla f(x^k))^\top. \tag{4.3.1}$$

While the minimization logic does not apply, we use (4.3.1) even when $H(x^k)$ is not positive definite. This is a weak point of Newton's method, but it is addressed in the refinements below.

The performance of the multivariate Newton method is similar to the one-dimensional version, as stated in theorem 4.3.1.

THEOREM 4.3.1 Suppose that $f(x)$ is C^3, minimized at x^*, and that $H(x^*)$ is nonsingular. Then there is some $\varepsilon > 0$ such that if $\|x^0 - x^*\| < \varepsilon$, then the sequence defined in (4.3.1) converges quadratically to x^*.

Proof See Luenberger (1984).

The multivariate Newton method can be expensive because computing and storing the Hessian, $H(x)$, takes $\mathcal{O}(n^3)$ time to compute and occupies $\mathcal{O}(n^2)$ space. In practice, the inversion step in (4.3.1) should never be executed. The critical fact is that the Newton step $s^k \equiv x^{k+1} - x^k$ is the solution to the linear system $H(x^k)s^k = -(\nabla f(x^k))^\top$. Therefore the actual procedure is to compute $H(x^k)$, solve the linear problem $H(x^k)s^k = -(\nabla f(x^k))^\top$ for s^k, and set $x^{k+1} = x^k + s^k$.

Theorem 4.3.1 states that convergence is quadratic for initial guesses sufficiently close to a local minimum. The multivariate Newton method is similar to the one-dimensional version also in terms of its problems. In particular, the multivariate Newton method is not globally convergent. The convergence problem is not surprising since Newton's method only uses the first-order optimization conditions. In particular, there is no assurance that the successive Hessians are positive definite; Newton's method could be generating iterates along which f is increasing. Even when the Hessians are positive definite, there is no assurance that the sequence x^k is moving downhill. Future sections will introduce methods that surely go downhill and get us to a minimum more reliably.

Stopping Rules

Even when Newton's method converges, we need a way to stop the process when it is close to a minimum. In the multivariate case we cannot resort to any bracketing method. We therefore must make a decision based on x^k, $f(x^k)$, $\nabla f(x^k)$, and $H(x^k)$. As in the one-dimension case, we typically use a twofold convergence test. The first thing is to determine if the sequence has converged. The convergence test is of the form

$$\|x^{k+1} - x^k\| < \varepsilon(1 + \|x^k\|). \tag{4.3.2}$$

Second, if the convergence test is satisfied, we determine if the latest iterate satisfies the first-order condition. The optimality test focuses on whether $\nabla f(x^k)$ is zero and takes the form

$$\|\nabla f(x^k)\| \leq \delta(1 + |f(x^k)|). \tag{4.3.3}$$

Again we add the 1 to $|f(x^k)|$ to deal with the case of $f(x^k) \approx 0$. If both (4.3.2) and (4.3.3) are satisfied, we stop and report success. Sometimes we may satisfy the convergence test (4.3.2) but not optimality, (4.3.3). This says that the sequence is changing slowly but not yet near an optimum, indicating that the quadratic approximations are not good locally. If this happens, we can restart with a smaller ε or change to another method.

The choices of ε and δ are tolerances that users can specify in most minimization software. The primary consideration in choosing δ is the accuracy with which one computes ∇f. One should never ask for tolerances smaller than the machine ε, and generally should use tolerances on the order of the square root of the machine ε. Also larger tolerances should be used if $f(x)$ is computed with error greater than the machine ε; generally, if f is computed with accuracy ε_f, then the ε and δ used in the stopping rules should be between $\varepsilon_f^{1/4}$ and $\varepsilon_f^{1/2}$. However, the best choices are problem dependent, and users should try several alternatives to learn the trade-off between the higher speed of large tolerances and the accuracy of smaller tolerances. Good software packages give users guidelines concerning these tolerances. Algorithm 4.4 summarizes Newton's method for R^n.

Algorithm 4.4   Newton's Method in R^n

Initialization. Choose initial guess x^0 and stopping parameters δ and $\varepsilon > 0$.

Step 1. Compute the Hessian, $H(x^k)$, and gradient, $\nabla f(x^k)$, and solve $H(x^k)s^k = -(\nabla f(x^k))^\top$ for the step s^k

Step 2. $x^{k+1} = x^k + s^k$.

Step 3. If $\|x^k - x^{k+1}\| < \varepsilon(1 + \|x^k\|)$, go to step 4; else go to step 1.

Step 4. If $\|\nabla f(x^k)\| < \delta(1 + |f(x^k)|)$, STOP and report success; else STOP and report convergence to nonoptimal point.

The key pieces of Newton's method are the Hessian and gradient computations. Since step 1 involves solving a linear system of equations, Newton's method inherits all the problems of linear systems. In particular, Newton's method will work well only if the Hessian is well-conditioned. Poorly conditioned Hessians will lead to large errors when computing s^k in step 1. If practical, one should estimate the condition number of $H(x)$ at the purported solution before accepting it. Of course we should also check that $H(x)$ satisfies second-order conditions at the purported solution.

Monopoly Example

To illustrate multivariate optimization algorithms, we use a simple monopoly problem. Suppose that a firm produces two products, Y and Z. Suppose that the demand for Y and Z is derived from the utility function

$$U(Y, Z) = (Y^\alpha + Z^\alpha)^{\eta/\alpha} + M$$

$$\equiv u(Y, Z) + M,$$

where M is the dollar expenditure on other goods. We assume that $\alpha = 0.98$ and $\eta = 0.85$. If the firm produces quantities Y and Z of the goods, their prices will be u_Y and u_Z. Hence the monopoly problem is

$$\max_{Y,Z} \Pi(Y,Z) \equiv Y u_Y(Y,Z) + Z u_Z(Y,Z) - C_Y(Y) - C_Z(Z), \qquad (4.3.4)$$

where $C_Y(Y)$ and $C_Z(Z)$ are the production costs of Y and Z. We assume that $C_Y(Y) = 0.62Y$ and $C_Z(Z) = 0.60Z$.

We immediately see a problem that can arise with any optimization method. In its search for the optimum, an algorithm may attempt to evaluate the profit function, (4.3.4), at a point where Y or Z is negative. Such attempts would cause most programs to crash, since fractional powers of negative numbers are generally complex. We need to make some change to avoid this problem. It is possible to perform all arithmetic as complex numbers, but that is generally impractical. The approach we take here is to restate the problem in terms of $y \equiv \ln Y$ and $z \equiv \ln Z$. When we make this substitution into (4.3.4), we find that the resulting problem is

$$\max_{y,z} \pi(y,z), \qquad (4.3.5)$$

where $\pi(y,z) \equiv \Pi(e^y, e^z)$; now Π is never evaluated at a negative argument. The system (4.3.5) will serve as our test problem, and has the solution $y^* = -0.58$ and $z^* = 1.08$.

We now discuss how Newton's method does in solving our test monopoly problem, (4.3.5). We will let x denote the log output vector, (y,z), and $f(x) = \pi(y,z)$ denote the objective. Table 4.1 displays the iterates for Newton's method. The second column contains $x^k - x^*$, the errors of the Newton iterates, beginning with $x^0 = (y_0, z_0) = (1.5, 2.0)$. Quadratic convergence is apparent. Column 1 contains the iteration counter, k. Column 2 contains the deviation of x^k from the optimal solution, x^*. Column 3 contains $f(x^k) - f(x^*)$, the "loss" from choosing x^k instead of x^*. Column 4 displays the steps taken by each iterate, $x^{k+1} - x^k$. Column 5 contains the coordinates of $\nabla f(x^k)/(1 + |f(x^k)|)$, the normed gradient used in step 4 of Newton's method.

The quadratic nature of convergence is demonstrated clearly in column 2 where the error at each iterate roughly equals the square of the error at the previous iterate once the error is less than 1. The properties of various convergence rules can be inferred. We see that if we only demanded that $\|\nabla f\| \le 0.001$, we would stop at $k = 5$, but that by also requiring $\|x^k - x^{k-1}\| \le 0.01$, we continue to $k = 7$ and reduce the error in x^k from 0.2 to 0.007. Notice that at $k = 9$, the error and the gradients were reduced to magnitudes close to machine ε.

Table 4.1
Newton's method applied to (4.3.5)

k	$x^k - x^*$	$f(x^k) - f(x^*)$	$x^k - x^{k-1}$	$\nabla f(x^k)/(1 + |f(x^k)|)$
0	(2.1, 0.92)	-0.4		$(-.43, -0.62)$
1	(1.5, 0.37)	-0.08	$(-0.61, -0.56)$	$(-0.13, -0.18)$
2	(0.98, -0.0029)	-0.012	$(-0.48, -0.37)$	$(-0.034, -0.04)$
3	(0.61, -0.12)	-0.0019	$(-0.36, -0.11)$	$(-0.0087, -0.0045)$
4	(0.28, -0.041)	-0.0003	$(-0.33, 0.075)$	$(-0.0028, -0.0022)$
5	(0.075, -0.0093)	$-1.9(-5)$	$(-0.2, 0.032)$	$(-6.1(-4), -6.5(-4))$
6	(0.0069, $-7.8(-4)$)	$-1.6(-7)$	$(-0.068, 0.0085)$	$(-5.3(-5), -6.4(-5))$
7	($6.3(-5), -7.0(-6)$)	$-1.3(-11)$	$(-0.0068, 7.7(-4))$	$(-4.8(-7), -6.0(-7))$
8	($5.4(-9), -6.0(-10)$)	$-3.2(-16)$	$(-6.3(-5), 7.0(-6))$	$(-4.1(-11), -5.1(-11))$
9	($-2.3(-15), 2.4(-15)$)	$-3.2(-16)$	$(-5.4(-9), 6.0(-10))$	$(-4.0(-17), -3.2(-16))$

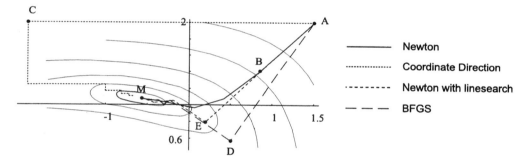

Figure 4.3
Various methods applied to (4.3.5)

Figure 4.3 displays the Newton iterates computed in table 4.1. The initial guess is at point A and the first iterate is B. After that the Newton iterates move along the solid line to the minimum at M.

Each step of Newton's method requires calculation of the Hessian, a step that is costly in large problem. One modification is to compute the Hessian only once at the initial point and use it to calculate each iteration; this is called the *modified Newton method*. The formal definition is to choose an initial guess, x^0, compute $H(x^0)$, and compute the sequence $x^{k+1} = x^k - H(x^0)^{-1}(\nabla f(x^k))^\top$. This will converge for sufficiently good initial guesses, but only linearly.

Although the modified Newton method may seem rather unappealing, there may be cases where it is useful if the Hessian is very difficult to compute. Also, when an application of the Newton method appears to be converging, one may want to switch to the modified Newton method, since the Hessian will not change much during the final iterations of Newton's method.

Notes on Computing Gradients and Hessians

In many optimization problems much computing time is devoted to computing gradients and Hessians. We must choose between finite difference methods and analytic computations. We will usually want to use finite difference methods, since analytic computation of derivatives by human hand is at best a tedious, error-laden process for most people. Fortunately finite-difference methods are often adequate. At the early stages of a computational project, we want to stick with finite differences because it is very costly to recompute derivatives each time the model is modified. For most problems the option of moving to analytic gradients and Hessians is relevant only at the final stage if more accuracy or speed is needed.

In some problems we cannot compute the true objective and must replace it with numerical approximations. This is the case, for example, whenever the objective includes an integral that must be computed numerically. We then must decide the accuracy needed for the objective. We will generally want to use a good approximation of the objective. Since the objective is only an approximation, any derivative we compute is also only an approximation. We could just approximate the derivatives of the true objective with the derivatives of the approximation we use for the objective. However, the question of how well we approximate the gradients and Hessians is independent of the approximation of the objective. To save time (remember, most of the running time in optimization problems is spent on gradient and Hessian computations), we may want to use lower-quality approximations for gradients and Hessians but use high-quality approximations for the objective.

Carter (1993) shows that high accuracy in computing Hessians and gradients is often not critical. He took a group of test optimization problems and used standard methods to solve them, but after computing gradients and Hessians analytically, he added random errors. These errors ranged from 1 to 80 percent of the true derivative. He showed that the optimization algorithms generally performed well even when he used 20 percent errors, and often did well even with 50 percent errors.

All this indicates that finite difference approximations of derivatives are generally adequate. In this book every problem can be successfully solved using finite differences unless it is explicitly stated otherwise; this text's attitude is that programmers have better things to do than taking difficult derivatives. Furthermore, if analytical derivatives are necessary, then they should be done by the computer using the symbolic software if possible.

4.4 Direction Set Methods

The most useful methods in optimization of smooth functions are direction set methods. Direction set methods pick a series of directions to search, performing a sequence of one-dimensional searches in each direction. If f is C^1 the first-order conditions of (4.2.1) state that the gradient of f vanishes at a local minimum, that is,

$$\nabla f \cdot u = 0 \qquad \forall u \in R^n. \tag{4.4.1}$$

Equation (4.4.1) holds for all $u \in R^n$ if $f \in C^2$ for n linearly independent vectors. The idea of direction set methods is to find a sequence of directions, and then, by repeated one-dimensional minimizations in those directions, to find a point where (4.4.1) holds. These methods reduce multidimensional optimization problems to a series of one-dimensional problems, which are easily solved. The hope is that eventually the process converges to a point where f is minimal in all directions.

The various direction set methods differ in terms of how they choose successive directions and approximants. However, they all roughly follow the same idea. First, given information about f at x^k, compute a search direction, s^k. Then find the scalar λ_k that minimizes f along the line $x^k + \lambda_k s^k$. The next iterate is $x^{k+1} = x^k + \lambda_k s^k$. If the derivatives of f at x^{k+1} and $\|\lambda_k s^k\|$ are close enough to zero, stop; otherwise, repeat.

Algorithm 4.5 Generic Direction Method

Initialization. Choose initial guess x^0 and stopping parameters δ and $\varepsilon > 0$.

Step 1. Compute a search direction s^k.

Step 2. Solve $\lambda_k = \arg\min_\lambda f(x^k + \lambda s^k)$.

Step 3. $x^{k+1} = x^k + \lambda_k s^k$.

Step 4. If $\|x^k - x^{k+1}\| < \varepsilon(1 + \|x^k\|)$, go to step 5; else go to step 1.

Step 5. If $\|\nabla f(x^k)\| < \delta(1 + f(x^k))$, STOP and report success; else STOP and report convergence to nonoptimal point.

Various direction set methods differ in how the directions are chosen. The directions may be confined to some specified set, or the search directions may vary as the algorithm proceeds. Some sensible choices are not good, but we will see that good direction sets can be derived. The main objective is that the search direction be a good descent direction at each iteration. This will force $f(x^{k+1})$ to be nontrivially less than $f(x^k)$ and impose the chance of convergence. This is not always true of Newton's method.

Table 4.2
Coordinate direction method applied to (4.3.5)

k	$x^k - x^*$	$x^k - x^{k-1}$	$\nabla f(x^k)/(1 + |f(x^k)|)$
0	(2.1, 0.92)		(−0.43, −0.62)
1	(−4.8, 0.92)	(−6.9, 0)	(5.4(−7), −0.39)
2	(−4.8, 0.16)	(0, −0.76)	(2.2(−4), 3.3(−10))
3	(−0.49, 0.16)	(4.3, 0)	(−3.5(−9), −2.0(−2))
4	(−0.49, 0.065)	(0, −0.096)	(1.8(−3), −6.7(−12))
5	(−0.18, 0.065)	(0.31, 0)	(1.0(−9), −6.7(−3))
6	(−0.18, 0.028)	(0, −0.037)	(8.9(−4), 3.5(−13))
7	(−0.074, 0.028)	(0.11, 0)	(6.1(−10), −2.7(−3))
8	(−0.074, 0.012)	(0, −0.016)	(4.1(−4), 1.1(−11))
9	(−0.032, 0.012)	(0.042, 0)	(2.4(−10), −1.1(−3))

Coordinate Directions

The coordinate direction method cycles over the set of unit coordinate vectors, $\{e^j : j = 1, \ldots, n\}$. That is, on iteration $mn + j + 1$, let λ^* minimize $f(x^{mn+j} + \lambda e^j)$, and make the next iterate $x^{mn+j+1} = x^{mn+j} + \lambda^* e^j$. The coordinate direction method will converge to a local minimum for smooth functions because it is always moving in a downhill direction, but it may converge slowly.

Table 4.2 displays the first ten iterates of the coordinate direction method applied to (4.3.5) with $x^0 = (y_0, z_0) = (1.5, 2.0)$. The format follows that of table 4.1. We see that convergence is rather slow. In fact the first iteration badly overshoots the solution in the x coordinate, but the algorithm recovers and heads to the optimal point. This is displayed in figure 4.3 by the dotted line beginning at A, proceeding to C, and then moving to the optimum. Even when close, the convergence is poor with the errors $x^k - x^*$ converging to zero slowly. The last column shows how each iteration sets one of the gradients close to zero, but then that gradient is nonzero in the next iterate. This is seen in figure 4.3 where the later iterates move right, then down, then right, and so on. At each corner one coordinate direction is tangent to the contour, but the other coordinate direction is orthogonal to the contour.

The coordinate direction method is one where we reduce a multivariate problem to a sequence of univariate ones. In this regard it is similar to the Gauss-Seidel approach to iteration discussed in section 3.6. We could also implement a block Gauss-Seidel extension of the coordinate direction method for optimization. This *block coordinate direction* method partitions the set of optimization variables into a collection of smaller sets and then optimizes over the variables in each smaller set, using the sets

Table 4.3
Steepest descent applied to (4.3.5)

k	$x^k - x^*$	$x^k - x^{k-1}$	$\nabla f(x^k)/(1 + f(x^k))$
0	(2.1, 0.92)		(−0.43, −0.62)
1	(1.1, −0.5)	(−1.0, −1.4)	(−0.014, 0.0098)
2	(0.38, −0.029)	(−0.68, 0.48)	(−0.0055, −0.0078)
3	(0.35, −0.084)	(−0.039, 0.055)	(−0.0026, 0.0018)
4	(0.26, −0.023)	(−0.088, 0.062)	(−0.003, −0.0043)
5	(0.24, −0.053)	(−0.021, −0.03)	(−0.0016, 0.0011)
6	(0.18, −0.017)	(−0.051, −0.036)	(−0.0019, −0.0027)
7	(0.17, −0.037)	(−0.014, −0.02)	(−0.0011, 0.00076)
8	(0.14, −0.013)	(−0.034, 0.024)	(−0.0013, −0.0019)
9	(0.13, −0.027)	(−0.0095, −0.014)	(−0.00077, 0.00054)

in succession. If each set of the partition is small enough, Newton's method can be used at each iteration, although it could not be used for the original problem. The advantage of a block approach is that we can exploit some of the multivariate structure in the objective without tackling all of the variables at once.

Steepest Descent

In the steepest descent method the search direction from a point x is taken to be that direction along which f falls most rapidly per unit length. The steepest ascent direction is the gradient. Therefore the steepest descent method chooses the search direction in step 1 in the generic direction method to be

$$s^{k+1} = -(\nabla f(x^k))^\top. \tag{4.4.2}$$

At first the steepest descent method appears promising. It will always be a descent direction, and locally it is the best direction to go. However, this local property does not hold globally. Steepest descent often has a slow rate of convergence.

Table 4.3 displays the first ten iterates of the steepest descent method applied to (4.3.5) with $x^0 = (1.5, 2.0)$; we follow the format of table 4.1. We see that convergence is much slower than Newton's method. We see that initially the method does well, but that near the solution it zigzags into the solution. It is trying to find the bottom of a valley, but it essentially bounces from valley side to side because the steepest descent direction never points in the direction of the true minimum. Newton's method does much better. It takes a more truly multivariate view of the problem and goes in a direction that is more globally optimal instead of the locally optimal direction.

Both coordinate search and steepest descent are sensible methods, but they are slow. They suffer from a common problem. The direction searched generally misses the true optimal point. While the steepest descent direction is the best direction locally, it is unlikely to be pointing in the direction of the global optimum. We need to find better directions.

Newton's Method with Line Search

Newton's method is a special case of a direction set method. It can be expressed in the form of the generic direction set method with the choices $s^k = -H(x^k)^{-1}(\nabla f(x^k))^\top$ and $\lambda_k = 1$. Therefore Newton's method is a direction set method with a fixed choice of $\lambda_k = 1$. Direction methods generally differ from Newton's method in both the direction examined and in their strategy of choosing λ_k.

The problem with Newton's method is that it takes the quadratic approximation too seriously, treating it as a global approximation of f. An alternative view is to think of the local quadratic approximation as telling us a good direction to use but to recognize that the quality of that approximation will decay as we move away from its base at x^k. In fact the Newton direction is a good direction initially if $H(x^k)$ is positive definite because $f(x)$ does fall as we move away from x^k in the Newton direction. When f is not a linear-quadratic function, the ray $s^k = -H(x^k)^{-1}(\nabla f(x^k))^\top$ may initially go downhill, though a full step may send it uphill again. In Newton's method with line search, we take the Newton step direction and use line search to find the best point in that direction. Therefore, in the generic direction method algorithm, we implement step 1 with

$$s^k = -H(x^k)^{-1}(\nabla f(x^k))^\top. \tag{4.4.3}$$

The advantage of this method over steepest descent is that it uses a direction that may be good globally. In fact, if we are close to the minimum or minimizing a nearly quadratic function, the Newton direction is the best possible direction. The advantage of this method over Newton's method is that the line search step guarantees that we will go downhill if f is smooth, and thereby guaranteeing convergence to a local minimum. In contrast, Newton's method ($\lambda_k = 1$) may overshoot the best point in the Newton direction and push the iteration uphill.

Unfortunately, convergence may be slower. First, there is the cost of doing the line search. Second, when we are close to the solution, we really want to use Newton's method, that is, have $\lambda_k = 1$, because that will guarantee quadratic convergence; if λ_k does not converge to unity, the asymptotic convergence rate will be less than quadratic. As we approach a minimum, it may be advisable to switch to Newton's method, since we know that λ_k will be unity.

Table 4.4
Newton's method with linesearch applied to (4.3.5)

k	$x^k - x^*$	$x^k - x^{k-1}$	$\nabla f(x^k)/(1 + \|f(x^k)\|)$	λ_k
0	$(2.1, 0.92)$		$(-0.43, -0.62)$	2.15
1	$(0.75, -0.28)$	$(-1.3, -1.2)$	$(-0.007, 0.0076)$	0.791
2	$(0.35, -0.022)$	$(-0.4, 0.26)$	$(-0.005, -0.0078)$	1.37
3	$(0.047, -0.019)$	$(-0.3, 0.0027)$	$(1.5(-5), 0.0017)$	0.966
4	$(8.5(-4), -1.5(-5))$	$(-0.046, 0.019)$	$(-8.7(-6), -2.1(-5))$	1.00
5	$(3.6(-7), -1.5(-7))$	$(-8.5(-4), 1.5(-5))$	$(2.6(-10), 1.4(-8))$	1.00
6	$(8.2(-13), -3.2(-13))$	$(-3.6(-7), 1.5(-7))$	$(4.0(-17), 2.9(-14))$	1.00
7	$(5.8(-15), -6.7(-16))$	$(-8.1(-13), 3.1(-13))$	$(4.0(-17), 3.2(-16))$	1.00
8	$(3.4(-15), 1.8(-15))$	$(-2.3(-15), 2.4(-15))$	$(-8.1(-17), -3.2(-16))$	

Table 4.4 displays the first ten iterates of Newton's method with line search applied to (4.3.5) with $x^0 = (1.5, 2.0)$; we follow the format of table 4.1, but we add a new column to display the λ_k sequence. Initially the step size parameter, λ_k, exceeds unity. As we get close, the quadratic approximation is quite good, and λ_k becomes 1, implying that the line search gives us the same point as would Newton's method. Figure 4.3 compares the Newton iterates and the iterates from Newton with line search, the latter beginning at A and proceeding along the finely broken line through B to the first iterate at E. Point E is clearly a better first iterate than B. In this case we want to overshoot the Newton iterate B because E has a lower objective value. From E we again use Newton with line search and converge to the solution more quickly than by Newton's method. Even though the line search feature will become less relevant as we get close, it will often substantially improve the initial progress.

There are potentially severe problems with any Newton-type method that uses $H(x)$. First, $H(x)$ which has n^2 elements can be quite costly to compute and store. Second, solving (4.4.3) will be costly if n is large. The next set of methods address these problems.

Quasi-Newton Methods

Quasi-Newton method takes Newton's method with line search and replaces the Hessian with another $n \times n$ matrix that performs the role of the Hessian in generating the search direction. This approximate Hessian is always positive semidefinite but easier to compute and invert. This means that at each iteration, we are looking for some easily computed, positive definite H_k that both generates a good search direction, $s^k = -H_k^{-1} (\nabla f(x^k))^\top$ which is like the Hessian in that

$$H_k^{-1}((\nabla f(x^k))^\top - (\nabla f(x^{k-1}))^\top) = x^k - x^{k-1},$$

and guarantees that s^k is a descent direction. Actually this last condition is assured if H_k is positive definite, since then $\nabla f(x^k)s^k = -\nabla f(x^k) H_k^{-1} (\nabla f(x^k))^\top < 0$. The key factor is the construction of a good H_k satisfying these first two conditions.

There are several good schemes for constructing H_k. One of the favorites is the Broyden-Fletcher-Goldfarb-Shanno (BFGS) update. The BFGS iteration is given in algorithm 4.6. The formula in (4.4.4) is the pure version of BFGS. However, to avoid overflow problems in (4.4.4), we set $H_{k+1} = H_k$ whenever $y_k^\top z_k$ is small relative to $\|y_k\|$.

Algorithm 4.6   BFGS Method

Initialization. Choose initial guess x^0, initial hessian guess $H^0 = 1$, and stopping parameters δ and $\varepsilon > 0$.

Step 1. Solve $H_k s^k = -(\nabla f(x^k))^\top$ for the search direction s^k.

Step 2. Solve $\lambda_k = \arg\min_\lambda f(x^k + \lambda s^k)$

Step 3. $x^{k+1} = x^k + \lambda_k s^k$.

Step 4. Update H_k:

$$z_k = x^{k+1} - x^k,$$

$$y_k = (\nabla f(x^{k+1}))^\top - (\nabla f(x^k))^\top,$$

$$H_{k+1} = H_k - \frac{H_k z_k z_k^\top H_k}{z_k^\top H_k z_k} + \frac{y_k y_k^\top}{y_k^\top z_k}. \tag{4.4.4}$$

Step 5. If $\|x^k - x^{k+1}\| < \varepsilon(1 + \|x^k\|)$, go to step 6; else go to step 1.

Step 6. If $\|\nabla f(x^k)\| < \delta(1 + |f(x^k)|)$, STOP and report success; else STOP and report convergence to nonoptimal point.

This H_k sequence is positive definite and symmetric as long as H_0 is. One common choice for H_0 is the identity matrix. In that case the initial step is the same as the steepest descent step. If a system is not too large, H_0 can be set equal to the Hessian at x^0, making the initial step equal to Newton's method with line search. Since all H_k are positive definite, Cholesky factorization can be used to solve for the search direction in step 1.

Equation (4.4.4) is the BFGS update. An older method is the simpler Davidon-Fletcher-Powell (DFP) update, which replaces (4.4.4) with (4.4.5):

$$H_{k+1} = H_k + \frac{(y_k - H_k z_k)y_k^\top + y_k(y_k - H_k z_k)^\top}{y_k^\top z_k}$$

$$- \frac{z_k^\top(y_k - H_k z_k)y_k y_k^\top}{(y_k^\top z_k)^2}. \tag{4.4.5}$$

General experience indicates that BFGS works more often than DFP but that DFP does better in some cases. Therefore it is best to be familiar with and have software for both methods.

In Hessian update algorithms the H_k sequence does not necessarily converge to the true Hessian at the solution. Therefore, if it is needed, the Hessian should be computed at the end. One such case is computing a maximum likelihood estimator where the Hessian is used for inference. Since the final Hessian must be computed anyway in these econometric contexts, one should switch to Newton's method once the optimization procedure has apparently converged. This has little cost: If the problem has converged, then one iteration of Newton's method should suffice; if more is needed, then that is evidence that the search should continue.

Table 4.5 displays the first ten iterates of the BFGS method applied to (4.3.5) with $x^0 = (1.5, 2.0)$ and H_0 being the true Hessian at x^0. We see that convergence is quite rapid, even though BFGS computes $H(x)$ only once. Figure 4.3 displays the BFGS method, beginning at A, proceeding along the steepest descent direction to D, and then converging to M. The first iterate of BFGS is better than the first Newton iterate at B, but not as good as the first iterate of Newton with line search at E. The Hessian approximation, though, allows BFGS to quickly catch up with Newton with line search, whereas continuing with the steepest descent direction method does less well.

Table 4.5
BFGS applied to (4.3.5)

k	$x^k - x^*$	$x^k - x^{k-1}$	$\nabla f(x^k)/(1 + |f(x^k)|)$	λ_k
0	$(2.1, 0.92)$		$(-0.43, -0.62)$	2.16
1	$(0.75, -0.28)$	$(-1.3, -1.2)$	$(-0.007, 0.0076)$	20.5
2	$(0.38, -0.026)$	$(-0.37, 0.25)$	$(-0.0055, -0.0081)$	5.75
3	$(0.15, -0.049)$	$(-0.23, -0.023)$	$(-3.3(-4), 0.0034)$	0.928
4	$(0.038, -0.0012)$	$(-0.11, 0.048)$	$(-0.0004, -8.9(-4))$	1.61
5	$(0.0015, -6.2(-4))$	$(-0.037, 5.9(-4))$	$(9.6(-7), 6.0(-5))$	0.93
6	$(4.6(-5), -1.1(-6))$	$(-0.0015, 6.2(-4))$	$(-4.6(-7), -1.1(-6))$	

Conjugate Directions

Newton and quasi-Newton methods carry around an estimate of the Hessian. This estimate may be large in high-dimensional problems, and a computer may not be able to store such a large matrix for large n. For example, personal computers today have no problem storing vectors with 1000 elements but cannot store a 1000×1000 matrix under normal conditions. To solve large problems, we need to develop methods that use less storage. Steepest descent and coordinate direction methods have small storage needs, storing only a gradient, but are rather poor methods.

Conjugate direction methods are direction set methods that store only a gradient, but they are successful because they implicitly keep track of curvature information in a useful way without storing a Hessian or keeping a history of past search directions. The key insight about conjugate direction methods comes from considering the failings of the steepest descent and coordinate direction methods. One reason they do poorly is that after they minimize f in one direction, u, they move along another direction, v, and likely end up at a point where f is no longer a minimum along the u direction. After moving in the u direction, the algorithm has solved one first-order condition, but moving in the v direction will lose optimality in the u direction. A better algorithm would choose v to maintain optimality in the u direction as it moves in the v direction.

The concept of conjugate directions makes this idea formal and implements it. Let us focus on the generic quadratic function $f(x) = \frac{1}{2}x^\top Ax + b^\top x + c$. The gradient of f is $\nabla f = (Ax + b)^\top$, and the change in ∇f as a point moves from x to $x + dx$ is $A\,dx$. After we minimize along a direction u, we get to a point, x, where

$$(Ax + b)^\top u = 0. \tag{4.4.6}$$

If we next move from x to $x + v$, the change in (4.4.6) is $v^\top Au$. If we want to keep the u-direction first-order condition (4.4.6) true, we must choose a direction v such that $0 = v^\top Au$. If u and v satisfy $v^\top Au = 0$, we say that u and v are *conjugate directions*.

We can now see a problem with applying the steepest descent and coordinate direction methods. In both cases the second direction, v, is orthogonal to the first, u, where v should instead be orthogonal to Au. In R^n there are many directions conjugate to u. There is a simple procedure that will generate a sequence of directions such that when applied to a quadratic problem, each direction is conjugate not only to the previous direction but to the previous $n - 1$ directions. We begin with a guess, x^0, and an initial search direction, $s^0 = -(\nabla f(x^0))$. Thereafter the iterative scheme proceeds as described in algorithm 4.7. This method also has a nice characterization relative to the steepest descent method. The conjugate direction step in (4.4.7) takes the steepest descent direction, $-(\nabla f(x^{k+1}))^\top$, and deflects it toward the last step, s^k.

Algorithm 4.7   Conjugate Gradient Method

Initialization. Choose initial guess x^0, $s^0 = -\nabla f(x^0)$ and stopping parameters δ and $\varepsilon > 0$.

Step 1. Solve $\lambda_k = \arg\min_\lambda f(x^k + \lambda s^k)$.

Step 2. Set $x^{k+1} = x^k + \lambda_k s^k$.

Step 3. Compute the search direction

$$s^{k+1} = -(\nabla f(x^{k+1}))^\top + \frac{\|\nabla f(x^{k+1})\|^2}{\|\nabla f(x^k)\|^2}\, s^k. \tag{4.4.7}$$

Step 4. If $\|x^k - x^{k+1}\| > \varepsilon(1 + \|x^k\|)$, go to step 1. Otherwise, if $\|\nabla f(x^k)\| < \delta(1 + |f(x^k)|)$, STOP and report success; else STOP and report convergence to non-optimal point.

In the conjugate direction algorithm there is no explicit Hessian calculation. Implicitly it differs from quasi-Newton methods in that it assumes that a single quadratic form is a valid approximation globally, whereas a quasi-Newton method knows it is tracking a moving target and changes its estimation of the current quadratic approximation. The implicit global approximation may break down and lead to successive conjugate directions being highly collinear. To keep the sequence of directions in a conjugate direction method from degenerating, we restart the iteration every so often (approximately every n steps, where n is the dimension of x) by setting the search direction equal to the steepest descent direction as in, for example, $s^{(kn)} = -(\nabla f(x^{(kn)}))^\top$.

Table 4.6 displays the first ten iterates of the conjugate gradient method applied to (4.3.5) with $x^0 = (1.5, 2.0)$. We see that convergence is initially rapid but slows down as expected.

4.5   Nonlinear Least Squares

Least squares problems are common in economics, particularly in econometric analysis. The typical problem has the form

$$\min_x \frac{1}{2}\sum_{i=1}^m f^i(x)^2 \equiv S(x),$$

Table 4.6
Conjugate gradient method applied to (4.3.5)

k	$x^k - x^*$	$x^k - x^{k-1}$	$\nabla f(x^k)/(1 + f(x^k))$
0	$(2.1, 0.92)$		$(-0.43, -0.62)$
1	$(1.1, -0.5)$	$(-1, -1.4)$	$(-0.014, 9.8(-3))$
2	$(0.34, -0.024)$	$(-0.73, 0.48)$	$(-4.5(-3), -6.9(-3))$
3	$(0.26, -0.068)$	$(-0.076, -0.045)$	$(-1.5(-3), 2.5(-3))$
4	$(0.2, -0.021)$	$(-0.061, 0.048)$	$(-2.0(-3), -2.6(-3))$
5	$(0.067, -0.025)$	$(-0.13, -3.7(-3))$	$(-5.6(-5), 2.0(-3))$
6	$(0.048, -0.006)$	$(-0.019, 0.019)$	$(-3.7(-4), -3.8(-4))$
7	$(0.041, -9.5(-3))$	$(-7.2(-3), -3.5(-3))$	$(-1.9(-4), 3.9(-4))$
8	$(0.02, -5.7(-4))$	$(-0.02, 8.9(-3))$	$(-2.1(-4), -4.8(-4))$
9	$(8.4(-3), -2.4(-3))$	$(-0.012, -1.8(-3))$	$(-2.4(-5), 1.6(-4))$

where $f^i \colon R^n \to R$ for $i = 1, \ldots, m$. Let $f(x)$ denote the column vector $(f^i(x))_{i=1}^m$. In econometric applications, $x = \beta$ and the $f^i(x)$ are $f(\beta, y^i)$, where β is the vector of unknown parameters and the y^i are the data. In these problems $f(\beta, y^i)$ is the residual associated with observation i, and $S(\beta)$ is the sum of squared residuals if β is the value of the parameters.

To solve a least squares problem, we can apply any general optimization method. However, there are methods that exploit the special structure of least squares problems. Let $J(x)$ be the Jacobian of $f(x) \equiv (f^1(x), \ldots, f^m(x))^\top$. Let $f_l^i \equiv \partial f^i / \partial x_l$ and $f_{jl}^i \equiv \partial^2 f^i / \partial x_j \partial x_l$. The gradient of $S(x)$ is $J(x)^\top f(x)$, with element l being $\sum_{i=1}^m f_l^i(x) f^i(x)$. The Hessian of $S(x)$ is $J(x)^\top J(x) + G(x)$, where the (j, l) element of $G(x)$ is

$$G_{jl}(x) = \sum_{i=1}^m f_{jl}^i(x) f^i(x).$$

Note the special structure of the gradient and Hessian. The $f_j^i(x)$ terms are necessary for computing the gradient of $S(x)$. If $f(x)$ is zero, then the Hessian reduces to $J(x)^\top J(x)$, which is composed of $f_j^i(x)$ terms only. The $J(x)^\top J(x)$ piece of the Hessian is much easier to compute than the whole Hessian. It involves no evaluations of f and its derivatives other than those necessary for computing the gradient, which is necessary to compute in almost all algorithms. A problem where $f(x)$ is small at the solution is called a *small residual problem*, and a *large residual problem* is one where $f(x)$ is large at the solution. For small residual problems the Hessian becomes nearly equal to $J(x)^\top J(x)$ near the solution. This means that we can compute a good, new approximation to the Hessian at each iteration at low cost.

This leads to the Gauss-Newton algorithm, which is Newton's method except that it uses $J(x)^\top J(x)$ as an estimate of the Hessian. The Gauss-Newton step is

$$s^k = -(J(x^k)^\top J(x^k))^{-1}(\nabla f(x^k))^\top. \qquad (4.5.1)$$

This results in considerable savings, for no second derivatives of f are evaluated. When it works, it works very well, far faster than Newton's method because there is no evaluation of second derivatives.

The Gauss-Newton approach has many problems. First, the product $J(x)^\top J(x)$ is likely to be poorly conditioned, since it is the "square" of a matrix. Second, $J(x)$ may be poorly conditioned itself, which is easily the case in statistical contexts. Third, the Gauss-Newton step may not be a descent direction.

These problems lead to the *Levenberg-Marquardt algorithm*. This method uses $J(x)^\top J(x) + \lambda I$ as an estimate of the Hessian for some scalar λ where I is the identity matrix. The Levenberg-Marquardt step is

$$s^k = -(J(x^k)^\top J(x^k) + \lambda I)^{-1}(\nabla f(x^k))^\top \qquad (4.5.2)$$

The extra term in the Hessian approximation reduces the conditioning problems. More important, the resulting step will be a descent direction for sufficiently large λ since s^k converges to the steepest descent direction for large λ.

Solving Multiple Problems

Sometimes we will want to solve several problems of the form $\min_x f(x; a)$, where a is a vector of parameters. The choice of initial conditions substantially affects the performance of any algorithm. In any Hessian updating method, the initial Hessian guess is also important. When we solve several such problems, it is convenient to use information about the solution to $\min_x f(x; a)$ when computing the solution to $\min_x f(x; a')$ for a' close to a. In Newton's method, the solution to $f(x; a) = 0$ will be a good initial guess when solving $\min_x f(x; a')$. In Hessian updating methods we can use both the final solution and the final Hessian estimate from $\min_x f(x; a)$ as the initial guesses when solving $\min_x f(x; a')$. In either case we call these *hot starts*. Because of the importance of initial guesses, solving N problems is generally cheaper than N times the cost of one problem. The order in which we solve a collection of problems will be important; it should be chosen to maximize the economies of scale from hot starts.

4.6 Linear Programming

The previous sections examined unconstrained optimization problems. We now begin our consideration of problems with constraints on the choice variables. A special case of constrained optimization is *linear programming* where both the objective and constraint functions are linear. A canonical form for linear programming problems is

$$\min_x a^\top x$$

$$\text{s.t.} \quad Cx = b, \tag{4.6.1}$$

$$x \geq 0.$$

This form may seem restrictive, since it does not explicitly include inequality constraints of the form $Dx \leq f$. But there is no restriction because we can add *slack variables*, s, and reformulate $Dx \leq f$ as $Dx + s = f, s \geq 0$.

Similarly constraints of the form $Dx \geq f$ can be replaced by $Dx - s = f, s \geq 0$, where now s is a vector of *surplus variables*. The constraint $x \geq d$ is handled by defining $y = x - d$ and reformulating the problem in terms of y. The case of x_i being free is handled by defining $x_i = y_i - z_i$, reformulating the problem in terms of y_i and z_i, and adding the constraints $y_i, z_i \geq 0$. With these transformation in hand, any linear programming problem can be expressed in the form in (4.6.1).

The basic method for linear programming is the *simplex method*. We will not go through the details here but its basic idea is simple. Figure 4.4 displays graphically the problem

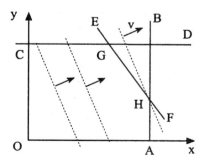

Figure 4.4
Linear programming

$$\min_{x,y} -2x - y$$

s.t. $x + y \le 4,$ $x, y \ge 0,$

   $x \le 3, y \le 2.$

We do not convert this problem into the form of (4.6.1) since we want to illustrate it in x-y space. The inequality constraints define a convex feasible set with a piecewise linear surface. In figure 4.4 those constraints are $x + y \le 4$, $x \le 3$, and $y \le 2$. The objective, $-2x - y$, is expressed as a series of dotted contour lines; the arrow points in the direction of decrease for the objective function.

The simplex method begins by finding some point on the surface of the constraint set, such as A in figure 4.4. We then move along the boundary of the feasible set to points that have a lower cost. The simplex method notes which constraints are active at A and points nearby. It then determines the feasible directions and determines which of these achieves the greatest rate of decrease in the objective. In figure 4.4 there are only two directions to go, one toward B and the other toward O, with the better one being toward B. The simplex algorithm follows that direction to the next vertex on the feasible set's boundary; more generally, it follows the direction of maximal decrease until a previously slack constraint becomes binding; in figure 4.4 that is point H. At H the set of binding constraints changes, and the simplex method notes this. With the new set of constraints at the new point, it repeats these steps to reach an even better point. This iteration continues until we reach a vertex from which all feasible movements increase the objective; in figure 4.4 that point is H. Since the constraint set is concave and the objective linear, this local minimum is also a global minimum. Since the simplex algorithm needs to visit only the finite set of vertices, it will converge in a finite number of steps.

The simplex method is an old and reliable way to solve linear programming problems, going back to Dantzig (1951). It is also fast; the average time for computing a solution is linear in the number of variables and constraints. The worst case running time is exponential, which is why the simplex algorithm is said to be exponential in time. Fortunately the worst-case scenario is unduly pessimistic in the case of the simplex method.

4.7   Constrained Nonlinear Optimization

Most economic optimization problems involve either linear or nonlinear constraints. Consumer optimization includes a budget constraint, optimal taxation problems include revenue constraints, and principal-agent problems face incentive constraints. In this section I outline basic approaches to numerical solutions to general constrained optimization problems.

Let us first recall the basic theory. Suppose that we want to solve

$$\min_x f(x)$$

$$\text{s.t.} \quad g(x) = 0, \tag{4.7.1}$$

$$h(x) \le 0,$$

where $f: R^n \to R$, $g: R^n \to R^m$, and $h: R^n \to R^l$, and f, g, and h are C^2. The nature of the solution is displayed in its Kuhn-Tucker representation. The Kuhn-Tucker theorem says that if there is a local minimum at x^* and a constraint qualification holds,[3] then there are multipliers $\lambda^* \in R^m$ and $\mu^* \in R^l$ such that x^* is a *stationary*, or *critical* point of $\mathscr{L}$, the *Lagrangian*,

$$\mathscr{L}(x, \lambda, \mu) = f(x) + \lambda^\top g(x) + \mu^\top h(x), \tag{4.7.2}$$

that is, $\mathscr{L}_x(x^*, \lambda^*, \mu^*) = 0$. The implied first-order conditions of the Lagrangian[4] tells us that the multipliers λ^* and μ^*, with the constrained minimum of (4.7.1), x^*, solve the system

$$f_x + \lambda^\top g_x + \mu^\top h_x = 0,$$

$$\mu_i h^i(x) = 0 \qquad i = 1, \dots, l,$$

$$g(x) = 0, \tag{4.7.3}$$

$$h(x) \le 0,$$

$$\mu \le 0.$$

A Kuhn-Tucker Approach

The following procedure reduces constrained optimization to a series of nonlinear equations. Let $\mathscr{I}$ be the set $\{1, 2, \dots, l\}$. For a subset $\mathscr{P} \subset \mathscr{I}$, define the $\mathscr{P}$ problem to be

3. As is typical in economic analysis, we ignore the constraint qualification condition in our discussion. However, it is a critical assumption in the foregoing. If one is not careful, it is easy to write down a problem where the constraint qualification fails.

4. Note that we assert only that x^* is a stationary point of $\mathscr{L}$; it is not necessarily a minimum.

$$g(x) = 0,$$

$$h^i(x) = 0, \qquad i \in \mathscr{P},$$

$$\mu^i = 0, \qquad i \in \mathscr{I} - \mathscr{P},$$

$$f_x + \lambda^\top g_x + \mu^\top h_x = 0.$$

(4.7.4)

This is a set of nonlinear equations.[5] For each subset $\mathscr{P}$ we have a different combination of binding and nonbinding inequality constraints, and we may have a solution; unfortunately, there may not be a solution to some of the combinations. Since there are just a finite number of such combinations, we can search over them to find the sets $\mathscr{P}$ with solutions to the Kuhn-Tucker conditions that satisfy all the constraints. There may be many such feasible solutions; we choose the one with the smallest objective value.

This procedure reduces the problem to solving nonlinear systems of equations. In some cases we may know that only some combinations of binding constraints are possible. Sometimes the resulting nonlinear equations may be simple to solve. In those cases this approach will have some advantages.

Penalty Function Method

Most constrained optimization methods use a *penalty function* approach. These are based on a simple idea: Permit anything to be feasible, but alter the objective function so that it is "painful" to make choices that violate the constraints. This approach replaces constraints with continuous penalty functions and forms an unconstrained optimization problem.

For example, consider the constrained problem

$$\min_x \ f(x)$$

$$\text{s.t.} \quad g(x) = a,$$

$$h(x) \le b.$$

(4.7.5)

We construct the penalty function problem

$$\min_x \ f(x) + \tfrac{1}{2} P \left(\sum_i (g^i(x) - a_i)^2 + \sum_j (\max[0, h^j(x) - b_j])^2 \right),$$

(4.7.6)

---

5. We defer discussing the details of solving nonlinear systems such as (4.7.4) until chapter 5.

where $P > 0$ is the penalty parameter. Denote the penalized objective in (4.7.6) $F(x; P, a, b)$; note that we are including the constraint constants a and b as parameters of the problem. If P is "infinite," then the two problems (4.7.5) and (4.7.6) are identical. For any P the penalty function will generally not have the same global minima as the constrained problem (4.7.5). However, for P large, their solutions will likely be close.

Unfortunately, we cannot directly solve (4.7.6) for very large P on real-world computers because, when P is large, the Hessian of F, F_{xx}, is likely to be ill-conditioned at points away from the solution, leading to numerical imprecision and slow progress at best. The solution is to solve a sequence of problems. We first solve $\min_x F(x; P_1, a, b)$ with a small choice of P_1, yielding a solution x^1. We then execute the iteration

$$x^{k+1} \in \arg \min_x F(x; P_{k+1}, a, b), \tag{4.7.7}$$

where the conditioning problem is alleviated by using x^k for the initial guess in the iteration $k + 1$ minimization problem in (4.7.7). At each iteration k the Hessian at the solution, $F_{xx}(x^k; P_k, a, b)$, will generally be well-conditioned because the constraint violations will be small. Then, if P_k does not rise too rapidly, the initial Hessian in the $k + 1$ iteration, $F_{xx}(x^k; P_{k+1}, a, b)$, will be close to $F_{xx}(x^k; P_k, a, b)$ and not be ill-conditioned, in which case convergence to x^{k+1} should be as rapid as expected given the minimization method used.

Not only does the x^k sequence converge to the solution, but we can also compute the shadow prices to (4.7.5). The shadow prices of the constraints in (4.7.5) correspond to the shadow prices of the parameters a and b in (4.7.6). The shadow price of a_i in (4.7.6) is $F_{a_i} = P(g^i(x) - a_i)$. The shadow price of b_j in (4.7.6) is F_{b_j}. F_{b_j} is zero if the corresponding constraint is not violated; otherwise, it equals $P(h^j(x) - b_j)$. In general, the shadow price of a binding constraint is approximated by the product of the penalty parameter and the constraint violation. Let $\lambda(P, a, b)$ be the shadow prices, (F_a, F_b), of the constraint constants (a, b) at a local solution to (4.7.6) with penalty parameter P. The following theorem states the properties of the penalty function method more precisely:

THEOREM 4.7.1   Let λ^* denote the vector of shadow prices of the constraints in (4.7.5) at a solution x^*. Suppose that the Jacobian of the active constraints at x^* is of full rank and that x^* is the unique solution to (4.7.5) on a compact set, C. Then, if $P_k \to \infty$, there is a sequence x^k satisfying (4.7.7) that asymptotically lies in C, and converges to x^*. Furthermore the shadow prices of the penalized problems converge to the constrained shadow price, namely $\lambda(P_k, a, b) \to \lambda^*$.

Since the shadow prices of the penalized problem converge to the constrained shadow prices, we conclude that $P(g^i(x) - a_i) \to \lambda_i^*$ and $P(h^j(x) - b_j) \to \lambda_j^*$. These limits show that constraint violations will asymptotically be inversely proportional to the penalty parameter. While theorem 4.7.1 is true for any unbounded sequence of penalty parameters, conditioning problems mean that in practice, we must keep the growth rate down. Typically we will choose $P_{k+1} = 10P_k$; however, we may occasionally need slower rates of increase in P_k.

From our description of penalty methods, we make an important practical observation. Constrained minimization routines will often examine f at infeasible points, so the objective function f and the constraint functions g and h must be defined everywhere. This may require some alteration of all these functions. If any of these functions is changed to extend its range, that extension should be smooth enough that derivative-based optimization methods can be used without fear of getting hung up on kinks. We will return to this domain problem in the next chapter.

We must be careful in how we interpret Theorem 4.7.1. Consider the problem $\min_{0 \leq x \leq 1} x^3$. This problem leads to the penalty function $x^3 + P[(\min[x, 0])^2 + \max[x - 1, 0])^2]$, which is unbounded below as $x \to -\infty$, but it does have a local minimum at $x = 0$. This example emphasizes the local nature of theorem 4.7.1 and penalty methods. In any use of penalty methods, one must still check that the constraints are not being violated.

We will illustrate the penalty function method by applying it to a basic problem. Suppose that the consumer has two products to consume, good y having a price of 1 and good z a price of 2. Also suppose that total income is 5. Suppose that utility is $u(y, z) = \sqrt{yz}$. The optimal consumption bundle is $(y^*, z^*) = (5/2, 5/4)$, and the shadow price on the budget constraint is $\lambda^* = 8^{-1/2}$. The constrained optimization problem is

$$\max_{y,z} \sqrt{yz}$$
$$\text{s.t.} \quad y + 2z \leq 5. \tag{4.7.8}$$

To solve this, we maximize the penalized objective $u(y, z) - \frac{1}{2}P(\max[0, y + 2z - 5])^2$. Table 4.7 displays the iterates as we increase P. Note that the errors do fall rapidly to give good approximations but that the process bogs down for large P. Note that the constraint violation, $y + 2z - 5$, is inversely proportional to P, as predicted above. The error in the estimated shadow price, $P(5 - y - 2z) - \lambda^*$, appears stuck at about 10^{-4}.

Sequential Quadratic Method

The Kuhn-Tucker and penalty methods are not generally useful methods by themselves. One popular method is the *sequential quadratic* method. It takes advantage

Table 4.7
Penalty function method applied to (4.7.8)

k	P_k	$(y, z) - (y^*, z^*)$	Constraint violation	Shadow error
0	10	$(8.8(-3), 0.015)$	$1.0(-1)$	$-5.9(-3)$
1	10^2	$(8.8(-4), 1.5(-3))$	$1.0(-2)$	$-5.5(-4)$
2	10^3	$(5.5(-5), 1.7(-4))$	$1.0(-3)$	$2.1(-2)$
3	10^4	$(-2.5(-4), 1.7(-4))$	$1.0(-4)$	$1.7(-4)$
4	10^5	$(-2.8(-4), 1.7(-4))$	$1.0(-5)$	$2.3(-4)$

of the fact that there are special methods that can be used to solve problems with quadratic objectives and linear constraints. Suppose that the current guesses are (x^k, λ^k, μ^k). The sequential quadratic method then solves the quadratic problem

$$\min_{s}(x^k - s)^\top \mathscr{L}_{xx}(x^k, \lambda^k, \mu^k)(x^k - s)$$

$$\text{s.t.} \quad g_x(x^k)(x^k - s) = 0, \tag{4.7.9}$$

$$h_x(x)(x^k - s) \leq 0,$$

for the step size s^{k+1}. The problem in (4.7.9) is a linear-quadratic problem formed from a quadratic approximation of the Lagrangian and linear approximations of the constraints. The next iterate is $x^{k+1} = x^k + s^{k+1}$; λ and μ are also updated but we do not describe the details here. The sequential quadratic algorithm proceeds through a sequence of quadratic problems. The sequential quadratic method inherits many of the desirable properties of Newton's method, including local convergence, and can similarly use quasi-Newton and line search adaptations.

Augmented Lagrangian methods combine sequential quadratic methods and penalty function methods by adding penalty terms to the Lagrangian function. Solving the constrained optimization problem (4.7.1) may be different from minimizing its Lagrangian, even using the correct multipliers, but adding penalty terms can make the optimization problem similar to unconstrained minimization of the augmented Lagrangian. This augmented Lagrangian may be used just during a line search step or may be included in the quadratic approximation as well. These extra terms help limit the extent to which the iterates violate the constraints.

Reduced Gradient Methods

The addition of Lagrangian and penalty terms increases the size and complexity of the objective. *Reduced gradient methods* instead follow a path close to the feasible set. The idea is to specify a set of independent variables, use the equality constraints and binding inequality constraints to solve for the remaining "dependent" variables, and then optimize over the independent variables subject to the nonbinding inequality constraints only. The idea of expressing the dependent variables in terms of the independent variables is a nonlinear problem, and it is executed at each step in terms of linear approximations. The set of independent variables will change between iterations, since we do not know which inequality constraints will bind at a solution. We refer the reader to Luenberger (1984) and Gill et al. (1981, 1989) for presentations of the details.

Active Set Methods

The difficulty with the direct Kuhn-Tucker approach is that there are too many combinations to check; some choices of $\mathscr{P}$ may have no solution, and there may be multiple local solutions to others. Penalty function methods will also be costly, since all constraints must be computed in the penalty function (4.7.5), even if we know that only a few bind at the solution. These problems are all addressed by active set methods, whose strategy is to consider a rationally chosen series of subproblems.

Again let $\mathscr{I}$ be the set $\{1, 2, \ldots, l\}$, and for $\mathscr{P} \subset \mathscr{I}$ we define the $\mathscr{P}$ problem to be

$$(\mathscr{P}) \quad \min_{x} f(x)$$
$$\text{s.t.} \quad g(x) = 0, \tag{4.7.10}$$
$$h^i(x) \le 0, \qquad i \in \mathscr{P}.$$

Active set methods solve a series of these subproblems. A typical algorithm chooses a set of constraints, $\mathscr{P}$, to consider, and begins to solve (4.7.10). However, as it attempts to solve this problem, it periodically checks to see if some of the constraints in $\mathscr{P}$ fail to bind, in which case they are dropped. It also periodically checks to see if some other constraints are being violated, and adds them if they are. As the algorithm progresses, the penalty parameters are increased and constraints are added and deleted as appropriate. Asymptotically such methods will converge to the true constrained optimum with appropriate choices of penalty parameters and strategies for choosing and changing $\mathscr{P}$. The simplex method for linear programing is really an active set method.

This discussion of constrained optimization has only scratched the surface. Modern algorithms use sophisticated combinations of penalty function, active set, reduced gradient, and Lagrangian ideas together with local approximation methods. In the following sections we will use simple penalty methods to illustrate constrained optimization ideas. However, any serious constrained optimization problem should be analyzed using the sophisticated software.

4.8   Incentive Problems

The literature on incentive problems provides us with a wealth of constrained optimization problems. In this section we will use penalty methods to solve two simple problems, the first a hidden action and the other a hidden information model where agents have asymmetric information. While these examples are the simplest possible of their kind, it is clear that the numerical methods we use here are applicable to a wide range of contract design, optimal regulation, multiproduct pricing, and security design problems under asymmetric information.

Principal-Agent Problems

In principal-agent problems a "principal" hires an "agent" who, after signing the contract, takes actions that affect the payoffs to the partnership but are not observable to the principal. More formally, final output, y, is a random quantity depending on the agent's effort, L. We assume that y takes on values $y_1 < y_2 \cdots < y_n$, effort takes on m values, $L_j, j = 1, \ldots, m$, and $\text{Prob}\{y = y_i \,|\, L\} = g_i(L)$ represents the effect of effort on output. The agent chooses his effort, but the principal observes only output. Therefore the uncertain payment, w, to the agent can be a function of output only; hence the wage is a random variable where $w = w_i$ if and only if $y = y_i$. The payment schedule is agreed upon when the agent is hired, and known by the agent when he makes his effort choice.

   The problem is for the principal to choose a level of effort and a wage schedule such that the agent will choose that level of effort and will prefer working for the principal to his best alternative, the utility of which is R. Let $U^P(\pi)$ be the principal's von Neumann-Morgenstern utility function over profit π, and let $U^A(w, L)$ be the agent's utility function over wage, w, and effort, L. The principal's problem is expressed as the constrained optimization problem

$$\max_{L, w_i} E\{U^P(y - w)\}$$

$$\text{s.t.}\quad L \in \arg\max_{L} E\{U^A(w, L)\}, \tag{4.8.1}$$

$$E\{U^A(w, L)\} \geq R.$$

The constraint on L in (4.8.1) can be represented as a collection of inequality constraints

$$E\{U^A(w, L)\} \geq E\{U^A(w, L_j)\}, \qquad j = 1, \ldots, m.$$

This is not an easy optimization problem; the difficulties are discussed in Grossman and Hart (1983).

We consider the following simple two-state case: First, we assume a risk-neutral principal, that is, $U^P(\pi) = \pi$. Output will be either 0 or 2: $y_1 = 0$, $y_2 = 2$. The agent chooses one of two effort levels: $L \in \{0, 1\}$. High output occurs with probability 0.8 if the effort level is high (Prob$\{y = 2 \,|\, L = 1\} = 0.8$) but with probability 0.4 otherwise (Prob$\{y = 2 \,|\, L = 0\} = 0.4$). We assume that the agent's utility is $U^A(w, L) = u(w) - d(L) = -e^{-2w} + 1 - d(L)$ and that the disutility of effort is $d(0) = 0$, $d(1) = 0.1$. We assume that the agent's best alternative job is equivalent to $w = 1$ and $L = 1$ surely, implying that the reservation utility level, R, is $u(1) - d(1)$.

Let

$$\Delta(w_1, w_2) = E\{u(w) - d(1) \,|\, L = 1\} - E\{u(w) - d(0) \,|\, L = 0\}$$

be the expected utility difference between choosing $L = 1$ and $L = 0$. The interesting case is where the principal wants[6] the agent to choose $L = 1$. This means that the wages must be such that $\Delta(w_1, w_2) \geq 0$. Furthermore the agents expected utility from working and choosing $L = 1$, $E\{u(w)\} - d(1)$, must exceed R. In this case the penalty function for (4.8.1) is

$$0.8(2 - w_1) - 0.2w_2 - P \max[0, -(E\{u(w) - d(1) \,|\, L = 1\} - R)]^2$$

$$- P \max[0, -\Delta(w_1, w_2)]^2. \tag{4.8.2}$$

We will again apply Newton's method to (4.8.2) as we increase P. Table 4.8 displays the iterates as we increase the penalty from 10 to 10,000. Note that the violations of the incentive and reservation value constraints, columns "IV" and "RV" in

Table 4.8
Principal-agent problem (4.10.2)

P	(w_1, w_2)	IV	RV
10	(0.7889, 0.4605)	0.2(−1)	0.1(0)
10^2	(1.1110, 0.5356)	0.6(−2)	0.1(−1)
10^3	(1.2142, 0.5452)	0.8(−3)	0.2(−2)
10^4	(1.2289, 0.5462)	0.9(−4)	0.2(−3)
10^5	(1.2304, 0.5463)	0.9(−5)	0.2(−4)

6. We leave it as an exercise to check if $L = 1$ is the principal's choice.

table 4.8, drop in proportion to P. One could stop at the fifth iterate where $P = 10^5$, since the constraint violations are all small relative to the rest of the problem.

Note some features of the problem. First, the expected wage is \$1.0937, compared to the \$1 certainty equivalent of the worker's reservation utility. This shows that the agent bears a risk that costs about 9.4 cents to him in utility. Note that the difference between success and failure for the agent is 69 cents, whereas the difference between success and failure for the project is 2; hence the agent receives only 35% of the marginal *ex post* profit from success.

Managerial Incentives

The solution to the principal-agent problem is trivial if the agent is risk-neutral, that is, $u(c) = c$. The solution is $w(y) = y - F$; that is, the agent "buys" the firm for F and then takes the output. Economists commonly use this case as a benchmark. The extent to which this is inappropriate is illustrated by the basic literature on managerial incentives.

Jensen and Murphy (1990) found that executives earn only about \$3 per extra \$1,000 of profits. They argued that executive compensation was not as connected to profits as desirable. Haubrich (1994), on the other hand, showed that the observed sharing rules were consistent with optimal contracting and risk-averse managers. Haubrich examined a broad range of numerical examples that showed that management would receive a small share of profits when one made reasonable assumptions concerning the risk-aversion of managers, the marginal product of their effort, and the riskiness associated with their decisions. His paper is a good example of where a numerical examination of a model yields answers dramatically different from results of a less realistic model with a closed-form solution.

Efficient Outcomes with Adverse Selection

The Rothschild-Stiglitz-Wilson (RSW) model of insurance markets with adverse selection is a simple model illustrating how asymmetric information affects equilibrium and efficient allocations. In this section we use the RSW model to study efficient allocations under asymmetric information.[7]

We examine a model of risky endowments where a type H agent has a probability π^H of receiving e_1 and probability $1 - \pi^H$ of receiving e_2 where $e_1 > e_2$. Similarly type L agents have a probability π^L of receiving e_1 where $\pi^H > \pi^L$. Let θ^H (θ^L) be the fraction of type H (L) agents. These risks are independent across agents; we assume an infinite number of each type and invoke a law of large numbers.

---

7. Readers not familiar with this model should consult Rothschild and Stiglitz (1976) and Wilson (1977).

Suppose that a social planner wants to help these agents deal with their risks through insurance contracts. He can observe whether an individual receives e_1 or e_2 but does not know whether he is a type H or L agent. The planner's budget constraint requires that he break even. We let $y = (y_1, y_2)$ denote an agent's net state-contingent income, combining endowment and insurance transfers; that is, he pays $e_1 - y_1$ to the insurer and consumes y_1 if the endowment is e_1, and receives a payment equal to $y_2 - e_2$ and consumes y_2 otherwise. Let

$$U^t(y^t) = \pi^t u^t(y_1^t) + (1 - \pi^t) u^t(y_2^t), \qquad t = H, L,$$

be the type t expected utility function of the type t net income, y^t.

The social planner would like to give different insurance policies to agents of different type but cannot observe an agent's type. Therefore the social planner offers a menu of insurance contracts and lets each agent choose the one best for him. The planner's profits are

$$\Pi(y^H, y^L) = \theta^H(\pi^H(e_1 - y_1^H) + (1 - \pi^H)(e_2 - y_2^H))$$
$$+ \theta^L(\pi^L(e_1 - y_1^L) + (1 - \pi^L)(e_2 - y_2^L)). \tag{4.8.3}$$

An allocation $y^H, y^L \in R^2$ in the RSW model is *constrained efficient* if it solves a constrained optimization problem of the form

$$\max \lambda U^H(y^H) + (1 - \lambda) U^L(y^L)$$

$$\text{s.t.} \quad U^H(y^H) \geq U^H(y^L),$$
$$U^L(y^L) \geq U^L(y^H), \tag{4.8.4}$$
$$\Pi(y^H, y^L) \geq 0,$$

where $0 \leq \lambda \leq 1$ is the welfare weight of type H agents. In (4.8.4), the social planner chooses an insurance contract for each type, but he is constrained by the revelation requirement that each type will prefer the contract meant for that type over the contracts meant for other types.

We adapt a penalty function approach to this problem. In table 4.9 we display the results for $e_1 = 1$, $e_2 = 0$, $\theta^H = 0.1, 0.75$, $\pi^H = 0.8$, and $\pi^L = 0.8, 0.79, 0.7, 0.6, 0.5$. This was computed by a penalty function implementation of (4.8.4) where $P_k = 10^{1+k/2}$. Note the slow increase in P_k; it was used because the $P_k = 10^k$ sequence did not work.

When we solve constrained optimization problems, we must keep in mind that the "solutions" often violate many of the constraints. The "IV" column gives the

Table 4.9
Adverse selection example (4.10.3)

π^L	θ^H	(y_1^H, y_2^H)	(y_1^L, y_2^L)	IV	Profit
0.80	0.1	0.8011, 0.7956	0.8000, 0.7999	$-1(-7)$	$-8(-7)$
0.79	0.1	0.8305, 0.6780	0.7900, 0.7900	$-6(-8)$	$-4(-8)$
0.70	0.1	0.8704, 0.5183	0.7000, 0.7000	$-8(-8)$	$-1(-7)$
0.60	0.1	0.8887, 0.4452	0.6000, 0.6000	$-2(-6)$	$-1(-7)$
0.50	0.1	0.9040, 0.3842	0.5000, 0.5000	$-0.9(-4)$	$-0.2(-3)$
0.80	0.75	0.8000, 0.8000	0.7995, 0.8021	$-4(-7)$	$-5(-7)$
0.79	0.75	0.7986, 0.7931	0.7974, 0.7975	$-2(-6)$	$-4(-8)$
0.70	0.75	0.7876, 0.7328	0.7699, 0.7699	$-1(-7)$	$-8(-9)$
0.60	0.75	0.7770, 0.6743	0.7306, 0.7306	$-9(-8)$	$-5(-9)$
0.50	0.75	0.6791, 0.6273	0.6862, 0.6862	$-2(-7)$	$-1(-7)$

violation in the incentive constraint, $U^L(y^L) \geq U^L(y^H)$; the other constraint is never violated. A small negative value here indicates that the bundle which the type L agents receives is slightly less than the value of y^H to them, implying that type L agents would actually choose y^H. It may seem objectionable to accept the results in table 4.9 as solutions; however, the results together with the underlying continuity of the problem's structure do indicate that there exist incentive compatible bundles near the solutions in table 4.9, and a local search would probably find some if that were desired. The "profit" column displays the firm's profit in the solution. It is always negative, indicating that the firm actually loses money. Again, however, the violations are small indicating that profitable allocations are nearby. Of course what we really need to know is that there are allocations near the "solutions" in table 4.9 that are both incentive compatible and profitable. This takes us into the constraint qualification issues which we typically ignore. We will follow standard practice here and not go through the details of actually finding the nearby feasible allocations in this problem, but one must keep in mind that perverse situations may arise in complex nonlinear constrained optimization problems.

The results do reflect the predictions of adverse selection theory. In the case where there were many fewer type H agents, each type receives an allocation that produces zero profits, and there is no cross-subsidy. When there are many more type H agents than type L, cross-subsidies arise where the numerous type H agents accept actuarially unfair allocations, but by doing so, they receive relatively risk-free allocations. Also theory predicts that type L agents always receive a risk-free allocation; this is true to four digits in all entries of table 4.9. Note how rapidly the contracts become different as we increase the gap between the two type's probabilities of a high endowment. In particular, the type H contract goes from $(0.80, 0.80)$ when $\pi^L = 0.8$ and to $(0.83, 0.68)$ when $\pi^L = 0.79$, a substantial increase in risk even when the probability gap is only 0.01. We return to this property in chapter 15.

4.9   Computing Nash Equilibrium

In this section we will discuss an optimization approach to computing Nash equilibria introduced by McKelvey (1992). We will closely follow McKelvey's notation and presentation of the method. We assume n players. Player i has a finite strategy set $S_i = \{s_{i1}, s_{i2}, \ldots, s_{iJ_i}\}$ of J_i strategies. Let $S = \Pi_{i=1}^n S_i$ denote the set of all possible strategy combinations. Player i has a payoff function $M_i : S \to R$. Therefore, if player 1 plays $s_1 \in S_1$, player 2 plays $s_2 \in S_2$, and so on, then player j receives $M_j(s_1, s_2, \ldots, s_n)$. A game is denoted by the pair (M, S).

A mixed strategy for player i is modeled by a mapping $\sigma^i : S_i \to [0, 1]$ which gives the probability that player i plays pure strategy $s_i \in S_i$; hence each σ^i must satisfy $\sum_{s_i \in S_i} \sigma^i(s_i) = 1$. The joint probability of a strategy profile $s \equiv (s_1, \ldots, s_n)$ will be denoted $\sigma(s) = \Pi_{i=1}^n \sigma^i(s_i)$. Let Δ_i be the set of all such mixed strategies for player i, and $\Delta \equiv \Pi_{i=1}^n \Delta_i$ be the set of all mixed strategy profiles.

The payoff functions, M_i must be extended over the joint mixed strategies; the extension is

$$M_i(\sigma) = \sum_{s \in S} \sigma(s) M_i(s).$$

Let $M_i(q_i, \sigma_{-i})$ be the payoff to player i from playing the mixed strategy q_i while each of the other players plays his component of σ.

DEFINITION   The vector of (possibly) mixed strategies $\sigma = (\sigma^1, \ldots, \sigma^n)$ is a *Nash equilibrium* for the game (M, S) if for $i = 1, \ldots, n$, and all strategies $q_i \in \Delta_i$, the payoff to i of playing q_i, $M_i(q_i, \sigma_{-i})$, does not exceed the return from playing σ, $M_i(\sigma)$.

Let $M_i(s_{ij}, \sigma_{-i})$ be the payoff to i of playing their jth pure strategy, while all other players play their components of σ. To compute a Nash equilibrium, we will construct a function over Δ whose global minima corresponds exactly to the Nash equilibria of the game. Consider the function

$$v(\sigma) = \sum_{i=1}^n \sum_{s_{ij} \in S_i} \left\{ \max[M_i(s_{ij}, \sigma_{-i}) - M_i(\sigma), 0] \right\}^2.$$

Obviously $v(\sigma)$ is a nonnegative function.

THEOREM 4.9.1 (McKelvey)   The global minima of $v(\sigma)$ where the elements of σ are probabilities (i.e., lie between 0 and 1, inclusive, and sum to unity) are the Nash equilibria of (M, S); they are also the zeros of $v(\sigma)$.

Theorem 4.9.1 says that we can reduce the computation of Nash equilibrium to a constrained minimization problem; hence it is called a *Lyapunov approach*. This method has the important feature of converging to any isolated equilibrium if it starts near enough. This Lyapunov approach together with extensive search can therefore find all Nash equilibria if there are only a finite number of equilibria.

One disadvantage is that this method may get stuck at some local minimum not corresponding to any Nash equilibrium. Fortunately there is no problem in determining whether a local minimum is a Nash equilibrium, since theorem 4.9.1 assures us that σ is a Nash equilibrium if and only if $v(\sigma) = 0$. Therefore, if we stop at a nonequilibrium σ, we will know that fact because $v(\sigma) \neq 0$, and we will then try a new initial guess and resume minimizing $v(\sigma)$.

We apply McKelvey's method to the simple coordination game:

II

1, 1	0, 0
0, 0	1, 1

I

We will let p_j^i denote the probability that player i plays his jth strategy in the coordination game. The equilibrium payoff for each player is $p_1^1 p_1^2 + p_2^1 p_2^2$. The Lyapunov function for this game is

$$v(p_1^1, p_2^1, p_1^2, p_2^2) = \sum_{i,j=1}^{2} \max[0, p_i^j - (p_1^1 p_1^2 + p_2^1 p_2^2)]^2.$$

The three global minima (and the three equilibria) are $p = (p_1^1, p_2^1, p_1^2, p_2^2) = (1, 0, 1, 0)$, $(0.5, 0.5, 0.5, 0.5)$, and $(0, 1, 0, 1)$. To deal with the constraint that the probabilities sum to 1, we minimize the function $V(p_1^1, p_1^2) \equiv v(p_1^1, 1 - p_1^1, p_1^2, 1 - p_1^2)$ which imposes the summation condition.

Table 4.10 displays the iterates of the BFGS procedure from section 4.4 applied to $V(p_1^1, p_1^2)$, with various initial guesses. The first three columns are examples where the algorithm converges quickly to an equilibrium. The fourth column is problematic. The algorithm is stuck at $(0.25, 0.25)$, which is not an equilibrium. The reason for converging to this point is that $V(p_1^1, p_1^2)$ has a saddle point at $(0.25, 0.25)$; here

Table 4.10
Coordination game

Iterate	(p_1^1, p_1^2)	(p_1^1, p_1^2)	(p_1^1, p_1^2)	(p_1^1, p_1^2)
0	(0.1, 0.25)	(0.9, 0.2)	(0.8, 0.95)	(0.25, 0.25)
1	(0.175, 0.100)	(0.45, 0.60)	(0.959, 8.96)	(0.25, 0.25)
2	(0.110, 0.082)	(0.471, 0.561)	(0.994, 0.961)	(0.25, 0.25)
3	(0, 0)	(0.485, 0.509)	(1.00, 1.00)	(0.25, 0.25)
4	(0, 0)	(0.496, 0.502)	(1.00, 1.00)	(0.25, 0.25)
5	(0, 0)	(0.500, 0.500)	(1.00, 1.00)	(0.25, 0.25)

the gradient is zero, and V is convex in the p_1^1 and p_1^2 axes but concave along the diagonal directions. This would be detected by testing the Hessian, and it is a good example of why one should always check the second-order conditions before accepting the output from an optimization routine.

4.10 A Portfolio Problem

We next describe basic portfolio problem. Suppose that an investor must allocate his current wealth across current consumption, c, which is also the numéraire, and n assets, where one unit of asset i is currently valued at p_i and will be worth Z_i tomorrow. In this section we assume that asset 1 is a safe asset with $p_1 = 1$; then $Z_1 = R > 0$ is the safe return and $r \equiv R - 1$ is the interest rate. Let the investor's endowment of asset i be e_i, $i = 1 \ldots, n$. The investor's portfolio optimization problem in

$$\max_{\omega_i} u(c) + E\left\{ u\left(\sum_{i=1}^{n} \omega_i Z_i \right) \right\}$$

$$\text{s.t.} \quad \sum_{i=1}^{n} p_i(\omega_i - e_i) + c = 0. \tag{4.10.1}$$

Note that (4.10.1) is an optimization problem with one equality constraint.

In order to solve (4.10.1), we need to specify the asset return distribution. This generally requires some sort of discretization. In general, we assume a finite number of possible states of the world, S, and that the final value of asset i has a finite number of possible values; specifically, state s occurs with probability π_s and $Z_i = z_i^s$ in state s. This reduces (4.10.1) to the finite, computable optimization problem

Table 4.11
Portfolio problem

a	-0.5	-1	-5.0
ω^*	$(-1.41, 0.80, 1.60)$	$(-0.21, 0.40, 0.80)$	$(0.76, 0.08, 0.16)$
Iterate	L^2 error		
0	1(0)	5(−1)	5(−1)
1	2(0)	9(−1)	2(−1)
2	1(−2)	7(−3)	1(−3)
3	2(−5)	3(−5)	7(−6)
4	4(−12)	2(−11)	4(−12)
5	2(−14)	2(−14)	7(−16)
cond. H	1(3)	1(3)	1(3)

$$\max_{\omega} \ u(c) + \sum_{s=1}^{S} \pi_s\, u\!\left(\sum_{i=1}^{n} \omega_i z_i^s \right)$$

$$\text{s.t.} \ \sum_{i=1}^{n} p_i(\omega_i - e_i) + c = 0. \tag{4.10.2}$$

We illustrate these ideas in a simple, three-asset problem. We assume that $u(c) = -e^{-ac}$, $a \in \{-0.5, -1, -5\}$. Asset 1 has $Z_1 = R = 2$. We assume that Z_2 is uniformly distributed over $\{0.72, 0.92, 1.12, 1.32\}$ and that Z_3 is uniformly distributed over $\{0.86, 0.96, 1.06, 1.16\}$. The asset returns of the two risky assets are assumed to be independent random variables. Hence there are 16 equiprobable states. The initial endowment is 2, which implies that consumption is about 1 in each period which in turn implies that relative risk aversion nearly equals the absolute risk aversion coefficient, a. Table 4.11 displays the results. In each case we begin with the initial guess $\omega_i = 0.33$, $i = 1, 2, 3$.

We then display the L^2 norms of the errors of the first ten iterates. Note the rapid convergence of all three cases. The final iterates are all very close, indicating convergence. We do not display the gradients at the solutions, but they are close to machine epsilon. We also display the condition number of the Hessian at the final solution; the small condition numbers indicate that the problems are well-behaved, and the solutions are close to the true optima.

Suppose that we slightly change the example and assume that the price of each of the two risky assets is 0.5 while the price of the safe asset remains 1. In this case each risky asset returns more than the safe asset in each state of the world, and both risky assets dominates the safe asset. At these prices there are arbitrage opportunities, since an investor with zero wealth can short the safe asset and use the proceeds to buy the risky assets and surely have positive final wealth. In this case there is no solution to (4.10.1). This shows that it is easy to construct a problem where there is no solution.

There are some ways to adjust (4.10.1) to avoid this problem. First, one could check for asset dominance, but that may not be convenient. Second, one could impose some constraints, as in

$$\max_{\omega_i} u(c) + E\left\{ u\left(\sum_{i=1}^{n} \omega_i Z_i \right) \right\}$$

$$\text{s.t.} \sum_{i=1}^{n} p_i(\omega_i - e_i) + c = 0, \tag{4.10.3}$$

$$\omega_i \geq \bar{\omega}_i, \qquad i = 1, \ldots, n,$$

where the $\bar{\omega}_i$ are often nonpositive to model shorting constraints. The new problem (4.10.3) has a solution. Unfortunately, it is a constrained optimization problem. A third idea is to smoothly penalize extreme portfolios. This can be accomplished by examining the problem

$$\max_{\omega_i} u(c) + E\left\{ u\left(\sum_{i=1}^{n} \omega_i Z_i \right) \right\} - P\sum_{i}^{n} \omega_i^2$$

$$\text{s.t.} \sum_{i=1}^{n} p_i(\omega_i - e_i) + c = 0, \tag{4.10.4}$$

where P is a positive penalty term. This is a smooth unconstrained problem and will have a solution under some conditions, in particular, when u is bounded. The penalty term is economically sensible, for it may model transaction costs which are related to total volume.

This simple portfolio problem can be generalized in several directions. There may be restrictions on the final portfolio. For example, we could add the constraint $\omega_i \geq 0$ to forbid short sales of asset i. Another restriction, often induced by tax laws or other regulations, is a maximum on the holding of asset i. Transaction costs could also be introduced into the problem, causing the budget constraint to be nonlinear.

4.11 A Simple Econometric Example

We will use a simple nonlinear least squares problem to illustrate the differences between Newton's method and the Gauss-Newton method. Consider the empirical model

$$y = \alpha x_1 + \beta x_2 + \beta^2 x_3 + \varepsilon, \tag{4.11.1}$$

where $\varepsilon \sim N(0, 1)$. The nonlinear relation between the coefficients on x_2 and x_3 creates a nonlinear least squares problem. The data (available in the archive for this book) consists of twenty values for the dependent variable, y, and each of the independent variables, (x_1, x_2, x_3). The values of the independent variables and the error were generated by a normal random variable with α and β both set equal to zero. The nonlinear least squares criterion with this data is

$$
\begin{aligned}
S(\alpha, \beta) &\equiv \sum_{i=1}^{20} (y_i - (\alpha x_1 + \beta x_2 + \beta^2 x_3))^2 \\
&= 38.5 - 5.24\alpha - 7.56\alpha^2 - 6.10\beta + 9.96\alpha\beta \\
&\quad - 3.44\beta^2 + 11.4\alpha\beta^2 + 11.6\beta^3 + 7.71\beta^4.
\end{aligned} \tag{4.11.2}
$$

We first illustrate the application of Newton's method to (4.11.2). The objective $S(\alpha, \beta)$ has two local minima, at $A = (-0.2194, 0.5336)$ and $B = (0.1475, -1.1134)$, plus a saddle point at $C = (0.4814, -0.3250)$; the global minimum is at A. Since the local minima and the saddlepoint satisfy the first-order conditions for a minimum, they are potential convergence points for Newton's method. The problem of multiple local minima occurs frequently in nonlinear least squares and maximum likelihood estimation. The only thing we know from theorem 4.3.1 is that if we begin with an initial guess close enough to the global minimum Newton's method will converge to the global minimum. Further analysis (see chapter 5) shows that we will converge to any point satisfying the first-order conditions if we begin close enough to it. Otherwise, we know nothing at all about the ability of Newton's method to converge, to say nothing of converging to the global minimum. In figure 4.5 we display the convergence behavior of Newton's method applied to (4.11.2). The white areas are sets of points such that if Newton's method begins, there it will converge to the global minimum after ten iterations. The light gray areas are points from which Newton's method will lead to the other local minimum. The dark gray areas are points from which Newton's method will lead to the saddlepoint. The black areas are points from which Newton's method will lead, after ten iterations, to points far from any critical point.

The patterns that emerge display several important points. First, the domain of convergence for each local optimum contains a nontrivial neighborhood of the criti-

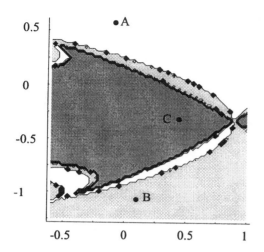

Figure 4.5
Domains of attraction for Newton's method applied to (4.11.2)

Table 4.12
Nonlinear least squares methods

Iterate	Newton	Gauss-Newton	Gauss-Newton	Gauss-Newton
0	(0, −0.5)	(0, −0.5)	(0, 1)	(0, −1.5)
1	(0.4956, −0.4191)	(0.4642, −0.7554)	(−0.6073, 0.7884)	(−0.0084, −1.2813)
2	(0.4879, −0.3201)	(0.2914, −1.0142)	(−0.3024, 0.6050)	(0.1192, −1.1524)
3	(0.4814, −0.3251)	(0.1741, −1.0914)	(−0.2297, 0.5426)	(0.1454, −1.1165)
4	(0.4814, −0.3251)	(0.1527, −1.1085)	(−0.2196, 0.5338)	(0.1475, −1.1134)
5	(0.4814, −0.3251)	(0.1487, −1.1123)	(−0.2194, 0.5336)	(0.1475, −1.1134)
6	(0.4814, −0.3251)	(0.1475, −1.1134)	(−0.2194, 0.5336)	(0.1475, −1.1134)

cal point, indicating that the closeness condition of theorem 4.3.1 is not a tightly binding restriction in practice.

Second, the regions are not connected. This is particularly the case near the boundaries of the convergence domains. Some initial guesses that cause Newton's method to converge to the global minimum are close to points that lead to the other local minimum, and some are close to points that lead nowhere. In some cases these boundary regions are actually fractal in nature, indicating the complexity and the erratic behavior of Newton's method in some cases.

We next examine the application of Gauss-Newton to solving (4.11.2). In table 4.12 we report the iterates of the Gauss-Newton method for various initial points.

Since Gauss-Newton does not have the quadratic convergence property, it is not as good as Newton in the later iterations. However, this is not important. The accuracy being attained at this point is not useful econometrically because of the nontrivial standard error.

Note that the Newton and Gauss-Newton methods may converge to different points even when they begin at the same point. Adding line search steps to these methods would improve both, and this is typically the way in which both are executed.

4.12   A Dynamic Optimization Problem

The previous examples have all been essentially static problems. Let us now examine a dynamic optimization problem. Many dynamic optimization problems require special methods because of the large number of choice variables. However, some have a special structure that can be exploited to improve speed.

We examine a simple life-cycle savings problem. Suppose that an individual lives for T periods, earns wages w_t in period $t, t = 1, \ldots, T$, consumes c_t in period t, earns interest on savings per period at rate r, and has the utility function $\sum_{t=1}^{T} \beta^t u(c_t)$. If we define S_t to be savings at the end of period t, then $S_{t+1} = (1 + r)S_t + w_{t+1} - c_{t+1}$. The constraint $S_T = 0$ expresses the dynamic budget constraint. Let us also assume that S_0, the initial asset level, is also zero. The substitution $c_t = S_{t-1}(1 + r) + w_t - S_t$ results in the problem

$$\max_{S_t} \sum_{t=1}^{T} \beta^t u(S_{t-1}(1 + r) + w_t - S_t) \equiv U(S)$$

$$\text{s.t.} \quad S_T = S_0 = 0$$

(4.12.1)

a problem with $T - 1$ choice variables. This may appear intractable for large T. However, there are two ways to exploit the special structure of this problem and to efficiently solve this problem.

First, one could use the conjugate gradient procedure. This has the advantage of computing only gradients. As long as $u(c)$ is concave, $U(S)$ is concave and the conjugate gradient procedure should proceed quickly to the solution. We will illustrate this in the case where $u(c) = -e^{-c}, \beta = 0.9, T = 6, r = 0.2, w_1 = w_2 = w_3 = w_4 = 1$ and $w_5 = w_6 = 0$. This models the case where the agent earns 1 per period in the first four periods of life, followed by two periods of no wage income which models retirement. Table 4.13 shows the result of applying the conjugate gradient method to (4.12.1) with these parameters and with the initial condition $S_1 = S_2 = S_3 = S_4 =$

Table 4.13
Conjugate gradient method for (4.14.1)

Iterate	S_1	S_2	S_3	S_4	S_5
1	0.4821	1.0170	1.015	1.326	0.7515
2	0.4423	0.7916	1.135	1.406	0.7270
3	0.3578	0.7631	1.120	1.446	0.7867
4	0.3680	0.7296	1.106	1.465	0.8258
5	0.3672	0.7351	1.100	1.468	0.8318
6	0.3710	0.7369	1.103	1.468	0.8370
7	0.3721	0.7447	1.110	1.476	0.8418
8	0.3742	0.7455	1.114	1.480	0.8427
9	0.3739	0.7456	1.114	1.480	0.8425

$S_5 = 0$. Row i of table 4.13 is the value of $(S_1, \ldots, S_5)$ produced by iteration i of the conjugate gradient method, with no restarts.

The rows in table 4.13 display several points. First, the method converged at the three-digit level after seven iterations and four digits after nine iterations. Those iterations were fast ones, avoiding any Hessian computation or storage. If the objective were quadratic, we would have convergence after five iterations. The objective in (4.12.1) is not quadratic, but the conjugate gradient method still converges quickly. Second, early iterates are surprisingly good approximations of the solution. For example, the worst component of iterate 3 has only a 10 percent error. This possibility is important, for in large problems with n variables we hope to be close after fewer than n iterations.

Third, the solution displays economically important properties. At early ages the worker saves, building up his assets. These assets are then dissaved during retirement. Given the solution for S, we can compute lifetime utility and any other index of interest. More complex versions of this model are frequently used in both theoretical and empirical work to analyze life-cycle savings and consumption patterns, and the conjugate gradient method can be used in these cases also. The ease with which we can solve this simple version numerically indicates that we can add much richness to our model and still solve it numerically with ease.

We can also use Newton's method to solve (4.12.1). Since Newton-like methods require a Hessian or an approximation to the Hessian, it would appear that they are not feasible, particularly if $T = 600$. However, consider the Hessian of $U(S)$; since S_t is separated from $S_{t-2}, S_{t-3}, \ldots$, and from $S_{t+2}, S_{t+3}, \ldots$, in $U(S)$ the Hessian is tridiagonal. Therefore computing a Newton step is easy, with a time and space cost of $\mathcal{O}(T)$. The key feature of (4.12.1) is that the objective is sum of functions, each of which depends only on successive pairs of the state variable, which in turn leads to a nearly diagonal Hessian. As long as the objective is representable in a similar, nearly separable, fashion, the Hessians of more complex problems will still be block diagonal and relatively easy to store and solve. Since these Hessians have special, tractable forms, any quasi-Newton method is also feasible.

4.13   Software

There are many optimization programs available. MINPACK contains basic optimization codes. Unfortunately, there is a cost to getting the best software, particulary if one wants sophisticated constrained optimization methods. The NPSOL and MINOS optimization packages are particularly noteworthy. Both are Fortran based and are among the best general purpose optimization packages available. The input interface of NPSOL is much more convenient. NPSOL is available in the NAG library. MINOS may be better for very large problems, since it has some sparse matrix capabilities. GAMS is a modeling language that accesses many algorithms. More and Wright (1993) is a very extensive review of optimization methods and available software packages, complete with instructions as to how to acquire them. The web site http://www.mcs.anl.gov/home/otc/Guide/SoftwareGuide/ contains links to many optimization software packages.

   The exercises below encourage the reader to implement the simple penalty function approach to constrained optimization. While this will be instructive, anyone who is going to solve many such problems should definitely get one of the sophisticated optimization packages. Many readers could write acceptable unconstrained optimization code, but it is much more difficult to write good, stable, reliable code for constrained optimization.

4.14   Further Reading and Summary

Optimization lies at the heart of most economic analyses. They range from the relatively simple problems of consumer demand to complex incentive mechanism design problems, multimodal maximum likelihood problems, and large dynamic optimization problems.

   The texts Bazaraa and Shetty (1979), Luenberger (1984), and Gill et al. (1981), and the surveys of Dennis and Schnabel (1989), Lemarachal (1989), and Gill, Murray, Saunders and Wright (1989) are excellent introductions to optimization theory and recent developments. The quadratic approximation idea of Newton's method and the Hessian-free approach of the conjugate gradient method are just two points on a continuum of possibilities. This is illustrated by some recent efforts in optimization theory. The tensor work of Schnabel and Chow (1985) goes beyond the quadratic approximation by adding higher-order terms. Greenblatt (1994) applies tensor methods to some econometric problems. All the methods we examined can give us only local optima. The global optimization literature is surveyed in Kan et al. (1989) and Horst and Pardalos (1995).

Linear programming is an important part of optimization theory; the reader is presumed to be familiar with the basics. Luenberger (1984) is an excellent text and Goldfarb and Todd (1989) surveys recent developments. Of particular interest are the new methods arising from Karmarkar (1984), which dominate the simplex method for large problems.

The McKelvey method is probably not the most efficient way for computing Nash equilibrium; however, it is the easiest to present and program. Alternative approaches are outlined in Wilson (1971), Lemke and Howson (1964), and Nagurney (1993); see also the McKelvey (1996) survey.

We finish this chapter by summarizing the lessons of numerical optimization. First, one should do a grid search if the nature of the objective is not known a priori. The grid search may include Hessian computations at the more promising points; this will alert one to possible ill-conditioning.

Then the proper choice of algorithm depends on the nature of the problem. If the objective is rough, a polytope method is advised, along with several restarts to avoid local solutions. If a problem is smooth and small, Newton's method is advised. If a problem is smooth but of moderate size, BFGS and DFP are advised to economize on Hessian computation. For large problems, the conjugate gradient method is available. If the objective is a sum of squares, then one should use specialized least squares methods.

Constrained problems are much more difficult than unconstrained methods, and one should use well-tested software. Linear programming problems are relatively simple to solve with the simplex method. In general, it is a good idea to make the constraints as linear as possible, putting nonlinearities in the objective function. General constrained problems are difficult, but there the sequential quadratic and reduced gradient methods are good methods that combine penalty function and local approximation ideas to solve them.

Exercises

1.   Use the polytope, steepest descent, Newton, Newton with line search, BFGS, and conjugate gradient methods to solve

$$\min_{x,y} 100(y - x^2)^2 + (1 - x)^2.$$

Which methods do well? poorly? Hint: Plot contours. Note that $(x, y) = (1, 1)$ is unique solution.

2. One of the classical uses of optimization in economics is the computation of the Pareto frontier. Consider the endowment economy with m goods and n agents. Assume that agent i's utility function over the m goods is

$$u^i(x) = \sum_{j=1}^{m} a_j^i x_j^{v_j^i + 1} (1 + v_j^i)^{-1}.$$

Suppose that agent i's endowment of good j is e_j^i. Assume that $a_j^i, e_j^i > 0 > v_j^i$, $i = 1, \ldots, n$, $j = 1, \ldots, m$. (For $v_j^i = -1$, we replace $x_j^{v_j^i + 1} (1 + v_j^i)^{-1}$ with $\ln x_j$.) Write a program (using the method of your choice) that will read in the v_j^i, a_j^i, and e_j^i values and the social weights $\lambda_i > 0$, and output the solution to the social planner's problem. First choose $m = n = 3$. For what preferences is convergence rapid? slow? Can your program handle $m = n = 5$? $m = n = 10$?

3. Solve the portfolio problem described in section 4.10. Table 4.11 used Newton's method. Implement the polytope, steepest descent, coordinate direction search, quasi-Newton method, BFGS, DFP, and conjugate gradient algorithms. Compare the performance of the methods.

4. Write a program for bimatrix games that implements McKelvey's Lyapunov approach to computing Nash equilibria. Compute equilibria for the following games:

Game 1

II

1, 1	5, 5	3, 0
1, 7	6, 4	1, 1
3, 0	2, 1	2, 2

I

Game 2

II

1, 1	4, 2	3, 2	0, 0
0, 3	2, 2	4, 1	0, 10
0, 0	5, 1	3, 3	10, 0
2, 1	5, 3	3, 1	4, 4

I

5. Use your program to solve figure 4.1.24 on page 39 and figure 4.2.5 on page 55 in Fudenberg and Tirole (1991) (FT). Generalize McKelvey's approach for subgame perfect equilibrium in two-stage games with perfect observation, and solve figure 4.3.3 in FT. Generalize this approach further to games with imperfect information and solve figures 3.4, 3.6, 3.15, 3.20, and 8.5 in FT.

6.   Solve the dynamic life-cycle consumption problem (4.12.1) where $w_t = 1 + 0.2t - 0.003t^2$ in year t, $T = 50$, $\beta = 0.96$, $r = 0.06$, $u(c) = -1/c$, and t is understood to be the year. Use both conjugate gradient method, and the Newton method with tridiagonal Hessian inversion. Compare the timing. Next solve the equivalent problem with a one-month time period with both methods, and again compare performance. Next assume that utility is $u(c) + v(l)$, where l is now labor supply; let $v(l) = -l^{1+\eta}/(1 + \eta)$, where $\eta = 1, 2, 10, 100$. Recompute the annual and monthly life-cycle problems.

7.   Write a program that computes Pareto-efficient allocations for the RSW model. Assume that all agents have the same utility but allow n risk types. Assume CRRA utility, and use the single-crossing property when specifying the constraint set. Next, write a program that solves any Paretian social planner's problem for a generalized RSW model that allows agents to differ in their (CRRA) utility function as well as in their probability of high income. Note that single crossing will not be useful here. Which incentive compatibility constraints now bind? Vary the social planner's weights. How does that affect which constraints bind?

5 Nonlinear Equations

Concepts of economic equilibrium are often expressed as systems of nonlinear equations. Such problems generally take two forms, zeros and fixed points. If $f : R^n \to R^n$, then a *zero of f* is any x such that $f(x) = 0$, and a *fixed point* of f is any x such that $f(x) = x$. These are essentially the same problem, since x is a fixed point of $f(x)$ if and only if it is a zero of $f(x) - x$. The existence of solutions is examined in Brouwer's theorem and its extensions.[1] In this chapter we examine numerical methods for solving nonlinear equations.

The Arrow-Debreu concept of general equilibrium reduces to finding a price vector at which excess demand is zero; it is the most famous nonlinear equation problem in economics. Other examples include Nash equilibria of games with continuous strategies and the transition paths of deterministic dynamic systems. More recently, economists have solved nonlinear dynamic problems in infinite-dimensional spaces by approximating them with nonlinear equations in finite-dimensional Euclidean spaces. Nonlinear equation solving is a central component in many numerical procedures in economics.

In this chapter we examine a wide range of methods for solving nonlinear equations. We first discuss techniques for one-dimensional problems. We then turn to several methods for solving general finite-dimensional problems, including Gauss-Jacobi, Gauss-Seidel, successive approximation, Newton's method, and homotopy methods. These methods offer a variety of approaches, each with its own strengths and weaknesses. We apply these methods to problems from static general equilibrium and oligopoly theory.

5.1 One-Dimensional Problems: Bisection

We first consider the case, $f : R \to R$, of a single variable and the problem $f(x) = 0$. This special case is an important one; it is also the basis of some multidimensional routines. We use this case to simply exposit ideas that generalize to n dimensions.

Bisection

The first method we examine is bisection, which is displayed in figure 5.1. Suppose f is continuous and $f(a) < 0 < f(b)$ for some a, b, $a < b$. Under these conditions, the intermediate value theorem (IVT) tells us that there is some zero of f in (a, b). The bisection method uses this result repeatedly to compute a zero.

Consider $c = \frac{1}{2}(a + b)$, the midpoint of $[a, b]$. If $f(c) = 0$, we are done. If $f(c) < 0$, the IVT says that there is a zero of f in (c, b). The bisection method then continues

---

1. For a review of fixed-point theory, see Border (1985).

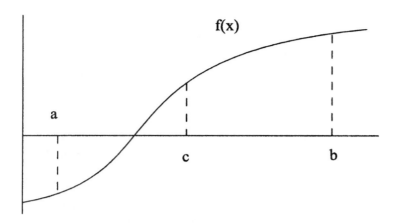

Figure 5.1
Bisection method

by focusing on the interval (c, b). If $f(c) > 0$, as in figure 5.1, there is a zero in (a, c), and the bisection method continues with (a, c). In either case, the bisection method continues with a smaller interval. There could be zeros in both (a, c) and (b, c), but our objective here is to find some zero, not all zeros. The bisection method applies this procedure repeatedly, constructing successively smaller intervals containing a zero.

Algorithm 5.1   Bisection Method

Objective: Find a zero of $f(x), f : R^1 \rightarrow R^1$.

Initialization. Initialize and bracket a zero: Find $x^L < x^R$ such that $f(x^L) \cdot f(x^R) < 0$, and choose stopping rule parameters $\varepsilon, \delta > 0$.

Step 1. Compute midpoint: $x^M = (x^L + x^R)/2$.

Step 2. Refine the bounds: If $f(x^M) \cdot f(x^L) < 0$, $x^R = x^M$ and do not change x^L; else $x^L = x^M$ and leave x^R unchanged.

Step 3. Check stopping rule: If $x^R - x^L \le \varepsilon(1 + |x^L| + |x^R|)$ or if $|f(x^M)| \le \delta$, then STOP and report solution at x^M; else go to step 1.

While the bisection algorithm is simple, it displays the important components of any nonlinear equation solver: Make an initial guess, compute iterates, and check if the last iterate is acceptable as a solution. We next address the stopping criterion of the bisection method.

Stopping Rules

Iterative schemes seldom land on the true solution. Furthermore, continuing the iteration is eventually of no value since round-off error in computing $f(x)$ will eventually dominate the differences between successive iterates. Therefore a critical component of any nonlinear equation solver is the stopping rule. A stopping rule generally computes some estimate of the distance to a solution, and then stops the iteration when that estimate is small. In the case of the bisection method, it is clear that $x^R - x^L$ is an overestimate of the distance to a solution since the zero is bracketed. Step 3 says to stop in either of two cases. First, we can stop whenever the bracketing interval is so small that we do not care about any further precision. This is controlled by the choice of ε, which need not be small. For example, if the problem is finding the equilibrium price for a market, there is little point in being more precise than finding the solution to within a penny if the equilibrium price is on the order of $1,000.

If we want high precision, we will choose small ε, but that choice must be reasonable. Choosing $\varepsilon = 0$ is nonsense, since it is unachievable; equally pointless is choosing $\varepsilon = 10^{-20}$ on a 12-digit machine where f can be calculated with at most 12 digits of accuracy. Note also that we use a relative step size condition in step 3 of the algorithm 5.1 for stopping because the computer can really detect only relatively small intervals. If x^L and x^R are of the order 10^{10}, demanding $x^R - x^L < 10^{-5}$ would be the same as choosing $\varepsilon = 0$ on a machine that has only 12-digit precision. This consideration alone would argue for a purely relative change test of the form $x^R - x^L < \varepsilon(|x^L| + |x^R|)$. Such a test would have problems in cases where the solution is close to $x = 0$ and x^L and x^R converges to 0. The "1" in the stopping criterion in step 3 avoids this problem.

Second, we must stop when round-off errors associated with computing f make it impossible to pin down the zero any further; that is, we stop when $f(x^M)$ is less than the expected error in calculating f. This is controlled in step 3 by δ; therefore δ should be at least the error expected in the computation of f. In some cases the computation of f may be rather complex and subject to a variety of numerical errors so that δ may be much larger than the machine precision. In other cases we may be satisfied with an x that makes $f(x)$ small but not zero. In those cases we should choose δ to be the maximal value for $f(x)$ that serves our purposes.

Convergence

If an iterative method is to be useful, it must converge to the solution and do so at a reasonable speed. Convergence properties for bisection are obvious. Bisection will always converge to a solution once we have found an initial pair of points, x^L and x^R, that bracket a zero.

Being essentially a linearly convergent iteration, bisection is a slow method. Suppose that you want to increase the accuracy by one significant decimal digit; that is, reduce the maximum possible error, $|x_k^L - x_k^R|$, by 90 percent. Since each iteration of bisection reduces the error by only 50 percent, it takes more than three iterations to add a decimal digit of accuracy.

5.2   One-Dimensional Problems: Newton's Method

While bisection is a reliable procedure, its slow speed makes it a poor method for solving one-dimensional equations. It is also a method that assumes only continuity of f. Newton's method uses smoothness properties of f to formulate a method that is fast when it works but may not always converge. Newton's method approximates $f(x)$ by a succession of linear functions, and it approximates a zero of f with the zeros of the linear approximations. If f is smooth, these approximations are increasingly accurate, and the successive iterates will converge rapidly to a zero of f. In essence Newton's method reduces a nonlinear problem to a sequence of linear problems, where the zeros are easy to compute.

Formally Newton's method is a simple iteration. Suppose that our current guess is x_k. At x_k we construct the linear approximation to f at x_k, yielding the function $g(x) \equiv f'(x_k)(x - x_k) + f(x_k)$. The functions $g(x)$ and $f(x)$ are tangent at x_k, and generally close in the neighborhood of x_k. Instead of solving for a zero of f, we solve for a zero of g, hoping that the two functions have similar zeros. Our new guess, x_{k+1}, will be the zero of $g(x)$, implying that

$$x_{k+1} = x_k - \frac{f(x_k)}{f'(x_k)}. \tag{5.2.1}$$

Figure 5.2 graphically displays the steps from x_1 to x_5. The new guess will likely not be a zero of f, but the hope is that the sequence x_k will converge to a zero of f. Theorem 2.1 provides a sufficient condition for convergence.

THEOREM 2.1   Suppose that f is C^2 and that $f(x^*) = 0$. If x_0 is sufficiently close to x^*, $f'(x^*) \neq 0$, and $|f''(x^*)/f'(x^*))| < \infty$, the Newton sequence x_k defined by (5.2.1) converges to x^*, and it is quadratically convergent, that is,

$$\limsup_{k \to \infty} \frac{|x_{k+1} - x^*|}{|x_k - x^*|^2} < \infty. \tag{5.2.2}$$

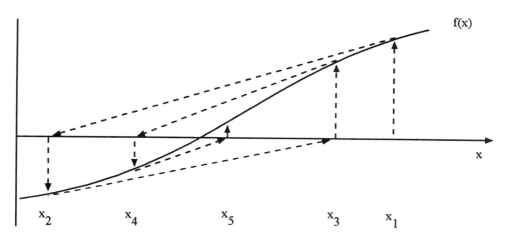

Figure 5.2
Newton method

Proof The proof of theorem 4.1.1 for Newton's method for optimization was really a proof that Newton's method for nonlinear equations converged when applied to the first-order conditions of an optimization problem. That proof applies here without change. In particular,

$$\lim_{k \to \infty} \frac{|x_{k+1} - x^*|}{|x_k - x^*|^2} = \frac{1}{2} \frac{|f''(x^*)|}{|f'(x^*)|} \tag{5.2.3}$$

which is finite if $f'(x^*) \neq 0$. ■

We see the usual trade-off when we compare Newton's method with bisection. Bisection is a safe method, always converging to a zero; unfortunately, it is slow. Newton's method sacrifices reliability for a substantial gain in speed if it converges. In choosing between the two methods, one must judge the relative importance of these features and the likelihood of Newton's method not converging.

Convergence Tests

Equation (5.2.1) is just the iterative portion of Newton's method. To complete the algorithm, we must append a convergence test, particularly since Newton's method does not bracket a zero. Typically an implementation of Newton's method applies a two-stage test in the spirit of the convergence tests discussed in chapter 2. First, we ask if the last few iterations have moved much. Formally we specify an ε and conclude that we have converged if $|x_k - x_{k-l}| < \varepsilon(1 + |x_k|)$ for $l = 1, 2, \ldots, L$; often we take $L = 1$.

Second, we ask if $f(x_k)$ is "nearly" zero. More precisely we stop if $|f(x_k)| \leq \delta$ for some prespecified δ. The tightness of this criterion is governed by the choice of δ, and the considerations here are the same as the choice of δ in bisection method. The full Newton algorithm is presented in algorithm 5.2.

Algorithm 5.2   Newton's Method

Objective: Find a zero of $f(x)$, $f : R^1 \to R^1$, $f \in C^1$.

Initialization. Choose stopping criterion ε and δ, and starting point x_0. Set $k = 0$.

Step 1. Compute next iterate: $x_{k+1} = x_k - f(x_k)/f'(x_k)$.

Step 2. Check stopping criterion: If $|x_k - x_{k+1}| \leq \varepsilon(1 + |x_{k+1}|)$, go to step 3. Otherwise, go to step 1.

Step 3. Report results and STOP: If $|f(x_{k+1})| \leq \delta$, report success in finding a zero; otherwise, report failure.

Even if we have found a point that satisfies both the ε and δ tests, it may still not be a zero, or close to one. Consider the case of $f(x) = x^6$. Appying step 1 to x^6 implies that $x_{k+1} = \frac{5}{6}x_k$, which is a slow, linearly convergent iteration. The problem is that x^6 is flat at its zero. More generally, if a function is nearly flat at a zero, convergence can be quite slow, and loose stopping rules may stop far from the true zero.

These stopping rule issues are more important in the case of nonlinear equations than in optimization problems. In optimization problems one is often satisfied with some point x that is nearly as good as the true optimum x^* in optimizing the objective, $F(x)$. In such cases one does not care if the error $x - x^*$ is large. We are often more demanding when solving nonlinear equations, requiring the error $x - x^*$ to be small. Therefore stopping rule issues are more important.

Importance of Units

At this point we turn to an important consideration in constructing equations and implementing the stopping criterion in step 3. In step 3 we declare success as long as we have found some x such that $f(x)$ is less than δ in magnitude. This is actually an empty test, for we can always take $f(x)$, multiply it by 10^{-k} for some large k, and have a new function with the same zeros. We may now find many x such that $10^{-k}f(x) < \delta$. While we would not do this intentionally, we could easily do this accidentally.

The general point is that we need to keep track of the units we are implicitly using, and formulate the problem and stopping rules in unit-free ways. Step 3 must be carefully formulated for it to be meaningful. For example, in computing the equilibrium price, p, of a good, let $f(p) = D(p) - S(p)$ be excess demand and assume that D and S can be computed with double precision accuracy. In this case the stopping rule in step 3 could be reformulated as $D(p) - S(p) < \delta D(p)$ with $\delta = 10^{-8}$. This stopping rule avoids all unit problems; it stops when excess demand is small relative to total demand. Simple adjustments to step 3 like this are ideal because they avoid unit problems without affecting the algorithm and can often be implemented.

Pathological Examples

Newton's method works well when it works, but it can fail. Consider the case of $f(x) = x^{1/3}e^{-x^2}$. The unique zero of f is at $x = 0$. However, Newton's method produces (see Donovan et al. 1993 for details) the iteration

$$x_{n+1} = x_n\left(1 - \frac{3}{1 - 6x_n^2}\right) \tag{5.2.4}$$

which has two pathologies. First, for x_n small, (5.2.4) reduces to $x_{n+1} = -2x_n$, showing that (5.2.4) converges to 0 only if $x_0 = 0$ is the initial guess. For large x_n, (5.2.4) becomes $x_{n+1} = x_n(1 + 2/x_n^2)$, which diverges but slowly. In fact, for any ε, $\delta > 0$, there will ultimately be large x_n and x_{n+1} such that $|f(x_{n+1})| < \delta$ and $|x_{n+1} - x_n| < \varepsilon$; reducing δ and ε will cause Newton's method to stop at a value even farther from the true zero.

What goes wrong? The divergence of Newton's method is due to the infinite value of $f''(0)/f'(0)$. The second problem arises because the e^{-x^2} factor squashes the function at large x, leading Newton's method, (5.2.4), to "think" that it is getting close to a zero; in some sense it is, since $f(\pm\infty) = 0$.

Newton's method can also converge to a cycle. Figure 5.3 illustrates how easy it is to construct such as case. To get Newton's method to cycle between, say, -1 and 1, we just need $f'(1) = 0.5 = f'(-1)$ and $f(1) = 1 = -f(-1)$. While these examples are contrived, their lessons should not be ignored. In particular one should be sure that $f'(x^*) \neq 0$ and $f''(x^*)$ are not too large. While this may seem trite, it is easy to write examples where some of the derivatives at the solution are very large, and the radius of convergence is small. In the less pathological case of figure 5.3, Newton's method will converge if we begin with $x \in [-0.5, 0.5]$, showing the importance of a good initial guess.

A General Equilibrium Example with the Limited Domain Problem

Our discussion has implicitly assumed that f is defined at each Newton iterate; this is not true in many economic examples. We have also not considered how multiple

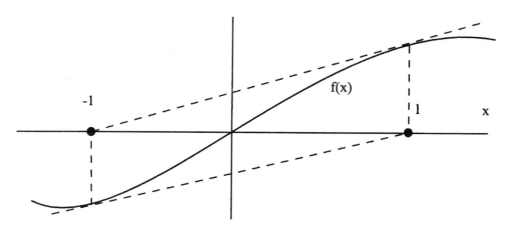

Figure 5.3
Newton method cycle

solutions affect the performance of Newton's method. We now examine both of these possibilities in the context of a simple equilibrium example.

Many economically interesting problems contain multiple solutions. This is illustrated in the following example of multiple equilibria taken from Kehoe (1991). Assume two goods and two consumers in an exchange economy. Agent i, $i = 1, 2$, has the utility function over consumption of goods 1 and 2:

$$u_i(x_1, x_2) = \frac{a_1^i x_1^{(\gamma_i + 1)}}{\gamma_i + 1} + \frac{a_2^i x_2^{(\gamma_i + 1)}}{\gamma_i + 1},$$

where $a_j^i \geq 0$, $\gamma_i < 0$. Let $\eta_i \equiv -1/\gamma_i$ be the constant elasticity of substitution in the utility function of agent i. If agent i has endowment $e^i \equiv (e_1^i, e_2^i)$ and the price of good j is p_j, then his demand function is $d_j^i(p) = \theta_j^i I^i p_j^{-\eta_i}$ where $I^i = p \cdot e^i$ is i's income and $\theta_j^i \equiv (a_j^i)^{\eta_i} / \sum_{l=1}^{2} (a_l^i)^{\eta_i} p_l^{(1-\eta_i)}$. Assume that $a_1^1 = a_2^2 = 1024$, $a_2^1 = a_1^2 = 1$, $e_1^1 = e_2^2 = 12$, $e_2^1 = e_1^2 = 1$, $\gamma_1 = \gamma_2 = -5$, implying that $\eta_1 = \eta_2 = 0.2$. An equilibrium is a solution to the system

$$\sum_{i=1}^{2} d_1^i(p) = \sum_{i=1}^{2} e_1^i, \qquad p_1 + p_2 = 1, \tag{5.2.5}$$

where the first equation imposes supply equals demand for good 1 and the second equation normalizes the price vector to lie on the unit simplex. The pair of equations

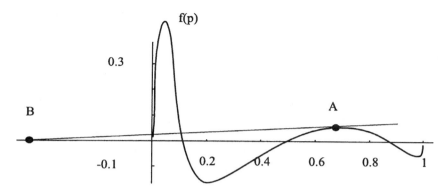

Figure 5.4
Excess demand function in (5.2.6)

in (5.2.5) suffice since Walras's law implies that supply will equal demand for good 2 at any solution to (5.2.5).

There are three equilibria to (5.2.5). They are $p^1 = (0.5, 0.5)$, the symmetric outcome, and two asymmetric equilibria at $p^2 = (0.1129, 0.8871)$ and $p^3 = (0.8871, 0.1129)$. We can reduce this problem to a one-variable problem when we make the substitution $p_2 = 1 - p_1$, yielding the problem

$$f(p_1) \equiv \sum_{i=1}^{2} d_1^i(p_1, 1 - p_1) - \sum_{i=1}^{2} e_1^i = 0. \tag{5.2.6}$$

The graph of f is displayed in figure 5.4.

We can use this example to examine the "dynamic" behavior of Newton's method. Each of the three equilibria are locally stable attraction points for Newton's method since the d_1^i have finite derivatives at each equilibrium.

However, between the equilibria Newton's method is not so well-behaved. A serious problem arises because the excess demand function f is defined only for positive p_1. Upon applying Newton's method to (5.2.6), one will often experience a severe problem; Newton's method will sometimes try to evaluate f at a negative price, where f is not defined. This *limited domain problem* is demonstrated in figure 5.4. If we began Newton's method at A, the next guess for p_1 would be B, outside the domain of f.

There are three approaches to deal with the limited domain problem. First, one could check at each iteration whether $f(x^{k+1})$ is defined, and if it is not, move x^{k+1} toward x^k until f is defined. This will prevent a crash due to undefined numerical operations. Unfortunately, this strategy requires access to the source code of the zero-finding routine, something that is often not possible. This new point may also generate an iterate outside the domain of f. With this strategy, one must be prepared to start over at a different initial guess.

Second, one could extend the definition of f so that it is defined at any price. Newton's method will now be globally defined. However, this is not generally easy. For Newton's method to have a good chance of getting back to the correct region, the extension should be a smooth extension of the existing function. In this case we also have the problem that demand is infinite at $p_1 = 0$, implying that any successful change must involve changing f for some region of positive p_1 values. One way to implement this *extension method* replaces f with $\tilde{f}(p_1)$, defined by

$$\tilde{f}(p_1) = \begin{cases} f(p_1), & p_1 > \varepsilon, \\ f(\varepsilon) + f'(\varepsilon)(p_1 - \varepsilon) + \dfrac{f''(\varepsilon)(p_1 - \varepsilon)^2}{2}, & p_1 \leq \varepsilon, \end{cases} \qquad (5.2.7)$$

for some small $\varepsilon > 0$. This replaces f with a C^2 function that agrees with f at most positive prices and is defined for all prices. We may have introduced extra solutions, but if Newton's method converges to a solution with a negative price, we should just try again with a different initial guess. The trick here is to choose ε so that there are no solutions to $f(p_1) = 0$ in $(0, \varepsilon)$, the set of positive prices where $\tilde{f}(p_1) \neq f(p_1)$. Outside of this region, any positive zero of $\tilde{f}$ is also a zero of f. This approach is easy to apply to single variable problems but not so easy to implement in multivariate problems.

Third, one can change the variable so that Newton's method stays in the appropriate region. This typically involves a nonlinear change of variables. In this case we want p_1 to stay within $[0, 1]$. If $P : R \rightarrow (0, 1)$ is C^2, monotonically increasing, and onto, then restating the problem in terms of $z \equiv P^{-1}(p_1)$ produces a new system, $f(P(z)) = 0$, which is defined for all $z \in R$ and whose zeros match one-to-one with the zeros of $f(p_1)$. In particular, one could use $p_1 = P(z) \equiv e^z/(e^z + e^{-z})$ with the inverse map $z = (1/2) \ln(p_1/(1 - p_1))$. Newton's method applied to

$$g(z) \equiv f(P(z)) = 0 \qquad (5.2.8)$$

results in the iteration

$$z_{k+1} = z_k - \frac{g(z_k)}{g'(z_k)}. \qquad (5.2.9)$$

Equation (5.2.9) implies the p_1 iteration

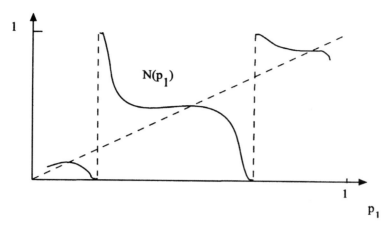

Figure 5.5
First iterate of Newton method applied to (5.2.6)

$$p_{1,k+1} = P\left(P^{-1}(p_{1,k}) - \frac{f(p_{1,k})}{f'(p_{1,k})P'(P^{-1}(p_{1,k}))}\right) \equiv N(p_{1,k}), \qquad (5.2.10)$$

where each iterate is positive.

The limited domain problem may arise in many numerical contexts. We touched on it briefly in the optimization chapter. The extension approach and nonlinear transformations will also work for domain problems that arise in optimization problems. Domain problems can arise in almost any kind of numerical problem. In general, one of these tricks will be necessary to construct a reliable algorithm when some function used by the algorithm is not globally defined.

Even after transforming the variable, Newton's method can behave strangely. We plot the transformed Newton's iteration (5.2.10) as $N(p_1)$ in figure 5.5. Note that it is discontinuous near $p_1 = 0.21$ and $p_1 = 0.7$. In this case let us consider the domains of attraction for each of the solutions. Figure 5.6 displays the fourth iterate of N. Figure 5.6 shows that (5.2.10) converges to some equilibrium after four iterates for most initial guesses but that the domains of attraction are not connected. In particular, we find that (5.2.10) converges to $p_1 = 0.1129$ from $p_1 \in [0, 0.2]$ and $p_1 \in [0.67, 0.70]$ but not from most intervening initial guesses. In particular, there is no reason to trust that Newton's method will converge to the equilibrium nearest the initial guess.

These examples illustrate both the power of and problems with Newton's method. Newton's method is very useful for solving nonlinear equations, but it must be

Figure 5.6
Fourth iterate of Newton method applied to (5.2.6)

applied carefully, with the user alert for the potential problems. These lessons will apply even more forcefully to the multivariate case studied below.

5.3   Special Methods for One-Dimensional Problems

We next consider two special one-dimensional methods. These do not directly generalize to multivariate problems but are quite useful in the single-variable case.

Secant Method

A key step in Newton's method is the computation of $f'(x)$, which may be costly. The *secant method* employs the idea of linear approximations but never evaluates f'. Instead, the secant method approximates $f'(x_k)$ with the slope of the secant of f between x_k and x_{k-1}, resulting in the iteration

$$x_{k+1} = x_k - \frac{f(x_k)(x_k - x_{k-1})}{f(x_k) - f(x_{k-1})}. \tag{5.3.1}$$

The secant method is the same as Newton's method except that step 1 uses equation (5.3.1) to compute the next iterate. The secant method suffers the same convergence problems as Newton's method, and when it converges, convergence is slower in terms of the number of required evaluations of f because of the secant approximation to the derivative. However, the running time can be much less because the secant method never evaluates f'. The convergence rate is between linear and quadratic.

THEOREM 3.1   If $f(x^*) = 0$, $f'(x^*) \neq 0$, and $f'(x)$ and $f''(x)$ are continuous near x^*, then the secant method converges at the rate $(1 + \sqrt{5})/2$, that is

$$\limsup_{k \to \infty} \frac{|x_{k+1} - x^*|}{|x_k - x^*|^{(1+\sqrt{5})/2}} < \infty. \tag{5.3.2}$$

Proof   See Young and Gregory (1988, vol. 1, pp. 150ff). ∎

Fixed-Point Iteration

As with linear equations, we can often rewrite nonlinear problems in ways that suggest a computational approach. In general, any fixed-point problem $x = f(x)$ suggests the iteration $x_{k+1} = f(x_k)$. Consider the problem

$$x^3 - x - 1 = 0. \tag{5.3.3}$$

Equation (5.3.3) can be rewritten in the fixed-point form $x = (x + 1)^{1/3}$, which suggests the iteration

$$x_{k+1} = (x_k + 1)^{1/3}. \tag{5.3.4}$$

The iteration (5.3.4) does converge to a solution of (5.3.3) if $x_0 = 1$. However, if we rewrite (5.3.3) as $x = x^3 - 1$, the suggested scheme

$$x_{k+1} = x_k^3 - 1 \tag{5.3.5}$$

diverges to $-\infty$ if $x_0 = 1$.

  The fixed-point iteration approach to solving nonlinear equations is often useful but not generally reliable. We have focused on the more reliable methods, but that does not mean that one should ignore fixed-point iteration schemes. Also we should be flexible, looking for transformations that can turn unstable schemes into stable schemes, just as we transformed (5.3.3) into (5.3.4). In economic analysis the objective is to solve the problem $f(x) = 0$; how one finds the solution is of secondary importance.

5.4   Elementary Methods for Multivariate Nonlinear Equations

Most problems have several unknowns, requiring the use of multidimensional methods. Suppose that $f : R^n \to R^n$ and that we want to solve $f(x) = 0$, a list of n equations in n unknowns:

$$f^1(x_1, x_2, \ldots, x_n) = 0,$$

$$\vdots \qquad\qquad\qquad\qquad\qquad\qquad (5.4.1)$$

$$f^n(x_1, x_2, \ldots, x_n) = 0.$$

This section examines simple methods for solving (5.4.1).

Gauss-Jacobi Algorithm

In chapter 3 we discussed Gauss-Jacobi and Gauss-Seidel iterative schemes for solving linear equations. Both of these methods can be generalized to nonlinear problems.

The simplest iteration method is the Gauss-Jacobi method. Given the known value of the kth iterate, x^k, we use the ith equation to compute the ith component of unknown x^{k+1}, the next iterate. Formally x^{k+1} is defined in terms of x^k by the equations in (5.4.2):

$$f^1(x_1^{k+1}, x_2^k, x_3^k, \ldots, x_n^k) = 0,$$

$$f^2(x_1^k, x_2^{k+1}, x_3^k, \ldots, x_n^k) = 0,$$

$$\vdots \qquad\qquad\qquad\qquad\qquad\qquad (5.4.2)$$

$$f^n(x_1^k, x_2^k, \ldots, x_{n-1}^k, x_n^{k+1}) = 0.$$

Each equation in (5.4.2) is a single nonlinear equation with one unknown, allowing us to apply the single-equation methods presented in the previous sections. The Gauss-Jacobi algorithm procedure reduces the problem of solving for n unknowns simultaneously in n equations to that of repeatedly solving n equations with one unknown.

The Gauss-Jacobi method is affected by the indexing scheme for the variables and equations. There is no natural choice for which variable is variable 1 and which equation is equation 1. Therefore there are $n!$ different Gauss-Jacobi schemes. It is difficult to determine which scheme is best, but some simple situations come to mind. For example, if some equation depends on only one unknown, then that equation should be equation 1 and that variable should be variable 1. In general, we should choose an indexing so that (5.4.2) "resembles" a nonlinear form of back-substitution.

Each step in the Gauss-Jacobi method is a nonlinear equation and is usually solved by some iterative method. There is little point in solving each one precisely, since we must solve each equation again in the next iteration. We could just approximately solve each equation in (5.4.2). This leads to the *linear Gauss-Jacobi method*, which takes a single Newton step to approximation the components of x^{k+1}. The resulting scheme is

$$x_i^{k+1} = x_i^k - \frac{f^i(x^k)}{f_{x_i}^i(x^k)}, \qquad i = 1, \dots, n. \tag{5.4.3}$$

Gauss-Seidel Algorithm

In the Gauss-Jacobi method we use the new guess of x_i, x_i^{k+1}, only after we have computed the entire vector of new values, x^{k+1}. The basic idea of the Gauss-Seidel method is to use the new guess of x_i as soon as it is available. In the general nonlinear case, this implies that given x^k, we construct x^{k+1} componentwise by solving the following one-dimensional problems in sequence:

$$f^1(x_1^{k+1}, x_2^k, x_3^k, \dots, x_n^k) = 0,$$

$$f^2(x_1^{k+1}, x_2^{k+1}, x_3^k, \dots, x_n^k) = 0,$$

$$\vdots \tag{5.4.4}$$

$$f^{n-1}(x_1^{k+1}, \dots, x_{n-2}^{k+1}, x_{n-1}^{k+1}, x_n^k) = 0,$$

$$f^n(x_1^{k+1}, \dots, x_{n-2}^{k+1}, x_{n-1}^{k+1}, x_n^{k+1}) = 0.$$

Again we solve $f^1, f^2, \dots, f^n$ in sequence, but we immediately use each new component. Now the indexing scheme matters even more because it affects the way in which later results depend on earlier ones. We can also implement a *linear Gauss-Seidel* method

$$x_i^{k+1} = x_i^k - \left(\frac{f^i}{f_{x_i}^i}\right)(x_1^{k+1}, \dots, x_{i-1}^{k+1}, x_i^k, \cdots x_n^k), \qquad i = 1, \dots, n, \tag{5.4.5}$$

to economize on computation costs at each iteration.

Gaussian methods are often used, but they have some problems. As in the linear case they are risky methods to use if the system is not diagonally dominant. One can apply extrapolation and acceleration methods to attain or accelerate convergence just as with linear equations. However, convergence is at best linear, and the discussion of convergence in chapter 3 applies here. The key fact for any iterative scheme

$x^{k+1} = G(x^k)$ is that the spectral radius of the Jacobian evaluated at the solution, $G_x(x^*)$, is its asymptotic linear rate of convergence.

Stopping Rule Problems for Multivariate Systems

We need to construct stopping rules for multivariate algorithms. We can use the same ideas we used for univariate problems, but implementing them is more difficult. We first need a rule for stopping. If we are using an iterative scheme $x^{k+1} = G(x^k)$ (e.g., Gauss-Jacobi) and we want to stop when $\|x^k - x^*\| < \varepsilon$, we must at least continue until $\|x^{k+1} - x^k\| \le (1 - \beta)\varepsilon$ where $\beta = \rho(G_x(x^*))$. Computing β directly would be impractical. To implement this test, we could estimate β with

$$\hat{\beta} = \max\left\{ \frac{\|x^{k-j+1} - x^k\|}{\|x^{k-j} - x^k\|} \mid j = 1, \dots, L \right\}$$

for some L. The estimate $\hat{\beta}$ should be close to $\rho(G_x(x^*))$ if $x^k \approx x^*$ and allow us to use the stopping rule $\|x^{k+1} - x^k\| \le (1 - \hat{\beta})\varepsilon$.

Even if x^k satisfies our stopping rule, we want to check that $f(x^k)$ is close to zero. A natural way to implement this is to require that $\|f(x^k)\| \le \delta$ for some small δ. As with univariate problems, we must be careful about units. Moreover the test $\|f(x^k)\| \le \delta$ implicitly makes trade-offs across the different equations. For example, some equations in f may be closer to zero at x^k than they are at x^{k+1}, but a stopping rule will choose x^{k+1} over x^k if $\|f(x^{k+1})\| \le \delta \le \|f(x^k)\|$. This would not happen if $\| \cdot \|$ is the supremum norm but could happen if one chooses the euclidean norm for $\| \cdot \|$. In either case the system f must be constructed so that δ is a reasonable approximation to zero for each component function.

In summary, we stop if $\|x^{k+1} - x^k\| < \varepsilon$, and we accept x^{k+1} as the solution if $\|f(x^{k+1})\| < \delta$ where $\delta > 0$ and $\varepsilon > 0$ are our stopping criterion parameters. Due to standard round-off problems, δ and ε should be about the square root of the error in computing f. In practice, nonlinear equation solvers give the user several options governing the stopping criterion to be used.

A Duopoly Example

We will use a two-player duopoly model to illustrate various multivariate methods for solving equations. We assume that there are two goods, Y and Z, and that the utility function over those goods and money M is

$$U(Y, Z) = u(Y, Z) + M$$

$$= (1 + Y^\alpha + Z^\alpha)^{\eta/\alpha} + M.$$

with $\alpha = 0.999$ and $\eta = 0.2$. We assume that the unit cost of Y is 0.07 and of Z is 0.08.

The Cournot duopoly game assumes that each firm simultaneously chooses its output, and each attempts to maximize its profits. If the firms choose outputs Y and Z, then $u_Y(Y, Z)$ is the price of Y and $u_Z(Y, Z)$ is the price of Z. Profit for the Y firm is $\Pi^Y(Y, Z) \equiv Y(u_Y(Y, Z) - 0.07)$ and for the Z firm is $\Pi^Z(Y, Z) \equiv Z(u_Z(Y, Z) - 0.08)$. Equilibrium is any pair of quantity choices (X, Y) that solves the problems

$$Y \in \arg \max_Y \Pi^Y(Y, Z),$$

$$Z \in \arg \max_Z \Pi^Z(Y, Z).$$

In practice, we compute equilibrium by finding (Y, Z) which solves each firm's first-order condition; that is, we solve the system

$$\Pi_1^Y(Y, Z) = 0, \tag{5.4.6a}$$

$$\Pi_2^Z(Y, Z) = 0. \tag{5.4.6b}$$

We can check the second-order conditions of each firm by checking

$$\Pi_{11}^Y(Y, Z), \Pi_{22}^Z(Y, Z) < 0,$$

but strictly speaking, we should check that each firm's choice is a global optimum of its problem.

This problem has the limited domain problem that utility is not defined for negative Y or Z. Since we need to keep Y and Z positive, we instead solve the system

$$\Pi_1^Y(e^y, e^z) = 0, \tag{5.4.7a}$$

$$\Pi_2^Z(e^y, e^z) = 0, \tag{5.4.7b}$$

for $y \equiv \ln Y$ and $z \equiv \ln Z$.

The game-theoretic examination of this problem often focuses on the reaction functions. Figure 5.7 displays the reaction function, $R_Y(z)$, which expresses the Y firm's choice of y if it expects the Z firm to choose log output equal to z; symmetrially, $R_Z(y)$ is the reaction function of firm Z to firm Y's choice of log output y. There is a unique Cournot-Nash equilibrium at the intersection of the reaction curves, $(y^*, z^*) = (-0.137, -0.576)$, or, equivalently, $(Y^*, Z^*) = (0.87, 0.56)$.

We will use the duopoly problem expressed in logarithmic terms, (5.4.7), to illustrate several iterative methods. Table 5.1 compares the performance of several Gaussian

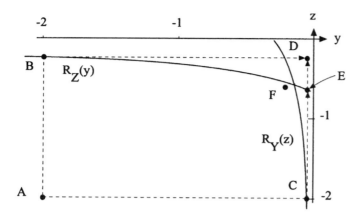

Figure 5.7
Solving the duopoly problem (5.4.7)

Table 5.1
Errors of Gaussian methods applied to (5.4.7)

Iteration	Gauss-Jacobi	Linear Gauss-Jacobi	Gauss-Seidel	Linear Gauss-Seidel
1	$(1(-1), 3(-1))$	$(1(0), 1(0))$	$(1(-1), -6(-2))$	$(1(0), -8(0))$
2	$(-7(-2), -6(-2))$	$(-8(-1), -1(-1))$	$(1(-3), -6(-3))$	$(-6(-1), 4(2))$
3	$(1(-2), 4(-2))$	$(2(-1), 1(-1))$	$(1(-4), -6(-4))$	*
4	$(-7(-3), -6(-3))$	$(-8(-1), -2(-1))$	$(1(-5), -6(-5))$	*
5	$(1(-3), 4(-3))$	$(1(-1), 3(-1))$	$(9(-6), -5(-6))$	*
6	$(-7(-4), -5(-4))$	$(-5(-2), -6(-2))$	$(9(-7), -5(-7))$	*
7	$(9(-5), 4(-4))$	$(9(-3), 3(-2))$	$(8(-8), -5(-8))$	*
8	$(-6(-5), -5(-5))$	$(-5(-3), -5(-3))$	$(8(-9), -5(-9))$	*

Note: The * means that the iterates became infinite.

methods. For example, if we use the initial guess $(y_0, z_0) = (-2, -2)$, point A in figure 5.7, the Gauss-Jacobi method generates the sequence of errors in column 2 of table 5.1; that is, the entry in row i, column 2 of table 5.1 equals $(y_i, z_i) - (y^*, z^*)$. In figure 5.7 the Gauss-Jacobi method computes C to be firm Y's reaction to firm Z's choice at A, and computes B to be Z's reaction to firm Y being at A. The Gauss-Jacobi method combines these reactions to take us to D. The next iteration of Gauss-Jacobi is F. The result is a slowly convergent sequence.

The Gauss-Seidel procedure is the more familiar alternating reaction sequence used in game theory. If we begin at A, then firm Y's reaction follows the broken line in figure 5.7 to $y = R_Y(Z)$ at C, and then firm Z's reaction to the situation at C follows the broken line to point E on R_Z. The amount of computation that takes us to E using Gauss-Seidel equals the computational effort in Gauss-Jacobi getting to D, an inferior approximation of equilibrium. Column 4 of table 5.1 contains the errors of the Gauss-Seidel iterates applied to (5.4.7). We see here that the Gauss-Seidel method converges more rapidly than Gauss-Jacobi.

The linearized methods display mixed performance. The linearized Gauss-Jacobi method converges relatively slowly, but the work per iteration is much less than with either Gauss-Jacobi or Gauss-Seidel. We also see that the linear Gauss-Seidel method blows up. The linearized Gauss-Seidel iterates do not keep us on the firms' reaction curves, for this method computes only the first step in a Newton computation of that reaction. Since the profit functions are significantly nonquadratic, this first step is not adequate, and the linear Gauss-Seidel method diverges even though the Gauss-Seidel method converges.

Fixed-Point Iteration

The simplest iterative procedure for solving the fixed point problem $x = f(x)$ is

$$x^{k+1} = f(x^k). \tag{5.4.8}$$

This process is called fixed-point iteration; it is also known as *successive approximation*, *successive substitution*, or *function iteration*. The process (5.4.8) generalizes to nonlinear equation systems the fixed-point iteration method discussed in section 3.6.

For a special class of functions, fixed-point iteration will work well.

DEFINITION   A *differentiable contraction map on D* is any C^1 $f : D \to R^n$ defined on a closed, bounded, convex set $D \subset R^n$ such that

1. $f(D) \subset D$, and
2. $\max_{x \in D} \|J(x)\|_\infty < 1$ where $J(x)$ is the Jacobian of f.

We have an exceptionally strong constructive existence theory for the fixed points of contraction mappings.

THEOREM 5.4.1 (Contraction mapping theorem)   If f is a differentiable contraction map on D, then

1. the fixed point problem $x = f(x)$ has a unique solution, $x^* \in D$;
2. the sequence defined by $x^{k+1} = f(x^k)$ converges to x^*;
3. there is a sequence $\varepsilon_k \to 0$ such that

$$\|x^* - x^{k+1}\|_\infty \leq (\|J(x^*)\|_\infty + \varepsilon_k)\|x^* - x^k\|_\infty.$$

The contraction mapping theorem uses a contraction condition to prove convergence of our simple iterative scheme (5.4.8), and shows that in the limit, fixed-point iteration converges linearly at the rate $\|J(x^*)\|_\infty$. If $D = R^n$, then we have a global contraction condition for global convergence and uniqueness. Theorem 5.4.2 is also a useful local result.

THEOREM 5.4.2   Suppose that $f(x^*) = x^*$ and is Lipschitz at x^*. If $\rho(J(x^*)) < 1$, then for x^0 sufficiently close to x^*, $x^{k+1} = f(x^k)$ is convergent.

Theorem 5.4.2 says that if the Jacobian at a fixed point is a contraction when viewed as a linear map in R^n, then iterating f will converge if the initial guess is good. The intuition is clear: Near a zero, a smooth function f is very nearly like its Jacobian at the zero and will inherit the iteration properties of the Jacobian. Furthermore a linear map is a contraction if and only if its spectral radius is less than 1. Hence the critical condition is $\rho(J(x^*)) < 1$. The convergence rate indicated in theorem 5.4.1 is linear. This is a lower bound on the rate of convergence, since fixed-point iteration methods may converge more rapidly. In fact Newton's method can be thought of as a successive approximation method, and it converges quadratically.

As with linear equations (see chapter 3) there are ways to accelerate convergence rates of convergent methods, even contraction mapping iterations, or stabilize unstable implementations of the fixed-point iteration method. The basic method is again *extrapolation*, where we add the parameter ω and form the system

$$x^{k+1} = \omega f(x^k) + (1 - \omega)x^k. \tag{5.4.9}$$

If the original system (5.4.8) is unstable, we try $\omega \in (0, 1)$ in (5.4.9) hoping to dampen the instabilities. If the original system (5.4.8) is converging too slowly, we try some $\omega > 1$ hoping to accelerate convergence.

We next apply fixed-point iteration to our duopoly example. Our example system (5.4.7) is written as a zero problem, but the fixed-point problem

$$\Pi_1^Y(e^y, e^z) + y = y,$$

$$\Pi_2^Z(e^y, e^z) + z = z,$$

is equivalent. Fixed-point iteration generates the sequence

$$y_{k+1} = \Pi_1^Y(e^{y_k}, e^{z_k}) + y_k,$$

$$z_{k+1} = \Pi_2^Z(e^{y_k}, e^{z_k}) + z_k. \tag{5.4.10}$$

Column 2 in table 5.2 displays the errors, $(y, z) - (y^*, z^*)$, of the iterates of fixed-point iteration applied to (5.4.7).

Table 5.2
Errors of fixed-point iteration in (5.4.11)

$\omega = 1.0$		$\omega = 0.9$	
Iterate	Error	Iterate	Error
20	$(-0.74(0), -0.47(0))$	5	$(-0.11(0), 0.42(-2))$
40	$(-0.31(0), -0.14(0))$	10	$(-0.14(-1), 0.20(-1))$
60	$(-0.13(0), -0.25(0))$	15	$(-0.31(-2), 0.67(-2))$
80	$(-0.62(-1), 0.87(-2))$	20	$(-0.82(-3), 0.20(-2))$
100	$(-0.30(-1), 0.15(-1))$	25	$(-0.23(-3), 0.57(-3))$

We can use extrapolation to improve the performance of (5.4.10). We introduce the parameter ω, form the system

$$y_{k+1} = \omega(\Pi_1^Y(e^{y_k}, e^{z_k}) + y_k) + (1 - \omega)y_k,$$
$$z_{k+1} = \omega(\Pi_2^Z(e^{y_k}, e^{z_k}) + z_k) + (1 - \omega)z_k, \tag{5.4.11}$$

and hope that for some ω, (5.4.11) will converge. Column 4 in table 5.2 contains the errors of the iterates of (5.4.11) for $\omega = 0.9$.

Fixed-point iteration may appear to be of limited usefulness due to the strong contraction conditions necessary for convergence. However, it forms the basis of many methods. The basic idea is to find another function that has the same zeros as f but for which fixed-point iteration converges. If possible, we find such a function that satisfies the conditions of theorems 5.4.2 or 5.4.3 and results in rapid convergence. We saw this in chapter 3 when we discussed stabilization and acceleration methods, and we will frequently return to this below when we examine applications. The most famous application of this idea is Newton's method, to which we now turn.

5.5 Newton's Method for Multivariate Equations

In Newton's method to solve (5.4.1), we replace f with a linear approximation, and then solve the linear problem to generate the next guess, just as we did in the one-dimensional case. By Taylor's theorem, the linear approximation of f around the initial guess x^0 is $f(x) \doteq f(x^0) + J(x^0)(x - x^0)$. We can solve for the zero of this linear approximation, yielding $x^1 = x^0 - J(x^0)^{-1}f(x^0)$. This zero then serves as the new guess around which we again linearize. The Newton iteration scheme is

$$x^{k+1} = x^k - J(x^k)^{-1}f(x^k) \tag{5.5.1}$$

THEOREM 5.5.1   If $f(x^*) = 0$, $\det(J(x^*)) \neq 0$, and $J(x)$ is Lipschitz near x^*, then for x^0 near x^*, the sequence defined by (5.5.1) satisfies

$$\lim_{k \to \infty} \frac{\|x^{k+1} - x^*\|}{\|x^k - x^*\|^2} < \infty . \tag{5.5.2}$$

As with the one-dimensional case, Newton's method is quadratically convergent. The critical assumption is that $\det(J(x^*)) \neq 0$. The basic approach of the proof [2] is to show that the map $g(x) = x - J(x)^{-1}f(x)$ is a contraction near x^*.

Algorithm 5.3   Newton's Method for Multivariate Equations

Initialization. Choose stopping criterion ε and δ, and starting point x^0. Set $k = 0$.

Step 1. Compute next iterate: Compute Jacobian $A_k = J(x^k)$, solve $A_k s^k = -f(x^k)$ for s^k, and set $x^{k+1} = x^k + s^k$.

Step 2. Check stopping criterion: If $\|x^k - x^{k+1}\| \leq \varepsilon(1 + \|x^{k+1}\|)$, go to step 3. Otherwise, go to step 1.

Step 3. STOP and report result: If $\|f(x^{k+1})\| \leq \delta$, report success in finding a zero; otherwise, report failure.

We again emphasize that f must be carefully defined if step 3 is to be meaningful. All the comments in section 5.2 concerning units apply here. One will typically use a package to solve $f(x) = 0$ and the user will define f to facilitate convergence. In such cases the package will apply a version of step 3 to that definition of f, which may not be the appropriate unit-free test; in that case, one applies step 3 to a unit-free version of the problem after the package has produced a candidate solution.

The rapid convergence of Newton's method is illustrated by our example system (5.4.7). Column 2 of table 5.3 contains errors, $(y_k, z_k) - (y^*, z^*)$, of the Newton iterates beginning at $(-2, -2)$. Note the rapid convergence, with each iteration doubling the number of accurate digits.

Secant Method (Broyden)

One would typically use finite differences to compute $J(x)$ in Newton's method but that requires n^2 evaluations of f. Explicit computation of the Jacobian is often costly to compute and code. One solution to the problem of Jacobian calculation is to begin with a rough guess of the Jacobian and use the successive evaluations of f and its

---

2. See, for example, Ortega and Rheinboldt (1970).

Table 5.3
Errors of Newton and Broyden methods applied to (5.4.7)

Iterate k	Newton	Broyden
0	$(-0.19(1), -0.14(1))$	$(-0.19(1), -0.14(1))$
1	$(0.55(0), 0.28(0))$	$(0.55(0), 0.28(0))$
2	$(-0.59(-1), 0.93(-2))$	$(0.14(-1), 0.65(-2))$
3	$(0.15(-3), 0.81(-3))$	$(-0.19(-2), 0.40(-3))$
4	$(0.86(-8), 0.54(-7))$	$(0.45(-3), 0.24(-3))$
5	$(0.80(-15), 0.44(-15))$	$(-0.11(-3), 0.61(-4))$
6	$(0, 0)$	$(0.26(-4), -0.14(-4))$
7	$(0, 0)$	$(-0.60(-5), 0.33(-5))$
8	$(0, 0)$	$(0.14(-5), -0.76(-6))$
9	$(0, 0)$	$(-0.32(-6), 0.18(-6))$
10	$(0, 0)$	$(0.75(-7), 0.41(-7))$

gradient to update the guess of J. In this way we make more use of the computed values of f and avoid the cost of recomputing J at each iteration.

The one-dimensional secant method did this, but the problem in n dimensions is more complex. To see this, suppose that we have computed f at y and z. In the one-dimensional case the slope, m, near y and z is approximated by the solution to the scalar equation $f(y) - f(z) = m(y - z)$, which is unique whenever $y \neq z$. The n dimension analogue to the slope, m, is the Jacobian, M, which near y and z approximately satisfies the multidimensional secantlike equation $f(y) - f(z) = M(y - z)$. There is no unique such matrix: Since $f(y) - f(z)$ and $y - z$ are column vectors, this equation imposes only n conditions on the n^2 elements of M. We need some way to fill in the rest of our estimate of M.

Broyden's method is the R^n version of the secant method. It produces a sequence of points x^k, and matrices A_k which serve as Jacobian guesses. Suppose that after k iterations our guess for x is x^k and our guess for the Jacobian at x^k is A_k. We use A_k to compute the Newton step; that is, we solve $A_k s^k = -f(x^k)$ for s^k, and define $x^{k+1} = x^k + s^k$. We next compute A_{k+1} to be our new approximation to $J(x^{k+1})$. If J is continuous, $J(x^{k+1})$ should be close to $J(x^k)$, which was approximated by A_k. The Broyden idea is to choose A_{k+1} consistent with the secant equation $f(x^{k+1}) - f(x^k) = A_{k+1} s^k$ but keep it as "close" to A_k as possible, where by "close" we refer to how it acts as a linear map. The basic property of the Jacobian is that $J(x)q$ should approximate $\delta(q, x) \equiv f(x + q) - f(x)$ for all directions q. For the specific direction $q = s^k$ we know $\delta(q, x^k) = f(x^{k+1}) - f(x^k)$. However, for any direction q orthogonal to s^k we have no information about $\delta(q, x^k)$. The Broyden method fixes A_{k+1} by assuming that $A_{k+1}q = A_k q$ whenever $q^\top s^k = 0$; that is, the predicted change in directions orthogonal to s^k under the new Jacobian guess, A_{k+1}, should equal the predicted change under the old Jacobian guess, A_k. Together with the secant condition this uniquely determines A_{k+1} to be

$$A_{k+1} = A_k + \frac{(y_k - A_k s^k)(s^k)^\top}{(s^k)^\top s^k},$$

where $y_k \equiv f(x^{k+1}) - f(x^k)$. Broyden discusses some alternative choices of A_{k+1}, but this one has been the most successful in practice. Algorithm 5.4 describes Broyden's method.

Algorithm 5.4   Broyden's Method

Initialization. Choose stopping criterion ε and δ, starting point x^0, and initial Jacobian guess $A_0 = I$. Set $k = 0$.

Step 1. Compute next iterate: Solve $A_k s^k = -f(x^k)$ for s^k, and set $x^{k+1} = x^k + s^k$.

Step 2. Update Jacobian guess: Set $y_k = f(x^{k+1}) - f(x^k)$ and

$$A_{k+1} = A_k + \frac{(y_k - A_k s^k)(s^k)^\top}{(s^k)^\top s^k}.$$

Step 3. Check stopping criterion: If $\|x^k - x^{k+1}\| \le \varepsilon(1 + \|x^{k+1}\|)$, go to step 4. Otherwise, go to step 1.

Step 4. STOP and report result: If $\|f(x^{k+1})\| \le \delta$, report success in finding a zero; otherwise, report failure.

The algorithm will stop when $f(x^k)$ is close to zero, or when the steps, s^k, become small. The last stopping condition is particularly desirable here, since the division in the computation of A_{k+1} will be problematic if s^k is small.

The convergence properties of Broyden's method are inferior to Newton's method, but still good.

THEOREM 5.5.3   There exists $\varepsilon > 0$ such that if $\|x^0 - x^*\| < \varepsilon$ and $\|A_0 - J(x^*)\| < \varepsilon$, then the Broyden method converges superlinearly.

Note that convergence is only asserted for the x sequence. The A sequence need not converge to the $J(x^*)$. Each iteration of the Broyden method is far less costly to compute because there is no Jacobian calculated, but the Broyden method will generally need more iterations than Newton's method. For large systems, the Broyden method may be much faster, since Jacobian calculation can be very expensive. For highly nonlinear problems the Jacobian may change drastically between iterations, causing the Broyden approximation to be quite poor. Of course that will also give Newton's method problems since the underlying assumption of any Newton method is that a linear approximation is appropriate, which is the same as saying that the Jacobian does not change much.

These features of the Broyden method is illustrated by our example system (5.4.7). Column 3 of table 5.3 contains the errors of the Broyden method. Note that convergence is slower than Newton's method, in terms of iterations required, but much faster than the Gaussian or fixed-point iteration methods.

Solving Multiple Problems

Sometimes we will want to solve several problems of the form $f(x; a) = 0$ for x where a is a vector of parameters. The choice of initial conditions substantially affects the performance of any algorithm. In the case of Broyden's method, we must also make an initial guess for the Jacobian. When we solve several problems, we can use the same hot start idea discussed in chapter 4 for optimization problems. In Newton's method the solution to $f(x; a) = 0$ will be a good initial guess when solving $f(x; a') = 0$ if $a' \approx a$. If we are using Broyden's method, we will want to use both the final solution and the final Jacobian estimate for $f(x; a) = 0$ as the initial guesses when solving $f(x; a') = 0$. As with optimization problems, hot starts can produce significant economies of scale when we want to solve several problems.

5.6 Methods That Enhance Global Convergence

Outside of the special case of contraction mappings, none of these methods is globally convergent. As we saw in the one-dimensional case, it is easy to construct cases where Newton's method cycles. There are systematic ways to enhance convergence to a zero that combine minimization ideas with the nonlinear equation approach.

Optimization Ideas and Nonlinear Equations

There are several strong connections between optimization problems and nonlinear equations. First, one can often be transformed into the other. For example, if $f(x)$ is C^2, then the solution to $\min_x f(x)$ is also a solution to the system of first-order conditions $\nabla f(x) = 0$. Newton's method for optimization in fact solves minimization problems by solving the first-order conditions.

We can also go in the opposite direction, converting a set of nonlinear equations into an optimization problem. Sometimes there is a function $F(x)$ such that $f(x) =$

$\nabla F(x)$, in which case the zeros of f are exactly the local minima of F. Such systems $f(x)$ are called *integrable*. Since we have globally convergent schemes for minimizing F we can use them to compute the zeros of f. In some economic contexts we can approach a problem in this fashion. For example, the real business cycle literature frequently computes dynamic equilibria by solving the equivalent social planner's problem. However, this approach is limited in its applicability because few systems $f(x)$ are integrable.

In one general sense any nonlinear equation problem can be converted to an optimization problem. Any solution to the system $f(x) = 0$ is also a global solution to

$$\min_x \sum_{i=1}^n f^i(x)^2, \tag{5.6.1}$$

and any global minimum of $\sum_{i=1}^n f^i(x)^2$ is a solution to $f(x) = 0$. While this approach is tempting, it has several problems. First, it is a global minimum problem because we are interested only in values of x that makes the objective in (5.6.1) zero. There may be local minima that are not near any solution to $f(x) = 0$.

Second, the condition number of the Hessian of (5.6.1) is roughly the square of the condition number of the Jacobian of $f(x) = 0$ at any solution. To see this, consider using (5.6.1) to solve the linear problem $Ax - b = 0$. The objective in (5.6.1) would become $x^\top A^\top A x - b^\top A x - x^\top A^\top b + b^\top b$, a function of x with a Hessian equal to $A^\top A$. Since the spectral condition number of $A^\top A$ is the square of the spectral condition number of A (or equivalently, the log condition number is doubled), the minimization problem is poorly conditioned relative to the matrix A. For example, if $\text{cond}_*(A) = 10^8$, the linear equation problem may be well-behaved, but the objective in (5.6.1) has a log condition number of 16, making it practically singular. This approach is used sometimes when A is sparse and positive definite, since then conjugate gradient methods can be used. Outside of small problems and special circumstances, the simple minimization approach in (5.6.1) is not a good method by itself.

There are ways in which solving (5.6.1) may assist. It is often difficult to find good initial guesses for a system of nonlinear equations, whereas optimization problems are not as sensitive to initial guesses. Furthermore the objective (5.6.1) may not be ill-conditioned away from a minimum. One way to find a reasonable guess is to solve (5.6.1) with a loose stopping rule. Hopefully the minimization process will move us toward a solution, but the loose stopping rule keeps us from wasting time dealing with poorly conditioned Hessians. Even with a loose stopping criterion, the outputted value for x produces a small value for $\sum_{i=1}^n f^i(x)^2$; therefore each component $f^i(x)$ is small, and x has a good chance of being a good initial guess for a conventional nonlinear solver.

Another situation where the minimization approach (5.6.1) may be useful is where there are many algebraic solutions to $g(x) = 0$ that are not of interest. Suppose that you only wanted solutions to $g(x) = 0$ at which all components of x were positive. Then one might solve the constrained problems

$$\min \sum_{i=1}^{n} g^i(x)^2$$

$$\text{s.t.} \quad x_i \geq 0, \qquad i = 1, \ldots, n.$$

(5.6.2)

Even when doing this, (5.6.2) should be solved with loose stopping rules, producing an initial guess for a good nonlinear equation algorithm.

Enhancing Convergence with Powell's Hybrid Method

The methods we have discussed present us with a choice. Newton's method will converge rapidly if it converges but it may diverge. On the other hand, the minimization idea in (5.6.1) will converge to something, but it may do so slowly, and it may converge to a point other than a solution to the nonlinear system. Since these approaches have complementary strengths and weaknesses, we are tempted to develop a hybrid algorithm combining their ideas. If we define $SSR(x) \equiv \sum_{i=1}^{n} f^i(x)^2$, then the solutions to the nonlinear equation $f(x) = 0$ are exactly the global solutions to the minimization problem (5.6.1). Perhaps we can use values of $SSR(x)$ to indicate how well we are doing and help restrain Newton's method when it does not appear to be working.

Powell's hybrid scheme is one such algorithm. Powell's method modifies Newton's method by checking if a Newton step reduces the value of SSR. More specifically, suppose that the current guess is x^k. The Newton step is then $s^k = -J(x^k)^{-1} f(x^k)$. Newton's method takes $x^{k+1} = x^k + s^k$ without hesitation; Powell's method checks $x^k + s^k$ before accepting it as the next iteration. In particular, Powell's method will accept $x^k + s^k$ as the next iteration only if $SSR(x^k + s^k) < SSR(x^k)$, that is, only if there is some improvement in SSR.

Powell's original proposal was to set $x^{k+1} = x^k + \lambda s^k$ for some $0 < \lambda < 1$ such that $SSR(x^k + \lambda s^k) < SSR(x^k)$. As long as $J(x^k)$ is nonsingular, there is such a λ. The idea is that we move in the Newton direction but only to the extent consistent with moving downhill in the sense of SSR.

Unfortunately, experience showed that this method may converge inappropriately to some point where J is singular. Powell then modified this procedure by choosing a direction equal to a combination of the Newton step and the gradient of $-SSR$, which is the steepest descent direction; Powell (1970) provides the details.

These methods will converge to a solution of $f(x) = 0$ or will stop if they come too near a local minimum of SSR. If there is no such local minimum then we will get global convergence. If we do get stuck near a local minimum x^m, we will know that we are not at the global solution, since we will know that $f(x^m)$ is not zero, and we can continue by choosing a new starting point.

Solving Overidentified Systems

Sometimes we may want to solve a nonlinear system $f(x) = 0$ where $f : R^n \to R^m$ and $n < m$; such a problem is likely not to have a solution. In these cases we could proceed as we did in section 3.14 with overidentified linear systems. Specifically, we solve the least squares problem

$$\min_x f(x)^\top f(x). \tag{5.6.3}$$

The result is typically a nonlinear least squares problem that can be solved using the optimization methods described in section 4.5. In particular, we may want to use a small residual method. While this may appear to be the same as using (5.6.1) to solve n equations in n variables, there is an important difference. Since there is likely no exact solution to an overidentified problem, the conditioning problems in (5.6.1) are not likely to occur. Therefore, for overidentified systems, a nonlinear least squares procedure is a sensible choice.

5.7 Advantageous Transformations

When solving nonlinear systems of equations, preliminary transformations of the equations may prove useful. The key assumption of Newton's method is that the system is well-approximated by a linear function. Changes in the equations can make that assumption more valid and help Newton's method to converge. We will examine the value of nonlinear transformations which turn a nonlinear system into an equivalent one easier to solve.

The general point can be illustrated in two simple examples. Suppose that we wants to solve

$$x^9 - 1 = 0. \tag{5.7.1}$$

Equation (5.7.1) has a unique real solution, $x = 1$. If we apply Newton's method directly to (5.7.1), with an initial guess of $x = 2$, we get the sequence 2, 1.778, 1.582, 1.409, 1.259, 1.137, 1.050, 1.009, 1.000.

Table 5.4
Newton's method applied to (5.7.2) and (5.7.3)

Iteration	(5.7.2)	(5.7.3)	(5.7.2)	(5.7.3)
0	(2, 2)	(2, 2)	(3, 3)	(3, 3)
1	(0.6118, 0.7992)	(0.9420, 1.0580)	(−0.2791, 0.3613)	(0.8122, 1.188)
2	(0.9259, 0.9846)	(0.9976, 0.9998)	*	(0.9791, 0.9973)
3	(0.9978, 0.9998)	(1.0000, 1.0000)	*	(0.9999, 1.0000)
4	(1.0000, 1.0000)	(1.0000, 1.0000)	*	(1.0000, 1.0000)

Note: The * indicates complex values.

On the other hand, (5.7.1) is equivalent to $x^9 = 1$, which is equivalent to $x = 1$ and $x - 1 = 0$. This transforms the highly nonlinear equation (5.7.1) into the trivial linear equation, $x - 1 = 0$, which has the same real solutions and which Newton's method will solve exactly after one iteration.

This is a trivial application of the idea, but it clearly illustrates the point that transformations can improve convergence of Newton's method. A more substantive example is the system

$$x^{0.2} + y^{0.2} - 2 = 0,$$
$$x^{0.1} + y^{0.4} - 2 = 0, \tag{5.7.2}$$

which has a solution $(x, y) = (1, 1)$. If we apply Newton's method directly to (5.7.2) with an initial guess of (2, 2), we get the (x, y) sequence in column 2 of table 5.4. If we instead apply Newton's method to the equivalent system

$$(x^{0.2} + y^{0.2})^5 - 32 = 0, \tag{5.7.3a}$$

$$(x^{0.1} + y^{0.4})^4 - 16 = 0, \tag{5.7.3b}$$

we get the sequence in column 3 of table 5.4. Equations (5.7.3) are useful because any solution of (5.7.2) is a solution of (5.7.3). Columns 4 and 5 report the results with a starting point of (3, 3). We see that if we use (5.7.2), we need to use complex arithmetic; most software would not use complex arithmetic and quit at iteration 2 when it tries to compute a root of a negative number. Newton's method applied to (5.7.3) starting at (3, 3) had no such problem. In general, we see that both sequences converge to (1, 1) more rapidly and more reliably for (5.7.3) than for (5.7.2).

The intuition for these results is clear. The transformed equation (5.7.3a) replaced $x^{0.2} + y^{0.2}$ with a CRTS function; in particular, the resulting function is linear along any line of the form $y = mx$. In (5.7.3b), the exponent 4 counters the "average" exponent 0.25 in the expression $x^{0.1} + y^{0.4}$. In both equations the exponents unwrap some of the nonlinearity of the expression to which it is applied.

These examples are only suggestive. The general idea is that a global nonlinear transformation may create an algebraically equivalent system on which Newton's method does better because the new system is more linear. Unfortunately, there is no general way to apply this idea; its application will be problem-specific. Fortunately simple and useful transformations are often suggested by the structure of the problem.

5.8   A Simple Continuation Method

No Newton-type method, nor any version of Gauss-Jacobi, Gauss-Seidel, or fixed-point iteration, is globally convergent; the best we are able to prove is that a method converges to a solution if we have a good initial guess or if the system of equations has some special structure. Also, for each regular zero, Newton's method has a non-trivial basin of attraction. These are good properties, but in practice, we often have no good guesses and only hope that a method will converge starting from our rough guesses. Sometimes we are not so lucky.

In this section we discuss a *continuation method* that uses the local convergence properties of a standard method to improve the chances of global convergence. The idea of all continuation methods is to construct a sequence of problems that ultimately leads to the problem of interest. Suppose that we want to solve $f(x; t) = 0$, where $f : R^n \times R \to R^n$, for some specific value $t = t^*$. This is natural structure in economic problems where x is a list of endogenous variables and t is a parameter of taste, technology, or policy. Further suppose that we do not have a solution for $f(x; t^*) = 0$ but we do know that for t^0, $f(x; t^0) = 0$ has a solution x^0. If t^* is near t^0, x^0 will be a good initial guess when trying to solve $f(x; t^*) = 0$. Furthermore, in methods where Jacobians are sequentially approximated such as with Broyden, an appropriate initial guess for the Jacobian for the t^* problem is the last approximation for the Jacobian of the t^0 problem.

If t^* is not close to t^0, we cannot rely on the local convergence property of the nonlinear equation method. We can still use this idea by constructing a sequence of problems of the form $f(x; t) = 0$ satisfying $t^0 \approx t^1 \approx t^2 \approx \cdots \approx t^n \approx t^*$. We set up a sequence of problems to which we can apply the hot start idea, using the solution from the t^k problem as the initial guess to the t^{k+1} problem. The hope is that each intermediate problem can be solved quickly and that we end up with a solution to $f(x; t^*) = 0$.

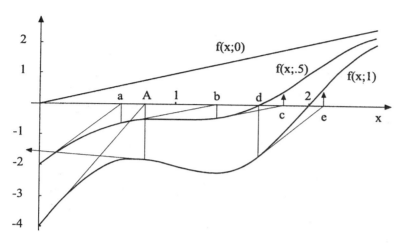

Figure 5.8
Continuation method for (5.8.1)

Algorithm 5.5   Simple Continuation Method

Objective: Find a zero of $f(x; t^*)$, $f : R^n \times R \to R^n$ where we know $f(x^0; t^0) = 0$.

Initialization. Form the sequence $t^0 \approx t^1 \approx t^2 \cdots \approx t^n = t^*$; set $i = 0$.

Step 1. Solve $f(x; t^{i+1}) = 0$ using x^i as the initial guess; set x^{i+1} equal to the solution.

Step 2. If $i + 1 = n$, report x^n as the solution to $f(x; t^*)$ and STOP; else go to step 1.

Consider the following example: Let

$$f(x; t) = (1 - t)x + t(2x - 4 + \sin(\pi x)). \tag{5.8.1}$$

In figure 5.8 we display the three problems corresponding to $t = 0, 0.5, 1.0$. Because of the oscillations in $\sin(\pi x)$, Newton's method applied to $f(x; 1) = 0$ starting with $x = 0$ will have problems. In fact the first iterate is $x = A$ in figure 5.8, but because the slope of $f(x; 1)$ is slightly negative at $(A, f(A; 1))$, the second iterate is negative, as illustrated in figure 5.8. On the other hand, the solution to the $t = 0$ problem, $x = 0$, is trivial. We proceed in two steps. We use $x = 0$, the solution to the $t = 0$ problem, as the initial guess for the $t = 0.5$ problem. Figure 5.8 illustrates the first three Newton iterates, points a, b, and c, after which Newton's method converges to the unique zero, $x = d$, for the $t = 0.5$ problem. We next take $x = d$ as the initial guess for the $t = 1$ problem and find that Newton's method leads us first to $x = e$ and

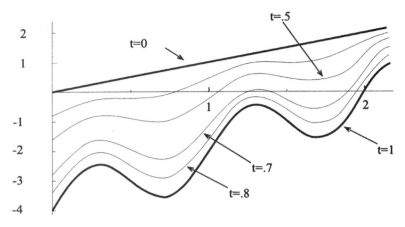

Figure 5.9
Graphs of (5.8.2)

then to the solution $x = 2$. Therefore Newton's method and simple continuation works well solving a problem starting at $x = 0$, whereas Newton's method alone starting at $x = 0$ would fail.

While this procedure is intuitive and will often work, it may fail. To see this, consider the slightly different example

$$H(x; t) = (1 - t)x + t(2x - 4 + \sin(2\pi x)). \qquad (5.8.2)$$

The only difference between f and H is that the sine argument is $2\pi x$ in H instead of πx. Figure 5.9 displays $H(x; t)$ for $t = \{0, 0.5, 0.7, 0.8, 1.0\}$. Again, if we try to solve for $H(x; 1) = 0$ with Newton's method with an initial guess $x = 0$, we will not do well. We will be tempted to try a simple continuation procedure. At $t = 0$ we start with the equation $x = 0$ and find the unique zero at $x = 0$. Suppose that we use the continuation approach and increase t in increments of 0.01. Note that $H(x; 0.70)$ has three zeros on $[0, 2]$. We will eventually come to the problem $H(x; 0.74) = 0$ and find the solution $x = 1.29$. We now encounter a difficulty. A solution to the problem $H(x; 0.74) = 0$ is $x = 1.29$, but the problem $H(x; 0.75) = 0$ has a unique solution of $x = 1.92$ and no solution near $x = 1.29$. If we use $x = 1.29$ as the initial guess for Newton's method for $H(x; 0.75) = 0$, the first five iterates are 1.29, 1.31, 1.23, 1.27, and 1.30, which do not appear to be converging to anything.

In figure 5.9 we see what went wrong. Close examination of $H(x; t)$ shows that $x = 1.28$ is close to a zero (it is actually close to two zeroes) of $H(x; 0.70)$ but is not close to any zero of $H(x; 0.75) = 0$. Therefore a small change in the problem causes a large change in the solution. This violates the basic premise of the simple continuation method. In the next section we will see how to improve on the continuation idea and construct a reliable algorithm.

5.9 Homotopy Continuation Methods

The idea behind continuation methods is to examine and solve a series of problems, beginning with a problem for which we know the solution and ending with the problem of interest. In reality we are deforming the problem as we progress. Homotopy methods formalize the notion of deforming a simple problem into a hard problem, computing a series of zeros of the intervening problems in order to end with a zero to the problem of interest. With homotopy methods, we finally have a globally convergent way to find zeros of $f : R^n \rightarrow R^n$.

We start by constructing homotopy functions, $H(x, t)$, $H : R^{n+1} \rightarrow R^n$, $H \in C^0(R^{n+1})$. A *homotopy function H* that continuously deforms g into f is any continuous function H where

$$H(x, 0) = g(x), \quad H(x, 1) = f(x). \tag{5.9.1}$$

In practice, we take $H(x, 0)$ to be a simple function with easily calculated zeros, and $H(x, 1)$ to be the function whose zeros we want. Let us consider some simple examples. The *Newton homotopy* is $H(x, t) = f(x) - (1 - t)f(x^0)$ for some x^0. At $t = 0$, $H = f(x) - f(x^0)$ which has a zero at $x = x^0$. At $t = 1$, $H = f(x)$. This is a simple homotopy, since the difference between $H(x, t)$ and $H(x, s)$ is proportional to $t - s$. The *fixed-point homotopy* is $H(x, t) = (1 - t)(x - x^0) + tf(x)$ for some x^0. It transforms the function $x - x^0$ into $f(x)$. A more general homotopy is the *linear homotopy*, $H(x, t) = tf(x) + (1 - t)g(x)$, which transforms g into f, since at $t = 0$, $H = g$, and at $t = 1$, $H = f$.

The basic object of our attention is the set

$$H^{-1}(0) = \left\{ (x, t) \mid H(x, t) = 0 \right\}.$$

If $H(x, 0)$ and $H(x, 1)$ have zeros, the hope is that there is a continuous path in $H^{-1}(0)$ which connects zeros of $H(x, 0)$ (the simple function) to zeros of $f(x) = H(x, 1)$. An example of such a zero set is displayed in figure 5.10. We return to the example in figure 5.9 for which simple continuation failed. We again take $f(x) = 2x - 4 + \sin(2\pi x)$ and construct the fixed-point homotopy

$$H(x, t) = (1 - t)x + t(2x - 4 + \sin(2\pi x)) \tag{5.9.2}$$

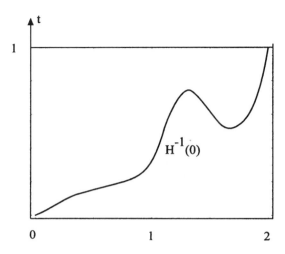

Figure 5.10
$H^{-1}(0)$ set for (5.9.2)

At $t = 0$ the unique zero is $x = 0$. Figure 5.9 displayed $H(x, t)$ for $t \in \{0, 0.5, 0.7, 0.8, 1.0\}$. Note that $H(x, 0.7)$ has three zeros and that $H(x, 1)$ has a unique zero at $x = 2$.

Figure 5.10 displays $H^{-1}(0)$ for (5.9.2) in (x, t) space. At each t we plot all x such that $H(x, t) = 0$. At $t = 0$ this is $x = 0$ only. For $t \in (0.53, 0.74)$ there are three zeros of $H(x, t)$. At $t = 1$ the unique zero is $x = 2$.

The key fact is that $H^{-1}(0)$ for (5.9.2) is a smooth curve connecting the zero of the $t = 0$ problem to the zero of the $t = 1$ problem. Homotopy methods focus on following paths in $H^{-1}(0)$ connecting the $t = 0$ problem to the $t = 1$ problem. These paths may not be simple. For example, in figure 5.10 the values of t are not monotonically increasing as we move along $H^{-1}(0)$ from $(0, 0)$ to $(2, 1)$. Simple continuation assumes that we can proceed from the zero of the $t = 0$ problem to the zero of the $t = 1$ problem by taking an increasing sequence of t values, a strategy that fails near $(x, t) = (1.31, 0.745)$ in figure 5.10. Homotopy methods instead follow the path $H^{-1}(0)$, tracing it wherever it goes and allowing t to increase and decrease as necessary to stay on $H^{-1}(0)$.

Before we indicate how this tracing is accomplished, we will discuss the forms $H^{-1}(0)$ may take for general homotopies $H : R^{n+1} \to R^n$. The path $H^{-1}(0)$ in figure 5.10 is not too bad. Figure 5.11 illustrates several possible features of $H^{-1}(0)$. $H^{-1}(0)$ generally consists of several pieces. Path AB is a simple, clean component of $H^{-1}(0)$

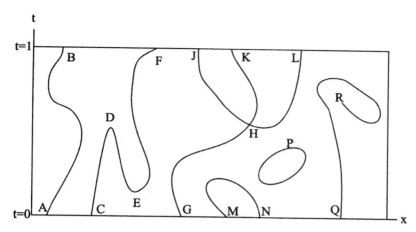

Figure 5.11
Possible $H^{-1}(0)$ sets

leading from $R^n \times \{0\}$, the bottom axis, to $R^n \times \{1\}$, the top axis. The key simplifying property of AB is that t is increasing along AB. The simple continuation method of the previous section will successfully traverse paths like AB if we take sufficiently small increments in t. The example in figure 5.8 has a $H^{-1}(0)$ set like AB.

Component $CDEF$ is quite different. Component $CDEF$ contains *turning points* at D and E, similar to the problematic path in figure 5.10. We can see here how the simple continuation method we described in the last section may have difficulty when it reaches a turning point. At a turning point there are no nearby solutions x to $H(x, t) = 0$ as we try to increase t. The component beginning at G presents even worse problems at the *branch point* H where three branches sprout, one for each of the solutions at J, K, and L. At branch points there are "too many" nearby solutions. At both turning and branch points, the Jacobian $H_x(x, t)$ is singular. Using Newton's method, or any other method, at such a point would send the iterates off in essentially random directions, and end any advantage of the continuation process.

Figure 5.11 also displays other kinds of problematic components. MN is a component that begins and ends at the $t = 0$ boundary. P is a closed curve touching neither the $t = 0$ nor $t = 1$ boundaries. QR begins with a solution to $H(x, 0) = 0$ at Q but ends at R before reaching the $t = 1$ boundary.

Despite the two-dimensional picture figure 5.11 represents the general case. Think of the bottom axis representing a compact subset of R^n. The paths pictured in figure 5.11 are one-dimensional threads that run through $x - t$ space where $x \in R^n$. The paths in the general case can be very complex, but we will see that we may restrict our attention to "nice" ones.

Parametric Path Following

Let us now consider how we trace out the path $H^{-1}(0)$. To follow paths like AB and $CDEF$, we view them as *parametric paths*. A parametric path is a set of functions $(x(s), t(s))$ that describes a path through (x, t) space. In particular, we want to construct parametric paths to traverse paths like AB and $CDEF$. Instead of parameterizing x in terms of t, the simple continuation method approach, we parameterize both x and t in terms of a third parameter, s.

The key advantage of parametric paths is that x and t are now viewed symmetrically, with both x and t being functions of some parameter s. The parametric path should satisfy $H(x(s), t(s)) = 0$ for all s. If we are on the path, the change in x and t necessary to maintain the condition $H(x(s), t(s)) = 0$ can be determined by implicit differentiation. Implicit differentiation of $H(x(s), t(s)) = 0$ with respect to s yields n conditions on the $n + 1$ unknowns,

$$\sum_{i=1}^{n} H_{x_i}(x(s), t(s))x_i'(s) + H_t(x(s), t(s))t'(s) = 0. \tag{5.9.3}$$

Because of the one dimension of indeterminacy, there are many solutions to the parametric equations in (5.9.3). However, we only care about $(x(s), t(s))$ pairs, not their dependence on s. Hence we need to find only one solution. If we define $y(s) = (x(s), t(s))$, then y obeys the system of differential equations

$$\frac{dy_i}{ds} = (-1)^i \det\left(\frac{\partial H}{\partial y}(y)_{-i}\right), \qquad i = 1, \ldots, n+1, \tag{5.9.4}$$

where $(\cdot)_{-i}$ means we remove the ith column.

Garcia and Zangwill (1981) call (5.9.4) the *basic differential equation*. When we reformulate the problem in this differential equation form, we immediately see a problem. If the $((\partial H/\partial y)(y)_{-i})$ matrices in (5.9.4) are ever all singular before $t(s) = 1$, then the system (5.9.4) will come to a stop. To avoid this, the $n \times (n+1)$ matrix $H_y = (H_x, H_t)$ must have full rank, that is, a rank of n, for all (x, t) on the path. Since the rank of $H_y(y)$ is so important, we have a special name for homotopies that have full rank:

DEFINITION The homotopy H is *regular* iff $H_y(y)$ is of full rank at all points in $H^{-1}(0)$, where $y \equiv (x, t)$.

Therefore, if a homotopy has full rank, the differential equation system (5.9.4) will have a solution that parameterizes a path leading to a solution of $H(x, 1) = 0$. The full rank condition is weaker than it may initially appear to be. H_y has full rank along simple path like AB but also at turning points like D and E in figure 5.11. This is substantial progress over simple continuation which requires H_x be nonsingular. Unfortunately, the homotopy is not regular at branch points like H in figure 5.11.

When we apply this method to our example (5.9.2), the system (5.9.4) becomes

$$\begin{pmatrix} dx/ds \\ dt/ds \end{pmatrix} = \begin{pmatrix} -H_t \\ H_x \end{pmatrix} = \begin{pmatrix} x - (2x - 4 + \sin(2\pi x)) \\ 1 - t + t(2 + 2\pi \cos(2\pi x)) \end{pmatrix}. \tag{5.9.5}$$

To find a zero of $H(x, 1)$ in (5.9.2), we start with $(x, t) = (0, 0)$ and then solve the differential equation (5.9.5) until we reach a s such that $t(s) = 1$. At that s, $x(s)$ will be a zero of $H(x(s), t(s)) = 0$.

We typically solve (5.9.4) numerically. We will discuss numerical methods for solving differential equations in chapter 10, but we will use a simple scheme to solve our example, (5.9.5). We let $s_i = i/1000$ for $i = 0, 1, \ldots, 720$, and define

$$x_{i+1} = x_i + h(x_i - (2x_i - 4 + \sin 2\pi x_i)),$$

$$t_{i+1} = t_i + h(1 - t_i + t_i(2 + 2\pi \cos 2\pi x_i)), \tag{5.9.6}$$

where $h = 0.001$ is the step size corresponding to ds and $x_0 = t_0 = 0$ are initial conditions. The iteration (5.9.6) approximates the solution to (5.9.5) at the s_i points. Table 5.5 displays several of these points as computed by (5.9.6).

The (t_i, x_i) pairs in table 5.5 are so close to the $H^{-1}(0)$ set graphed in figure 5.10 that a graph cannot distinguish them. The value $t = 1$ is achieved between $i = 711$ and $i = 712$; the natural estimate of the zero of $2x - 4 + \sin 2\pi x$ is 2.003, since $t = 1$ is halfway between t_{711} and t_{712}. This answer is correct to three significant digits. Furthermore, once we have the estimate of 2.003 for the root, we can use it as an initial guess for Newton's method, which will quickly converge to the true solution $x = 2.0$ in this case.

Good Homotopy Choices

Figure 5.11 illustrates several possible paths, some do connect the $t = 0$ line to the $t = 1$ line, but many others don't. We will choose homotopies that avoid the bad possibilities. Some problems are easily avoided. For example, MN in figure 5.11 turns back to the $t = 0$ line, something that is possible only if $H(x, 0)$ has multiple zeros. To avoid this, we just choose a homotopy where $H(x, 0)$ has a unique zero.

Table 5.5
Homotopy path following in (5.9.6)

Iterate i	t_i	x_i	True solution $H(x, t_i) = 0$
50	0.05621	0.16759	0.16678
100	0.11130	0.30748	0.30676
200	0.15498	0.64027	0.64025
300	0.35543	1.02062	1.01850
400	0.69540	1.23677	1.23288
500	0.67465	1.41982	1.42215
600	0.51866	1.68870	1.69290
650	0.61731	1.84792	1.84391
700	0.90216	1.97705	1.97407
711	0.99647	2.00203	1.99915
712	1.00473	2.00402	2.00114

Closed curves are no problem as long as there are components that join the $t = 0$ and $t = 1$ cases.

The more serious problems arise from branch points. They can be avoided if we do a good job constructing our homotopy. A basic theorem is the next one:

THEOREM 5.9.1   Suppose that $f \in C^2$. Let D be compact with nonempty interior. Define

$$H(x, t) = (1 - t)(x - x^0) + tf(x).$$

If H is regular, and $H(x, t) \neq 0$ for all $0 \leq t < 1$ and $x \in \partial D$, then f has a zero that is at the end of a path joining $t = 0$ and $t = 1$ in $H^{-1}(0)$.

A key assumption in this method is that H is regular. In figure 5.11 the presence of the branch point at H or a dead end at QR means that the homotopy is not regular. Determining that a homotopy is regular is a computational task as demanding as finding zeros. It would appear that we have not made any progress. Fortunately the following theorems tell us that many simple homotopies are regular:

THEOREM 5.9.2 (Chow et al. 1978)   If $B^n \equiv \{x \in R^n \mid |x| < 1\}$ and $f : \overline{B^n} \to \overline{B^n}$ is C^1, then the homotopy

$$H : B^n \times (0, 1) \times B^n \to R^n,$$

$$H(a, t, x) = (1 - t)(x - a) + t(x - f(x)),$$

is regular and for almost all $a \in B^n$, $H^{-1}(0)$ is a smooth curve joining $(0, a)$ to a fixed point of f at $t = 1$.

THEOREM 5.9.3 (Mas-Colell) There is an open and dense subset of C^2 functions, $\mathscr{F}$, such that for $f \in \mathscr{F}$, $H^{-1}(0)$ is a smooth curve for the homotopy $H(x, t) = tf(x) - x$.

We should comment that $H^{-1}(0)$ still could have infinite length and oscillate as $t \to 1$. However, that is of only moderate practical concern. Indeed, by continuity of f, we will reach a point where $|f(x) - x| < \varepsilon$ in finite time for any $\varepsilon > 0$.

When we put together the ideas above, we arrive at one simple homotopy solution method to find a fixed point for $f(x) = x$. Remember that theorem 5.9.2 says that it will work with probability one; if the algorithm appears to be failing, then start over at the initialization step of algorithm 5.6 with another a.

Algorithm 5.6 Generically Convergent Euler Homotopy Method

Initialization. Choose an $a \in R^n$ and form the homotopy. $H(a, t, x) = (1 - t)(x - a) + t(x - f(x))$. Let $x_0 = a$, $s_0 = 0$, and $t_0 = 0$. Choose step size $\varepsilon > 0$.

Step 1. Given x_i, s_i, and t_i, compute x_{i+1} and t_{i+1} using (5.9.4). Let $s_{i+1} = s_i + \varepsilon$.

Step 2. If $t_{i+1} > 1$ go to step 3; else go to step 1.

Step 3. Stop and return the last iterate of x as the solution.

Theorems 5.9.2 and 5.9.3 say that we may still have to handle the curves like *CDEF* in Figure 5.11 where the index t is not monotonic but that for many simple homotopies we won't have to worry about paths with branch points. These theorems essentially say that the homotopy methods are almost surely convergent. This high degree of reliability is good, but it comes at a high cost, since tracking one of these curves may involve a great deal of calculation.

While theorems 5.9.2 and 5.9.3 present cases of generic regularity, we could first try more natural homotopies. An alternative approach is to let $H(x, t) = (1 - t)g(x) + tf(x)$ where $g(x)$ is similar to $f(x)$. For example, if $f(x)$ is a system of excess demand equations, we could let $g(x)$ be a system of excess demand equations with a known solution. Constructing such a $g(x)$ is often easy; for example, we could let $g(x)$ be the case where each agent has the same endowment and tastes with the common endowment and tastes being the "average" endowment and tastes behind the excess demand system in $f(x)$. There is also no requirement that $H(x, t)$ be linear in t. While these approaches may lead to problems with branch points, they may also be much faster. As always in numerical analysis, it sometimes pays to try approaches that do not fall into the safe categories; novel ones may be turn out to be very effective and one can always go back to the safe methods.

Simplicial Homotopy Methods

Homotopy methods using differential equations still need to compute or approximate Jacobians. That will become increasingly impractical as the problem size increases.

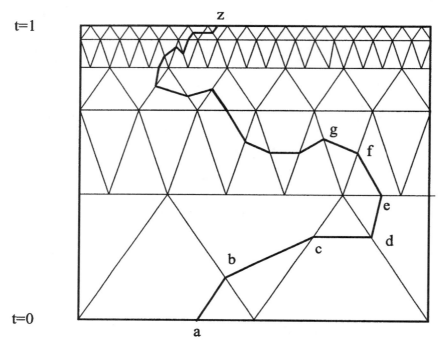

Figure 5.12
Piecewise-linear homotopy

Simplicial homotopy methods continue to use the continuation ideas but depend on a "rougher" deformation of $H(x,0)$ into f. The resulting method uses only function evaluations of f.

We will first describe a simple version of simplicial methods. We begin with a homotopy function $H(x,t)$. Next, divide (x,t) space into simplices, such as the triangular decomposition in figure 5.12. The next, and defining, step is to define a new function $\hat{H}(x,t)$, agreeing with H at the simplicial nodes but linear within each simplex. We then construct the path of zeros of $\hat{H}$. Figure 5.12 shows such a simplicial division and path of zeros $abcdefg\ldots$ that leads to a solution at z.

In a simplicial method we let the piecewise linear function $\hat{H}(x,t)$ deform $\hat{H}(x,0)$ into $\hat{H}(x,1)$ which is a piecewise linear approximation of f. The advantage of this method is that the computation of $\hat{H}^{-1}(0)$ is relatively easy, since $\hat{H}$ is locally linear and each of the $\hat{H}^{-1}(0)$ is piecewise linear. The cost is that the final zero is a zero of $\hat{H}(x,1)$, not f. A potential problem is that $\hat{H}^{-1}(0)$ may lead to points that are not near zeros of f, or that the path may lead nowhere. The following theorem says that the method will work if the simplicial decomposition of (x, t) space is sufficiently fine:

THEOREM 5.9.4   For all ε there is an δ such that if the simplices in $\hat{H}$ are less than δ on each edge, then $\hat{H}^{-1}(0)$ is within ε of some path in H^{-1}.

Combining Homotopy Methods and Newton's Method

Homotopy methods have good convergence properties, but they may be slower than alternatives. In many homotopy methods each step involves computing a Jacobian; in such cases each step is as costly as a Newton step. This observation suggests that we first use a homotopy method to compute a rough solution and then use it as the initial guess for Newton's method.

The slow convergence of homotopy methods also implies that it is difficult to satisfy the tough convergence criterion. In such cases applying Newton's method to the final iterate of a homotopy method is a natural step to improve on the homotopy result. In either case we can implement this by switching to Newton's method at some $t < 1$.

5.10   A Simple CGE Problem

One of the classical uses of nonlinear equations in economics is the computation of competitive equilibrium. In this section we will consider the computation of equilibrium in a simple endowment economy.

Assume that there are m goods and n agents. Assume that agent i's utility function over the m goods is $u^i(x)$, $x \in R^m$. Suppose that agent i's endowment of good j is e^i_j. Economic theory proceeds in the following fashion: First, we "construct" the demand function for each agent; that is, we define

$$d^i(p) = \arg \max_x u^i(x) \tag{5.10.1}$$

$$\text{s.t.} \quad p \cdot (x - e^i) = 0,$$

where $p \in R^m$ is the price vector. We then construct the excess demand function, $E : R^m \to R^m$, defined by $E(p) = \sum_i^n (d^i(p) - e^i)$. Equilibrium is any $p \in R^m$ such that $E(p) = 0$. By the degree zero homogeneity of demand in prices, if $p \in R^m$ is an equilibrium price, so is λp for any $0 \neq \lambda \in R$; in particular, there is an equilibrium on the unit simplex.

To prove existence of an equilibrium price vector, we construct a map $g(p)$ on the unit simplex $S^{m-1} = \{p | \sum_{j=1}^m p_j = 1\}$ such that at any fixed point of $g(p)$, say p^*, we have $E(p^*) \leq 0$. One such function (see Varian 1978) is

$$g_j(p) = \frac{p_j + \max(0, E_j(p))}{1 + \sum_{j=1}^{m} \max(0, E_j(p))}. \tag{5.10.2}$$

Since $g : S^{m-1} \to S^{m-1}$ is continuous, it has a fixed point.

We have several alternative computational approaches to compute a equilibrium price vector. We will now discuss the various methods below.

Fixed-Point Iteration

We could use fixed-point iteration to compute the equilibrium price. Since all equilibria are solutions to the fixed-point problem $p = g(p)$, we could execute the iteration $p^{k+1} = g(p^k)$. If we have closed-form expressions for the individual demand functions, then this approach is particularly easy to implement and avoids the complications of computing Jacobians. Since the map g has range in the unit simplex, there is no chance that some p_k iterate falls outside the permissible range of prices. Of course there is no assurance that the fixed-point iteration approach will converge.

$E(p) = 0$ as a Nonlinear System

One approach is to solve the system $E(p) = 0$ for p. If we can analytically solve for the individual demand functions, then we can construct a routine that explicitly computes the excess demand function and feeds it to a nonlinear equation solver. However, we must take into account the degree zero homogeneity of E. Strictly speaking, if there is one solution, then there is a continuum of solutions. One way to deal with this is to add an equation forcing the prices to lie on the unit simplex, $\sum_{i=1}^{m} p_i = 1$. This gives us one more equation than unknown, but Walras's law tells us that if p satisfies $E(p) = 0$ for $m - 1$ components of E, then the mth component of E is also zero. Hence the system of equations we send to a nonlinear equation solver is

$$E_1(p) = 0,$$

$$\vdots$$

$$E_{m-1}(p) = 0,$$

$$\sum_{i=1}^{m} p_i = 1.$$

In this form we can use Newton's method or a homotopy method to solve for equilibrium.

Hierarchical Numerical Methods

Our discussion has implicitly assumed that we can express $E(p)$ in closed form. If we don't have closed-form expressions for the individual demand functions, then we will have to solve for the individual demands numerically. For each price p we will have to solve a constrained optimization problems for each agent. This produces a hierarchical structure in the resulting algorithm. Suppose that we use the fixed-point iteration approach to find a fixed point of $g(p)$ defined in (5.10.2). At each price iterate p^k, we will need to compute $g(p^k)$. To compute this excess demand vector, the algorithm will have to call upon an optimization routine to solve the demand problem, (5.10.2), for each agent with prices p^k and then use these solutions to compute aggregate excess demand and $g(p^k)$. More generally, we must construct a subroutine $E(p)$ to compute excess demand. In the end the nonlinear equation solver calls a routine for $E(p)$ that in turn calls an optimization routine.

This hierarchical structure generates some new problems. Convergence of any nonlinear equation solution method applied to $E(p)$ depends on the accuracy with which we solve the individual demand problems, which in turn is determined by the convergence factors we choose in the optimization algorithm chosen to solve (5.10.1). The convergence criterion of the nonlinear equation solver and the optimization routine must be consistent. We generally will demand a tight convergence criterion for the optimization routine because it uses an analytical representation for $u(x)$. That optimization problem will have some error in excess of machine precision. Since the convergence criterion for the nonlinear equation solver depends on the error with which $E(p)$ is computed, we need to impose a looser criterion for the nonlinear equation solver than we do for the optimization routine called by $E(p)$. In general, the outer routine of any hierarchical numerical approach must have looser convergence criterion so that it can tolerate the numerical errors generated by the inner numerical procedure.

First-Order Conditions and Market Balance

An alternative approach simultaneously solves for the individual demands and the equilibrium in one large nonlinear system. To do this, we specify a long list of equations, combining the first-order conditions of the individual optimization problem, their budget constraints, and the equilibrium conditions. In an m-good, n-agent example this results in combining the first-order conditions for each good and each agent

$$u_j^i(x^i) = p_j \lambda^i, \qquad i = 1, \ldots, n, \; j = 1, \ldots, m, \tag{5.10.3}$$

the budget constraint for each agent

$$p \cdot (x^i - e^i) = 0, \qquad i = 1, \ldots, n, \tag{5.10.4}$$

the supply equals demand conditions for goods[3] 1 through $m - 1$,

$$\sum_{i=1}^{n} (x_j^i - e_j^i) = 0, \qquad j = 1, \ldots, m - 1, \tag{5.10.5}$$

and the simplex condition for prices

$$\sum_{j} p_j = 1 \tag{5.10.6}$$

to yield a system of nonlinear equations in the unknowns p, x^i, and $\lambda^i, i = 1, \ldots, n$. The system (5.10.3–5.10.6) can be sent to a nonlinear equation solver to determine the equilibrium value of λ and x as well as p.

This joint approach appears to be inefficient because of the large number of unknowns and equations. However, the Jacobian of the resulting joint system will be sparse. This approach is also easy to program, an advantage that may be decisive in small problems.

Negishi Method

A final procedure exploits the first theorem of welfare economics. This theorem states that any competitive equilibrium in an Arrow-Debreu model of general equilibrium is Pareto efficient; that is, for any equilibrium there is a set of nonnegative social welfare weights, $\lambda^i, \ i = 1, \ldots, n$, such that the equilibrium allocation of final consumption, $x^i, i = 1, \ldots, n$, is the solution to the social welfare problem

$$\max_{x^1, x^2, \ldots} \sum_{i=1}^{n} \lambda^i u^i(x^i)$$

$$\tag{5.10.7}$$

$$\text{s.t.} \quad \sum_{i=1}^{n} (e^i - x^i) = 0.$$

In the Negishi approach to computing general equilibrium, we look for the set of social welfare weights, $\lambda^i, \ i = 1, \ldots, n$, such that the solution to (5.10.7) is an equi-

---

3. Recall that if supply equals demand for all but one market, and all budget constraints are satisfied, then supply equals demand for the last market.

librium allocation. Since prices are proportional to marginal utilities, the equilibrium condition can be written $\sum_j u_j^i(x^i)(x_j^i - e_j^i) = 0$ for $i = 1, \ldots, n$.

We proceed as follows: For any vector of social welfare weights, λ, we compute the allocation, $X(\lambda) \in R^{m \times n}$, which solves (5.10.7). We next compute the prices, constrained to lie in the unit simplex, implied by the allocation $X(\lambda)$. These prices are defined by[4]

$$p_j = \frac{u_{x_j^1}^1(X^1(\lambda))}{\sum_{l=1}^m u_{x_l^1}^1(X^1(\lambda))} \equiv P_j(\lambda).$$

We then ask, for each agent i if he can afford his allocation, $X^i(\lambda)$, at the prices $P(\lambda)$ by computing the excess wealth function $W_i(\lambda) \equiv P(\lambda) \cdot (e^i - X^i(\lambda))$. If $W_i(\lambda)$ is nonnegative, then agent i can afford $X^i(\lambda)$ at prices $P(\lambda)$ and have $W_i(\lambda)$ in "wealth" left over. If $W_i(\lambda) = 0$ for each i, the prices $P(\lambda)$ are equilibrium prices, and $X(\lambda)$ is the equilibrium final allocation. Therefore the Negishi approach boils down to solving the system of nonlinear equations

$$W_i(\lambda) = 0, \qquad i = 1, \ldots, n, \tag{5.10.8}$$

for λ, and we then compute $P(\lambda)$ at the solution to (5.10.8) to get the equilibrium prices.

The Negishi approach has substantial advantages if there are fewer agents than goods and individual demands are analytically computable, since the number of unknowns equal the number of agents. It may also be useful even if we must numerically compute demands. When we have a single representative agent, then this approach is particularly appropriate because the competitive equilibrium just maximizes the representative agent's utility. This fact is heavily exploited in many aggregate models.

5.11 Software

There is some software available for nonlinear equations, but there is not nearly the variety and quantity as that available for optimization. HYBRD, a program available as part of MINPACK, combines Powell's method for enhancing convergence with Broyden's procedure for updating the Jacobian. The result is a generally reliable

---

4. We need only compute the relative prices for one agent since any solution to (5.10.7) will equate marginal rates of substitutions across agents.

algorithm for solving nonlinear equations. HOMPACK, available from Netlib, uses differential equation homotopy approaches. Aluffi-Pentini, F., V. Parisi, and F. Zirilli (1984) presents a differential equation approach to solving nonlinear equations. Allgower and Georg (1990) is a recent presentation of homotopy methods, and it offers readers software to implement both piecewise-continuous and piecewise-linear algorithms. The web site http://www.mcs.anl.gov/home/otc/Guide/SoftwareGuide/ Categories/nonlinequ.html contains links to many nonlinear equation packages. Kalaba and Tesfatsion (1991) extend the homotopy method to include a complex tracing variable in order to maneuver around and over branch points. More and Wright (1993) provide references to some nonlinear equation packages.

5.12 Further Reading and Summary

This chapter has presented the basic methods for solving nonlinear equations. One-dimensional problems are easily solved, reliably by comparison methods and often very quickly by Newton's method. Nonlinear systems of nonlinear equations are more difficult. Solving systems of nonlinear equations reduces to an iterative search guided generally by the Jacobian or diagonal portions of the Jacobian. For small systems we generally use Newton's method because of its good local convergence properties. Large systems are generally solved by breaking the system into smaller systems as in Gauss-Jacobi and Gauss-Seidel methods and their block versions.

Newton and Gaussian methods need good initial guesses, but finding good initial guesses is often an art and usually conducted in an ad hoc fashion. Powell's hybrid method combines Newton's method with optimization ideas to create a more reliable algorithm, but it too may not converge. Homotopy methods generically converge from any initial guess, and they are necessary to use when we can't easily generate good initial conditions. Unfortunately, homotopy methods are slower, and their use is limited to systems of small to moderate size. Of course what we consider "small" and "moderate" grows as computer power increases.

Nonlinear equation solving presents problems not present with linear equations or optimization. In particular, the existence problem is much more difficult for nonlinear systems. Unless one has an existence proof in hand, a programmer must keep in mind that the absence of a solution may explain a program's failure to converge. Even if there exists a solution, all methods will do poorly if the problem is poorly conditioned near a solution. Transforming the problem will often improve performance. After computing a solution, the condition number of the Jacobian should be computed if possible to get an estimate of the error.

The literature on nonlinear equations and computation of economic equilibrium is substantial. Ortega and Rheinboldt (1970) is a classic introduction to nonlinear equations. There is a large literature on computational general equilibrium; Johansen (1960) and Scarf and Hansen (1973) are classics in the area, and Shoven and Whalley (1992) and Dixon and Parmenter (1996) are comprehensive surveys of the literature. Scarf's method is a historically important method. It was the first globally convergent algorithm for solving nonlinear equations, but it has seldom been a competitive method in practice.

The Kakutani fixed-point theorem generalizes the Brouwer fixed-point theorem to correspondences, which allows for a more general theorem; Eaves (1971) discusses methods to solve such problems. Brown, DeMarzo, and Eaves (1994) and Schmedders (1996) have developed algorithms for computing equilibrium in general equilibrium models with incomplete asset markets. Actual homotopy solution methods are more complicated and efficient than (5.9.4). See Eaves (1972), Algower and Georg (1990), and Garcia and Zangwill (1981) for discussions of homotopy methods.

The game theory literature contains much related material on computing Nash equilibrium. The numerical literature begins with Lemke and Howson's (1964) treatment of two-person games, and Wilson (1971) generalized this to n players. Wilson (1992) presents an algorithm for finding stable components of Nash equilibria. McElvey (1996) surveys this literature. Wilson (1996) presents methods for solving nonlinear pricing problems.

Variational inequalities are problems that encompass both optimization and nonlinear equations. Nagurney (1993) contains a clear introduction to this topic.

Exercises

1. Solve $\sin 2\pi x - 2x = 0$ using bisection, Newton's method, the secant method, and fixed-point iteration. For what values of the initial guess $x_0 \in [-2, 2]$ does each of these methods converge? Repeat for $\sin 2\pi x - x = 0$. Repeat for $\sin 2\pi x - .5x = 0$.

2. Compute and compare the domains of convergence of Newton's method applied to (5.7.2) and (5.7.3) for initial guesses in $[0, 2]^2$. Did the nonlinear transformation in (5.7.3) increase the domain of convergence? Also, is the average rate of convergence over these domains greater for (5.7.2) or (5.7.3)? To do this exercise, develop your own concept of the "average rate of convergence" over a domain. Also use a graphical presentation similar to that in figure 5.7 in section 5.4.

3. Consider the CGE problem in section 5.10 with

$$u^i(x) = \sum_{j=1}^{m} a_j^i x_j^{v_j^i + 1} (1 + v_j^i)^{-1}.$$

Assume that $a_j^i, e_j^i > 0 > v_j^i$, $i = 1, \ldots, n$, $j = 1, \ldots, m$. Write programs that take the a_j^i, v_j^i, and e_j^i coefficients as inputs, and compute the pure exchange equilibrium price vector p_j, $j = 1, \ldots, m$, and consumption of good j for agent i, c_j^i. For purposes of testing, make random choices for $a_j^i \in [1, 10]$, $v_j^i \in [-0.5, -3]$, and $e_j^i \in [1, 5]$. Initially start with two goods and two agents. Then try larger systems. Can you handle $m = n = 5$? $m = n = 10$?

a. Write a program using Newton's method applied to the first-order conditions. How often do you get convergence?

b. Find a program using Powell's hybrid method (e.g., HYBRD in Minpack) applied to the first-order conditions. Compare the performance of Newton's method and the hybrid method.

c. Write a program using the Negishi approach.

d. Write a program using the function iteration approach applied to g defined in (5.10.2).

e. If all agents are identical, then it is trivial to compute equilibrium. Write a program that uses simple continuation to move from an identical agent case to the inputted case. Does simple continuation usually work?

(For $v_j^i = -1$, we replace $x_j^{v_j^i + 1} (1 + v_j^i)^{-1}$ with $\ln x_j$. If you do not want to program this special case, you can approximate $v_j^i = -1$ with, for example, $v_j^i = -1.01$.)

4.   Assume there are n individual investors and m assets with asset j paying Z_s^j dollars with probability π_s^j, $s = 1, \ldots, S$, in state s. Let e_j^l denote agent l's endowment of asset j. Assume that asset 1 is safe, paying R dollars tomorrow per unit held today. Suppose that investor l maximizes expected utility, $E\{u_l(W)\}$, over final wealth, W; let $u_l(W) = W^{1+\gamma_l}/(1 + \gamma_l)$ where $\gamma_l < 0$. Write a program that reads in data on tastes, returns, and endowments, and computes the equilibrium price of the assets and the expected utility of each investor. Begin with three agents ($n = 3$), one safe asset paying 1, and two risky assets ($m = 3$). Assume that one risky asset pays 0.8, 1.0, 1.1, or 1.2 with equal probability, that the other risky asset pays 0.1, 0.8, 1.1, or 1.3 with equal probability, and that the two risky assets are independent.

5.   Repeat the duopoly example of section 5.4, but assume three firms, concave, increasing utility functions of the form $u(x, y, z) = (a + x^\alpha + y^\beta + z^\gamma)^\delta + M$, and unit cost equaling 1. Compute and compare the Bertrand and Cournot outcomes for a variety of combinations of $a \in [0.1, 2]$ and $\alpha, \beta, \gamma, \delta \in [0.1, 0.9]$. Compute the change in profits for firms x and y if they merge; compare the results for the Bertrand and Cournot cases.

6 Approximation Methods

Many computational problems require us to approximate functions. In some cases we have a slow and complex way to compute a function and want to replace it with a simpler, more efficient approximating function. To do this, we compute the value of the function at only a few points and make guesses about its values elsewhere. In many interesting cases the function of interest is unknown; we then approximate it by generating a finite amount of information about it and use the information to construct an approximating function. Choosing the best way to accomplish this is often an essential aspect of an efficient computational strategy.

We examine three types of approximation problems in this chapter, representing three different kinds of data and objectives. A *local approximation* takes as data the value of a function f and its derivatives at a point x_0 and constructs a function that matches those properties at x_0 and is (hopefully) a good approximation of f near x_0. Taylor series and Padé expansions are the major local approximation methods.

An L^p *approximation* finds a "nice" function g that is "close to" a given function f over some interval in the sense of a L^p norm. To compute an L^p approximation of f, we ideally need the entire function, an informational requirement that is generally infeasible. *Interpolation* is any procedure that finds a "nice" function that goes through a collection of prescribed points. Interpolation and L^p approximation are similar except that the data in interpolation are a finite set of points; in fact interpolation uses n facts to fix n free parameters.

Regression lies between L^p approximation and interpolation in that it uses m facts to fix n parameters, $m > n$, producing an approximation that only nearly fits the data. Regression methods are more stable but use more information than interpolation methods, and they are less accurate in that they use less information than the full L^p approximation.

In this chapter we will present the formal implementations of these ideas. In all cases we need to formalize the notions of "nice" and "close to." We introduce orthogonal polynomials, splines, and their approximation properties. Economists often deal with functions that they know to be nonnegative, or concave, for example; we present methods that preserve such information about shape. Much of approximation theory is based on linear methods. Flexible, nonlinear approximation is a difficult topic, but one promising approach is *neural networks*. We discuss neural networks and their approximation properties.

6.1 Local Approximation Methods

Local approximation methods use information about a function $f: R \to R$ only at a point, $x_0 \in R$, but that information may include several derivatives of f at x_0 as well as $f(x_0)$. The objective is to produce locally good approximations with little effort; for many important classes of functions, these local procedures produce approximations that are also globally useful. The two most common such procedures are Taylor series and Padé approximation.

Taylor Series Approximation

The theoretical basis for all local approximations is Taylor's theorem, theorem 1.6.1. The basic point of Taylor's theorem is that we can take a n-times differentiable function, f, form the polynomial approximation

$$f(x) \doteq f(x_0) + (x - x_0)f'(x_0) + \frac{(x - x_0)^2}{2} f''(x_0) + \cdots$$

$$+ \frac{(x - x_0)^n}{n!} f^{(n)}(x_0)$$

(6.1.1)

and be assured that the error is $\mathcal{O}(|x - x_0|^{n+1})$ and hence asymptotically smaller than any of the terms. The *degree n Taylor series approximation to f* is the right-hand side of (6.1.1). Taylor series approximations of f are polynomials that agree with f to a high order near x_0. Taylor's theorem only says that this approximation is good near x_0; its accuracy may decay rapidly as we move away from x_0.

As we take $n \rightarrow \infty$ (assuming that $f \in C^\infty$), (6.1.1) is potentially a power series representation for f near x_0. The key fact about power series is that if $\sum_{n=0}^\infty a_n z^n$ converges for z_0, then it converges absolutely for all complex numbers z such that $|z| < |z_0|$. If we define

$$r = \sup\left\{ |z| : \left| \sum_{n=0}^\infty a_n z^n \right| < \infty \right\},$$

then r is called the *radius of convergence*, and $\sum_{n=0}^\infty a_n z^n$ converges for all $|z| < r$ and diverges for all $|z| > r$.

The properties of power series are studied extensively in complex analysis. We will give some basic definitions from complex analysis and state some basic theorems without proof. We provide them so that we can discuss various aspects of approximation in a precise fashion. First, let Ω be any nonempty, connected open set in the complex plane. A function $f: \Omega \subset C \rightarrow C$ on the complex plane C is *analytic* on Ω iff for every $a \in \Omega$, there is an r and a sequence c_k such that $f(z) = \sum_{k=0}^\infty c_k (z - a)^k$ whenever $\|z - a\| < r$. A *singularity of f* is any point a such that f is analytic on $\Omega - \{a\}$ but not on Ω. A point $a \in C$ is a *pole of f* iff a is a singularity of f, but

$f(z)(z-a)^m$ is analytic on Ω for some m. The pole has *multiplicity m* iff $f(z)(z-a)^m$ is analytic on Ω, but $f(z)(z-a)^{m-1}$ is not. A function $f: C \to C$ is *meromorphic* iff it is analytic on an open set in the complex plane outside of a nowhere dense set of poles.

The following theorem states a basic property of analytic functions:

THEOREM 6.1.2   Let f be analytic at $x \in C$. If f or any derivative of f has a singularity at $z \in C$, then the radius of convergence in the complex plane of the Taylor series based at x_0, $\sum_{n=0}^{\infty}((x-x_0)^n/n!)f^{(n)}(x_0)$, is bounded above by $\|x_0 - z\|$.

Theorem 6.1.2 tells us that the Taylor series at x_0 cannot reliably approximate $f(x)$ at any point farther away from x_0 than any singular point of f. This fact will be important for economic applications, since utility and production functions often satisfy an Inada condition, a singularity, at some point. Note that it is distance that matters, not direction. Therefore, if $f(x) = x^{-1/2}$, the singularity at $x = 0$ means that the Taylor series based at $x_0 = 1$ cannot be accurate for $x > 2$. Also even a singularity at a complex point affects convergence for real x.

We illustrate the quality of a Taylor expansion with a function familiar to economists. Suppose that $f(x) = x^\alpha$, where $0 < \alpha < 1$. This function has its only singularity at $x = 0$, implying that the radius of convergence for the Taylor series around $x = 1$ is only unity. The coefficients in the Taylor series decline slowly, since

$$a_k = \frac{1}{k!}\frac{d^k}{dx^k}(x^\alpha)\Big|_{x=1} = \frac{\alpha(\alpha-1)\cdots(\alpha-k+1)}{1\cdot 2 \cdots k}.$$

For example, if $\alpha = 0.25$, then for $k < 50$, $|a_k| > 0.001$. Table 6.1 displays the error, $|x^{1/4} - \sum_{k=0}^{N} a_k(x-1)^k|$, for various values of x and N.

Table 6.1 shows that the Taylor series is very good near $x = 1$ but that its quality falls sharply as x falls away from $x = 1$. Even a 50th-order Taylor series approximation achieves only two-digit accuracy at $x = 0.05$. Also note that the Taylor series is worthless for $x > 2$. In fact outside $[0, 2]$ the error grows as we increase the degree; for example, the error at $x = 3$ is of order 10^{12} for the 50th-order expansion.

Rational Approximation

The kth-degree Taylor series approximation is the degree k polynomial that matches f at x_0 up to the kth derivative. When stated this way, we are led to ask if we can do better by matching some other functional form to f and its derivatives at x_0. *Padé approximation* is a powerful alternative that uses the local information to construct a *rational function*, a ratio of polynomials, to approximate f at x_0.

Table 6.1
Taylor series approximation errors for $x^{1/4}$

x	N 5	10	20	50	$x^{1/4}$
3.0	5(−1)	8(1)	3(3)	1(12)	0.9457
2.0	1(−2)	5(−3)	2(−3)	8(−4)	0.9457
1.8	4(−3)	5(−4)	2(−4)	9(−9)	0.9457
1.5	2(−4)	3(−6)	1(−9)	0(−12)	0.9457
1.2	1(−6)	2(−10)	0(−12)	0(−12)	0.9457
0.80	2(−6)	3(−10)	0(−12)	0(−12)	0.9457
0.50	6(−4)	9(−6)	4(−9)	0(−12)	0.8409
0.25	1(−2)	1(−3)	4(−5)	3(−9)	0.7071
0.10	6(−2)	2(−2)	4(−3)	6(−5)	0.5623
0.05	1(−1)	5(−2)	2(−2)	2(−3)	0.4729

DEFINITION   A (m, n) Padé approximant of f at x_0 is a rational function

$$r(x) = \frac{p(x)}{q(x)},$$

where $p(x)$ and $q(x)$ are polynomials, the degree of p is at most m, the degree of q is at most n, and

$$0 = \frac{d^k}{dx^k}(p - f\,q)\,(x_0), \qquad k = 0, \ldots, m + n.$$

One usually chooses $m = n$ or $m = n + 1$. The defining conditions can be rewritten as $q(x_0) = 1$ and

$$p^{(k)}(x_0) = (f\,q)^{(k)}(x_0), \qquad k = 0, \ldots, m + n, \tag{6.1.2}$$

which are linear in the $m + 1$ unknown coefficients of p and the $n + 1$ coefficients of q once the derivatives of f at x_0 are computed. The $m + n + 1$ conditions in (6.1.2) together with the normalization $q(x_0) = 1$ form $m + n + 2$ linear conditions on the $m + n + 2$ coefficients of p and q. The linear system may be singular; in that case one reduces n or m by 1 and tries again.

In practice, we replace f by its degree $m + n$ Taylor series and equate the coefficients of like powers; that is, if $t(x)$ is the degree $m + n$ Taylor series of f based at x_0, then we find $p(x)$ and $q(x)$ such that $p^{(k)}(x_0) = (t(x)q(x))^{(k)}(x_0)$ for all $k = 0, \ldots, m + n$, which is equivalent to finding $p(x)$ and $q(x)$ such that the coefficients of

Table 6.2
Padé approximation errors for $x^{1/4}$

x	(3, 2)	(5, 5)	(10, 10)	(9, 1)	(4, 1)
			(m, n)		
3.0	7(−4)	1(−6)	2(−12)	1(−2)	6(−3)
2.0	5(−5)	6(−9)	0(−12)	2(−4)	2(−4)
1.8	2(−5)	1(−9)	0(−12)	2(−6)	8(−5)
1.5	2(−6)	2(−11)	0(−12)	2(−8)	8(−6)
1.2	1(−8)	0(−12)	0(−12)	2(−12)	5(−8)
0.80	4(−8)	0(−12)	0(−12)	5(−12)	1(−7)
0.50	3(−5)	4(−9)	0(−12)	3(−7)	7(−5)
0.25	1(−3)	5(−6)	1(−10)	1(−4)	2(−3)
0.10	1(−2)	6(−4)	8(−7)	4(−3)	2(−2)
0.05	4(−2)	4(−3)	5(−5)	2(−2)	5(−2)

$1, x, x^2, \ldots, x^{m+n}$ in $p(x) - t(x)q(x)$ are all zero. To illustrate the method, we compute the (2, 1) Padé approximation of $x^{1/4}$ at $x = 1$. We first construct the degree $2 + 1 = 3$ Taylor series for $x^{1/4}$ at $x = 1$:

$$t(x) = 1 + \frac{(x-1)}{4} - \frac{3(x-1)^2}{32} + \frac{7(x-1)^3}{128}.$$

If $p(x) \equiv p_0 + p_1(x-1) + p_2(x-1)^2$, and since $q_0 = 1$, $q(x) \equiv 1 + q_1(x-1)$, we are searching for p_0, p_1, p_2, and q_1 such that

$$p_0 + p_1(x-1) + p_2(x-1)^2 - t(x)(1 + q_1(x-1)) = 0 \tag{6.1.3}$$

Combining coefficients of like powers in (6.1.3) implies a set of linear equations for p_0, p_1, p_2, and q_1 that produces, after multiplying p and q by 40, the (2, 1) Padé approximation

$$\frac{21 + 70x + 5x^2}{40 + 56x}. \tag{6.1.4}$$

In table 6.2 we report the errors of various Padé approximants to $x^{1/4}$ based at $x_0 = 1$. Comparing these results to those in table 6.1 shows that both are excellent for x close to x_0 but that the Padé approximant is much better for x farther from x_0 even for $x = 2$ and $x = 3$. The range of validity for the Padé approximant on $[1, \infty)$ is not limited by the singularity at $x = 0$.

The straightforward linear equation approach we used to solve for the Padé coefficients in (6.1.4) is satisfactory for some cases but may lead to poorly conditioned linear systems if we use high-degree polynomials in the numerator and denominator. See Cuyt and Wuytack (1986) for better methods of constructing higher-order approximations.

The general experience is that Padé approximants of "well-behaved" functions are better global approximants than Taylor series approximations; that is, the error grows less rapidly as we move away from x_0. The following theorem from Cuyt and Wuytack[1] covers some important cases.

THEOREM 6.1.3   Let $P_{m,n}$ be the (m, n) Padé approximant of $f(z)$, a meromorphic function on $B \equiv \{z \mid \|z\| \leq r\} \subset C$. Then for every $\delta, \varepsilon > 0$ there is a k such that for all $j > k$ the Lebesgue measure of $\{z: \|f(z) - P_{j,1}(z)\| > \varepsilon\}$ is less than δ. Furthermore, if the poles of f are finite in number and have total multiplicity of n, then the sequence $P_{j,n}$ converges uniformly as $j \to \infty$ to f on every closed and bounded subset of B outside of the poles.

These are useful results confirming the convergence of Padé approximants for important classes of functions. For example, it applies to $x^{1/4}$ on the right half of the complex plane; since its only pole is at the origin, the convergence of $P_{m,1}$ to $x^{1/4}$ as m increases is assured on each bounded interval on the positive real line. Table 6.2 shows that Padé approximation generally works well for $x^{1/4}$. We would like stronger results, such as $P_{m,m-1}$ converging on the real line, but the full convergence theory of Padé approximation is beyond the scope of this text; see Cuyt and Wuytack (1986) and Braess (1986) for treatments of these issues. In practice, we construct Padé expansions for a function and then check its quality, usually finding that it does well.

Log-Linearization, Log-Quadraticization, etc.

Economists often want to express results in unit-free form in terms of elasticities and shares. One way to accomplish this is to *log-linearize* an equation at a point. Suppose that we know a solution $f(x_0, \varepsilon_0) = 0$, and we want to compute the elasticity $(dx/x)/(d\varepsilon/\varepsilon)$ at $x = x_0$ and $\varepsilon = \varepsilon_0 \neq 0$. By implicit differentiation, $f_x dx + f_\varepsilon d\varepsilon = 0$, which implies that

$$\hat{x} = \frac{dx}{x} = -\frac{\varepsilon f_\varepsilon}{x f_x}\frac{d\varepsilon}{\varepsilon} = -\frac{\varepsilon f_\varepsilon}{x f_x}\hat{\varepsilon},$$

where we use the caret notation, $\hat{z} \equiv dz/z$. The term $\varepsilon f_\varepsilon / x f_x$ evaluated at $x = x_0$ and $\varepsilon = \varepsilon_0$ is unit-free, and generally can be decomposed into elasticities and shares.

---

1. See discussion in Cuyt and Wuytack (1986, pp. 97–99).

Since $\hat{x} = d(\ln x)$, log-linearization implies the log-linear approximation

$$\ln x - \ln x_0 \doteq -\frac{\varepsilon_0 f_\varepsilon(x_0, \varepsilon_0)}{x_0 f_x(x_0, \varepsilon_0)} (\ln \varepsilon - \ln \varepsilon_0). \tag{6.1.5}$$

The log-linear expression in turn implies that

$$x \doteq x_0 \exp\left(-\frac{\varepsilon_0 f_\varepsilon(x_0, \varepsilon_0)}{x_0 f_x(x_0, \varepsilon_0)} (\ln \varepsilon - \ln \varepsilon_0)\right), \tag{6.1.6}$$

which is a constant elasticity approximation of $x(\varepsilon)$ for ε near ε_0. The expressions (6.1.5) and (6.1.6) can be compared to the linear approximation

$$x \doteq x_0 + (\varepsilon - \varepsilon_0)\left(-\frac{f_\varepsilon(x(\varepsilon_0), \varepsilon_0)}{f_x(x(\varepsilon_0), \varepsilon_0)}\right).$$

The log-linear approximation has the advantage of producing expressions based on shares and elasticities; this is useful when deriving qualitative formulas and in empirical work where one wants to express results in terms of shares and elasticities. However, there is no general reason for either the linear or log-linear approximation being a more accurate approximation than the other. They may appear to provide us with different information, but the differences concern higher-order information about f which is not contained in the first-order information used in (6.1.5) and (6.1.6).

It may appear difficult to extend the "log-linearized" first-order method to a "log-quadraticized" second-order approximation. However, once we realize that both methods are essentially the same, we see that we can arbitrarily generalize log-linearization.

The key observation is that we are just using a nonlinear change of variables. Suppose that we have $Y(X)$ implicitly defined by $f(Y(X), X) = 0$. Define $x = \ln X$ and $y = \ln Y$, then $y(x) = \ln Y(e^x)$. Furthermore the equation $f(Y(X), X) = 0$ is equivalent to $f(e^{y(x)}, e^x) \equiv g(y(x), x) = 0$. Implicit differentiation of $g(y(x), x) = 0$ will produce $y'(x) = (d \ln Y)/(d \ln X)$ and the log-linear approximation (6.1.5) applies. The expression $\ln Y(X) = y(x)$ suggests the second-order approximation

$$\ln Y(X) = y(x) \doteq y(x_0) + y'(x)(x - x_0) + y''(x_0)\frac{(x - x_0)^2}{2}, \tag{6.1.7}$$

which expresses $\ln Y$ in terms of a polynomial in $x = \ln X$. Again we have no reason to prefer (6.1.7) over a quadratic expansion in X. In any specific case they may differ; it may be sensible to compute both and then pick whichever one does better at satisfying the implicit relation $f(Y(X), X) = 0$.

These ideas can also be applied to constructing Padé expansions in terms of the logarithm. One could construct approximations that are ratios of polynomials in the logarithm. We also see that there is nothing special about log function. We could take any monotonic $h(\cdot)$, define $x = h(X)$ and $y = h(Y)$, and use the identity

$$f(Y, X) = f(h^{-1}(h(Y)), h^{-1}(h(X)))$$

$$= f(h^{-1}(y), h^{-1}(x)) \equiv g(y, x).$$

The log expansion where $h(z) = \ln z$ is natural for economists, since it delivers expressions in terms of elasticities and shares. However, it is not the only possibility, and others may be better when we are using Taylor series expansions as numerical approximations.

6.2   Ordinary Regression as Approximation

Economists are familiar with one common form of global approximation, that being least squares regression. In this section we discuss ordinary regression as an approximation method, the statistical context with which we are most familiar, and show how it can be adjusted to form efficient approximation methods in numerical contexts.

Regression analysis studies the function $f(x) = E\{y|x\}$, the expectation of the dependent variable, $y \in R$, conditional on the variables, $x \in R^k$. The task of econometric analysis is to derive an approximation of f using n data points, $(y_i, x^i) \in R \times R^k$, $i = 1, \ldots, n$, and $m < n$ functions, $\phi_j : R^k \to R, j = 1, \ldots, m$. *Ordinary least squares regression* (OLS) fits the data with the functions ϕ_j by solving the problem

$$\min_{a_1, a_2, \ldots, a_m} \sum_{i=1}^{n} \left(a_1 \phi_1(x^i) + a_2 \phi_2(x^i) + \cdots + a_m \phi_m(x^i) - y_i \right)^2. \tag{6.2.1}$$

The a_j coefficients that solve (6.2.1) defines a function, $\hat{f}(x) \equiv \sum_{j=1}^{m} a_j \phi_j(x)$ such that $\hat{f}(x^i)$ is "close to" y_i for each i. Generally, $y_i \neq \hat{f}(x^i)$, but the coefficients are chosen to minimize the sum of squared errors. More generally, $\hat{f}(x)$ is a curve that hopefully approximates the true function $f(x)$ over all points x in some region of interest.

In numerical analysis we will also want to generate approximations, $\hat{f}(x)$, to unknown or known functions and, as with OLS, do so with only the finite amount of information represented by (y_i, x^i) points. We could use simple regression. However, we can generally do much better because the context of our numerical approximation problems differs substantially from the statistical context of econometric problems.

The first key difference is that the econometrician has no control over the x^i points in his data set, whereas the numerical analyst will be able to choose the x^i he uses. Second, the econometrician has to deal with significant error in the (y_i, x^i) data, since $y_i - f(x^i)$ will generally be nontrivial; in numerical analysis we will be able to control this error, often making it trivial.

These features allow us to do things in numerical analysis that are unacceptable in econometrics. For example, econometricians would never solve (6.2.1) with $m = n$; the resulting approximations would generally be silly and unreliable. However, we will see that when the error $y_i - f(x^i)$ is small, we can often construct reliable exact fits through *careful* choices of the x^i values.

In the rest of the chapter we describe several approximation methods available. Even in one dimension we find that they do significantly better than simple regression; in several dimensions the advantage increases exponentially. These more powerful methods build on the same basic ideas as ordinary least squares approximation; therefore much of this material will be familiar. We will see, however, that by pushing these ideas a bit and analyzing them in the context of numerical, not statistical, problems, we can develop much more efficient approximation methods.

6.3 Orthogonal Polynomials

We next use basic vector space ideas to construct representations of functions that lead to good approximations. Since the space of continuous functions is spanned by the monomials, x^n, $n = 0, 1, 2, \ldots$, it is natural to think of the monomials as a basis for the space of continuous functions. However, good bases for vector spaces possess useful orthogonality properties. We will develop those orthogonality ideas to construct *orthogonal polynomials*.

DEFINITION A *weighting function, $w(x)$, on $[a, b]$* is any function that is positive almost everywhere and has a finite integral on $[a, b]$. Given a weighting function $w(x)$, we define the inner product

$$\langle f, g \rangle = \int_a^b f(x)\, g(x)\, w(x)\, dx.$$

The family of polynomials $\{\varphi_n(x)\}$ is *mutually orthogonal* with respect to the weighting function $w(x)$ if and only if $\langle \varphi_n, \varphi_m \rangle = 0$ for $n \neq m$. They are *mutually orthonormal* if they are mutually orthogonal and $\langle \varphi_n, \varphi_n \rangle = 1$ for all n. The inner product defines a norm $\|f\|^2 = \langle f, f \rangle$ on the functions f for which $\langle f, f \rangle$ is finite.

Table 6.3
Common families of orthogonal polynomials

Family	$w(x)$	$[a,b]$	Definition
Legendre	1	$[-1,1]$	$P_n(x) = \dfrac{(-1)^n}{2^n n!}\dfrac{d^n}{dx^n}[(1-x^2)^n]$
Chebyshev	$(1-x^2)^{-1/2}$	$[-1,1]$	$T_n(x) = \cos(n\cos^{-1}x)$
General Chebyshev	$\left(1-\left(\dfrac{2x-a-b}{b-a}\right)^2\right)^{-1/2}$	$[a,b]$	$T_n\left(\dfrac{2x-a-b}{b-a}\right)$
Laguerre	e^{-x}	$[0,\infty)$	$L_n(x) = \dfrac{e^x}{n!}\dfrac{d^n}{dx^n}(x^n e^{-x})$
Hermite	e^{-x^2}	$(-\infty,\infty)$	$H_n(x) = (-1)^n e^{x^2}\dfrac{d^n}{dx^n}(e^{-x^2})$

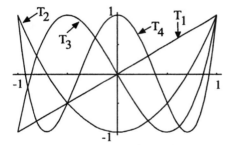

Figure 6.1
Chebyshev polynomials

We assume that all the nonnegative powers of x are integrable with respect to w. Since the resulting orthogonal polynomial families are orthogonal bases of the space of polynomials, they can be generated using the Gram-Schmidt procedure. Below we will find simpler ways to generate orthogonal polynomials.

There are several examples of orthogonal families of polynomials, each defined by a different weighting function. Some common ones are described in table 6.3.

Figures 6.1 through 6.4 display the degree 1, 2, 3, and 4 members of the first four of four orthogonal families. The first member of each family is the constant function $x = 1$; we do not display it in these figures. Note that each Chebyshev polynomial has a maximum of 1 and a minimum of -1. Legendre polynomials are roughly similar to Chebyshev polynomials in appearance, but they do not bounce between 1 and -1. Both the Laguerre and Hermite polynomials are defined over infinite domains and diverge as $|x| \to \infty$. This divergence is not important in their respective inner prod-

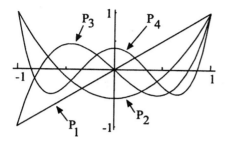

Figure 6.2
Legendre polynomials

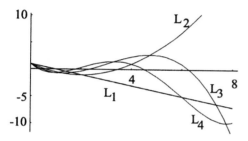

Figure 6.3
Laguerre polynomials

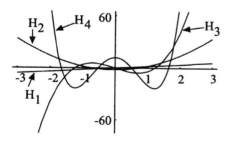

Figure 6.4
Hermite polynomials

ucts because the exponentially vanishing weighting functions will dominate any polynomial divergence.

Recursion Formulas

The formulas defining orthogonal families in table 6.3 are complex and too costly to compute; in fact some of the expressions in table 6.3 don't look like polynomials. Fortunately each family satisfies a simple recursive scheme. First note that $P_0(x) = T_0(x) = L_0(x) = H_0(x) = 1$, $P_1(x) = T_1(x) = x$, $L_1(x) = 1 - x$, and $H_1(x) = 2x$ are the first and second members of the Legendre, Chebyshev, Laguerre, and Hermite families. With these initial choices, these orthogonal polynomial families satisfy the following recursive schemes:

$$P_{n+1}(x) = \frac{2n+1}{n+1} \, x \, P_n(x) - \frac{n}{n+1} \, P_{n-1}(x), \qquad (6.3.1)$$

$$L_{n+1}(x) = \frac{1}{n+1} \, (2n+1-x) \, L_n(x) - \frac{n}{n+1} \, L_{n-1}(x), \qquad (6.3.2)$$

$$T_{n+1}(x) = 2x \, T_n(x) - T_{n-1}(x), \qquad (6.3.3)$$

$$H_{n+1}(x) = 2x \, H_n(x) - 2n \, H_{n-1}(x). \qquad (6.3.4)$$

Recursive formulas yield efficient ways of evaluating orthogonal polynomials which are faster than the direct definitions given in table 6.3. Algorithm 6.1 illustrates the procedure for evaluating a finite sum of Chebyshev polynomials, $\sum_{i=0}^n a_i T_i(x)$, at a single point, x.

Algorithm 6.1   Chebyshev Evaluation Algorithm

Objective: Evaluate $\sum_{i=0}^n a_i T_i(x)$.

Step 1. Evaluate the Chebyshev polynomials at x by recursion:

$$T_0(x) = 1; \qquad T_1(x) = x,$$

$$T_{i+1}(x) = 2x T_i(x) - T_{i-1}(x), \qquad i = 1, \ldots, n.$$

Step 2. Construct the sum at x, $\sum_{i=0}^n a_i T_i(x)$.

This recursive approach is a relatively efficient way to compute $\sum_{i=0}^n a_i T_i(x)$. For example, if one wanted the value of the first twelve Chebyshev polynomials at x, only twenty multiplications and ten subtractions are needed. If one instead evaluated each polynomial separately using the trigonometric formula in table 6.3, the operation count would be much worse at ten cosine and ten arc cosine evaluations. If one is to compute $\sum_{i=0}^{n} a_i T_i(x)$ for many values of x, it may seem better to compute the b_i coefficients such that $\sum_{i=0}^{n} a_i T_i(x) = \sum_{i=0}^{n} b_i x^i$. Computing $\sum_{i=0}^{n} a_i T_i(x)$ in the manner above is often more accurate because of round-off error problems, particularly if n is large. If that is not important, then using the $\sum_{i=0}^{n} b_i x^i$ representation is better because Horner's method can be used.

One can generally use the recursive schemes in (6.3.1)–(6.3.4) to accurately compute the polynomials in table 6.3. The recursive definitions for these orthogonal families are not special since recursion formulas exist for any orthogonal family, as demonstrated in theorem 6.3.1.

THEOREM 6.3.1 Let $\{\varphi_n(x)\}_{n=0}^{\infty}$ be an orthogonal family on $[a, b]$ relative to an inner product $\langle \cdot, \cdot \rangle$, $\varphi_0(x) = 1$, and $\varphi_1(x) = x - \langle x, 1 \rangle / \langle x, x \rangle$. Then $\{\varphi_n(x)\}_{n=0}^{\infty}$ satisfies the recursive scheme

$$\varphi_{n+1}(x) = (x - \delta_n)\varphi_n(x) - \gamma_n \varphi_{n-1}(x) \tag{6.3.5}$$

where δ_n and γ_n are defined by

$$\delta_n = \frac{\langle x\varphi_n, \varphi_n \rangle}{\langle \varphi_n, \varphi_n \rangle}, \qquad \gamma_n = \frac{\langle \varphi_n, \varphi_n \rangle}{\langle \varphi_{n-1}, \varphi_{n-1} \rangle}.$$

Proof See Young and Gregory (1988, pp. 319–21). ∎

If one were using a special purpose basis different from one of the standard families, then theorem 6.3.1 produces the corresponding recursion formulas.

6.4 Least Squares Orthogonal Polynomial Approximation

Before describing approximation algorithms, we first develop the critical concepts and theory. In the next two sections, we ask how well orthogonal polynomials can approximate functions. This material will give us a language with which we can discuss approximation ideas and also give us some idea of how well we can do.

Given $f(x)$ defined on $[a, b]$, one approximation concept is least squares approximation. That is, given $f(x)$, the *least squares polynomial approximation of f with respect to weighting function* $w(x)$ is the degree n polynomial that solves

$$\min_{\deg(p) \le n} \int_a^b (f(x) - p(x))^2 \, w(x) \, dx. \tag{6.4.1}$$

In this problem the weighting function $w(x)$ indicates how much we care about approximation errors as a function of x. For example, if we have no preference over where the approximation is good (in a squared-error sense), then we take $w(x) = 1$.

The connections between orthogonal polynomials and least squares approximation are immediately apparent in solving for the coefficients of $p(x)$ in the least squares approximation problem. If $\{\varphi_n\}_{n=0}^{\infty}$ is an orthogonal sequence with respect to a weighting function on $[a, b]$, $w(x)$, the solution to (6.4.1) can be expressed

$$p(x) = \sum_{k=0}^{n} \frac{\langle f, \varphi_k \rangle}{\langle \varphi_k, \varphi_k \rangle} \varphi_k(x). \tag{6.4.2}$$

Note the similarity between least squares approximation and regression. The formula for $p(x)$ is essentially the same as regressing the function $f(x)$ on $n + 1$ orthogonal regressors that are the $\varphi_k(x)$ functions; the coefficient of the kth regressor, $\varphi_k(x)$, equals the "covariance" between f and the kth regressor divided by the "variance" of the kth regressor. This is no accident, since regression is a least squares approximation. The difference in practice is that regression is limited to those observations of the regressors, the $\varphi_k(x)$, that real data give the analyst, whereas in L^p approximation (6.4.2) evaluates the regressors at all x.

Any polynomial can be easily expressed as a linear sum of orthogonal polynomials. Specifically, if $\{\varphi_n(x)\}_{n=0}^{\infty}$ is an orthogonal collection of polynomials with $\deg(\varphi_n) = n$, then for any polynomial $f(x)$ of degree n,

$$f(x) = \sum_{k=0}^{n} \frac{\langle f, \varphi_k \rangle}{\langle \varphi_k, \varphi_k \rangle} \varphi_k(x). \tag{6.4.3}$$

Fourier Approximation

One common form of least squares approximation is Fourier approximation. Fourier approximation theorems tell us that if f is continuous on $[-\pi, \pi]$ and $f(-\pi) = f(\pi)$, then

$$f(\theta) = \frac{1}{2}a_0 + \sum_{n=1}^{\infty} a_n \cos(n\theta) + \sum_{n=1}^{\infty} b_n \sin(n\theta) \tag{6.4.4}$$

where the *Fourier coefficients* are defined by

$$a_n = \frac{1}{\pi} \int_{-\pi}^{\pi} f(\theta) \cos(n\theta)\, d\theta, \quad b_n = \frac{1}{\pi} \int_{-\pi}^{\pi} f(\theta) \sin(n\theta)\, d\theta,$$

and convergence in (6.4.4) is uniform. Since the sine and cosine functions satisfy the necessary orthogonality conditions on $[-\pi, \pi]$, trigonometric polynomials fit our orthogonal function framework. A *trigonometric polynomial* is any function of the form in (6.4.4).

Fourier approximation is particularly important when we are approximating a *periodic function*, that is, a function $f: R \rightarrow R$ such that for some ω, $f(x) = f(x + \omega)$ for all x, which is also smooth. Nonperiodic functions may also be approximated by their Fourier series, (6.4.4). However, convergence is not uniform, and many terms are needed for good fits.

Chebyshev Least Squares Approximation

Chebyshev polynomials are a special class of polynomials with many useful strong properties. One hint of their special position is given by the formula $T_n(x) = \cos(n \cos^{-1} x)$. Note that $T_n(\cos \theta) = \cos n\theta$ is an orthogonal sequence on $[0, 2\pi]$ with respect to $w(x) = 1$. This is closely related to Fourier analysis, the dominant way to approximate smooth periodic functions. Given this connection, it is not surprising that Chebyshev approximations are good for smooth nonperiodic functions. The next theorem states this precisely.

THEOREM 6.4.1   Assume $f \in C^k [-1, 1]$. Let

$$c_j \equiv \frac{2}{\pi} \int_{-1}^{1} \frac{f(x) \, T_j(x)}{\sqrt{1 - x^2}} \, dx, \tag{6.4.5}$$

$$C_n(x) \equiv \frac{1}{2} c_0 + \sum_{j=1}^{n} c_j T_j(x). \tag{6.4.6}$$

Then there is a $B < \infty$ such that for all $n \geq 2$,

$$\|f - C_n\|_\infty \leq \frac{B \ln n}{n^k}. \tag{6.4.7}$$

Hence $C_n \rightarrow f$ uniformly as $n \rightarrow \infty$. We next present a useful theorem on Chebyshev coefficients.

THEOREM 6.4.2   If $f \in C^k [-1, 1]$ has a Chebyshev representation

$$f(x) = \frac{1}{2} c_0 + \sum_{j=1}^{\infty} c_j T_j(x), \tag{6.4.8}$$

then there is a constant c such that

$$|c_j| \le \frac{c}{j^k}, \qquad j \ge 1. \tag{6.4.9}$$

Hence the Chebyshev coefficients eventually drop off rapidly for smooth functions.

In practice, we never have the infinite series (6.4.8), and we never have a perfect way to calculate f. In practice, we must approximate f with a finite sum, $(1/2)c_0 + \sum_{j=1}^{n} c_j T_j(x)$ for some n. The growth condition on the coefficients (6.4.9) can be useful in choosing n. If the c_k coefficients, $k < n$, are rapidly falling and c_n is small, then we can be more confident that the ignored coefficients make a trivial contribution, and that the $(n + 1)$-term finite series is an acceptable approximation to f. If c_n is not much less than c_{n-1}, then we should extend the series beyond the T_n term. This is done even if c_n is small. The reason is that if the coefficients are not trailing off rapidly, the sequence of coefficients that are ignored, c_k, $k > n$, may add up to be important. We often will not know the character of the f that we are approximating; therefore, if the Chebyshev coefficients are not dropping off rapidly, that may indicate that f is not as smooth as required by theorem 6.4.2. In that case we should move to a different approximation approach, such as splines.

At this point, we should note that computing Chebyshev least squares coefficients is difficult because the integral in (6.4.5) generally does not have an analytic solution. The numerical solution of integrals is taken up in the next chapter.

Approximations over General Intervals

We usually need to find polynomial approximations over intervals other than $[-1, 1]$. Suppose that we have a function, $f(y)$, $f: [a, b] \to R$ and want to compute an orthogonal polynomial approximation over $[a, b]$ that corresponds to the orthogonal family over $x \in [-1, 1]$ with weighting function $w(x)$. To do this, we define the transformation $X(y) = -1 + 2(y-a)/(b-a) = (2y - a - b)/(b - a)$ and the inverse transform $Y(x) = ((x + 1)(b - a))/2 + a$. We define the function $g(x) = f(Y(x))$. If $g(x) = \sum_{i=0}^{\infty} a_i \varphi_i(x)$ where the φ_i are orthogonal over $[-1, 1]$ with respect to $w(x)$, then

$$f(y) = \sum_{i=0}^{\infty} a_i \varphi_i(X(y)) \tag{6.4.10}$$

is an orthogonal representation with respect to the weight $w(X(y))$ over $[a, b]$ since $\int_a^b \varphi_i(X(y))\varphi_j(X(y))w(X(y)) \, dy = 0$ for $i \ne j$. The a_i coefficients in (6.4.10) are therefore defined by

$$a_i = \frac{\langle g(x), \varphi_i(x) \rangle}{\langle \varphi_i(x), \varphi_i(x) \rangle} = \frac{\int_{-1}^{1} f(Y(x)) \varphi_i(x) w(x) \, dx}{\int_{-1}^{1} \varphi_i(x)^2 w(x) \, dx}$$

$$= \frac{\int_a^b f(y) \varphi_i(X(y)) w(X(y)) \, dy}{\int_a^b \varphi_i(X(y))^2 w(X(y)) \, dy}.$$
(6.4.11)

In table 6.3 we include a line for the general case of Chebyshev polynomials on the general interval $[a, b]$. We could do the same for Legendre polynomials. Similar linear transformations of Laguerre and Hermite polynomials allow us to create orthogonal polynomial families with weighting function $e^{-(ax+b)}$ on the interval $[d, \infty)$ and families with weighting function $e^{-(ax^2+bx+c)}$ on $(-\infty, \infty)$.

6.5 Uniform Approximation

The previous sections showed how to approximate functions in L^2 norms. Unfortunately, convergence in L^2 puts no restriction on the approximations at any individual point. We often instead want to approximate f *uniformly* well with polynomials; that is, we want to find a sequence, $p_n(x)$, such that

$$\lim_{n \to \infty} \max_{x \in [a,b]} |f(x) - p_n(x)| = 0.$$
(6.5.1)

Uniform approximations are good approximations of f at each x, whereas least squares approximations attempt to have small total error. Uniform approximation is more demanding than least squares approximation in that it attempts to be a good pointwise approximation. The Weierstrass theorem tells us that there exists such a sequence of approximations for continuous functions.

THEOREM 6.5.1 (Weierstrass theorem)   If $f \in C[a, b]$, then for all $\varepsilon > 0$, there exists a polynomial $p(x)$ such that

$$\forall x \in [a, b], |f(x) - p(x)| \le \varepsilon.$$
(6.5.2)

Furthermore, if $f \in C^k[a, b]$ then there exists a sequence of polynomials, p_n, where the degree of p_n is n, such that

$$\lim_{n \to \infty} \max_{x \in [a,b]} |f^{(l)}(x) - p_n^{(l)}(x)| = 0$$
(6.5.3)

for $l \le k$.

One proof (see Powell 1981, ch. 6) constructs the *Bernstein polynomials* on $[0, 1]$,

$$p_n(x) \equiv \sum_{k=0}^{n} \binom{n}{k} f\left(\frac{k}{n}\right) x^k (1 - x)^{n-k} \tag{6.5.4}$$

and, by noting the properties of the binomial distribution and the law of large numbers, shows that $\lim_{n \to \infty} p_n(x) = f(x)$ for all $x \in [0, 1]$. Furthermore the Bernstein polynomials also satisfy the stronger convergence conditions for the derivatives of f expressed in (6.5.3).

The Weierstrass theorem is conceptually valuable but not important from a practical point of view. For example, Bernstein polynomial approximations converge slowly. This is not surprising, since the derivatives of the Bernstein polynomial approximations also converge uniformly to the derivatives of f. We next turn to more efficient methods of generating uniformly convergent approximations of f.

Minimax Approximation

In *minimax approximation* we attempt to find that polynomial that best approximates a function uniformly. More precisely, we define $\rho_n(f)$ to be the infimum of the L^∞ errors of all degree n polynomial approximations of f:

$$\rho_n(f) \equiv \inf_{\deg(q) \le n} \|f - q\|_\infty. \tag{6.5.5}$$

Theorem 6.5.2 tells us that there is a polynomial that achieves this lower bound.

THEOREM 6.5.2 (Equioscillation theorem)   If $f \in C[a, b]$, then there is a unique polynomial of degree n, $q_n^*(x)$, such that $\|f - q_n^*\|_\infty = \rho_n(f)$. The polynomial q_n^* is also the unique polynomial for which there are at least $n + 2$ points $a \le x_0 < x_1 < \cdots < x_{n+1} \le b$ such that for $m = 1$ or $m = -1$,

$$f(x_j) - q_n^*(x_j) = m(-1)^j \rho_n(f), \qquad j = 0, \ldots, n + 1. \tag{6.5.6}$$

The property (6.5.6) is called the *equioscillation property*. Geometrically it says that the maximum error of a cubic approximation, for example, should be achieved at least five times and that the sign of the error should alternate between these points. The equioscillation principle is illustrated in figure 6.5 where we plot the error of the minimax cubic polynomial approximation of $(x + 0.1)^{0.1}$ on $[0, 1]$. This picture is important to remember because it shows us the desired shape of the error when we want L^∞ approximation. If we plot the error and have a very different shape, we know that it is theoretically possible to do better. Knowing what the best possible error looks like helps us to know when to stop looking for something better.

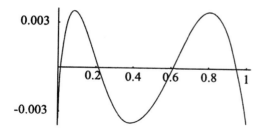

Figure 6.5
Equioscillation example

When using an L^∞ approximation of a function f, one should always keep in mind that it is only the values of f that are being approximated, not any of its derivatives. In fact the derivatives may be poorly approximated. This is illustrated in figure 6.5 where the slope of the approximation error, which equals the difference between the slopes of f and its approximation and is clearly greater and more volatile than the size of the approximation error.

The quality of the $q_n^*(x)$ approximation is addressed by Jackson's theorem.

THEOREM 6.5.3 (Jackson's theorem)   For all k, if $f \in C^k[a, b]$, then for $n \geq k$,

$$\rho_n(f) \leq \frac{(n-k)!}{n!} \left(\frac{\pi}{2}\right)^k \left(\frac{b-a}{2}\right)^k \|f^{(k)}\|_\infty. \tag{6.5.7}$$

Proof   This is implied in Powell (1981, p. 197, eq. 16.50). ∎

Jackson's theorem says two important things. First, the quality of $q_n^*(x)$ improves polynomially as we increase n; that is, use higher degree polynomials. Second, the polynomial rate of convergence is faster for smoother functions. Unfortunately, computing $q_n^*(x)$ can be difficult. Instead of developing these algorithms, we discuss a least squares approximation procedure that also does very well in creating uniform approximations.

Near-Minimax Approximation

Because minimax approximation is difficult, we commonly use Chebyshev least squares approximation to compute a good substitute. The special property of Chebyshev least squares approximation is that it is nearly the same as the minimax polynomial approximation.

THEOREM 6.5.4   If $C_n(x)$ is the nth degree Chebyshev least squares approximation to $f \in C^1[-1, 1]$, then

$$\rho_n(f) \le \|f - C_n\|_\infty \le \left(4 + \frac{4}{\pi^2} \ln n\right) \rho_n(f) \tag{6.5.8}$$

Proof   See Rivlin (1990, p. 167, thm. 3.3).   ∎

By theorem 6.5.4, we conclude that least squares Chebyshev approximations are not much worse than the best polynomial approximation in the L^∞ norm. This is convenient, since constructing L^2 approximations involves only a few linear operations on the data. The fact that this can be done with Chebyshev polynomials is due to the Chebyshev weighting function, $w(x) = (1 - x^2)^{-1/2}$.

Other methods will also yield a good sequence of approximations but will tend to have nonuniform errors. For example, Legendre approximation implicitly uses a constant weighting function, and tends to have larger errors at the end points. The reasons are intuitive. With a constant loss function, making an approximation good at $x = 0$ also makes it good at nearby points to the right and left, whereas making an approximation good at $x = 1$ makes it good only at points to its left. Minimizing the sum of squared errors will therefore concentrate at making the approximation good for central values by sacrificing accuracy at the end points. The Chebyshev weighting function counters this tendency by penalizing errors at the end points more than it penalizes errors in the center.

The $\ln n$ factor is a troublesome term in (6.5.8). Fortunately $\rho_n(f)$ goes to zero fast by Jackson's theorem, yielding an important convergence theorem.

THEOREM 6.5.5   For all k, for all $f \in C^k[a, b]$,

$$\|f - C_n\|_\infty \le \left(4 + \frac{4}{\pi^2} \ln n\right) \frac{(n - k)!}{n!} \left(\frac{\pi}{2}\right)^k \left(\frac{b - a}{2}\right)^k \|f^{(k)}\|_\infty, \tag{6.5.9}$$

and hence $\lim_{n \to \infty} \|f - C_n\|_\infty = 0$ uniformly.

The proof of theorem 6.5.5 follows from combining Jackson's theorem with the estimate of $\rho_n(f)$ above.

We illustrate these properties with some simple examples. Table 6.4 contains the Chebyshev coefficients of approximations to e^{x+1}, $(x + 1)^{1/4}$, $\max[0, x^3]$, and $\min[\max[-1, 4(x - 0.2)], 1]$ on $[-1, 1]$. Also next to the nth coefficient is the L^∞ error of the degree n Chebyshev approximation. Note that the patterns are consistent with the theory. For e^{x+1} the coefficients drop very rapidly, and low-order approximations

Table 6.4
Chebyshev coefficients

$f(x)$:	e^{x+1}	$(x+1)^{1/4}$	$\max[0, x^3]$	$\min[\max[-1, 4(x-0.2)], 1]$
c_0	6.88	1.81	0.424	-0.259
c_1	3.07	0.363	0.375	1.23
c_2	0.738	-0.121	0.255	0.241
c_3	0.121	0.065	0.125	-0.314
c_4	$1.49(-2)$	-0.042	0.036	-0.192
c_5	$1.48(-3)$	0.030	0	0.100
c_6	$1.22(-4)$	-0.023	-0.004	0.129
c_7	$8.69(-6)$	0.018	0	-0.015
c_8	$5.42(-7)$	-0.015	0.001	-0.068
c_9	$3.00(-8)$	0.012	0	-0.010
c_{10}	$1.50(-9)$	0.011	$-4.2(-4)$	0.025

do quite well. On the other hand, convergence for $\max[0, x^3]$ is much slower. The function $(x+1)^{1/4}$ is an intermediate case. It is $C^\infty(0, 1]$, but all derivatives at $x = -1$ are infinite, making our error estimates useless.

Chebyshev Economization

Suppose that $q(x)$ is an mth degree polynomial. Then q can be written

$$q(x) = \sum_{k=0}^{m} a_k T_k(x).$$

Since it is a polynomial, computing the Chebyshev least squares approximation is easy. In fact, once we have the Chebyshev polynomial expansion of q, the nth degree least squares approximation for $n < m$ can be written

$$p_n(x) = \sum_{k=0}^{n} a_k T_k(x).$$

This is called the nth degree *Chebyshev economization* of q. Furthermore $p_n(x)$ is the minmax degree n polynomial approximation of q. In this way we can approximate a high-degree polynomial very well with a lower-degree polynomial.

While these results are of interest, they do not yet yield a reliable and simple approximation method since computing the Chebyshev least squares approximation is costly, involving the evaluation of several integrals. Since almost all approximations are ultimately based on only a finite number of evaluations of $f(x)$, we next consider interpolation as an approximation scheme. The past two sections have described basic approximation theory. With these ideas in mind, we will now move to actual methods constructing approximations.

6.6 Interpolation

Interpolation is any method that takes a finite set of conditions and constructs a "nice" function that satisfies these conditions. In this section we will interpolate with polynomials, our collection of "nice functions," but it will be clear that many of the ideas will also work with other families of "nice" functions.

Lagrange Interpolation

The most demanding but feasible version of one-dimensional polynomial interpolation is to take a collection of n points in R^2, $D = \{(x_i, y_i)|i = 1, \ldots, n\}$, where the x_i are distinct, and find a degree $n - 1$ polynomial, $p(x)$, such that $y_i = p(x_i)$, $i = 1, \ldots, n$. The collection D is called the *Lagrange data*, and this is called the *Lagrange interpolation* problem.

We can explicitly construct the interpolating polynomial. Define

$$l_i(x) = \prod_{j \neq i} \frac{x - x_j}{x_i - x_j}. \tag{6.6.1}$$

Note that $l_i(x)$ is unity at $x = x_i$ and zero at $x = x_j$ for $j \neq i$. This property implies that the *Lagrange interpolation polynomial*

$$p(x) = \sum_{i=1}^{n} y_i l_i(x) \tag{6.6.2}$$

interpolates the data, that is, $y_i = p(x_i)$, $i = 1, \ldots, n$.

The Lagrange interpolation formula is not practical in general. The reason for computing the interpolant p is to evaluate p at $x \neq x_i$, but to evaluate (6.6.2) at an arbitrary x would require a large number of operations. The Lagrange formula uses (roughly) $3n$ additions, $2n$ divisions, and $2n$ multiplications even when done most efficiently. Recall that Horner's method shows that evaluating a degree $n - 1$ polynomial needs only $n - 2$ additions and $n - 1$ multiplications. To make the Lagrange formula useful, we need to compute the coefficients of the interpolating polynomial, that is, to find the a_i such that $p(x) = \sum_{i=0}^{n-1} a_i x^i$. This is easily accomplished using symbolic math software.

A theoretically useful way to "compute" the coefficients of the interpolating polynomial is to solve the linear system

$$a_0 + a_1 x_i + a_2 x_i^2 + \cdots + a_{n-1} x_i^{n-1} = y_i, \qquad i = 1, \ldots, n. \tag{6.6.3}$$

If we define the *Vandermonde matrix* for x_i, $i = 1, \ldots, n$, to be

$$V = \begin{pmatrix} 1 & x_1 & x_1^2 & \cdots & x_1^{n-1} \\ 1 & x_2 & x_2^2 & \cdots & x_2^{n-1} \\ \vdots & \vdots & \vdots & \ddots & \vdots \\ 1 & x_n & x_n^2 & \cdots & x_n^{n-1} \end{pmatrix}, \tag{6.6.4}$$

then the coefficient vector $a = (a_0, a_1, \ldots, a_{n-1})^\top$ of $p(x)$ solves $Va = y$.

THEOREM 6.6.1   If the points $x_1, \ldots, x_n$ are distinct, then there is a unique solution to the Lagrange interpolation problem.

Proof   The Lagrange formula implies existence. To show uniqueness, suppose that $\hat{p}(x)$ is another polynomial of degree at most $n - 1$ that interpolates the n data points. Then $p(x) - \hat{p}(x)$ is a polynomial of at most degree $n - 1$ and is zero at the n interpolation nodes. Since the only degree $n - 1$ polynomial with n distinct zeros is the zero polynomial, $p(x) - \hat{p}(x) = 0$ and $p(x) = \hat{p}(x)$. Note that this shows V is nonsingular iff the x_i are distinct. ∎

Using (6.6.3) to directly compute the coefficients of the interpolating polynomial is not practical for the reason that the condition number of V is generally large. In any case, solving the linear equation $Va = y$ has a time cost of $O(n^3)$. The simplest way to compute the a_i coefficients is to compute the coefficients of the Lagrange polynomial in (6.6.2), and then combine the coefficients of like powers of x.

Hermite Interpolation

We may want to find a polynomial p that fits slope as well as level requirements. Suppose that we have data

$$p(x_i) = y_i, \ p'(x_i) = y_i', \qquad i = 1, \ldots, n, \tag{6.6.5}$$

where the x_i are distinct. Since we have $2n$ conditions, we are looking for a degree $2n - 1$ polynomial that satisfies these conditions; this is the *Hermite interpolation problem*.

We construct the unique solution, $p(x)$. First define the functions

$$\tilde{h}_i(x) = (x - x_i)\, l_i(x)^2,$$

$$h_i(x) = (1 - 2l_i'(x_i)(x - x_i))\, l_i(x)^2. \tag{6.6.6}$$

The critical properties of h_i and $\tilde{h}_i$ are

$$h_i'(x_j) = \tilde{h}_i(x_j) = 0, \qquad 1 \le i, j \le n,$$

$$h_i(x_j) = \tilde{h}_i'(x_j) = \begin{cases} 0, & i \ne j, \\ 1, & i = j. \end{cases} \tag{6.6.7}$$

Hence h_i is a function that is zero at all interpolation nodes except x_i, where it is unity, and its derivative is zero at all x_j, $j = 1, \ldots, n$; the reverse is true for $\tilde{h}_i(x)$. The properties (6.6.7) allow us to simply construct the *Hermite interpolating polynomial* as a weighted sum of the h_i and $\tilde{h}_i$ functions with the weights being the prescribed values for $p(x)$ and $p'(x)$ at the interpolation nodes:

$$p(x) = \sum_{i=1}^{n} y_i\, h_i(x) + \sum_{i=1}^{n} y_i'\, \tilde{h}_i(x) \tag{6.6.8}$$

As with Lagrange interpolation, the formulas generated by Hermite interpolation are inefficient. If one were to use these formulas, one would simplify (6.6.8) by combining like powers.

Cardinal Function Interpolation

Lagrange and Hermite interpolation are special cases of a general approach to interpolation. Suppose that we have a set of interpolation nodes, x_i, and linearly independent functions $\phi_i(x)$, $i = 1, \ldots, n$, that satisfy

$$\phi_i(x_j) = \delta_i^j \equiv \begin{cases} 1 & \text{if } i = j, \\ 0 & \text{if } i \ne j. \end{cases} \tag{6.6.9}$$

Such a collection is called a *cardinal function basis*. With such a basis, we can directly write an interpolating function with Lagrange data as

$$p(x) = \sum_i y_i \phi_i(x). \tag{6.6.10}$$

In the case of Lagrange interpolation, the functions $\phi_i(x) = \prod_{j \ne i} (x - x_j)/(x_i - x_j)$

comprise the cardinal basis. The advantages of cardinal bases is that the data are the coefficients. The disadvantages are that the basis functions may be costly to compute and that any evaluation of $p(x)$ requires the evaluation of each of the $\phi_i(x)$.

6.7 Approximation through Interpolation and Regression

We often have some qualitative information about a function, such as smoothness properties, and can evaluate the function at many points, but at a nontrivial cost per point. In such a case, computing the least squares approximation (6.4.2) is not possible because the critical integrals cannot be evaluated exactly. In this section we turn to methods that use a finite number of points to compute an approximation to $f(x)$.

We could use Lagrange interpolation. If the result is to be a good approximation of f, we also want some assurance that the interpolating function agrees with the function more generally. This is a much more difficult problem because it requires some information about the function globally.

Unfortunately, interpolation does not always work even on well-behaved, simple functions. Examine figure 6.6. The solid line is a graph of the function $f(x) = (1 + x^2)^{-1}$ over the interval $[-5, 5]$, whereas the dotted line is the tenth-degree polynomial Lagrange interpolation of f at the 11 uniformly spaced nodes, including the end points. Note that the interpolating polynomial does a very poor job of approximating f. This is not an aberration; in fact the degree $n - 1$ interpolation at n uniformly spaced points, $p_n(x)$, gets *worse* as we use more points, since, for $|x| > 3.64$, $\lim \sup_{n \to \infty} |f(x) - p_n(x)| = \infty$. Therefore, for a seemingly well-behaved C^∞ function, interpolation at the uniformly spaced nodes does not improve as we use more

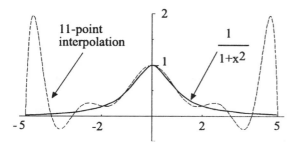

Figure 6.6
Nonconvergence of interpolation example

points.[2] This example shows that this interpolation scheme may not work; we will next ask whether there are any dependable interpolation schemes.

Interpolation Error

The last example may discourage one from approximating a function through interpolation. While it does indicate that caution is necessary, there are some procedures that reduce the likelihood of perverse behavior by interpolants. Recall that we defined $l_i(x) = \prod_{j \neq i}(x - x_j)/(x_i - x_j)$, and that the Lagrange polynomial interpolating f at points x_i is $p_n(x) = \sum_{i=1}^{n} f(x_i) l_i(x)$. Define

$$\Psi(x; x_1, \ldots, x_n) = \prod_{k=1}^{n}(x - x_k).$$

The following theorem uses smoothness conditions to compute a bound on the error of the Lagrange interpolation polynomial:

THEOREM 6.7.1   Assume that $a = x_1 < \cdots < x_n = b$. Then for all $x \in [a, b]$ there is some $\xi \in [a, b]$ such that

$$f(x) - \sum_{j=1}^{n} f(x_j) l_j(x) = \Psi(x; x_1, \ldots, x_n) \frac{f^{(n)}(\xi)}{n!}.$$

Proof   See Atkinson (1989, p. 134, thm. 3.2).   ∎

Theorem 6.7.1 implies that if $p_n(x) \equiv \sum_{j=1}^{n} f(x_j) l_j(x)$, then

$$\sup_{x \in [a,b]} |f(x) - p_n(x)| \leq \frac{\|f^{(n)}\|_\infty}{n!} \sup_{x \in [a,b]} \Psi(x; x_1, \ldots, x_n) \tag{6.7.1}$$

is an upper bound on the error of the interpolant, $p_n(x)$, through $x_1, \ldots, x_n$. We want $p_n(x)$ to be an increasingly good approximation for $f(x)$ as $n \to \infty$. Suppose that we interpolate at uniformly distributed points. The example in figure 6.6 showed that convergence may fail with a uniform grid, implying that (6.7.1) does not shrink to zero. Using Hermite interpolation does not improve matters. If $p(x)$ is a Hermite interpolant given by (6.6.8), the Hermite interpolation error is bounded above by

$$|f(x) - p(x)| \leq (\Psi(x; x_1, \ldots, x_n))^2 \frac{|f^{(2n)}(\xi)|}{(2n)!} \tag{6.7.2}$$

---

2. This failure may not be so surprising if we take into account some elementary complex analysis: $(1 + x^2)^{-1}$ has poles at $\pm i$, implying that it has no power series representation on $[-5, 5]$.

for some ξ between x and x_1. Since Ψ again is the critical piece, this error bound will not shrink to zero if we use uniform grids, even for $f \in C^\infty$.

Chebyshev Minimax Property

The challenge of approximation through interpolation is to choose the interpolation nodes, x_i, so as to be assured of a small interpolation error. The key result is the minimax property of Chebyshev polynomials.

THEOREM 6.7.2   For $n > 0$, consider

$$s_n = \inf_p \left[\max_{-1 \le x \le 1} |x^n + p(x)| \right]$$

s.t. $\deg(p) \le n - 1$.

Then $s_n = 2^{1-n}$ and is attained when $x^n + p(x) = (1/2)^{n-1} T_n(x)$.

Proof   See Powell (1981, p. 78, thm. 7.3).   ∎

Hence $(1/2)^{n-1} T_n(x)$ is the polynomial with a leading term equal to x^n which has the smallest maximum magnitude.

Chebyshev Interpolation

We will next combine the interpolation error formula with the Chebyshev minimax property to determine a good collection of interpolation nodes. Equation (6.7.1) demonstrates that this error is no more than

$$\left(\max_{x \in [a,b]} \Psi(x; x_1, \ldots, x_n) \right) \| f^{(n)} \|_\infty (n!)^{-1}.$$

Note the three components. The term $n!$ is a function of only n, and $\| f^{(n)} \|_\infty$ depends only on f. Both of these are independent of the interpolation points. Our choice of $\{x_i\}_{i=1}^n$ affects only the maximum value of $\Psi(x)$, which in turn does not depend on f. So if we want to choose interpolation points so as to minimize their contribution to (6.7.1), the problem is

$$\min_{x_1, \ldots, x_n} \max_{x \in [a,b]} \Pi_{k=1}^n (x - x_k). \tag{6.7.3}$$

Note that the zeroes of $\Psi(x; x_1, \ldots, x_n)$ are the x_k and that the leading term is x^n. Hence the minimax property of Chebyshev polynomials tells us that the choice of $\Psi(x)$ must be $T_n(x)/2^{n-1}$. Furthermore we conclude that the x_k, the zeros of

$\Psi(x; x_1, \ldots, x_n)$, must be the zeros of T_n. Hence

$$x_k = \cos\left(\frac{2k-1}{2n}\pi\right), \qquad k = 1, \ldots, n, \tag{6.7.4}$$

are the interpolation nodes that minimize the error bound computed above.

The next question is whether interpolation at the zeros of Chebyshev polynomials leads to asymptotically valid approximations of f.

THEOREM 6.7.3   Suppose that function $f: [-1, 1] \to R$ is C^k for some $k \geq 1$, and let I_n be the degree n polynomial interpolation of f based at the zeros of $T_n(x)$. Then

$$\|f - I_n\|_\infty \leq \left(\frac{2}{\pi}\log(n+1) + 1\right)\frac{(n-k)!}{n!}\left(\frac{\pi}{2}\right)^k\left(\frac{b-a}{2}\right)^k\|f^{(k)}\|_\infty \tag{6.7.5}$$

Proof   See Rivlin (1990, p. 14).

Theorem 6.7.3 shows that Chebyshev interpolation will work for C^1 smooth functions. This result is not quite as good as the Fourier theory. For periodic functions Fourier series are used, and one gets pointwise convergence almost everywhere for any piecewise C^0 function.

It may appear unnatural not to include the end points in an interpolation scheme for $[-1, 1]$. In fact for x near -1 and 1 the Chebyshev approximation is really an extrapolation of the data, not an interpolation. For such points the Chebyshev interpolant often does poorly. If one wants to include -1 and 1 as interpolating nodes, then let

$$x_i = \sec\left(\frac{\pi}{2n}\right)\cos\left(\frac{2i-1}{2}\frac{\pi}{n}\right), \qquad i = 1, \ldots, n, \tag{6.7.6}$$

be the set of n points used. This is called the *expanded Chebyshev array* and is practically as good as the Chebyshev array (see Rivlin 1990, p. 23).

Approximation and Regression

When the number of data points substantially exceeds the number of unknown coefficients in a representation, then least squares methods can be used to find an approximation. These are essentially regression methods. In our approximation problems, regression lies between the pure least squares approximation method, as solved in (6.4.2), and interpolation. Least squares approximation, (6.4.2), implicitly uses all the value of $f(x)$ at all x, whereas interpolation methods use only n points to find n parameters. In regression methods we use m points to find $n < m$ parameters in some approximation. We will generally underfit the data, resulting in some approximation error. However, using more points than free parameters makes the approximation method better behaved. Furthermore the convergence results in theorem 6.7.3 hold also for regression.

We can adapt Chebyshev least squares approximation and Chebyshev interpolation ideas to come up with a general *Chebyshev regression* algorithm. We compute the degree $m - 1$ interpolation formula but use only the degree n truncation, essentially dropping the degree $n + 1$ through $m - 1$ terms. The omitted terms are high-degree polynomials that may produce undesirable oscillations; this is an application of Chebyshev economization. The result is a smoother function that approximates the data. The Algorithm 6.2 summarizes the procedure for constructing a degree n polynomial that approximately computes the function f for $x \in [a, b]$ using $m > n$ points. If $m = n + 1$, the algorithm reduces to Chebyshev interpolation.

Algorithm 6.2 Chebyshev Regression Algorithm

Objective: Choose m nodes and use them to construct a degree $n < m$ polynomial approximation of $f(x)$ on $[a, b]$.

Step 1. Compute the $m \geq n + 1$ Chebyshev interpolation nodes on $[-1, 1]$:

$$z_k = -\cos\left(\frac{2k - 1}{2m} \pi\right), \qquad k = 1, \ldots, m.$$

Step 2. Adjust the nodes to the $[a, b]$ interval:

$$x_k = (z_k + 1)\left(\frac{b - a}{2}\right) + a, \qquad k = 1, \ldots, m.$$

Step 3. Evaluate f at the approximation nodes:

$$y_k = f(x_k), \qquad k = 1, \ldots, m.$$

Step 4. Compute Chebyshev coefficients, $a_i, i = 0, \ldots, n$:

$$a_i = \frac{\sum_{k=1}^{m} y_k T_i(z_k)}{\sum_{k=1}^{m} T_i(z_k)^2}$$

to arrive at the approximation for $f(x), x \in [a, b]$:

$$\hat{f}(x) = \sum_{i=0}^{n} a_i T_i\left(2\frac{x - a}{b - a} - 1\right).$$

6.8   Piecewise Polynomial Interpolation

Lagrange interpolation computes a C^∞ function to interpolate the given data. An alternative is to construct a function that is only piecewise smooth. This section presents two simple methods.

Piecewise Linear Interpolation

The simplest way to interpolate is the kindergarten procedure of "connecting the dots," that is, draw straight lines between successive data points of the Lagrange data. If we have Lagrange data (x_i, y_i), then the *piecewise linear interpolant* $\hat{f}(x)$ is given by the formula

$$\hat{f}(x) = y_i + \frac{x - x_i}{x_{i+1} - x_i} (y_{i+1} - y_i), \qquad x \in [x_i, x_{i+1}]. \tag{6.8.1}$$

Piecewise linear interpolants are spanned by B-splines, which we discuss below.

Hermite Interpolation Polynomials

Suppose that we want to interpolate both level and slope information at $x_1, \ldots, x_n$, but we only use piecewise cubic polynomials. *Piecewise Hermite polynomial interpolation* will do this. First, for an arbitrary interval $[a, b]$, define the four cubic polynomials

$$\varphi_1(x) = 1 - 3t^2 + 2t^3, \quad \varphi_2(x) = (b - a)t(t - 1)^2,$$

$$\varphi_3(x) = t^2(3 - 2t), \quad \varphi_4(x) = (b - a)t^2(t - 1), \tag{6.8.2}$$

where $t \equiv (x - a)/(b - a)$. The polynomial

$$p(x) = y_1\varphi_1(x) + y_2\varphi_3(x) + y_1'\varphi_2(x) + y_2'\varphi_4(x) \tag{6.8.3}$$

interpolates the data

$$y_1 = p(a), \quad y_2 = p(b), \quad y_1' = p'(a), \quad y_2' = p'(b).$$

Next, suppose that we have this level and slope information at several points. Within each interval we construct the polynomial in (6.8.3). The collection of interval-specific interpolations constitute our piecewise polynomial approximation. The resulting function is a cubic polynomial almost everywhere and is C^1 everywhere.

6.9 Splines

A particularly powerful and widely used piecewise polynomial interpolation scheme uses *splines*. A spline is any smooth function that is piecewise polynomial but also smooth where the polynomial pieces connect. Formally a function $s(x)$ on $[a, b]$ is a *spline of order n* if s is C^{n-2} on $[a, b]$, and there is a grid of points (called nodes) $a = x_0 < x_1 < \cdots < x_m = b$ such that $s(x)$ is a polynomial of degree $n - 1$ on each subinterval $[x_i, x_{i+1}]$, $i = 0, \ldots, m - 1$. Note that an order 2 spline is just the common piecewise linear interpolant in equation (6.8.1).

Cubic Splines

Since the *cubic spline* (a spline of order 4) is the most popular, we will describe in detail one way to construct a cubic spline interpolant; the procedure can be applied analogously to compute a spline of any order. Suppose that the Lagrange data set is $\{(x_i, y_i) | i = 0, \ldots, n\}$. The x_i will be the nodes of the spline, and we want to construct a spline, $s(x)$, such that $s(x_i) = y_i, i = 0, \ldots, n$. On each interval $[x_{i-1}, x_i]$, $s(x)$ will be a cubic $a_i + b_i x + c_i x^2 + d_i x^3$. A cubic spline is represented in a computer as a list of the a_i, b_i, c_i, and d_i coefficients along with a list of the x_i nodes. We therefore have n intervals, $n + 1$ data points, and $4n$ unknown coefficients, $a_i, b_i, c_i, d_i, i = 1, \ldots, n$.

The interpolating conditions plus continuity at the interior nodes implies $2n$ conditions on the coefficients:

$$y_i = a_i + b_i x_i + c_i x_i^2 + d_i x_i^3, \qquad i = 1, \ldots, n, \tag{6.9.1}$$

$$y_i = a_{i+1} + b_{i+1} x_i + c_{i+1} x_i^2 + d_{i+1} x_i^3, \qquad i = 0, \ldots, n - 1. \tag{6.9.2}$$

Since the approximation is to be C^2 at the interior nodes, the first and second derivatives must agree at the nodes, implying $2n - 2$ more conditions:

$$b_i + 2c_i x_i + 3d_i x_i^2 = b_{i+1} + 2c_{i+1} x_i + 3d_{i+1} x_i^2, \qquad i = 1, \ldots, n - 1, \tag{6.9.3}$$

$$2c_i + 6d_i x_i = 2c_{i+1} + 6d_{i+1} x_i, \qquad i = 1, 2, \ldots, n - 1. \tag{6.9.4}$$

Note that (6.9.1)–(6.9.4) are linear equations in the unknown parameters, a, b, c, and d.

This exhausts the interpolation and smoothness conditions, leaving us two conditions short of fixing the unknown coefficients. Various splines are differentiated by the two additional conditions imposed. One way to fix the spline is to pin down $s'(x_0)$ and $s'(x_n)$. For example, the *natural spline* imposes $s'(x_0) = 0 = s'(x_n)$. A natural spline is of special interest because it minimizes the total curvature, defined to be $\int_{x_0}^{x_n} s''(x)^2\, dx$, of all cubic splines that interpolate the data.

Another way to fix $s(x)$ is to make the interpolation good in some other sense. For example, we may know, or have a good guess, about the slope at x_0 and x_n. For example, we may reject the natural spline if we want a concave $s(x)$. If we know the true slopes for the function being approximated are y_0' and y_n' at the end points, we can then impose $s'(x_0) = y_0'$ and $s'(x_n) = y_n'$; the resulting spline is called the *Hermite spline*. If we want to use a slope approach but do not have the true values, we can use the slopes of the secant lines over $[x_0, x_1]$ and $[x_{n-1}, x_n]$; that is, we choose $s(x)$ to make $s'(x_0) = (s(x_1) - s(x_0))/(x_1 - x_0)$ and $s'(x_n) = (s(x_n) - s(x_{n-1}))/(x_n - x_{n-1})$. We call this the *secant Hermite spline*. With natural, secant, and Hermite splines, the two extra conditions are linear. To solve for the coefficients, we just add two slope conditions to the system (6.9.1)–(6.9.4), and solve the combined system of linear equations.

Theorem 6.9.1 displays some useful error formulas that indicate the quality of spline approximation.

THEOREM 6.9.1 If $f \in C^4[x_0, x_n]$ and s is the Hermite cubic spline approximation to f on $\{x_0, x_1, \ldots x_n\}$ and $h \geq \max_i\{x_i - x_{i-1}\}$, then

$$\|f - s\|_\infty \leq \frac{5}{384} \|f^{(4)}\|_\infty h^4$$

and

$$\|f' - s'\|_\infty \leq \left[\frac{\sqrt{3}}{216} + \frac{1}{24}\right] \|f^{(4)}\|_\infty h^3.$$

Proof See Prenter (1989, p. 112). ∎

These error bounds indicate the rapid rate of convergence of spline interpolation. In general, order $k + 2$ splines will yield $\mathcal{O}(n^{-(k+1)})$ convergence for $f \in C^{k+1}[a, b]$.

Splines are excellent for approximations for two general reasons. First, evaluation is cheap, since splines are locally cubic. To evaluate a spline at x one must first find which interval $[x_i, x_{i+1}]$ contains x, look at some table to find the coefficients for the particular polynomial used over $[x_i, x_{i+1}]$, and evaluate that polynomial at x. The only possible difficulty is determining which interval $[x_i, x_{i+1}]$ contains x. If there are n intervals, then it will take at most $\lceil \log_2 n \rceil$ comparisons to determine which one contains x. Even that cost can be avoided if the nodes are carefully chosen. For example, if the nodes are evenly spaced, that is, $x_i = a + ih$ for some h, then finding the relevant interval for x uses the fact that $x \in [x_i, x_{i+1}]$ if and only if $i = \lfloor (x - a)/h \rfloor$. In general, if the nodes are created according to some invertible formula, the inverse can be used to quickly determine the interval to which x belongs.

The second reason for using splines is that good fits are possible even for functions that are not C^∞ or have regions of large higher-order derivatives. This is indicated for cubic splines by the error formulas above, which depend only on $f^{(4)}(x)$ implying that badly behaved $f^{(5)}(x)$ will not adversely affect the performance of a cubic spline.

B-Splines

The discussion above assumes that a spline is represented by the collection of nodes, x_i, and of interval specific coefficients, a_i, b_i, c_i and d_i, $i = 0, \ldots, n$. The space of splines with nodes on a prescribed grid comprise a finite vector space. The B-splines form a basis for splines.

Suppose that we have a grid of knots at $x_{-k} < \cdots < x_{-1} < x_0 < \cdots < x_{n+k}$. Order 1 splines implement step function interpolation and are spanned by the B^0-splines. The typical B^0-spline is

$$B_i^0(x) = \begin{cases} 0, & x < x_i, \\ 1, & x_i \le x < x_{i+1}, \\ 0, & x_{i+1} \le x, \end{cases} \tag{6.9.5}$$

for $i = -k, \ldots, n$. Note that the B_i^0 are right-continuous step functions. Linear splines implement piecewise linear interpolation and are spanned by the B^1-splines, with a typical B^1-spline being

$$B_i^1(x) = \begin{cases} 0, & x \le x_i \text{ or } x \ge x_{i+2}, \\ \dfrac{x - x_i}{x_{i+1} - x_i}, & x_i \le x \le x_{i+1}, \\ \dfrac{x_{i+2} - x}{x_{i+2} - x_{i+1}}, & x_{i+1} \le x \le x_{i+2}. \end{cases} \tag{6.9.6}$$

The B_i^1-spline is the tent function with peak at x_{i+1} and is zero for $x \le x_i$ and $x \ge x_{i+2}$. Both B^0- and B^1-splines form cardinal bases for interpolation at the x_i's.

Higher-order B-splines are defined by the recursive relation

$$B_i^k(x) = \left(\frac{x - x_i}{x_{i+k} - x_i} \right) B_i^{k-1}(x) + \left(\frac{x_{i+k+1} - x}{x_{i+k+1} - x_{i+1}} \right) B_{i+1}^{k-1}(x). \tag{6.9.7}$$

These B-spline families can be used to construct arbitrary splines.

THEOREM 6.9.2   Let S_n^k be the space of all order $k + 1$ spline functions on $[x_0, x_n]$ with knots at $\{x_0, x_1, \ldots, x_n\}$. Then 1–4 follow:

1. The set

$$\{B_i^k|_{[x_0, x_n]} : -k \leq i \leq n - 1\}$$

forms a linearly independent basis for S_n^k, which has dimension $n + k$.

2. $B_i^k(x) \geq 0$, and the support of $B_i^k(x)$ is (x_i, x_{i+k+1}).

3. $(d/dx)B_i^k(x) = (k/x_{i+k} - x_i) B_i^{k-1}(x) - (k/x_{i+k+1} - x_{i+1}) B_{i+1}^{k-1}(x)$.

4. If we have Lagrange interpolation data, $(z_i, y_i), i = 1, \ldots, n + k$, and

$$\max[x_0, x_{i-k-1}] < z_i < \min[x_i, x_n], \quad 1 \leq i \leq n + k,$$

then there is an interpolant S in S_n^k such that $y_i = S(z_i), i = 1, \ldots, n + k$.

These properties form the basis for computations using B-splines. The general theory of B-splines is laid out in de Boor (1978), and the necessary programs are also presented there.

6.10   Examples

We next illustrate various approximation methods for some simple functions. We examine each of these functions on the interval $[-1, 1]$. To make the comparisons "fair," we will use methods which have five free parameters. Therefore we explore fourth-degree least squares approximations and interpolations at five different points. The spline approximations are all cubic splines where we use the secant Hermite method to fix the free end points.

First, we examine e^{2x+2}. This is a C^∞ function; in fact, it is analytic on the complex plane, a very well-behaved function. Figure 6.7 displays the approximation error for four different approximation methods: Legendre least squares, Chebyshev interpolation, spline, and polynomial interpolation on a uniform grid. Over $[-1, 1]$, e^{2x+2} ranges in value from 1 to 54, and its derivative ranges from 1 to 109. Despite this substantial variation, all methods did so well in approximating e^{2x+2} that graphs of e^{2x+2} and its approximations are indistinguishable. Figure 6.7 displays the approximation errors. The Chebyshev interpolation approximation had the smallest maximum error and most nearly satisfied the equioscillation property, as predicted by our theorems.

Next figure 6.8 displays the spline, Chebyshev, and uniform interpolation approximations of $(x + 1)^{1/4}$ on $[-1, 1]$. This function has a singularity at $x = -1$. Note

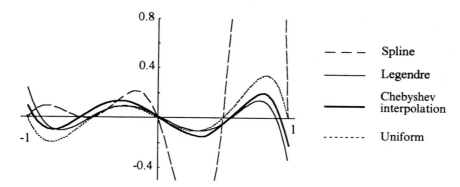

Figure 6.7
Approximation errors for e^{2x+2} approximations

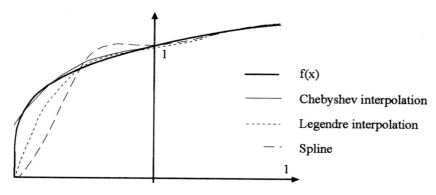

Figure 6.8
Approximations for $(x+1)^{0.25}$

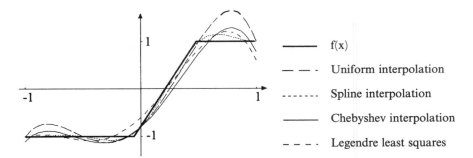

Figure 6.9
Approximations of $\min[\max[-1, 4(x - 0.2)], 1]$

that the approximations do well except near the singular point, $x = -1$. This is expected, since all the derivatives of $(x + 1)^{1/4}$ are infinite at $x = -1$. Since the spline and uniform approximants interpolate $(x + 1)^{1/4}$ at $x = -1$, they do poorly on $[-1, -0.5]$ because $(x + 1)^{1/4}$ initially has infinite slope, a feature that no low-order polynomial can match. In an effort to catch up with the fast-rising $(x + 1)^{1/4}$ the spline and uniform interpolants overshoot it at $x = -0.5$. In contrast, the Chebyshev interpolant ignores the value at $x = -1$, avoiding the high curvature there by instead interpolating at a point to the right of $x = -1$, and it does well almost everywhere else. Even though $(x + 1)^{1/4}$ is C^∞ and locally analytic, the singularity at $x = -1$ makes approximation more difficult. Note how the spline and uniform interpolant approximations have convex regions even though $(x + 1)^{1/4}$ is concave over $[-1, 1]$. This shows how our methods will fail at preserving qualitative properties, such as concavity, even while producing good L^∞ approximations. Also one should be very careful using any of these methods near singularities.

Figure 6.9 displays the results for $f(x) = \min[\max[-1, 4(x - 0.2)], 1]$, a much more difficult case. The problem in approximating this function lies in trying to approximate the two kink points with polynomials.[3] The key point is that all of these approximations are bothered by the kinks. Since they can use only low-order polynomials, they have difficulty in "turning the corners," which are essentially points of infinite curvature. In order to make any turn through a kink, all of the approximations oscillate around $f(x)$ on both sides of the kink. Even the spline does not do well, though the piecewise polynomial structure of splines would seem to make them

---

3. The first kink was put at $x = -0.05$ so that it would not be an interpolation point.

better for dealing with kinks. The problem here is that cubic splines are C^2, which is much smoother than the function being approximated, and five free parameters are not enough for the flexibility of splines to be exploited. In this case, though, it is surprising that any of the methods, particularly the interpolation methods, do as well as they do.

6.11 Shape-Preserving Approximation

All of the procedures above find an approximation that is close to f in some norm. Sometimes we may be less concerned with closeness and more interested in other properties. In particular, we may care more about getting a visually pleasing approximation, one that looks right. For example, in figure 6.8, we had L^2 approximations to a concave function that were not themselves concave. Instead, they fluctuated around the function being approximated. In fact the equioscillation property of L^∞ approximation methods shows that methods that are good in the L^∞ sense necessarily yield such oscillations around the true function. The spline approximations can also fail to produce concave approximations in those cases. Not only can these approximations fail to preserve curvature, but it is possible that an increasing function is approximated by a function that is decreasing in some places. We refer to the curvature and monotonicity properties of a function as aspects of its shape. In some cases it is important to construct approximations that preserve shape as well as are accurate. We now turn to some basic methods for preserving shape.

Piecewise-Linear Interpolation

Piecewise-linear interpolation obviously preserves positivity, monotonicity, and concavity. However, it is not differentiable. This violates our desire to use smooth functions to approximate smooth functions.

Shape-Preserving Quadratic Spline Interpolation

We next present the shape-preserving quadratic spline of Schumaker (1983) which produces a smooth function which both interpolates data and preserves some shape. We first examine the Hermite interpolation version and then discuss the Lagrange version.

Let us consider the shape-preservation problem on an interval. The basic Hermite problem on the single interval $[t_1, t_2]$ takes the data z_1, z_2, s_1, s_2, and constructs a piecewise-quadratic function $s \in C^1[t_1, t_2]$ such that

$$s(t_i) = z_i, \; s'(t_i) = s_i, \qquad i = 1, 2. \tag{6.11.1}$$

We first examine the nongeneric case where a quadratic polynomial works.

LEMMA 6.11.1   If $(s_1 + s_2)/2 = (z_2 - z_1)/(t_2 - t_1)$, then the quadratic function

$$s(t) = z_1 + s_1(t - t_1) + \frac{(s_2 - s_1)(t - t_1)^2}{2(t_2 - t_1)} \tag{6.11.2}$$

satisfies (6.11.1).

The shape-preserving properties of this construction are clear. First, if $s_1 \cdot s_2 \geq 0$, then $s'(t)$ has the same sign as s_1 and s_2 throughout $[t_1, t_2]$. Therefore, if the data indicate a monotone increasing (decreasing) function on $[t_1, t_2]$, then $s(t)$ is similarly monotone. Second, $s_1 < s_2$ indicates a convex function, which $s(t)$ satisfies since $s''(t) = (s_2 - s_1)/(t_2 - t_1)$. Similarly, if $s_1 > s_2$, then $s(t)$ and the data are concave.

In general, lemma 6.11.1 does not apply. The typical strategy is to add a knot to the interval $[a, b]$ and then construct a spline with the desired properties. Lemma 6.11.2 first constructs a quadratic spline that satisfies (6.11.1).

LEMMA 6.11.2   For every $\xi \in (t_1, t_2)$, there is a unique quadratic spline solving (6.11.1) with a knot at ξ. It is

$$s(t) = \begin{cases} A_1 + B_1(t - t_1) + C_1(t - t_1)^2, & t \in [t_1, \xi], \\ A_2 + B_2(t - \xi) + C_2(t - \xi)^2, & t \in [\xi, t_2], \end{cases} \tag{6.11.3}$$

$$A_1 = z_1, \quad B_1 = s_1, \quad C_1 = \frac{\bar{s} - s_1}{2\alpha},$$

$$A_2 = A_1 + \alpha B_1 + \alpha^2 C_1, \quad B_2 = \bar{s}, \quad C_2 = \frac{s_2 - \bar{s}}{2\beta},$$

$$\bar{s} = \frac{2(z_2 - z_1) - (\alpha s_1 + \beta s_2)}{t_2 - t_1},$$

$$\alpha = \xi - t_1, \quad \beta = t_2 - \xi.$$

Lemma 6.11.2 constructs a quadratic spline once we choose ξ. Note that ξ is a free node in that we do not know $s(\xi)$; $s(\xi)$ is allowed to be whatever is convenient.

We will now choose ξ to satisfy desirable shape properties. First, if $s_1, s_2 \geq 0$, then $s(t)$ is monotone if and only if $s_1 \bar{s} \geq 0$, which is equivalent to

$$2(z_2 - z_1) \geq (\xi - t_1)s_1 + (t_2 - \xi)s_2 \quad \text{if } s_1, s_2 \geq 0,$$

$$2(z_2 - z_1) \leq (\xi - t_1)s_1 + (t_2 - \xi)s_2 \quad \text{if } s_1, s_2 \leq 0.$$

To deal with curvature, we compute $\delta = (z_2 - z_1)/(t_2 - t_1)$, the average slope between t_1 and t_2. If $(s_2 - \delta)(s_1 - \delta) \geq 0$, there must be an inflection point in $[t_1, t_2]$, and we can have neither a concave nor convex interpolant. If $|s_2 - \delta| < |s_1 - \delta|$, and ξ satisfies

$$t_1 < \xi \leq \bar{\xi} \equiv t_1 + \frac{2(t_2 - t_1)(s_2 - \delta)}{s_2 - s_1}, \tag{6.11.4}$$

then $s(t)$ in (6.11.3) is convex (concave) if $s_1 < s_2(s_1 > s_2)$. Furthermore, if $s_1 s_2 > 0$, it is also monotone. If $|s_2 - \delta| > |s_1 - \delta|$ and

$$t_2 + \frac{2(t_2 - t_1)(s_1 - \delta)}{s_2 - s_1} \equiv \underline{\xi} \leq \xi < t_2, \tag{6.11.5}$$

then $s(t)$ in (6.11.3) is convex (concave) if $s_1 < s_2(s_1 > s_2)$, and if $s_1 s_2 > 0$, s is monotone. Inequalities (6.11.4) and (6.11.5) give us a range of ξ that can be used to preserve shape conditions. These facts imply the following algorithm for finding a value for ξ such that $s(t)$ defined in (6.11.3) is a shape preserving interpolant on the interval $[t_1, t_2]$ of the data in (6.11.1):

Algorithm 6.3   Schumaker Shape-Preserving Interpolation for (6.11.1)

Initialization. Check if lemma 6.11.1 applies; if so, $\xi = t_2$, (6.11.3) gives $s(t)$, and STOP.

Step 1. Compute $\delta = (z_2 - z_1)/(t_2 - t_1)$.

Step 2. If $(s_1 - \delta)(s_2 - \delta) \geq 0$, set $\xi = (1/2)(t_1 + t_2)$ and STOP else, if $|s_2 - \delta| < |s_1 - \delta|$, then compute $\bar{\xi}$ using (6.11.4), set $\xi = (1/2)(t_1 + \bar{\xi})$, and STOP; if $|s_2 - \delta| \geq |s_1 - \delta|$, then compute $\underline{\xi}$ using (6.11.5), set $\xi = (1/2)(t_2 + \underline{\xi})$, and STOP.

This algorithm for ξ solves the problem for a single interval, $[t_1, t_2]$. We next consider a general interpolation problem. If we have Hermite data, namely we have $\{(z_i, s_i, t_i) | i = 1, \ldots, n\}$, we then apply the shape-preserving interpolant algorithm to each interval to find $\xi_i \in [t_i, t_{i+1}]$. If we have Lagrange data, $\{(z_i, t_i) | i = 1, \ldots, n\}$, we must first add estimates of the slopes and then proceed as we do with Hermite data. Schumaker suggests the following formulas for estimating slopes s_1 through s_n:

$$L_i = \left[(t_{i+1} - t_i)^2 + (z_{i+1} - z_i)^2\right]^{1/2}, \qquad i = 1, \ldots, n-1,$$

$$\delta_i = \frac{z_{i+1} - z_i}{t_{i+1} - t_i}, \qquad i = 1, \ldots, n-1,$$

$$s_i = \begin{cases} \dfrac{L_{i-1}\delta_{i-1} + L_i\delta_i}{L_{i-1} + L_i} & \text{if } \delta_{i-1}\delta_i > 0 \\ 0, & \text{if } \delta_{i-1}\delta_i \le 0 \end{cases}, \qquad i = 2, \ldots, n-1, \qquad (6.11.6)$$

$$s_1 = -\frac{3\delta_1 - s_2}{2}, \qquad s_n = \frac{3\delta_{n-1} - s_{n-1}}{2}.$$

Once we have the level and slope information data, the latter either given or computed, we can then proceed locally, choosing ξ_i which causes (6.11.3) to be a shape-preserving spline on each interval $[t_i, t_{i+1}] \equiv I_i$. The result of this scheme is a quadratic spline that is globally monotone if the data are monotone. Similarly for convexity and concavity. Furthermore the resulting spline is *co-monotone*, that is, s is increasing (decreasing) on I_i iff $z_i < z_{i+1}$ ($z_i > z_{i+1}$). This property follows from the local monotonicity of (6.11.3) and our imposing $s_i = 0$ wherever the slope changes. Preserving local curvature is also accomplished. If $\delta_i < \delta_{i+1} < \delta_{i+2} < \delta_{i+3}$ the data appear to be convex on I_{i+1}, and our construction is convex on I_{i+1}, since $s_{i+1} < s_{i+2}$ by construction; hence the Shumaker scheme is *co-convex*.

In table 6.5 we display the results of applying the Schumaker procedure to some familiar functions. We use uniformly spaced nodes on the indicated intervals. Note the small errors in approximating both f and f'. The first four columns display L^∞ and L^2 norms for the error in the approximation to f, first using estimated slopes from (6.11.6) and then using the true slopes. The last two columns display error

Table 6.5
Shape-preserving interpolation

| | | f errors | | | | f' errors | |
| | | Estimated slopes | | True slopes | | True slopes | |
Function	Nodes	L^∞	L^2	L^∞	L^2	L^∞	L^2
$\sqrt{x}$ on $[1, 2]$	3	6($-$3)	2($-$3)	3($-$5)	1($-$5)	1($-$3)	5($-$5)
	4	4($-$3)	1($-$3)	1($-$5)	6($-$6)	7($-$4)	3($-$5)
	5	2($-$3)	7($-$4)	8($-$6)	3($-$6)	5($-$4)	2($-$5)
$\sqrt{x}$ on $[1, 20]$	3	3($-$1)	1($-$1)	2($-$2)	5($-$3)	3($-$2)	1($-$3)
	4	2($-$1)	8($-$2)	1($-$2)	3($-$3)	3($-$2)	8($-$4)
	5	2($-$1)	5($-$2)	8($-$3)	2($-$3)	2($-$2)	6($-$4)
$\sin x$ on $[0, 2\pi]$	5	3($-$1)	9($-$2)	2($-$2)	8($-$3)	7($-$2)	1($-$3)
	7	1($-$1)	4($-$1)	7($-$3)	3($-$3)	4($-$2)	7($-$4)
	10	5($-$2)	1($-$1)	3($-$3)	1($-$3)	2($-$2)	4($-$4)

norms for the implied estimate of f' where we use the true slopes of f. Using the true slopes helps substantially, and the resulting approximations are very good at approximating both f and f'.

6.12 Multidimensional Approximation

Most problems require us to approximate multidimensional functions. When we move beyond one dimension, several difficulties present themselves. We will discuss multidimensional interpolation and approximation methods, first by generalizing the one-dimensional methods via product formulations and then by constructing inherently multidimensional schemes.

General Theory of Multidimensional Approximation

We next present two basic theorems in multidimensional approximation. We first present Stone's theorem. Suppose that X is a compact metric space. The space of real-valued continuous functions, $C[X]$, is a linear vector space. It is also an algebra when we add multiplication, $*$; that is, the operations $+$ and $*$ over $C[X]$ satisfy distributivity and associativity, and for scalar $a \in R$, $(a*f)*g = a*(f*g)$. We say that $S \subset C[X]$ is a *subalgebra* if it is closed under $+$ and $*$; furthermore a subalgebra S *separates points* if for all distinct $x, y \in X$, there is $f \in S$ such that $f(x) \neq f(y)$.

THEOREM 6.12.1 (Stone's theorem) If X is a compact metric space and $(S, +, *)$ is a subalgebra of $(C[X], +, *)$ which contains the function $f(x) = 1$ and separates points in X, then S is dense in $C[X]$.

Proof See Cheney (1966, pp. 191–92).   ∎

The Weierstrass theorem is a special case of Stone's theorem, since the ordinary polynomials form a subalgebra of $C[R]$ and the linear monomial $f(x) = x$ separates any two points in R. Since any two points in R^n can be separated by some linear monomial, Stone's theorem implies that the ordinary multivariate polynomials are dense in $C[R^n]$, as are the tensor product bases of orthogonal polynomials. Stone's theorem can be used to show completeness of many linear approximation schemes, including ones built from nonpolynomial functions.

While linear approximation theory is very well developed, there are nonlinear schemes of approximation. We saw how Padé approximations effectively used rational approximations. A totally different approach to approximation is the subject of the remarkable Kolmogorov's theorem.

THEOREM 6.12.2 (Kolmogorov's theorem)   For any n there exists an $\alpha \in [0,1]^n$ and $2n + 1$ strictly monotone Lipschitz functions, $\varphi_l : [0,1] \to R$, $l = 1, \ldots, 2n+1$, such that for any $f \in C[0,1]^n$ there is a $\psi \in C[0,n]$ such that

$$f(x) = \sum_{l=1}^{2n+1} \psi \left(\sum_{i=1}^{n} \alpha_i \varphi_l(x_i) \right). \tag{6.12.1}$$

This is a striking theorem. It breaks down a multivariate function into a special sequence of addition, multiplication, and univariate operations. The whole approach is fundamentally different from linear procedures, focusing not on a sequence of nonlinear but on univariate function evaluations. One key difference between (6.12.1) and an orthogonal polynomial approach is that division is a permissible operation in ψ and φ_l, whereas it is not used when evaluating any polynomial. In practice, this is the key difference, for the computer only does division, multiplication, and addition. Therefore (6.12.1) is operationally equivalent to a special class of rational functions.

Unfortunately, implementation of Kolmogorov's theorem is difficult; the φ's are nondifferentiable functions and very difficult to compute. While the direct practical usefulness of Kolmogorov's theorem is questionable, it does give us reason to examine alternative approaches to approximation. One such alternative are artificial neural networks, which we examine in a later section.

Lagrange Interpolation

Multidimensional Lagrange interpolation takes a finite set of conditions (the Lagrange data), $D \equiv \{(x_i, z_i)\}_{i=1}^{N} \subset R^{n+m}$, where $x_i \in R^n$ and $z_i \in R^m$, and finds a function $f : R^n \to R^m$ such that $z_i = f(x_i)$. Section 6.6 examined the case where $n = m = 1$. The multidimensional problem is much more complex, and occasionally impossible. For example, suppose that data at the four points are $\{P_1, P_2, P_3, P_4\} \equiv \{(1,0), (-1,0), (0,1), (0,-1)\}$ in R^2, and we want to interpolate using linear combinations of the functions $\{1, x, y, xy\}$. Let $z_i = f(P_i), i = 1, 2, 3, 4$. The linear set of conditions for a polynomial $f(x, y) = a + bx + cy + dxy$ to satisfy $f(P_i) = z_i$ is

$$\begin{pmatrix} 1 & 1 & 0 & 0 \\ 1 & -1 & 0 & 0 \\ 1 & 0 & 1 & 0 \\ 1 & 0 & -1 & 0 \end{pmatrix} \begin{pmatrix} a \\ b \\ c \\ d \end{pmatrix} = \begin{pmatrix} z_1 \\ z_2 \\ z_3 \\ z_4 \end{pmatrix},$$

which is a singular system due to the column of zeros. Hence interpolation over these four points using $\{1, x, y, xy\}$ is not generally possible.

If we want to interpolate in R^n, then we must proceed carefully. Interpolation is possible on many grids. To determine that, we form the linear system as we did above, and check if it is nonsingular. By standard genericity logic, interpolation is possible on most grids. That is not good enough. We also want grids that do a good job and produce well-conditioned procedures.

Tensor Product Bases

Linear approximations begin with a basis of functions. We can use *tensor products* of univariate functions to form bases of multivariate functions. If A and B are sets of functions over $x \in R^n$, $y \in R^m$, their tensor product is

$$A \otimes B = \{\varphi(x)\psi(y) | \varphi \in A, \psi \in B\}. \tag{6.12.2}$$

Given a basis for functions of the single variable x_i, $\Phi^i = \{\varphi_k^i(x_i)\}_{k=0}^\infty$, we can build the *n-fold tensor product* basis for functions of n variables $(x_1, x_2, \ldots, x_n)$ by taking all possible n-term products of φ_k^i. The resulting basis is

$$\Phi = \left\{ \prod_{i=1}^n \varphi_{k_i}^i(x_i) \;\middle|\; k_i = 0, 1, \ldots, i = 1, \ldots, n \right\} \tag{6.12.3}$$

One problem with tensor product bases is their size. We will only want to use finite subsets of the full tensor product basis. It will be natural to take the first m elements (typically those of degree less than m) of each univariate basis and construct the tensor product of these subbases. If Φ is a basis for univariate functions and $\Psi \subset \Phi$ has m elements, then the n-dimensional tensor product of Ψ, has m^n elements. This exponential growth in dimension makes it quite costly to use the full tensor product subbasis.

Multidimensional versions of splines can also be constructed through tensor products; here B-splines would be useful. There are more sophisticated methods available, but the details are more complex. We refer the interested reader to Nurnberger (1989).

Our discussion of orthogonal polynomials and least squares approximation generalizes directly to the multivariate case. To compute n-dimensional least squares approximation, we need only note that the basis Φ from (6.12.3) inherits the orthogonality properties of the individual Φ^i. Hence, if the elements of Φ^i are orthogonal with respect to the weighting function $w_i(x_i)$ over the interval $[a_i, b_i]$, then the least squares approximation of $f(x_1, \ldots, x_n)$ in Φ is

$$\sum_{\varphi \in \Phi} \frac{\langle \varphi, f \rangle}{\langle \varphi, \varphi \rangle} \varphi, \tag{6.12.4}$$

where the product weighting function

$$W(x_1, x_2, \ldots, x_n) = \prod_{i=1}^{n} w_i(x_i) \tag{6.12.5}$$

defines $\langle \cdot, \cdot \rangle$ over $D = \prod_i [a_i, b_i]$ in

$$\langle f(x), g(x) \rangle = \int_D f(x)g(x)W(x)\, dx. \tag{6.12.6}$$

The following procedure for Chebyshev approximation in R^2 illustrates how one adapts one-dimensional methods to higher dimensions:

Algorithm 6.4   Chebyshev Approximation Algorithm in R^2

Objective: Given a function $f(x, y)$ defined on $[a, b] \times [c, d]$, find its Chebyshev polynomial approximation $p(x, y)$.

Step 1. Compute the $m \geq n + 1$ Chebyshev interpolation nodes on $[-1, 1]$:

$$z_k = -\cos\left(\frac{2k-1}{2m}\pi\right), \qquad k = 1, \ldots, m.$$

Step 2. Adjust the nodes to the $[a, b]$ and $[c, d]$ intervals:

$$x_k = (z_k + 1)\left(\frac{b-a}{2}\right) + a, \qquad k = 1, \ldots, m,$$

$$y_k = (z_k + 1)\left(\frac{d-c}{2}\right) + c, \qquad k = 1, \ldots, m.$$

Step 3. Evaluate f at the approximation nodes:

$$w_{k,l} = f(x_k, y_l), \qquad k = 1, \ldots, m, \quad l = 1, \ldots, m.$$

Step 4. Compute Chebyshev coefficients, $a_{ij}, i, j = 0, \ldots, n$:

$$a_{ij} = \frac{\sum_{k=1}^{m} \sum_{l=1}^{m} w_{k,l} T_i(z_k) T_j(z_l)}{(\sum_{k=1}^{m} T_i(z_k)^2)(\sum_{l=1}^{m} T_j(z_l)^2)}$$

to arrive at the approximation for $f(x, y), x \in [a, b]; y \in [c, d]$:

$$p(x, y) = \sum_{i=0}^{n} \sum_{j=0}^{n} a_{ij} T_i\left(2\frac{x-a}{b-a} - 1\right) T_j\left(2\frac{y-c}{d-c} - 1\right).$$

Complete Polynomials

Tensor product collections have the disadvantage of growing exponentially as the dimension increases. We will now turn to bases that grow only polynomially as the dimension increases and see why they can be quite good even though they have far fewer members. Recall that Taylor's theorem for many dimensions produces the approximation

$$f(x) \doteq f(x^0) + \sum_{i=1}^{n} \frac{\partial f}{\partial x_i}(x^0)(x_i - x_i^0)$$

$$\vdots$$

$$+ \frac{1}{k!} \sum_{i_1=1}^{n} \cdots \sum_{i_k=1}^{n} \frac{\partial^k f}{\partial x_{i_1} \cdots \partial x_{i_k}}(x_0)(x_{i_1} - x_{i_1}^0) \cdots (x_{i_k} - x_{i_k}^0).$$

Notice the terms used in the kth-degree Taylor series expansion. For $k = 1$, Taylor's theorem for n dimensions used the linear functions $\mathscr{P}_1^n \equiv \{1, x_1, x_2, \ldots, x_n\}$. For $k = 2$, Taylor's theorem used

$$\mathscr{P}_2^n \equiv \mathscr{P}_1^n \cup \{x_1^2, \ldots, x_n^2, x_1 x_2, x_1 x_3, \ldots, x_{n-1} x_n\}.$$

$\mathscr{P}_2^n$ contains some product terms, but not all; for example, $x_1 x_2 x_3$ is not in $\mathscr{P}_2^n$. In general, the kth-degree expansion of n dimensional functions uses functions in

$$\mathscr{P}_k^n \equiv \left\{ x_1^{i_1} \cdots x_n^{i_n} \,\middle|\, \sum_{l=1}^{n} i_l \leq k, \, 0 \leq i_1, \ldots, i_n \right\}.$$

The set $\mathscr{P}_k^n$ is called the *complete set of polynomials of total degree k in n variables.*

Using complete sets of polynomials will give us a way of constructing bases for multivariate approximation that are often more efficient than tensor products. If $\Psi_k \equiv \{1, x, \ldots, x^k\}$ is the collection of kth-degree basis functions, then its n-dimensional tensor product contains many more elements than $\mathscr{P}_k$. For example, table 6.6 compares the size of $\mathscr{P}_k^n$ to the tensor product.

The key difference is that the tensor product basis grows exponentially in dimension n for fixed k, but the set of complete polynomials grows polynomially. However, from the perspective of the rate of convergence, many of the elements in a tensor product are excessive. Taylor's theorem tells us that the elements of $\mathscr{P}_k^n$ will yield an approximation near x^0 which has kth-degree convergence asymptotically. The n-fold tensor product of Ψ_k can give us only kth-degree convergence, since it does not

Table 6.6
Sizes of alternative bases

Degree k	$\mathscr{P}_k^n$	Tensor product Ψ_k^n
2	$1 + n + \dfrac{n(n+1)}{2}$	3^n
3	$1 + n + \dfrac{n(n+1)}{2} + n^2 + \dfrac{n(n-1)(n-2)}{6}$	4^n

contain all terms of total degree $k + 1$. Therefore, in terms of asymptotic convergence, the complete polynomials will give us as good an approximation as the tensor product with far fewer elements. We use complete polynomials of finite degree in the hope that this asymptotic behavior holds for polynomials of practical degree.

6.13   Finite Element Approximations

A finite element approach to approximation uses basis functions that are zero over most of the domain. It is a local approach to approximation, in contrast to orthogonal polynomial approach where the basis elements are each nonzero everywhere. We present two two-dimensional examples.

Bilinear Interpolation

Bilinear interpolation constructs an approximation that interpolates the data linearly in both coordinate directions. Suppose that we have the values of $f(x,y)$ at $(x,y) = (\pm 1, \pm 1)$. Then the following four functions form a cardinal interpolation basis on $[-1,1]^2$:

$$\varphi_1(x,y) = \tfrac{1}{4}(1-x)(1-y), \quad \varphi_2(x,y) = \tfrac{1}{4}(1+x)(1-y),$$
$$\varphi_3(x,y) = \tfrac{1}{4}(1+x)(1+y), \quad \varphi_4(x,y) = \tfrac{1}{4}(1-x)(1+y). \tag{6.13.1}$$

Notice that each of these functions is zero at all but one of the points $(\pm 1, \pm 1)$. Therefore the approximation to f on the square $[-1,1] \times [-1,1]$ is

$$f(-1,-1)\varphi_1(x,y) + f(1,-1)\varphi_2(x,y)$$
$$+ f(1,1)\varphi_3(x,y) + f(-1,1)\varphi_4(x,y) \tag{6.13.2}$$

The basis function φ_1 is graphed in figure 6.10; note the mixed curvature of the surface. In particular, it is linear only on the edges, and has a saddle point curvature on

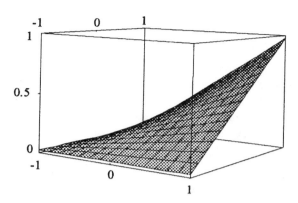

Figure 6.10
Typical bilinear element

the interior; that is, it is convex in the $(-1, -1)$ to $(1, 1)$ direction, as can be seen in figure 6.10, and concave in the $(-1, 1)$ to $(1, -1)$ direction. This is true of each of the basis functions in (6.13.1).

If we have data at the vertices of a rectangle other than $[-1, 1] \times [-1, 1]$ we can interpolate using the φ_i in (6.13.1) after a linear change of variables. If the data are at the vertices $[a, b] \times [c, d]$, then the linear map

$$l(x, y) = \left(-1 + 2\frac{x - a}{b - a}, \ -1 + 2\frac{y - c}{d - c}\right)$$

maps $[a, b] \times [c, d]$ onto $[-1, 1] \times [-1, 1]$, and the functions $\psi_i(x, y) \equiv \varphi_i(l(x, y))$, $i = 1, 2, 3, 4$, are cardinal basis functions for bilinear interpolation over $[a, b] \times [c, d]$ based on $f(a, c)$, $f(a, d)$, $f(b, c)$, and $f(b, d)$.

If we have Lagrange data on a two-dimensional lattice, we compute the interpolants on each square and piece them together. While this is similar to how we constructed piecewise-polynomial approximations on R, we must be more careful here because of the extra difficulties created by the higher dimensionality. Since we are trying to compute a continuous interpolant, we must be sure that the individual pieces meet continuously at common edges. In the piecewise-polynomial case, this was ensured by the fact that the intervals had common nodes. That is not enough, in general, in higher dimensions because adjacent regions share faces as well as vertices. Therefore interpolants in neighboring regions must agree along all common faces, edges, and vertices. In bilinear interpolation this will happen because any two approximations overlap only at the edges of rectangles, and on those edges the approximation is the linear interpolant between the common end points. Higher-order interpolation generates much more complex problems, which we will not cover here.

An equivalent approach to bilinear interpolation is to take the linear interpolation basis in each dimension, the tent functions, and construct the tensor product, which will also be a cardinal function basis. This fact is useful but misleading, since finite element approximation does not generally reduce to a tensor product formulation. In either case the result has a pockmarked shape, like a golf ball, because of the mixed curvature inside each rectangle.

Simplicial 2-D Linear Interpolation

While bilinear interpolation is used sometimes, many prefer simplicial triangular elements. We start by triangulating the x-y plane. Let $P_1 P_2 P_3$ be the canonical linear triangular element, where $P_1 = (0,0)$, $P_2 = (0,1)$, and $P_3 = (1,0)$. We are looking for linear functions $\varphi_i(x,y)$ such that $\varphi_i(P_i) = 1$ and $\varphi_i(P_j) = 0$ for $i \neq j$, $i, j = 1, 2, 3$. The functions $\varphi_1(x,y) = 1 - x - y$, $\varphi_2(x,y) = y$, and $\varphi_3(x,y) = x$ satisfy the cardinal interpolation conditions on the set $\{P_1, P_2, P_3\}$. If we examine $P_2 P_3 P_4$ where $P_4 = (1,1)$, then $\varphi_4(x,y) = 1 - x$, $\varphi_5(x,y) = 1 - y$, and $\varphi_6(x,y) = x + y - 1$ are cardinal basis functions on the set $\{P_2, P_3, P_4\}$. Therefore, on the square $P_1 P_2 P_4 P_3$, the interpolant, $\hat{f}$, is

$$\hat{f}(x,y) = \begin{cases} f(0,0)(1 - x - y) + f(0,1)y + f(1,0)x & \text{if } x + y \leq 1, \\ f(0,1)(1 - x) + f(1,0)(1 - y) + f(1,1)(x + y - 1), & \text{if } x + y \geq 1. \end{cases}$$

(6.13.3)

Elementary considerations show that piecewise-planar approximation is no worse than bilinear approximation. Since bilinear interpolation uses only $1, x, y$, and xy, the highest degree of completeness is 1. Therefore, as the rectangles get smaller, we only get linear convergence, the same as linear triangular elements.

Multidimensional Linear Interpolation

Both the bilinear and simplicial interpolation methods can be extended to arbitrarily high dimensions. Weiser and Zarantonello (1988) develop simple recursive formulas for both methods. We describe both methods.

Without loss of generality, we can assume that we are working with the hypercube $\mathscr{C} \equiv \{x \in R^n | 0 \leq x_i \leq 1, i = 1, \ldots, n\}$. We also assume that we have Lagrange data on the vertices of $\mathscr{C}$, $V \equiv \{x \in \mathscr{C} | x_i \in \{0,1\}, i = 1, \ldots, n\}$. Therefore we know $f(x)$ for $x \in V$ and want to compute an interpolating function $f(x)$ for $x \in \mathscr{C}$.

The multilinear interpolant, $\hat{f}(x)$ is defined recursively by a sequence of linear interpolations in successive dimensions. The first step is to define f by linear interpolation in dimension n:

$$\hat{f}(x_1, \ldots, x_n) = \hat{f}(x_1, \ldots, x_{n-1}, 0)$$
$$+ x_n(\hat{f}(x_1, \ldots, x_{n-1}, 1) - \hat{f}(x_1, \ldots, x_{n-1}, 0)),$$

where the elements on the lefthand side of (6.13.4) are now $(n-1)$-dimensional interpolants. These in turn are inductively defined by successive interpolation on the next lower dimension:

$$\hat{f}(x_1, \ldots, x_l, j_{l+1}, \ldots, j_n) = \hat{f}(x_1, \ldots, x_{l-1}, 0, j_{l+1}, \ldots, j_n)$$
$$+ x_l(\hat{f}(x_1, \ldots, x_{l-1}, 1, j_{l+1}, \ldots, j_n) - \hat{f}(x_1, \ldots, x_{l-1}, 0, j_{l+1}, \ldots, j_n))$$

where the $j_i = 0, 1$ for $i = l+1, \ldots, n$. This scheme ends when each component of $\hat{f}$ is either 0 or 1, in which case the point is in V, and we know the value from the Lagrange interpolation data. This scheme is rather costly, requiring roughly 2^n multiplications to evaluate the interpolation at just one point. The general curvature is also complex and difficult to perceive. These considerations make this a poor method.

We next generalize the simplicial 2-D linear interpolation method above to R^n. The idea is to pick a simplicial subdivision of $\mathscr{C}$ and compute the linear interpolation on each simplex. This sounds difficult, but the following simple scheme computes a piecewise-linear simplicial interpolant.

Suppose that we want to compute $f(x)$ where $x \in [0,1]^n$. We first need to determine the simplex which contains x. To do this, we find the permutation π of the indexes such that

$$0 \le x_{\pi(1)} \le x_{\pi(2)} \le \cdots \le x_{\pi(n)} \le 1. \tag{6.13.6}$$

This is done by sorting the components of x according to the value of each component. The complete procedure is summarized in algorithm 6.5, where e^i denotes the vector with 1 in component i and zero elsewhere:

Algorithm 6.5   Multidimensional Simplicial Interpolation

Objective: Given x on V, compute $f(x)$ for $x \in \mathscr{C}$.

Initialization. Construct the permutation π satisfying (6.13.4). Let $s^0 = (1, \ldots, 1)$, $y_0 = f(s^0)$.

Step 1. For $i = 1, \ldots, n$, $s^i = s^{i-1} - e^{\pi(i)}$ and $y_i = y_{i-1} + (1 - x_{\pi(i)})(f(s^i) - f(s^{i-1}))$.

Step 2. Report y_n as the value of $f(x)$ and STOP.

This procedure can be adapted, through linear transformations, to compute the simplicial interpolant at any point x in any hypercube. Because of the linearity of the approximation, interpolants of different hypercubes will match at common points, resulting in a continuous interpolation globally. The simplicial interpolation method is less costly than multilinear interpolation and has simpler curvature.

6.14 Neural Networks

The previous approximation procedures are based on linear combinations of polynomial and trigonometric functions. Neural networks use simple but powerful nonlinear approximation schemes. Below we state the important definitions and results.

Neural Network Functional Form

For our purposes, a neural network is a particular type of functional form used in approximation. A *single-layer* neural network is a function of the form

$$F(x;\beta) \equiv h\left(\sum_{i=1}^{n} \beta_i g(x_i)\right), \tag{6.14.1}$$

where $x \in R^n$ is the vector of inputs and h and g are scalar functions. A common form assumes that $g(x) = x$, reducing (6.14.1) to the form $h(\beta^\top x)$. A *single hidden-layer feedforward* network has the form

$$F(x;\beta,\gamma) \equiv f\left(\sum_{j=1}^{m} \gamma_j h\left(\sum_{i=1}^{n} \beta_i^j g(x_i)\right)\right), \tag{6.14.2}$$

where h is called the *hidden-layer activation function*.

   The source of this terminology is displayed in figure 6.11. Figure 6.11b displays (6.14.2). Each input is processed by a node, where each node is some function. The output of each node is then fed to one more node for further processing that produces the output. In figure 6.11a we illustrate the single hidden-layer structure.

Neural Network Approximation

The data for a neural network consists of (y_i, x^i) pairs such that y_i is supposed to be the output of a neural network if x^i is the input. This requirement imposes conditions on the parameter matrix β in (6.14.1) and β and γ in (6.14.2). Indeed, when we use

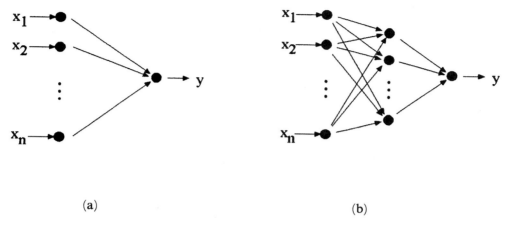

(a)   (b)

Figure 6.11
Neural networks

single-layer neural networks, the objective is to find β to solve

$$\min_{\beta} \sum_j (y_j - F(x^j; \beta))^2,$$

and when we use a single hidden-layer feedforward network, our objective is to find β and γ to solve

$$\min_{\beta, \gamma} \sum_j (y_j - F(x^j; \beta, \gamma))^2.$$

These objectives are just instances of nonlinear least squares fitting. Because of the nonlinearity, we do not have simple formula for the β and γ coefficients. Instead, we must use general minimization methods. Experience also informs us that there often are several local minima.

Neural networks are useful for approximation since they are flexible enough to fit general functions. The power of neural network approximation is indicated by the following theorem of Horni, Stinchcombe and White (1989).

THEOREM 6.14.1 Let G be a continuous function, $G: R \to R$, such that either (1) $\int_{-\infty}^{\infty} G(x)dx$ is finite and nonzero and G is L^p for $1 \le p < \infty$ or (2) G is a *squashing function* $G: R \to [0, 1]$; that is, G is nondecreasing, $\lim_{x\to\infty} G(x) = 1$, and $\lim_{x\to-\infty} G(x) = 0$. Define

$$\Sigma^n(G) = \left\{ g: R^n \to R \mid g(x) = \sum_{j=1}^{m} \beta_j G(w^j \cdot x + b_j), \ b_j, \beta_j \in R^{\cdot}, \right.$$

$$\left. w^j \in R^n, w^j \neq 0, \ m = 1, 2, \cdots \right\}$$

to be the set of all possible single hidden-layer feedforward neural networks, using G as the hidden layer activation function. Let $f: R^n \to R$ be continuous. Then for all $\varepsilon > 0$, probability measures μ, and compact sets $K \subset R^n$, there is a $g \in \Sigma^n(G)$ such that

$$\sup_{x \in K} |f(x) - g(x)| \leq \varepsilon$$

and

$$\int_K |f(x) - g(x)| \, d\mu \leq \varepsilon.$$

The class of functions covered by theorem 6.14.1 is quite broad. The functions that fit (1) in theorem 6.14.1 include all probability density functions with compact support. Note that any squashing function is a cumulative distribution function, and vice versa. A common choice for G is the *sigmoid function*, $G(x) = (1 + e^{-x})^{-1}$. Also note that the form of the functions in $\Sigma^n(G)$ is a simple case of (6.14.2).

Theorem 6.14.1 is a universal approximation result that justifies the use of neural network approximation and helps to explain its success. Note the simplicity of the functional forms; this simplicity makes neural network approximations easy to evaluate. Barron (1993) shows that neural networks are efficient functional forms for approximating multidimensional functions. It is unclear if this efficiency is sufficient compensation for the operational problems of finding a fit. The theoretical development of neural networks is proceeding but is inherently difficult because of the nonlinearity of this approach.

Note the strong similarities between neural networks and the universal approximators in Kolmogorov's theorem. Both proceed by successive application of addition, multiplication, and scalar functions. In both cases the innermost one-dimensional functions are monotonic. However, there are differences. In neural networks the innermost function, $g(x)$, is fixed, whereas there are $2n + 1$ innermost functions in Kolmogorov's representation. Neural networks fit functions by different choices of weights γ_j and β_i^j, whereas the Kolmogorov approximation alters only the $2n + 1$ innermost weights and the $\psi(x)$ function. However, these distinctions are small from a practical point of view, and both methods are quite different from the approach implicit in the Stone-Weierstrass theorem.

6.15 Further Reading and Summary

This chapter has presented basic methods for constructing approximations of functions. These methods use various kinds of data including function values, derivative values, and a priori shape information. Many approximation methods resemble statistical techniques; however, we can do much better than statistical methods typically do because we have control over the values of the independent variables. The major software libraries, such as IMSL and NAG, contain many programs for constructing polynomial, spline, and rational approximations.

Many of the interpolation ideas described above, such as polynomial interpolation, were presented in simple ways which are often ill-conditioned and inefficient. More efficient methods are presented in most numerical analysis texts, such as Atkinson (1989), Rice (1983), and de Boor (1978).

There is a large literature on finite element approximations of multidimensional functions. Burnett (1987) gives a very readable presentation of the basic methods. Because the finite element method is largely aimed at engineers, it is most highly developed for one-, two-, and three-dimensional problems. For higher dimensions, economists will have to adapt existing methods, but the basic ideas will still hold: low-order approximations within elements, simplicial or rectangular, with smoothness conditions across the boundaries of elements.

There is a large literature on shape-preserving splines, much of it spurred on by the demand for efficient computer graphics methods. Rasch and Williamson (1990) present a general discussion and comparison of several shape-preserving schemes in the one-dimensional case. There has also been success in producing shape-preserving interpolants for data over R^2; Costantini and Fontanella (1990) is a recent example. Again this literature is concerned with at most three-dimensional problems, presumably because of the focus on "visually appealing" approximations. Economists need shape-preserving approximation methods for higher dimensions as well.

The sections above have relied on polynomials to approximate functions over an interval. We saw that rational functions were useful in constructing approximations based at a point and had some advantages over polynomial approximations. We can also compute minimax rational approximations of functions over compact intervals. As with Padé approximations rational approximants are often superior for a given number of free parameters. An important difficulty is that rational approximations are not linear functions of the data. The absence of a vector space formulation makes them more cumbersome to compute and make the theory much more difficult. For these reasons rational approximation methods have not been used as much as orthogonal polynomial and piecewise polynomial approximations.

The neural network literature is growing rapidly, but the potential value of neural networks is not clear. White (1992) presents the basic ideas, and universal approximation results, such as those of Barron (1993), Gallant and White (1988), and Hornik et al. (1989, 1990), indicate that neural network approximations can produce efficient approximations. Unfortunately, solving the least squares solution to the fitting problem is quite difficult because of multiple local minima. Golomb (1959) discusses Kolmogorov's theorem.

Exercises

1. Compute the degrees 1, 2, and 3 Taylor expansions for $f(x) = (x^{1/2} + 1)^{2/3}$ near $x_0 = 1$. Compute the log-linear approximation, the log-quadratic approximation, and the log-cubic approximation of f near $x_0 = 1$. Compute the $(1, 1)$ Padé approximation based at $x_0 = 1$. Compare the quality of these approximations for $x \in [0.2, 3]$.

2. Compute the condition number of the Vandermonde matrix for $x_i = i/n$ for $n = 3, 5, 10, 20, 50$.

3. Write a program to compute the coefficients of the Lagrange interpolating polynomial $p(x)$ given $\{y_i, x_i\}_{i=1}^n$ data. Write another program that uses those coefficients and computes $p(x)$. Use these programs to interpolate the values of $f(x) = x^{1/3}$ on the set $X = \{i/5 | i = 1, 2, 3, 4, 5\}$, and compare $x^{1/3}$ and this interpolant on $[0.1, 0.5]$.

4. Write a program to compute the coefficients of the Hermite interpolating polynomial $p(x)$ given $\{y_i, y_i', x_i\}_{i=1}^n$ data. Write another program that uses those coefficients and computes $p(x)$. Apply this to the values of $x^{1/3}$ and its derivatives on $[0.1, 0.5]$ to construct the degree 9 Hermite interpolant on the set $X = \{i/5 | i = 1, 2, 3, 4, 5\}$. Compare $x^{1/3}$, this Hermite interpolant on $[0.1, 0.5]$, and the Lagrange interpolant constructed in exercise 3.

5. Compute the n-term Legendre approximation for $f(x)$ on $[-1, 1]$ for the following cases:

    a. $f(x) = (x + 2)^{.5}$, $n = 3, 4, 5$
    b. $f(x) = (x + 2)^{-2}$, $n = 3, 4, 5$

    In both cases compute the L^∞ and L^2 errors over $[-1, 1]$.

6. Express the orthogonal polynomial family with weighting function 1 on the interval $[a, b]$ in terms of Legendre polynomials. Express the orthogonal polynomial family with weighting function $e^{-(ax+b)}$ on the interval $[d, \infty)$ in terms of Laguerre polynomials. Express the orthogonal polynomial family with weighting function $e^{-(ax^2+bx+c)}$ on $(-\infty, \infty)$ in terms of Hermite polynomials.

7. Compute the linear minmax approximation to e^x on $[0, 1]$. Compare it to the Legendre approximation and the Chebyshev approximation.

8. Compute the upper bound for $\rho_n(f)$ given by Jackson's theorem for $f(x) = x^{1/2}$ on the interval $[0.1, 2.0]$. Compare it to the bound on the interval $[0, 2.0]$.

9. Compute the natural cubic spline approximation to $x^{1/4}$ on $[1, 10]$. Plot L^2 and L^∞ errors against the number of nodes used.

10. Compute tables 6.1 and 6.2 for x^γ for $\gamma = -0.5, -2$, and -5. Also use neural networks to approximate these functions over $[1, 10]$. Plot the errors using equi-spaced Lagrange data.

11. Newton's method uses a sequence of linear approximations to converge to a zero of $f(x) = 0, x \in R$. Develop an algorithm that uses a sequence of $(1,1)$ Padé approximations to solve $f(x) = 0$. Compare the methods' performances for solving $x^2 - 2$ with the initial guess $x = 0$. What are the apparent rates of convergence?

12. Write a program to implement Schumaker's quadratic shape-preserving approximation. Apply it to the function $V(k) = k^\alpha$ on $[0, 10]$ for $\alpha = 0.01, 0.25, 0.80$. Compare the results when you use slope information to the results when you just approximate the slopes. Compare the results with Chebyshev interpolation.

13. Write a program that takes an increasing function $f(x)$ and computes the inverse function. Use Lagrange, Hermite, and shape-preserving interpolation schemes, and test the program on the functions x^3, $\sin \pi x/2$, and e^x on $[0, 2]$ using the points $\{0, 0.5, 1.0, 1.5, 2.0\}$.

14. Let $f(k, l) = (k^{1/2} + l^{1/2})^2$. Compute its quadratic Taylor expansion around $(1, 1)$. Plot the error over $[0, 2.5] \times [0, 2.5]$.

15. Construct an interpolant of the function $V(x, y) = (x^\alpha + y^\alpha)^{\gamma+1}/(\gamma + 1)$ on $[a, b] \times [c, d]$ using the triangular element approach. Let $\alpha = 0.1, 0.3, 0.5, 0.9$, $\gamma = -0.5, -1.1, -3, -5$, $a, c = 0.1, 1, 1$, $b = 2a$, $10a$, $d = 2c, 10c$.

16. Let

$$V(k_1, k_2, k_3) = (k_1 + k_2 + k_3)^{1/4} - (k_1 - k_2)^2 - (k_1 - 3k_3)^2 - (k_2 - 2k_3)^2.$$

Compute $V(k)$ on the uniform grid of 11^3 points on $[1, 3]^3$. Use these points to compute neural network approximations and Chebyshev approximations for $V(k)$. Which type of approximation does best (smallest error in supremum norm) per floating operation?

17. Consider a two-person, two-good exchange economy with total endowment of each good being $(1, 1)$. Assume agent one's utility function is $x^{1/3}y^{2/3}$ and agent two's utility function is $\sqrt{x} + 2\sqrt{y}$. Approximate the contract curve with (a) a Chebyshev polynomial, (b) a cubic spline, and (c) a Schumaker quadratic shape-preserving spline.

7 Numerical Integration and Differentiation

Numerical evaluation of a definite integral is a frequent problem encountered in economic modeling. If a firm pays a continuous stream of dividends, $d(t)$, and the interest rate is r, then the present value of the dividends equals $\int_0^\infty e^{-rt} d(t)\, dt$. If the random variable X is distributed $N(0, 1)$, then the expectation of $f(X)$ is $(2\pi)^{-1/2} \int_{-\infty}^\infty f(x) e^{-x^2/2}\, dx$. In Bayesian statistics, if one's prior belief over the parameter space, Θ, has density $f(\theta)$, if the data are X, and if $g(X|\theta)$ is the density of X conditional on θ, then the posterior mean belief is $(\int \theta g(X|\theta) f(\theta) d\theta)/(\int g(X|\theta) f(\theta)\, d\theta)$. Not only do integrals arise naturally in formulations of economic and econometric problems, but we will often introduce them as part of our numerical procedures. For example, computing the coefficients of orthogonal polynomial approximations in chapter 6 involves computing integrals.

The general problem in numerical integration, also called *quadrature* or *cubature*, is to compute $\int_D f(x)\, dx$ where $f: R^n \to R$ is an integrable function over the domain $D \subset R^n$. All numerical integration formulas use a finite number of evaluations of the integrand, f, and use a weighted sum of those values to approximate $\int_D f(x)\, dx$.

We examine several methods in this chapter and the next two. The reason for our studying quadrature so intensively is that analysts typically will have to choose among several alternatives. The most generally applicable methods are slow. Alternative methods are very efficient, but they require strong conditions on the integrand. Knowing when one can use the efficient methods can improve running times by orders of magnitude. Also analysts will frequently code the integration methods themselves. Since so many decisions must be made by the analyst, he must be aware of the critical mathematical factors. Of course one could economize on thinking and choose a simple method; however, the returns to careful analysis are particularly high in the case of quadrature.

Quadrature methods differ in how they choose where to evaluate the integrand and how to use the evaluations. The first quadrature methods we examine use ideas from approximation and interpolation theory. The second class of methods are called sampling methods and are examined in the next two chapters.

7.1 Newton-Cotes Formulas

The *Newton-Cotes quadrature formulas* use ideas from piecewise-polynomial approximation theory. They evaluate f at a finite number of points, use this information to construct a piecewise-polynomial approximation of f, and then integrate this approximation of f to approximate $\int_D f(x)\, dx$. This section will present various Newton-Cotes formulas and their error properties.

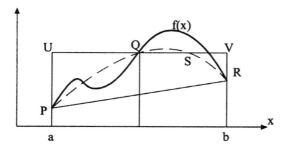

Figure 7.1
Newton-Cotes rules

Consider the graph in figure 7.1. Suppose that f is the solid curve through the points P, Q, and R. The integral $\int_a^b f(x)\, dx$ is the area under the function f and above the horizontal axis. Three approximations are immediately apparent. The box $aUQVb$ approximates f with a constant function equaling f at Q, which is the midpoint of $[a, b]$. The trapezoid $aPRb$ approximates f with a straight line through points P and R. The area under the broken curve $PQSR$ approximates f with a parabola through P, Q, and R. These approximations are based on one, two, and three evaluations of f, respectively, which are used to compute interpolating polynomials of degree one, two, and three. This approach yields *Newton-Cotes* quadrature formulas. We will now examine particular cases.

Midpoint Rule

The simplest quadrature formula is the *midpoint rule*, implied by (7.1.1):

$$\int_a^b f(x)\, dx = (b - a)f\left(\frac{a + b}{2}\right) + \frac{(b - a)^3}{24} f''(\xi) \tag{7.1.1}$$

for some $\xi \in [a, b]$. We will express many integration formulas in the fashion of (7.1.1), where the first terms comprise the integration rule and the last term is the error of the integration rule. Hence the midpoint rule is the first term on the RHS of (7.1.1), and the second term is its error term. Equation (7.1.1) is proved by applying Taylor's theorem and the intermediate value theorem. The midpoint rule is the simplest example of an *open rule*, which is a rule that does not use the end points.

This approximation is too coarse to be of value generally. Instead, we break the interval $[a, b]$ into smaller intervals, approximate the integral over each of the smaller intervals, and add those approximations. The result is a *composite rule*. Let $n \geq 1$

be the number of intervals, $h = (b - a)/n$, and $x_j = a + (j - \frac{1}{2})h$, $j = 1, 2, \ldots, n$. Then the *composite midpoint rule* derives from the equation

$$\int_a^b f(x)\, dx = h \sum_{j=1}^n f(x_j) + \frac{h^2(b-a)}{24} f''(\xi) \tag{7.1.2}$$

for some $\xi \in [a, b]$. Notice that the error is proportional to h^2; doubling the number of quadrature nodes will halve the step size h and reduce the error by about 75 percent. Therefore the composite midpoint rule[1] converges quadratically for $f \in C^2$.

Trapezoid Rule

The trapezoid rule is based on the linear approximation of f using only the value of f at the endpoints of $[a, b]$. The trapezoid rule is

$$\int_a^b f(x)\, dx = \frac{b - a}{2} [f(a) + f(b)] - \frac{(b-a)^3}{12} f''(\xi) \tag{7.1.3}$$

for some $\xi \in [a, b]$. The trapezoid rule is the simplest example of a *closed rule*, which is a rule that uses the end points. Let $h = (b - a)/n$, and $x_i = a + ih$, and let f_j denote $f(x_j)$; the composite trapezoid rule is

$$\int_a^b f(x)\, dx = \frac{h}{2} [f_0 + 2f_1 + \cdots + 2f_{n-1} + f_n] - \frac{h^2(b-a)}{12} f''(\xi) \tag{7.1.4}$$

for some $\xi \in [a, b]$,

Simpson's Rule

Piecewise-linear approximation of f in the composite trapezoid rule is unnecessarily coarse if f is smooth. An alternative is to use a piecewise-quadratic approximation of f which uses the value of f at a, b, and the midpoint, $\frac{1}{2}(a + b)$. The result is Simpson's rule over the interval $[a, b]$. Simpson's rule is

$$\int_a^b f(x)\, dx = \left(\frac{b-a}{6}\right) \left[f(a) + 4f\left(\frac{a+b}{2}\right) + f(b) \right] - \frac{(b-a)^5}{2880} f^{(4)}(\xi) \tag{7.1.5}$$

for some $\xi \in [a, b]$.

We next construct corresponding $(n + 1)$-point composite rule over $[a, b]$. Let $n \geq 2$ be an even number of intervals; then $h = (b - a)/n$, $x_j = a + jh$, $j = 0, \ldots, n$,

---

1. The term "composite" is often dropped, and the term "midpoint rule" includes the composite version. The same is true for the rules below.

Table 7.1
Some simple integrals

Rule	Number of points	$\int_0^1 x^{1/4}\,dx$	$\int_1^{10} x^{-2}\,dx$	$\int_0^1 e^x\,dx$	$\int_{-1}^{-1}(x+0.05)^+\,dx$
Trapezoid	4	0.7212	1.7637	1.7342	0.6056
	7	0.7664	1.1922	1.7223	0.5583
	10	0.7797	1.0448	1.7200	0.5562
	13	0.7858	0.9857	1.7193	0.5542
Simpson	3	0.6496	1.3008	1.4662	0.4037
	7	0.7816	1.0017	1.7183	0.5426
	11	0.7524	0.9338	1.6232	0.4844
	15	0.7922	0.9169	1.7183	0.5528
Gauss-Legendre	4	0.8023	0.8563	1.7183	0.5713
	7	0.8006	0.8985	1.7183	0.5457
	10	0.8003	0.9000	1.7183	0.5538
	13	0.8001	0.9000	1.7183	0.5513
Truth		0.80000	0.90000	1.7183	0.55125

and the composite Simpson's rule is

$$S_n(f) = \frac{h}{3}[f_0 + 4f_1 + 2f_2 + 4f_3 + \cdots + 4f_{n-1} + f_n] - \frac{h^4(b-a)}{180} f^{(4)}(\xi) \qquad (7.1.6)$$

for some $\xi \in [a, b]$. The composite Simpson's rule essentially takes three consecutive x_j nodes, uses the interpolating quadratic function to approximate f, and integrates the interpolating quadratic to approximate the integral over that interval.

Notice that by using a locally quadratic approximation to f we have an error of order h^4, whereas the locally linear approximation yields the trapezoidal rule which has error of order h^2. As with any local approximation of smooth functions, higher-order approximations yield asymptotically smaller error.

We illustrate these rules by applying them to integrals with known values. Table 7.1 displays Newton-Cotes approximations for $\int_0^1 x^{1/4}dx$, $\int_1^2 x^{-2}dx$, $\int_0^{10} e^{-x}dx$, and $\int_{-1}^1 \max[0, x + 0.05]\,dx$.

The trapezoid and Simpson rules do fairly well for $\int_0^1 e^x dx$, but thirteen points are needed to get five-digit accuracy for the Simpson rule. Both rules have difficulty with $\int_1^{10} x^{-2}dx$ because the integrand's curvature varies greatly within $[1, 10]$, but both converge with Simpson doing so more rapidly. Similar problems arise with $\int_0^1 x^{1/4}\,dx$ where the integrand is singular at $x = 0$, making the error bounds infinite and hence useless. Both the trapezoid and Simpson rules have difficulty with the integral in the last column because of the kink at $x = -0.05$. If instead the kink were at $x = 0$ as in $\int_{-1}^1 \max(0, x)\,dx$, then any trapezoid rule with an odd number of points would compute the integral exactly. This, however, would be an accident, and the case in table 7.1 is more typical of real life. In general, Simpson's rule does converge in table 7.1 as predicted by theory, but convergence may be quite poor if too few points are used.

Change of Variables Formula and Infinite Integration Domains

The integrals above were defined over finite domains. We will often want to compute integrals with infinite domains. We can adapt Newton-Cotes rules via the change of variables formula to derive integration formulas for some integrals with infinite domains. Since the resulting integral approximations vary substantially in quality, we develop some ideas concerning good choices for the change of variables.

Suppose that we want to integrate $\int_0^\infty f(x)\,dx$. First, we need to be sure that such an integral exists. Such improper integrals are defined by

$$\int_0^\infty f(x)\,dx \equiv \lim_{b\to\infty} \int_0^b f(x)\,dx \tag{7.1.7}$$

whenever the limit exists. The limit may fail to exist because of divergence, as in the case of $\int_0^\infty 1 \cdot dx$, or because of oscillations, as in the case of $\int_0^\infty \sin x\,dx$. The doubly infinite integral is defined by

$$\int_{-\infty}^\infty f(x)\,dx = \lim_{\substack{a\to-\infty \\ b\to\infty}} \int_a^b f(x)\,dx,$$

where the limit is defined if it does not depend on how a and b diverge to $-\infty$ and ∞.

If (7.1.7) exists, then $f(x) \to 0$ as $x \to \infty$. This indicates that we can approximate (7.1.7) by computing $\int_0^b f(x)\,dx$ as long as b is large enough. We can similarly use $\int_a^b f(x)\,dx$ to approximate $\int_{-\infty}^\infty f(x)\,dx$ if b is large and positive, and a large and negative. These are direct, but slow, ways to approximate integrals with infinite domains.

One way to integrate an improper integral is to transform it into an integral with finite bounds. The following theorem facilitates this.

THEOREM 7.1.2 (Change of variables) If $\phi: R \to R$ is a monotonically increasing, C^1 function on the (possibly infinite) interval $[a, b]$, then for any integrable $g(x)$ on $[a, b]$,

$$\int_a^b g(y)\,dy = \int_{\phi^{-1}(a)}^{\phi^{-1}(b)} g(\phi(x))\phi'(x)\,dx. \tag{7.1.8}$$

Equation (7.1.8) is called the *change of variables formula*, since it converts an integral in the variable y into an equivalent one with variable x where y and x are related by the nonlinear relation $y = \phi(x)$. When we refer to a function $\phi(x)$ as a "change of variables," we mean that it satisfies the necessary conditions of theorem 7.1.2.

We can use (7.1.8) to approximate integrals of the form (7.1.7). Suppose that we introduce a change of variables, $x(z)$. If $x(0) = 0$ and $x(1) = \infty$, then theorem 7.1.2 implies

$$\int_0^\infty f(x)\,dx = \int_0^1 f(x(z))\,x'(z)\,dz. \tag{7.1.9}$$

Once we have the new integral defined on $[0, 1]$ we can use any Newton-Cotes formula on this new, equivalent integral.

There are many changes of variables which can be used. The objective is to come up with a $x(z)$ function such that $\int_0^1 f(x(z))\,x'(z)\,dz$ can be easily and accurately computed. One such map is $x(z) = z/(1 - z)$ with derivative $x'(z) = 1/(1 - z)^2$, implying that

$$\int_0^\infty f(x)\,dx = \int_0^1 f\left(\frac{z}{1 - z}\right)(1 - z)^{-2}\,dz. \tag{7.1.10}$$

In this form we see that we may have a problem. As $z \to 1$, the term $(1 - z)^{-2}$ diverges. The divergent terms make it unclear if the error bounds of the Newton-Cotes quadrature rules imply that the Newton-Cotes formulas applied to (7.1.10) converge to the true value of (7.1.10). In general, if we choose the $x(z) = z/(1 - z)$ transformation to approximate (7.1.7), f must be such that $f(x(z))x'(z)$ has some bounded derivatives.

Even with these considerations in mind, $x(z) = z/(1 - z)$ may be a good choice for interesting integrands $f(x)$. Consider the integral $\int_0^\infty e^{-t}t^2\,dt$. The transformation $t = z/(1 - z)$ results in the integral

$$\int_0^1 e^{-z/(1-z)}\left(\frac{z}{1 - z}\right)^2(1 - z)^{-2}\,dz. \tag{7.1.11}$$

The derivative of the integrand in (7.1.11) is

$$-e^{-z/(1-z)}(1 - z)^{-6}z(2z^2 + z - 2), \tag{7.1.12}$$

which converges to 0 as $z \to 1$. Similar calculations show that all derivatives of the integrand of (7.1.11) are bounded on $[0, 1)$. Hence any Newton-Cotes error bound formula applies.

Another example would be the integral

$$\int_{-\infty}^\infty e^{-x^2}f(x)\,dx, \tag{7.1.13}$$

which equals $\sqrt{\pi} E\{f(X)\}$ if $X \sim N(0, \frac{1}{2})$. In this case we need a monotonic, smooth transformation $x: (0, 1) \to (-\infty, \infty)$ such that $x(0) = -\infty$ and $x(1) = \infty$. One candidate for this is $x(z) = \ln(z/(1 - z))$. With its derivative $x'(z) = (z(1 - z))^{-1}$, it replaces (7.1.13) with

$$\int_0^1 e^{-(\ln(z/(1-z)))^2} f\left(\ln\left(\frac{z}{1-z}\right)\right) \frac{dz}{(1-z)z}$$

$$= \int_0^1 \left(\frac{1-z}{z}\right)^{\ln(z/(1-z))} f(\ln(z/(1-z))) \frac{dz}{z(1-z)}. \tag{7.1.14}$$

Again, as long as f is exponentially bounded in its growth, all the derivatives of the integrand in (7.1.14) are bounded.

Not every transformation is appropriate. For example, the map $x(z) = (\ln z/(1 - z))^{1/3}$ also maps $(0, 1)$ onto $(-\infty, \infty)$. However, using it when applying (7.1.8) to (7.1.13) will result in an integral whose integrand has unbounded derivatives.

The change of variable strategy is commonly used to convert a difficult integral into a more manageable one. The best change of variables depends on the context, but the basic objective is always the same: The new form of the integral should be suitable for the application of some integration method.

7.2 Gaussian Formulas

Newton-Cotes formulas use a collection of low-order-polynomial approximations on small intervals to derive piecewise-polynomial approximations to f. Gaussian quadrature instead builds on the orthogonal polynomial approach to functional approximation. All Newton-Cotes rules are of the form

$$\int_a^b f(x)\, dx \doteq \sum_{i=1}^n \omega_i f(x_i) \tag{7.2.1}$$

for some *quadrature nodes* $x_i \in [a, b]$ and *quadrature weights* ω_i. The key feature of Newton-Cotes formulas is that the x_i points are chosen arbitrarily, usually being the uniformly spaced nodes on $[a, b]$, and the ω_i weights are chosen so that if f is locally a low-degree polynomial then the approximation (7.2.1) will be correct. In contrast, Gaussian formulas are constructed by efficient choices of both the nodes and weights. In general, the Gaussian approach is to find points $\{x_i: i = 1, \ldots, n\}$ and weights $\{\omega_i: i = 1, \ldots, n\}$ so as to make the approximation (7.2.1) of $\int f$ a "good" one.

In order to accomplish this, we must define what we mean by a "good" quadrature formula. The criterion we use is *exact integration* for a finite-dimensional collection of functions. More specifically, we choose the weights and nodes so that the approximation is exactly correct when f is a low-order polynomial. The remarkable feature of Gaussian quadrature is that it accomplishes this for spaces of degree $2n - 1$ polynomials using only n nodes and n weights.

Furthermore Gaussian quadrature is more general than (7.2.1). For any fixed nonnegative weighting function $w(x)$ Gaussian quadrature creates approximations of the form

$$\int_a^b f(x)\, w(x)\, dx \doteq \sum_{i=1}^n \omega_i f(x_i) \tag{7.2.2}$$

for some nodes $x_i \in [a, b]$ and positive weights ω_i, and the approximation (7.2.2) is exact whenever f is a degree $2n - 1$ polynomial. Specifically, given a nonnegative function $w(x)$ and the $2n$-dimensional family $\mathscr{F}_{2n-1}$ of degree $2n - 1$ polynomials, we can find n points $\{x_i\}_{i=1}^n \subset [a, b]$, and n nonnegative weights $\{\omega_i\}_{i=1}^n$ such that

$$\int_a^b f(x)\, w(x)\, dx = \sum_{i=1}^n \omega_i f(x_i) \tag{7.2.3}$$

for all $f \in \mathscr{F}_{2n-1}$. The following theorem summarizes the discussion in Davis and Rabinowitz (1984).

THEOREM 7.2.1   Suppose that $\{\varphi_k(x)\}_{k=0}^{\infty}$ is an orthonormal family of polynomials with respect to $w(x)$ on $[a, b]$. Furthermore define q_k so that $\varphi_k(x) = q_k x^k + \cdots$. Let x_i, $i = 1, \ldots, n$ be the n zeros of $\varphi_n(x)$. Then $a < x_1 < x_2 < \cdots < x_n < b$, and if $f \in C^{(2n)}[a, b]$, then

$$\int_a^b w(x) f(x)\, dx = \sum_{i=1}^n \omega_i f(x_i) + \frac{f^{(2n)}(\xi)}{q_n^2 (2n)!}$$

for some $\xi \in [a, b]$, where

$$\omega_i = -\frac{q_{n+1}/q_n}{\varphi_n'(x_i)\, \varphi_{n+1}(x_i)} > 0.$$

Furthermore the formula $\sum_{i=1}^n \omega_i f(x_i)$ is the unique Gaussian integration formula on n nodes that exactly integrates $\int_a^b f(x)\, w(x)\, dx$ for all polynomials in $\mathscr{F}_{2n-1}$.

We can develop a Gaussian quadrature scheme over any interval $[a, b]$ using any weighting function. A key substantive result in theorem 7.2.1 is that Gaussian quadrature uses the zeros of the orthogonal polynomials and that they lie in the interval $[a, b]$. Furthermore the ω_i weights are always positive, avoiding the precision problems of high-order Newton-Cotes formulas. The formulas in theorem 7.2.1 tell us how to compute the necessary nodes and weights. Typically one does not do the computation indicated in theorem 7.2.1. Instead, there are some Gaussian quadrature formulas that are particularly useful, and the values of the nodes and weights are kept in tables.

Gauss-Chebyshev Quadrature

Integrals of the form $\int_{-1}^{1} f(x)(1 - x^2)^{-1/2} \, dx$ have the weighting function $(1 - x^2)^{-1/2}$, which is the weighting function defining Chebyshev polynomials. To evaluate such integrals, we use the *Gauss-Chebyshev quadrature formula*, defined by the formula,

$$\int_{-1}^{1} f(x)(1 - x^2)^{-1/2} \, dx = \frac{\pi}{n} \sum_{i=1}^{n} f(x_i) + \frac{\pi}{2^{2n-1}} \frac{f^{(2n)}(\xi)}{(2n)!} \tag{7.2.4}$$

for some $\xi \in [-1, 1]$, where the quadrature nodes are

$$x_i = \cos\left(\frac{2i - 1}{2n} \pi\right), \qquad i = 1, \ldots, n. \tag{7.2.5}$$

The Gauss-Chebyshev rule is particularly easy because of the constant weight, π/n, for each node and the easy formula for the quadrature nodes. We will see below that integrals of this form arise naturally when solving various functional equations.

We generally will not be computing integrals of the form $\int_{-1}^{1} f(x)(1 - x^2)^{-1/2} dx$; instead, we will often need to compute integrals of the form $\int_{a}^{b} f(x) \, dx$ where the range of integration is $[a, b]$ rather than $[-1, 1]$, and where the weight function, $(1 - x^2)^{-1/2}$, is missing in the integrand. To apply Gauss-Chebyshev quadrature, we use the linear change of variables $x = -1 + 2(y - a)/(b - a)$ to convert the range of integration to $[-1, 1]$, and multiply the integrand by $(1 - x^2)^{-1/2}/(1 - x^2)^{-1/2}$. This identity implies that

$$\int_{a}^{b} f(y) \, dy = \frac{b - a}{2} \int_{-1}^{1} f\left(\frac{(x + 1)(b - a)}{2} + a\right) \frac{(1 - x^2)^{1/2}}{(1 - x^2)^{1/2}} \, dx. \tag{7.2.6}$$

We then use Gauss-Chebyshev quadrature to evaluate the RHS of (7.2.6) producing the approximation

$$\int_a^b f(y)\, dy \doteq \frac{\pi(b-a)}{2n} \sum_{i=1}^n f\left(\frac{(x_i+1)(b-a)}{2}+a\right)(1-x_i^2)^{1/2}, \qquad (7.2.7)$$

where the x_i are the Gauss-Chebyshev quadrature nodes over $[-1,1]$.

Gauss-Legendre Quadrature

Integrals over $[-1,1]$ could use the trivial weighting function, $w(x)=1$, resulting in *Gauss-Legendre quadrature* formula

$$\int_{-1}^1 f(x)\, dx = \sum_{i=1}^n \omega_i f(x_i) + \frac{2^{2n+1}(n!)^4}{(2n+1)!\,(2n)!} \cdot \frac{f^{(2n)}(\xi)}{(2n)!} \qquad (7.2.8)$$

for some $-1 \le \xi \le 1$. The n-point Gauss-Legendre weights, ω_i, and nodes, x_i, are listed in table 7.2 for various n.

A linear change of variables is necessary to apply Gauss-Legendre quadrature to general integrals. In general,

$$\int_a^b f(x)\, dx \doteq \frac{b-a}{2} \sum_{i=1}^n \omega_i f\left(\frac{(x_i+1)(b-a)}{2}+a\right), \qquad (7.2.9)$$

where the ω_i and x_i are the Gauss-Legendre quadrature weights and nodes over $[-1,1]$.

The Gauss-Legendre formula is typical of the rapid convergence of Gaussian quadrature schemes. Applying Stirling's formula, $n! \doteq e^{-n-1}\, n^{n+(1/2)}\, \sqrt{2\pi n}$, to the error term in (7.2.8), we find that the error is bounded above by $\pi 4^{-n} M$, where

Table 7.2
Gauss—Legendre quadrature

N	x_i	ω_i	N	x_i	ω_i
2	0.5773502691	0.1000000000(1)	7	0.9491079123	0.1294849661
3	0.7745966692	0.5555555555		0.7415311855	0.2797053914
	0.0000000000	0.8888888888		0.4058451513	0.3818300505
4	0.8611363115	0.3478548451		0.0000000000	0.4179591836
	0.3399810435	0.6521451548	10	0.9739065285	0.6667134430(−1)
5	0.9061798459	0.2369268850		0.8650633666	0.1494513491
	0.5384693101	0.4786286704		0.6794095682	0.2190863625
	0.0000000000	0.5688888888		0.4333953941	0.2692667193
				0.1488743389	0.2955242247

Source: Stroud and Secrest (1966).
Note: $a(k)$ means $a \times 10^k$. An (x,ω) entry for N means that $\pm x$ are quadrature nodes in the N-point formula, and each gets weight ω.

$$M = \sup_{m} \left[\max_{-1 \le x \le 1} \frac{f^{(m)}(x)}{m!} \right].$$

For many functions, such as analytic functions, M is finite. This bound shows that if M is finite, the convergence of Gauss-Legendre quadrature is of exponential order as the number of quadrature nodes goes to infinity. Since Newton-Cotes formulas are only polynomial in convergence, Gauss-Legendre quadrature is much better when f is C^∞ and its derivatives are tame. The same considerations show that the Gauss-Chebyshev error is also proportional to $4^{-n}M$.

Gauss-Legendre integration can be used to compute discounted sums over finite horizons. For example, suppose that consumption at time t equals $c(t) = 1 + t/5 -7(t/50)^2$, where $0 \le t \le 50$. The discounted utility is $\int_0^{50} e^{-\rho t}u(c(t))\,dt$, where $u(c)$ is the utility function and ρ is the pure rate of time preference. Let $\rho = 0.05$ and $u(c) = c^{1+\gamma}/(1+\gamma)$. We can approximate the discounted utility with (7.2.9). Table 7.3 displays the result for these methods.

Gauss-Hermite Quadrature

Gauss-Hermite quadrature arises naturally because Normal random variables are used often in economic problems. To evaluate $\int_{-\infty}^{\infty} f(x)\,e^{-x^2}dx$ using n points, the Gauss-Hermite quadrature rule uses the weights, ω_i, and nodes, $x_i, i = 1, \ldots, n$, indicated in table 7.4, and is defined by

$$\int_{-\infty}^{\infty} f(x)e^{-x^2}dx = \sum_{i=1}^{n} \omega_i f(x_i) + \frac{n!\sqrt{\pi}}{2^n} \cdot \frac{f^{(2n)}(\xi)}{(2n)!}$$

for some $\xi \in (-\infty, \infty)$.

Gauss-Hermite quadrature will be used in connection with Normal random variables. In particular, if Y is distributed $N(\mu, \sigma^2)$, then

Table 7.3
Errors in computing $-\int_0^{50} e^{-0.05t}\left(1 + \frac{t}{5} - 7\left(\frac{t}{50}\right)^2\right)^{1-\gamma} dt$ with Gauss-Legendre rule

γ:		0.5	1.1	3	10
Truth:		1.24431	0.664537	0.149431	0.0246177
Nodes:	3	5(−3)	2(−3)	3(−2)	2(−2)
	5	1(−4)	8(−5)	5(−3)	2(−2)
	10	1(−7)	1(−7)	2(−5)	2(−3)
	15	1(−10)	2(−10)	9(−8)	4(−5)
	20	7(−13)	9(−13)	3(−10)	6(−7)

Table 7.4
Gauss–Hermite quadrature

N	x_i	ω_i	N	x_i	ω_i
2	0.7071067811	0.8862269254	7	0.2651961356(1)	0.9717812450(−3)
3	0.1224744871(1)	0.2954089751		0.1673551628(1)	0.5451558281(−1)
	0.0000000000	0.1181635900(1)		0.8162878828	0.4256072526
4	0.1650680123(1)	0.8131283544(−1)		0.0000000000	0.8102646175
	0.5246476232	0.8049140900	10	0.3436159118(1)	0.7640432855(−5)
5	0.2020182870(1)	0.1995324205(−1)		0.2532731674(1)	0.1343645746(−2)
	0.9585724646	0.3936193231		0.1756683649(1)	0.3387439445(−1)
	0.0000000000	0.9453087204		0.1036610829(1)	0.2401386110
				0.3429013272	0.6108626337

Source: Stroud and Secrest (1966).
Note: $a(k)$ means $a \times 10^k$. An (x, ω) entry for N means that $\pm x$ are quadrature nodes in the N-point formula, and each gets weight ω.

$$E\{f(Y)\} = (2\pi\sigma^2)^{-1/2} \int_{-\infty}^{\infty} f(y)e^{-(y-\mu)^2/2\sigma^2} dy.$$

However, one must remember that to use Gauss-Hermite quadrature to compute such expectations, it is necessary to use the linear change of variables, $x = (y - \mu)/\sqrt{2}\sigma$, and use the identity

$$\int_{-\infty}^{\infty} f(y)e^{-(y-\mu)^2/(2\sigma^2)} dy = \int_{-\infty}^{\infty} f(\sqrt{2}\,\sigma x + \mu)e^{-x^2}\sqrt{2}\,\sigma \, dx. \tag{7.2.10}$$

Hence the general Gauss-Hermite quadrature rule for expectations of functions of a normal random variable is

$$E\{f(Y)\} = (2\pi\sigma^2)^{-1/2} \int_{-\infty}^{\infty} f(y)e^{-(y-\mu)^2/(2\sigma^2)} dy$$

$$\doteq \pi^{-1/2} \sum_{i=1}^{n} \omega_i f(\sqrt{2}\,\sigma x_i + \mu), \tag{7.2.11}$$

where the ω_i and x_i are the Gauss-Hermite quadrature weights and nodes over $[-\infty, \infty]$.

Examples of using Gauss-Hermite quadrature to compute expectations arise naturally in portfolio theory. For example, suppose that an investor holds one bond which will be worth 1 in the future and equity whose value is Z, where $\ln Z \sim N(\mu, \sigma^2)$. If he consumes his portfolio at a future date and his future utility is $u(c)$, then his expected utility is

Table 7.5
Errors in computing the certainty equivalent of (7.2.12) with Gauss-Hermite rule

Nodes	γ				
	-0.5	-1.1	-2.0	-5.0	-10.0
2	$1(-4)$	$2(-4)$	$3(-4)$	$6(-3)$	$3(-2)$
3	$1(-6)$	$3(-6)$	$9(-7)$	$7(-5)$	$9(-5)$
4	$2(-8)$	$7(-8)$	$4(-7)$	$7(-6)$	$1(-4)$
7	$3(-10)$	$2(-10)$	$3(-11)$	$3(-9)$	$1(-9)$
13	$3(-10)$	$2(-10)$	$3(-11)$	$5(-14)$	$2(-13)$

$$U = (2\pi\sigma^2)^{-1/2} \int_{-\infty}^{\infty} u(1 + e^z)e^{-(z-\mu)^2/2\sigma^2} \, dz \tag{7.2.12}$$

and the certainty equivalent of (7.2.12) is $u^{-1}(U)$.

Table 7.5 displays the errors of various methods applied to (7.2.12) with $\mu = 0.15$ and $\sigma = 0.25$, and $u(c) = c^{1+\gamma}/(1+\gamma)$ for various values of γ. The error that we display is the difference of the certainty equivalent of the approximation and the certainty equivalent of the true value of (7.2.12). We do this so that the error is expressed in economically meaningful terms. Since the certainty equivalent of (7.2.12) with $\mu = 0.15$ and $\sigma = 0.25$ is $2.34\ldots$, the errors in table 7.5 are also roughly half the relative errors.

Gauss-Laguerre Quadrature

Exponentially discounted sums are used often in economic problems. To approximate integrals of the form $I = \int_0^\infty f(x)e^{-x}dx$, we use *Gauss-Laguerre quadrature*. In this case $w(x) = e^{-x}$, and the appropriate weights, ω_i, and nodes, x_i, $i = 1, \ldots, n$, to use in (7.2.2) are listed in table 7.6 for various choices of n. The Gauss-Laguerre formulas are defined by

$$\int_0^\infty f(x)e^{-x} \, dx = \sum_{i=1}^n \omega_i f(x_i) + (n!)^2 \frac{f^{(2n)}(\xi)}{(2n)!}$$

for some $\xi \in [0, \infty)$.

To compute the more general integral, $\int_a^\infty f(y)e^{-ry}dy$, we must use the linear change of variables $x = r(y - a)$, implying that

$$\int_a^\infty e^{-ry}f(y)dy \doteq \frac{e^{-ra}}{r} \sum_{i=1}^n \omega_i f\left(\frac{x_i}{r} + a\right), \tag{7.2.13}$$

Table 7.6
Gauss-Laguerre quadrature

N	x_i	ω_i	N	x_i	ω_i
2	0.5857864376	0.8535533905	7	0.1930436765	0.4093189517
	0.3414213562(1)	0.1464466094		0.1026664895(1)	0.4218312778
3	0.4157745567	0.7110930099		0.2567876744(1)	0.1471263486
	0.2294280360(1)	0.2785177335		0.4900353084(1)	0.2063351446(−1)
	0.6289945082(1)	0.1038925650(−1)		0.8182153444(1)	0.1074010143(−2)
4	0.3225476896	0.6031541043		0.1273418029(2)	0.1586546434(−4)
	0.1745761101(1)	0.3574186924		0.1939572786(2)	0.3170315478(−7)
	0.4536620296(1)	0.3888790851(−1)	10	0.1377934705	0.3084411157
	0.9395070912(1)	0.5392947055(−3)		0.7294545495	0.4011199291
5	0.2635603197	0.5217556105		0.1808342901(1)	0.2180682876
	0.1413403059(1)	0.3986668110		0.3401433697(1)	0.6208745609(−1)
	0.3596425771(1)	0.7594244968(−1)		0.5552496140(1)	0.9501516975(−2)
	0.7085810005(1)	0.3611758679(−2)		0.8330152746(1)	0.7530083885(−3)
	0.1264080084(2)	0.2336997238(−4)		0.1184378583(2)	0.2825923349(−4)
				0.1627925783(2)	0.4249313984(−6)
				0.2199658581(2)	0.1839564823(−8)
				0.2992069701(2)	0.9911827219(−12)

Source: Stroud and Secrest (1966).
Note: $a(k)$ means $a \times 10^k$. An (x, ω) entry for N means that x is a quadrature node in the N-point formula, weight ω.

where the ω_i and x_i are the Gauss-Laguerre quadrature weights and nodes over $[0, \infty]$.

Gauss-Laguerre quadrature can be used to compute the present value of infinitely long streams of utility or profits. For example, suppose that a monopolist faces a demand curve $D(p) = p^{-\eta}$, $\eta > 1$, and has unit cost of $m(t)$ at time t. If unit costs change over time, say $m(t) = a + be^{-\lambda t}$, and the interest rate is r, then discounted profits equal

$$\eta \left(\frac{\eta - 1}{\eta} \right)^{\eta - 1} \int_0^\infty e^{-rt} m(t)^{1-\eta} dt. \tag{7.2.14}$$

In table 7.7 we display the errors of several rules in computing (7.2.14) with $a = 2$, $b = -1$, and $\eta = 0.8$.

The errors in table 7.7 follow the expected pattern. Since we are using the Laguerre formula, the critical piece of the integrand is $m(t)^{1-\eta}$. Gauss-Laguerre integration implicitly assumes that $m(t)^{1-\eta}$ is a polynomial. When $\lambda = 0.05$, $m(t)$ is nearly constant, but when $\lambda = 0.20$, $m(t)^{1-\eta}$ is not constant and becomes less polynomial-like. Therefore it is not surprising that the errors are much larger when $\lambda = 0.20$.

Table 7.7
Errors in computing (7.2.14) with Gauss-Laguerre rule

		$r = 0.05$ $\lambda = 0.05$	$r = 0.10$ $\lambda = 0.05$	$r = 0.05$ $\lambda = 0.20$
Truth:		49.7472	20.3923	74.4005
Nodes:	4	3(−1)	4(−2)	6(0)
	5	7(−3)	7(−4)	3(0)
	10	3(−3)	6(−5)	2(−1)
	15	6(−5)	3(−7)	6(−2)
	20	3(−6)	8(−9)	1(−2)

General Applicability of Gaussian Quadrature

If $f(x)$ is not C^∞, we can still use Gaussian quadrature. Even when the asymptotic rate of convergence for Gaussian quadrature is no better than the comparable Newton-Cotes formula, experience shows that Gaussian formulas often outperform the alternative Newton-Cotes formula. For general integrable functions, we have theorem 7.2.2, proved in Davis and Rabinowitz (1984).

THEOREM 7.2.2 (Gaussian quadrature convergence) If f is Riemann Integrable on $[a, b]$, the error in the n-point Gauss-Legendre rule applied to $\int_a^b f(x)\,dx$ goes to 0 as $n \to \infty$.

We now illustrate Gauss-Legendre integration by applying it to the integrals computed by the Newton-Cotes formulas in table 7.1. We find that the Gauss-Legendre approximations are much better than either the trapezoid or Simpson rules. This is the case even for $\int_{-1}^{1} \max(x + .05, 0)\,dx$ where the integrand has a kink at $x = -0.05$ and is not even C^1. The four-point formula computes $\int_0^1 e^x\,dx$ with five-digit accuracy. This is not surprising, for e^x is a very well-behaved integrand.

Interpolatory Rules

The formulas investigated above used values of $f(x)$, the integrand. We next investigate rules that also use derivatives of $f(x)$ to approximate $\int_a^b f(x)\,dx$. These rules, known as *interpolatory quadrature rules*, take the form

$$\int_a^b f(x)w(x)\,dx \doteq \sum_{i=1}^{n} \sum_{j=0}^{m} \omega_{ij} f^{(j)}(x_i), \tag{7.2.15}$$

where the x_i are the nodes and the ω_{ij} are the weights for the various derivatives. This generalizes the standard Gaussian form where $m = 0$ implicitly. We generally choose the nodes and weights so that the rule correctly integrates low-order polynomials. A formula of form (7.2.15) is a *degree l interpolatory rule* if it exactly integrates all polynomials of degree l and less. To determine these rules, we need to solve a system of nonlinear equations that expresses these exactness requirements.

For example, suppose that we want to derive a degree 11 interpolatory rule for $[-1, 1]$ which uses three points. We examine a formula of the form

$$\hat{I}(f) \equiv \omega_0 f(0) + \omega_1 (f(-x) + f(x))$$

$$+ \omega_2 (f'(-x) - f'(x))$$

$$+ \omega_3 (f''(-x) + f''(x))$$

$$+ \omega_4 f''(0), \tag{7.2.16}$$

where the six unknown parameters are the nodal distance, x, and the five weights, $\omega_i, i = 0, \ldots, 4$. Note that $\hat{I}(x^m) = 0 = \int_{-1}^{1} x^m \, dx$ for any odd m and for any values of the ω parameters. To determine the six parameters in (7.2.16), we impose the six conditions $\hat{I}(x^m) = I(x^m)$ for $m = 0, 2, 4, 6, 8, 10$, resulting in six nonlinear equations in six unknowns. Fortunately there is a real-valued solution, which is

$$x = 0.81444, \quad \omega_0 = 0.93337, \quad \omega_1 = 0.53332,$$

$$\tag{7.2.17}$$

$$\omega_2 = -0.03116, \quad \omega_3 = 0.00411, \quad \omega_4 = 0.02213.$$

To test the quality of the resulting formula, we apply it to three functions. Table 7.8 compares the error of our interpolatory formula with the errors of the five point (degree 9) and six-point (degree 11) Legendre formulas applied to integrals of $\cos 3x$, e^{3x}, and $(x + 1.1)^{1/2}$. We see that the degree 11 interpolatory rule defined by (7.2.16) and (7.2.17) is better than the degree 9 Legendre rule and close to the degree 11 Legendre rule, even though the interpolatory rule uses f at only 3 points.

At first, derivative rules may not appear to offer any advantages, since computing derivatives often involve substantial extra computation. In fact, if one uses finite dif-

Table 7.8
Interpolatory rule errors

$f(x)$	$\cos 3x$	e^{3x}	$(x + 1.1)^{1/2}$
Interpolatory rule	1.9(−6)	2.6(−6)	1.2(−4)
Five-point Legendre rule	4.0(−5)	5.7(−5)	3.6(−4)
Six-point Legendre rule	7.0(−7)	9.6(−7)	4.7(−5)

ferences to evaluate derivatives, then interpolatory quadrature rules are not advantageous. However, computing a derivative may be much cheaper than computing a function value, particularly, if we can use automatic differentiation. Interpolatory rules are not used much, but as automatic differentiation software becomes more common, these rules may gain in popularity.

7.3   Singular Integrals

We have focused on integrals with bounded integrands and used error formulas that assume that the integrand's derivatives are also bounded. In this section we consider $\int_0^1 f(x)\,dx$ where either f or f' is unbounded on $[0, 1]$. Without loss of generality we can assume that the singular point of f is $x = 1$; otherwise, if there is a singularity at $a \in (0, 1)$, we separately consider terms in the equivalent sum $\int_0^a f(x)\,dx + \int_a^1 f(x)\,dx$. In all cases we assume that $\int_0^1 f(x)\,dx$ exists and is finite, facts that one must establish independent of any numerical computations.

Ignore the Singularities

We can often just use the standard Newton-Cotes or Gaussian rules. The following theorem makes a precise statement concerning this approach.

THEOREM 7.3.1   If there is a continuous monotonically increasing $g: [0, 1] \to R$ such that $\int_0^1 g(x)\,dx < \infty$ and $|f(x)| \le g(x)$ on $[0, 1]$, then Newton-Cotes rules (in which we set $f(1) = 0$ to avoid the singular value) and the Gauss-Legendre quadrature rule converge to $\int_0^1 f(x)\,dx$ as $n \to \infty$.

Proof   See Davis and Rabinowitz (1984, pp. 180–82), and citations therein.   ■

Our examples in table 7.1 included the integral $\int_0^1 x^{1/4}\,dx$ which is singular at $x = 0$. The trapezoid and Simpson rules do fairly well, but not as well as for non-singular integrals. The Gauss-Legendre approximations are very good even for handling the singularity in $x^{1/4}$ at 0 and the high curvature of x^{-2} over $[1, 10]$.

The major problem with using standard methods is that the convergence is generally much slower. In fact the standard error formulas are worthless, since $\| f^{(k)} \|_\infty$ is infinite for $k \ge 1$ for singular $f(x)$. Hence, if we want to have useful error bounds, we must use methods tailored to deal with the singularity.

Standard Methods Adapted to the Singularity

We can take standard methods of interpolation and orthogonal polynomials and adapt them to a particular singularity. Suppose that we have an integral of the form

$$\int_0^1 f(x) x^{-1/2}\, dx. \tag{7.3.1}$$

If $0 < x_0 < x_1 < \cdots < x_n \le 1$ are the $n+1$ fixed quadrature nodes, we can derive rules that will exactly integrate any degree n polynomial. For $n = 1$, $x_0 = 1/4$, and $x_1 = 3/4$, we are looking for weights w_1, w_2 such that

$$w_1 + w_2 = \int_0^1 x^{-1/2} \cdot 1\, dx = 2,$$
$$\tfrac{1}{4} w_1 + \tfrac{3}{4} w_2 = \int_0^1 x^{-1/2} \cdot x\, dx = \tfrac{2}{3}. \tag{7.3.2}$$

This linear system has the solution $w_1 = 5/3$ and $w_2 = 1/3$, which implies the rule

$$\int_0^1 f(x) x^{-1/2}\, dx \doteq \frac{5}{3} f\left(\frac{1}{4}\right) + \frac{1}{3} f\left(\frac{3}{4}\right). \tag{7.3.3}$$

In general, this approach will lead to extensions of Newton-Cotes to this singularity. Similarly one could view $x^{-1/2}$ as a weighting function over $[0, 1]$ and construct an orthogonal polynomial family and corresponding Gaussian quadrature rules. This approach has been applied to several kinds of singularities; see the references in Davis and Rabinowitz (1984). The weakness of this strategy is that one must derive the quadrature formulas anew for each different singularity. However, this would be a fixed, one-time cost, well worth the effort if it reduced the marginal cost of evaluating a common singular integral.

Change of Variables

A singularity can sometimes be eliminated by a change of variable. For example,

$$\int_0^1 x^{-1/p} f(x)\, dx = p \int_0^1 y^{p-2} f(y^p)\, dy \tag{7.3.4}$$

eliminates the singularity at $x = 0$ with the change of variables $y^p = x$. Note that the second integral has no singularity for $p \ge 2$ as long as f has no singularities. Also the change of variables $y^q = x$ implies that

$$\int_0^1 x^{p/q} f(x)\, dx = q \int_0^1 y^{p+q-1} f(y^q)\, dy, \tag{7.3.5}$$

which eliminates the singular contribution of $x^{p/q}$ at zero if $p + q - 1 > 0$.

One example of this approach is the computation of Chebyshev coefficients. It is convenient to use the change of variables $x = \cos\theta$, which leads to the identity

$$\int_{-1}^{1} \frac{f(x) T_n(x)}{\sqrt{1 - x^2}} \, dx = \int_{0}^{\pi} f(\cos \theta) \cos n\theta \, d\theta. \tag{7.3.6}$$

The first integral's integrand diverges at both $x = -1$ and $x = 1$. The second integral in (7.3.6) is much better behaved since it has no singularities, and this is the preferred way to compute Chebyshev coefficients.

These devices will often deal satisfactorily with singularities in integrals. There are no general rules for singular integrals; one should always be looking for clever transformations that eliminate or tame the singularity.

7.4 Adaptive Quadrature

The fact that a quadrature formula will converge for large N is comforting, but in actual problems the analyst must decide on how many points to use. It is difficult to say how many points suffice to get a good approximation before one begins to compute an integral. For example, if f is monotonically increasing and its high-order derivatives are small, Gaussian rules with few points will likely suffice. If instead f is oscillatory, many points will be needed. For many complicated functions, one will not know whether f is easy or difficult to integrate. Unless one knows f to be well-behaved, one must be prepared to deal with difficult integrands.

To deal with poorly behaved integrands or integrands about which we know little, we use *adaptive rules*. An adaptive rule takes a simple rule and progressively refines it until the estimates don't change "much." Simple examples include the trapezoid and Simpson rules where we first use an interval size h, then $h/2$, then $h/4$, and so forth, proceeding until the approximations appear to be converging. Such rules are robust and recommended if one does not know much about the shape of f. Unfortunately, these rules are conservative and relatively costly to use. The reader who feels he needs such procedures should consult Davis and Rabinowitz (1984). Also QUADPACK, described in Piessens et al. (1983), is an integration package that contains many such routines. However, one should first try to see if Newton-Cotes or Gaussian rules are applicable because the savings can be substantial.

7.5 Multidimensional Quadrature

If we only had to deal with one-dimensional integrals, the choice of method would not be of great importance. However, many interesting problems in economics involve the integration of multidimensional functions. Unfortunately, many economists appear to believe that Monte Carlo integration (a method we examine in the next chapter) is the only practical way to do multidimensional integration. In this section and in chapter 9, we will consider procedures for multidimensional integration, many of which often dominate Monte Carlo integration for integrals arising in economics.

One approach is to directly extend the one-dimensional methods via product rules. This approach yields formulas that require a rapidly growing number of function evaluations as the dimension increases. Fortunately many of the ideas used in one-dimensional quadrature can be applied to multidimensional integrals without incurring the "curse of dimensionality"; we will describe those methods in the sections below. For high-dimension problems, we often switch to sampling methods, which will be discussed in the next two chapters.

Product Rules

Suppose that we want to compute $\int_{[-1,1]^d} f(x)\, dx$. We can form product rules based on any one-dimensional quadrature rule. Let x_i^l, ω_i^l, $i = 1, \ldots, m$, be one-dimensional quadrature points and weights in dimension l from a Newton-Cotes rule or the Gauss-Legendre rule. The *product rule* approximates the integral $\int_{[-1,1]^d} f(x)\, dx$ with the sum

$$\sum_{i_1=1}^{m} \cdots \sum_{i_d=1}^{m} \omega_{i_1}^1 \omega_{i_2}^2 \cdots \omega_{i_d}^d f(x_{i_1}^1, x_{i_2}^2, \ldots, x_{i_d}^d). \tag{7.5.1}$$

We can also use this idea for any Gaussian quadrature formula. If $w^l(x)$ is a scalar weighting function in dimension l, let

$$W(x) \equiv W(x_1, \ldots, x_d) = \prod_{l=1}^{d} w^l(x_l) \tag{7.5.2}$$

be a d-dimensional weighting function. Then the integral $\int_{[-1,1]^d} f(x) W(x)\, dx$ can be computed using (7.5.1) where the $\omega_{i_l}^l$ and $x_{i_l}^l$ choices are the weights and nodes for the one-dimensional formula for the weighting function $w^l(x)$.

A difficulty of this approach is that the number of functional evaluations is m^d for a d-dimensional problem if we take m points in each direction. Notice that as d increases, the amount of work rises exponentially—the "curse of dimensionality." This exponential growth in cost restricts product rules to low-dimension integrals. Product versions of Newton-Cotes formulas are particularly limited, for more points are required in each dimension with Newton-Cotes than Gaussian quadrature to attain a target level of accuracy.

Monomial Formulas: A Nonproduct Approach

The reason for the exponential growth rate for product formulas is that they are exactly integrating tensor product bases of function. We next use the Gaussian idea of finding a rule that exactly integrates a family of polynomials, but we focus on a smaller family, such as the set of complete polynomials, to determine the rule's nodes and weights. This approach yields *monomial* rules.

Consider the case of degree l monomials over $D \subset R^d$. A monomial rule uses N points $x^i \in D$ and associated weights, ω_i, so that

$$\sum_{i=1}^{N} \omega_i p(x^i) = \int_D p(x)\, dx \tag{7.5.3}$$

for each polynomial $p(x)$ of total degree l; recall that $\mathcal{P}_l$ was defined in chapter 6 to be the set of such polynomials. Any such formula is said to be *complete for degree l*, or, a *degree l formula* for short. For the case $l = 2$, this implies the following system of monomial equations:

$$\sum_{i=1}^{N} \omega_i = \int_D 1 \cdot dx,$$

$$\sum_{i=1}^{N} \omega_i x_j^i = \int_D x_j\, dx, \qquad j = 1, \ldots, d, \tag{7.5.4}$$

$$\sum_{i=1}^{N} \omega_i x_j^i x_k^i = \int_D x_j x_k\, dx, \qquad j, k = 1, \ldots, d.$$

While the system (7.5.4) is easy to express, the algebra associated with its analysis is more problematic than in the one-dimensional case. Since there are $1 + d + \frac{1}{2}d(d+1)$ basis elements of $\mathcal{P}_2$, we have $1 + d + \frac{1}{2}d(d+1)$ equations in (7.5.4). The unknowns are the N weights ω_i and the N nodes x^i each with d components, yielding a total of $(d+1)N$ unknowns. If $(d+1)N$ exceeds $1 + d + \frac{1}{2}d(d+1)$, we would expect there to be solutions, but given the nonlinearity in our system, that is not guaranteed. Furthermore there may be many solutions. As we increase l, the problems only increase.

Solutions are known for some simple cases. Recall that $e^j \equiv (0, \ldots, 1, \ldots, 0)$ where the "1" appears in column j. One rule that uses $2d$ points and exactly integrates all elements of $\mathcal{P}_3$ over $[-1, 1]^d$ is

$$\int_{[-1,1]^d} f \doteq \omega \sum_{i=1}^{d} (f(ue^i) + f(-ue^i)), \tag{7.5.5}$$

where

$$u = \left(\frac{d}{3}\right)^{1/2}, \quad \omega = \frac{2^{d-1}}{d}.$$

For $\mathscr{P}_5$ the following scheme works:

$$\int_{[-1,1]^d} f \doteq \omega_1 f(0) + \omega_2 \sum_{i=1}^{d} (f(ue^i) + f(-ue^i))$$

$$+ \omega_3 \sum_{\substack{1 \le i < d, \\ i < j \le d}} (f(u(e^i \pm e^j)) + f(-u(e^i \pm e^j))), \tag{7.5.6}$$

where

$$\omega_1 = 2^d (25d^2 - 115d + 162), \quad \omega_2 = 2^d (70 - 25d),$$

$$\omega_3 = \frac{25}{324} 2^d, \quad u = \left(\frac{3}{5}\right)^{1/2}.$$

Unfortunately, these weights get large and are of mixed sign for $d \ge 3$, both undesirable features for quadrature formulas. This is typical of simple monomial rules.

Another scheme for $\mathscr{P}_5$ on $[-1, 1]^2$ is the Radon seven-point formula:

$$\int_{[-1,1]^2} f(x, y)\, dx\, dy = \omega_1 f(P_1)$$

$$+ \omega_2[f(P_2) + f(P_3) + f(P_4) + f(P_5)]$$

$$+ \omega_3[f(P_6) + f(P_7)], \tag{7.5.7}$$

where

$$P_1 = (0, 0),$$

$$P_2, P_3, P_4, P_5 = (\pm s, \pm t), \quad s = \sqrt{\frac{1}{3}}, \quad t = \sqrt{\frac{3}{5}},$$

$$P_6, P_7 = (\pm r, 0), \quad r = \sqrt{\frac{14}{15}},$$

$$\omega_1 = \frac{8}{7},$$

$$\omega_2 = \frac{5}{9},$$

$$\omega_3 = \frac{20}{63}.$$

This rule exactly integrates all elements of $\mathscr{P}_5$ with positive weights.

Despite the weaknesses of these examples, there is theoretical evidence that the monomial approach has potential. Tchakaloff's theorem and its extension by Mysovskikh tell us that there are good quadrature formulas.

THEOREM 7.5.1 (Tchakaloff) Let B be a closed, bounded set in R^2 with positive area. Then there exists at least one collection of $N \le \frac{1}{2}(m+1)(m+2)$ points in B, $P_1, \ldots, P_N$, and N positive weights, $\omega_1, \ldots, \omega_N$, such that

$$\int_B f(x,y)\, dx\, dy = \sum_{i=1}^{N} \omega_i f(P_i)$$

for all f polynomial in x, y of total degree $\le m$.

In the following theorem a *multi-index* α is a vector of nonnegative integers $(\alpha_1, \ldots, \alpha_d)$; the norm of the multi-index α, $|\alpha|$, equals the sum of the components, $\sum_{i=1}^{d} \alpha_i$. For $x \in R^d$ the term x^α is shorthand for the monomial $x_1^{\alpha_1} \cdots x_d^{\alpha_d}$.

THEOREM 7.5.2 (Mysovskikh) Let $w(x)$ be a nonnegative weighting function on $D \subset R^d$ such that each moment

$$\int_D w(x) x_1^{i_1} \cdots x_d^{i_d} dx_1 \cdots dx_d$$

exists for $i_1, \ldots, i_d \ge 0$, $i_1 + \cdots + i_d \le m$. Then, for some $N \le (m+d)!/(m!d!)$, there exists N positive weights, ω_i, and N nodes, x^i, such that for each multi-index $|\alpha| \le m$,

$$\int_D w(x) x^\alpha\, dx = \sum_{i=1}^{N} \omega_i (x^i)^\alpha.$$

The problem with the Tchakaloff and Mysovskikh theorems is that they are purely existential, giving us no efficient procedure to find such points and weights. However, we should not be deterred by their nonconstructive nature. The Tchakaloff and

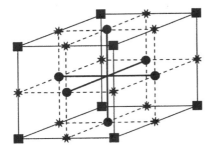

Figure 7.2
Nodes for monomial rules over $[-1, 1]^3$

Mysovskikh theorems essentially reduce the problem of finding good quadrature formulas to solving a set of nonlinear equations, (7.5.3). While that system may have multiple solutions over any particular domain, and some solutions may use negative weights, these theorems tells us that good solutions exist and will (presumably) be found if we search through all the solutions to the monomial equations. If there are better formulas than guaranteed by Tchakaloff and Mysovskikh, we will also find them. For example, Radon's seven-point formula is much better than what is guaranteed by Tchakaloff's theorem.

If one is willing to impose conditions on the points and weights, then one can sometimes derive monomial formulas in a straightforward fashion. Stroud (1971) examines symmetric domains and imposes symmetry restrictions that considerably simplify the monomial equations. There is no assurance that such solutions exist, but this approach often yields good formulas.

The first step in constructing monomial formulas is choosing a set of quadrature nodes. Figure 7.2 illustrates some alternatives for the case of the three-dimensional cube. We often choose a set of points with some symmetry properties. We would usually include the center of the cube. A seven-point formula may use the center plus the six points that are the centers of the cube's faces, the points which are circles in figure 7.2. A nine-point formula might use the center and the eight vertices, the square points in figure 7.2. A twelve-point formula might use the centers of the cube's edges, the stars in figure 7.2. Other formulas might use some combinations of the squares, circles, and stars. Of course, if we use all 27 points (including the center) in figure 7.2, then we would have the collection of points used by the three-dimensional product formula with three points in each dimension. Once we have chosen a collection of points, the weights are chosen so that some important collection of functions is integrated exactly.

We will review a few examples now. They are taken from Stroud (1971) which contains a large collection of such formulas. We first consider integrals of the form

$$\int_{R^d} f(x) e^{-\Sigma_{i=1}^d x_i^2} dx \tag{7.5.8}$$

which arise naturally when computing expectations of functions of multivariate normal random variables. The following is a degree 3 formula using $2d$ points for the integral (7.5.8):

$$\frac{V}{2d} \sum_1^d f(\pm re^i), \qquad r = \sqrt{\frac{d}{2}}, \quad V = \pi^{d/2}. \tag{7.5.9}$$

The following formula is also degree 3 but uses 2^d points:

$$\frac{V}{2^d} \sum f(\pm re^1, \ldots, \pm re^d), \qquad r = \sqrt{\frac{1}{2}}, \quad V = \pi^{d/2}. \tag{7.5.10}$$

The following is a degree 5 rule using $2d^2 + 1$ points:

$$Af(0,\ldots,0) + B \sum_{i=1}^d (f(re^i) + f(-re^i)) + D \sum_{i=1}^{d-1} \sum_{j=i+1}^d f(\pm se^i \pm se^j), \tag{7.5.11}$$

where

$$r = \sqrt{1 + \frac{1}{2}d}, \quad s = \sqrt{\frac{1}{2} + \frac{1}{4}d}, \quad V = \pi^{d/2},$$

$$A = \frac{2}{d+2} V, \quad B = \frac{4-d}{2(d+2)^2} V, \quad D = \frac{V}{(d+2)^2}.$$

For $\int_{[-1,1]^d} f(x)$ we have the rule

$$Af(0,\ldots,0) + B \sum_{i=1}^d (f(re^i) + f(-re^i)) + D \sum_{x \in C} f(x), \tag{7.5.12}$$

where $C = \{x \mid \forall i (x_i = \pm 1)\}$ and

$$r = \sqrt{\frac{2}{5}}, \quad V = 2^d, \quad A = \frac{8 - 5d}{9} V, \quad B = \frac{5}{18} V, \quad D = \frac{1}{9}.$$

This is a degree 5 rule using $2^d + 2d + 1$ points.

These formulas are just a few examples of what is available. Stroud (1971) displays many other formulas and discusses methods for generating such formulas.

Multivariate Changes of Variables

All the formulas above assume that integrals are in some standard form. Most integrals that arise in economic contexts are not in these canonical forms. We must transform them into integrals in the canonical forms with a change of variables transformation. The key theorem is the following one:

THEOREM 7.5.3 (Change of variables in R^n)   Assume that $\Phi: X \subset R^n \to R^n$ is C^1 and that there is a C^1 inverse map $\Phi^{-1}: Y \subset R^n \to X$ where $Y = \Phi(X)$ and Y and X are open. If f is integrable on X, then

$$\int_Y f(y)\, dy = \int_X f(\Phi(x))|\det J(\Phi)(x)|\, dx, \tag{7.5.13}$$

where $J(\Phi)(x)$ is the Jacobian of Φ at x.

Change of variable formulas have many uses. For example, they can be used to convert nonstandard integration domains into the canonical domains used by the methods above. For example, consider the integral

$$\int_a^b \int_c^x f(x, y)\, dy\, dx. \tag{7.5.14}$$

The domain of integration in (7.5.14) is a trapezoid if $c < a$ or $c > b$, or a "bowtie" region if $a < c$. The change of variable $y = c + (x - c)(z - c)/(b - c)$ converts (7.5.14) into

$$\int_a^b \int_c^b f\left(x, c + \frac{(x - c)(z - c)}{(b - c)}\right) \frac{x - c}{b - c}\, dz\, dx,$$

which has a rectangular domain to which we can apply standard formulas.

A particularly important application of theorem 7.5.3 arises in connection with multivariate normal random variables. To evaluate a multivariate normal expectation, we use the Cholesky decomposition of the variance-covariance matrix together with a linear change of variables. Specifically, suppose that $Y \sim N(\mu, \Sigma)$, and we want to compute $E\{f(Y)\}$. First, we note that

$$E\{f(Y)\} = |\Sigma|^{-1/2}(2\pi)^{-n/2} \int_{R^n} f(y) \exp[-\tfrac{1}{2}(y - \mu)^\top \Sigma^{-1}(y - \mu)]\, dy$$

Second, Σ has a Cholesky decomposition since Σ is symmetric positive definite. Let $\Sigma = \Omega\Omega^\top$ be that decomposition. Since $\Sigma^{-1} = (\Omega^{-1})^\top\Omega^{-1}$, the linear change of variables $x = \Omega^{-1}(y-\mu)/\sqrt{2}$ implies that $y = \sqrt{2}\Omega x + \mu$ and that

$$\int_{R^n} f(y)e^{-1/2(y-\mu)^\top\Sigma^{-1}(y-\mu)}\,dy$$

$$= \int_{R^n} f(\sqrt{2}\Omega x + \mu)e^{-\sum_{i=1}^n x_i^2}|\det\Omega|\,2^{n/2}dx \tag{7.5.15}$$

which, is in the form required by (7.5.8).

7.6   Example: Portfolio Problems

In chapter 4 we introduced the general portfolio choice problem. In the examples there we assumed a discrete distribution. We now move to problems with a continuous distribution and use quadrature rules to approximate the integrals that arise when we compute the objective and its derivatives. The portfolio optimization problem with neither transaction costs nor shorting constraints is

$$\max_{\omega_i} E\left\{u\left(\sum_{i=1}^n \omega_i Z_i\right)\right\}$$

$$\text{s.t.} \quad \sum_{i=1}^n p_i(\omega_i - e_i) = 0 \tag{7.6.1}$$

(see section 4.12). Throughout this example we assume the CRRA utility function $u(c) = c^{1+\gamma}/(1+\gamma)$. This example shows both the power and pitfalls of Gaussian quadrature.

We investigate the individual investor problem. To simplify matters, we assume only two assets. Suppose that each asset costs \$1 per unit. Asset 1 is a safe asset with future value R, and the log of the future value of asset 2 is $Z_2 \sim N(\mu, \sigma^2)$. We assume that the initial endowment is $e_1 = W$ and $e_2 = 0$. If the utility function is $u(c)$, we use the substitution $\omega_1 = W - \omega_2$ and let $\omega = \omega_2$ be the choice variable. Then $c = R(W - \omega) + \omega e^z$ and the problem reduces to the unconstrained problem

$$\max_\omega E\{u(R(W-\omega) + \omega e^z)\}.$$

This objective has the derivatives $U'(\omega) = E\{u'(c)(e^z - R)\}$ and $U''(\omega) = E\{u''(c)(e^z - R)^2\}$, where $U(\omega) \equiv E\{u(c)\}$. The objective and its derivatives are integrals that usually must be numerically approximated.

Table 7.9
Portfolio solutions

	Rule				
γ	GH3	GH4	GH5	GH6	GH7
-3	2.75737	2.57563	2.54240	2.53343	2.53035
-4	2.02361	1.95064	1.94533	1.94503	1.94502
-5	1.59369	1.56166	1.56200	1.56210	1.56209

Note: GHn denotes Gauss-Hermite rule with n nodes.

We first compute the value of various portfolios, $U(\omega)$. Without loss of generality, we let $W = 2$. We examine five cases of the utility function, $\gamma = -0.5, -1.1, -2, -5$, and -10. We assume that $(\mu, \sigma) = (0.4, 0.3)$. Recall table 7.5. The integrand examined there, (2.12), is the value of the portfolio here with one unit of each asset with $R = 1$ and $\omega = 1$ as computed by various Gauss-Hermite rules. Table 7.5 reports the certainty equivalent of expected utility and the integration errors, since we want to report these quantities in economically meaningful units. The errors in table 7.5 are small even when we use only a few points.

We next compute the optimal portfolios. We use Newton's optimization method to maximize $U(\omega)$ and use Gauss-Hermite integration to evaluate $U(\omega)$. Table 7.9 indicates the optimal choice of ω for various integration rules and various values for γ. One important detail is that we need to use enough points so that we capture the problem correctly. For example, the two-point rule for $R = 1.1$, $\mu = 0.4$, $\sigma = 0.3$, approximates $U(\omega)$ with

$$\frac{0.9[(2.2 + 0.005\,\omega)^{1+\gamma} + (2.2 + 0.9\omega)^{1+\gamma}]}{1 + \gamma},$$

which is a monotonically increasing function of ω, whereas we know that $U(\omega)$ is concave and eventually decreasing. The three-point rule produces the approximation

$$\frac{0.3(2.2 - 0.2\,\omega)^{1+\gamma} + 1.2(2.2 + 0.4\,\omega)^{1+\gamma} + 0.3(2.2 + 1.4\,\omega)^{1+\gamma}}{1 + \gamma},$$

which does have a maximum. If we are to use quadrature to maximize $U(\omega)$, we clearly need to choose enough integration points so that the objective's approximation has a maximum value.

Table 7.9 displays the maximizing value of ω when we approximate $U(\omega)$ with various Gauss-Hermite formulas. We assume that $\gamma = -3, -4, -5$. The results for $\gamma = -3$ are disturbing, since with $W = 2$ the choice of any $\omega > 2$ implies a positive

Table 7.10
Portfolio Optimization

Iterate	Rule		
	GH3	GH4	GH7
1	0.46001	0.45908	0.45905
2	1.05932	1.05730	1.05737
3	1.51209	1.51197	1.51252
4	1.57065	1.56270	1.56248
5	1.56031	1.56209	1.56209
9	1.56211	1.56209	1.56209

Note: GHn denotes Gauss-Hermite rule with n nodes.

probability that $R(W - \omega) + \omega e^Z$ will be negative, an impermissible case for any CRAA utility function. The reason for the perverse results in table 7.9 is that the Gauss-Hermite rules used did not include enough points to properly treat the extreme cases where e^Z is nearly zero. For $\gamma = -3$ it appears that we would need many points to avoid the problem. This example shows how one must be careful when using quadrature to approximate integrals. These problems are not difficult to avoid; here the problem is that some choices of ω cause singularities to arise, a fact that we should see before attempting to solve this problem. The other solutions are not affected by these considerations because they do not cause any singularities in either the expected utility or expected marginal utility integrals.

We next consider issues associated with the approximation of gradients and Hessians in the portfolio problem. In chapter 4 we discussed the possibility of using low-quality gradients and Hessians to improve performance. We can examine this issue in the portfolio problem, since the objective and any of its derivatives must be computed in an approximate fashion. In table 7.10 we indicate the Newton iterates for the $\gamma = -5$ case using a variety of quadrature rules for the first and second derivatives. Note that the convergence is rapid even when we use the three point formula for U'' (we use GH7 for U'). This one-dimensional example shows that we can save considerably with less precise derivatives. This phenomenon is of even greater value in higher dimensions.

7.7 Numerical Differentiation

Numerical differentiation is used frequently in numerical problems. We use finite-difference approximations of gradients, Hessians, and Jacobians in optimization and nonlinear equation problems. In fact, as emphasized above, these objects are frequently computed numerically, since analytic computation of derivatives is difficult and time-consuming for the programmer. Numerical derivatives are also important in some differential equation methods. In this section we examine the general approach to developing numerical derivative formulas.

The derivative is defined by

$$f'(x) = \lim_{\varepsilon \to 0} \frac{f(x+\varepsilon) - f(x)}{\varepsilon}.$$

This suggests the formula

$$f'(x) \doteq \frac{f(x+h) - f(x)}{h} \tag{7.7.1}$$

to approximate $f'(x)$. How big should h be? It would seem that h should be as small as possible. But here the subtraction problem is obviously problematic for small h.

Suppose that f is computed with accuracy ε; that is, if $\hat{f}(x)$ is the computed value of $f(x)$, then $|f(x) - \hat{f}(x)| \le \varepsilon$. If we apply (7.7.1) to estimate $f'(x)$ but use the computed function $\hat{f}$, then $D(h) = (\hat{f}(x+h) - \hat{f}(x))/h$ is the computed approximation to $f'(x)$, and the error is

$$\left| D(h) - \frac{f(x+h) - f(x)}{h} \right| \le \frac{2\varepsilon}{h}.$$

But by Taylor's theorem,

$$f'(x) = \frac{f(x+h) - f(x)}{h} - \frac{h}{2} f''(\xi)$$

for some $\xi \in [x, x+h]$. Suppose that $M_2 > 0$ is an upper bound on $|f''|$ near x. Then the error in $D(h)$ is bounded above:

$$|f'(x) - D(h)| \le \frac{2\varepsilon}{h} + \frac{h}{2} M_2. \tag{7.7.2}$$

This upper bound is minimized by choosing $h = h^*$ where

$$h^* = 2 \sqrt{\frac{\varepsilon}{M_2}} \tag{7.7.3}$$

and the upper bound equals $2\sqrt{\varepsilon M_2}$.

Two-Sided Differences

Sometimes the one-sided difference will not be accurate enough for our purposes. Our upper bound formula says that for $M_2 \sim 1$ it gives only $d/2$ significant digits for the derivative when we know the function values to d digits. This may not be good enough for some purposes. Since we generally don't want to compute analytic derivatives, we seek better finite-difference formulas.

A better approximation is the two-sided formula

$$f'(x) \doteq \frac{f(x+h) - f(x-h)}{2h}, \tag{7.7.4}$$

which differs from $f'(x)$ by $(h^2/6)f'''(\xi)$ for some $\xi \in [x - h, x + h]$. The round-off error of the approximation error is ε/h, resulting in an upper bound for the error of $(M_3 h^2)/6 + \varepsilon/h$ if M_3 is an upper bound on $|f'''|$ near x. In this case the optimal h is $h^* = \left(3\varepsilon/M_3\right)^{1/3}$ where the upper bound is $2\varepsilon^{2/3} M_3^{1/3} 9^{1/3}$. Using the two-sided formula, we reduce the error from order $\varepsilon^{1/2}$ to order $\varepsilon^{2/3}$. For example, on a twelve-digit machine, the one-sided formula yields (roughly) six-digit accuracy and the two-sided formula yields eight-digit accuracy.

General Three-Point Formulas

We next discuss the general procedure for generating three-point formulas for f' and f''. Suppose that we know $f(x)$ at x_1, x_2, and x_3, and we want to approximate $f'(x_1)$ and $f''(x_1)$ with quadratic accuracy. More specifically, we want to find constants a, b, and c such that

$$af(x_1) + bf(x_2) + cf(x_3) = f'(x_1) + o((x_1 - x_2)^2 + (x_1 - x_3)^2). \tag{7.7.5}$$

By Taylor's theorem, for $i = 2, 3$,

$$f(x_i) = f(x_1) + f'(x_1)(x_i - x_1) + \frac{f''(x_1)(x_i - x_1)^2}{2} + \frac{(x_i - x_1)^3 f'''(\xi_i)}{6}$$

for some ξ_i between x_1 and x_i. If we substitute these expansions into (7.7.5), drop the cubic terms, and then match the coefficients of $f(x_1)$, $f'(x_1)$, and $f''(x_1)$, we find that

$$a + b + c = 0,$$

$$b(x_2 - x_1) + c(x_3 - x_1) = 1, \tag{7.7.6}$$

$$b(x_2 - x_1)^2 + c(x_3 - x_1)^2 = 0,$$

which is a linear system in the unknown a, b, and c. As long as the x_i are distinct, (7.7.6) will have a unique solution for a, b, and c. In the symmetric two-sided case where $x_2 < x_1 < x_3$, and $x_3 - x_1 = x_1 - x_2 = h$, the solution is $a = 0$, $c = -b = 1/(2h)$, the two-point formula. Since we dropped only cubic terms from (7.7.5), this approximation has an error proportional to $(x_1 - x_2)^3 + (x_3 - x_1)^3$. Sometimes, we don't have the symmetric case. Suppose that we instead have x_2 and x_3 positioned to the right of x_1 with $x_2 = x_1 + h$, and $x_3 = x_1 + 2h$. Then $a = -3/(2h)$, $b = 2/h$, and $c = -1/(2h)$ produces a formula with a possibly larger cubic error.

The same approach can be used to compute a three-point formula for $f''(x_1)$ with a quadratic error. Similarly higher-order formulas can be derived for first and second derivatives.

7.8 Software

There is some integration software available in the public domain. Elhay and Kautsky's IQPACK is a Fortran program, available from Netlib, that will compute the Gaussian quadrature and interpolatory quadrature nodes and weights for a large variety of weighting functions. Instead of carrying around a large table of nodes and weights, it is convenient to have a program compute the necessary nodes and weights for a specified interval and weighting function. This generally takes little time and increases the flexibility of a program. QUADPACK, presented in Piessens et al. (1983), is a large package of integration routines for univariate problems, with a focus on adaptive routines.

7.9 Further Reading and Summary

This chapter presented the classical topics in numerical quadrature. Many of the integrals encountered in economics have very well-behaved integrands with many derivatives and simple shape properties such as monotonicity, concavity, and unimodality. This gives economists a variety of formulas to use. The importance of integration in economics will encourage economists to find good integration formulas aimed at integrating the sets of functions they need to integrate.

Davis and Rabinowitz (1984) is the classic in numerical quadrature, but it is a bit dated in its evaluations which are based on technology available at the time. Evans (1993) and Zwillinger (1992) are recent books that cover some recent developments. One new approach is to use the computer to find good integration formulas, substituting computer power for clever algebra and analysis; Cohen and Gismalla (1985, 1986) give some useful examples.

Exercises

1. The least squares orthogonal polynomial approximations discussed in chapter 6 require the evaluation of integrals. Use Gauss-Legendre quadrature to compute the n-term Legendre approximation for x^α on $[a, b]$ for $n = 3, 6, 15$, $\alpha \in \{0.5, 1\}$, $a \in \{0.2, 1\}$, and $b = \{2, 5\}$. In all cases compute the L^∞ and L^2 errors of the polynomial approximations over $[a, b]$.

2. Using the transformation (7.3.7) and appropriate numerical integration rules, compute the n-term Chebyshev least-squares approximation for x^α on $[a, b]$ for $n = 3, 6, 15$, $\alpha \in \{0.5, 1\}$, $a \in \{0.2, 1\}$, and $b \in \{2, 5\}$. In all cases compute the L^∞ and L^2 errors over $[a, b]$.

3. Simpson's rule is based on a local quadratic approximation of the integrand. Derive the corresponding cubic and quartic approximations.

4. Compute three-point approximations for $f'(a)$ and $f''(a)$ using $f(x)$ at $x = a + h, a + 2h$, and $a + 3h$. Next, compute five-point approximations for $f'(a)$ and $f''(a)$ using $f(x)$ at $x = a$, $a \pm h$, and $a \pm 2h$.

5. Compute $\int_0^\infty e^{-\rho t} u(1 - e^{-\lambda t}) \, dt$ for $\rho \in \{0.04, 0.25\}$, $u(c) = -e^{-ac}$, $a \in \{0.5, 1.0, 2.0, 5.0\}$, $\lambda \in \{0.02, 0.05, 0.10, 0.20\}$, using Gauss-Laguerre quadrature. Use changes of variables to find an equivalent integral over $[0, 1)$, and devise a Newton-Cotes approach to the problem. Compare the Gauss-Laguerre and Newton-Cotes approaches for 3, 5, and 10 node formulas.

6. The Tchakaloff and Mysovskikh theorems tell us that good monomial quadrature formulas exist. Write a program that will search for Tchakaloff nodes and weights for hypercubes of dimension d and valid for monomials with total degree m for $m \in \{4, 5\}$, $d \in \{3, 4, 5\}$.

7. Assume that there n individual investors and m assets with asset j paying a random amount Z^j. Let e_j^l denote agent l's endowment of asset j. Suppose that investor l's objective is to maximize expected over utility, $E\{u_l(W)\}$ over final wealth, W. Write a program that reads in data on tastes, returns, and endowments, and computes the equilibrium price of the assets and the expected utility of each investor. First, let $u_l(W) = -e^{-a_l W}$ where $a_l > 0$. Begin with three agents $(n = 3)$, one safe asset paying 1 and two risky assets $(m = 3)$. Assume that the two risky assets are normally distributed with variance-covariance matrix Σ and mean μ; try $\mu^\top = (1.1, 1.2)^\top$ and $\Sigma = \begin{pmatrix} 0.1 & 0.02 \\ 0.02 & 0.2 \end{pmatrix}$. Use Gauss-Hermite quadrature and two-dimensional monomial formulas, and compare the results to the true solution.

8. Compute the discounted utility integral
    $$\int_0^\infty e^{-\rho t} u(c(t), l(t)) \, dt,$$
    where $c(t) = 1 - e^{-\mu_1 t}$, $l(t) = 1 - e^{-\mu_2 t}$, and $u(c, l) = (c^\sigma + l^\sigma)^{(\gamma+1)/\sigma}/(\gamma + 1)$. Let $\gamma \in \{-0.5, -1.1, -3, -10\}$, $\sigma \in \{0.5, 2.0\}$, $\mu_1 \in \{0.05, 0.1, 0.2\}$, $\mu_2 \in \{0.05, 0.1, 0.2\}$, and $\rho = 0.05$. Use both Simpson's rule and Gauss-Laguerre rules. How do the choices of γ, σ, μ_1, and μ_2 affect accuracy?

9. Suppose that a firm's output at time t is $q = 3 - (1 + t + t^2)e^{-t}$, price is $P(q) = q^{-2}$, cost is $C(q) = q^{3/2}$, and the interest rate is 0.1. What are profits over the interval $[0, 10]$? What are profits over $[0, \infty)$? Use several methods for each integral. Which do best?

8 Monte Carlo and Simulation Methods

In this chapter we discuss various sampling methods that are intuitively based on probability ideas. We will use such sampling methods to solve optimization problems, solve nonlinear equations, and compute integrals. These methods are often called *Monte Carlo* methods, but they also include *stochastic approximation, genetic algorithms,* and *simulated annealing.*

Monte Carlo methods have features that distinguish them from most of the methods we have studied in previous chapters. First, they can handle problems of far greater complexity and size than most other methods. The robustness and simplicity of the Monte Carlo approach are its strengths. Second, Monte Carlo methods are intuitively based[1] on laws of large numbers and central limit theorems. Since most readers are already acquainted with these probability results, the marginal cost of learning Monte Carlo methods is low. This combination of general applicability and low marginal cost of learning help explain the popularity of Monte Carlo methods.

The probabilistic nature of Monte Carlo methods has important implications. The result of any Monte Carlo procedure is a random variable. Any numerical method has error, but the probabilistic nature of the Monte Carlo error puts structure on the error that we can exploit. In particular, the accuracy of Monte Carlo methods can be controlled by adjusting the sample size. With Monte Carlo methods we can aim for answers of low but useful accuracy as well as for answers of high accuracy, and we can easily estimate the cost of improved accuracy.

In this chapter we will present basic examples of Monte Carlo approaches to a wide variety of problems. In the next chapter we examine the logical basis of Monte Carlo methods, a discussion that naturally leads to consideration of the more general category of sampling methods. Together these chapters provide us with a collection of tools and ideas that allow us to examine problems too complex and large for more conventional methods.

8.1 Pseudorandom Number Generation

We should first deal with some semantic (some might say metaphysical) but substantive issues. Strictly speaking, Monte Carlo procedures are almost never used since it is difficult to construct a random variable. There have been attempts to construct "true" random variables,[2] but such methods are costly and awkward. Furthermore it

---

1. We will later see that the true logical and mathematical foundation for the methods actually used in practice is quite different.

2. One old procedure was to examine the computer's clock time and use the least significant digits as a random variable; however, this practice could easily degenerate into a cycle if a computer's programs became too synchronized. Another approach used geiger counter readings. True randomness may be an important feature of future computing, since results of quantum computation would often be random (under the Heisenberg interpretation). However, current technology avoids true randomness.

is not generally practical to replicate calculations that have truly random features, since replication would require one to store all the realizations of the random variables, a task that would often exceed a computer's storage capacity.

Constructing random variables can also drag one into side issues of little interest to numerical analysis. For example, suppose that you generate a random sequence and use it in a problem, but you also record the sequence on paper. A tricky question arises when you later use the recorded sequence in another problem. Is the second result produced deterministically because you deterministically read the recorded sequence, or is it stochastic because the sequence originally came from a stochastic process? If you say stochastic, would your answer change if told that that random process produced a constant string of zeros? And, finally, what mathematical property of the recorded sequence is changed if I next told you that I had lied and that the sequence had been constructed according to a deterministic rule?

Because of the practical difficulties, truly random variables are seldom used in Monte Carlo methods. This fact makes discussions related to randomness and the advantages of random over deterministic approaches of no practical value. In this chapter we will follow the standard practice in economics of using probabilistic language and ideas to describe and analyze Monte Carlo methods; however, the reader should be aware of the fact that this is not a logically valid approach to analyzing methods that don't use true random variables.

Almost all implementations of Monte Carlo methods actually use *pseudorandom sequences*, that is, deterministic sequences, X_k, $k = 1, 2, \ldots, N$, that *seem* to be random. "Pseudorandom" essentially means that a sequence displays *some* properties satisfied by random variables. Two basic properties generally demanded of pseudorandom sequences are zero serial correlation and the correct frequency of *runs*. A run is any sequential pattern, such as "five draws below 0.1" or "six draws each greater than the previous draw." The zero serial correlation condition demands that if we take a finite subsequence of length $n < N$, X_k, $k = 1, n$, and we regress X_{k+1} on X_k, the regression coefficient is not "statistically significantly" different from zero. No real statistics is involved because the sequence X_k is deterministic; what we mean is that if we apply statistical techniques to X_k acting as if X_k were random, we would find no statistical evidence for serial correlation. More generally, a candidate pseudorandom sequence should display zero serial correlation at all lags. The serial correlation properties are only linear properties. Analyzing the frequency of runs allows us to examine some nonlinear aspects of X_k. For example, if X_k is i.i.d., then it is unlikely that there is a run of ten draws each greater than its predecessor, but there should be a few in a long sequence. These tests are described in more detail in Rubinstein (1981).

However, no pseudorandom sequence satisfies *all* properties of an i.i.d. random sequence. Any pseudorandom sequence would be found to be deterministic by the methods described in Brock et al. (1986, 1988, 1991). We should keep in mind Lehmer's point that such a pseudorandom sequence is "a vague notion ... in which each term is unpredictable to the *uninitiated* and whose digits pass a *certain number* of tests traditional with *statisticians*." Keeping these distinctions in mind, we refer to pseudorandom number generators as random number generators.

Uniform Random Number Generation

The simplest pseudorandom number generators use the *linear congruential method* (LCM) and take the form

$$X_{k+1} = aX_k + c \,(\text{mod } m). \tag{8.1.1}$$

One popular example chooses $a = \pm 3 \,(\text{mod } 8)$ and close to $2^{b/2}$, $c = 0$, X_0 odd, and $m = 2^b$, where b is the number of significant binary bits available on the computer. This will generate a sequence with period 2^{b-2}. If we want a multidimensional uniform pseudorandom number generator, we assign successive realizations to different dimensions. For example, the collection of points $Y_n \equiv (X_{2n+1}, X_{2n+2})$ is a pseudorandom two-dimensional set of points.

The graph of a typical LCM generator is illustrated in figure 8.1. Note the steep slope of the function at each point and the numerous discontinuities. Figure 8.2 gives a typical two-dimensional collection of 1,500 pseudorandom points. Note that the scatter resembles what we expect from a random number generator. The scatter is not uniform. There are some areas where there are too many points and some areas where there are too few, as predicted by the central limit theorem.

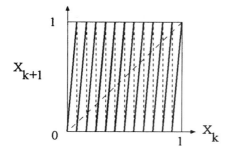

Figure 8.1
Graph of LCM rule

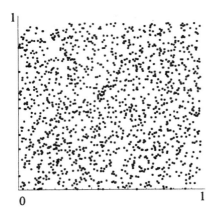

1

0   1

Figure 8.2
Initial 1,500 pseudorandom points

In general, LCM generators have fallen into disfavor. Marsaglia (1968) showed that successive d-tuples of numbers generated by LCM generators live in a few planes in $[0,1]^d$. Specifically, if we have $X_{k+1} = aX_k + c \,(\text{mod } m)$, and form the d-tuples $Y_k \equiv (X_k, X_{k+1}, \ldots, X_{k+d})$, the Y_k points lie on at most $(d!m)^{1/d}$ hyperplanes. For example, if $m = 2^{31}$ and $d = 6$, the successive d-tuples lie on at most 108 hyperplanes. This implies that moderate-dimensional Monte Carlo methods that rely on LCM generators are really sampling from relatively few hyperplanes, a fact that could lead to poor results. The problem also becomes more severe for higher dimensions.

The response to these problems has been to develop more complex generators. A simple example of this is the multiple prime random number generator (MPRNG) from Haas (1987). Algorithm 8.1 displays Fortran code, taken from Haas, that generates a sequence of NSAMP values for IRAND:

Algorithm 8.1   MPRNG Algorithm

```
M=971;IA=11113;IB=104322;IRAND=481
DO I=1,NSAMP
  M=M+7;IA=IA+1907;IB=IB+73939
  IF(M.GE.9973)M=M-9871
  IF(IA.GE.99991)IA=IA-89989
  IF(IB.GE.224729)IB=IB-96233
  IRAND=MOD[IRAND*M+IA+IB,100000]/10
ENDDO
```

This method generates integers[3] between 0 and 9999 for IRAND; to generate numbers with more digits (and more precision) one just concatenates two successive iterates to get one eight digit number. We use IRAND/10,000 as a pseudorandom variable to approximate the uniform random variable on $[0, 1]$. In this algorithm the multiplier M and the increments IA and IB are constantly changing, in contrast to the linear congruential method where they are constant. This mixing results in a method that avoids many of the problems of other methods and results in a large period of over 85 trillion.

There are many other ways to generate pseudorandom sequences. One can use nonlinear congruential methods that take the form $X_{k+1} = f(X_k) \bmod m$. One old method was the Fibonacci generator $X_k = (X_{k-1} + X_{k-2}) \bmod m$. This sequence has a number of poor properties. In particular, if X_{k-1} and X_{k-2} are small relative to m, so will be X_k. However, an updated version that begins with 55 odd numbers and computes

$$X_k = (X_{k-24} \cdot X_{k-55}) \bmod 2^{32} \tag{8.1.2}$$

is much better, having a period length of approximately 10^{25} and passing many randomness tests.

Nonuniform Random Number Generation

The random number generators constructed above yield approximations to the uniform random variable on $[0, 1]$. We use them to construct random number generators approximating other random variables.

The most general method is called *inversion*. Suppose that we want to simulate a scalar random variable with distribution $F(x)$ and U is a uniform random variable. Then $F^{-1}(U)$ has distribution function $F(x)$. Therefore, to approximate a random variable with distribution $F(x)$, we need only approximate F^{-1} and use $y = F^{-1}(U)$ where U is generated by a pseudorandom sequence. For example, suppose that we want to generate a random variable that has density proportional to x^2 on $[1, 2]$. Since $\int_1^2 x^2 \, dx = 7/3$, the density function is $3x^2/7$, the distribution function is $F(x) = \frac{3}{7} \int_1^x z^2 \, dz = (x^3 - 1)/7$, and $F^{-1}(u) = (7u + 1)^{1/3}$. Therefore $X \equiv (7U + 1)^{1/3}$ is a random variable over $[1, 2]$ with density $3x^2/7$. Notice that the inversion method allows us to translate all random variables into nonlinear functions of $U[0, 1]$. Sometimes one cannot analytically determine F^{-1}. Approximating F^{-1} is just a problem in approximation, solvable by using the methods of chapter 6. Of

---

3. The division in the MPRNG algorithm is integer division that drops any noninteger piece of the result.

particular importance here would be preserving the monotonicity of F^{-1}; hence a shape-preserving method is advised if other methods fail to preserve shape.

Some random variables can be constructed more directly. A popular way to generate $X \sim N(0, 1)$ is the *Box-Muller method*. If U_1 and U_2 are two independent draws from $U[0, 1]$, then

$$
\begin{aligned}
X_1 &= \cos(2\pi U_1)\sqrt{-2\ln U_2}, \\
X_2 &= \sin(2\pi U_1)\sqrt{-2\ln U_2},
\end{aligned}
\tag{8.1.3}
$$

are two independent draws from $N(0, 1)$.

Gibbs Sampling

Some random variables are difficult to simulate, particularly in multivariate cases. The *Gibbs sampling method* constructs a Markov chain that has a useful ergodic distribution.

Suppose that $f: R^d \to R$ is the probability density for the random variable X, and let $f(z|y)$ denote the density of $Z \in R^l$ conditional on $y \in R^m$ where $l + m = d$. We construct a sequence, x^k, in a componentwise fashion. We start with an arbitrary x^0. Then given x^k, we construct x^{k+1} componentwise from a sequence of d draws satisfying the densities in (8.1.4):

$$
\begin{aligned}
x_1^{k+1} &\sim f(x_1 | x_2^k, \ldots, x_d^k), \\
x_2^{k+1} &\sim f(x_2 | x_1^{k+1}, x_3^k, \ldots, x_d^k), \\
&\vdots \\
x_d^{k+1} &\sim f(x_d | x_1^{k+1}, \ldots, x_{d-1}^{k+1}).
\end{aligned}
\tag{8.1.4}
$$

Each component of x^{k+1} is constructed by a univariate random draw conditional on the most recent draws of the other variates. These univariate draws can be performed by the inversion method or an appropriate direct method.

The key theorem is due to Gelfand and Smith (1990).

THEOREM 8.1.1   Let $g: R^d \to R$ be measurable, and let the sequence x^k be generated by (8.1.4). Then

$$
\lim_{n \to \infty} \frac{1}{n} \sum_{j=1}^{n} g(x^j) = \int g(x) f(x) \, dx = E\{g(X)\}.
\tag{8.1.5}
$$

The key component to a Gibbs sampler is the collection of conditional random variates. If they are easy to generate, then the Gibbs method is quite practical. Theorem 8.1.1 says that eventually the x^k sequence becomes sufficiently uncorrelated that it satisfies (8.1.5), which is similar to a law of large numbers. This occurs despite the substantial correlation between x^k and x^{k+1}. If we want a sequence of x^k with nearly zero serial correlation, we take x^1, x^{K+1}, x^{2K+1}, and so on, for a large K. This then provides us with a method for creating nearly independent draws from X.

Gibbs sampling is a powerful tool in many dynamic contexts. We do not develop any of its uses here; see Geweke (1996) for discussion of Gibbs sampling and its applications.

8.2   Monte Carlo Integration

When the dimension is high, simple numerical integration methods, such as product formulas, are likely to be impractical. Each of those methods would do well for smooth integrands if one can evaluate the integrand at enough points. Unfortunately, the minimal necessary number can be very high, and results using fewer points are of no value. Monte Carlo methods for computing integrals can deliver moderately accurate solutions using a moderate number of points. As with the quadrature methods discussed in chapter 7, we select points at which we evaluate the integrand and then add the resulting values. The differentiating feature of Monte Carlo methods is that the points are selected in a "random" fashion instead of according to a strict formula.

The law of large numbers (LLN) motivates Monte Carlo integration. Recall that if X_i is a collection of i.i.d. random variables with density $q(x)$ and support $[0, 1]$, then

$$\lim_{N \to \infty} \frac{1}{N} \sum_{i=1}^{N} X_i = \int_0^1 xq(x)\, dx, \qquad a.s.$$

Furthermore

$$\mathrm{var}\left(N^{-1} \sum_{i=1}^{N} X_i\right) = \frac{\sigma_x^2}{N},$$

where $\sigma_x^2 = \mathrm{var}(X_1)$. If σ_x^2 is not known a priori, an unbiased estimator is

$$\hat{\sigma}_x^2 \equiv (N-1)^{-1} \sum_{i=1}^{N} (X_i - \bar{X})^2,$$

where $\bar{X}$ is the sample mean, $\bar{X} \equiv N^{-1} \sum_{i=1}^{N} X_i$.

The LLN immediately suggests a numerical integration procedure. Suppose that one wants to compute $I_f \equiv \int_0^1 f(x)\, dx$. If $X \sim U[0, 1]$, then

$$E\{f(X)\} = \int_0^1 f(x)\,dx;$$

that is, $\int_0^1 f(x)\,dx$ equals the mean of $Y \equiv f(X)$. Hence one way to approximate $\int_0^1 f(x)\,dx$ is to estimate $E\{Y\}$. The *crude Monte Carlo* method generates N draws from $U[0, 1]$, $\{x_i\}_{i=1}^N$, and takes

$$\hat{I}_f \equiv \frac{1}{N} \sum_{i=1}^N f(x_i)$$

as an estimate of $\int_0^1 f(x)\,dx$.

Monte Carlo procedures differs substantially from our earlier methods in that the approximation is itself a random variable, $\hat{I}_f$, with variance

$$\sigma_{\hat{I}_f}^2 = N^{-1} \int_0^1 \left(f(x) - I_f\right)^2 dx = N^{-1}\sigma_f^2.$$

An estimate of the variance of $f(X)$ is

$$\hat{\sigma}_f^2 = (N-1)^{-1} \sum_{i=1}^N \left(f(x_i) - \hat{I}_f\right)^2.$$

Since σ_f^2 is unknown, we take $\hat{\sigma}_f^2$ as an estimate of σ_f^2. The standard error of $\hat{I}_f$ is $\sigma_f/\sqrt{N}$.

These variance calculations are central to any Monte Carlo procedure. Since Monte Carlo quadrature procedures yields a random variable, any estimate of $\hat{I}_f$ should be accompanied with an estimate of $\sigma_{\hat{I}_f}^2$. Presenting an estimate of $\hat{I}_f$ without reporting $\hat{\sigma}_{\hat{I}_f}^2$ is like presenting a parameter estimate without also reporting a confidence interval.

The crude Monte Carlo method is seldom used without modification. Although this method is unbiased, its variance is too large. There are a variety of simple techniques that can substantially reduce the variance of the integral estimate but retain the unbiasedness of the estimator.

Stratified Sampling

The first variance reduction technique is *stratified sampling*. The observation is that the variance of f over a subinterval of $[0, 1]$ is often less than over the whole interval. Suppose that we divide $[0, 1]$ into $[0, \alpha]$ and $[\alpha, 1]$. Then, if we have N points sampled over $[0, \alpha]$ and N over $[\alpha, 1]$, we form the estimate

$$\hat{I}_f = \frac{\alpha}{N} \sum_i f(x_{1i}) + \left(\frac{1-\alpha}{N}\right) \sum_i f(x_{2i}),$$

where $x_{1i} \in [0, \alpha]$ and $x_{2i} \in [\alpha, 1]$, $i = 1, \ldots, N$. Its variance is

$$\frac{\alpha}{N} \int_0^\alpha f^2 + \frac{(1-\alpha)}{N} \int_\alpha^1 f^2 - \frac{\alpha}{N} \left(\int_0^\alpha f\right)^2 - \frac{(1-\alpha)}{N} \left(\int_\alpha^1 f\right)^2.$$

A good α equates the variance over $[0, \alpha]$ with that over $[\alpha, 1]$.

Note that the basic idea of stratified sampling is to keep the draws from clumping in one region. This feature is typical of acceleration schemes.

Antithetic Variates

A popular acceleration method is that of antithetic variates. The idea is that if f is monotonically increasing, then $f(x)$ and $f(1-x)$ are negatively correlated. One way to apply this idea to reduce the variance of $\hat{I}_f$ for monotone f is to estimate I_f with the antithetic estimate

$$\hat{I}_f^a = \frac{1}{2N} \sum_{i=1}^N (f(x_i) + f(1-x_i)).$$

The antithetic estimate is an unbiased estimate of I_f but will have smaller variance than the crude estimate whenever the antithetic summands are negatively correlated. The antithetic variate method is particularly valuable for monotonic functions f; in particular, if f is linear (one-dimensional) function, then antithetic variates will integrate $\int_0^1 f(x) \, dx$ exactly.

Control Variates

The third method is that of *control variates*. Suppose that we know of a function, φ, that is similar to f but easily integrated. Then the identity $\int f = \int \varphi + \int (f - \varphi)$ reduces the problem to a Monte Carlo integration of $\int (f - \varphi)$ plus the known integral $\int \varphi$. The variance of $f - \varphi$ is $\sigma_f^2 + \sigma_\varphi^2 - 2 \operatorname{cov}(f, \varphi)$. So if $\operatorname{cov}(f, \varphi)$ is large, the N-point variance of the crude methods applied to $f - \varphi$ is smaller than $(1/N)\sigma_f^2$, the variance of the crude method. Therefore the control variate method estimates I_f with $\int \varphi$ plus a Monte Carlo estimate of $\int (f - \varphi)$.

Importance Sampling

The crude method to estimate $\int_0^1 f(x) \, dx$ samples $[0, 1]$ in a manner unrelated to the integrand $f(x)$. This can be wasteful, since the value of f in some parts of $[0, 1]$ is much more important than in other parts. Importance sampling tries to sample $f(x)$ where its value is most important in determining $\int_0^1 f(x)\,dx$. If $p(x) > 0$, and $\int_0^1 p(x)\,dx = 1$, then $p(x)$ is a density and

$$I_f = \int_0^1 f(x)\,dx = \int_0^1 \frac{f(x)}{p(x)}\,p(x)\,dx.$$

The key idea behind importance sampling is that if x_i is drawn with density $p(x)$, then

$$\hat{I}_f^p = \frac{1}{N}\sum_{i=1}^N \frac{f(x_i)}{p(x_i)}.$$

is an unbiased estimate of I, and its variance is

$$\sigma_{\hat{I}_f^p}^2 = \frac{1}{N}\left(\int_0^1 \frac{f(x)^2}{p(x)}\,dx - \left(\int_0^1 f(x)\,dx\right)^2\right).$$

If $f(x) > 0$ and $p(x) = f(x)/\int_0^1 f(x)$, then $f(x) = I_f p(x)$ and $\sigma_{\hat{I}_f^p}^2 = 0$. If $f(x)$ is negative somewhere but bounded below by $B < 0$, we can integrate $f(x) - B$ in this way. Of course, if we could construct this $p(x)$, we would have solved the problem. This example points out that we want to use a $p(x)$ that similar to $f(x)$ in shape, thereby minimizing the variance of $f(x)/p(x)$.

The construction of $\hat{I}_f^p$ is called *importance sampling* because we sample more intensively where f is large, which is where $f(x)$ makes the greatest contribution to the integral $\int f(x)\,dx$. The cost of this method is that it may take some effort to construct a nonuniform random variable that has a density similar to $f(x)$. We must trade this off against the cost of evaluating $f(x)$ at a larger number of points.

A key problem with importance sampling is clear from the $\sigma_{\hat{I}_f^p}^2$ formula. Note that the key integrand is $f(x)^2/p(x)$; if p goes to zero more rapidly than f^2 as x approaches points where p is zero, then this integrand will go to infinity. This is the case if f has fat tails and p has thin tails. Since a popular choice for p is the thin-tailed normal distribution, this *thin tails problem* arises easily. We must choose p to avoid this problem.

Importance Sampling and Changes of Variables

Importance sampling is usually described in probabilistic terms, giving the impression that importance sampling is probabilistic in nature. The truth is that importance sampling is really an application of the change of variables (COV) theorem discussed in section 7.1. This observation helps us understand importance sampling and its relation to other integration tools.

To see the connection between importance sampling and changes of variables, let $x(u): [0, 1] \to D$ be a monotone increasing map, and let $u(x)$ be its inverse. Then $u = u(x(u))$, $1 = u'(x(u)) x'(u)$, and the COV theorem implies that

$$\int_D f(x)\, dx = \int_0^1 f(x(u)) x'(u)\, du = \int_0^1 \frac{f(x(u))}{u'(x(u))}\, du = E\left\{ \frac{f(x(U))}{u'(x(U))} \right\},$$

where $U \sim U[0, 1]$.

Consider the maps $u(x)$ and its inverse $x(u)$. Then $1/x'(u(x)) = u'(x)$ and $X = x(U)$ has density $p(x) = u'(x)$. This last equivalence is particularly on point, since it shows that any monotonic map $x: [0, 1] \to R$ can be used to transform $\int_R f(x)\, dx$ to an equal integral over $[0, 1]$, which in turn has the probabilistic interpretation as the expectation of a function of U. However, any method can be used to compute the resulting integral over $[0, 1]$, not just Monte Carlo.

The key task in importance sampling, or any COV method, lies in choosing the map $x(u)$. If one ultimately uses Monte Carlo, it is natural to choose a map that leaves the $\text{var}[f(x(U))/u'(x(U))]$ as small as possible, since our error estimates are expressed in terms of this variance. In practice, the objective is to find a $x(u)$ that leaves $f(x(u))/u'(x(u))$ nearly flat. We also want to avoid the thin tails problem that arises if $f(x(u))/u'(x(u))$ is not bounded for $u = 0$ or $u = 1$. This is avoided by choosing $x(u)$ so that the implied density $u'(x(U))$ does not go off to zero too rapidly as U goes to zero or one.

Sometimes the choice of sampling distribution is suggested by the integrand. If the integrand can be expressed in the form $\int_D g(x)f(x)\, dx$ where $f \geq 0$ on D, then we would like to create a random variable X with density proportional to $f(x)$. Such an X would have density $f(x)/\int_D f(x)\, dx$, which has distribution function $F(x)$. Then $X = F^{-1}(U)$ has density proportional to $f(x)$ on D, and

$$\int_D g(x)f(x)\, dx = \left(\int_D f(x)\, dx \right) E\{g(X)\}.$$

For example, suppose that $D = [0, 1]$ and $f(x) = x^3$. Then $\int_D x^3\, dx = \frac{1}{4}$, $F(x) = 4\int_0^x z^3\, dz = x^4$, and $X = (U)^{1/4}$ has density $4x^3$. Hence

$$\int_0^1 g(x)x^3\, dx = \frac{1}{4} E\{g(U^{1/4})\},$$

which we approximate with the finite sum $4N^{-1} \sum_{j=1}^N g(u_i^{1/4})$ where the u_i are generated by a uniform pseudorandom number generator.

A few final points need to be made about these acceleration methods. First, despite the use of the term "acceleration," the *rate* of convergence is still proportional to $N^{-1/2}$ as with crude Monte Carlo. All that is achieved is a reduction in the proportionality constant, not the convergence rate. Second, these methods replace $\int f$ with $\int g$ which has the same value but smaller variance when we apply the crude Monte Carlo method; hence, in some way, we always end up using crude Monte Carlo.

8.3 Optimization by Stochastic Search

Some optimization problems involve objectives that are rough and have many local extrema. Polytope methods can handle nonsmooth objectives, but they are purely local search methods and will stop at the first local extremum found. To solve these ill-behaved problems, one must adopt procedures that rely neither on smoothness nor on local comparisons. In this section we will examine a variety of stochastic search methods commonly used to solve general optimization problems. In practical terms, these are the only general, globally convergent optimization methods we have.

Optimization by Random Search

One simple procedure for optimization is to evaluate the objective at a random collection of numbers and take the best. The law of large numbers assures us that we will almost surely converge to the optimum as we take larger samples. This method is slow. However, we can substantially improve its performance if each randomly generated point is also used to begin a more standard optimization procedure. One such example would be to apply a fixed number of iterations of some standard method to each randomly drawn point. The points generated by the standard optimization procedure are included in the total collection when we choose the best. Combining a random search with standard methods takes advantage of each method's strengths: The randomness makes sure that we don't get stuck at a bad point, and if one of these randomly chosen points is close to the optimum, a locally convergent standard method will send us to the optimum.

In problems where Newton's method and other derivative-based procedures are not effective or not applicable, random search methods are more useful. However, searching the choice set in a serially uncorrelated fashion is seldom efficient. The following procedures learn from past draws to focus their search on regions more likely to contain the solution.

Genetic Algorithms

Genetic algorithms are one class of random search optimization methods that has recently received much attention. The intuition behind genetic methods arises from biological ideas of evolution, fitness, and selection, as will be clear from the terminology. The reader is encouraged to read manuscripts such as Holland (1975) and Goldberg (1989) for the history of these ideas. I will just present a formal description of the method, using basic mathematical ideas to guide our intuition.

Suppose that we want to solve

$$\max_{x \in S} f(x), \tag{8.3.1}$$

where $f: R^n \to R^n$ and S is a subset of R^n, of the form $S = S_1 \times S_2 \times \cdots \times S_n$, $S_i = [a_i, b_i]$. Since f is to model "fitness," it is natural that it be nonnegative. If f is not nonnegative everywhere on S, then we replace it with a function of the form $\max\{0, f(x) - f(c)\}$ for some $c \in S$ where $f(c) < 0$. Such a replacement in (8.3.1) will leave the problem essentially unchanged.

A genetic algorithm keeps track of f at a set of points, with that set evolving so as to keep points with high values of f. We start with choosing m points from S to construct $X_1 = \{x^1, \ldots, x^m\}$. We construct a sequence of such sets; let X_k denote the set of x's generated at stage k. The initial points may reflect some information about where the maxima of f are likely to lie, or can be chosen "at random." The choice of m is important. Large m will make the search more global and reduce the likelihood of premature convergence, but at the cost of more evaluations of f.

The basic idea is to evaluate f at each $x \in X_k$. The points x are called "chromosomes," and the value of f at x is a measure of the fitness of x. We then "mate" pairs of $x \in X_k$ to produce new chromosomes, such mating involving both "recombination" and "mutation." Some of these new chromosomes then replace some of the initial chromosomes to create a new population, X_{k+1}. The algorithm produces a sequence of populations in this fashion and ends either when time runs out or when we have a point, x^*, that appears to be as good as possible. The details arise in specifying the mating rules, the rate of mutation, and rules for replacing old points with new points. In the following we will describe the implementation used in Dorsey and Mayer (1992).

Given the values of f at $x \in X_k$, we need to determine the mating process. We want those x with high f values to be "selected." Therefore we take some nonnegative, increasing $T: R \to R$ and define

$$p_i = \frac{T(f(x^i))}{\sum_{x \in X_k} T(f(x))} \tag{8.3.2}$$

to be the probability that $x^i \in X_k$ is selected to participate. Dorsey and Mayer (1992) choose $T(y) = y + a$, where a may be altered between iterations to keep the probabilities p_i from being either too diffuse or too concentrated. Using the probabilities in (8.3.2), we make m draws from X_k with replacement, producing a set Y_k of m chromosomes that will participate in mating.

Next draw two points y^1, y^2 from Y_k without replacement. We want to "mate" y^1 and y^2 to produce two new vectors, z^1 and z^2. To do so, we select $i \in \{1, 2, \ldots, n\}$ at random and have y^1 and y^2 "crossover" at position i, that is

$$
\begin{aligned}
z^1 &= (y_1^1, \ldots, y_i^1, y_{i+1}^2, \ldots, y_n^2), \\
z^2 &= (y_1^2, \ldots, y_i^2, y_{i+1}^1, \ldots, y_n^1).
\end{aligned}
\tag{8.3.3}
$$

We keep drawing pairs y^1 and y^2 from Y_k without replacement until we have exhausted Y_k.

This specification of crossover in (8.3.3) is just one possible way to specify the mating process. Another choice would be to construct z_i^1 (z_i^2) by adding the integer part of y_i^1 (y_i^2) to the fractional part of y_i^2 (y_i^1), $i = 1, \ldots n$. There are practically an infinity of ways to specify the mating process, each one revolving around a "schema," that is, a way to code points in S. See Holland (1975) for the general theory and description of schemas.

Let Z_k consist of the m resulting z's constructed after reproduction and crossover. We next "mutate" the points. For example, we could, with probability q, replace z_i^j with a random number drawn from $[a_i, b_i]$ (e.g., with the uniform distribution). We do this independently at all $j = 1, \ldots, m$, $i = 1, \ldots, n$. X_{k+1}, the next generation of points, then consists of the mutations of the Z_k.

The fundamental result, called the Schema theorem, asserts that if we make good choices for the mating and mutation process, the average value of f over X_{k+1} will generally be greater than the average value over X_k. Of course we cannot allow the process to go forever. One kind of rule is to stop when progress has been small for the last j iterations. More precisely, we stop at iteration k if

$$\left| \max_{x \in X_l} f(x) - \max_{x \in X_m} f(x) \right| < \delta$$

and

$$\left\| \arg\max_{x \in X_l} f(x) - \arg\max_{x \in X_m} f(x) \right\| < \varepsilon$$

for $l, m = k - j, \ldots, k - 1, k$.

There are numerous alternative ways to implement a genetic algorithm. We examine the Dorsey-Mayer implementation above because it is simple. Dorsey and Mayer applied this genetic algorithm to reestimate a variety of econometric analyses where the original estimation used standard optimization methods. Their reestimation using this genetic algorithm sometimes yielded point estimates statistically superior to and economically different from those published. We may initially wonder why the genetic algorithm did better than standard methods. Even when econometricians use standard optimization methods for estimation, they typically restart their computations at several points in order to find the global optimum. Therefore there is no inherent advantage in the genetic algorithm as long as users of standard methods do *enough* restarts. The reason why Dorsey and Mayer's genetic algorithm estimates were better is that their genetic algorithm took a more global view and was more exhaustive in its search than were the computations behind the original estimates. The basic lesson from the Dorsey and Mayer study is that we must be more careful concerning multiple local solutions than is the apparent standard practice, and we should make greater use of procedures that intensively look for global solutions. The genetic algorithm is one possible scheme that learns from experience and searches intelligently.

The most powerful approach may be a *hybrid genetic method*. In such hybrid methods, one begins with a collection of points and mates them to produce a new set, but then allows a standard optimization procedure to proceed for a fixed number of iterations from each of these points. This produces a new collection of parents that will be mated, and so on. The advantage of the hybrid method is that the standard procedures will move toward nearby local optima, and the resulting mating process will give preference to the better local optima. In this marriage of standard and genetic methods, we see that the genetic component is essentially providing a more systematic approach to restarts than random guesses.

Simulated Annealing

Suppose that $f(x)$ is defined over some domain X; X can be discrete or continuous. Simulated annealing is, similar to the genetic algorithm, a method that uses the objective function $f(x)$ to create a nonhomogeneous Markov chain process that will asymptotically converge to the minimum of $f(x)$. We first create a *neighborhood system* covering X; that is, for each $x \in X$ there is a set $V_x \subset X$ such that $x \in V_x$ and for all $x, y \in X, x \in V_y$ iff $y \in V_x$. Essentially V_x is the set of points that are neighbors of x. A further requirement is that any two points, x and y, can be linked by a sequence of points, x_i, such that $x_0 = x, x_{i+1} \in V_{x_i}, i = 0, 1 \ldots, n$, and $x_{n+1} = y$. One simple example would be $X = \{l/n : l = 0, 1, \ldots, n\}$ for some integer n with $V_x = (x - \varepsilon, x + \varepsilon) \cap X$ for some $\varepsilon > 1/n$. Simulated annealing is commonly used on combinatorial problems, such as the traveling salesman problem, where X is discrete and finite.

We will construct a Markov process on X. The idea is that the process can move from x to any of the neighbors of x; the linkage condition ensures that the process can ultimately visit any point in X. The Markov process we construct has two stages to each step. If x_n is the nth realization, then we first draw a $y \in V_{x_n}$ which will be our candidate for the next value. However, the final choice of x_{n+1} is governed by the rules

$$f(y) < f(x_n) \Rightarrow x_{n+1} = y,$$

$$f(y) \geq f(x_n) \Rightarrow \begin{cases} \mathrm{Prob}\{x_{n+1} = y\} = e^{-(f(y) - f(x_n))/T_n}, \\ \mathrm{Prob}\{x_{n+1} = x_n\} = 1 - \mathrm{Prob}\{x_{n+1} = y\}. \end{cases}$$

Hence, if $f(y) < f(x_n)$, we surely jump to y, but if $f(y) \geq f(x_n)$, we do so only probabilistically. T_n is called the temperature, and it depends on n, the position in the sequence. If T_n is large, then a jump to y almost always occurs, but as T_n falls, uphill jumps become less likely. Once we have determined the value of x_{n+1}, we then make a random draw $y \in V_{x_{n+1}}$, and proceed to compute x_{n+2}.

This process constructs a sequence x_n that is the realization of a (time-varying) Markov process on X which we hope converges to the minimum of f. The key theorem is that if $T_n > R/\log n$ for sufficiently large R, then x_n will almost surely converge to a global minimum of f. This kind of choice for T_n is called *exponential cooling*, which, assuming X is finite, has the property

$$\Pr\{x_n \notin f_{\min}\} = \mathcal{O}\left(\left(\frac{K}{n}\right)^\alpha\right),$$

where $f_{\min}$ is the set of x which minimize $f(x)$, and K and α are positive constants.

Simulated annealing will be slow on conventional optimization problems, such as continuous functions on R^n. However, it has a good chance of producing good results in many complex situations where conventional methods (which focus on getting the perfect answer) may be impractical or in problems, such as those arising in integer programming and combinatorial optimization, where conventional methods do not apply.

8.4 Stochastic Approximation

Frequently the objective of an optimization problem includes integration. Specifically, suppose that the objective is $f(x) = E\{g(x, Z)\}$, and we want to solve

$$\min_{x} E\{g(x, Z)\}, \tag{8.4.1}$$

where Z is a random variable. A conventional way to proceed would use a high-accuracy integration rule to compute $E\{g(x, Z)\}$. That may be quite costly[4]. In this section we discuss procedures that work well with low-quality evaluations of $E\{g(x, Z)\}$ and/or its gradients.

Stochastic approximation is designed to deal with such problems. We begin with an initial guess x^1. Suppose that we take a draw, z^1, from Z. The gradient $g_x(x^1, z^1)$ is an unbiased estimate of the gradient $f_x(x^1)$. In the steepest descent method we would let the next guess be $x^1 - \lambda_1 f_x(x^1)$ for some $\lambda_1 > 0$. In the *stochastic gradient method*, we execute the iteration

$$x^{k+1} = x^k - \lambda_k g_x(x^k, z^k), \tag{8.4.2}$$

where $\{z^k\}$ is a sequence of i.i.d. draws from Z and λ_k is a changing step size. Also we are constrained to remain in some set U; if this step crosses ∂U, then we bounce back into the interior of U in the normal direction.

THEOREM 8.4.1   Suppose that f is C^2. If $\lambda_k \to 0$, $\sum_{k=1}^{\infty} \lambda_k = \infty$, and $\sum_{k=1}^{\infty} \lambda_k^2 < \infty$, then the sequence x^k generated by the stochastic gradient method, (8.4.2), confined to U will almost surely have a subsequence that converges to a point either on ∂U or at a (possibly local) minimum of f.

The basic idea behind the stochastic gradient method is clear. First, since λ_k decreases to 0, it is small after an initial period. Even though $g_x(x, z)$ is a poor estimate of the gradient $f_x(x)$, it does have some information, and taking a small step in that direction will not affect x much. The only way x will move appreciably is if a long sequence of z's pushes it in a particular direction. By the law of large numbers, the most likely direction in which it will be pushed is, to a first approximation, the

---

4. Econometricians frequently fix a set of z's, say S, and minimize $\sum_{z \in S} g(x, z)$, an application of the crude Monte Carlo method to $E\{g(x, Z)\}$ that requires a large set S to yield an acceptable result.

Table 8.1
Statistics of (8.4.3) for 25 runs

Iterate	Average x_k	Standard deviation
1	0.375	0.298
10	0.508	0.143
100	0.487	0.029
200	0.499	0.026
500	0.496	0.144
1,000	0.501	0.010

true gradient. The condition that $\sum_{k=1}^{\infty} \lambda_k = \infty$ keeps λ_k from becoming small too quickly and forces the process to be patient before converging. As k increases, λ_k falls, and it takes more iterations for x to make a nontrivial step, strengthening the power of the law of large numbers. The condition that $\sum_{k=1}^{\infty} \lambda_k^2 < \infty$ forces the x^k sequence to settle down eventually, yielding an accumulation point somewhere almost surely. That such an accumulation point be at a local minimum of f is not surprising, for if it wandered close to such a point, the gradients will, on average, push x toward the minimum.

The performance of stochastic approximation is rough. For example, suppose that we want to solve $\min_{x \in [0,1]} E\{(Z - x)^2\}$ where $Z \sim U[0, 1]$. The solution is $x = 0.5$. If we use the sequence $\lambda_k = 1/k$, the scheme (8.4.2) becomes

$$x_{k+1} = x_k + \frac{2}{k}(z_k - x_k), \tag{8.4.3}$$

where the z_k are i.i.d. and distributed $U[0, 1]$. In table 8.1 we display the result of 25 runs of (8.4.3) with random x_1. At iterate k we display the mean of the x_k and the variance. We see that the means are close to the correct solution. However, the variance is nontrivial even at iterate 1,000.

Equation (8.4.2) is really just solving for the zero of a nonlinear equation. In general, stochastic approximation is a stochastic process of the form

$$x^{k+1} = x^k - \lambda_k h(x^k, z^k). \tag{8.4.4}$$

If (8.4.4) converges to a limit x^*, then x^* is a zero of $E\{h(x, Z)\}$. Therefore we could use (8.4.4) to find zeros of such functions. This is really a stochastic form of successive approximation. In fact we can rewrite (8.4.4) as

$$x^{k+1} = (1 - \lambda_k)x^k + \lambda_k(x^k - h(x^k, z^k)), \tag{8.4.5}$$

which for small λ_k resembles a heavily damped extrapolation version of successive approximation applied to finding a zero of $h(x, z)$. The difference is that z is varying randomly in (8.4.5), and this turns the problem into finding a zero of $E\{h(x, Z)\}$.

Neural Network Learning

Stochastic approximation is often used to compute the coefficients of a neural network. Neural network coefficients are chosen to minimize a loss function. While one could directly minimize the loss function, most users of neural networks determine the coefficients using stochastic approximation methods to model a dynamic process of observation and learning.

Suppose that we have a neural network with weights θ. If we have a set of N data points (generated at random or otherwise), $(y_l, X^l), l = 1, \ldots, N$, we want to find θ such that the L^2 error, $\sum_{l=1}^{N}(y_l - f(X^l, \theta))^2$, is small. In *back-propagation*, a sequence of weights, θ^k, are computed in an adaptive fashion; specifically

$$\theta^{k+1} = \theta^k + \lambda_k(\nabla f(X^k, \theta^k))^T(y_k - f(X^k, \theta^k)), \qquad (8.4.6)$$

where λ_k is the learning rate sequence (consistent with theorem 8.4.1) and $\nabla f \equiv \partial f / \partial \theta$. The gradient of f tells us the direction of maximal increase and $y_k - f(X^k, \theta^k)$ is the approximation error for (y_k, X^k) with neural network weights θ^k. This adjustment formula tells us to change θ in the direction of maximal improvement given the values of θ^k and data (y_k, X^k), and in proportion to the current error. Ideally the process in (8.4.6) continues indefinitely; in practice, it continues for $k = 1, 2, \ldots, M$, where $M >> N$.

While stochastic approximation has some intuitive value in describing dynamic learning processes, experiments indicate that it is not an efficient way to compute the neural network coefficients. To get good results using (8.4.6), one usually runs the data through (8.4.6) many times. Straightforward nonlinear least squares is often superior. However, both methods have problems with multiple local minima.

8.5 Standard Optimization Methods with Simulated Objectives

In this section we continue our discussion of problems of the form

$$\min_{x \in U} E\{g(x, Z)\} = f(x) \qquad (8.5.1)$$

for some random variable Z. For many problems of the form in (8.5.1), the objective $f(x)$ and its derivatives can be computed only with nontrivial error. When solving problems of the form (8.5.1), we need to determine how well we need to approximate the integral. Stochastic approximation was one way to solve (8.5.1). We will now consider standard optimization approaches that use simulation ideas.

The general idea is to take a sample of size N of Z, and replace $E\{g(x, Z)\}$ in (8.5.1) with its sample mean $1/N \sum_{i=1}^N g(x, Z_i)$. For example, suppose that we want to solve

$$\min_{x \in [0,1]} E\{(Z - x)^2\}, \tag{8.5.2}$$

where $Z \sim U[0, 1]$. To solve (8.5.2), we take, say, three draws from $U[0, 1]$; suppose that they are 0.10, 0.73, and 0.49. We then minimize the sample average of $(Z - x)^2$,

$$\min_{x \in [0,1]} \tfrac{1}{3}((0.10 - x)^2 + (0.73 - x)^2 + (0.49 - x)^2). \tag{8.5.3}$$

The solution to (8.5.3) is 0.43, a rough approximation of the true solution to (8.5.2) of 0.5.

We illustrate this approach to solving problems of the form (8.5.1) with a simple portfolio problem. In fact the use of Monte Carlo integration is quite natural for such problems, since we are essentially simulating the problem. For this example, assume that there are two assets and that the utility function is $u(c) = -e^{-c}$. Assume that the safe asset has total return $R = 1.01$, and the risky asset has return $Z \sim N(\mu, \sigma^2)$ with $\mu = 1.06$ and $\sigma^2 = 0.04$. The portfolio problem reduces to

$$\max_{\omega} -E\{e^{-((1-\omega)R + \omega Z)}\}. \tag{8.5.4}$$

With our parameter values, the optimal ω, denoted ω^*, equals 1.25. The Monte Carlo approach to solve (8.5.4) is to use Monte Carlo integration to evaluate the integral objective. Specifically we make N draws of $Z \sim N(\mu, \sigma^2)$, generating a collection $Z_i, i = 1, \ldots, N$, and replace (8.5.4) by

$$\max_{\omega} -\frac{1}{N} \sum_{i=1}^N e^{-((1-\omega)R + \omega Z_i)}. \tag{8.5.5}$$

The solution to (8.5.5) is denoted $\hat{\omega}^*$ and hopefully approximates the solution to (8.5.4), ω^*.

The quality of this procedure depends on the size of N and how well the integral in (8.5.4) is approximated by the random sample mean in (8.5.5). We perform two experiments to examine the error. First, we set $\omega = 1.25$ and compute $-E\{e^{-((1-\omega)R + \omega Z)}\}$ using m samples of N draws. Columns 2 and 3 of table 8.2 display the mean estimate of these m estimates, and the standard deviation of these m

Table 8.2
Portfolio choice via Monte Carlo

N	$N^{-1} \sum_{i=1}^{N} u(c_i)$		$\hat{\omega}^*$	
	Mean	Standard deviation	Mean	Standard deviation
100	−1.039440	0.021362	1.2496	0.4885
1,000	−1.042647	0.007995	1.2870	0.1714
10,000	−1.041274	0.002582	1.2505	0.0536

estimates, for $m = 100$, and $N = 100$, 1,000, and 10,000. Notice that the mean estimates are all close to the true certainty equivalent of 1.04125; furthermore the standard errors are roughly 2, 0.8, and 0.2 percent. From these experiments one may conclude that using 1000 points will yield integral approximations with roughly 1 percent error.

We next turn to solving the optimization problem (8.5.4) and determine the number of points needed to solve (8.5.4). To do that, we solve (8.5.5) for $\hat{\omega}^*$ for m draws of 100, 1,000, and 10,000 points. The average $\hat{\omega}^*$ is close to the true value of 1.25, as shown in column 4 of table 8.2. However, the standard deviation of these solutions was 0.49 for $N = 100$, 0.17 for $N = 1,000$, and 0.05 for $N = 10,000$. Even for the largest sample size of 10,000, the standard error in computing the optimal ω was still 4 percent, which may be unacceptable. The key fact is that the error in computing ω^* is much larger, ten to twenty times larger, than the error in computing an expectation.

The conclusions of these exercises show that one must be much more careful in evaluating integrals when they are not of direct interest but computed as part of solving an optimization problem. Since individual optimization problems are important in equilibrium analysis, the same warning applies to the use of Monte Carlo in equilibrium analysis.

8.6 Further Reading and Summary

Monte Carlo methods are popular because of their ability to imitate random processes. Since they rely solely on the law of large numbers and the central limit theorem, they are easy to understand and robust. This simplicity and robustness comes at a cost, for convergence is limited to the rate $N^{-1/2}$.

There are several books on the generation of random variables and stochastic processes, including Ross (1990), Ripley (1987), Rubinstein (1986), Bratley, Fox, and

Schrage (1987), and Devroye (1986). Dwyer (1997) discusses the topic for econo-mists. Ermoliev and Wets (1988), and Beneveniste, Métivier, and Priouret (1990), Kushner and Clark (1979), and Ljung and Soderstrom (1983), and Kushner and Huang (1979, 1980) discuss stochastic approximation. Gibbs sampling is being used to efficiently solve difficult empirical problems. Geweke (1994) discusses many topics in Monte Carlo simulation including Gibbs sampling. Bayesian methods often rely on Monte Carlo methods. John Geweke's web site http://www.econ.umn.edu/bacc/ provides information about integration methods in Bayesian methods. Bootstrapping is an important computation intensive technique in statistics. The Efron (1994), and Lepage and Billard (1992) books present the basic ideas and applications.

Monte Carlo simulation is particularly useful in understanding economies where agents use particular learning strategies. This is discussed in Cho and Sargent (1996). Marimon et al. (1990), Arifovic (1994), and Marks (1992) are early applications of genetic algorithms to learning processes.

Goffe et al. (1992, 1994) presents applications of simulated annealing methods in econometrics. These papers demonstrate that simulated annealing is more robust than most alternative optimization schemes when there are multiple optima. This is particularly important in maximum likelihood problems. Aarts and Korst (1990) give an introduction to simulated annealing in general.

Exercises

1. Write a program that implements the MPRNG random number generator. Compute the correla-tion between X_t and X_{t-l} for $l = 1, 2, 3, 4$ using samples of size $10, 10^2, 10^4$, and 10^6. Repeat this for (8.1.2).

2. Write a program that takes a vector of probabilities, p_i, $i = 1, \ldots, n$, and generates a discrete ran-dom variable with that distribution.

3. Apply crude Monte Carlo integration to x, x^2, $1 - x^2$, and e^x over the interval $[0, 1]$, using $N = 10, 10^2, 10^3$, and 10^4. Next apply antithetic variates using the same sample sizes, and compare errors with crude Monte Carlo.

4. Use random search, simulated annealing, genetic algorithms, and stochastic approximation con-fined to $x \in [-5, 5]$ to solve

    $$\max_{x \in R} \left(\frac{\cos x}{\sqrt{x^2 + a}} \right)$$

    for various choices of $a \in [0.1, 10]$. Then do the same for the multivariate version

    $$\max_{x \in R^n} \Pi_{i=1}^n \left(\frac{\cos x_i}{\sqrt{x_i^2 + a_i}} \right)$$

    for $x \in [-5, 5]^n$, $n = 2, 3, 5, 10$ and random $a_i \in [0.1, 10]$.

5.   Suppose that there are three agents, each initially holding $1 and $\frac{1}{3}$ share of stock. Assume that the stock will be worth $Z \sim N(\mu, \sigma^2)$ tomorrow and a $1 bond will be worth R surely. If agent i has the utility function $-e^{-a_i c}$ over future consumption, compute the equilibrium price of the equity. Let $a_i \in [0.2, 5]$, $R \in [1.01, 1.5]$, $\mu \in [1.05, 2.0]$ and $\sigma \in [0.001, 0.1]$. Use Monte Carlo integration of various sizes to compute the necessary integrals.

6.   Use stochastic approximation to solve the asset demand example of section 8.5.

7.   Use stochastic approximation to solve problem 5 above.

8.   Use the inversion method to develop a random number generator for exponential distribution, for the Poisson distribution, and for the Normal distribution. Use suitable approximation methods from chapter 6.

9.   Suppose X and Y are independent and both $U[0, 1]$, and $Z = (X^{0.2} + Y^{0.5})^{0.3}$. Compute polynomial approximations of the conditional expectation $E\{Y|Z\}$. What size sample do you need to get the average error down to .01.

10. Use Monte Carlo methods to compute the ergodic distributions for $x_{t+1} = \rho x_t + \varepsilon_t$ for $\rho = 0.1, 0.5, 0.9$, and $\varepsilon_t \sim U[-1, 1]$. Next compute the ergodic distribution for $x_{t+1} = \rho \sqrt{x_t} + \varepsilon_t$ for $\rho = 0.1, 0.5, 0.9$, and $\varepsilon_t \sim U[0, 1]$. Repeat these exercises with $\ln \varepsilon_t \sim N(0, 1)$.

9 Quasi–Monte Carlo Methods

We next discuss *quasi–Monte Carlo* methods for integration and simulation. In contrast to Monte Carlo ideas, they rely on ideas from number theory and Fourier analysis, and they are often far more powerful than Monte Carlo methods. In this chapter we present the basic quasi–Monte Carlo ideas and methods.[1] Before we get to the details, we first make some general points.

To understand the basic idea behind quasi–Monte Carlo methods, it is useful to realize what Monte Carlo methods really are in practice. As we pointed out in chapter 8, pseudorandom sequences are generally used in practice instead of truly "random" (whatever that means) sequences. Despite their similarities, pseudorandom sequences are deterministic, not random, sequences. Mathematicians have long known this; according to John von Neumann, anyone who believes otherwise "is living in a state of sin." Since they are not probabilistically independent, neither the law of large numbers nor the central limit theorem[2] apply to pseudorandom sequences. The fact that neither linear statistical techniques nor the human eye can distinguish between random numbers and pseudorandom number sequences is of no logical relevance and has no impact on mathematical rates of convergence.

These issues are often confusingly discussed in the Monte Carlo literature. For example, Kloek and van Dijk (1978) contrast the Monte Carlo convergence rate of $N^{-1/2}$ with Bahravov's theorem showing that the convergence rate for deterministic schemes for d-dimensional C^1 integrable functions is $N^{-1/d}$ at best. However, they then go on to use pseudorandom number generators in their Monte Carlo experiments. This is typical of the Monte Carlo literature where probability theorems are often used to analyze the properties of algorithms that use *deterministic* sequences. Strictly speaking, procedures that use pseudorandom numbers are not Monte Carlo schemes; when it is desirable to make the distinction, we will refer to Monte Carlo schemes using pseudorandom sequences as *pseudo–Monte Carlo* (pMC) methods.

Even though experimental evidence of pseudo–Monte Carlo methods shows that they work as predicted by the Monte Carlo theory, this does not validate the invalid use of probabilistic arguments. Pseudorandom methods are instead validated by a substantial literature (Niederreiter 1992 and Traub and Wozniakowski 1992 are recent good examples) which explicitly recognizes the determinism of pseudorandom sequences. These analyses rely on the properties of the deterministic pseudorandom

---

1. In this chapter we frequently use Fourier expansions wherein the letter i will denote the square root of -1. To avoid confusion, we do not use it as an index of summation.

2. I here refer to the law of large numbers as stated in Chung (1974, theorem 5.2.2), and the central limit theorem as stated in Chung (1974, theorem 6.4.4). These theorems rely on independence properties of random variables, not just on zero correlation. There may exist similar theorems that rely solely on the serial correlation and runs properties of pseudorandom sequences, but I don't know of any.

generators, not on probability theory. More important, since pseudorandom sequences are deterministic, their success tells us that there are deterministic sequences that are good for numerical integration. Furthermore the random versus deterministic distinction is of no practical importance in numerical analysis. In fact it is damaging, for it may keep a reader from considering other deterministic schemes. Therefore the real questions for our purposes are, How can *deterministic* sequences yield good approximations to integrals, which *deterministic* sequences yield the most rapidly convergent quadrature schemes, and how can good *deterministic* sequences be constructed? This perspective leads to a new set of concepts, and also to *quasi–Monte Carlo* (qMC) methods.

These observations still raise a logical problem: Why do the *deterministic* schemes used in Monte Carlo applications satisfy the $N^{-1/2}$ prediction of *probability* theorems, and avoid the $N^{-1/d}$ convergence rate of *deterministic* schemes? There is no problem once one knows the norms that are being used in these comparisons. Monte Carlo methods have an *expected* error proportional to $N^{-1/2}$, whereas the *worst-case* error for deterministic schemes is $N^{-1/d}$. Furthermore, if we confine our attention to functions of bounded variation, as is usually the case for applications of Monte Carlo methods, then there exist deterministic schemes with convergence rate N^{-1}. In this chapter we present a unified analysis of error bounds for Monte Carlo, pseudo–Monte Carlo, and quasi–Monte Carlo schemes and find that this confusion disappears when one uses the *same* metric and focus on relevant spaces of functions to compare alternative methods.

When we dispense with the irrelevant random versus deterministic distinction, we find that quasi–Monte Carlo methods schemes do far better asymptotically than any Monte Carlo method for many problems. For example, in September 1995, IBM announced that it had developed software for pricing financial derivatives based on quasi–Monte Carlo methods that outperformed Monte Carlo methods by a factor of 1,000.

Before proceeding, we make two distinctions. First, a *sampling* method is any method that "samples" the domain of integration and uses an (usually unweighted) average of the integrand's values at the sample as an estimate of an integral's value. The Monte Carlo method is a sampling method. Second, we define quasi–Monte Carlo methods in a negative way: *Quasi–Monte Carlo methods* are sampling methods that do not rely on probabilistic ideas and pseudorandom sequences for constructing the sample and analyzing the estimate. Quasi–Monte Carlo methods are frequently called *number theoretic methods* because they often explicitly rely on number theory ideas. The term "quasi–Monte Carlo" is misleading because the methods covered under that umbrella have nothing to do with probability theory; on the other hand, the use of the prefix "pseudo"—which, according to *Webster's Third New International Dictionary*, means "false, feigned, fake, counterfeit, spurious, illusory"—to describe pseudorandom numbers is totally appropriate. The key idea is sampling, and the various methods, pseudo- and quasi-, are distinguished by the particular deterministic scheme used to generate the sample.

9.1 Equidistributed Sequences

Up to nonlinear changes of variables, Monte Carlo integration methods ultimately rely on the properties of sequences of uniformly distributed i.i.d. random variables. The ex ante uniformity of the samples make the Monte Carlo estimate of an integral unbiased. However, probability theory does not apply to pseudorandom sequences. In order to analyze deterministic sampling schemes, including pseudorandom numbers, we need to develop concepts for analyzing errors and convergence.

We next introduce the concept for deterministic sequences which (up to measure zero) generalizes the key properties of Monte Carlo samples.

DEFINITION   A sequence $\{x_j\}_{j=1}^{\infty} \subset R$ is *equidistributed* over $[a, b]$ iff

$$\lim_{n \to \infty} \frac{b-a}{n} \sum_{j=1}^{n} f(x_j) = \int_{a}^{b} f(x) \, dx \tag{9.1.1}$$

for all Riemann-integrable $f(x)$. More generally, a sequence $\{x^j\}_{j=1}^{\infty} \subset D \subset R^d$ is *equidistributed* over D iff

$$\lim_{n \to \infty} \frac{\mu(D)}{n} \sum_{j=1}^{n} f(x^j) = \int_{D} f(x) \, dx \tag{9.1.2}$$

for all Riemann-integrable $f(x) : R^d \to R$, where $\mu(D)$ is the Lebesgue measure of D.

Equidistribution formalizes the idea of a uniformly distributed sequence. One key property is that an equidistributed sequence is ex post uniformly distributed, not just uniform in expectation. Equidistribution is exactly the property that a sequence will give us an asymptotically valid approximation to any integral. Here we focus directly on constructing sequences that do well at integration.

Unfortunately, it is not easy to construct equidistributed sequences. For example, one might think that the sequence $0, \frac{1}{2}, 1, \frac{1}{4}, \frac{3}{4}, \frac{1}{8}, \frac{3}{8}, \frac{5}{8}, \frac{7}{8}$, etc., would be equidistributed over $[0, 1]$. This is not the case, since the finite sums $\frac{1}{n} \sum_{j=1}^{n} f(x_j)$ for, say, $f(x) = x$, do not converge to $\int_{0}^{1} x \, dx = \frac{1}{2}$, nor to anything else. Certain subsequences of the finite sums will converge properly; in particular, if we average over the first 5 terms,

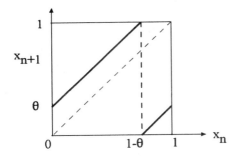

Figure 9.1
Graph of a Weyl rule

then the first 9, then 17, 33, $\ldots, 2^k + 1$, etc., the averages will converge to $\frac{1}{2}$. Hence the true integral is a limit point. However, if we average over the first 7, then 13, 25, etc., the limit is $\frac{3}{8}$. This is because the first 7 terms contain two terms greater than 0.5 and four below 0.5, and a similar two-to-one ratio holds for the first 13, 25, 49, etc. The definition of equidistributed sequences, however, requires convergence of the sequence *and all subsequences* of finite sums to the integral, not just a subsequence. The failure of this simple sequence to be equidistributed shows that equidistribution is a strong property.

The simplest example of a sequence equidistributed over $[0, 1]$ is a *Weyl sequence*

$$x_n = \{n\theta\}, \qquad n = 1, 2, \ldots, \tag{9.1.3}$$

for θ irrational, where the expression $\{x\}$ is called the *fractional part of* x and is defined by $\{x\} \equiv x - \max\{k \in Z \mid k \leq x\}$. The $\{x\}$ notation is a bit odd since $\{\cdot\}$ has other uses. In this chapter we try to avoid confusion by limiting use of $\{\cdot\}$ to this fractional part function. Figure 9.1 displays the graph of $x_{n+1} = f(x_n)$ implied by (9.1.3). Note that the slope is unity and there is only one discontinuity. This function is notably different from the typical LCM generator in figure 8.1.

One should be careful when calculating $\{x\}$. This calculation is determined by the digits of x of lowest significance, making it very sensitive to roundoff error. For example, suppose that we have a machine with six-digit precision. To six digits, $\sqrt{2} = 1.41421$. On such a machine, $\{100\sqrt{2}\} = 0.421$, which is only the first three significant digits of the six-digit accurate value 0.421356. In general, if $\theta \in [0, 1]$, $\{n\theta\}$ will have $\log_{10} n$ fewer significant digits than machine precision. Such sequences will have successively less precision as n increases. If this is a concern, then $\{n\theta\}$ should be calculated using quadruple precision or multiple precision software.

Table 9.1
Equidistributed sequences in R^d

Name	Formula for x^n
Weyl	$(\{np_1^{1/2}\}, \ldots, np_d^{1/2}\})$
Haber	$\left(\left\{\dfrac{n(n+1)}{2}p_1^{1/2}\right\}, \ldots, \left\{\dfrac{n(n+1)}{2}p_d^{1/2}\right\}\right)$
Niederreiter	$(\{n2^{1/(d+1)}\}, \ldots, \{n2^{d/(d+1)}\})$
Baker	$(\{ne^{r_1}\}, \ldots, \{ne^{r_d}\}), r_j$ rational and distinct

This example can be generalized to construct multidimensional equidistributed sequences. If θ_j, $j = 1, \ldots, d$, are linearly independent irrational numbers over the rationals, that is, if $\forall \alpha \in Z^d$ $(\sum_{j=1}^{d} \alpha_j \theta_j \neq 0)$, then the points

$$x^n = (\{n\theta_1\}, \ldots, \{n\theta_d\}), \qquad n = 1, 2, \ldots,$$

are equidistributed over $[0, 1]^d$.

Many equidistributed sequences rely on the properties of primes; let $p_1, p_2, \ldots,$ denote the sequence of prime numbers $2, 3, 5, \ldots$. Table 9.1 contains a number of examples of equidistributed sequences.

The connections between equidistributed sequences and Monte Carlo ideas should be noted. First, the law of large numbers essentially says that a sequence of i.i.d. draws is almost surely equidistributed. However, pseudorandom sequences, such as those of the linear congruential form, are not equidistributed since they eventually cycle. Second, the sequence (9.1.3) can be generated by the iteration $x_{n+1} = (x_n + \theta) \bmod 1$, a form similar to the schemes used to generate pseudorandom numbers.

The more relevant distinction between pseudorandom sequences and equidistributed sequences is that there is no attempt to make equidistributed sequences "look like" random numbers. In fact they generally display substantial nonzero serial correlation. We begin to see why quasi–Monte Carlo methods may outperform Monte Carlo methods when it comes to integration. Equidistributed sequences are designed from the outset to do integration accurately, and they are not encumbered by other requirements associated with "randomness." The only purpose served by the "random" character of pseudorandom sequences is that it tempts us to invoke the law of large numbers in convergence arguments. If there is some other way of showing (9.1.1) or (9.1.2), then we can jettison "randomness," which is needed for applications of LLN and CLT. In fact we will see that by attacking the integration problem directly we will do much better than Monte Carlo.

9.2   Low-Discrepancy Methods

In Monte Carlo methods the ex post sample is not uniformly distributed. The deviations from uniformity lead to errors proportional to $N^{-1/2}$, in accord with the CLT. If deterministic pseudo–Monte Carlo methods have a similar error, then something other than the CLT is at work. We saw in the previous section that equidistribution was the key to a valid quadrature method. In this section we introduce the concepts that are used to analyze the properties of all deterministic sequences, pseudorandom and quasi–Monte Carlo, for integration. These concepts allow us to rank various equidistributed sequences and compare them to Monte Carlo sequences.

Discrepancy

We need to define a measure of how dispersed a collection of points is; this leads us to concepts of *discrepancy*. Let $x_j \in I \equiv [0,1]$, $j = 1, \ldots, N$, be a sequence of scalars. If $S \subset I$, define the cardinality of a set X in a set S, $\mathrm{card}(S \cap X)$, to be the number of elements of X which are also in S. We define two notions of discrepancy for finite sets.[3]

DEFINITION   The *discrepancy* D_N of the set $X \equiv \{x_1, \ldots, x_N\} \subset [0,1]$ is

$$D_N(X) = \sup_{0 \leq a < b \leq 1} \left| \frac{\mathrm{card}([a,b] \cap X)}{N} - (b-a) \right|.$$

DEFINITION   The *star discrepancy* D_N^* of the set $X \equiv \{x_1, \ldots, x_N\} \subset [0,1]$ is

$$D_N^*(X) = \sup_{0 \leq t \leq 1} \left| \frac{\mathrm{card}([0,t] \cap X)}{N} - t \right|$$

We can extend these concepts to sequences.

DEFINITION   If X is a sequence $x_1, x_2, \cdots \subset [0,1]$, then $D_N(X)(D_N^*(X))$ is $D_N(X^N)$ $(D_N^*(X^N))$ where $X^N = \{x_j \in X \,|\, j = 1, \ldots, N\}$.

These definitions allow us to measure the deviations from uniformity of both sets and initial segments of sequences. We focus on the behavior of D_N and D_N^* as N increases. The difference between D_N and D_N^* is that D_N examines all subintervals, whereas D_N^* examines only initial segments, $[0,t)$. Even though a continuum of

---

3. Authors differ in their definitions of D and D^*; we use the definitions in Niedereitter (1992). Despite the possible confusion, all results concerning rates of convergence are the same for D^* and D.

intervals is used in the definitions, we need only to check open intervals of the form (x_l, x_j), $1 \le l, j \le N$, for D_N, and $(0, x_l)$, $1 \le l \le N$, for D_N^*. The star discrepancy is far easier to compute, but both are useful concepts measuring dispersion. The smallest possible value for D_N and D_N^* is $1/(N + 1)$, which is the discrepancy of $\{1/(N + 1), 2/(N + 1), \ldots, N/(N + 1)\}$, the most dispersed set of N points possible in $[0, 1]$. The dimension one theory of discrepancy is trivial. We next consider multi-dimensional versions of these concepts.

DEFINITION   The star discrepancy D_N^* of the set $X = \{x_1, \ldots, x_N\} \subset I^d$ is

$$D_N^*(X) = \sup_{0 \le t_1, \ldots, t_d \le 1} \left| \frac{\text{card}([0, t_1) \times \cdots \times [0, t_d) \cap X)}{N} - \Pi_{j=1}^d t_j \right|$$

and $D_N^*(X)$ for sequences in I^d is defined as in the case $d = 1$. $D_N(X)$ is generalized similarly from $d = 1$.

A small discrepancy says that the sequence evenly fills up the hypercube I^d. As N increases, the discrepancy should go down. Not all equidistributed sequences have the same discrepancy. We want to find equidistributed sequences with initial segments having small discrepancy, a property that will lead to smaller errors in integration applications.

One set of particular interest is the uniformly distributed lattice points. More specifically, if we define

$$U_{d,m} = \left\{ \left(\frac{2m_1 - 1}{2m}, \ldots, \frac{2m_d - 1}{2m} \right) \middle| 1 \le m_j \le m, j = 1, \ldots, d \right\}$$

to be the lattice with m points in each of the d directions in I^d, then $U_{d,m}$ has $N = m^d$ points and $D_N^*(U_{d,m}) = \mathcal{O}(N^{-1/d}) = \mathcal{O}(m^{-1})$. (See Hua and Wang 1981.) For the uniform lattice the discrepancy falls very slowly as the number of points increases, and more slowly as d increases.

Random sequences have smaller discrepancies than $U_{d,m}$ on average. Let x^j, $j = 1, \ldots, N$, be an i.i.d. sequence uniformly and independently distributed over I^d. Chung (1949) and Kiefer (1961) prove that the star discrepancy of such a collection of N points is almost surely $\mathcal{O}(N^{-1/2}(\log \log N)^{1/2})$, where the proportionality constant depends on dimension. Note that this is essentially $\mathcal{O}(N^{-1/2})$, the familiar Monte Carlo rate of convergence.

There are also results that put lower limits on D_N^*. Roth (1954) and Kuipers and Niederreiter (1974) showed that for any collection of N points in I^d,

$$D_N^* > 2^{-4d}((d - 1) \log 2)^{(1-d)/2} N^{-1} (\log N)^{(d-1)/2}. \tag{9.2.1}$$

Notice that this lower bound is considerably below the Chung-Kiefer result on randomly generated point sets. This bound applies to all sets, even to those generated "randomly."

No one has yet constructed a sequence that achieves the lower bound in (9.2.1). Some good sequences are constructed using the *radical-inverse function*. Suppose that p is a prime number. Any positive integer n has a base p expansion $n = \sum_{j=0}^k a_j p^j$. Given the coefficients, a_j, the radical-inverse function, $\varphi_p(n)$, is defined by

$$\varphi_p(n) = \sum_{j=0}^k a_j p^{-j-1}. \tag{9.2.2}$$

The *van der Corput sequence* is the sequence $\varphi_2(n)$ for $n = 1, 2, \ldots$, and has discrepancy $D_N^* < (\frac{1}{3} \log_2 N + 1)/N$.

In d dimensions, $d \geq 2$, the *Hammersley set* of N points is the set

$$\left\{ \left(\frac{n}{N}, \varphi_{p_1}(n), \ldots, \varphi_{p_{d-1}}(n) \right) \middle| n = 1, \ldots, N \right\},$$

where $p_1, \ldots, p_{d-1}$ are $d-1$ relatively prime integers. Because it is finite, the Hammersley set is not an equidistributed sequence. The *Halton sequence* in I^d is

$$\{(\varphi_{p_1}(n), \varphi_{p_2}(n), \ldots, \varphi_{p_d}(n))\}_{n=1}^\infty, \tag{9.2.3}$$

where $p_1, \ldots, p_d$ are d distinct primes, and has discrepancy

$$ND_N < \frac{d}{N} + \prod_{j=1}^d \left(\frac{p_j - 1}{2 \log p_j} \log N + \frac{p_j + 1}{2} \right). \tag{9.2.4}$$

The discrepancy bounds in (9.2.1), (9.2.4) hold for all N, but is useful only for their asymptotic information since $(\log N)^d$ can be quite large. In fact, for a fixed value of d, $(\log N)^d$ will grow faster than N for moderate N, implying that D_N can be small for only very large N. Therefore, while the asymptotic properties of these bounds are good, they kick in at only impractically large N if the dimension d is not small.

Figure 9.2 displays a two-dimensional set of equidistributed points. Figure 9.2 is a plot of the first 1,500 Weyl points with $d = 2$. Note that this sample is more uniform than the set of pseudorandom points seen earlier in figure 8.2. This illustrates the point that quasi-random points aim to construct a uniform set of points, not one that looks random.

The weakness of these simple equidistributed sequences lies in their poor small sample properties. Of course some pseudo–Monte Carlo methods have similar

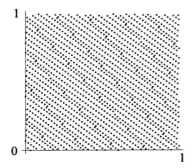

Figure 9.2
Initial 1,500 Weyl points

problems. It may appear easier to avoid small sample problems with pseudo–Monte Carlo schemes, but new quasi–Monte Carlo methods, cited in section 9.7, produce good small samples.

Variation and Integration

To apply the notions of discrepancy to integration, we need a measure of how variable a function is. This is easy in the one-dimensional case.

DEFINITION   The *total variation* of f, $V(f)$, on $[0,1]$ is

$$V(f) = \sup_n \sup_{0 \le x_0 < x_1 < \cdots < x_n \le 1} \sum_{j=1}^{n} |f(x_j) - f(x_{j-1})|.$$

The next theorem ties together the total variation and the discrepancy concepts to compute an upper bound on a quadrature formula.

THEOREM 9.2.1 (Koksma)   If f has bounded total variation, namely $V(f) < \infty$, on I, and the sequence $x_j \in I$, $j = 1, \ldots, N$, has discrepancy D_N^*, then

$$\left| N^{-1} \sum_{j=1}^{N} f(x_j) - \int_0^1 f(x)\, dx \right| \le D_N^* V(f) \tag{9.2.5}$$

The quadrature approximation $N^{-1} \sum_{j=1}^{N} f(x_j)$ in theorem 9.2.1 is essentially the composite midpoint rule except for the fact that here the x_j nodes need not be evenly distributed. However, (9.2.5), tells us that the best choice of $\{x_1, \ldots, x_N\}$ would be the uniform collection since that set has the smallest D_N^*. Therefore the one-dimensional case leads us essentially back to the midpoint rule.

Note the kind of the quadrature error analysis implicit in Koksma's theorem. Monte Carlo methods use the variance of a function to get probabilistic estimates of error. Quasi–Monte Carlo methods use variation measures to generate worst-case error bounds. Since Monte Carlo methods also use quadrature approximations of the kind in (9.2.5), the worst-case error bound in (9.2.5) also applies to Monte Carlo errors. This observation gives us more information about Monte Carlo integration. Koksma's theorem combined with the Chung-Kiefer bound on D_N^* of a random set of points in R tells us that the worst-case error for Monte Carlo integration is almost surely $\mathcal{O}(N^{-1/2}(\log \log N)^{1/2})$. Of course the absolute worst-case error is $\mathcal{O}(1)$, since there are sequences that won't converge.

While these results are aesthetically interesting and provide insight as to how these methods work, they have little practical value since the convergence rate is the same as for the midpoint rule. No one seriously uses Monte Carlo or quasi–Monte Carlo methods for one-dimensional integrals of smooth functions.

The real interest lies in multidimensional applications. To extend these ideas to R^d, we need a multidimensional version of total variation. Suppose that $H = [a_1^1, a_2^1] \times [a_1^2, a_2^2] \times \cdots \times [a_1^d, a_2^d]$ is a subset of I^d. A measure of how much f varies over H is

$$\Delta(f; H) \equiv \sum_{j_1=1}^{2} \cdots \sum_{j_d=1}^{2} (-1)^{j_1 + \cdots + j_d} f(a_{j_1}^1, \ldots, a_{j_d}^d).$$

A partition $\mathscr{P}$ of I^d is any collection of hyper-rectangles that is pairwise disjoint but covers I^d. Our first measure of total variation is

$$V^V(f) = \sup_{\mathscr{P}} \sum_{H \in \mathscr{P}} |\Delta(f; H)|.$$

If f has enough derivatives, then $V^V(f) = \int_{I^d} |\partial^d f / \partial x_1 \ldots \partial x_d| \, dx$. If $V^V(f)$ is finite, then f is *of bounded variation on I^d in the sense of Vitali*.

From the derivative version, we immediately see a problem with $V^V(f)$. The dth cross-partial of f for $d > 2$ will be zero even for functions that vary substantially, such as $\sum_{j=1}^{d-1} x_j x_{j+1}$. The Vitali concept of variation ignores variation on lower-dimensional subspaces. To address this problem, we measure $V^V(f)$ on those lower-dimensional subspaces and include it in the measure of total variation. Suppose that $J \subset \{1, \ldots, d\}$. Define f^J to be the function equal to f but restricted to $I^J \equiv \{x \in I \mid x_j = 1, j \in J\}$. If J is the empty set, f^J is f; otherwise, f^J is the restriction of f to a $(d - |J|)$-dimensional subspace of I^d, and $V^V(f^J)$ is the variation of f on that subspace. The *variation in the sense of Hardy and Krause* is defined by the formula

$$V^{HK}(f) = \sum_{J \subset \{1,\ldots,d\}} V^V(f^J).$$

The following theorem generalizes Koksma to multiple dimensions.

THEOREM 9.2.2 (Hlawka)   If $V^{HK}(f)$ is finite and $\{x^j\}_{j=1}^N \subset I^d$ has discrepancy D_N^*, then

$$\left| \frac{1}{N} \sum_{j=1}^N f(x^j) - \int_{I^d} f(x)\,dx \right| \le V^{HK}(f) D_N^*.$$

The Hlawka theorem is a much more useful result. Again it tells us to use sets with small D_N^*, but that does not point to any simple rule we saw before. The product trapezoid rule essentially uses the uniform grid point set, $U_{d,m}$, with star-discrepancy $\mathcal{O}(N^{-1/d})$. Instead, we should use one of the sequences that had much smaller discrepancies, such as the Halton sequence or one of those in table 9.1.

Monte Carlo versus Quasi–Monte Carlo

We next compare "stochastic" sampling methods and quasi–Monte Carlo methods of sampling. In terms of asymptotic performance for smooth functions of bounded variation, there is no contest. For all dimensions d we know of sequences such that the rate of convergence of the worst-case error for quasi–Monte Carlo methods is of order $N^{-1}(\log N)^d$, whereas the *expected* error of Monte Carlo integration methods is of order $N^{-1/2}$.

Furthermore, even though the worst-case measures used to evaluate quasi–Monte Carlo methods differ in spirit from the average-case measure implicitly used in Monte Carlo analyses, there is no difference for this problem. Wozniakowski (1991) showed that the average convergence rate for the optimal deterministic sampling method is the same as the worst-case rate, that being $N^{-1}(\log N)^{(d-1)/2}$.

We have examined the theoretical issue of rate of convergence of Monte Carlo and quasi–Monte Carlo sampling schemes. We will next show that these asymptotic results do appear at reasonable sample sizes and are of practical importance.

Tables 9.2 and 9.3 concretely illustrate our asymptotic results. These tables examine two integrals, displaying the errors of various quadrature formulas for versions of each in various dimensions. In table 9.2 we examine an integral that has no interaction across variables but does contain kinks. First note that for $d = 10$, the errors appear to be following the predicted asymptotic behavior, with all procedures converging at roughly rate N^{-1}. At both dimensions we see that the Monte Carlo procedure (we invoked a library Fortran random number generator) was inferior to

Table 9.2
Integration errors for $\int_{I^d} d^{-1} \sum_{j=1}^{d} |4x_j - 2| \, dx$

N	MC	Weyl	Haber	Niederreiter
$d = 10$				
10^3	1(−3)	3(−4)	4(−4)	4(−4)
10^4	2(−4)	6(−5)	1(−3)	3(−5)
10^5	1(−3)	7(−6)	2(−4)	2(−6)
10^6	4(−5)	6(−7)	2(−4)	2(−7)
$d = 40$				
10^3	3(−3)	4(−4)	3(−3)	2(−4)
10^4	3(−4)	6(−5)	1(−3)	2(−6)
10^5	4(−6)	5(−6)	3(−4)	9(−6)
10^6	1(−4)	6(−7)	1(−5)	4(−7)

Table 9.3
Integration errors for $\int_{I^d} \prod_{j=1}^{d} \left(\frac{\pi}{2} \sin \pi x_j \right) dx$

N	MC	Weyl	Haber	Niederreiter
$d = 10$				
10^3	1(−2)	6(−2)	8(−2)	9(−3)
10^4	3(−2)	8(−3)	5(−3)	5(−4)
10^5	9(−3)	2(−3)	1(−3)	6(−4)
10^6	2(−3)	3(−5)	6(−3)	2(−4)
$d = 40$				
10^3	4(−1)	5(−1)	5(−2)	7(−1)
10^4	2(−1)	4(−1)	4(−1)	8(−2)
10^5	1(−2)	2(−1)	3(−3)	5(−2)
10^6	3(−2)	2(−1)	3(−2)	4(−3)

two of the three quasi-random sequences. All procedures did less well for the high-dimension case, but the Monte Carlo procedure seems to be the most sensitive to the dimensionality problems, whereas the Haber and Niederreiter quasi-random sequences have small errors converging at the theoretical rate even for $d = 40$.

Table 9.3 displays results for integrals with more interactions and higher total variation. For $d = 10$ the errors are small and falling, but for $d = 40$ it appears that the asymptotic bounds are not operating except for the largest sample sizes. Monte Carlo seems to be the best behaved in terms of avoiding very large errors but begins to be dominated by quasi-random sequences at large samples. The Niederreiter sequence appears to be the most reliable one, almost always dominating Monte Carlo for large samples.

Tables 9.2 and 9.3 apply equidistributional sequences to integration problems. They can also be used for optimization problems. Section 8.3 discussed using pseudorandom sequences to solve optimization problems by search. Equidistributional sequences can be substituted for the pseudorandom sequences and optimization implemented by *quasi-random search*; see Niederreiter and McCurley (1979) for a discussion.

These experiments are consistent with the theory in that Monte Carlo schemes are dominated by quasi–Monte Carlo schemes asymptotically but may enjoy finite sample advantages. The finite sample advantages of Monte Carlo methods are greater as the dimension increases. Therefore the choice of method depends on the dimension of the problem and the sample size used. In the past, such as when Davis and Rabinowitz (1984) wrote, sensible sample sizes were small. As computing speeds increase, the typical sample size will increase, likely increasing the dominance of quasi-random sequences over Monte Carlo methods. Also, as we develop equidistributional schemes better than the simple ones used in tables 9.2 and 9.3, even these small sample advantages of Monte Carlo schemes will be reduced and likely disappear.

9.3 Fourier Analytic Methods

Quasi–Monte Carlo integration methods which rely on low-discrepancy sequences can be used for any integrable function of finite variation. Despite these weak restrictions the results of the previous section show that small discrepancy quasi–Monte Carlo methods are able to construct integration methods with $\mathcal{O}(N^{-1+\varepsilon})$ convergence rates for any positive ε.

However, the methods of the previous section are often not the best for our purposes. In particular, their finite sample behavior is not acceptable for large dimensions. Fortunately we can do better by exploiting a function's properties. Most of the functions we use in economics are much better behaved than just being of bounded variation. Bringing this good behavior to our analysis can dramatically improve sampling approaches to quadrature just as it did in Gaussian quadrature. In this section we will see that we can do much better when we apply Fourier methods to periodic integrands.

The power of Fourier methods is illustrated by the integral $\int_0^1 \cos 2\pi x \, dx = 0$ and its finite-sum approximation $N^{-1} \sum_{n=1}^{N} \cos 2\pi x_n$ where $x_n = \{n\alpha\}$. The periodicity of $\cos x$ implies that $\cos 2\pi \{n\alpha\} = \cos 2\pi n\alpha$ and allows us to drop the fractional part notation from the finite-sum expressions. Periodicity of $\cos 2\pi x$ also implies the existence of a convergent Fourier series representation; from de Moivre's theorem, the Fourier series for $\cos 2\pi x$ is $\cos 2\pi x = \frac{1}{2}(e^{2\pi i x} + e^{-2\pi i x})$. Since the integral $\int_0^1 \cos 2\pi x \, dx$ equals zero, the magnitude of any finite-sum approximation is the error and equals

$$\left| \frac{1}{N} \sum_{n=1}^{N} \frac{1}{2}(e^{2\pi i n \alpha} + e^{-2\pi i n \alpha}) \right| \leq \frac{1}{2N} \left(\left| \frac{e^{2\pi i N \alpha} - 1}{e^{2\pi i \alpha} - 1} \right| + \left| \frac{e^{-2\pi i N \alpha} - 1}{e^{-2\pi i \alpha} - 1} \right| \right)$$

$$\leq \frac{1}{2N} \left| \frac{2}{|e^{2\pi i \alpha} - 1|} + \frac{2}{|e^{-2\pi i \alpha} - 1|} \right| \leq \frac{C}{N} \qquad (9.3.1)$$

for a finite C as long as $e^{2\pi i \alpha} \neq 1$, which is true for any irrational α. Since the error is at most C/N, the convergence rate is N^{-1}. This is much better than the $N^{-1/2}$ promised by Monte Carlo methods, and also better than the $N^{-1} \ln N$ rate of using any of the sequences in table 9.1. The calculation in (9.3.1) is valid for any $f(x)$ which is a finite sum of $e^{2\pi i k x}$ terms. It can also be generalized to functions with arbitrary Fourier expansions.

We next want to apply this method to periodic functions over arbitrary dimension. To do this, we need to use some notation from Fourier analysis.

DEFINITION   Suppose that $f : [0,1]^d \to R$ is bounded. f is *periodic* if

$$f(x_1, \ldots, x_{j-1}, 0, x_{j+1}, \ldots, x_d) = f(x_1, \ldots, x_{j-1}, 1, x_{j+1}, \ldots, x_d)$$

for $j = 1, \ldots, d$, and for all $x \in I^d$. For $h \in Z^d$ and $x \in I^d$, let $h \cdot x$ denote $\sum_{l=1}^{d} h_l x_l$, and define.

$$\hat{f}(h) \equiv \int_{[0,1]^d} f(x) e^{-2\pi i h \cdot x} \, dx \qquad (9.3.2)$$

to be the *order h Fourier coefficient* of the periodic function f. Define

$$r(h) = \prod_{j=1}^{d} \max(1, |h_j|) \qquad (9.3.3)$$

for $h \in Z^d$. For a scalar $C > 0$, define $\mathscr{E}^k(C)$ to be the set of all periodic functions f such that its Fourier series representation

$$f(x) = \sum_{h \in Z^d} \hat{f}(h) e^{2\pi i h \cdot x} \qquad (9.3.4)$$

is absolutely convergent and that for all $h \neq 0$ the coefficients $\hat{f}(h)$ in (9.3.2) satisfy $|\hat{f}(h)| < Cr(h)^{-k}$. $\mathscr{E}^k$ is the set of functions which belong to $\mathscr{E}^k(C)$ for some $C > 0$.

The growth condition for the Fourier coefficients of $\mathscr{E}^k$ functions is certainly satisfied for any k by any finite Fourier series. We would like to have an easy way to determine if a function is a member of $\mathscr{E}^k$. Korobov proved the following important theorem (reported in Davis and Rabinowitz):

THEOREM 9.3.1 (Korobov)   Suppose, for some integer k, that $f: [0,1]^d \to R$ satisfies the following two conditions:

1. All partial derivatives

$$\frac{\partial^{m_1 + \cdots + m_d} f}{\partial x_1^{m_1} \cdots \partial x_d^{m_d}}, \qquad 0 \leq m_j \leq k - 1, \ 1 \leq j \leq d,$$

exist and are of bounded variation in the sense of Hardy and Krause.

2. All partial derivatives

$$\frac{\partial^{m_1 + \cdots + m_d} f}{\partial x_1^{m_1} \cdots \partial x_d^{m_d}}, \qquad 0 \leq m_j \leq k - 2, \ 1 \leq j \leq d,$$

are periodic on $[0,1]^d$.
   Then $f \in \mathscr{E}^k$.

Korobov's theorem is useful. It is impractical to compute Fourier series coefficients of multidimensional functions. Korobov tells us that we don't need to do this. All we need to check are smoothness, periodicity, and bounded variation; that is, if a function and enough of its derivatives are bounded and periodic, then its Fourier coefficients disappear at rate $r(h)^{-k}$. These derivative conditions are generally easy to check, and therefore Korobov's theorem makes it practical to use the $\mathscr{E}^k$ property.

The importance of periodicity is illustrated in Richtmeyer's (1952) theorem.

THEOREM 9.3.2 (Richtmeyer)   Suppose that $f: [0,1]^d \to R$ is periodic and $\theta_1, \ldots, \theta_d$, are d linearly independent irrational numbers in $[0,1]$. If f is C^1 with ∇f being bounded and of bounded variation in the sense of Hardy and Krause, then

$$\left| \int_{[0,1]^d} f \, dx - \frac{1}{N} \sum_{n=1}^{N} f(\{n\theta_1\}, \ldots, \{n\theta_d\}) \right| \leq \frac{A}{N}$$

for some $A \in R$.

This is a significant improvement, since we have eliminated the $(\log N)^d$ terms which appear in even the best versions of Hlawka's theorem. This theorem shows that we can get rapid convergence with moderate-size samples as long as f is periodic and smooth.

Periodization

At first theorems 9.3.1 and 9.3.2 may seem of little use because they assume that f is periodic. This can be remedied at relatively small cost. To use these rules for nonperiodic functions, we replace $f(x)$ with a periodic function, $\tilde{f}(x)$ such that $\int_{[0,1]^d} f = \int_{[0,1]^d} \tilde{f}$. One simple example of such a transformation is

$$\tilde{f}(x_1, \ldots, x_d) = f(1 - 2|x_1 - \tfrac{1}{2}|, \ldots, 1 - 2|x_d - \tfrac{1}{2}|).$$

Since this transformation will not preserve differentiability, $\tilde{f}$ cannot belong to any C^k.

If we want Richtmeyer's theorem to apply, we must preserve differentiability. Suppose that we want to compute $\int_0^1 f(x)dx$ where $f(x)$ is C^∞ but not periodic. To accomplish this, we use a change of variables. Let $x = g(u)$ be a C^∞ nonlinear change of variables with $g(0) = 0$ and $g(1) = 1$. Then

$$\int_0^1 f(x)dx = \int_0^1 f(g(u))g'(u)du \equiv \int_0^1 h(u)du,$$

where $h(u) \equiv f(g(u))g'(u)$. If $g'(0) = g'(1) = 0$, then $h(0) = h(1) = 0$ and $h(u)$ is continuous and periodic. Furthermore, if $g''(0) = g''(1) = 0$, then we can show that $h'(u)$ is also continuous and periodic. In these cases g has transformed $\int_0^1 f(x)dx$ into an integral with a periodic integrand.

The following family of transformations accomplish periodization:

$$\tilde{f}_m(x_1, \ldots, x_d) = f(\psi_m(x_1), \ldots, \psi_m(x_d))\, \psi'_m(x_1) \cdots \psi'_m(x_d),$$

where

$$\psi_m(u) \equiv (2m - 1)\binom{2m - 2}{m - 1} \int_0^u t^{m-1}(1 - t)^{m-1}\, dt.$$

In general, if f is C^m on a compact domain, then $\tilde{f}_m$ will be in $\mathscr{E}^{m+2}$. Each transformation can be easily computed. In particular, $\psi_2(u) = 3u^2 - 2u^3$ and $\psi_3(u) = 10u^3 - 15u^4 + 6u^5$.

This is again the application of the change of variables idea. In this case we want to use formulas designed for periodic functions; therefore we find a change of variables such that the new integrand is periodic. This periodization technique is also useful for the next class of rules we examine.

9.4 Method of Good Lattice Points

The procedures outlined in sections 9.2 and 9.3 use infinite sequences that are equi-distributed. The advantage of such methods is that one has flexibility concerning the size of the sample to be taken. However, they have finite sample problems. Instead, the *method of good lattice points* first fixes the sample size, and then chooses a good collection of points of that size. This method is due to Korobov (1959, 1960) and makes powerful use of the $\mathscr{E}^k$ property to construct quadrature formulas that converge at rate $N^{-k+\varepsilon}$ for $f \in \mathscr{E}^k$.

The method of good lattice points begins with an integer N and a vector $g \in \{0, 1, \ldots, N-1\}^d$, forms the finite collection of points

$$x_l = \left\{ \frac{l}{N} g \right\}, \qquad l = 1, \ldots, N, \tag{9.4.1}$$

and computes the quasi–Monte Carlo approximation

$$\int_{I^d} f(x)dx \doteq \frac{1}{N} \sum_{l=1}^{N} f(x_\ell). \tag{9.4.2}$$

This approach uses a sample of fixed size N; extending (9.4.1) beyond N is pointless, since $x_{N+l} = x_\ell$.

The task is to find combinations of N and g such that the approximation in (9.4.2) is good. To do this, we apply Fourier series methods. Suppose that f is periodic on I^d, with an absolutely convergent Fourier series (9.3.4). Next note that $\hat{f}(0) = \int_{I^d} f(x)dx$. Using the Fourier series (9.3.4), the error in the approximation (9.4.2) can be written

$$\frac{1}{N} \sum_{l=1}^{N} \sum_{h \in Z^d} \hat{f}(h) e^{(2\pi i l/N)h \cdot g} - \hat{f}(0). \tag{9.4.3}$$

In (9.4.3) we note that $e^{2\pi i x}$ is periodic on I^d and drop the fractional part notation from $\{(l/N)g\}$. By changing the order of summation, we can rewrite (9.4.3) as

$$\frac{1}{N} \sum_{h \in Z^d} \hat{f}(h) \sum_{l=1}^{N} e^{(2\pi i l/N)h \cdot g} - \hat{f}(0). \tag{9.4.4}$$

The key insight revolves around the inner sum, $\sum_{l=1}^{N} e^{(2\pi i l/N)(h \cdot g)}$. If $h \cdot g$ is a multiple of N, then $e^{(2\pi i l/N)(h \cdot g)} = 1$ for all l, and $\sum_{l=1}^{N} e^{(2\pi i l/N)(h \cdot g)} = N$. If $h \cdot g$ is not a multiple of N, then $h \cdot g = m \bmod N$ for some $m \neq 0$. The inner sum in (9.4.4) reduces to $\sum_{l=1}^{N} e^{2\pi i l m/N}$, which equals 0 when $m \neq 0$. Hence the error (9.4.3) reduces to

$$\sum_{\substack{0 \neq h \in Z^d \\ h \cdot g = 0 \bmod N}} \hat{f}(h). \tag{9.4.5}$$

which is a sum of some of the Fourier coefficients of $f(x)$. This error is bounded above by $\sum_{\substack{h \neq 0 \\ h \cdot g = 0 \bmod N}} |\hat{f}(h)|$ which is finite whenever the Fourier series is absolutely convergent. Since the low-order terms of (9.3.4) make the major contribution to (9.4.5), good choices of N and g will make $h \cdot g = 0 \bmod N$ for low-order choices of h. Furthermore, if the Fourier coefficients decline rapidly, then this error bound will also decline rapidly as we choose g and N that leave fewer of the low-order terms in (9.4.5). Therefore good choices for g and N will result in quadrature formulas that converge rapidly as N increases.

These ideas lead to informal notions of what are "good lattice points." Since $r(h)$ is a measure of the degree ("complexity") of e^{ihx}, we use it to create a sense of order to the Fourier coefficients. Hence we want $r(h)$ to be large if $h \cdot g \equiv 0 \bmod N$. In this case the error bound for the integration approximation is small.

Computation of Good Lattice Points

The computation of good lattice points is a difficult task; see Hua and Wang (1981) for some derivations. We include some examples of good lattice points, g, in table 9.4. In table 9.4, N is the sample size corresponding to a good lattice point. The good lattice points in table 9.4 have the form $g^d = (1, g_2^d, \ldots, g_d^d) \in R^d$ for $d = 3, 4, 5, 6$.

Unfortunately, the tables in existing books and papers are limited in their coverage. A serious user of lattice point methods would want to have a way to compute good lattice points for any sample size and dimension. A strategy pursued by Korobov and others is to examine lattice points that are simply generated and evaluate their performance in integrating certain test functions with known integrals. Two test functions that are particularly valuable are

$$F_1(x) = \prod_{j=1}^{d} (1 - 2\ln(2\sin \pi x_j)),$$

$$F_2(x) = \prod_{j=1}^{d} \left(1 - \frac{\pi^2}{6} + \frac{\pi^2}{2}(1 - 2\{x_j\})^2\right),$$

Table 9.4
Good lattice points

N	g_2^3	g_3^3	g_2^4	g_3^4	g_4^4
101	40	85			
1,069	136	323	71	765	865
10,007	544	5,733	1,206	3,421	2,842
100,063	53,584	37,334	92,313	24,700	95,582

N	g_2^5	g_3^5	g_4^5	g_5^5
1,069	63	762	970	177
10,007	198	9,183	6,967	8,507
33,139	32,133	17,866	21,281	32,247
10,063	90,036	77,477	27,253	6,222

N	g_2^6	g_3^6	g_4^6	g_5^6	g_6^6
3,001	233	271	122	1,417	51
10,007	2,240	4,093	1,908	931	3,984
33,139	18,236	1,831	19,143	5,522	22,910
100,063	43,307	15,440	39,114	43,534	39,955

which are both defined on I^d and integrate to 1. Their Fourier coefficients are $\hat{F}_1(h) = r(h)^{-1}$ and $\hat{F}_2(h) = r(h)^{-2}$. Therefore F_k is the function in $\mathscr{E}^k$, $k = 1, 2$, which Fourier coefficients converge at the slowest possible rate.

The first procedure is due to Korobov (1960). We choose a prime, p, to be the sample size N in (9.4.1), and choose the integer $a \in \{1, \ldots, p - 1\}$ that minimizes

$$H_1(a) \equiv \frac{3^d}{p} \sum_{k=1}^{p} \prod_{j=1}^{d} \left(1 - 2\left\{k\frac{a^{j-1}}{p}\right\}\right)^2.$$

$H_1(a)$ is the lattice integration formula (9.4.2) applied to $F_2(x)$ where we construct the lattice point g from the powers of $a \bmod p$ by $g_j = a^{j-1} \bmod p$, $j = 1, \ldots, d$. Since the Fourier coefficients of F_2 are all positive, the error is always positive. Therefore the Korobov method is to find a lattice point consisting of powers of $a \bmod p$ that minimizes $H_1(a)$, one of the worst-behaved functions in $\mathscr{E}^2$. We call such a point a *Korobov good lattice point*.

We can do this for each prime p to get a p-point lattice quadrature formula. There is no assurance that the formulas are monotonically better as we increase p, the number of points. Therefore, in constructing a sequence of lattice formulas, one should keep only those formulas that do better in integrating F_2 than formulas with fewer points.

The Korobov procedure for finding lattice points can be rather inefficient, requiring up to $O(dp^2)$ operations. Keast (1973) offers a more general procedure with lower computational cost. He first chooses J distinct primes, p_j, $j = 1, \ldots, J$, and lets their product p be the sample size N. He then chooses a sequence of integers a_j, $j = 1, \ldots, J$. First, a_1 is chosen to minimize

$$\frac{3^d}{p_1} \sum_{k=1}^{p_1} \prod_{j=1}^{d} \left(1 - 2\left\{k\frac{a^{j-1}}{p}\right\}\right)^2$$

over $a \in \{1, \ldots, p_1 - 1\}$. More generally, for $l = 1, \ldots, J$, a_l minimizes

$$H_l(a) \equiv \frac{3^d}{p_1 \cdots p_l} \sum_{k=1}^{p_1 \cdots p_l} \prod_{j=1}^{d} \left(1 - 2\left\{k\left(\frac{a_1^{j-1}}{p_1} + \cdots + \frac{a_{l-1}^{j-1}}{p_{l-1}} + \frac{a^{j-1}}{p}\right)\right\}\right)^2$$

for $a \in \{1, \ldots, p_l - 1\}$. The *Keast good lattice point* g is then defined to be

$$g_j = \sum_{l=1}^{J} \frac{p}{p_l} a_l^{j-1}, \qquad j = 1, \ldots, d.$$

This approach has the advantage of requiring at most $\mathcal{O}(d(p_1 \cdot p_1 + (p_1 p_2) \cdot p_2 + \cdots + pp_J))$ operations. Again $H_J(g)$ serves as a performance index to rank various lattice point rules. The Korobov and Keast procedures are capable of generating lattice integration rules with a wide variety of accuracy, size, and dimensions.

We next state precisely how good "good lattice points" are.

THEOREM 9.4.1 (Korobov, Keast) For each d there is a constant, α, such that the following is true for all N: The error in integrating $f \in \mathscr{E}^k(C)$ with a Korobov or Keast good lattice point with sample size N is bounded above by $\alpha C N^{-k} (\ln N)^{kd}$.

Note the very rapid asymptotic convergence rate as the sample size, N, increases; in fact we do better than $N^{-k+\varepsilon}$ convergence for every $\varepsilon > 0$. The presence of the logarithms and the dimensional factor may indicate that the asymptotics take longer to bite at higher dimensions and in the less smooth classes of functions, or it may just indicate that these error bounds are not good for small N. The practical value of these rules depends on whether these error bounds are tight, an issue best examined by numerical experimentation.

The method of good lattice points requires $f(x)$ to be periodic. The periodization methods discussed in section 9.3 can be used here to apply lattice methods to nonperiodic $f(x)$.

9.5 Estimating Quasi–Monte Carlo Errors

One purported advantage of Monte Carlo quadrature rules is the joint computation of an estimate for an integral and an estimate for the variance of such estimates, resulting in a confidence interval for the estimate. We now show that one can similarly estimate the error in a quasi–Monte Carlo approximation.

The basic idea is to add a small degree of randomness to provide an error estimate. This is referred to as the *randomization of a quasi–Monte Carlo rule*, and originated with Cranley and Patterson (1976). The general idea is to take a quadrature rule, $Q(f)$, and construct a continuum of related rules, $Q(f;\beta)$, parameterized by β, such that each rule is of "equal quality." While the equal quality requirement is ambiguous, the essential necessity is that the error of the quadrature rule $Q(f;\beta)$ is not systematically related to β and that these β rules are accurate "on average." More precisely, we require that

$$I(f) \equiv \int_D f(x)\,dx = E\{Q(f;\beta)\} \tag{9.5.1}$$

for some distribution of β.

One simple case is where (9.5.1) holds when β is uniformly distributed on $[0,1]$. Then, if we take a sample, $\beta_1,\dots,\beta_m$, the estimate

$$\hat{I} \equiv \frac{1}{m}\sum_{j=1}^{m} Q(f;\beta_j) \tag{9.5.2}$$

is an unbiased estimator of $I(f)$. Furthermore the standard deviation of $\hat{I}$, $\sigma_{\hat{I}}$, is approximated by

$$\hat{\sigma}_{\hat{I}}^2 \equiv \frac{\sum_{j=1}^{m}(Q(f;\beta_j) - \hat{I})^2}{m-1} \tag{9.5.3}$$

From the Chebyshev inequality $Pr\{|\hat{I} - I(f)| < k\sigma_{\hat{I}}\} \geq 1 - 1/k^2$, we can estimate confidence intervals. Here, as in Monte Carlo integration, the crucial step is to formulate the problem in such a fashion that we have an estimate of the standard deviation.

We can apply this to many quasi–Monte Carlo methods. Recall that number theoretic methods approximate $\int_{I^d} f(x)\,dx$ with rules of the form $Q^g(f) \equiv (1/N)\sum_{n=1}^{N} f(\{(n/N)\,g\})$ which has an error (9.4.5). Similarly the β shifted approximation $Q^g(f;\beta) \equiv 1/n\sum_{n=1}^{N} f(\{(n/N)\,g + \beta\})$ has error

$$\sum_{\substack{0 \neq h \in Z^d \\ h \cdot g = 0 \bmod N}} \hat{f}(h) e^{2\pi i \beta}, \tag{9.5.4}$$

which has the same absolute convergence properties as (9.4.5), since the formulas are identical except that each $\hat{f}(h)$ in (9.5.4) is multiplied by a complex number of norm one. Obviously the condition (9.5.1) holds when β is uniform. We can also use this procedure for any quasi–Monte Carlo integration scheme that relies on an equidistributed sequence, since if x_j is equidistributed on $[0, 1]$, then so is $x_j + \beta$.

9.6 Acceleration Methods and qMC Schemes

In the previous chapter we saw how we could improve the performance of Monte Carlo methods through a variety of acceleration methods. We can also use the same methods to improve quasi–Monte Carlo methods. The point of the acceleration methods was to replace $f(x)$ with a function that had the same integral but reduced variance. Since qMC methods do better with functions with reduced variation, acceleration schemes can also help qMC schemes.

For example, consider antithetic variates applied to $\int_0^1 x^2$. The total variation of $f(x) = x^2$ on $[0, 1]$ is 1, whereas the total variation of $\frac{1}{2}(x^2 + (1 - x)^2) = x^2 - x + \frac{1}{2}$ is $\frac{1}{2}$. Therefore applying a sampling scheme to $\frac{1}{2}(x^2 + (1 - x)^2)$ instead of x^2 will reduce the Koksma error bound, (9.2.5), by half. Similarly control variates are applicable whether we use MC or qMC to integrate the residual $f - \varphi$. We can also incorporate "importance sampling" into qMC schemes because it is just a change of variables scheme. We proceed just as in importance sampling for Monte Carlo integration except now we use a quasi–Monte Carlo sequence instead of a Monte Carlo scheme.

This observation holds for each of the acceleration methods discussed in chapter 8. Despite their probabilistic motivations, each acceleration method is basically a way to reduce total variation, which will reduce the maximum error of any deterministic sampling scheme, pseudo– or quasi–Monte Carlo.

9.7 Further Reading and Summary

This chapter has described sampling methods for integration and optimization that are based on number theoretic and Fourier analytic ideas. These methods realize an asymptotic convergence rate of N^{-1}, far faster than Monte Carlo methods. However, these asymptotic properties may not apply at reasonable sample sizes, and Monte

Carlo methods may dominate existing quasi–Monte Carlo methods for small sample sizes.

We have focused on the simpler quasi–Monte Carlo methods. The Sobol sequence, as implemented in Bratley and Fox (1988), is better than the equidistributed sequences displayed in tables 9.1. The (t, m, s) sequences described in Niederreiter (1992) dominate the Fourier analytic methods we discussed. This is an active area of ongoing research that is continuing to produce even better quasi–Monte Carlo methods.

The past three chapters have focused on integration methods. There is no one method that is always best. Gaussian methods dominate for low-dimensional integrals, say two to four, with smooth integrands. Monomial rules are likely to be competitive for integrals of moderate dimension, five to eight, with polynomial-like integrands. For smooth integrands and moderate dimension, quasi–Monte Carlo methods will also do well. If the dimension is large, the integrand not smooth, and the sample size is limited to a relatively small size (e.g., under a million), then Monte Carlo methods are likely the only ones that can give even a rough estimate.

Quasi–Monte Carlo methods have not been extensively used in economic analysis or econometrics. They have, however, received substantial attention in the financial literature, even the financial press, due to Paskov (1994) and Paskov and Traub (1995). Two web pages on quasi–Monte Carlo methods are http://www.mat.sbg.ac.at/schmidw/links.html/ and http://www.math.hkbu.edu.hk/qmc/qmc.html.

Exercises

1. Write programs that compute the Weyl, Haber, and Niederreiter sequences. Write them so as to keep down round-off errors. Compute serial correlation properties for the first 10^5 points.

2. Redo the example solving (8.5.4) in the preceding chapter, but use equidistributed sequences. Are the errors less?

3. Write programs implementing Korobov's and Keast's method for generating good lattice points. How well do they do on the integrals in tables 9.2, and 9.3?

4. Write a program to compute the star discrepancy of a set of points from I^n. Generate several random sets of 1,000 points in I^n, for $n = 3, 4, 5$, and compute their star discrepancy.

5. Devise a way to compute a set of points from I^n with low discrepancy. Use it to find a set of 100 points with $n = 2, 3, 5, 10, 20$. Do your sets have lower discrepancy than 100 random points? than 500 random points? Repeat this for 1,000 points.

6. Solve exercise 8.5 using Monte Carlo and quasi–Monte Carlo methods. Compare performance.

7. Redo exercise 8.9 using quasi–Monte Carlo samples.

8. Redo exercise 8.4 with equidistributional sequences. Compare the performance of Monte Carlo and quasi–Monte Carlo methods for this problem.

9. Repeat Exercise 8.10 using quasi–Monte Carlo methods.

III NUMERICAL METHODS FOR FUNCTIONAL PROBLEMS

10 Finite-Difference Methods

A wide variety of economic problems lead to differential, difference, and integral equations. Ordinary differential equations appear in models of economic dynamics. Integral equations appear in dynamic programming problems and asset pricing models. Discrete-time dynamic problems lead to difference equations. These examples are all examples of dynamic problems. However, other problems also reduce to differential equations, such as equilibria of signaling models. Furthermore differential and difference equations are just examples of what is more generally called functional equations. Many functional equations that arise naturally in economics lie outside the usual families. As economic analysis of dynamic problems becomes more advanced, even more complex functional equations will appear. In this and the next chapter we examine basic ways to solve functional equations.

In this chapter we examine basic methods for solving ordinary differential equations and linear Fredholm integral equations. The key common feature is that they discretize the independent variable. We begin with finite-difference methods for ordinary differential equations, and discuss applications to continuous-time optimal control models.

We first describe basic methods for solving initial value problems and apply them to a signaling problem. We then discuss shooting methods, which combine initial value problem methods with nonlinear equation methods to solve boundary value problems. Optimal control problems are boundary value problems, which we illustrate with a life-cycle examples. Simple shooting is often numerically unstable in economic applications. We introduce *reverse shooting* and show how it can do very well in optimal control problems by replacing "shooting" *for* a steady state with "shooting" *from* a steady state. We then examine integral equation solution methods that discretize the state space.

10.1 Classification of Ordinary Differential Equations

A *first-order ordinary differential equation* (ODE) has the form

$$\frac{dy}{dx} = f(y, x),$$ (10.1.1)

where $f: R^{n+1} \to R^n$ and the unknown is the function $y(x): [a, b] \subset R \to R^n$. When $n = 1$, we have a single differential equation, whereas if $n > 1$, we call (10.1.1) a *system of differential equations*.

In addition to (10.1.1) we need side conditions to tie down the unknown function $y(x)$. If we impose the condition $y(x_0) = y_0$ for some x_0, we have an *initial value problem* (IVP). A simple condition is $y(a) = y_0$; that is, we fix the value of y at the initial point, $x = a$. The IVP classification is also appropriate if we impose the terminal condition $y(b) = y_0$; the key fact is that $y(x)$ is pinned down at one $x_0 \in [a, b]$.

If we have a single differential equation, we can fix y at only one x; hence a first-order differential equation in one variable is an IVP by default. When $n > 1$, the auxiliary conditions could fix different components of y at various x's. A *two-point boundary value problem* (2PBVP) imposes n conditions on y of the form

$$g_i(y(a)) = 0, \qquad i = 1, \ldots, n',$$
$$g_i(y(b)) = 0, \qquad i = n' + 1, \ldots, n, \tag{10.1.2}$$

where $g \colon R^n \to R^n$. More generally, a BVP imposes

$$g_i(y(x_i)) = 0 \tag{10.1.3}$$

for a set of points, x_i, $a \le x_i \le b, 1 \le i \le n$. We often take $b = \infty$ in which case we impose some condition on $\lim_{x \to \infty} y(x)$. In both (10.1.2) and (10.1.3) we implicitly assume that the possibly nonlinear functions g do constitute n independent conditions. Despite the use of the words "initial" and "boundary," the critical difference between IVPs and BVPs is whether the auxiliary conditions concern the solution at one point, as in IVPs, or whether the auxiliary conditions concern the solution at several points, as in BVPs.

A simple transformation makes all these definitions apply even when higher derivatives of y are used. For example, when presented with the second-order differential equation

$$\frac{d^2 y}{dx^2} = g\left(\frac{dy}{dx}, y, x\right)$$

for $x, y \in R$, we define $z = dy/dx$ and study the system

$$\frac{dy}{dx} = z, \qquad \frac{dz}{dx} = g(z, y, x),$$

of two first-order differential equations. Similarly we can transform an nth-order differential equation to n first-order equations.

The same descriptions of IVP and BVP apply to discrete-time systems, and we can focus on first-order systems. For example, we can convert the second-order system $x_{t+1} = g(x_t, x_{t-1}, t)$ into the first-order system

$$z_{t+1} = \begin{pmatrix} x_{t+1} \\ x_t \end{pmatrix} = \begin{pmatrix} g(x_t, x_{t-1}, t) \\ x_t \end{pmatrix} = G(z_t).$$

This stacking trick allows first-order notation to denote arbitrary dynamic systems.

10.2 Solution of Linear Dynamic Systems

We review basic results from linear system theory. These are special cases but cases that arise frequently and are important.

One-Dimensional Linear Problems

The general linear differential equation in R is

$$\dot{x} + a(t)x = b(t), \quad x(0) = x_0, \tag{10.2.1}$$

and has the solution

$$x(t) = x_0 e^{-\int_0^t a(s)\,ds} + \int_0^t e^{-\int_s^t a(z)\,dz} b(s)\,ds. \tag{10.2.2}$$

We can also solve linear finite-difference equations. The equation

$$x_{t+1} = a_t x_t + b_t \tag{10.2.3}$$

with x_0 given has the solution

$$x_{t+1} = \left(\prod_{s=0}^t a_s\right) x_0 + \sum_{s=0}^t \left(\prod_{j=s}^{t-1} a_j\right) b_s. \tag{10.2.4}$$

Linear Systems with Constant Coefficients

The special case of linear systems of ordinary differential equations with constant coefficients is also important. We will need to know the basic methods in later chapters. Suppose that $x \in R^n$ and

$$\dot{x} = Ax, \quad x(0) = x_0. \tag{10.2.5}$$

The solution to (10.2.5) is

$$x(t) = e^{At} x_0. \tag{10.2.6}$$

A useful representation of the solution (10.2.6) is to take the Jordan canonical form of A, $A = N^{-1}DN$, and write the solution (10.2.6) as

$$x(t) = e^{At} x_0 = e^{N^{-1}DNt} x_0 = N^{-1} e^{Dt} N x_0,$$

which, if the eigenvalues of A are distinct, expresses the solution $x(t)$ as a weighted sum of the fundamental solutions, $e^{\lambda_i t}$ for $\lambda_i \in \sigma(A)$. This form shows that the solution (10.2.6) is bounded only if all eigenvalues of A have negative real part. If the eigenvalues are not distinct, the Jordan canonical form is the same and the solution in (10.2.6) is unchanged; the only alteration is that e^{Dt} is not simply the diagonal matrix of $e^{\lambda_i t}$ terms.[1]

Discrete-time systems can be similarly solved. Suppose that $x \in R^n$, and we want to solve[2]

$$x_{t+1} = Ax_t. \tag{10.2.7}$$

The solution to (10.2.7) is

$$x_t = A^t x_0. \tag{10.2.8}$$

Again we take the Jordan canonical form of A and rewrite the solution as

$$x_t = A^t x_0 = (N^{-1}DN)^t x_0 = N^{-1}D^t N x_0,$$

which, in the case of distinct eigenvalues, expresses the solution x_t as a weighted sum of the fundamental solutions, λ_i^t where $\lambda_i \in \sigma(A)$. Here the solution is stable only if all $\lambda \in \sigma(A)$ has modulus less than one.

Equations (10.2.5) and (10.2.7) are examples of initial value problems. Linear boundary value problems also arise frequently in economics. Specifically we often need to solve problems of the form

$$\dot{x} = Ax,$$

$$x \equiv \begin{pmatrix} y \\ z \end{pmatrix}, \tag{10.2.9}$$

$$y(0) = y_0, \quad \lim_{t \to \infty} |z(t)| < \infty,$$

where y are called the *predetermined variables* and the z are free variables. To solve such problems, we replace A with its Jordan form, resulting in the system

$$\frac{d}{dt} \begin{pmatrix} y \\ z \end{pmatrix} = N^{-1}DN \begin{pmatrix} y \\ z \end{pmatrix},$$

which we rewrite as

---

1. For a discussion of linear differential equations, see Hirsch and Smale (1974).
2. We will use the conventional notation in dynamic analysis and let subscripts denote different vectors.

$$\frac{d}{dt}\left(N\begin{pmatrix} y \\ z \end{pmatrix}\right) = DN\begin{pmatrix} y \\ z \end{pmatrix}. \tag{10.2.10}$$

Without loss of generality, we can assume that $D \equiv \begin{pmatrix} D_1 & 0 \\ 0 & D_2 \end{pmatrix}$, where D_1 has the eigenvalues of D with negative real parts and D_2 has the eigenvalues of D with positive real parts.[3]

At this point we need to discuss determininacy issues. We want (10.2.9) to have a unique solution. That holds if and only if D_1 is square with the same size as the length of y, which is the number of predetermined variables, and the size of the square matrix D_2 equals the number of free variables. If we define

$$N \equiv \begin{pmatrix} N_{11} & N_{12} \\ N_{21} & N_{22} \end{pmatrix}, \quad \bar{x} = \begin{pmatrix} \bar{y} \\ \bar{z} \end{pmatrix} \equiv N\begin{pmatrix} y \\ z \end{pmatrix},$$

the system (10.2.10) reduces to $d\bar{x}/dt = D\bar{x}$, which implies the solution

$$\bar{x} = \begin{pmatrix} \bar{y} \\ \bar{z} \end{pmatrix} = \begin{pmatrix} e^{D_1 t} \\ e^{D_2 t} \end{pmatrix} = e^{Dt}. \tag{10.2.11}$$

We must choose $z(0)$ so that $z(t)$ is asympotically bounded. Since the eigenvalues of D_2 are unstable, $\bar{x}$ can be stable only if $0 = \bar{z}(0) = N_{21}y(0) + N_{22}z(0)$, which implies the solution

$$z(0) = -N_{22}^{-1}N_{21}y(0). \tag{10.2.12}$$

Therefore, to solve (10.2.9), we compute the matrix of eigenvectors, N, decompose it, and compute $z(0)$. Since $\bar{z}(t) = 0$ for all t, we actually have $z(t) = -N_{22}^{-1}N_{21}y(t)$ and $y(t) = (N_{11} - N_{12}N_{22}^{-1}N_{21})^{-1}e^{D_1 t}$.

Discrete-time boundary value problems are also handled in this fashion. Suppose that we have the problem

$$x_{t+1} = Ax_t,$$

$$x_t \equiv \begin{pmatrix} y_t \\ z_t \end{pmatrix}, \tag{10.2.13}$$

$$y_0 \text{ given}, \quad \lim_{t \to \infty} |z_t| < \infty.$$

---

3. We are ignoring the more complicated case of eigenvalues with zero real part.

We again replace A with its Jordan form and examine the system

$$N \begin{pmatrix} y_{t+1} \\ z_{t+1} \end{pmatrix} = DN \begin{pmatrix} y_t \\ z_t \end{pmatrix}.$$

Without loss of generality, we can assume that $D \equiv \begin{pmatrix} D_1 & 0 \\ 0 & D_2 \end{pmatrix}$, where now D_1 has the eigenvalues of D which have modulus less than one and D_2 has the other eigenvalues. Notice that the decomposition of D differs in the discrete-time case because the notion of a stable eigenvalue has changed.

We again have to deal with determinacy issues. If we have a unique solution to (10.2.13), then D_1 has the same size as the length of y, the number of predetermined variables, and the size of the square matrix D_2 equals the number of free variables. If we define $N \equiv \begin{pmatrix} N_{11} & N_{12} \\ N_{21} & N_{22} \end{pmatrix}$, and $\bar{x} = \begin{pmatrix} \bar{y} \\ \bar{z} \end{pmatrix} \equiv N \begin{pmatrix} y \\ z \end{pmatrix}$, the system (10.2.13) reduces to $\bar{x}_{t+1} = D\bar{x}_t$, which has the solution

$$\bar{x} = \begin{pmatrix} \bar{y} \\ \bar{z} \end{pmatrix} = \begin{pmatrix} D_1^t \bar{y}_0 \\ D_2^t \bar{z}_0 \end{pmatrix}. \tag{10.2.14}$$

Since z_t is asympotically bounded and the eigenvalues of D_2 are unstable, $\bar{x}$ can be stable only if $0 = \bar{z}_0 = N_{21} y_0 + N_{22} z_0$, which in turn implies the solution

$$z_0 = -N_{22}^{-1} N_{21} y_0. \tag{10.2.15}$$

Therefore, to solve (10.2.13), we compute the matrix of eigenvectors, N, decompose it, and compute z_0. Since $\bar{z}_t = 0$ for all t, we have $z_t = -N_{22}^{-1} N_{21} y_t$ and $y_t = (N_{11} - N_{12} N_{22}^{-1} N_{21})^{-1} D_1^t$ for all t.

10.3 Finite-Difference Methods for Initial Value Problems

Finite-difference methods are frequently used to solve the IVP

$$y' = f(x, y), \quad y(x_0) = y_0. \tag{10.3.1}$$

A finite-difference method first specifies a grid for x, $x_0 < x_1 < \cdots < x_i < \cdots$. In this chapter we assume that the grid has the form $x_i = x_0 + ih, i = 0, 1, \ldots, N$ where h is the step size. The intent is to find for each i a value Y_i which approximates $y(x_i)$. Therefore we construct a difference equation on the grid, such as $Y_{i+1} = F(Y_i, Y_{i-1}, \ldots, x_{i+1}, x_i, \ldots)$, similar to the differential equation, and solve the difference equation for $Y_1, \ldots, Y_i, \ldots$, in sequence, where Y_0 is fixed by the initial con-

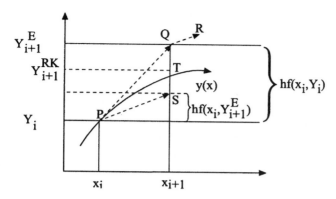

Figure 10.1
Euler and Runge-Kutta rules

dition, $Y_0 = y(x_0) = y_0$. Finite-difference methods approximate the solution at the grid points. To approximate the solution at other points, one could use any of a variety of interpolation methods.

Euler's Method

The simplest finite-difference scheme for (10.3.1) is the *Euler method*. Euler's method is the difference equation

$$Y_{i+1} = Y_i + hf(x_i, Y_i), \tag{10.3.2}$$

where Y_0 is fixed by the initial condition, $Y_0 = y(x_0) = y_0$. Figure 10.1 displays the geometric content of (10.3.2). Suppose that the current iterate is $P = (x_i, Y_i)$ and $y(x)$ is the true solution. At $P, y'(x_i)$ is the tangent vector $\vec{PQ}$. Euler's method follows that direction until $x = x_{i+1}$ at Q. The Euler estimate of $y(x_{i+1})$ is then Y_{i+1}^E.

The Euler scheme can be motivated by a Taylor series argument. Suppose that $y(x)$ is the true solution. Then expanding $y(x)$ around x_i shows that

$$y(x_{i+1}) = y(x_i) + hy'(x_i) + \frac{h^2}{2} y''(\xi)$$

for some $\xi \in [x_i, x_{i+1}]$. If we drop the h^2 term, assume $y'(x_i) = f(x_i, Y_i)$ and $Y_i = y(x_i)$, we get the Euler formula. If h is small, $y(x)$ should approximately solve this truncated Taylor expansion, allowing us to consider the Y_i generated by (10.3.2) to be a good approximation of $y(x_i)$. This derivation of the Euler scheme implicitly approximates $y(x)$ on the interval $[x_i, x_{i+1}]$ with a linear function with slope $f(x_i, Y_i)$.

We could also motivate the Euler scheme with a simple integration argument. The fundamental theorem of calculus implies that

$$y(x_{i+1}) = y(x_i) + \int_{x_i}^{x_{i+1}} f(t, y(t)) \, dt. \qquad (10.3.3)$$

If we approximate the integral in $(10.3.3)$ with $hf(x_i, y(x_i))$, that is, we approximate the integral with the box having width h and height $f(x_i, y(x_i))$, then $(10.3.3)$ reduces to $y(x_{i+1}) \doteq y(x_i) + hf(x_i, y(x_i))$ which implies $(10.3.2)$ if $Y_i \doteq y(x_i)$. This derivation of the Euler scheme also approximates $y(x)$ with a linear function $[x_i, x_{i+1}]$ of slope $f(x_i, Y_i)$.

As the step size h decreases, one hopes that the approximate solutions produced by the Euler method become better. To understand how the error of the Euler procedure depends on h, consider the differential equation $y'(x) = y(x)$, $y(0) = 1$. The solution is $y(x) = e^x$. The Euler method reduces to the finite-difference equation $Y_{i+1} = Y_i + hY_i = (1 + h) Y_i$ which has the solution $Y_i = (1 + h)^i$ and implies the approximation $Y(x) = (1 + h)^{x/h}$. The relative error is

$$\ln \left| \frac{Y(x)}{y(x)} \right| = \frac{x}{h} \ln(1 + h) - x = \frac{x}{h}(h - h^2 + \cdots) - x = -xh + \cdots,$$

where the excluded terms are of higher order than h. This exercise shows that the relative error in the Euler approximation to $y(x)$ is proportional to h. Clearly, as h goes to zero, $Y(x)$ converges to the true solution $y(x)$.

The last example was a particular example, but it does indicate the general result. The next theorem states that, in general, the error of the Euler method is proportional to h, the step size, displaying *linear convergence*.

THEOREM 10.3.1   Suppose that the solution to $y'(x) = f(x, y(x))$, $y(0) = y_0$, is C^3 on $[a, b]$, that f is C^2, and that f_y and f_{yy} are bounded for all y and $a \leq x \leq b$. Then the error of the Euler scheme with step size h is $\mathcal{O}(h)$; that is, it can be expressed as

$$y(x_i) - Y_i = D(x_i)h + \mathcal{O}(h^2)$$

where $D(x)$ is bounded on $[a, b]$ and solves the differential equation

$$D'(x) = f_y(x, y(x)) D(x) + \tfrac{1}{2} y''(x), \quad D(x_0) = 0$$

Proof   See Atkinson (1989, pp. 352–53).   ∎

Theorem 10.3.1 shows that in the limit as the step size h goes to zero, the Euler scheme will produce $y(x)$, since the function $D(x)$ is finite and independent of h.

We generally need to make a choice between the rate of convergence and the amount of calculation per step. A higher rate of convergence will allow a larger choice of h and fewer total iterations. For example, if the error target is 0.0001, and the error equals h, then h must be 0.0001 or less, but if the error is h^2, then $h = 0.01$ is adequate, reducing the number of iterations by a factor of 100. Quadratically convergent methods generally use more calculations per step, but it is clear that more rapidly schemes will be preferred unless the extra calculation burden is large.

The Euler scheme is an example of an *explicit method*. Explicit schemes are those that calculate Y_{i+1} explicitly in terms of x_i and Y_i. Explicit schemes are easy to program but often have stability problems unless h is small.

Implicit Euler Method

An alternative to the Euler scheme is the *implicit Euler method*. One way to derive the Euler scheme was to compute Y_{i+1} by using the Taylor expansion of y around x_i. Suppose instead that we expand around x_{i+1}. This yields the approximation

$$y(x_i) \doteq y(x_{i+1}) - hy'(x_{i+1}) = y(x_{i+1}) - hf(x_{i+1}, y(x_{i+1})),$$

which motivates the implicit Euler method

$$Y_{i+1} = Y_i + hf(x_{i+1}, Y_{i+1}). \tag{10.3.4}$$

This is a more difficult problem, for now Y_{i+1} is defined only implicitly in terms of x_i and Y_i. Each step of the implicit Euler scheme will need to solve a nonlinear equation in the unknown Y_{i+1}. This may appear to make the implicit Euler scheme inferior. On the other hand, the approximation scheme underlying the implicit Euler scheme is better in that it is more global in nature. The value of Y_{i+1} depends not only on Y_i and x_{i+1} but also on the behavior of f at (x_{i+1}, Y_{i+1}), whereas the explicit Euler's method depended only on f at (x_i, Y_i). Experience shows that the approximation considerations are often important and that we may do *much* better with the implicit Euler scheme. The extra computing time used in the nonlinear equation solving is often compensated by the ability to use larger h.

The primary difficulty with (10.3.4) is that it is a nontrivial numerical problem. To solve for Y_{i+1} in the nonlinear equation (10.3.4), we begin with $Y_{i+1}^0 = Y_i$, and construct a sequence, Y_{i+1}^j, of approximations to Y_{i+1} iteratively by using either fixed-point iteration,

$$Y_{i+1}^{j+1} = Y_i^j + hf(x_{i+1}, Y_{i+1}^j). \tag{10.3.5}$$

or Newton's method,

$$Y_{i+1}^{j+1} = Y_{i+1}^j - \frac{Y_{i+1}^j - Y_i^j - hf(x_{i+1}, Y_{i+1}^j)}{1 - hf_y(x_{i+1}, Y_{i+1}^j)}, \tag{10.3.6}$$

and stop when successive guesses are close. Fixed-point iteration is convenient to program but requires $|hf_y| < 1$ for convergence. Newton's method may also have convergence problems but should do better for *stiff* problems, that is, where f_y is large.

Trapezoid Rule

Another improvement on the Euler scheme is to use the integral approximation approach with a better quadrature formula. The fundamental theorem of calculus says that

$$y(x_{i+1}) = y(x_i) + \int_{x_i}^{x_{i+1}} f(t, y(t)) \, dt$$

$$\doteq y(x_i) + \frac{h}{2}[f(x_i, y(x_i)) + f(x_{i+1}, y(x_{i+1}))] - \frac{h^3}{12} y'''(\xi) \tag{10.3.7}$$

for some $\xi \in [x_i, x_{i+1}]$. This motivates the difference equation

$$Y_{i+1} = Y_i + \frac{h}{2}[f(x_i, Y_i) + f(x_{i+1}, Y_{i+1})], \tag{10.3.8}$$

which is called the *trapezoid method*, has quadratic convergence, and is an implicit single-step method.

Runge-Kutta Methods

The Runge-Kutta method is one of many that first use a simple formula to look where the solution is going, but then check it and implement a correction when needed. In figure 10.1 we illustrate the typical iteration. Y_i and x_i are given by previous calculations, and we next want to compute Y_{i+1}. We first calculate the Euler step, $hf(x_i, Y_i)$, and the Euler approximation, $Y_{i+1}^E = Y_i + hf(x_i, Y_i)$. We then check the slope of the vector field at the point (x_i, Y_{i+1}^E), which is $f(x_i, Y_{i+1}^E)$. The Euler approximation implicitly assumes that the slope at (x_i, Y_{i+1}^E) is the same as the slope at (x_i, Y_i), a bad assumption in general. For example, if $y(x)$ is concave, this estimate of Y_{i+1} will overshoot $y(x_{i+1})$. If instead we use the slope at (x_i, Y_{i+1}^E) to estimate Y_{i+1}, we would end up at $Y_i + h f(x_i, Y_{i+1}^E)$, point S in figure 10.1. That estimate implicitly assumes that the slope of the vector field is always $f(x_i, Y_{i+1}^E)$ between x_i and x_{i+1}, an equally bad assumption, but in the opposite direction. For concave $y(x)$

this estimate of Y_{i+1} will undershoot $y(x_{i+1})$. The *first-order Runge-Kutta formula* (RK1) takes the average of these two estimates to arrive at a superior estimate displayed as T in figure 10.1. This geometrical argument yields the formula

$$Y_{i+1} = Y_i + \frac{h}{2}\left[f(x_i, Y_i) + f(x_{i+1}, Y_i + hf(x_i, Y_i))\right]. \tag{10.3.9}$$

The Runge-Kutta method in (10.3.9) converges quadratically to the true solution as $h \to 0$, using only two evaluations of f per step. Compared to the Euler method, Runge-Kutta achieves a higher order of convergence with only twice as much calculation per step.

A refinement of this approach will yield the *fourth-order Runge-Kutta method* (RK4), a more accurate Runge-Kutta scheme. RK4 executes the following iteraton:

$$z_1 = f(x_i, Y_i),$$

$$z_2 = f\left(x_i + \tfrac{1}{2}h, \ Y_i + \tfrac{1}{2}hz_1\right),$$

$$z_3 = f\left(x_i + \tfrac{1}{2}h, \ Y_i + \tfrac{1}{2}hz_2\right), \tag{10.3.10}$$

$$z_4 = f(x_i + h, \ Y_i + hz_3),$$

$$Y_{i+1} = Y_i + \frac{h}{6}[z_1 + 2z_2 + 2z_3 + z_4].$$

This scheme converges at the rate h^4, and evaluates f only four times per step. The extra computation per step is amply rewarded by the higher rate of convergence.

Systems of Differential Equations

Many problems reduce to a system of differential equations of the form

$$y_1'(x) = f_1(x, y_1, y_2, \ldots y_n),$$

$$\vdots \tag{10.3.11}$$

$$y_n'(x) = f_n(x, y_1, y_2, \ldots, y_n).$$

To solve a system of differential equations, one can just apply a single-equation method to each equation. For example, the explicit Euler method for this system is

$$Y_l^{i+1} = Y_l^i + hf_l(x_i, Y_1^i, \ldots, Y_n^i), \qquad l = 1, \ldots, n. \tag{10.3.12}$$

Again it yields error proportional to h asymptotically. The implicit Euler method produces the system

$$Y_l^{i+1} = Y_l^i + hf_l(x_{i+1}, Y_1^{i+1}, \ldots, Y_n^{i+1}), \qquad l = 1, \ldots, n, \tag{10.3.13}$$

which would make each iteration an n-dimensional system of nonlinear equations.

Runge-Kutta methods can also be adapted to solve systems. RK1 applied to (10.3.11) results in the vector difference system

$$Y^{i+1} = Y^i + \frac{h}{2}[f(x_i, Y^i) + f(x_{i+1}, Y^i + hf(x_i, Y^i))]. \tag{10.3.14}$$

RK4 applied to (10.3.11) results in the difference system

$$z^1 = f(x_i, Y^i),$$

$$z^2 = f\left(x_i + \tfrac{1}{2}h, Y^i + \tfrac{1}{2}hz^1\right),$$

$$z^3 = f\left(x_i + \tfrac{1}{2}h, Y^i + \tfrac{1}{2}hz^2\right), \tag{10.3.15}$$

$$z^4 = f(x_i + h, Y^i + hz^3),$$

$$Y^{i+1} = Y^i + \frac{h}{6}[z^1 + 2z^2 + 2z^3 + z^4].$$

Systems of differential equations lead to stability problems, which don't arise in one-dimensional problems. As with single equations, implicit methods have superior stability properties, and one can use larger h. While the formulas are similar for systems, stability problems are more likely, since it only takes one explosive dimension to destabilize the entire solution. Stability problems are particularly severe in *stiff systems*. A system $dy/dx = f(y, x)$ is stiff if, along the solution path, the Jacobian of f, f_y, has negative eigenvalues that are much larger in magnitude than the other eigenvalues; such conditions can arise in optimal control problems. We do not discuss these problems here for two reasons. First, they do not appear to have been a major problem in economic problems so far, nor in the examples we discuss. Second, the methods discussed in the next chapter will also solve differential equations and do avoid these difficulties.

10.4 Economic Examples of IVPs

We will now examine a few examples of IVPs that arise in economic models. The first is Spence's signaling model. In the second example we return to homotopy continuation methods for solving nonlinear equations.

Signaling Equilibrium

One of the simplest initial value problems in economics is the education signaling model of Spence (1974). In this section we will describe the Spence model and numerically solve it with various methods.

The Spence model assumes that workers vary in their ability, each worker knowing that his ability is n for some $n \in [n_m, n_M]$, but cannot be directly observed by anyone else. Workers acquire y years of education, paying a total cost of $C(y, n)$; they then get a job. The output of a worker, $S(y, n)$, is a function of a worker's skill level, n, and his education, y, where $S_n, S_y, C_y > 0 > C_n$, and C is (weakly) concave in y. The critical assumption is that the employer sees only y, not output nor ability. Therefore wages are a function only of the education that a worker obtains. The problem is to compute the equilibrium wage schedule $w(y)$. Let $N(y)$ be the worker type that chooses education level y. Spence showed that in equilibrium $N(y)$ satisfies the first-order nonlinear differential equation

$$N'(y) = \frac{C_y(y, N(y)) - S_y(y, N(y))}{S_n(y, N(y))}. \tag{10.4.1}$$

Note that in this formulation of the problem, we take the education y as the independent variable and the type, n, as the dependent variable. While this may seem odd since y is endogenous and n is exogenous, it is nonetheless an equivalent formalization of the problem, since the only important feature is the presence of a monotonic functional relation between n and y, not which is endogenous and which is exogenous.

We assume that the lowest-ability individuals choose the socially efficient level of education; hence $N(y_m) = n_m$, where y_m, is fixed by the efficiency condition

$$S_y(y_m, n_m) = C_y(y_m, n_m). \tag{10.4.2}$$

The condition $N(y_m) = n_m$ gives us the initial condition we need to solve the Spence signaling equation (10.4.1).

In the case $S(y, n) = ny^\alpha$ and $C(y, n) = y/n$ the differential equation (10.4.1) reduces to

$$N'(y) = \frac{N(y)^{-1} - \alpha N(y) y^{\alpha - 1}}{y^\alpha}, \tag{10.4.3}$$

and (10.4.2) implies that

$$N(y_m) = n_m, \tag{10.4.4}$$

Table 10.1
Signaling model results

	h										
	Euler				RK				RK4		
$y - y_m$	0.1	0.01	0.001	0.0001	0.1	0.01	0.001	0.0001	0.1	0.01	0.001
0.1	4(−1)	3(−2)	1(−3)	1(−4)	4(−1)	1(−3)	1(−4)	1(−6)	3(−2)	3(−3)	2(−6)
0.2	1(0)	2(−2)	1(−3)	1(−4)	3(−1)	1(−3)	5(−4)	1(−6)	2(−2)	2(−3)	1(−6)
0.4	7(−1)	1(−2)	7(−4)	7(−5)	2(−1)	4(−4)	3(−4)	4(−7)	1(−2)	1(−3)	6(−7)
1.0	4(−1)	6(−3)	4(−4)	4(−5)	8(−2)	2(−4)	1(−4)	2(−7)	4(−3)	4(−4)	3(−7)
2.0	2(−1)	4(−3)	3(−4)	3(−5)	4(−2)	1(−4)	7(−5)	1(−7)	2(−3)	2(−4)	1(−7)
10.0	6(−2)	1(−3)	1(−4)	1(−5)	1(−2)	2(−5)	2(−6)	0(−7)	6(−4)	6(−5)	0(−7)
Time	0.01	0.11	1.15	9.17	0.02	0.16	1.49	14.4	0.02	0.27	2.91

	h										
	Implicit Euler–fixed-point iteration				Implicit Euler–Newton				Trapezoid		
$y - y_m$	0.1	0.01	0.001	0.0001	0.1	0.01	0.001	0.0001	0.1	0.01	0.001
0.1	2(0)	1(−1)	1(−3)	1(−4)	1(−1)	1(−2)	1(−3)	1(−4)	3(−3)	1(−4)	2(−6)
0.2	2(0)	5(−2)	1(−3)	1(−4)	1(−1)	1(−2)	1(−3)	1(−4)	2(−3)	7(−5)	8(−7)
0.4	2(0)	3(−2)	7(−2)	7(−5)	7(−2)	8(−3)	7(−4)	7(−5)	1(−3)	4(−5)	5(−7)
1.0	3(0)	1(−2)	4(−3)	4(−5)	5(−2)	5(−3)	5(−4)	4(−5)	4(−4)	2(−5)	2(−7)
2.0	3(0)	6(−3)	3(−3)	3(−5)	3(−2)	3(−3)	3(−4)	3(−5)	2(−4)	9(−6)	1(−7)
10.0	6(0)	1(−3)	1(−4)	1(−5)	1(−2)	1(−3)	1(−4)	1(−5)	6(−5)	2(−6)	0(−7)
Time	0.02	0.22	2.14	15.87	0.11	0.50	4.12	45.1	0.44	3.02	22.91

where $y_m = (n_m^2 \alpha)^{1/(1-\alpha)}$ is the efficient level of education for type n_m individuals. The closed-form solution is

$$N(y) = y^{-\alpha} \left(\frac{2(y^{1+\alpha} + D)}{1 + \alpha} \right)^{1/2}, \tag{10.4.5}$$

where $D = ((1 + \alpha)/2)(n_m / y_m^{-\alpha})^2 - y_m^{1+\alpha}$.

Since we have a closed-form solution for this case, we can compare the true solution to the solutions produced by our discretization methods. In table 10.1 we display the results for $\alpha = 0.25$. We choose $n_m = 0.1$, which fixes $y_m = 0.00034$. The first column lists a variety of education levels; specifically it expresses $y - y_m$ for various values of y. We then display the magnitude of the error, that is, the difference between $N(y)$ and the computed approximation to the solution of (10.4.1), for several choices of method and h. We report the absolute error; since $n_m = 0.1 = N(y_m)$ is the smallest ability level, the relative errors are generally more but by one order of magnitude at most. The first collection of four columns indicate the results when the Euler method was used and $h = 0.1, 0.01, 0.001$, and 0.0001. The errors are initially nontrivial but decline roughly in proportion to h. The simple Runge-Kutta method has smaller errors and appears to be converging more rapidly. RK4 does even better.

Implicit methods are also considered. The implicit Euler method using Newton's method to solve the nonlinear equation appears to dominate the fixed-point iteration implementation for $h = 0.1, 0.01$, and 0.001 but is slower with the same error for $h = 0.0001$. At $h = 0.0001$, fixed-point iteration converges quickly, and its simplicitly makes it faster than Newton's method. The trapezoid method is very good for $h \leq 0.01$. In this example, the best method was RK4 with $h = 0.0001$, since it achieved six-digit accuracy in under three seconds. The times in seconds are for a 33 MHz 486 computer; however, the important and robust feature is the relative time across methods.

Table 10.1 gives us an idea as to how small h needs to be to get good solutions. We find that good solutions can be computed for moderate values of h and that they need rather little computer time. We also see that the solutions do settle down quickly as h becomes smaller; apparently the convergence properties that the theory gives us begin to take effect at reasonable values of h. While numerical methods are unnecessary for the special case examined here, they would be needed for more general choices of S and C. While table 10.1 does not directly apply to these more general cases, it gives us assurances that these methods should do well for the more general cases.

Homotopy Solution Methods

In chapter 5 we saw that homotopy methods of solving nonlinear systems of equations naturally lead to systems of differential equations. Recall that the basic differential equation (5.9.4) is

$$\frac{dy_i}{ds} = (-1)^i \det\left(\frac{\partial H}{\partial y}(y)_{-i}\right), \qquad i = 1, \dots, n+1, \tag{10.4.6}$$

where $(.)_{-i}$ means we remove the ith column, $y = (x, t)$, and $H: R^n \times [0, 1] \to R^n$ is a homotopy with $H(0, 0) = 0$. With the initial conditions $t(0) = 0$ and $H(x(0), 0) = 0$, the solution to (10.4.6) is a parametric path $(x(s), t(s))$ which passes through a solution to $H(x, 1) = 0$, that is, for some $s > 0$, $t(s) = 1$ and $H(x(s), 1) = 0$.

In chapter 5 we used the Euler equation method in an example of the homotopy solution method. In that example we used a small step size and attained three-digit accurate answer to the solution of $H(x, 1) = 0$. More typically we would use a better differential equation solver. See Garcia and Zangwill (1981), and Allgower (1990) for extensive discussions of such methods.

10.5 Boundary Value Problems for ODEs: Shooting

Initial value problems are relatively easy to solve because the solution at each point depends only on local conditions. This allows us to use methods that are also local in nature, as are both the explicit and implicit procedures. In contrast, boundary value problems impose conditions on the solution at multiple points. We lose the local nature of the problem, and the numerical methods we use must become correspondingly global in nature. In this section we will discuss basic methods for solving BVPs.

Suppose that we have the two-point boundary value problem:

$$\dot{x} = f(x, y, t),$$

$$\dot{y} = g(x, y, t), \qquad\qquad\qquad (10.5.1)$$

$$x(0) = x^0, \quad y(T) = y^T,$$

where $x \in R^n$, $y \in R^m$, and $\dot{x}$ and $\dot{y}$ are dx/dt and dy/dt.

A basic method for solving two-point boundary value problems is *shooting*. We know only $x(0)$, not $y(0)$. If we knew $y(0)$, then we could solve the equation by an initial value method. The idea of shooting is to guess the value of $y(0)$ and use an initial value method to see what that guess implies about $y(T)$. Usually the resulting value of $y(T)$ will not be consistent with the terminal condition, $y(T) = y^T$. So we make new guesses for $y(0)$ until we find a value for $y(0)$ that is consistent with the terminal condition.

When we consider the details, we see that the shooting algorithm has two basic pieces. First, for any guess $y(0) = y^0$, we solve the IVP differential equation in (10.5.2)

$$\dot{x} = f(x, y, t),$$

$$\dot{y} = g(x, y, t), \qquad\qquad\qquad (10.5.2)$$

$$x(0) = x^0, \quad y(0) = y^0,$$

to get the corresponding value of $y(T)$; call that value $Y(T, y^0)$ to make explicit its dependence on y^0. Therefore the first piece of any BVP method is a method for solving the IVP (10.5.2) that arises when we make a guess for $y(0)$. This can be done by using finite-difference methods.

The second piece of a BVP method involves finding the correct y^0. Most guesses for y^0 will be wrong in that the terminal value $Y(T, y^0)$ won't equal y^T. We are interested in finding the y^0 such that $y^T = Y(T, y^0)$. This is a nonlinear equation in the unknown y^0. Therefore the second piece of a BVP method is a method for solving nonlinear equations.

Algorithm 10.1   Generic Shooting Algorithm

Objective: Solve two-point BVP (10.5.1).

Initialization. Guess $y^{0,i}$. Choose stopping criterion $\varepsilon > 0$.

Step 1. Solve (5.2) for $(x(T), y(T))$ given initial condition $y^0 = y^{0,i}$.

Step 2. If $\| y(T) - y^T \| < \varepsilon$, STOP. Else choose $y^{0,i+1}$ based on $y^{0,i}$, $y^{0,i-1}$, etc., and go to step 1.

This generic shooting method is an example of a two-layer algorithm. The inner layer, represented here in step 1, uses an IVP method that solves $Y(T, y^0)$ for any y^0. This could be the Euler method, a Runge-Kutta method, or any of the other IVP methods. The accuracy of any of these methods depends on the choice of the step size h and will have errors substantially greater than machine zero. At the outer layer, step 2 here, we solve the nonlinear equation $Y(T, y^0) = y^T$. One can use any nonlinear equation method to choose the next iterate, $y^{0,i+1}$, based on previous iterates, $y^{0,i}, y^{0,i-1}, \ldots$, and/or derivatives of $Y(T, y^0)$. Therefore we implement this in practice by defining a subroutine to compute $Y(T, y^0) - y^T$ as a function of y^0 and then send that subroutine to a zero-finding program. Our admonitions in chapter 5 about two-layer algorithms apply here; since the inner procedure is numerical, its error may require one to use a loose stopping criterion in the outer procedures.

10.6   Finite-Horizon Optimal Control Problems

Optimal control problems generally lead to boundary value problems and will be extensively studied in future chapters. We will review them now, focusing on the important computational aspects. The canonical problem is[4]

$$\max_u \int_0^T e^{-\rho t} \pi(x, u, t) \, dt + W(x(T))$$
$$\text{s.t.} \quad \dot{x} = f(x, u, t), \tag{10.6.1}$$
$$x(0) = x_0,$$

---

4. There are several variations of this problem. See Kamien and Schwartz (1981) for a catalogue of optimal control problems and the associated necessary conditions.

where $x \in R^n, u \in R^m$; that is, we have n state variables and m controls, ρ is the rate of discount, $\pi: R^n \times R^m \times R \to R$ is the flow rate of payoff, $W(x)$ is the value of the terminal state, and $f: R^n \times R^m \to R^n$ is the law of motion. To examine this problem, we form the current-value Hamiltonian

$$H(x, u, \lambda, t) = \pi(x, u, t) + \lambda^\top f(x, u, t), \tag{10.6.2}$$

where $\lambda \in R^n$ is the vector of shadow prices for x. The costate equations are

$$\dot{\lambda} = \rho\lambda - (\pi_x + \lambda^\top f_x). \tag{10.6.3}$$

and the maximum principle implies that

$$u(t) \in \arg \max_u H(x, u, \lambda, t). \tag{10.6.4}$$

The resulting collection of equations constitute a differential equation problem once we see how to use the maximum principle. The maximum principle produces an algebraic relation among the state, costate, and control variables which allows us to express the control variables as functions of the state and costate variables. If H is C^2 and concave in u, there is a unique selection in (10.6.4), $U(x, \lambda, t)$, defined by the first-order condition

$$0 = H_u(x, U(x, \lambda, t), \lambda, t). \tag{10.6.5}$$

Using the substitution $u(t) = U(x, \lambda, t)$, the solution to (10.6.1) satisfies (10.6.6):

$$\dot{x} = f(x, U(x, \lambda, t), t),$$
$$\dot{\lambda} = \rho\lambda - (\pi_x(x, U(x, \lambda, t), t) + \lambda^\top f_x(x, U(x, \lambda, t), t)), \tag{10.6.6}$$

plus boundary conditions, which for this problem are the initial condition on the state

$$x(0) = x_0 \tag{10.6.7}$$

plus the transversality condition

$$\lambda(T) = W'(x(T)). \tag{10.6.8}$$

Another common problem sets $W(x(T)) = 0$ in (10.6.1) and imposes the terminal condition $x(T) = x^T$. In these problems the state and costate equations are the same as for (10.6.1) but the terminal condition replaces (10.6.8) with

$$x(T) = x^T. \tag{10.6.9}$$

The typical optimal control problem leads to the boundary value problem system of equations consisting of (10.6.6)–(10.6.7) and either (10.6.8) or (10.6.9). Numerical solution of the resulting system requires methods to deal with differential equations obviously but also needs to deal with the function $U(x, \lambda, t)$. Sometimes U can be determined analytically but more frequently one will have to solve (10.6.5) numerically. The direct approach is to solve (10.6.4) for u at the values of x and λ that arise at each step of solving (10.6.6).

Life-Cycle Model of Consumption and Labor Supply

The life-cycle model is a simple example of an important BVP in economics. A simple case of this is the problem

$$\max_c \int_0^T e^{-\rho t} u(c)\, dt$$

$$\text{s.t.} \quad \dot{A} = f(A) + w(t) - c(t), \tag{10.6.10}$$

$$A(0) = A(T) = 0.$$

$u(c)$ is the concave utility function over consumption c, $w(t)$ is the wage rate at time t, $A(t)$ is assets at time t, and $f(A)$ is the return on invested assets. We assume assets are initially zero and terminally zero.

The Hamiltonian of the agent's problem is $H = u(c) + \lambda(f(A) + w(t) - c)$. The costate equation is $\dot{\lambda} = \rho\lambda - \lambda f'(A)$. The maximum principle implies the first-order condition $0 = u'(c) - \lambda$, which implies consumption function $c = C(\lambda)$. The final system of differential equations describing life-cycle consumption is

$$\dot{A} = f(A) + w - C(\lambda),$$

$$\dot{\lambda} = \lambda(\rho - f'(A)), \tag{10.6.11}$$

with the boundary conditions

$$A(0) = A(T) = 0. \tag{10.6.12}$$

It is often convenient to convert a state-costate system into one that consists of observable variables, such as assets and consumption. The relation $u'(c) = \lambda$ implies that (10.6.11) can be replace by

$$\dot{c} = -\frac{u'(c)}{u''(c)}(f'(A) - \rho),$$

$$\dot{A} = f(A) + w - c, \tag{10.6.13}$$

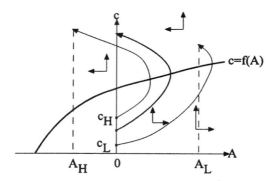

Figure 10.2
Shooting in a life-cycle problem

with boundary conditions (10.6.12), which is a system for the observables c and A.

Figure 10.2 gives a phase diagram representation of (10.6.10) assuming that $f'(A) > \rho$ for all A. The consumption path must obey the vector field defined by the system (10.6.10). The terminal condition is represented by the requirement that the consumption path begins and ends on the $A = 0$ line. We know neither the initial nor terminal λ values.

To solve this problem, the shooting method is a natural one to use. Figure 10.2 displays the implications of alternative guesses for $c(0)$. If $A(T) < 0$ when we guess $c(0) = c_H$, but $A(T) > 0$ when we guess $c(0) = c_L$, then we know that the correct $c(0)$ lies between c_L and c_H. We can find the true $c(0)$ by using the bisection method presented in algorithm 5.1. We formalize these steps in algorithm 10.2.

Algorithm 10.2   Life-Cycle Shooting

Objective: Solve (10.6.11) and (10.6.12) for $c(t)$ and $A(t)$ paths.

Initialization. Find some c_H such that $c(0) = c_H$ implies $A(T) < 0$ and c_L such that $c(0) = c_L$ implies $A(T) > 0$; choose a stopping criterion $\varepsilon > 0$. Set $c_0 = (c_L + c_H)/2$.

Step 1. Solve (using Runge-Kutta, Euler, or any other IVP scheme) the IVP consisting of (10.6.11) with the initial conditions $c(0) = c_0$, $A(0) = 0$ to compute $c(T)$, $A(T)$.

Step 2. If $|A(T)| < \varepsilon$, STOP. If $A(T) > \varepsilon$, then set $c_L = c_0$; else set $c_H = c_0$; set $c_0 = (c_L + c_H)/2$ and go to step 1.

10.7   Infinite-Horizon Optimal Control and Reverse Shooting

The canonical infinite-horizon autonomous optimal control problem is

$$\max_u \int_0^\infty e^{-\rho t} \pi(x, u)\, dt$$

s.t. $\dot{x} = f(x, u),$ (10.7.1)

   $x(0) = x_0,$

which again will imply conditions (10.6.3)–(10.6.6). The difference lies in the boundary conditions. We still have $x(0) = x_0$, but we no longer have (10.6.8). In the examples we use in this book, (10.6.8) will be replaced by the transversality condition at infinity (TVC_∞)

$$\lim_{t \to 0} e^{-\rho t}|\lambda(t)^\top x(t)| < \infty.$$

   Shooting methods have only limited value in solving infinite-horizon optimal control problems. It is particularly difficult to solve long-horizon models with shooting methods, since they involve integrating the differential equations over long time periods, and $x(T)$ is very sensitive to $\lambda(0)$ when T is large. To deal with these problems we must develop a better approach.

   Let us go back to the basic problem. The difficulty with simple shooting is that the terminal state is excessively sensitive to the initial guess. However, this implies the reverse result that the initial state corresponding to any terminal state is relatively insensitive to the terminal state. Therefore, instead of making a guess as to the value of the unspecified initial conditions and integrating forward, we will make a guess as to the value of the unspecified terminal conditions and integrate *backward*; we will call that *reverse shooting*. We will illustrate it in some problems related to infinite-horizon control.

Optimal Growth

The simplest infinite-horizon economic problem is the continuous-time optimal growth model with one good and one capital stock. It is

$$\max_c \int_0^\infty e^{-\rho t} u(c)\, dt$$

s.t. $\dot{k} = f(k) - c,$ (10.7.2)

   $k(0) = k_0,$

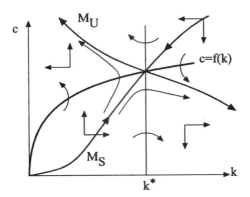

Figure 10.3
Shooting in a saddle-point problem

where k is the capital stock, c consumption, and $f(k)$ the aggregate net production function. The differential equations governing $c(t)$ and $k(t)$ reduce to

$$\dot{c} = \frac{u'(c)}{u''(c)} \, (\rho - f'(k)),$$

$$\dot{k} = f(k) - c,$$

(10.7.3)

and the boundary conditions are

$$k(0) = k_0, \quad 0 < \lim_{t \to \infty} |k(t)| < \infty.$$

Figure 10.3 is a phase diagram of this system when we assume that u and f are concave. The steady state is $k = k^*$, where $f'(k^*) = \rho$, and $c^* = f(k^*)$. There is a stable manifold, M_S, and an unstable manifold, M_U, making the steady state *saddle point stable*. Both M_U and M_S are *invariant manifolds* because, if the system begins on a point on M_S (M_U), the resulting path will remain on M_S (M_U). M_S is "stable," since any path beginning on M_S will converge to the steady state, and M_U is "unstable" because any path beginning on M_U will diverge from the steady state.

We first try to use shooting to compute the stable manifold. We must adjust shooting to accomodate the infinite horizon. We want k and c to equal their steady state values at $t = \infty$, but that is impossible to accomplish. Instead, we try to find a $c(0)$ that produces a $(c(t), k(t))$ path that comes close to the steady state. This idea leads to algorithm 10.3 for $k_0 < k^*$. Observe that if $c(0)$ is too large, then the path crosses the $\dot{k} = 0$ curve and ultimately implies a falling capital stock, but that a deficient $c(0)$ results in a path that crosses the $\dot{c} = 0$ line and implies a falling consumption level. These observations produce algorithm 10.3.

Algorithm 10.3   Infinite-Horizon Forward Shooting

Objective: Solve (10.7.3) for $c(t)$ and $k(t)$ paths for $t \in [0, T]$ and $k_0 < k^*$.

Initialization. Set c_H equal to $f(k_0)$, and set $c_L = 0$; choose a stopping criterion $\varepsilon > 0$.

Step 1. Set $c_0 = (c_L + c_H)/2$.

Step 2. Solve (using Runge-Kutta, Euler, or any other IVP scheme) the IVP consisting of (10.7.3) with initial conditions $c(0) = c_0$, $k(0) = k_0$; stop the IVP algorithm at the first t when $\dot{c} < 0$ or $\dot{k} < 0$, and denote it T.

Step 3. If $|c(T) - c^*| < \varepsilon$, STOP. If $\dot{c} < 0$, then set $c_L = c_0$; else set $c_H = c_0$; go to step 1.

From the phase diagram it is clear why numerical solutions will have difficulty computing the path corresponding to the stable manifold. We see that any small deviation from M_S is magnified and results in a path that increasingly departs from M_S. However, suppose that we wanted to compute a path on M_U; note that the flow actually pushes points toward M_U, and small deviations are squashed. For example, if we solve the differential equation system beginning at a point near the steady state, the solution will move toward M_U. Therefore, if we were interested in computing a path that lies on M_U, we would just choose a point near the steady state for the initial condition and integrate the system.

Even though we don't want to compute the unstable manifold, we can use this observation to compute the stable manifold. The idea is to change the system so that the stable manifold becomes the unstable manifold. This is accomplished easily by reversing the direction of time, yielding the system

$$\dot{c} = -\frac{u'(c)}{u''(c)} (\rho - f'(k)),$$

$$\dot{k} = -(f(k) - c).$$

(10.7.4)

The phase diagram of this system is the same as figure 10.3 but *with the arrows turned 180 degrees*. Therefore the unstable manifold of (10.7.4) is M_U in figure 10.4.

The stable manifold of (10.7.3) has a particularly important interpretation. Since calendar time plays no role in this problem, the choice of consumption at time t depends solely on the current capital stock. We express this by defining a policy function, $C(k)$, such that $c(t) = C(k(t))$. Since optimality requires the capital stock to converge to the steady state, the only optimal (c, k) pairs are those on the stable

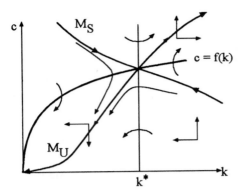

Figure 10.4
Reverse shooting in a saddle-point problem

manifold. Hence the stable manifold is the consumption policy function, $C(k)$. Furthermore $(10.7.3)$ implies that $C(k)$ satisfies the differential equation

$$C'(k) = \frac{\dot{c}}{\dot{k}} = \frac{u'(C(k))}{u''(C(k))} \frac{\rho - f'(k)}{f(k) - C(k)}, \tag{10.7.5}$$

which can also be written

$$C'(k)(f(k) - C(k)) - \frac{u'(C(k))}{u''(C(k))}(\rho - f'(k)) = 0. \tag{10.7.6}$$

One application of reverse shooting is to compute the stable manifold of $(10.7.3)$. We first compute $C'(k)$ at k^*. At the steady state, $(10.7.5)$ reduces to $0/0$. By l'Hôpital's rule

$$C'(k^*) = -\frac{f''(k^*))}{f'(k^*) - C'(k^*)} \frac{u'(C(k^*))}{u''(C(k^*))},$$

which is a quadratic equation in $C'(k^*)$. Since consumption is increasing in k, we choose the positive root:

$$C'(k^*) = \frac{f'(k^*)}{2}\left(1 + \sqrt{1 + 4\frac{u'(c^*)}{u''(c^*)} \frac{f''(k^*)}{f'(k^*)f'(k^*)}}\right). \tag{10.7.7}$$

With reverse shooting, $C(k)$ can be calculated by solving two IVPs. For $k > k^*$ we begin with $k = k^* + h$, using the approximate initial condition

Table 10.2
Optimal growth with reverse shooting

		Errors		
k	c	$h = 0.1$	$h = 0.01$	$h = 0.001$
0.2	0.10272	0.00034	3.1(−8)	3.1(−12)
0.5	0.1478	0.000025	3.5(−9)	4.1(−13)
0.9	0.19069	−0.001	−3.5(−8)	1.8(−13)
1.	0.2	0	0	0
1.1	0.20893	−0.00086	−5.3(−8)	−1.2(−12)
1.5	0.24179	−0.000034	−1.8(−9)	−2.1(−14)
2.	0.2784	−9.8(−6)	−5.0(−10)	3.6(−15)
2.5	0.31178	−5.0(−6)	−2.6(−10)	−1.3(−14)
2.8	0.33068	−3.8(−6)	−1.9(−10)	−1.2(−14)

$$C(k^* + h) \doteq c^* + hC'(k^*),$$

and then proceed via some IVP method applied to (10.7.5) to compute $C(k)$ for $k = k^* + nh, n = 2, 3, 4, \ldots$. For $k < k^*$ the initial condition is

$$C(k^* - h) \doteq c^* - hC'(k^*),$$

and we proceed via some IVP method applied to (10.7.5) to compute $C(k)$ for $k = k^* - nh, n = 2, 3, 4, \ldots$. The total result is an approximation to $C(k)$ for k above and below k^*.

Table 10.2 illustrates results of reverse shooting applied to (10.7.6) for the case $\rho = 0.05$, $f(k) = 0.2k^{0.25}$, and $u(c) = -c^{-1}$. The first column is capital stock k, and the second column is the computed consumption for k when $h = 10^{-5}$, a step size so small that we take the answer as the true solution. Columns 3 through 5 display the errors when we use RK4 with $h = 0.1, 0.01$, and 0.001. Note that the consumption values appear to be converging at the rate h^4 to the $h = 10^{-5}$ solution, the convergence predicted by theory. It is not surprising that the solution is so accurate for k near 1; table 10.2 also shows that the solution is quite accurate even for the extreme values of $k = 0.2$ and $k = 2.8$. The uniformity of the error illustrates the stability of the reverse shooting approach.

We often want to express the policy function, $C(k)$ in a simple form. The points $\{(c_i, k_i) \mid i = -N, \ldots, N\}$ generated by reverse shooting are all supposedly on or near the graph of $c = C(k)$. Therefore we could use the least squares approach

$$\min_{\beta} \sum_{i=-N}^{N} \left(c_i - \sum_{j=0}^{m} \beta_j \varphi_j(k_i) \right)^2$$

to approximate $C(k)$ with $\hat{C}(k) \equiv \sum_{j=0}^{m} \beta_j \varphi_j(k)$ for some basis functions $\varphi_j(k)$.

Multidimensional Reverse Shooting

To further illustrate reverse shooting, we next consider the multidimensional profit maximization problem

$$\max \int_0^\infty e^{-rt} \left(\pi(k) - \sum_{i=1}^{n} I_i - \sum_{i=1}^{n} \frac{\gamma_i I_i^2}{2} \right) dt,$$

$$\dot{k}_i = I_i, \qquad i = 1, \dots, n,$$

$$k(0) = k^0,$$

where $k \in R^n$ represents n capital stocks, $\pi(k)$ is the profit flow, r the interest rate, and I_i the net investment rate of stock i. The adjustment costs for stock i equal $\gamma_i I_i^2/2$. The costate equation is $\dot{\lambda}_i = r\lambda_i - \pi_i$, $i = 1, \dots, n$. The maximum principle yields $0 = -(1 + \gamma_i I_i) + \lambda_i$, $i = 1, \dots, n$, which implies the investment rules $I_i = (\lambda_i - 1)/\gamma_i$, $i = 1, \dots, n$. The resulting system is

$$\dot{k}_i = \frac{\lambda_i - 1}{\gamma_i}, \qquad i = 1, \dots, n,$$

$$\dot{\lambda}_i = r\lambda_i - \pi_i(k), \qquad i = 1, \dots, n,$$

(10.7.9)

with the initial condition $k(0) = k^0$. The steady state is defined by $\dot{k} = \dot{\lambda} = 0$, which implies that $\lambda_i = 1$ and $\pi_i = r$ in the steady state for $i = 1, \dots, n$. We assume that π is strictly concave and that there exists a unique steady state at $k = k^*$. This is a simple system, but we use it to illustrate the basic ideas.

We first need to deal with the problem of having an infinite horizon. One way to deal with the infinite horizon is to replace it with a long, finite horizon and solve the problem

$$\max \int_0^T e^{-rt} \left(\pi(k) - \sum_{i=1}^{n} I_i - \sum_{i=1}^{n} \frac{\gamma_i I_i^2}{2} \right) dt,$$

$$\dot{k}_i = I_i, \qquad i = 1, \dots, n,$$

$$k(0) = k^0, \qquad k(T) = k^*,$$

for some large T. The terminal conditions on $k(T)$ make sure that we approximate a path to the steady state. The system (10.7.9) still describes the optimal path.

The standard shooting procedure would guess λ^0 and integrate the system (10.7.9) to compute $k(T)$, which is a function, say $K(T, \lambda^0)$, of λ^0. It then solves the equation $K(T, \lambda^0) - k^* = 0$ to determine the correct λ^0. Since small changes in λ^0 will produce large changes in $k(T)$, this approach is poor. In reverse shooting, we also take $k(T) = k^*$ as fixed and try to choose a $\lambda^T \in R^n$ consistent with $k(0) = k_0$. To do this, we guess a value for λ^T, then compute $k(0)$ by integrating the time-reversed system of (10.7.9), expressed as

$$\dot{k}_i = -(\lambda_i - 1)\gamma_i^{-1}, \qquad i = 1, \ldots n,$$
$$\dot{\lambda}_i = -r\lambda_i + \pi_i(k), \qquad i = 1, \ldots, n, \tag{10.7.10}$$

together with the initial conditions[5] $k(T) = k^*$ and $\lambda(T) = \lambda^T$. In this case it is $k(0)$ which is a function of λ^T, say $K(0, \lambda^T)$, and our task is to compute a solution to the equation

$$K(0, \lambda^T) - k^0 = 0. \tag{10.7.11}$$

This is more likely to work, since small changes in λ^T will, hopefully, generate only small changes in the implied value of $k(0)$.

We must be flexible with the terminal time. If T is too small, we will find that the λ^T that solves (10.7.11) will differ substantially from λ^*. Since we want λ^T be close to λ^*, we increase T until the λ^T solution to (10.7.11) is close to λ^*.

We could use the result of reverse shooting to compute policy functions in the multidimensional case. To generate the necessary data, we would have to apply reverse shooting to several choices of $k(0)$. This will generate points on several threads on the stable manifold, points that can be used in a least squares approximation of the policy function.

In this problem the reverse shooting method is generally far more stable than the forward shooting method. There is no guarantee that it will always be better for arbitrary optimal control problems; this will depend on the character of steady state convergence. We offer it as an alternative to the more common forward shooting method.

---

5. We need an initial guess for $\lambda(T)$. Ideally we would like to use $\lambda(T) = \lambda^*$ as the initial guess, but then the system (10.7.9) would go nowhere. Instead we could use, for example, $\lambda(T) = 0.99\lambda^*$.

10.8 Integral Equations

Integral equations arise naturally in dynamic economic analyses. The general integral equation can be written

$$0 = \varphi\left(g(x), f(x), \int_a^b H(x, z, f(z))\, dz\right),\tag{10.8.1}$$

where $f(x)$ is the unknown function, and $g(x)$ and $H(x, z, y)$ are known functions.

This general formulation has some special forms of particular interest. A *linear Fredholm equation of the first kind* has the form

$$f(x) = \int_a^b K(x, z) f(z)\, dz.\tag{10.8.2}$$

The function $K(x, z)$ is called the *kernel* of the integral equation. This is a linear equation because the RHS is linear in the unknown function f. A *linear Fredholm equation of the second kind* has the form

$$f(x) = g(x) + \int_a^b K(x, z) f(z)\, dz.\tag{10.8.3}$$

Volterra equations of the first and second kind are special cases of Fredholm equations. Suppose that $K(x, z) = 0$ for $x < z$; then $\int_a^b K(x, z) f(z)\, dz = \int_a^x K(x, z) f(z)\, dz$, and the linear Fredholm equations of first and second kind can be written

$$f(x) = \int_a^x K(x, z) f(z)\, dz\tag{10.8.4}$$

and

$$f(x) = g(x) + \int_a^x K(x, z) f(z)\, dz,\tag{10.8.5}$$

which are *linear Volterra equations of first and second kind*. Volterra integral equations and ordinary differential equations are closely related, since the differential equation $f'(x) = K(x, f(x))$ for $x \in [a, b]$ is equivalent to the nonlinear Volterra integral equation

$$f(x) = f(a) + \int_a^x K(z, f(z))\, dz,$$

where $f(a)$ is the initial condition.

Linear Fredholm Equations

A general approach to solving linear Fredholm integral equations of the second kind arise naturally from quadrature methods. In equations like (10.8.2) and (10.8.3), the item needing approximation is the integral, $\int_a^b K(x,z)f(z)\,dz$. For each x this is an integral over z. Furthermore, if $K(x,z)$ is continuous in z for each x, we can replace the integral with a good quadrature rule. Any such rule has a weighting function, $w(x)$, (which is $w(x) = 1$ in the case of Newton-Cotes formulas), nodes $x_i \in [a,b]$, $i = 1,\ldots,n$, and weights, $\omega_i > 0$, $i = 1,\ldots,n$, and, at each x, yields the approximation

$$\int_a^b K(x,z)f(z)\,dz \doteq \sum_{j=1}^n \frac{\omega_j K(x,x_j)f(x_j)}{w(x_j)}. \tag{10.8.6}$$

This sum approximates $\int_a^b K(x,z)f(z)\,dz$ for any x, in particular, for the quadrature nodes x_i, $i = 1,\ldots,n$. If we make the substitutions $x = x_i$ for $i = 1,\ldots,n$, in the Fredholm equation and apply (10.8.6), we arrive at the set of n linear equations for the n values $f(x_i)$:

$$f(x_i) = g(x_i) + \sum_{j=1}^n \frac{\omega_j K(x_i, x_j)f(x_j)}{w(x_j)}, \qquad i = 1,\ldots,n, \tag{10.8.7}$$

which is linear in the $f(x_i)$. This use of a quadrature formula in the integral equation reduces the problem of estimating the function f to that of estimating f at the quadrature nodes.

Integral equation methods differ in their choice of the weights and nodes. One choice is to set $w(x) = 1$, $x_i = a + (i-1)(b-a)/(n-1)$, and choosing the ω_i according to a Newton-Cotes formula; this leads to the linear system

$$f(x_i) = g(x_i) + \sum_{j=1}^n \omega_j K(x_i, x_j)f(x_j), \qquad i = 1,\ldots,n. \tag{10.8.8}$$

An alternative is the Gauss-Legendre set of nodes and weights, which also assumes $w(x) = 1$ and leads to a similar formula.

Sometimes an efficient choice will suggest itself. For example, if $K(x,z) = H(x,z)e^{-z^2}$, $-a = b = \infty$, and $H(x,z)$ is polynomial-like in z, then a Gauss-Hermite approximation of the integral is suggested. This leads to the linear system

$$f(x_i) = g(x_i) + \sum_{j=1}^n \omega_j H(x_i, x_j)f(x_j), \qquad i = 1,\ldots,n, \tag{10.8.9}$$

where the x_i and ω_i are the Gauss-Hermite nodes and weights. One can apply any Gaussian quadrature formula. In applying Gaussian quadrature corresponding to the weighting function $w(z)$, one uses the corresponding Gaussian rule's weights, ω_i and nodes, x_i and solve the system (10.8.8).

The solution to (10.8.9) produces values for $f(x)$ at the $x_i, i = 1, \ldots, n$. We really want a function that approximates the solution to (10.8.3) at all $x \in [a, b]$. To construct this approximation, we form $\hat{f}(x)$, where

$$\hat{f}(x) = g(x) + \sum_{j=1}^{n} \frac{\omega_j K(x, x_j) f(x_j)}{w(x_j)}. \tag{10.8.10}$$

This is called the *Nystrom extension*. It is an approximation to the unknown function, not just an approximation to a finite set of values.

Markov Chains: Approximations and Ergodic Distributions

One example of integral equation is the computation of an ergodic distribution of a discrete-time, continuous-state Markov process. Suppose that a random variable obeyed the law $\Pr\{x_{t+1} \leq x | x_t\} = F(x | x_t)$ where F has a density $f(x | x_t)$. We are often interested in the ergodic distribution

$$H(x) = \lim_{T \to \infty} P\{x_T \leq x | x_0\}.$$

If $H(x)$ has a density $h(x)$, then $h(x)$ satisfies the integral equation

$$h(x) = \int h(z) f(x | z) \, dz. \tag{10.8.11}$$

Since $H(\cdot)$ is a distribution, $h(\cdot)$ also must satisfy $\int h(z) \, dz = 1$. To solve (10.8.11), we pick a weighting function $w(x)$, and an appropriate quadrature rule with weights ω_i and nodes x_i, and form the linear system of equations

$$h(x_i) = \sum_{j=1}^{n} \frac{\omega_j h(x_j) f(x_i | x_j)}{w(x_j)}. \tag{10.8.12}$$

This system is linear and homogeneous in the unknown $h(x_i)$ values. To eliminate the indeterminacy arising from the homogeneity, we replace one of the equations with

$$\sum_{j=1}^{n} \frac{\omega_j h(x_j)}{w(x_j)} = 1, \tag{10.8.13}$$

which states that $h(x)$ is a probability density.

The linear problem (10.8.12) has a suggestive interpretation. Equation (10.8.12) examines only the value of h on the x_i grid. Tauchen and Hussey (1991) show how we can approximate the continuous-state Markov chain with a finite-state chain. They begin as we do with a grid of x_i points and a weight function. They then define

$$\pi(x_k|x) = \frac{f(x_k|x)}{s(x)w(x_k)}\,\omega_k$$

where

$$s(x) = \sum_{i=1}^{n} \frac{f(x_i|x)}{w(x_i)}\,\omega_i$$

For each x, $\pi(x_k|x)$ is a probability measure over the x_k, constructed by replacing the integral with a sum to compute the relative probabilities and then normalizing to attain true probabilities. These probabilities have the advantage of being approximations to the conditional expectation operator, since

$$E\{g(x,y)|x\} = \int g(x,y)f(y|x)dy \doteq \sum_{k=1}^{n} g(x,x_k)\pi(x_k|x).$$

Furthermore, when we restrict $\pi(x_k|x)$ to the x_i grid, we have a Markov chain on the x_i. This should serve as a good approximation to the continuous-space chain as long as it is constructed to be a good approximation to all the conditional expectations operators. As a result many authors use this finite-state approximation to model continuous-state processes.

10.9 Further Reading and Summary

Finite difference methods are powerful techniques to solve ldifferential equations and have been extensively developed. Lick (1989) is a recent presentation of basic finite-difference methods. We did not discuss partial differential equations because most economists are unaware of them and special methods dominate in those areas where PDEs do arise. The next chapter presents simpler, more intuitive, and more robust numerical methods for PDEs and applies them in continuous-time dynamic stochastic contexts. A reader interested in finite-difference methods for PDEs is referred to Ames (1977), Botha and Pinder (1983), and Lapidus and Pinder (1982). PDEs are used in option pricing models; see Hull (1989) for the key references.

Since optimal control is so pervasive in the analysis of deterministic dynamic economic systems, the boundary value problems discussed here arise frequently.

Shooting methods have been used; in particular, see Lipton et al. (1982) for a discussion of multiple shooting. Other methods have also been utilized. Ascher et al. (1988), Kubicek and Hlavacek (1983), and Roberts and Shipman (1971) are the standard references for boundary value problems.

Exercises

1. Consider the Solow growth model $\dot{k} = sf(k) - \delta k$ with $s = 0.2$, $\delta = 0.1$, $f(k) = k^{\alpha}$, $\alpha = 0.25$, and $k(0) = 0.5$. Compute the numerical solutions using the Euler method, Runge-Kutta, and RK4 with $h = 1, 0.1, 0.01$. Compare these solutions with the exact solution.

2. Consider the life-cycle problem (10.6.10). Suppose that $u(c) = c^{\gamma+1}/(\gamma + 1)$. Suppose that the lending rate is r but that the borrowing rate of interest is $r(1 + \theta A^2)$ expressing the costs and limitations of borrowing. Suppose that wages follow the pattern $w(t) = 1$ for $M \leq t \leq R$ and zero otherwise. Compute solutions for $c(t)$ and $A(t)$ for $\rho = 0.04$, $r \in \{0.05, 0.06, 0.08, 0.10\}$ $\theta \in \{0, 0.04, 0.2, 1.0\}$, $T = 55$, $M = 5, 10$, $R = 40, 45$, and $h = 0.01, 0.1, 1.0$.

3. Use the path-following homotopy method to solve the general equilibrium problem posed in equation (5.2.6). Which solution do you get to? Can you find other homotopies that find the other equilibrium? Apply homotopy path-following to solve instances of exercise 5.3. How large can the step sizes be before you have problems? Does RK4 do better than the Euler finite-difference method?

4. Using the approach exposited before theorem 10.3.1, compute the error of applying the implicit Euler, RK, RK4, and trapezoid methods to the differential equation $y'(x) = y(x)$, $y(0) = 1$.

5. Consider the optimal growth problem with adjustment costs

    $$\max_{I} \int_{0}^{\infty} e^{-\rho t} u(f(k) - I - \gamma I^2) \, dt$$

    s.t. $\dot{k} = I$,

    for $\rho = 0.05$, $u(c) = \log c$, $f(k) = 0.2k^{0.25}$, $\gamma = 100$. Compute both the time path with $k(0) = 0.5$, and the optimal policy function.

6. Consider the learning curve problem

    $$\max_{q} \int_{0}^{\infty} e^{-\rho t} \pi(q, Q) \, dt$$

    s.t. $\dot{Q} = q - \dfrac{Q}{100}$,

    where $\rho = .04$, $\pi(q, Q) = q - q^2/2 - (Q + 1)^{-0.2} q$. Compute both the optimal time path with $Q(0) = 0$ and the optimal policy function.

7. Write programs using shooting and reverse shooting to solve the multidimensional growth problem

    $$\max_{I \in R^n} \int_{0}^{\infty} e^{-\rho t} u\left(\sum_{i=1}^{n} f_i(k_i) - \sum_{i=1}^{n} (I_i + \gamma_i I_i^2) \right) dt$$

    s.t. $\dot{k}_i = I_i$, $i = 1, \ldots, n$,

for $\rho = 0.05$, $u(c) = \log c$, and $f_i(k_i) = \rho k_i^{\alpha_i} / \alpha_i$. Solve the problem for $n = 2, 3, 5, 10$ and for several combinations of $\alpha_i \in \{0.25, 0.4\}$, and $\gamma_i \in \{10, 50, 100, 250\}$, and $k_i(0) \in \{0.5, 0.8, 1.0, 1.2, 1.5\}$. Compute the optimal policy functions for several cases.

8. Solve the two-sector optimal growth problem

$$\max_{I_c, I_I, l_c, l_I} \int_0^\infty e^{-\rho t} u(f_c(k_c, l_c), l_c + l_I) \, dt$$

s.t. $\dot{k}_c = I_c$,

$\dot{k}_I = I_I$,

$$0 = I_c + \gamma_c I_c^2 + I_I + \frac{\gamma_I I_I^2}{100} - f_I(k_I, l_I),$$

where $f_i(k_i, l_i)$ is the output of sector i with capital input k_i and labor input l_i, $i = c$ denotes the consumption sector, and $i = I$ denotes the investment sector. Make Cobb-Douglas choices for the f functions and CRRA choices for u. Compute the steady state. Compute the optimal path with initial conditions equal to ± 5 and ± 10 percent of the steady state. Plot the optimal k_c and k_I paths in (k_c, k_I) space from these various initial conditions.

9. Repeat Exercise 8.10 using integral equation methods.

11 Projection Methods for Functional Equations

Finite-difference methods have been useful for solving ordinary differential equations in economics; they can be used to solve partial differential equations and a wide variety of other equations. However, many problems in economics lead to functional equations that are not of a standard type. For example, the functional equations that arise in discrete-time growth models involve composition of functions, a feature that cannot be handled directly by finite-difference methods. The complexity of the equations that arise in economics forces us to use more sophisticated methods from numerical functional analysis.

In this chapter we study *projection methods*. The underlying approach of projection methods is substantially more general than finite-difference methods, and this more general approach will allow us to solve problems for which there are no easy finite-difference methods. The advantage of the projection approach is that it is so intuitive; it gives a general way to solve functional equations of almost any description. In fact the typical economist's acquaintance with regression will make these methods feel natural. Moreover many of the ad hoc solution methods that have been developed by economists to solve economic problems turn out to be particular implementations of the projection method. By learning the general projection method, we will understand better how these methods work, how to improve on existing methods, and how to apply the projection method to more complex problems.

In this chapter we will first display the projection method applied to linear ordinary and partial differential equations. We then give a general description of projection methods in terms of the functional analytic basics. From this description, it is obvious that projection methods are potentially useful in solving almost any functional equation in economics. We demonstrate their flexibility in this chapter by showing how to use projection methods to solve boundary value problems, life-cycle and optimal growth problems, implicit function problems, and conditional expectations. Projection methods will also be used extensively in later chapters on solving dynamic economic models.

11.1 An Ordinary Differential Equation Example

The projection method is a general method using approximation methods and finite-dimensional methods to solve problems with unknown functions. In section 11.3 we will define it abstractly in functional analytic terms. Since that description will be rather abstract, we first present examples of projection methods applied to a simple ordinary differential equation and to a simple partial differential equation. These examples will make the later abstract discussion more understandable.

Consider the differential equation

$$y' - y = 0, \quad y(0) = 1 \tag{11.1.1}$$

which has the solution $y = e^x$. We will use projection methods to solve it over the interval $0 \leq x \leq 3$.

The first point is that projection methods view the problem differently than finite-difference methods. Finite-difference methods focus on approximating the value of y at a finite number of specified points; that is, at a prespecified collection of x_i, we compute approximations Y_i. Finite-difference methods proceed by solving a finite set of equations linking these x_i and Y_i values. In contrast, projection methods take a functional analytic view of a problem, focusing on finding a *function* that approximately solves the *functional* equation expressed in (11.1.1). While the differences appear to be slight at this point, the change in focus leads to a much more flexible approach.

To formulate (11.1.1) in a functional way, we define L

$$Ly \equiv y' - y. \tag{11.1.2}$$

L is an operator, a function that maps functions to functions. The domain of L includes all C^1 functions, and its range is C^0. The differential equation $y' = y$ combined with the initial condition $y(0) = 1$ can be viewed as the problem of finding a C^1 function y that satisfies the initial condition $y(0) = 1$ and is mapped by L to the zero function. Another way of viewing it is to define the set $Y = \{y(x) \,|\, y \in C^1, y(0) = 1\}$; that is, Y is the set of C^1 functions that satisfies the initial condition $y(0) = 1$. Then (11.1.1) is the problem of finding a $y \in Y$ such that $Ly = 0$.

Since the focus in projection methods is on finding an approximate function, not just a sequence of values, we must find a way to represent functions in the computer. One way is to use polynomials. We know from the Weierstrass theorem that any C^1 function can be approximated well by large sums of polynomial terms. We cannot represent infinite series on the computer, but we can represent finite sums. We will let the finite list a_i, $i = 1, \ldots, n$, represent the polynomial $\sum_{j=1}^{n} a_j x^j$. For each choice for the values of the a_i, we define the function

$$\hat{y}(x; a) = 1 + \sum_{j=1}^{n} a_j x^j. \tag{11.1.3}$$

The set of such functions created by letting the a_j coefficients range over R creates an affine subset of the vector space of polynomials. Note that $\hat{y}(0; a) = 1$ for any choice of a, implying that $\hat{y}$ satisfies the boundary condition of (11.1.1) no matter what a is chosen. Hence $\hat{y}(\cdot \,; a) \in Y$ for any a.

We will try to choose a so that $\hat{y}(x; a)$ "nearly" solves the differential equation (1.1). To determine how well $\hat{y}$ does this, we compute the *residual function*

$$R(x; a) \equiv L\hat{y} = -1 + \sum_{j=1}^{n} a_j(jx^{j-1} - x^j) \qquad (11.1.4)$$

The residual function is the deviation of $L\hat{y}$ from zero, the target value. A projection method adjusts a until it finds a "good" a that makes $R(x; a)$ "nearly" the zero function. Different projection methods are generated by varying how one operationalizes the notions "good" and "nearly." We will now review the basic implementations.

For this example we initially take $n = 3$. We need to calculate the three coefficients, a_1, a_2, and a_3. A natural procedure for economists is the *least squares* method. In this method we find a that minimizes the total squared residual over the interval of interest; that is, it solves

$$\min_{a} \int_0^3 R(x; a)^2 dx. \qquad (11.1.5)$$

The objective is quadratic in the a's, and the first-order conditions reduce to the linear problem

$$\begin{pmatrix} 6 & \dfrac{9}{2} & -\dfrac{54}{5} \\[2ex] \dfrac{9}{2} & \dfrac{36}{5} & 0 \\[2ex] \dfrac{54}{5} & 0 & 41\dfrac{23}{35} \end{pmatrix} \begin{pmatrix} a_1 \\[1ex] a_2 \\[1ex] a_3 \end{pmatrix} = \begin{pmatrix} -3 \\[1ex] 0 \\[1ex] \dfrac{27}{2} \end{pmatrix}. \qquad (11.1.6)$$

The solution is displayed on the first row of table 11.1.

Table 11.1
Solutions for coefficients in (11.1.3)

Scheme	a_1	a_2	a_3
Least squares	1.290	−0.806	0.659
Galerkin	2.286	−1.429	0.952
Subdomain	2.500	−1.500	1.000
Chebyshev collocation	1.692	−1.231	0.821
Uniform collocation	1.000	−1.000	0.667
Power series	1.000	0.500	0.167
Optimal L^2	1.754	−0.838	0.779

Another concept of $R(\cdot\,; a)$ being nearly zero is that it is zero on average. Since we have three unknowns, we need to find three averages. One way is to decompose $[0, 3]$ into three intervals

$$[0, 3] = [0, 1] \cup [1, 2] \cup [2, 3] \equiv D_1 \cup D_2 \cup D_3.$$

We then use the three conditions

$$0 = \int_{D_i} R(x; a)\, dx, \qquad i = 1, 2, 3, \tag{11.1.7}$$

to fix a. This yields the linear conditions

$$\begin{pmatrix} \dfrac{1}{2} & \dfrac{2}{3} & \dfrac{3}{4} \\[2mm] -\dfrac{1}{2} & \dfrac{2}{3} & \dfrac{13}{4} \\[2mm] -\dfrac{3}{2} & -\dfrac{4}{3} & \dfrac{11}{4} \end{pmatrix} \begin{pmatrix} a_1 \\ a_2 \\ a_3 \end{pmatrix} = \begin{pmatrix} 1 \\ 1 \\ 1 \end{pmatrix}. \tag{11.1.8}$$

This procedure is called the *subdomain* method. The solution to (11.1.8) appears on the row in table 11.1 labeled "subdomain."

If $R(x; a)$ were the zero function, then the integral of its product with any other function would also be zero. This observation leads us to the *method of moments* which fixes a by using powers of x to generate projection conditions. Since we have three unknowns, we use the first three powers:

$$0 = \int_0^3 R(x; a)\, x^j\, dx, \qquad j = 0, 1, 2. \tag{11.1.9}$$

Continuing for $j = 1, 2$, we end up with a linear system in a:

$$\begin{pmatrix} -\dfrac{3}{2} & 0 & \dfrac{27}{4} \\[2mm] -\dfrac{9}{2} & -\dfrac{9}{4} & \dfrac{243}{20} \\[2mm] -\dfrac{45}{4} & \dfrac{81}{10} & \dfrac{243}{10} \end{pmatrix} \begin{pmatrix} a_1 \\ a_2 \\ a_3 \end{pmatrix} = \begin{pmatrix} 3 \\ \dfrac{9}{2} \\ 6 \end{pmatrix}. \tag{11.1.10}$$

Our approximation is built up from weighted sums of x, x^2, and x^3. If $R(x; a)$ were the zero function, then the integral of its product with each of these functions would be zero. This observation leads us to the *Galerkin method* which fixes a by using the functions used in the approximation to impose the three moment conditions

$$0 = \int_0^3 R(x;a)\, x^j dx, \qquad j = 1,2,3.$$

This is the same as the method of moments except that here we use x, x^2, and x^3 instead of 1, x, and x^2. However, the motivation is different; in the method of moments we use x^k because it is a moment, but in the Galerkin we use x^k because it is used in the construction of the approximation. In general, there will be substantial differences between these methods.

The preceding methods all involve integrals of the residual function. In this problem these integrals are easy to compute directly; that is not true generally. In contrast, *collocation* methods proceed by choosing a so that $R(x;a)$ is zero at a finite set of x values. Since we have three unknowns, we will choose three collocation points. If we choose the three points $0, 3/2, 3$, and set $R(x;a)$ equal to zero at these values for x, the linear conditions on a are

$$R(0;a) = 0 = -1 + a_1$$

$$R(1.5;a) = 0 = -1 - \frac{1}{2}a_1 + \frac{3}{4}a_2 + \frac{27}{8}a_3 \qquad (11.1.11)$$

$$R(3;a)0 = -1 - 2a_1 - 3a_2$$

Although a uniform grid is natural, our discussion of interpolation in chapter 6 indicates that it is not a good choice. If we were told that $R(x_i;a) = 0$, $i = 1,2,3$, then the quadratic interpolant for $R(x;a)$ given these data would be the zero function. Collocation implicitly assumes (hopes) that if a is such that $R(x_i;a) = 0$, $i = 1,2,3$, then $R(x;a) = 0$ for all $0 \le x \le 3$. In order for this interpolation argument to be as reliable as possible, what x_i's should be chosen? In chapter 6 we saw that a uniform grid may be a poor choice, in that there are functions with modest curvature that are zero on the uniform grid but vary substantially otherwise.

However, we saw that if a smooth, well-behaved function were zero at the zeros of some Chebyshev function on $[-1, 1]$, then the function is close to zero on all of $[-1, 1]$. When we are on intervals other than $[-1, 1]$, we must make an appropriate linear change of variable, discussed in section 6.4. In this context, this implies that the x_i should be the zeros of $T_3(x)$ adapted to $[0, 3]$, which is the set

$$\left\{ \frac{3}{2}\left(\cos\frac{\pi}{6} + 1\right), \frac{3}{2}, \frac{3}{2}\left(\cos\frac{5\pi}{6} + 1\right) \right\}.$$

Collocation at zeros of Chebyshev polynomials adapted to the interval of interest called *Chebyshev collocation*.

Another way to compute an approximate solution is the *power series* method. The power series method uses information about y and its derivatives at $t = 0$ to compute a. Since $y' - y = 0$ at $t = 0$, we know that $y'(0) = 1$. But $\hat{y}' = a_1 + 2a_2 x + 3a_3 x^2$ and $\hat{y}'(0) = a_1$. Hence $a_1 = 1$. We can also fix a_2 and a_3 in this way. Assuming a smooth solution, we can differentiate the differential equation to find $y'' - y' = 0$. Since this holds at $t = 0$, $y''(0) = y'(0) = 1$. However, $\hat{y}'' = 2a_2 + 6a_3 x$ and $\hat{y}''(0) = 2a_2$. Hence $a_2 = 1/2$. Similarly $y''' - y'' = 0$, $\hat{y}'''(0) = 1 = 6a_3$, implying that $a_3 = 1/6$. The final approximation is

$$\hat{y} \cong 1 + x + \frac{x^2}{2} + \frac{x^3}{6},$$

which indeed are the first four terms of the Taylor series expansion of e^x.

The power series method will produce an approximation that is very good near 0. In fact, since the error is $\mathcal{O}(x^4)$, this cubic approximation is the best possible cubic approximation near 0. As we move away from 0 the quality of the approximation will decay rapidly because the error is $\mathcal{O}(x^4)$. We discuss the power series method here because it is also a well-known method for solving ordinary differential equations which produces an approximating function.

The rows in table 11.1 show that the coefficients generated by these procedures differ substantially from each other. They often differ from the coefficients of the least squares fit of a cubic polynomial satisfying the boundary condition to the function e^x. These coefficients are displayed in the row labeled "optimal L^2."

The L^2 errors for these methods for $n = 3, 4, \ldots, 10$, are summarized in table 11.2. table 11.2 demonstrates several aspects of these methods. First, they all do better as

Table 11.2
Errors of projection methods applied to (11.1.2)

n	Uniform collocation	Chebyshev collocation	Least squares	Galerkin	Subdomain	Taylor series	Optimal L^2
3	5.3(0)	2.2(0)	3.2(0)	5.3(−1)	1.4(0)	3.8(0)	1.7(−1)
4	1.3(0)	2.9(−1)	1.5(−1)	3.6(−2)	1.4(−1)	1.8(0)	2.4(−2)
5	1.5(−1)	2.5(−2)	4.9(−3)	4.1(−3)	2.2(−2)	7.7(−1)	2.9(−3)
6	2.0(−2)	1.9(−3)	4.2(−4)	4.2(−4)	2.0(−3)	2.9(−1)	3.0(−4)
7	2.2(−3)	1.4(−4)	3.8(−5)	3.9(−5)	2.7(−4)	9.8(−2)	2.8(−5)
8	2.4(−4)	9.9(−6)	3.2(−6)	3.2(−6)	2.1(−5)	3.0(−2)	2.3(−6)
9	2.2(−5)	6.6(−7)	2.3(−7)	2.4(−7)	2.3(−6)	8.2(−3)	1.7(−7)
10	2.1(−6)	4.0(−8)	1.6(−8)	1.6(−8)	1.6(−7)	2.1(−3)	1.2(−8)

one uses more terms. Since both collocation methods are based on interpolation ideas, we cannot be assured of this. The Taylor series method is generally the worst. Its poor performance is not too surprising, for it is a local method. Uniform collocation is inferior to the integral methods, an expected result since collocation uses information at so few points. Least squares and Galerkin do best and yield similar results. Their solutions are almost as good as the polynomial that minimizes the sum of squared errors over $[0, 3]$. Chebyshev collocation does nearly as well as Galerkin and better than subdomain. This is strong evidence of how good Chebyshev collocation can be.

11.2   A Partial Differential Equation Example

We will now apply projection methods to a simple partial differential equation to illustrate projection methods in a different context. Readers who are unfamiliar with partial differential equations should not despair; the point of this example is to show how one can use projection methods even when one is not expert about the kind of equation being considered.

Consider the simple heat equation

$$\theta_t - \theta_{xx} = 0 \tag{11.2.1}$$

on the domain $0 \le x \le 1$ and $0 \le t < \infty$. We assume the initial condition

$$\theta(x, 0) = \sin \pi x \tag{11.2.2}$$

and impose the boundary conditions

$$\theta(0, t) = 0, \quad \theta(1, t) = 0, \qquad 0 \le t < \infty. \tag{11.2.3}$$

The problem is to find a function on $[0, 1] \times [0, \infty)$ that satisfies the partial derivative conditions in (11.2.1) and also satisfy (11.2.2) for $t = 0$ and (11.2.3) at $x = 0, 1$. There is a unique solution, $\theta(x, t) = e^{-\pi^2 t} \sin \pi x$.

We will take a projection approach to solve this problem. We begin by forming the polynomial approximation

$$\hat{\theta}(x, t) = \theta_0(x) + \sum_{j=1}^{n} a_j(t)\, (x - x^j), \tag{11.2.4}$$

where

$$\theta_0(x) = \sin \pi x$$

is the initial condition. Note how we handled the boundary condition, (11.2.3). The approximation in (11.2.4) consists of weighted sums of $x - x^j$ terms. Since $x - x^j$ is zero at $x = 0, 1$, $\hat{\theta}$ will satisfy the boundary conditions in (11.2.3) for any $a_j(t)$ functions. Initial conditions for initial value ODEs are easy to specify, since they just involve the value of a function at a point. Modeling boundary conditions for PDE's generally requires more ingenuity.

When we substitute $\hat{\theta}$ into $\theta_t - \theta_{xx} = 0$, we get the residual function:

$$R(x, t) = -\theta_{0xx}(x, t) + \sum_{j=1}^{n} (\dot{a}_j(t) (x - x^j) - a_j(t) (-j)(j - 1)x^{j-2}). \qquad (11.2.5)$$

We have n unknown functions, $a_j(t)$. Let $\langle \cdot, \cdot \rangle$ be the inner product $\langle u, v \rangle = \int_0^1 uv \, dx$. As in the previous example, we solve out for the unknown $a_j(t)$ functions by imposing, at each t, n projection conditions of the form

$$\langle R(x, t), \psi_j(x) \rangle = 0, \qquad j = 1, \ldots, N, \qquad (11.2.6)$$

for some collection of functions $\psi_j(x)$. This will result in a system of linear differential equations of the form

$$M\dot{A} + BA + C = 0, \qquad (11.2.7)$$

where

$$A(t) = \begin{pmatrix} a_1(t) \\ \vdots \\ a_n(t) \end{pmatrix},$$

$$M_{jk} = \langle x - x^j, \psi_k \rangle,$$

$$B_{jk} = -\langle j(j - 1)x^{j-2}, \psi_k \rangle,$$

$$C_k = -\langle \theta_{0xx}, \psi_k \rangle.$$

Since $\theta(x, 0) = \theta_0(x)$, $A(0) = 0$ is the initial condition. Rewrite (11.2.7) as $\dot{A} = -M^{-1}BA - M^{-1}C$. Since M, B, and C are constant with respect to time, the result is a linear ordinary differential equation in A with constant coefficients and with initial condition $A = 0$. This could be solved for arbitrary t once we calculate the eigenvalues of $M^{-1}B$.

We have not yet specified the ψ_j functions. The ψ_j could be the $x - x^j$ functions, but the rows of M and B would be somewhat collinear, creating the possibility of

$M^{-1}B$ being poorly conditioned. A better choice may be the Legendre polynomials adapted to the interval $[0, 1]$. The main requirement is that the ψ_j be chosen so that the ψ_j can be easily computed and the linear systems to be solved be well-conditioned.

Note that the projection conditions reduced the partial differential equation to a system of ordinary differential equations in the coefficient functions $a_j(t)$. These equations could be solved using finite-difference methods. We could go one step further and eliminate all derivatives. Suppose that we want to solve $\theta(x, t)$ over the compact domain $0 \leq x \leq 1$ and $0 \leq t \leq 1$. We can approximate θ in both the x and t dimensions with a finite polynomial sum:

$$\theta(x, t) = \theta_0(x) + \sum_{i=1}^{n} \sum_{j=1}^{m} a_{ij} (x - x^i) t^j. \tag{11.2.8}$$

Then the residual function is a function of both space and time, equaling

$$R(x, t) = -\theta_{0xx}(x) + \sum_{i=1}^{n} \sum_{j=1}^{m} \left(a_{ij} (x - x^i) j t^{j-1} - a_{ij} (-i)(i - 1) x^{i-2} t^j \right). \tag{11.2.9}$$

We now have only scalar unknowns, the a_{ij}. To determine those nm scalar constants, we impose the nm projection conditions:

$$\langle R(x, t), \psi_{ij}(x, t) \rangle = 0, \qquad i = 1, \ldots, n, \; j = 1, \ldots, m, \tag{11.2.10}$$

where $\psi_{ij}(x, t) = (x - x^i) t^j$ is a collection of nm basis functions. Equations (11.2.10) form a system of linear algebraic equations in the unknown coefficients a_{ij}.

We will not go further with this example. These manipulations show how to convert a linear partial differential equation into a linear ordinary differential equation or even into a linear algebraic system. Such transformations can be used generally to construct powerful solution methods. We next describe the projection method for general problems.

11.3 General Projection Method

In the previous two sections we applied projection ideas to familiar problems. We now describe the projection method in a more generally applicable fashion. The ability to do this is a strength of projection methods. We give a step-by-step overview of the approach; then we highlight the critical issues for each step and discuss how the pieces interact.

General Projection Approach

Suppose that we want a solution to the operator equation

$$\mathcal{N}(f) = 0, \tag{11.3.1}$$

where $\mathcal{N}: B_1 \to B_2$, with B_1 and B_2 complete normed vector spaces of functions $f: D \subset R^n \to R^m$, and where $\mathcal{N}$ is a continuous map. In our simple ordinary differential equation example (11.1.1), $D = [0, T]$, $f: D \to R$, $\mathcal{N} = d/dt - I$ where I is the identity operator, B_1 is the space of C^1 functions, and B_2 is the space of C^0 functions. In this example, B_2 contained B_1, and both are contained in the space of measurable functions. More generally, f is a list of functions in the definition of equilibrium, such as decision rules, price functions, value functions, and conditional expectations functions, and the $\mathcal{N}$ operator expresses equilibrium conditions such as market clearing, Euler equations, Bellman and HJB equations, and rational expectations.

Since we are focused on describing the computational method, we will specify the topological details only to the extent implicit in the computational details. For example, we do not say exactly what norms and inner products are being implicitly used in the ODE and PDE examples in the previous sections. While these topological details are important, they lie far beyond the scope of this book. This may make some readers uncomfortable, particularly when we note that the topological aspects of many of our applications are not well-understood. Some comfort can be taken in the fact that we always check the validity of our solutions, and those checks may keep us from accepting projection method solutions in cases where the underlying functional analytic structure does not support the use of such methods. The reader can also see Zeidler (1986) and Krasnosel'ski and Zabreiko (1984) for serious discussions of those issues, and is encouraged to apply the methods there to economic problems.

The first step is to decide how to represent approximate solutions to $\mathcal{N}(f) = 0$. One general way is to assume that our approximation, $\hat{f}$, is built up as a linear[1] combination of simple functions from B_1. We will also need concepts of when two functions are close or far apart. Therefore, the first step is to choose bases and concepts of distance:

STEP 1   Choose a basis over B_1, $\Phi = \{\varphi_i\}_{i=1}^{\infty}$ and a norm, $\|\cdot\|$. Similarly choose a basis over B_2, $\Psi = \{\psi_i\}_{i=1}^{\infty}$ and an inner product, $\langle \cdot, \cdot \rangle_2$ over B_2.

---

1. Nonlinear combinations are also possible, but we stay with linear combinations here, since linear approximation theory is a much more developed theory than nonlinear approximation theory.

When B_1 and B_2 are subsets of another space, we will often use a basis of the larger space as the basis of B_1 and an inner product norm of the larger space as the norm on B_2. Our approximation to the solution of $\mathcal{N}(f) = 0$ will be denoted $\hat{f}$; we next decide how many of these basis elements we will use.

STEP 2   Choose a degree of approximation, n, and define[2] $\hat{f} \equiv \sum_{i=1}^{n} a_i \varphi_i(x)$.

Step 1 lays down the structure of our approximation, and step 2 fixes the flexibility of the approximation. Once we have made these basic decisions, we begin our search for an approximate solution to (11.3.1). Since the only unknown part of the approximation is the vector a, we have reduced the original infinite-dimensional problem to a finite-dimensional one. If our diagnostic tests leave us dissatisfied with that approximation, we can return to step 2 and increase n in hopes of getting an improved approximation. If that fails, we can return to step 1 and begin again with a different basis.

Since the true solution f satisfies $\mathcal{N}(f) = 0$, we will choose as our approximation some $\hat{f}$ that makes $\mathcal{N}(\hat{f})$ nearly equal to the zero function, where by near we refer to properties defined by the norm in B_2, $\|\cdot\|_2$, which corresponds to the inner product $\langle \cdot, \cdot \rangle_2$. Since $\hat{f}$ is parameterized by a, the problem reduces to finding an a which makes $\mathcal{N}(\hat{f})$ nearly zero. In many cases computing $\mathcal{N}(\hat{f})$ is also challenging, such as when $\mathcal{N}(f)$ involves integration of f; in those cases we need to approximate the $\mathcal{N}$ operator.

STEP 3   Construct a computable approximation, $\hat{\mathcal{N}}$, to $\mathcal{N}$, and define the residual function

$$R(x; a) \equiv (\hat{\mathcal{N}}(\hat{f}(\cdot\,; a)))(x).$$

Steps 2 and 3 transform an operation in an infinite-dimensional space into a computable finite-dimensional one. We need next to specify our notion of $\hat{f}$ nearly solving $\mathcal{N}(f) = 0$.

STEP 4   Either compute the norm of $R(\cdot\,; a)$, $\|R(\cdot\,; a)\| \equiv \langle R(\cdot\,; a), R(\cdot\,; a) \rangle$, or choose a collection of l *test functions* in B_2, $p_i: D \to R^m$, $i = 1, \ldots, l$, and for each guess of a compute the l projections, $P_i(\cdot) \equiv \langle R(\cdot\,; a), p_i(\cdot) \rangle$.

Step 4 creates the projections we will use. The choices made in step 4 generally give the projection method its name. Projection methods are also called "weighted

---

2. The convention is that the φ_i increase in "complexity" and "nonlinearity" as i increases, and that the first n elements are used. In the case of standard families of orthogonal polynomials, φ_i is the degree $i - 1$ polynomial.

residual methods," since the criteria in step 4 weigh the residuals. Once we have chosen our criterion, we can determine the value of the unknown coefficients, a.

STEP 5   Find $a \in R^n$ that either minimizes $\|R(\cdot; a)\|$ or solves $P(a) = 0$.

When we have our solution, $\hat{f}$, we are not done. It is only a candidate solution, and we must test the quality of our solution before accepting it.

STEP 6   Verify the quality of the candidate solution by approximating $\mathcal{N}(\hat{f})$.

We accomplish step 6 by computing the norm $\|\mathcal{N}(\hat{f})\|$ and/or projections of $\mathcal{N}(\hat{f})$ against test functions not used in step 4. If $\mathcal{N}$ must be approximated, we should, if feasible, use a better approximation in step 6 than that constructed in step 3. Ideally all of these quantities will be zero; in practice, we choose target quantities for these diagnostics that imply that the deviations from zero are not economically significant.

This general algorithm breaks the numerical problem into several distinct steps. It points out the many distinct techniques of numerical analysis which are important. First, in steps 1 and 2 we choose the finite-dimensional space wherein we look for approximate solutions, hoping that within this set there is something "close" to the real solution. These steps require us to think seriously about approximation theory methods. Second, step 4 will involve numerical integration if we cannot explicitly compute the integrals that define the projections, and step 3 frequently involves numerical integration in economics applications. Third, step 5 is a third distinct numerical problem, involving the solution of a nonlinear set of simultaneous equations or the solution of a minimization problem. We will now consider each of these numerical problems in isolation.

Choice of Basis and Approximation Degree

There are many criteria that the basis and inner product should satisfy. The full basis Φ for the space of candidate solutions should be "rich," flexible enough to approximate any function relevant to the problem. The best choice of n cannot be determined a priori. Generally, the only correct choice is $n = \infty$. If the choice of the basis is good, then larger n will yield better approximations. We are most interested, however, in the smallest n that yields an acceptable approximation. We initially begin with small n and increase n until some diagnostic indicates little is gained by continuing. Computational considerations also play a role in choosing a basis. The φ_i should be simple to compute, and all be similar in size to avoid scaling problems.

Of course, the number of basis elements needed will depend greatly on the basis being used; using a basis that is well-suited to a problem can greatly improve performance. Approximation theory, discussed in chapter 6, can be used to evaluate alternative bases because ultimately we are trying to approximate the solution f with a finite combination of simple known functions. The basis elements should look something like the solution so that only a few elements can give a good approximation. While asymptotic results such as the Stone-Weierstrass theorem may lull one into accepting polynomial approximations, practical success requires a basis where only a few elements will do the job. The individual terms should also be "different"; ideally they should be orthogonal with respect to the inner product $\langle \cdot, \cdot \rangle$. The reasons are essentially the same as why one wants uncorrelated explanatory variables in a regression. Nonorthogonal bases will reduce numerical accuracy just as multicollinear regressors enlarge confidence intervals. Algorithms that solve for the unknown coefficients a solve several linear systems of equations, and the accuracy of these solutions depends on the rows and columns not being collinear. Orthogonal bases will help avoid ill-conditioned matrices in these intermediate steps.

From chapter 6 we know that there are several possible bases. First, let us consider the ordinary polynomials, $\{1, x, x^2, x^3, \ldots\}$. If B_1 is the set of bounded measurable functions on a compact set then the Stone-Weierstrass theorem assures us of their completeness in the L_1 norm. However, they may not be a good choice since they are too similar. For example, they are all monotonically increasing and positive on R^+, and they will not be orthogonal in any natural inner product on R^+. They will also vary a great deal in size over most intervals D. The ordinary polynomials will sometimes be adequate, as they were in our simple examples, because we needed few terms to get a good solution.

These considerations do not mean that we cannot use ordinary polynomials, just that it is preferable to use polynomial bases that are orthonormal with respect to the inner product. A generally useful choice are systems of Chebyshev polynomials, which were discussed in chapter 6. Nonpolynomial alternatives include various sequences of trigonometric and exponential functions. The choice depends on the range, D, computational demands, and the expected shape of a solution. In physics, trigonometric bases such as $\{1, \sin x, \sin 2x, \sin 3x, \ldots\}$ are often used, since solutions are often periodic, allowing for Fourier series techniques. In economic problems, however, it is better to use nontrigonometric bases, since solutions are generally not periodic and periodic approximations to nonperiodic functions require many terms.

We can use the full array of approximation methods discussed in chapter 6. Some families of projection methods are known by their method of approximation. *Spectral methods* use bases where each element is nonzero almost everywhere, such as in trigonometric bases and orthogonal polynomials. *Finite element* methods use bases where each element has small support, as discussed in section 6.13.

Most interesting problems in economics involve more than one state variable—physical versus human capital, capital stocks of oligopolistic competitors, wealth distribution across investor groups, and so on. The tensor product methods discussed in Chapter 6 build up multidimensional basis functions from simple one-dimensional basis functions. The curse of dimensionality, a problem that arises with tensor product bases, can be avoided by using the complete polynomials as a basis instead.

We are not limited to the conventional approaches described in chapter 6. If we have some reason to believe that a solution will look like some nonconventional functions, then we should try them. We may want to orthogonalize the family, and we may need to develop the corresponding Gaussian quadrature formulas, but all that is just a straightforward application of the methods discussed in chapters 6 and 7. This may be quite important in multidimensional problems because we will need to economize on basis elements. In chapter 15 we will discuss formal ways to generate good problem-specific bases. Even though we will focus here on using standard approximation methods, the ideas of projection methods generalize directly to more idiosyncratic choices.

Choice of Projection Conditions

As we have seen in our examples, projection techniques include a variety of special methods. In general, we specify some inner product, $\langle \cdot, \cdot \rangle$, of B_2, and use $\langle \cdot, \cdot \rangle$ to measure the "size" of the residual function, R, or its projection against the test functions. We can use inner products of the form

$$\langle f(x), g(x) \rangle \equiv \int_D f(x)g(x)w(x)\,dx$$

for some weighting function $w(x)$, but there is no reason why we are limited to them. In choosing the norm, one should consider exactly what kind of error should be small and find a norm that will be sensitive to the important errors. There are several ways to proceed.

The general *least squares projection method* computes the L^2 norm of the residual function, namely $\langle R(x; a), R(x; a) \rangle$, and chooses a so as to minimize the "sum of squared residuals":

$$\min_a \langle R(x; a), R(x; a) \rangle.$$

We have thereby reduced the problem of solving a functional equation to solving a nonlinear minimization problem in R^n, a more tractable problem. Of course, the standard difficulties will arise. For example, there may be local minima which are not global solutions. However, there is no reason for these problems to arise more often here than in any other context, such as maximum likelihood estimation, where minimization problems are solved numerically.

The least squares method is a direct implementation of the idea to make small the error of the approximation. In general, one could develop alternative implementations by using different norms. However, most projection techniques find a good-fitting approximation in less direct fashions. For these techniques the basic idea is that the true solution would have a zero residual error function; in particular, its projection in all directions is zero. Therefore one way to find the n components of a is to fix n projections and choose a so that the projection of the resulting residual function in each of those n directions is zero. Formally these methods find a such that $\langle R, p_i \rangle = 0$ for some specified collection of test functions, p_i. Different choices of the p_i defines different implementations of the projection method.

It is clear that the least squares and alternative implementations of projection ideas are similar since one way to solve the least squares approach is to solve the nonlinear set of equations generated by its first-order conditions, $\langle R, \partial R / \partial a_i \rangle = 0$. Seeing the least squares method expressed as a system of projection equations gives us some indication why other methods may be better. The projection directions in the least squares case, the gradients of the residual function, could be highly correlated. Furthermore the projection directions depend on the guess for a. This lack of control over the implicit projection directions is not a good feature. Also in economic problems we may have a preference for approximations that have zero projections in certain directions, such as the average error in an Euler equation. Many of the alternative techniques will naturally include that condition.

One such alternative technique is the *Galerkin* method, also known as the *Bubnov-Galerkin* or *Galerkin-Petrov* method. In the Galerkin method we use the first n elements of the basis for the projection directions, where we are making the weak assumption that Φ, our basis of B_1, lies in B_2. Therefore a is chosen to solve the following set of equations:

$$P_i(a) \equiv \langle R(x; a), \varphi_i(x) \rangle = 0, \qquad i = 1, \ldots, n.$$

Notice that here we have reduced the problem of solving a differential equation to one of solving a set of nonlinear equations. In some cases the Galerkin projection equations are the first-order conditions to some minimization problem, as is often the case in linear problems from physics. When we have such an equivalence, the Galerkin method is also called the *Rayleigh-Ritz* method. This is not as likely to happen in economics problems because of nonlinearities.

The method of moments, subdomain, and collocation procedures can be applied to the general setting. If $D \subset R$, then the *method of moments* chooses the first n polynomials for the projection directions; that is, we find a that solves the system

$$P_i(a) \equiv \langle R(x;a), x^{i-1} \rangle = 0, \qquad i = 1, \ldots, n.$$

If D is of higher dimension, then we project R against a sufficient number of low-order multivariate monomials. In the *subdomain method* the idea is to find an approximation that is good on average on a collection of subsets that cover the whole domain. More specifically, we choose a so that

$$P_i(a) \equiv \langle R(x;a), I_{D_i} \rangle = 0, \qquad i = 1, \ldots, n,$$

where $\{D_i\}_{i=1}^n$ is a sequence of intervals covering D, and I_{D_i} is the indicator function for D_i.

The *collocation method* chooses a so that the functional equation holds exactly at n fixed points. That is, we choose a to solve

$$R(x_i; a) = 0, \qquad i = 1, \ldots, n,$$

where $\{x_i\}_{i=1}^n$ are n fixed points from D. This is a special case of the projection approach, since $R(x_i; a)$ equals $\langle R(x;a), \delta(x - x_i) \rangle$, the projection of $R(x;a)$ against the Dirac delta function at x_i.

Orthogonal collocation is the method where the x_i are the n zeros of the nth orthogonal polynomial basis element and the basis elements are orthogonal with respect to the inner product. It is a particularly powerful application of projection ideas when used with a Chebyshev polynomial basis. This is not a surprise in light of the Chebyshev interpolation theorem. Suppose that $D = [-1, 1]$ and $R(z_i^n; a) = 0$, $i = 1, \ldots, n$, where the z_i^n are the n zeros of T_n. As long as $R(x;a)$ is smooth in x, the Chebyshev interpolation theorem says that these zero conditions force $R(x;a)$ to be close to zero for all $x \in [-1, 1]$. The optimality of Chebyshev interpolation also says that if one is going to use collocation, these are the best possible points to use. Even after absorbing these considerations, it is not certain that even Chebyshev collocation is a reliable method. We will see below that its performance is surprisingly good.

Collocation can be used for bases other than orthogonal polynomials. *Spline collocation* methods use spline bases. The collocation points could be the spline nodes themselves or some other set of points, such as the midpoints of the spline mesh. The key objective is keeping the Jacobian of the collocation equation system well-conditioned.

Evaluation of Projections

The meat of the problem is step 4 whose the major computational task is the computation of those projections. The collocation method is fastest in this regard because it only uses the value of R at n points. More generally, the projections will involve integration. In some cases one may be able to explicitly perform the integration. This is generally possible for linear problems, and possible for special nonlinear problems. However, our experience with the economic applications below is that this will generally be impossible for nonlinear economic problems. We instead need to use quadrature techniques to compute the integrals associated with the evaluation of $\langle \cdot, \cdot \rangle$. A typical quadrature formula approximates $\int_a^b f(x)\, w(x)\, dx$ with a finite sum $\sum_{i=1}^n \omega_i f(x_i)$ where the x_i are the quadrature nodes and the ω_i are the weights. Since these formulas also evaluate R at just a finite number of points, quadrature-based projection techniques are essentially weighted collocation methods. The advantage of quadrature formulas is that information at more points is used to compute a more accurate approximation of the projections.

Finding the Solution

Step 5 uses either a minimization algorithm or a nonlinear algebraic equation solver. If the system $P(a) = 0$ is overidentified or if we are minimizing $\|R(\cdot; a)\|$, we may invoke a nonlinear least squares algorithm. The nonlinear equations associated with Galerkin and other inner product methods can be solved by the variety of methods discussed in chapter 5. While fixed-point iteration appears to be popular in economics, Newton's method and its refinements have often been successful. Homotopy methods can also be used if one has no good initial guesses.

Initial Guesses

Good initial guesses are important since projection methods involve either a system of nonlinear equations or optimizing a nonlinear, possibly multimodal, objective. Fortunately this is generally not a big problem. Often there are degenerate cases for which we can find the solution, which in turn will be a good guess for the problem we want to solve. The perturbation methods discussed in chapers 13 and 14 often generate good initial guesses. In some problems there are problem-specific ways of generating good initial guesses.

There is one general approach which is often useful. The least squares approach may not be a good one to use for high-quality approximations. However, it may yield low-quality approximations relatively quickly, and, since the least squares method is an optimization method, convergence to a local extrema is ensured even if one has no good initial guess. Furthermore, by adding terms to the least squares objective, one can impose sensible restrictions on the coefficients to eliminate economically nonsensical extrema. These facts motivate a two-stage approach. First, one uses a least squares approach with a loose convergence criterion to quickly compute a low-quality approximation. Second, one uses this approximation as the initial guess for a projection method attempting to compute a higher-order approximation. With some luck the least squares solution will be a good initial guess for the second computation. If it is difficult to find good initial guesses, then one can use homotopy methods that are globally convergent.

Coordination among Steps 1–5

We now see what is needed for efficiency. The key is to choose elements for the separate steps that work well together. We need basis functions that are easy to evaluate because they will be frequently evaluated. Any integration in steps 3 and 4 must be accurate but fast. Therefore we should use quadrature formulas that work well with the basis. The nonlinear equation solver in step 5 needs to be efficient and should be able to use all the information arising from step 4 calculations. Step 5 will typically use gradient information about the integrals of step 4. It is therefore important to do those gradient calculations quickly, doing them analytically when practical.

A particularly important interaction is that between the choice of a basis and the solution of the nonlinear problem in R^n. Most methods for solving the system $P(a) = 0$ will use its Jacobian, $P_a(a) = 0$. If this matrix is nearly singular near the solution, accuracy will be poor due to round-off error and convergence will be slow. Choosing an orthogonal basis, or nearly orthogonal basis (as is the case with B-splines), will substantially reduce the likelihood of a poorly conditioned Jacobian, even in nonlinear problems.

Most methods used in numerical analysis of economic models fall within the general description for projection methods. We will see these connections below when we compare how various methods attack a common problem. The key fact is that the methods differ in their choices of basis, fitting criterion, and integration technique.

Evaluating a Solution

As with operator equation methods in general, the projection algorithm does not automatically evaluate the quality of the candidate approximate solution. One of the advantages of the projection approach is the ease with which one can do the desired evaluation. The key observation is that we typically use an approximation to $\mathcal{N}$, $\hat{\mathcal{N}}$, when searching for the approximate solution, $\hat{f}$. For example, we use numerical integration methods to compute conditional expectations and to compute projections. To economize on computer time, we use the least amount of information possible to compute $\hat{f}$.

This is a risky but acceptable strategy, since we accept $\hat{f}$ only after we strenuously test the candidate $\hat{f}$. Therefore we use better quadrature rules here to evaluate $\hat{f}$, and we check if $0 = (\hat{\mathcal{N}}(\hat{f}))(x)$ at many points that were not used in the derivation of $\hat{f}$. We also use a finite number of test functions in constructing $\hat{f}$, leaving an infinite number of test functions that we can use to evaluate $\hat{f}$. While this discussion is abstract here, the actual implementation will be quite intuitive in actual applications.

Existence Problems

Projection methods are useful ways to transform infinite-dimensional problems into finite-dimensional problems. However, these transformations present problems that we have not faced in previous methods—existence. In previous chapters we investigated methods that were more similar to the problem being analyzed. For example, in chapter 5 we examined nonlinear equations, where there is a solution to the numerical problem if and only if there is a solution to the original, pure problem. This can be different here. Sometimes the finite-dimensional problem generated by a projection method will not have a solution even when the original, pure problem does have a solution. Therefore, if one is having difficulty solving a projection equation system for a particular basis and particular n, the problem may go away just by trying another n or another basis. For well-behaved problems, choosing a sufficiently large n will work.

One way to ensure existence of a solution but gain some of the advantages of the projection methods is to construct a least squares objective from the projections. For example, in the case of the Galerkin method, one could solve the least squares problem

$$\min_a \sum_{i=1}^{n} \langle R(x; a), \varphi_i(x) \rangle^2.$$

One could use an *overidentification* approach and solve the problem

$$\min_a \sum_{i=1}^{m} \langle R(x; a), \varphi_i(x) \rangle^2$$

for some $m > n$. These combinations of least squares and projection ideas are compromises. Existence of the finite-dimensional approximation is assured as long as the objectives are continuous, and optimization methods can be reliably used to find solutions.

In beginning a numerical analysis of a model, it is important to maintain flexibility as to which method to use. Since the projection methods are so similar, it is easy to change from one to another. Experimentation with several methods is the only way to find out which will be best.

Consistency

When using numerical procedures, it is desirable to know something concerning the error of the solution. As we discussed in chapter 2, an important focus of theoretical numerical analysis is deriving error bounds and proving that methods are asymptotically valid. For example, we would like to know that the errors of a projection method go to zero as we enlarge the basis; this property is called *consistency*. There has been little work on proving that the algorithms used by economists are asymptotically valid.

The absence of convergence theorems does not invalidate the projection approach. The compute and verify approach will help avoid bad approximations. Even if we had a consistent method, we would have to develop a stopping criterion for n, the degree of the approximation, which itself would be a verification procedure. This is in keeping with our philosophy that a convergence theorem is not necessary for a procedure to be useful nor do convergence theorems make any particular result more reliable. In practice, we must use a method which stops at some finite point, and any candidate solution produced by any method must be tested before it is accepted.

11.4   Boundary Value Problems

Boundary value problems are commonly solved by projection methods. In this section we will apply projection methods to solve continuous-time boundary value problems arising in life-cycle problems.

Consider the two-point boundary value problem for $x, y \in R$:

$$\dot{x} = f(x, y, t),$$

$$\dot{y} = g(x, y, t), \tag{11.4.1}$$

$$x(0) = x_0, \quad y(T) = y_T.$$

To solve this, we approximate $x(t)$ and $y(t)$ with polynomials

$$\hat{x}(t) = \sum_{i=0}^{n} a_i t^i, \quad \hat{y}(t) = \sum_{i=0}^{n} b_i t^i. \tag{11.4.2}$$

To fix a and b, we first impose the boundary conditions

$$x_0 = \hat{x}(0) = a_0,$$

$$y_T = \hat{y}(T) = \sum_{i=0}^{n} b_i T^i. \tag{11.4.3}$$

Since a and b contain $2n + 2$ unknown parameters, we also impose the $2n$ projection conditions

$$\int_0^T \left(\frac{d}{dt} (\hat{x}(t)) - f(\hat{x}(t), \hat{y}(t), t) \right) \varphi_i(t) w(t) \, dt = 0, \qquad i = 1, \dots, n,$$

$$\tag{11.4.4}$$

$$\int_0^T \left(\frac{d}{dt} (\hat{y}(t)) - g(\hat{x}(t), \hat{y}(t), t) \right) \varphi_i(t) w(t) \, dt = 0, \qquad i = 1, \dots, n,$$

for some functions $\varphi_i(t)$ and some weighting functions $w(t)$. Equations (11.4.3) and (11.4.4) give us a total of $2n + 2$ conditions that hopefully pin down the $2n + 2$ parameters.

There are many kind of BVP's which can be treated in the same way. For example, the boundary conditions could be $x(0) = x_0$ and $x(T) = x_T$; in this case (11.4.3) becomes $x_0 = \hat{x}(0) = a_0$ and $x_T = \hat{x}(T) = \sum_{i=0}^{n} a_i T^i$. Whatever the boundary conditions in (11.4.1), simple substitution can be used to produce the numerical conditions in (11.4.3).

Continuous-Time Life-Cycle Consumption Models

We next use simple projection methods to solve a simple life-cycle version of the life-cycle problem (10.6.10) with utility function $u(c) = c^{1+\gamma}/(1 + \gamma)$ and asset return function $f(A) = rA$. After some manipulation the optimal c and A paths are characterized by the boundary value problem

$$\dot{c} = \gamma^{-1} c(\rho - r),$$

$$\dot{A} = rA + w - c, \tag{11.4.5}$$

$$A(0) = 0 = A(T).$$

Projection methods are often used to solve boundary value problems. We next turn to a particular case of (11.4.5) with $\rho = 0.05$, $r = 0.10$, $\gamma = -2$, $w(t) = 0.5 + t/10 - 4(t/50)^2$, and $T = 50$. We will use degree 10 approximations for both $c(t)$ and $A(T)$:

$$A(t) = \sum_{i=0}^{10} a_i T_i \left(\frac{t-25}{25} \right),$$

$$c(t) = \sum_{i=0}^{10} c_i T_i \left(\frac{t-25}{25} \right),$$

(11.4.6)

where $T_i(x)$ is the degree i Chebyshev polynomial. We use a linear transformation in the argument of the T_i functions that maps $t \in [0, 50]$ into $[-1, 1]$, the domain of the Chebyshev polynomials. The functions $c(t)$ and $A(t)$ must approximately solve the two point BVP

$$\dot{c}(t) = -\tfrac{1}{2} c(t)(0.05 - 0.10),$$

$$\dot{A}(t) = 0.1A(t) + w(t) - c(t),$$

(11.4.7)

$$A(0) = A(T) = 0.$$

We define the two residual functions

$$R_1(t) = \dot{c}(t) - 0.025c(t)$$

$$R_2(t) = \dot{A}(t) - \left(0.1A(t) + \left(0.5 + \frac{t}{10} - 4\left(\frac{t}{50}\right)^2 \right) - c(t) \right).$$

(11.4.8)

We want to choose coefficients a_i, $i = 0, 1, \ldots, 10$, and c_i, $i = 0, 1, \ldots, 10$, so that the residual functions are nearly zero and so that the boundary conditions $A(0) = A(T) = 0$ are satisfied. Since the boundary conditions impose two conditions, we need 20 more conditions to determine the 22 unknown coefficients. We next determine the collocation points for our residuals. Since we need 20 conditions for the two equations, we need only 10 collocation points. We will therefore use the 10 zeros of $T_{10}((t-25)/25)$, which are $\mathscr{C} \equiv \{0.31, 2.72, 7.32, 13.65, 21.09, 28.91, 36.35, 42.68, 47.28, 49.69\}$. We then choose the a_i and c_i coefficients, which solve

$$R_1(t_i) = 0, \qquad t_i \in \mathscr{C}, \; i = 1, \ldots, 10,$$

$$R_2(t_i) = 0, \qquad t_i \in \mathscr{C}, \; i = 1, \ldots, 10,$$

$$A(0) = \sum_{i=1}^{10} a_i(-1)^i = 0,$$

(11.4.9)

$$A(50) = \sum_{i=1}^{10} a_i = 0.$$

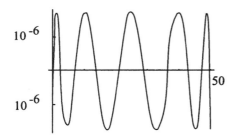

Figure 11.1
Residuals of Chebyshev collocation applied to (11.4.7): $\dot{c}$ equation

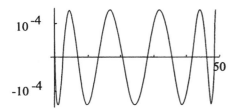

Figure 11.2
Residuals of Chebyshev collocation applied to (11.4.7): k equation

These are 22 linear equations in 22 unknowns. The system is nonsingular; therefore there is a unique solution. The true solution to the system (11.4.7) can be solved since it is a linear problem. Figures 11.1 to 11.4 illustrate the accuracy of the collocation procedure. Figures 11.1 and 11.2 display the residuals for both the consumption and asset equations. Note the near-equioscillation property of the residuals. This is almost expected because we are using Chebyshev ideas to approximate the residuals directly. The fact that the residuals nearly satisfy equioscillation implies that the implicit polynomial approximation is nearly optimal in the L^∞ sense. Figure 11.3 illustrates the relative errors in the consumption solution, and figure 11.4 displays the errors of the asset solution relative to the maximum asset level in the true solution. The consumption error is less than 0.05 of 1 percent. The asset error is similarly small. The fact that the errors in the asset and consumption paths also nearly satisfy equioscillation implies that their approximations are also close to being optimal. The fact that the amplitudes are not equal says that they are not the best possible, but that is not critical. The fact that we have the desired amount of oscillation is most critical. If instead the errors were linear without any oscillation, then we would know that we

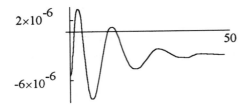

Figure 11.3
Relative error of Chebyshev collocation consumption solution of (11.4.7)

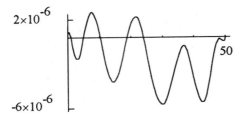

Figure 11.4
Relative error of Chebyshev collocation asset solution of (11.4.7)

could do much better. These graphs illustrate the importance and usefulness of the equioscillation theorem of chapter 6.

11.5   Continuous-Time Growth Model

We again consider the canonical continuous-time optimal growth problem for an economy with one good and one capital stock:

$$\max_{c} \int_{0}^{\infty} e^{-\rho t} u(c)\, dt$$

s.t. $\dot{k} = f(k) - c.$

In chapter 10 we noted that the optimal policy function, $C(k)$, satisfied the differential equation

$$0 = C'(k)(f(k) - C(k)) - \frac{u'(C(k))}{u''(C(k))}(\rho - f'(k)) \equiv \mathcal{N}(C) \tag{11.5.1}$$

together with the boundary condition that $C(k^*) = f(k^*)$, where k^* is the steady state capital stock and is fixed by the condition $f'(k^*) = \rho$.

We use (11.5.1) to solve for $C(k)$. We assume that $f(k) = \rho k^\alpha / \alpha$ and that $u(c) = c^{1+\gamma}/(1+\gamma)$ with $\rho = 0.04$, $\alpha = 0.25$ and $\gamma = -2$; this implies a steady state $k^* = 1$. We use a basis of Chebyshev polynomials to approximate $C(k)$, and compute $C(k)$ for $k \in [0.25, 1.75]$. With the approximation $\hat{C}(k; a) \equiv \sum_{i=1}^n a_i T_i((k-1)/0.75)$ and the definition $R(k; a) = \mathcal{N}(\hat{C}(\cdot; a))(k)$ a collocation method can solve for a, by solving the system of equations

$$R(k_i; a) = 0, \qquad i = 1, \ldots, n,$$

where the k_i are the n zeros of $T_n((k-1)/0.75)$.

The performance of the algorithm is very good, independent of the details of the implementation. The only critical element is the choice of the initial guess. However, the crude approximation consisting of the linear policy that consumes nothing at a zero capital stock and consumes all output at the (easily computed) steady state serves as a satisfactory initial guess. Tenth-order polynomial approximations are easily found in a few seconds and all diagnostics (e.g., the location of the steady state and slope at the steady state) all indicated a very good approximation. This algorithm easily outperformed the more commonly used shooting approach to the problem.

In table 11.3 we display the solution for various polynomial degrees and capital stocks. $\hat{C}^j(k)$ is the degree j collocation solution and $\hat{E}^j(k)$ equals the residual function of the degree j solution divided by $\rho C^j(k)$ to take out the units. Table 11.3 shows that the degree 12 solution has residuals little larger than machine zero, and that the degree 5 and 8 solutions are also very good. We did not use the fact that we know $C(k^*) = 0.2$. Also we do not use the point $k = k^*$ as a collocation point when computing the fifth-degree approximation. Note that the degree 8 and 12 solutions agree to six digits on the points used in table 11.3. All of these diagnostics indicate that the approximation is quite good. In fact all three solutions do an excellent job at getting $C(k^*)$ right when we compare the projection method results with the reverse shooting results.

11.6 Computing Conditional Expectations

Many problems in economics require us to compute conditional expectation functions. If Y and X are random variables, the *conditional expectation of Y given X*, denoted $E\{Y|X\}$, is a function of X, $\psi(X)$, such that

$$E\{(Y - \psi(X)) g(X)\} = 0 \tag{11.6.1}$$

Table 11.3
Projection methods applied to (11.5.1)

k	$\hat{C}^2(k)$	$\hat{E}^2(k)$	$\hat{C}^5(k)$	$\hat{E}^5(k)$	$\hat{C}^8(k)$	$\hat{E}^8(k)$	$\hat{C}^{12}(k)$	$\hat{E}^{12}(k)$
0.6	0.158905	$-9(-3)$	0.159640	$-2(-3)$	0.159638	$4(-6)$	0.159638	$-9(-9)$
0.8	0.180273	$-2(-2)$	0.180924	$-2(-4)$	0.180922	$-2(-6)$	0.180922	$-1(-8)$
1.0	0.200000	$5(-16)$	0.199991	$-2(-4)$	0.200000	$-5(-16)$	0.200000	$5(-16)$
1.2	0.218086	$1(-2)$	0.217543	$1(-4)$	0.217543	$1(-6)$	0.217543	$7(-9)$
1.4	0.234531	$4(-3)$	0.233944	$-9(-5)$	0.233941	$-2(-6)$	0.233941	$7(-9)$

for all continuous functions g. This says that the error $Y - \psi(X)$ is uncorrelated with all functions of X.

We seek a function $\hat{\psi}(X)$ which approximates $E\{Y|X\}$. To do so, we construct

$$\hat{\psi}(X;a) = \sum_{i=0}^{n} a_i\varphi_i(X), \tag{11.6.2}$$

where $\{\varphi_i(X)\}_{i=0}^{\infty}$ is a basis for continuous functions of X. This reduces the problem to finding the a coefficients in $\hat{\psi}$. Suppose that there is a random variable Z such that $Y = g(Z)$ and $X = h(Z)$. Then the least squares coefficients a solve

$$\min_{a} E\{(\hat{\psi}(h(Z);a) - g(Z))^2\}. \tag{11.6.3}$$

There are two ways to compute the unknown coefficients. First, the Monte Carlo approach generates a sample of (Y, X) pairs, then regresses the values of Y on X. More precisely, we construct a random number generator tuned to model the joint distribution (Y, X) and use it to produce the set of pairs, $\{(y_i, x_i) \mid i = 1, \ldots, N\}$. We then fix a by solving the least squares problem

$$\min_{a} \sum_{i} (\hat{\psi}(x_i;a) - y_i)^2. \tag{11.6.4}$$

The second approach uses projection ideas instead of probabilistic ideas. Since $\psi(X) = E\{Y|X\}$, then the projection condition $E\{(g(Z) - \psi(h(Z)))\varphi_i(h(Z))\} = 0$ holds for all i. To fix the coefficients a in an approximation $\hat{\psi}(\cdot\,;a)$, we impose the $n + 1$ projection conditions

$$E\{(g(Z) - \hat{\psi}(h(Z);a))\varphi_i(h(Z))\} = 0, \qquad i = 0, \ldots, n. \tag{11.6.5}$$

The system (11.6.5) is a linear equation in the a coefficients. Each of the equations in (11.6.5) involves an integral; we use deterministic quadrature methods to evaluate them.

The two methods are related. The least-squares problem in (11.6.3) leads to first-order conditions similar to (11.6.5) and the integrals in (11.6.5) could be approximated by pseudo–Monte Carlo methods. Of course quasi–Monte Carlo methods could also be used to compute the integrals in (11.6.5).

To indicate the relative quality of these procedures, we apply them to a simple example. Let $Y, W \sim U[0,1]$ and $X = \varphi(Y, W) = (Y + W + 1)^2$; then $E\{Y|X\} = (X^{1/2} - 1)/2$. We let $N = 1,000$ and produce $1,000$ (y, w) pairs. We compute the $1,000$ values of $x = \varphi(y, w)$. We then regress y on $1, x, x^2, x^3$, and x^4, producing

$$\hat{\psi}_{MC}(x) = -0.1760 + 0.2114x - 0.0075x^2 - 0.0012x^3 + 0.0001x^4. \tag{11.6.6}$$

Straightforward calculation shows that the L^2 norm of $\hat{\psi}_{MC} - \psi$ is 0.0431.

We next try a projection approach. We project the prediction error $\hat{\psi}(\varphi(y, w); a) - y$ against the polynomials $1, x, x^2, x^3, x^4$, and x^5 by forming the five equations

$$\int_0^1 \int_0^1 (\hat{\psi}(\varphi(y, w); a) - y)\, \varphi(y, w)^k \, dw \, dy = 0 \tag{11.6.7}$$

for $k = 0, 1, 2, 3, 4$. Since $\hat{\psi}$ is linear in a, (11.6.7) is a linear system of equations in the unknown coefficients a. Moreover the integrals in (11.6.7) are easy to compute analytically; even if they weren't analytically integrable, the integrals in (11.6.7) can be efficiently approximated by deterministic methods since φ is smooth. The solution to (11.6.7) implies the approximate conditional expectation function

$$\hat{\psi}_P = -0.2471 + 0.2878x - 0.0370x^2 + 0.0035x^3 - 0.0001x^4.$$

The L^2 norm of $\hat{\psi}_P - \psi$ is 0.0039, ten times less than the L^2 error of the $\hat{\psi}_{MC}$ approximation displayed in (11.6.6). Furthermore $\hat{\psi}_P$ is faster to compute than $\hat{\psi}_{MC}$.

We see that the projection method is far more efficient than Monte Carlo sampling in computing the conditional expectation $E(Y|X)$. The reason is that the conditional expectation is a smooth function of X, and can be well-approximated by a polynomial, in which case we know from chapters 6 and 11 that we only need a few well-chosen points to determine the unknown function. The Monte Carlo approach (or a pseudo–Monte Carlo approach) generates (y, x) pairs in a disorganized and inefficient way, and leads to an inferior approximation of $E\{Y|X\}$.

11.7 Further Reading and Summary

Projection methods are powerful alternatives to discretization methods. The basic idea is to choose a parameterization of the critical functions and then use either optimization or nonlinear equation solution methods to fix the parameterization's coefficients. Some implementations resemble nonlinear least squares procedures, but we can often do much better. We have seen that the basic ideas can be applied to a variety of mathematical and economic problems. Their flexibility and the ease with which they can be applied to new problems make them particularly valuable in economics where many problems do not fit into the standard differential and integral equation classifications.

Boyd (1989) is a reader-friendly introduction to spectral projection methods, whereas Canuto et al. (1988), Fletcher (1984), and Gottlieb and Orszag (1977) are more formal. We have focused on spectral methods. Finite element methods are the focus of Akin (1982), Burnett (1987), and White (1985). Judd (1992) presents the basic ideas in the context of a few simple dynamic growth problems, and Gaspar and Judd (1997) examine some multidimensional problems.

Exercises

1.   Solve the Spence signaling example in equation (10.4.5) and table 6.1 using projection methods.

2.   Solve the problem (11.2.1–3) using the method in (11.2.10) for Chebyshev, Legendre, and ordinary polynomial bases.

3.   Solve the life-cycle problem

$$\max_{c,l} \int_0^T e^{-\rho t} \left(u(c) - v(l) \right) dt$$

s.t. $\dot{A} = rA + wl - c,$

$\quad\quad A(0) = 0 = A(T),$

where

$$w(t) = 1 - \left(\frac{t - T/2}{T/2} \right)^2, \quad u(c) = \frac{c^{1+\gamma}}{\gamma + 1}, \quad v(l) = \frac{l^{\eta+1}}{\eta + 1}.$$

Assume that $\rho = 0.04$, $r = 0.08$, $T = 50$, $\gamma \in \{-0.5, -1.1, -2.0, -5.0\}$, and $\eta \in \{0.1, 1, 2\}$.

a. Compute average wealth over the life-cycle.

b. Suppose interest income is taxed at rate τ. Compute resulting utility and present value of revenue. Plot the trade-off between utility and revenue.

c. Repeat b for a proportional wage tax.

d. Compare the welfare cost of wage income taxation and interest income taxation.

4.   Use the projection approach to solve the discrete-time life-cycle problem

$$\max_c \sum_0^T \beta^t u(c_t)$$

s.t. $A_{t+1} = (1+r)A_t + w_t - c_t,$

$A(0) = A(T) = 0,$

with $u(c) = c^{1+\gamma}/(1+\gamma)$.

5. Solve exercise 10.5 using projection methods.

6. Solve exercise 10.6 using projection methods.

7. Solve exercise 10.7 using projection methods.

8. Solve exercise 10.8 using projection methods.

12 Numerical Dynamic Programming

Dynamic programming is a fundamental tool of dynamic economic analysis. Theoretical properties are well-understood (see Bertsekas 1976, 1995, Bertsekas and Shreve 1978; Puterman 1995). Stokey and Lucas (1989) develop the theory of dynamic programming and present some applications of dynamic programming in economic analysis.

Various numerical techniques have been developed in the operations research literature. This chapter examines the two basic numerical approaches to dynamic programming problems. We first discuss finite-state problems. These problems are straightforward, with much of the work reducing to basic matrix operations. We describe the value function iteration method for finite-state problems and various accelerations. Finite-state problems can be used to approximate continuous-state problems via discretization, but this approach is often inefficient. This motivates the second approach of using continuous methods, building on the approximation methods of chapter 6, for dynamic programming problems with continuous state spaces.

12.1 Discrete-Time Dynamic Programming Problems

In dynamic programming we are concerned with controlling a dynamic process that takes on several possible states, can be influenced by the application of controls, and yields a stream of state- and control-dependent payoffs. We first specify the problem in each period. Let X be the set of states, and $\mathscr{D}$ the set of controls. The flow of payoffs to the controller in period t is $\pi(x, u, t)$ if $x \in X$ is the state at the beginning of period t, and the control $u \in \mathscr{D}$ is applied in period t. There may be time- and state-contingent constraints on the controls; let $D(x, t) \subseteq \mathscr{D}$ be the nonempty set of controls which are feasible in state x at time t. We let x_t and u_t denote the state and control in period t.

We next specify the dynamics of the process. If x is the state at the beginning of period t and u is the control, then let $F(A; x, u, t)$ be the probability that $x_{t+1} \in A \subset X$. We assume that $F(\cdot; x, u, t)$ describes a probability measure over the states X for each state x, control u, and time t.

Finite-Horizon Problems

In the finite-horizon case we assume that the objective of the controller is to maximize expected total returns over a $T + 1$ period horizon,

$$E\left\{ \sum_{t=1}^{T} \pi(x_t, u_t, t) + W(x_{T+1}) \right\}, \tag{12.1.1}$$

where $W(x)$ is the terminal valuation and x_1, the initial state, is given. The analysis of a dynamic programming problem revolves around the *value function*, $V(x, t)$, which is defined to be the greatest feasible total expected payoff from time t forward if the time t state is x. More precisely, let $\mathcal{U}(x, t)$ be the set of all feasible rules for choosing u at time s, $s \geq t$, beginning from state x in period t. Then V is defined by

$$V(x, t) \equiv \sup_{\mathcal{U}(x,t)} E\left\{ \sum_{s=t}^{T} \pi(x_s, u_s, s) + W(x_{T+1}) \mid x_t = x \right\}. \tag{12.1.2}$$

The fundamental result is that the optimal policy and value function are *memoryless*; that is, the value and optimal policy at time s depends only on x_s, and the value function satisfies the Bellman equation

$$V(x, t) = \sup_{u \in D(x,t)} \pi(x, u, t) + E\{V(x_{t+1}, t+1) \mid x_t = x, u_t = u\}. \tag{12.1.3}$$

with terminal condition

$$V(x, T+1) = W(x). \tag{12.1.4}$$

The value function always exists by backward induction: the terminal valuation is given by (12.1.4), and for any $V(x, t)$, $V(x, t-1)$ exists because the supremum in the right-hand side of (12.1.3) exists as long as $D(x, t)$ is nonempty.

The value function is the least upper bound on the possible payoff. We also want to know how to achieve this value. To that end, we attempt to compute the *optimal policy function*, $U(x, t)$, which is an optimal choice of control in state x at time t; if it exists, it solves

$$U(x, t) \in \arg\max_{u \in D(x,t)} \pi(x, u, t) + E\{V(x_{t+1}, t+1) \mid x_t = x, u_t = u\}.$$

The existence of the optimal policy function in state x at time t depends on the existence of a control which achieves the supremum in (12.1.3). Even when there is no such control, we can construct nearly optimal controls. This is because for any ε there is a policy function that comes within ε of achieving the value function; this fact follows from the definition of supremum.

The concept of value function in (12.1.2) is a bit limited. Note that the value function defined in (12.1.2) is the total utility of following the optimal policy. Sometimes we will want to examine nonoptimal policies and their values. In general, if we are at the state (x, t) and we are going to use the policy U, the resulting expected total utility equals $V^U(x, t)$, which is defined recursively by

$$V^U(x, t) = \pi(x, U(x, t), t) + E\{V^U(x_{t+1}, t+1) \mid x_t = x, u_t = U(x, t)\} \qquad (12.1.5)$$

Equation (12.1.5) is the general equation defining the value of a policy U and is linear in the unknown function V^U. The usual value function defined in (12.1.2) is the value of the optimal policy.

The notion of state variable is flexible since there are often many variables in a problem which can serve as the state variable. The only requirement is that the state vector must be a sufficient description of the problem at some moment during a period. In particular, it is sometimes useful to focus on an end-of-period state variable instead of the beginning-of-period specification. Suppose that y is a beginning-of-period state variable, u a control that is implemented in the middle of the period, $\pi(y, u, t)$ the payoff, and $x \equiv g(y, u)$ an end-of-period state variable. One could let (y, u) be the end-of-period state variable; fortunately there is often a more parsimonious end-of-period state variable. Let $F(\cdot; x_t, t)$ be the probability measure over y_{t+1} conditional on x_t. The end-of-period value function $V(x, t)$ is

$$V(x, t) = E\left\{ \sup_{\mathcal{U}(y_{t+1}, t+1)} \sum_{s=t+1}^{T} \pi(y_s, u_s, s) + W(y_{T+1}) \mid x_t = x \right\}, \qquad (12.1.6)$$

and it satisfies the Bellman equation

$$V(x, t) = E\left\{ \sup_{u \in D(y_{t+1}, t+1)} \pi(y_{t+1}, u, t+1) + V(x_{t+1}, t+1) \mid x_t = x \right\}, \qquad (12.1.7)$$

together with the terminal condition $V(x, T) = E\{W(y_{T+1}) \mid x_T = x\}$.

From a theoretical perspective there is no difference between a beginning-of-period state variable formulation of the value function and an alternative end-of-period formulation. However, there may be substantial computational differences that argue for one formulation over the other. We will see this below in the commodity storage problem.

Infinite-Horizon Problems

We frequently use infinite-horizon, discounted, time-separable, autonomous dynamic programming problems to analyze long-run economic problems. The calendar time t does not enter into the problem directly; therefore the payoff function is $\pi(x, u)$, and $D(x)$ is the nonempty set of feasible controls for the current state x. The state in the "next" period will be denoted x^+, and it depends on the current state and action in a possibly stochastic, but autonomous, fashion: Let $F(A; x, u)$ be the time-independent probability that $x^+ \in A$ if the current state is x and the current control is u.

For time-separable, autonomous problems the objective of the controller is to maximize discounted expected returns $E\{\sum_{t=0}^{\infty} \beta^t \pi(x_t, u_t)\}$ given a fixed initial value, x_0, and $\beta < 1$, the discount factor. The value function is defined by

$$V(x) \equiv \sup_{\mathscr{U}(x)} E\left\{ \sum_{t=0}^{\infty} \beta^t \pi(x_t, u_t) \mid x_0 = x \right\}, \qquad (12.1.8)$$

where $\mathscr{U}(x)$ is the set of all feasible strategies starting at x. The value function satisfies the Bellman equation

$$V(x) = \sup_{u \in D(x)} \pi(x, u) + \beta E\{V(x^+) \mid x, u\} \equiv (TV)(x), \qquad (12.1.9)$$

and the policy function, $U(x)$, solves

$$U(x) \in \arg \max_{u \in D(x)} \pi(x, u) + \beta E\{V(x^+) \mid x, u\}.$$

The key theorem in infinite horizon dynamic programming is the contraction mapping theorem applied to the Bellman equation. We first need two definitions.

DEFINITION   A map $T: Y \to Z$ on ordered spaces Y and Z is *monotone* if and only if $y_1 \geq y_2$ implies $Ty_1 \geq Ty_2$.

DEFINITION   A map $T: Y \to Y$ on a metric space Y is *a contraction with modulus $\beta < 1$* if and only if $\|Ty_1 - Ty_2\| \leq \beta \|y_1 - y_2\|$.

The critical theorem, due to Denardo (1967), is the contraction mapping theorem for dynamic programming.

THEOREM 12.1.1   If X is compact, $\beta < 1$, and π is bounded above and below, then the map

$$TV = \sup_{u \in D(x)} \pi(x, u) + \beta E\{V(x^+) \mid x, u\} \qquad (12.1.10)$$

is monotone in V, is a contraction mapping with modulus β in the space of bounded functions, and has a unique fixed point.

The boundedness and compactness assumptions in theorem 12.1.1 may appear limiting but not for us, since numerically feasible dynamic programming problems can generally examine only compact state spaces. The task we address here is the computation of $V(x)$ and $U(x)$.

The formulation in (12.1.9) assumes that x is the beginning-of-period state. Infinite-horizon problems can also be formulated in terms of an end-of-period state. If y is the beginning-of-period state, $\pi(y, u)$ the payoff function, $x = g(y, u)$ the end-of-period state, and y^+ is the next period's beginning-of-period state then the end-of-period value function, $V(x)$, is defined to be

$$V(x) = E\left\{ \sup_{\mathscr{U}(y_1)} \sum_{s=1}^{\infty} \beta^s \pi(y_s, u_s) \mid x_0 = x \right\},$$

and Bellman's equation is

$$V(x) = \beta E\left\{ \sup_{u \in D(y)} \pi(y^+, u) + V(g(y^+, u)) \mid x \right\}. \tag{12.1.11}$$

Theorem 12.1.1 applies also to problems of this kind. We now present a few examples of dynamic programming applied to familiar problems.

Wealth Accumulation Examples

The most common examples of dynamic programming models are simple wealth accumulation models. We describe them here and use them in examples.

The simplest wealth accumulation model is the deterministic growth model. The rate of consumption is denoted by c, and $f(k)$ is the net-of-depreciation output when capital stock is k, implying that capital evolves according to $k_{t+1} = k_t + f(k_t) - c_t$. We let $F(k)$ denote $f(k) + k$. We assume the time-separable utility function $\sum_{t=0}^{\infty} \beta^t u(c)$ where $\beta < 1$ is the discount factor. The discrete-time optimal growth problem becomes

$$\max_{c_t} \sum_{t=0}^{\infty} \beta^t u(c_t) \tag{12.1.12}$$

s.t. $k_{t+1} = F(k_t) - c_t,$

where k_0 is given. If c_t and k_t are consumption and capital at time t, the first-order conditions for the optimal path are $u'(c_t) = \beta u'(c_{t+1}) F'(k_{t+1})$ for all t. The dynamic programming version of (12.1.12) is

$$V(k) = \max_{c} u(c) + \beta V(F(k) - c). \tag{12.1.13}$$

The optimal policy function, also called the control law, $C(k)$, obeys the first-order conditions

$$0 = u'(C(k)) - \beta V'(F(k) - C(k)). \tag{12.1.14}$$

The envelope theorem applied to (12.1.13) implies that $V'(k) = \beta V'(F(k) - c)F'(k)$, which together with (12.1.14) implies that

$$0 = u'(C(k))F'(k) - V'(k). \tag{12.1.15}$$

Therefore the solution to (12.1.13) is a policy function $C(k)$ and a value function $V(k)$ that satisfy (12.1.15) and

$$V(k) = u(C(k)) + \beta V(F(k) - C(k)). \tag{12.1.16}$$

Note that (12.1.16) defines the value of an arbitrary policy function $C(k)$, not just for the optimal $C(k)$. The pair (12.1.15) and (12.1.16) combines the definition of the value function of a policy (12.1.16) with a first-order condition for optimality (12.1.15).

When labor, l, is supplied elastically, the net production function is $f(k,l)$, $F(k,l) = k + f(k,l)$, and the utility function becomes $u(c,l)$. The discrete-time dynamic programming problem becomes

$$V(k) = \max_{c,l} u(c,l) + \beta V(F(k,l) - c). \tag{12.1.17}$$

Combining the first-order conditions and the envelope theorem, we find that the control laws $C(k)$ and $L(k)$ satisfy

$$0 = u_c(C(k), L(k))F_k(k, L(k)) - V'(k),$$

$$0 = u_l(C(k), L(k)) + F_l(k, L(k))u_c(C(k), L(k)). \tag{12.1.18}$$

The solution to (12.1.17) are functions $C(k)$ and $V(k)$ that satisfy (12.1.18) and

$$V(k) = u(C(k, L(k))) + \beta V(F(k, L(k)) - C(k)). \tag{12.1.19}$$

While this example is motivated by an optimal growth model, that is only one interpretation. For example, (12.1.17) can also be interpreted as the dynamic programming problem of a monopolistic firm. In the monopolistic firm application, c is dividends, $u(c,l) = c$, l is the amount of labor hired, k is both the capital stock and total assets, and $F(k,l)$ is the profit flow if the monopolist has k units capital and hires l units of labor. We can also interpret (12.1.17) as a dynamic problem of an individual, where u is the utility function, k is individual wealth, and $F(k,l)$ is asset plus labor income. It would be most natural to use the finite horizon version in this case, make F and u depend on age, and require $k \geq 0$ at death. The problem in (12.1.17) is quite general. There is an endogenous state variable, k, and controls, c

and l, that enter into the payoff and the law of motion. Our interpretations are not as general as possible, since the payoff function does not depend on the state. However, the use of growth model terms and notation does not imply that we are limited to studying those problems since we will not utilize any of their special features.

Stochastic Accumulation Problems

We next consider a stochastic model of accumulation. Let θ denote the current productivity level and $f(k, l, \theta)$ denote net income; define $F(k, l, \theta) = k + f(k, l, \theta)$, and assume that θ follows $\theta_{t+1} = g(\theta_t, \varepsilon_t)$ where the ε_t are i.i.d. disturbances. The infinite-horizon discrete-time optimization problem becomes

$$V(k, \theta) = \max_{c_t, l_t} E \left\{ \sum_{t=0}^{\infty} \beta^t u(c_t, l_t) \right\}$$

$$\text{s.t.} \quad k_{t+1} = F(k_t, l_t, \theta_t) - c_t, \tag{12.1.20}$$

$$\theta_{t+1} = g(\theta_t, \varepsilon_t),$$

$$k_0 = k, \ \theta_0 = \theta.$$

The Euler equation for (12.1.20) is

$$u_c(c_t, l_t) = \beta E\{u_c(c_{t+1}, l_{t+1}) F_k(k_{t+1}, l_{t+1}, \theta_{t+1}) \mid k_t, \theta_t\}.$$

In (12.1.20), k is no longer a sufficient description of the problem because the value of today's θ provides us information about tomorrow's value of θ. Therefore both the beginning-of-period capital stock and the current value of θ are needed for a sufficient description of the state. The dynamic programming formulation is

$$V(k, \theta) = \max_{c, l} u(c, l) + \beta E\{V(F(k, l, \theta) - c, \theta^+) \mid \theta\}, \tag{12.1.21}$$

where θ^+ is next period's θ realization. The control laws $c = C(k, \theta)$ and $l = L(k, \theta)$ satisfy the first-order conditions

$$0 = u_c(C(k, \theta), L(k, \theta)) F_k(k, L(k, \theta), \theta) - V_k(k, \theta),$$

$$0 = u_l(C(k, \theta), L(k, \theta)) + F_l(k, \theta) u_c(C(k, \theta), L(k, \theta)). \tag{12.1.22}$$

The Euler equation implies that the control laws also satisfy

$$0 = u_c(C(k, \theta), L(k, \theta)) - \beta E\{u_c(C(k^+, \theta^+), l^+) F_k(k^+, l^+, \theta^+) \mid \theta\}, \tag{12.1.23}$$

where

$$k^+ \equiv F(k, L(k, \theta), \theta) - C(k, \theta),$$

$$l^+ \equiv L(k^+, \theta^+),$$

represent the next period's capital stock and labor supply.

Again this example has many economic interpretations. In the life-cycle interpretation, θ is a state variable that may affect either asset income, labor income, or both. In the monopolist interpretation, θ may reflect shocks to costs, demand, or both.

Stochastic Transition Problems

In the preceding examples the current control fixes the next period's state exactly. For example, by an appropriate choice of consumption, one can fix the end-of-period capital stock in (12.1.20). In such cases we get a simple Euler equation for the policy function. We will see that such Euler equations allow us to compute the policy function directly without any reference to the value function. When the controls can't fix the state exactly, we need the value function. We present one simple example of that here.

Suppose that a firm has profits $\pi(x)$ that depend on productivity x, where productivity can have several possible values, x_i, $i = 1, \ldots, n$. Suppose that an investment expenditure of I will control the transition probability of the productivity state according to $\text{Prob}\{x^+ = x_i \mid x = x_j\} = q(I, i, j)$ where $0 \leq q \leq 1$ and $\sum_i q(I, i, j) = 1$ for all I and j. In productivity state x gross profits will be $\pi(x)$. The resulting dynamic programming problem will be

$$V(x_j) = \max_I \pi(x_j) - I + \beta \sum_i q(I, i, j) V(x_i), \tag{12.1.24}$$

which implies the first-order condition

$$0 = -1 + \beta \sum_i q_I(I, i, j) V(x_i), \tag{12.1.25}$$

Note that in this problem the value function is an essential component of the first-order condition, a feature absent in (12.1.23). This is an important difference for computational purposes.

12.2 Continuous-Time Dynamic Programming Problems

We can also formulate dynamic programming problems in continuous time. Here we must deal specifically with the stochastic structure. Most problems in economics assume a Brownian motion or jump process, or a combination, to model the stochastic elements. We will consider only Brownian motion examples here; see Malliaris and Brock (1982) for a more complete discussion of stochastic control.

The canonical deterministic discounted optimal control problem is

$$V(x_0, t) = \max_u \int_t^T e^{-\rho(s-t)} \pi(x, u, s)\, ds + W(x(T), T)$$

$$\text{s.t.} \quad \dot{x} = f(x, u, s), \tag{12.2.1}$$

$$x(t) = x_0,$$

where $x \in R^n$ and $u \in R^m$. The Bellman equation for this problem is

$$\rho V(x, t) - V_t(x, t) = \max_u \pi(x, u, t) + \sum_{i=1}^n V_{x_i}(x, t) f^i(x, u, t), \tag{12.2.2}$$

with the terminal condition

$$V(x, T) = W(x, T). \tag{12.2.3}$$

If π depends only on x and u, and $T = \infty$, we have the autonomous case, wherein $V(x, t) = V(x)$ and the Bellman equation

$$\rho V(x) = \max_u \pi(x, u) + \sum_{i=1}^n V_{x_i}(x) f^i(x, u) \tag{12.2.4}$$

characterizes the current value function.

Wealth Accumulation Examples

The continuous-time optimal accumulation problem is

$$\max_c \int_0^\infty e^{-\rho t} u(c)\, dt \tag{12.2.5}$$

$$\text{s.t.} \quad \dot{k} = f(k) - c,$$

which was studied in chapter 10. The dynamic programming formulation of (12.2.5) is

$$0 = \max_c u(c) + V'(k)(f(k) - c) - \rho V(k), \tag{12.2.6}$$

and the control law $c = C(k)$ obeys the first-order condition

$$0 = u'(C(k)) - V'(k). \tag{12.2.7}$$

The continuous-time dynamic programming problem with elastic labor supply becomes

$$0 = \max_{c,l} u(c,l) + V'(k)(f(k,l) - c) - \rho V(k), \tag{12.2.8}$$

and the control laws $C(k)$ and $L(k)$ satisfy the first-order conditions

$$0 = u_c(C(k), L(k)) - V'(k),$$
$$0 = u_l(C(k), L(k)) + f_l(k,l) V'(k). \tag{12.2.9}$$

The solution to (12.2.8) are functions $C(k)$, $L(k)$, and $V(k)$ that satisfy (12.2.9) and

$$0 = u(C(k), L(k)) + V'(k)(f(k, L(k)) - C(k)) - \rho V(k). \tag{12.2.10}$$

Stochastic Dynamic Programming

We next examine the continous-time case with white noise disturbances. Suppose that $x \in R^n, u \in R^m$ are the state and controls, $u \in D(x, t)$ describes the control constraint, and the law of motion is

$$dx = f(x, u, t)\, dt + \sigma(x, u, t)\, dz, \tag{12.2.11}$$

where $f(x, u, t) \in R^n$ is the instantaneous drift, dz is "white noise," and $\sigma(x, u, t)$ is the $n \times n$ matrix function representing the instantaneous standard deviation of the x process at (x_t, u_t); we let $\sigma^2(x, u, t)$ denote the corresponding variance-covariance matrix. The value function is defined

$$V(x, t) = \max_{u \in \mathcal{U}(x,t)} E_t \left\{ \int_t^T e^{-\rho(s-t)} \pi(x, u, t)\, ds + W(x_T) \right\}, \tag{12.2.12}$$

where $\mathcal{U}(x, t)$ is the set of feasible feedback controls if the state is x at time t. If $x \in R$, then the Hamilton-Jacobi-Bellman (HJB) equation for V is

$$\rho V(x, t) - V_t(x, t) = \max_{u \in D(x,t)} \pi(x, u, t) + V_x(x, t) f(x, u, t) + \tfrac{1}{2} V_{xx}(x, t)\sigma^2(x, u, t), \tag{12.2.13}$$

with the terminal condition

$$V(x, T) = W(x). \tag{12.2.14}$$

If $x \in R^n$, then the HJB equation is

$$\rho V(x,t) - V_t(x,t) = \max_{u \in D(x,t)} \pi(x,u,t) + \sum_{i=1}^{n} V_{x_i}(x,t)f^i(x,u,t)$$

$$+ \tfrac{1}{2}\mathrm{Tr}[\sigma(x,u,t)\,\sigma(x,u,t)^\top V_{xx}(x,t)], \qquad (12.2.15)$$

where $\mathrm{Tr}[A]$ is the trace of the matrix A. In the autonomous infinite-horizon case, tastes and technology do not depend on t; hence the value function depends solely on x and (12.2.13) reduces to

$$\rho V(x) = \max_{u \in D(x,t)} \pi(x,u) + V'(x)f(x,u) + \tfrac{1}{2}\sigma^2(x,u)V''(x) \qquad (12.2.16)$$

and (12.2.15) reduces to

$$\rho V(x) = \max_{u \in D(x,t)} \pi(x,u) + \sum_{i=1}^{n} V_{x_i}(x)f^i(x,u) + \tfrac{1}{2}\mathrm{Tr}[\sigma(x,u)\sigma(x,u)^\top V_{xx}(x)] \qquad (12.2.17)$$

12.3 Finite-State Methods

The simplest dynamic programming problems have a finite number of states. We discuss these problems for three reasons. First, some problems are naturally discrete. Second, discrete approximations are often used in the economics literature. Third, discrete problems allow us to clearly illustrate important aspects of the common numerical dynamic programming methods.

Finite-Horizon Problems

Let X be the set x_i, $i = 1, \ldots, n$, of n states, and $\mathcal{D} = \{u_i \mid i = 1, \ldots, m\}$ the set of m controls for a finite-state problem. Each control induces a Markov transition rule for the states, which can be summarized by the probabilistic law $q_{ij}^t(u)$; that is, for each control u, $q_{ij}^t(u)$ is the probability of a transition to state x_j if the state is x_i and control is u in period t. The collection of probabilities specifies a Markov transition matrix at time t for each u, which we will denote $Q^t(u)$. For control u and state x_i, row i in $Q^t(u)$ is the probability distribution of the state at time $t+1$ if the time t state is x_i and the controller applies control u.

This formulation is general, including a wide variety of problems. For example, deterministic transition laws can be modeled by permitting only zero and unit entries in the transition matrix, $Q^t(u)$, for each control u. State-dependent constraints on controls can be modeled by creating an extra absorbing state with a constant payoff of $-\infty$ and making the process move to that state whenever an inappropriate control is chosen. Hence, when we deal with finite-state, finite-control problems, we will drop the control constraints, assuming that any such constraints are expressed in the payoff function.

The analysis of a dynamic programming problem generally concentrates on the value function. In the finite-horizon case we inductively use (12.1.3) to compute the value function at each time t, beginning with the terminal value function, $V(x, T+1) = W(x)$. Since we have just a finite number of states, the value function $V(x, t)$ at time t is really just a finite list of values. If we define $V_i^t \equiv V(x_i, t)$, the Bellman (12.1.3) equation becomes

$$V_i^t = \max_u \left[\pi(x_i, u, t) + \beta \sum_{j=1}^n q_{ij}^t(u) V_j^{t+1} \right], \qquad i = 1, \dots, n, \qquad (12.3.1)$$

with the terminal condition

$$V_i^{T+1} = W(x_i), \qquad i = 1, \dots, n. \qquad (12.3.2)$$

Therefore finite-horizon dynamic programming reduces to (12.3.2) combined with the induction step (12.3.1), where each induction step in (12.3.1) consists of several optimization problems. At this point it is clear that the most demanding task is solving the maximization problems in (12.3.1). If there is no useful structure and there are only a finite number of controls, the only way to solve each of the maximization problems in (12.3.1) is to check out each possible control at each state. In any case each step in (12.3.1) is finitistic, and this procedure will terminate in a finite amount of time.

If u is a continuous variable, then the maximization problems in (12.3.1) must be solved using an appropriate optimization method. Define

$$h(u; x_i, t) \equiv \pi(x_i, u, t) + \beta \sum_{j=1}^n q_{ij}^t(u) V_j^{t+1} \qquad (12.3.3)$$

to be the specific optimization problem at state x_i in period t with period $t+1$ value function V^{t+1}. The proper choice of optimization algorithm depends on how h depends on u. If $h(u; x_i, t)$ is a smooth function of u for each x_i and t, then we may use Newton's method or some variant; however, if h is not smooth in u, then we may need to use a comparison method such as the polytope method. If $h(u; x_i, t)$ is multimodal, then we must use global optimization methods. It is this maximization step that will often consume most of the computing time and will be a focus of efforts below to create efficient algorithms.

Infinite-Horizon Problems

In infinite-horizon problems with a finite number of states, the infinite-horizon Bellman equation (12.1.9) still imposes definitive conditions on the value function. Since we have just a finite number of states, the value function is really just a finite list of values, a value vector. If we define $V_i \equiv V(x_i)$ to be the vector of values then the Bellman equation (12.1.9) becomes a system of nonlinear equations:

$$V_i = \max_u \left[\pi(x_i, u) + \beta \sum_{j=1}^n q_{ij}(u)\, V_j \right], \qquad i = 1, \ldots, n. \tag{12.3.4}$$

Let V^* denote the solution to (12.3.4).

By the contraction theorem, this equation does fix a unique solution, V^*. Unfortunately, it is a nonlinear equation because of the maximization step. However, we can decompose the problem into a linear problem and a sequence of optimization problems. First we note that we can easily compute the value of any specific policy. Suppose that in state x_i, the control is $U_i \in \mathcal{D}$, $i = 1, \ldots, n$; then the vector $U \equiv (U_1, \ldots, U_n)$ is the policy function and the return in state i is $P_i^U \equiv \pi(x_i, U_i)$. The induced transition rule for the states, Q^U, is defined by $Q_{ij}^U = q_{ij}(U_i)$; that is, the row i column j element of Q^U is $q_{ij}(u)$ if $U_i = u$. In terms of P^U and Q^U, the equation defining the value of following the policy U forever reduces to the vector equation $V^U = P^U + \beta Q^U V^U$ which has the solution

$$V^U = (I - \beta Q^U)^{-1} P^U. \tag{12.3.5}$$

Since Q^U is a probability matrix, $I - \beta Q^U$ is invertible, and V^U is well-defined in (12.3.5). Therefore, to compute the value of the control law U, one constructs the induced Markov chain, Q^U, and the induced state-contingent payoff vector, P^U, and computes (12.3.5), a linear algebra calculation.

If V^* is the value function for the problem, then it is the value of following the optimal policy, U^*. The optimal policy also satisfies the optimality condition

$$U_i^* \in \arg\max_u \left[\pi(x_i, u) + \beta \sum_j q_{ij}(u)\, V_j \right], \qquad i = 1, \ldots, n. \tag{12.3.6}$$

The optimal control policy and the value function for the problem are the U and V that jointly satisfy (12.3.5) and (12.3.6). If there are only a finite number of possible control policies, one could find V by computing the value of all possible policies. However, that is an impractical approach, and usually avoidable.

Before considering various schemes for calculating V and U, we will define two useful maps. The map T takes next period's value function, V^+, creates the current value function, V, and is defined by

$$V_i = \max_u \left[\pi(x_i, u) + \beta \sum_{j=1}^n q_{ij}(u) V_j^+ \right] \equiv (TV^+)_i, \qquad i = 1, \ldots, n, \qquad (12.3.7)$$

We also define a selection for today's control given next period's value

$$U_i \in \arg\max_u \left[\pi(x_i, u) + \beta \sum_{j=1}^n q_{ij}(u) V_j^+ \right] \equiv (\mathscr{U}V^+)_i, \qquad i = 1, \ldots, n. \qquad (12.3.8)$$

These maps have useful interpretations. If V^+ is tomorrow's value function, then $V = TV^+$ is today's value function, and $\mathscr{U}V^+$ is today's policy function.[1] With the mappings T and $\mathscr{U}$ we can describe a variety of computation methods. We next turn to two iterative schemes for solving (12.3.4).

Value Function Iteration

The simplest numerical procedure for finding V^*, *value function iteration*, is motivated by the contraction properties of the Bellman equation. Value function iteration computes the sequence

$$V^{l+1} = TV^l, \qquad l = 0, 1, 2, \ldots. \qquad (12.3.9)$$

By the contraction mapping theorem, V^l will converge to the infinite-horizon value function for any initial guess V^0. The sequence of control rules, U^l, defined by $U^{l+1} = \mathscr{U}V^l$ will also converge to the optimal control rule.

The iterative scheme (12.3.9) will converge to the solution V^∞ only asymptotically. In practice, one iterates until the successive V^l change little, and the successive U^l do not change. When one believes that the U^l series has converged, one should compute the final approximation of V^*, $V^{U^l} = (I - \beta Q^{U^l})^{-1} P^{U^l}$. This will ensure that the computed value function is the value corresponding to the computed policy, and it is often a faster way to compute V^* than continued iteration of the value function equation. If V^{U^l} satisfies $V = TV$, then one is done. Otherwise, the iteration (12.3.9) should continue from V^{U^l}. Since the contraction theorem applies and there

1. Since $\mathscr{U}V$ is uniquely defined for generic V and for many common economic problems, we will not explicitly consider the multiplicity problem. Furthermore, if there are multiple optimal policies, they lead to the same value function and the planner is indifferent among them.

are only a finite number of possible control laws, this process will converge in finite time.

It is also advisable to choose a V^0 which is close to and similar to the final solution. For example, if one knows some bounds on V^*, then V^0 should also satisfy those bounds. Also, if V_i is increasing in i, then a good choice of V_i^0 would also be increasing in i. It is well worth the effort to think about the initial guess; the better the initial guess, the fewer iterations needed for convergence. In summary, the value function algorithm is presented in algorithm 12.1.

Algorithm 12.1   Value Function Iteration Algorithm

Objective: Solve the Bellman equation, (12.3.4).

Initialization. Make initial guess V^0; choose stopping criterion $\varepsilon > 0$.

Step 1. For $i = 1, \ldots, n$, compute

$$V_i^{l+1} = \max_{u \in D}\ \pi(x_i, u) + \beta \sum_{j=1}^{n} q_{ij}(u) V_j^l.$$

Step 2. If $\| V^{l+1} - V^l \| < \varepsilon$, then go to step 3; else go to step 1.

Step 3. Compute the final solution, setting

$$U^* = \mathcal{U} V^{l+1},$$

$$P_i^* = \pi(x_i, U_i^*), \qquad i = 1, \ldots, n,$$

$$V^* = (I - \beta Q^{U^*})^{-1} P^*,$$

and STOP.

Error Bounds

Once we compute an approximate solution to a dynamic programming problem, we would like to have some idea as to the possible error. The special structure of the Bellman equation implies that we can compute error bounds on (12.3.9). The contraction property implies that the iterates of value function iteration satisfy the inequality

$$\| V^* - V^k \|_\infty \leq \frac{1}{1 - \beta} \| V^{k+1} - V^k \|_\infty. \tag{12.3.10}$$

Therefore, if we want to be sure that we have a value function V^k which is within ε^V of the solution V^*, we stop the value function iteration process at the first iterate V^k such that

$$\|V^{k+1} - V^k\|_\infty \le \varepsilon^V (1 - \beta). \tag{12.3.11}$$

Inequality (12.3.11) becomes the convergence rule given our ε^V goal, implying that we set $\varepsilon = \varepsilon^V (1 - \beta)$ in the initialization step of algorithm 12.1.

This is one of the few cases where our convergence criterion also gives us an upper bound on how far we are from the true solution. Note that this bound applies only to the value function, not the policy function. In some cases the inequality (12.3.11) also gives us information about the error in the policy function, but that requires problem-specific analysis.

Exploiting Concavity and Monotonicity

The maximization step in value iteration is a costly step. Anything that can econo-mize on this step will help convergence. In some cases we have a priori information that can be exploited. We here explore two such examples.

For example, if F and u in (12.1.12) are concave then $V(k)$ is also concave. In such cases we should begin with a concave initial guess, since then each value iteration will also be concave. We consider methods to exploit this in the general case. Define

$$h(u; x) \equiv \pi(x, u) + \beta E\{V(x^+) \mid x, u\}$$

to be the objective function in the maximization step at state x, and suppose that we know that V is concave in x and $h(u; x)$ is concave in u. Suppose that D is finite; then each maximization problem in the maximization step would normally be solved by trying all possible $u \in D$. However, if the objective, $h(u; x)$ is concave in u, then we need not try all such u. Instead, we need only compute $h(u_1; x), h(u_2; x), h(u_3; x), \ldots$, for an increasing sequence of u's until the $h(u_i; x)$ values begin to decrease. As soon as $h(u_{j+1}; x) < h(u_j; x)$, we know that u_j is the optimal solution since $h(u, x)$ is concave in u. We will call this the *concave stopping rule*, since it gives us a useful stopping rule for concave problems. If u is a continuous control, then Newton's method is likely to be a good choice for problems where h is concave and smooth in u.

In some problems, such as concave versions of (12.1.13), theory tells us that the optimal control is monotone increasing in the state and that we only need to examine monotone increasing U; we can also exploit this to economize on comparisons in step 1 of value function iteration. If u_j maximizes $h(u; x_i)$, then when we analyze $x_l > x_i$, we know that $u_j < U_l$. The monotonicity of U then tells us we only need to consider $h(u_j; x_l), h(u_{j+1}; x_l), \ldots$. This is an example of the solution of one optimization problem being a good initial guess to another optimization problem. Clearly the order in which we solve the various $\max_u h(u; x)$ problems is important in exploiting these properties.

This discussion of concavity and monotonicity makes the general point that anything that helps us solve the maximization step will help the value iteration algorithm. When solving dynamic programming problems, there often is special structure that can be exploited to reduce running time.

Adaptive Control Choices and Optimization Rules

We next discuss two more ideas that can help for infinite-horizon problems. The basic idea is that since initial iterates of the value iteration algorithm are only interim approximations, they need not be computed with great accuracy. Only as we approach the final solution do we really need to make the effort to exactly solve the maximization problem.

One way to implement this idea is to initially examine only a subset of the controls in D; that is, solve the optimization problem for $u \in D' \subset D$ in the early iterations and then solve it for all $u \in D$ in later iterations. Another idea is to initially solve the problem for a subset of the states, and solve the problem for all states only in the final iterations.

The value function iteration method implicitly assumes that the maximization step (12.3.7) can be solved exactly. If $\mathscr{D}$ is finite, then (12.3.7) can be solved by checking all possibilities, but if $\mathscr{D}$ is infinite (which usually means continuous), then one must use an appropriate optimization method. We are implicitly assuming that (12.3.7) can be solved. Since it is the only nontrivial calculation in (12.3.9), it is critical that (12.3.7) be solved efficiently.

We should also note that these ideas to economize on the optimization step also work if u is a continuous variable. In particular, use a loose convergence criterion for the maximization step in the early iterations when accuracy is not as important, and tighten the convergence criterion in later iterations. Also, after solving the maximization problem for state x_i, one can use that solution for u along with any gradient and Hessian information to produce a hot start for solving the maximization step for state x_{i+1}. Of course, in order to make this effective, the states should be ordered so that x_i is close to x_{i+1} for most i.

12.4 Acceleration Methods for Infinite-Horizon Problems

Value function iteration is a slow procedure for infinite-horizon problems since V^l converges only linearly at the rate β, and at each iteration we solve as many optimization problems as there are states. In the finite-horizon case, V^0 in the initialization step of value function iteration is just the terminal value function, and the later iterates produce the value and policy functions for each period before the terminal time. In finite-horizon problems, all of this is a necessary part of the final solution, and we can do no better than value function iteration. However, in infinite-horizon problems, we want only the stationary optimal policy and value function. Since the intermediate iterates computed by value function iteration are of no intrinsic value, we would like to economize on their computation. In this section we consider acceleration methods that solve infinite-horizon problems much faster than value function iteration.

Policy Function Iteration

The first acceleration method is the *policy function iteration* method. Policy iteration economizes by making more use of each new computed policy function. More specifically, each time a new policy function is computed, policy function iteration computes the value function which would occur if the new policy function were used forever; in contrast, value function iteration assumes that the new policy is used only for one period. Then, with this new value function, we compute a new optimal policy function and continue the iteration. Using our definitions of T and $\mathscr{U}$, the iteration scheme is expressed in algorithm 12.2.

Algorithm 12.2   Policy Function Algorithm

Objective: Solve the Bellman equation, (12.3.4).

Initialization. Choose stopping criterion $\varepsilon > 0$. EITHER make initial guess, V^0, for the value function and go to step 1, OR make initial guess, U^1, for the policy function and go to step 2.

Step 1. $U^{l+1} = \mathscr{U} V^l$

Step 2. $P_i^{l+1} = \pi(x_i, U_i^{l+1}), \quad i = 1, \cdots, n$

Step 3. $V^{l+1} = (I - \beta Q^{U^{l+1}})^{-1} P^{l+1}$

Step 4. If $\| V^{l+1} - V^l \| < \varepsilon$, STOP; else go to step 1.

Note that in the initialization step we are given a choice: We may begin either with an initial guess for the policy or value function. Sometimes we may have a good guess for V but not U, but other times we may have a good guess for U but not V. Having a good initial guess is important; we choose between these alternatives depending on the relative quality of our initial guesses for V and U.

Policy iteration often takes only a few iterations. Unfortunately, the computation of $(I - \beta Q^{U^{l+1}})^{-1}$ may be expensive, making each iteration costly. A second acceleration procedure, *modified policy iteration with k steps*, implements the basic idea of policy iteration without computing $(I - \beta Q^{U^{l+1}})^{-1}$. Modified policy iteration replaces step 3 of policy function iteration with

$$V^{l+1} = \sum_{t=0}^{k} \beta^t (Q^{U^{l+1}})^t P^{l+1} + \beta^{k+1} (Q^{U^{l+1}})^{k+1} V^l. \tag{12.4.1}$$

The expression in (12.4.1) is actually implemented by the steps

$$W^0 = V^l,$$

$$W^{j+1} = P^{l+1} + \beta Q^{U^{l+1}} W^j, \qquad j = 0, \ldots, k, \tag{12.4.2}$$

$$V^{l+1} = W^{k+1}.$$

The modified policy iterate V^{l+1} defined in (12.4.2) is the value of following the policy U^{l+1} for $k + 1$ periods after which the problem has value V^l. Policy iteration is the limiting case of modified policy iteration as k becomes infinite. The following theorem summarizes what we know about convergence rates of modified and unmodified policy iteration:

THEOREM 4.1 (Putterman and Shin)   The successive iterates of modified policy iteration with k steps, (12.4.1), satisfy the error bound

$$\frac{\|V^* - V^{l+1}\|}{\|V^* - V^l\|} \le \min \left[\beta, \frac{\beta(1 - \beta^k)}{1 - \beta} \|U^l - U^*\| + \beta^{k+1} \right]. \tag{12.4.3}$$

Theorem 4.1 points out that as the policy function gets close to U^*, the linear rate of convergence approaches β^{k+1}. Hence convergence accelerates as the iterates converge.

Gaussian Iteration Methods

The value and policy function iteration methods have strong dynamic intuitions. The value function iteration is exactly the limit of backward iteration. However, recall that the problem being solved,

$$V_i = \max_u \pi(x_i, u) + \beta \sum_{j=1}^{n} q_{ij}(u) V_j, \qquad i = 1, \ldots, n, \tag{12.4.4}$$

is just a nonlinear system of equations in the unknowns V_i. We next examine iteration methods that are motivated by standard nonlinear equation solution methods.

Value function iteration is also called *pre–Gauss-Jacobi* since its definition

$$V_i^{l+1} = \max_u \; \pi(x_i, u) + \beta \sum_{j=1}^n q_{ij}(u) V_j^l \tag{12.4.5}$$

is similar to the Gauss-Jacobi iteration examined in chapters 3 and 5. When we apply the full nonlinear Gauss-Jacobi method to (12.4.4), we have the *Gauss-Jacobi iteration method*

$$V_i^{l+1} = \max_u \frac{\pi(x_i, u) + \beta \sum_{j \neq i} q_{ij}(u) V_j^l}{1 - \beta q_{ii}(u)}. \tag{12.4.6}$$

The difference between (12.4.5) and (12.4.6) is the $1 - \beta q_{ii}(u)$ term, which is essentially 1 unless there is significant chance that the optimal control results in no change in state.

In both pre–Gauss-Jacobi and Gauss-Jacobi, we do not use the new state i value, V_i^{l+1}, until we have computed all components of V^{l+1}. In the *pre–Gauss-Seidel* method we use the new value immediately but in a value function iteration fashion:

$$V_i^{l+1} = \max_u \; \pi(x_i, u) + \beta \sum_{j < i} q_{ij}(u) V_j^{l+1} + \beta \sum_{j \geq i} q_{ij}(u) V_j^l, \qquad i = 1, 2, \ldots . \tag{12.4.7}$$

This is the same as value function iteration except that we use the new approximation V_i^{l+1} immediately when computing V_j^{l+1} for $j > i$. The *Gauss-Seidel* method is

$$V_i^{l+1} = \max_u \frac{\pi(x_i, u) + \beta \sum_{j < i} q_{ij}(u) V_j^{l+1} + \beta \sum_{j > i} q_{ij}(u) V_j^l}{1 - \beta q_{ii}(u)}, \qquad i = 1, 2, \ldots . \tag{12.4.8}$$

We would like to know that these methods converge. All of the procedures are obviously monotone in the sense that the solutions for the V_i^{l+1} in (12.4.7) and (12.4.8) are increasing in the V_i^l values. Therefore, if the initial guess for the value function is uniformly less than (uniformly greater than) $\min_{x,u} \pi(x, u)$ ($\max_{x,u} \pi(x, u)$), then the iterates of each of these methods will converge monotonically to the true value function. Since we have $\beta < 1$, the Gauss-Jacobi and Gauss-Seidel iterations are contraction mappings.

Upwind Gauss-Seidel

The methods discussed in the previous section accelerate convergence by exploiting ideas from nonlinear equation solving. The Gauss-Seidel methods in (12.4.7) and

(12.4.8) can be further refined since they depend on the ordering of the states. In this section we will describe Gauss-Seidel methods in which the ordering is endogenous, chosen to enhance convergence.

To illustrate the basic idea, we consider a trivial two-state model. Suppose that there are two states, x_1 and x_2, and two controls, u_1 and u_2, where control u_i causes the state to move to $x_i, i = 1, 2$, and

$$\pi(x_1, u_1) = -1, \quad \pi(x_1, u_2) = 0,$$
$$\pi(x_2, u_1) = 0, \quad \pi(x_2, u_2) = 1.$$
(12.4.9)

We assume that $\beta = 0.9$. Since the only time when the payoff is positive is when the state is x_2 and the control is u_2, and since u_2 keeps the state in state x_2, it is clear that the optimal policy is to choose control u_2 in both states. This implies the solution

$$V(x_1) = 9, \quad V(x_2) = 10.$$

Under the optimal policy, x_2 is the unique stable steady state; that is, once we get there the optimal policy keeps us there, and if we are in any other state we use a control which takes us to the steady state.

We will now illustrate value iteration and policy function iteration for (12.4.9). If we use value iteration with $V^0(x_1) = V^0(x_2) = 0$ the first three iterates are

$$V^1(x_1) = 0, \quad V^1(x_2) = 1, \quad U^1(x_1) = 2, \quad U^1(x_2) = 2,$$
$$V^2(x_1) = 0.9, \quad V^2(x_2) = 1.9, \quad U^2(x_1) = 2, \quad U^2(x_2) = 2,$$
$$V^3(x_1) = 1.71, \quad V^3(x_2) = 2.71, \quad U^3(x_1) = 2, \quad U^3(x_2) = 2,$$

and further iterates will converge at the linear rate prescribed by theory. The first iteration produces the optimal policy function and the successive iterates are necessary only to get V right.

Policy iteration applied to (12.4.9) produces the sequence

$$V^1(x_1) = 0, \quad V^1(x_2) = 1, \quad U^1(x_1) = 2, \quad U^1(x_2) = 2,$$
$$V^2(x_1) = 9, \quad V^2(x_2) = 10, \quad U^2(x_1) = 2, \quad U^2(x_2) = 2,$$

converging after two iterations. This rapid convergence arises because the first iterate produces the optimal policy function. Since the policy iteration method then immediately computes the value of that policy, we converge at the end of the second iterate. In this case we execute the maximization step in value function iteration only

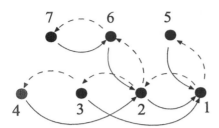

Figure 12.1
Downwind and upwind directions

twice and get the exact answer, whereas value function iteration requires much more computation to get answers that are only approximately accurate.

The key observation to make about this problem is that we have a very good idea about the value at x_2, since it is an absorbing state under the optimal policy. The value function at absorbing states is trivial to compute: If s is an absorbing state when the optimal policy constantly applies control u, then $V(s) = \pi(s,u)/(1-\beta)$. Once we know the value of an absorbing state we can easily compute the value of any state that sends the system to the absorbing state under the optimal policy. In our example, we know that x_2 is an absorbing state under the optimal policy; then $V(x_2) = 10$. When we examine state x_1, we find that the optimum is to choose u_2. Therefore the system will be in state x_1 for one period when control u_2 is applied, sending the system to state x_2. This implies that $V(x_1) = \beta V(x_2) = 9$. We have therefore computed the infinite horizon value function *in just one pass* through the state space.

Figure 12.1 illustrates the general idea. Suppose we have a seven-state, infinite horizon dynamic programming problem, and suppose that a policy induces the motion indicated by the solid arrows. State 1 is the absorbing state for all initial conditions. The value of the policy can be easily computed at state 1, since it is the steady state. The value at states 2, 3, and 5 can be directly computed once we know the value at state 1, after which we can compute the value at states 4 and 6, and then finally state 7 can be valued. We see here that if the state flows in the directions of the solid arrows, the proper direction for us the construct the value function is in the opposite, "upwind," direction.[2] Another way to express this is that information nat-

---

2. We use the term "upwind" because it expresses the critical role played by the flow of the state. Also the same idea is behind the "upwind differencing" finite-difference method often used in fluid mechanics problems.

urally flows in the upwind direction. For example, information about state 1 tells us much about states 2 and 5, but we can evaluate state 1 without knowing anything about states 2 and 5. Again, a single pass through the states will determine the value of the indicated policy.

While the speed achieved in these simple examples is unusual, it does suggest a more general approach. In general, once we ascertain the value of the problem at the stable steady states, we can determine the value at the remaining states. To accomplish this, the *upwind Gauss-Seidel (UGS)* algorithm makes a policy guess, constructs an upwind sequence of states, and then updates the value of those states in the reverse order.

Algorithm 12.3   Upwind Gauss-Seidel (UGS)

Objective: Solve the Bellman equation (12.3.4).

Initialization. Make initial guess for policy, U^0, and set $V^0 = 0$; choose stopping criterion $\varepsilon > 0$.

Step 1. Reorder the states to produce a new indexing, $x_1, x_2, \ldots,$ such that $q_{i,i+1}(U_i^k) \geq q_{i+1,i}(U_{i+1}^k)$.

Step 2. Construct V^{k+1}: Set $W = V^k$. Then build W by iterating

$$W_i = \max_{u \in D} \pi(x_i, u) + \beta \sum_{j=1}^{n} q_{ij}(u) W_j, \qquad i = n, n-1, \ldots, 1,$$

where, at each i, we set U_i^{k+1} equal to a maximizing choice of u.

Step 3. Set $V^{k+1} = W$. If $\| V^k - V^{k+1} \| < \varepsilon$, STOP. Otherwise, go to step 1.

The key details are the reordering in step 1 and the construction of W in step 2. The reordering requirement in step 1 just requires that it is more likely that we move from state x_i to x_j, than vice versa, if $i > j$. In step 2 note that new values of W_i are used to compute the new values of W_j for $j < i$. It is the combination of the reordering of the states and the construction of W which implements the upwind idea. The contraction mapping theorem shows that V^k will converge to V^* no matter what order is chosen in step 1.

However, it may be difficult in step 1 of the UGS method to find an appropriate order for traversing the states. We next explore two ideas that attempt to deal with this problem. First, we describe the *alternating sweep* method. Formally, we first fix an ordering of the states, x_1, x_2, etc. The alternating sweep Gauss-Seidel method then traverses the states first in increasing order and then in decreasing order. Step 1 in UGS would be eliminated, and step 2 in UGS would be replaced by

$$W = V^k,$$

$$W_i^+ = \max_u \pi(x_i, u) + \beta \sum_{j=1}^{i-1} q_{ij}(u) W_j^+ + \beta \sum_{j=i}^{n} q_{ij}(u) W_j, \qquad i = 1, 2, 3, \ldots,$$

$$W_i^{++} = \max_u \pi(x_i, u) + \beta \sum_{j=1}^{i} q_{ij}(u) W_j^+ + \beta \sum_{j=i+1}^{n} q_{ij}(u) W_j^{++}, \qquad i = n, n-1, \ldots,$$

$$V^{k+1} = W^{++}.$$

The alternating sweep method has the advantage of trying two opposite orders in alternation; at each state, one of the orders will, with any luck, be useful. In one-dimensional problems, this is likely but in multidimensional cases the effectiveness will depend critically on the indexing.

The key idea in upwind updating is to find a sequence of communicating states and traverse them in an upwind fashion. One way is to accomplish this is by simulation. In this approach, called *simulated upwind Gauss-Seidel*, we start with a state, x_{i_1}, then simulate the dynamic process of the dynamic programming problem under the current policy rule, U^l, to generate a sequence of states, $x_{i_2}, x_{i_3}, x_{i_4}$, etc., such that in the simulation the process moves from x_{i_j} to $x_{i_{j+1}}$. We simulate the process for T periods. We take this simulation as evidence that $q_{i_1 i_2}(U_{i_1}^l)$ exceeds $q_{i_2 i_1}(U_{i_2}^l), q_{i_2 i_3}(U_{i_2}^l)$ exceeds $q_{i_3 i_2}(U_{i_3}^l)$, etc., the desired feature of step 1 of UGS. Then we apply Gauss-Seidel updating to state x_{i_T}, next to state $x_{i_{T-1}}$, then $x_{i_{T-2}}$, etc., updating x_{i_1} last; that is, we update the states in the reverse order. The resulting procedure is displayed in algorithm 12.4.

In our simple example, (12.4.9), SUGS does much better than value function iteration. After an iteration of value function iteration, we arrive at the optimal policy, $U^1(x_1) = 2$, $U^1(x_2) = 2$. If we begin our simulation with x_1 and simulate a five-period process, we arrive at the sequence $\{x_1, x_2, x_2, x_2, x_2, x_2\}$. We then apply value function iteration to x_2 five times, followed by one value function iteration applied to x_1. This produces a second iterate of

$$V^2(x_1) = 4.68, \qquad V^2(x_2) = 4.21$$

which is exactly what the sixth iterate of value function iteration would achieve but only after applying value function at x_2 five times instead of once. This clearly shows how computing the downwind states first may result in substantial savings in computing the upwind states.

Algorithm 12.4   Simulated Upwind Gauss-Seidel Algorithm (SUGS)

Objective: Solve the Bellman equation (12.3.4).

Initialization. Make initial guess for policy, U, and value, V^0, functions; choose stopping criterion $\varepsilon > 0$.

Step 1. Set $I = \varnothing$, $W = V^k$.

Step 2. Simulate the problem under U for T periods beginning with some $x_{i_1} \notin I$ to produce a sequence $x_{i_2}, x_{i_3}, \ldots, x_{i_T}$. Add the realized states to the set I.

Step 3. Recompute value function at the realized states in the upwind Gauss-Seidel direction:

$$W_l = \max_{u \in D} \pi(x_l, u) + \beta \sum_{j=1}^{n} q_{ij}(u) W_j, \qquad l = i_T, i_{T-1}, \ldots, i_1.$$

At each l set U_l equal to the maximizing choice of u.

Step 4. If $I \neq X$, go to step 2; otherwise, go to step 5.

Step 5. Set $V^{k+1} = W$. If $\| V^{k+1} - V^k \| < \varepsilon$, go to step 6; else go to step 2.

Step 6. Compute the final solutions:

$$U^* = \mathscr{U} V^{k+1},$$

$$P_i^* = v(x_i, U_i^*), \qquad i = 1, \ldots, n,$$

$$V^* = (I - \beta Q^{U^*})^{-1} P^*.$$

and STOP.

Linear Programming Approach

Another approach to finite-state, finite-control dynamic programming is to reformulate it as a linear programming problem. It is clear the (12.3.4) is equivalent to the linear program

$$\min_{V_i} \sum_{i=1}^{n} V_i$$

$$\text{s.t.} \quad V_i \geq \pi(x_i, u) + \beta \sum_{j=1}^{n} q_{ij}(u) V_j, \qquad \forall i, u \in \mathscr{D}, \tag{12.4.10}$$

where $\mathscr{D}$ is finite. This linear program finds the smallest value function that satisfies the inequalities implied by (12.3.4) which are here the constraints. While (12.4.10) may be a large problem, the critical fact is that all components are linear in the V_i

values. This transformation allows us to use linear programming to solve dynamic programming.

This approach has not been viewed favorably in the operations research literature. However, it may have value for some problems we see in economics. Once we have reformulated the problem in this fashion, we can utilize acceleration methods for linear programming problems; Trick and Zin (1997) pursued one such approach with success.

12.5 Discretization Methods for Continuous-State Problems

In many economic applications, both the state and control variables are naturally continuous. One way to approximately solve such problems is to specify a finite-state problem that is "similar" to the continuous problem, and solve the finite problem using finite-state methods. In this section we will examine the details of this approach.

Single-State Optimal Growth

We examine the deterministic growth model exposited in (12.1.12) with the Bellman equation

$$V(k) = \max_c \; u(c) + \beta V(F(k) - c). \tag{12.5.1}$$

Discretizing this problem is fairly easy but not trivial. We first replace the continuous-state variable, k, with a finite set, $K = \{k_1, \ldots, k_n\}$, of permissible values. We next need to choose a collection of values for c, the control variable, that are consistent with the discretization of the state variable. Specifically, since V will be defined only for $k \in K$, those c values must be such that they keep the capital stock on that grid. Therefore the set of permissible c choices varies with the state k. To deal with this difficulty, we rewrite this problem as

$$\max_{I_t} \; \sum_{t=0}^{\infty} \beta^t u(F(k_t) - I_t) \tag{12.5.2}$$

s.t. $k_{t+1} = I_t,$

where now the control is the next period's state. This kind of transformation is not always possible, but when possible, it is convenient to have the control variable be the next period's state.

The Bellman equation for (12.5.2) becomes

$$V(k) = \max_{k^+} \; u(F(k) - k^+) + \beta V(k^+) \tag{12.5.3}$$

where tomorrow's capital stock, k^+, is the control. The consumption choice equals $F(k) - k^+$. In this form it is now easy to create a discrete version of (12.5.3) since the future state is the control. We let K be both the set of states, X, and the set of permissible controls, D, and solve the finite-state, finite-control problem

$$V(k_i) = \max_{k_j \in K} u(F(k_i) - k_j) + \beta V(k_j), \qquad i = 1, \ldots, n. \tag{12.5.4}$$

Some care is necessary in choosing K. The finiteness of K implies that there is a minimum, k^m, and a maximum, k^M, value in K. Therefore we are really discretizing the problem

$$\max_{c_t} \sum_{t=0}^{\infty} \beta^t u(c_t)$$

$$\text{s.t.} \quad k_{t+1} = F(k_t) - c_t, \tag{12.5.5}$$

$$k^m \le k_t \le k^M.$$

We want to choose values in K such that the problems (12.5.1) and (12.5.5) are nearly the same. Theory tells us that if $u(c)$ and $F(k)$ are concave the solution to (12.5.1) will converge to a steady state capital stock, k^{ss}, defined by $\beta F'(k^{ss}) = \beta(1 + f'(k^{ss})) = 1$. The constraints $k^m \le k_t \le k^M$ will not bind as long as $k_0, k^{ss} \in [k^m, k^M]$; hence we should choose k^m and k^M so that $k^m < k_0, k^{ss} < k^M$. In general, one should choose a range $[k^m, k^M]$ such that the optimal solution to (12.5.1) begins and stays in $[k^m, k^M]$. Otherwise, the constraints implicit in the discretization will cause the solution to (12.5.1) to differ from the solution to (12.5.5).

We will now examine the performance of various methods when applied to (12.5.2). Specifically, we choose $u(c) = c^{\gamma+1}/(\gamma + 1)$, and $F(k) = k + f(k) \equiv k + ((1 - \beta)/\alpha\beta)k^\alpha$. This implies a steady state at $k = 1$. We will focus on the interval $[0.8, 1.2]$. We choose $\gamma = -2$, $\alpha = 0.25$, and $\beta = 0.96$. Our discretization in general will be $k_i = 0.8 + (i - 1)\kappa$, for some κ. We first choose $\kappa = 0.001$, which implies 401 capital stocks between $k = 0.8$ and $k = 1.2$.

We first explore value iteration. Table 12.1 displays the results at a few capital stocks. The first two columns. labeled V^* and U^*, display the optimal value and policy for the $\kappa = 0.001$ case. In this problem there is a good initial guess. One of the feasible policies here is zero net saving, that is, $k^+ = k$. Under this policy the utility flow at state k is $u(f(k))$ forever, yielding a discounted value of $u(f(k))/(1 - \beta)$. Therefore we know that the function $V^c(k) \equiv u(f(k))/(1 - \beta)$ is a feasible value function and hence less than the value function of the optimal policy. However, since savings is probably small at any particular k, $V^c(k)$ is probably not too far away

Table 12.1
Dynamic programming solutions to (12.5.2)—Value iteration

	Solution		Case 1					Case 2				
k	V^*	U^*	V^0	U^1	V^1	U^{10}	V^{10}	V^0	U^1	V^1	U^{10}	V^{10}
0.8	−23.7454	0.816	−23.7908	0.826	−23.7772	0.817	−23.7475	0	0.8	−2.38	.811	−15.5
0.9	−23.0906	0.908	−23.1005	0.913	−23.0976	0.908	−23.0911	0	0.8	−1.88	.901	−14.8
1.0	−22.5000	1.000	−22.5000	1.000	−22.5000	1.000	−22.5000	0	0.8	−1.55	.991	−14.3
1.1	−21.9623	1.092	−21.9702	1.097	−21.9681	1.092	−21.9628	0	0.8	−1.32	1.081	−13.8
1.2	−21.4689	1.184	−21.4945	1.174	−21.4899	1.183	−21.4706	0	0.8	−1.16	1.170	−13.3

Table 12.2
Dynamic programming solutions to (12.5.2)—Policy iteration

	Case 1					Case 2				
k	V^0	U^1	$V^{1,50}$	U^2	$V^{2,50}$	V^0	U^1	V^1	$V^{1,50}$	U^5
0.8	−23.79	0.826	−23.75	0.820	−23.7459	0	0.8	−2.38	−23.68	0.818
0.9	−23.10	0.913	−23.09	0.908	−23.0907	0	0.8	−1.88	−23.17	0.917
1.0	−22.50	1.000	−22.50	1.000	−22.5000	0	0.8	−1.55	−22.85	0.993
1.1	−21.97	1.087	−21.96	1.092	−21.9624	0	0.8	−1.32	−22.63	1.091
1.2	−21.50	1.174	−21.47	1.185	−21.4691	0	0.8	−1.16	−22.46	1.194

from the true value function. Hence let $V^0(k) = V^c(k)$ be the initial guess. We display the results in case 1 of table 12.1. This initial guess is close to the solution, and the subsequent iterates are quite good. Also, even the first policy iterate U^1 is quite good.

We also tried the initial guess $V^0 = 0$. This is a general purpose initial guess but seldom a good one. We display the results in case 2 of table 12.1. The initial guess $V^0 = 0$ implies the constant policy $U^1 = 0.8$, choosing 0.8, the minimal capital stock, for next period's capital stock no matter what the current k is. This policy is a poor one; a larger grid would have produced an even worse U^1, since U^1 will always choose maximal consumption if $V^0 = 0$. Even the tenth iterates are rather poor. Comparisons of the two initial guesses used in table 12.1 shows the value of a good initial guess.

We next examine policy and modified policy iteration in table 12.2. The value function $V^{1,50}$ is the value function at the end of the first iteration in (12.4.1) when we take 50 policy iterations in (12.4.1). We will again use the initial guesses $V^0 = V^c$ and $V^0 = 0$. The results are displayed in table 12.2. The combination of a good initial guess and policy iteration is impressive; in fact U^2 is correct to 0.001 in case 1 where

$V^0 = V^c$. The $V^0 = 0$ initial guess again leads to slow progress in case 2, but far better than the value iteration scheme.

We now use the upwind Gauss-Seidel procedure to solve (12.5.2) rapidly and illustrate convergence properties as we take finer discretizations. Theory tells us that both $C(k)$ and $F(k) - C(k)$ are monotonically increasing. These properties imply that the solution is stable with the optimal policy moving the capital stock toward the steady state capital stock, whose value we know. Therefore from any capital stock we know the downwind direction in which the state will move, telling us the upwind direction in which we should compute the solution.

This means that the growth problem (12.5.1) has the same structure as the example in (12.4.9), and that we can develop a one-pass algorithm for computing the value and policy functions. We choose F and β so that $k^* = 1$. Since the steady state is an absorbing state, we know $V(k^*) = u(f(k^*))/(1 - \beta)$. Next consider the capital stock just below the steady state, $1 - \kappa$. Since it is less than the steady state, the optimal policy will either choose zero net saving, in which case the capital stock will stay at $1 - \kappa$ forever, or it will choose investment equal to κ and move the capital stock up to the steady state level, where it will stay forever. This exhausts all of the possibilities for the optimal policy since, due to the monotonicity of C and $F - C$, it is not optimal to overshoot the steady state and later retreat to it, nor it is optimal to reduce the capital stock and later climb to the steady state. We can compute the value of these two choices and know that the correct value is the greater of the two. Hence from the steady state we can calculate the value function at the next lower capital stock. Proceeding in this way, we can calculate the value and policy at $1 - i\kappa, i = 2, 3, \ldots$, down to $k = 0.1$. Symmetric considerations show that we can also compute the value function at capital stocks in excess of the steady state, starting at $k = 1.0$ and proceeding to $k = 1.9$ in steps of κ. This produces the value function in just one pass.

Table 12.3 displays the results for the case $\alpha = 0.33333$, $\gamma = -2$, and $\beta = 0.95$ and we choose $\kappa = 10^{-4}, 10^{-5}$, and 10^{-6}, implying 18,001 to 1,800,001 capital stocks in $[0.1, 1.9]$. The results show that the computed policy functions converge smoothly. In fact, for most capital stocks, the computed optimal policy at $\kappa = 10^{-4}$ and $\kappa = 10^{-5}$ equals the optimal policy for $\kappa = 10^{-6}$ rounded to the nearest point in the coarser discretizations. For example, the optimal saving policy at $k = 0.9$ is 0.003036 if $\kappa = 10^{-6}$, 0.00304 if $\kappa = 10^{-5}$, and 0.0030 if $\kappa = 10^{-4}$. Therefore it appears that the computed savings function is as accurate as possible given the discretization κ.

All of the policy functions in table 12.3 were computed in a few minutes on a 90-MHz Pentium, including the case with 1,800,001 capital stocks. This efficiency is due to the one-pass nature of the UGS scheme we used, which in turn relied on our knowing the steady state. This is not essential. If we begin with the initial guess of

Table 12.3
UGS solution to (12.5.2) with $\alpha = 1/3$, $\gamma = -2$

	κ		
k	10^{-4}	10^{-5}	10^{-6}
1.9	−0.028700	−0.028690	−0.028692
1.5	−0.015800	−0.015750	−0.015752
1.1	−0.003100	−0.003090	−0.003086
1.0	0	0	0
0.9	0.003000	0.003040	0.003036
0.5	0.014300	0.014260	0.014261
0.1	0.019200	0.019240	0.019241

zero net saving, then the optimal value of any steady state is computed correctly. If we then apply the alternating sweep Gauss-Seidel procedure we will correctly compute the optimal value function after visiting each capital stock only twice. Hence, even if we did not know the steady state, we could solve the problem in at most twice the time of a single-pass scheme.

The final issue we will analyze is the size of the error due to discretization. The value function computed in table 12.3 is clearly a lower bound since the policy function it uses would continue to be feasible in the continuous k case. We would like an upper bound for V. To do that, we examine the dynamic programming problem

$$V^u(k) = \max_{k^+} u(F(k) - k^+ + \kappa) + \beta V^u(k^+) \tag{12.5.6}$$

where, recall, κ is the difference between successive k's in our discretization. The problem (12.5.6) allows an individual to consume an extra κ units of consumption in each period. Suppose that k were allowed to be continuous and $k^+ = I(k)$ were the optimal policy. An individual would attain greater utility if, in the continuous k case, he chose k^+ instead to be the next highest value in K above $I(k)$, say k_j, and consumed $f(k) + k - k_j + \kappa$; but that is now a policy which keeps k on the discrete grid in (12.5.2), and feasible in (12.5.6). Therefore V^u exceeds the value function of the continuous state problem, but can be solved exactly since it is a discrete problem. By combining the error estimates for the solution of the discrete problems, we can compute upper and lower bounds for the true value function.

Commodity Storage Problems

We next describe the optimal commodity stockpiling problem which agricultural economists have studied intensively. This problem goes back to the analysis of

Gustafson (1958), to which we will return later. Here we focus on the dynamic programming analysis.

The commodity storage model assumes that a crop is harvested each year, with the yield allocated between current consumption and changes in inventory. The state variable is the inventory, which can never be negative. The social planner also chooses inputs for the next year's production. We include *convenience value*, that is, the value to having a positive level of inventory. Specifically $u(c_t)$ is the per-period utility function, expressed in dollars, over consumption of grain in time t, c_t, $L(y_t)$ is the dollar cost of input choice (e.g., labor effort) y_t at the end of period t, and I_t is the nonnegative beginning-of-period-t inventory. We assume that output in period $t+1$, q_{t+1}, equals $y_t\theta_{t+1}$, where θ_{t+1} is a serially uncorrelated productivity shock. We first let the total amount of grain available *after* harvest, including inventories, be the state variable; let $x_t \equiv I_t + q_t$ denote the state. After harvest, the grain supply is allocated between consumption and inventories, $x_t = c_t + I_{t+1}$, and input, y_t, is chosen. The convenience value in period t of the inventory I_{t+1} is $g(I_{t+1})$. This implies the dynamic programming problem

$$V(x) = \max_{0 \le y, I \le x} u(x - I) + g(I) - L(y) + \beta E\{V(I + \theta y)\}. \tag{12.5.7}$$

This problem is novel because of the nonnegativity constraint on I. In this form it is also an example of where we can discretize neither the state nor control space because we have no guarantee that $I + \theta y$ will lie on the prescribed grid. This difficulty can easily arise in stochastic problems.

To apply discretization methods, one must develop a reformulation that allows discretization. In this case we may proceed by changing the definition of state variable and focusing on a function other than $V(x)$. Consider the inelastic supply case with no convenience value, modeled here as $y = 1$ and $g(I) = 0$. In this case we proceed as follows: First, consider the dynamic programming problem which uses I, the *end-of-period* stock, as both the state and control variable:

$$W(I) = \beta E\left\{ \max_{0 \le I^+ \le I + \theta} u(I + \theta - I^+) + W(I^+) \right\},$$

where I^+ is the next period's inventory chosen after θ is observed. To keep matters simple, we will assume that θ is uniformly distributed over $[\theta_m, \theta_M]$. If we choose a grid of I values, $I_i, i = 1, \ldots, n_I$, and a uniform grid of θ values on $[\theta_m, \theta_M]$, θ_j, $j = 1, \ldots, n_\theta$, we arrive at the discrete-state problem

$$W(I_i) = \frac{1}{n_\theta} \beta \sum_{j=1}^{n_\theta} \left\{ \max_{0 \le I^+ \le I_i + \theta_j} u(I_i + \theta_j - I^+) + W(I^+) \right\}.$$

In this discretization, for each I_i, we cycle through the θ_j values, where for each θ_j we solve

$$\max_{0 \leq I^+ \leq I_i + \theta_j} u(I_i + \theta_j - I^+) + W(I^+)$$

and then take the average of these maximal values over the θ values to arrive at our approximation to $W(I_i)$. When we have done this for each I_i, we have our new approximation for the value function W. We can apply policy iteration to accelerate convergence as long as we store the policy function approximations, $\mathscr{I}^+(I_i, \theta_j)$, along the way.

We can also use this procedure for the elastic supply case; here the end-of-period state vector is (I, y), and Bellman's equation is

$$W(I, y) = \beta E \left\{ \max_{0 \leq y^+, I^+ \leq I + \theta} u(I + y\theta - I^+) - L(y^+) + W(I^+, y^+) \right\}.$$

Again we can discretize I, y, and θ to arrive at a discrete-state approximation of $W(I, y)$.

This example shows why we must be careful in formulating dynamic programming problems when developing computational strategies. While all formulations of a dynamic programming problem are theoretically equivalent, they may differ substantially in their numerical properties. Here we find that when we use a different state variable and rewrite the problem, we can go from a formulation where discretization is not possible to one where discretization can be applied.

Limits of Discretization Methods

Discretization procedures are of limited value even if one fully uses a priori information about the solution. They are often inefficient since, in order to have any hope of realistically approximating an agent's flexibility and the stochastic law of motion, a large number of points are required. Multidimensional problems are practically impossible since the "curse of dimensionality" is particularly vexing for this method; if N points are used for a one-dimensional problem, then it would be natural to use N^k points for a k-dimensional problem. Since N must be large, N^k is infeasible for even small k. This problem would be reduced by using more efficient grids motivated by multidimensional quadrature methods, such as monomial formulas and low-discrepancy sets of points. For multidimensional problems with continuous state variables and smooth value functions, there are alternatives to discretization. We will now turn to those methods.

12.6 Methods for Solving Linear-Quadratic Problems

A special case of dynamic programming is the class of linear-quadratic problems. This class is used extensively in dynamic economic analyses because it is relatively tractable. We also study it here because it is a simple example of a different approach to solving dynamic programs. When we solve any dynamic programming problem, we focus on solving the decision rule and/or the value function. In the case of linear-quadratic problems, we know that the value function is a quadratic form and the decision rule is linear in the state. Therefore, to solve for these unknown functions, we solve for the unknown coefficients of the quadratic value function or linear decision rule. This is an obvious approach to take in the linear-quadratic case since we know the form of the solution. We will see that it is also a natural approach in general, providing an alternative to discretization methods.

The discrete-time linear-quadratic optimal control problem assumes a payoff flow function $\pi(x, u, t) = \frac{1}{2}x^\top Q_t x + u^\top R_t x + \frac{1}{2}u^\top S_t u$, a discount factor of $\beta \in [0, 1)$, a law of motion $x_{t+1} = A_t x_t + B_t u_t$, and a terminal valuation $\frac{1}{2}x^\top W_{T+1}x$. Without loss of generality, we can assume that Q_t, S_t, and W_{T+1} are symmetric; we will also assume here that $\pi(x, u, t)$ is concave in (x, u), implying that we have a well-behaved concave dynamic optimization problem. This is a general representation once we adopt the convention that the first component in x is the constant 1. With these specifications the problem is

$$\max_{u_t} \sum_{t=0}^{T} \beta^t(\tfrac{1}{2}x_t^\top Q_t x_t + u_t^\top R_t x_t + \tfrac{1}{2}u_t^\top S_t u_t) + \tfrac{1}{2}x_{T+1}^\top W_{T+1} x_{T+1} \tag{12.6.1}$$

s.t. $x_{t+1} = A_t x_t + B_t u_t$,

and the Bellman equation becomes

$$V(x, t) = \max_{u_t} \tfrac{1}{2}x^\top Q_t x + u_t^\top R_t x + \tfrac{1}{2}u_t^\top S_t u_t + \beta V(A_t x + B_t u_t, t + 1). \tag{12.6.2}$$

If we make the guess that $V(x, t) = \frac{1}{2}x^\top W_t x$, then (12.6.2) implies that

$$0 = S_t u_t + R_t x + \beta B_t^\top W_{t+1}(A_t x + B_t u_t),$$

which in turn implies the control law

$$u_t = -(S_t + \beta B_t^\top W_{t+1} B_t)^{-1}(R_t + \beta B_t^\top W_{t+1} A_t)x \equiv U_t x. \tag{12.6.3}$$

After some manipulation we find that

$$W_t = Q_t + \beta A_t^\top W_{t+1} A_t + (\beta A_t^\top W_{t+1} B_t + R_t^\top) U_t. \tag{12.6.4}$$

Equation (12.6.4) is referred to as the *Riccati equation*.

Solving the finite-horizon problem is easy. Since we know W_{T+1}, we can iteratively apply (12.6.4) to solve for the W_t; under the assumption of strict concavity of π and W_{T+1}, the necessary inverses in (12.6.4) exist. The iteration in (12.6.4) is essentially the basic value function iteration method.

The infinite-horizon case is a bit more difficult. Suppose that $T = \infty$, $R_t = R$, $Q_t = Q$, $S_t = S$, $A_t = A$, and $B_t = B$ in (12.6.1). Then the value function becomes autonomous; in particular, $V(x) \equiv \frac{1}{2} x^\top W x$ for some W which is a solution to the *algebraic Riccati equation*

$$W = Q + \beta A^\top W A - (\beta A^\top W B + R^\top)(S + \beta B^\top W B)^{-1}(\beta B^\top W A + R). \tag{12.6.5}$$

Solving (12.6.5) for W is not simple because it is a quadratic matrix equation. Our dynamic programming intuition for the concave case does produce a method. The value function iteration approach to solving (12.6.5) is to choose some initial negative definite guess W_0 and compute the sequence

$$W_{k+1} = Q + \beta A^\top W_k A - (\beta A^\top W_k B + R^\top)(S + \beta B^\top W_k B)^{-1}(\beta B^\top W_k A + R). \tag{12.6.6}$$

The W_k iterates will converge to the solution, W, of (12.6.5).

We can also use policy iteration to help solve (12.6.5). Suppose that we begin with our initial guess, W_0, and perform one value function iteration; a by-product of such is a guess of the policy function,

$$U = -(S + \beta B^\top W_0 B)^{-1}(R + \beta B^\top W_0 A).$$

Given the terminal value function W_0 and the policy rule U, the Bellman equation implies that the current value function is

$$\tfrac{1}{2} x^\top W_1 x = \tfrac{1}{2} x^\top Q x + (Ux)^\top R x + \tfrac{1}{2}(Ux)^\top S U x + \beta \tfrac{1}{2} x^\top W_0 x.$$

If we followed the policy U forever, the resulting value function would be $\frac{1}{2} x^\top W x$ with

$$W = \frac{\tfrac{1}{2} Q + \tfrac{1}{2} U^\top S U + U^\top R}{1 - \beta}.$$

Hence policy iteration for linear-quadratic problems is summarized by the iteration

$$U_{i+1} = -(S + \beta B^\top W_i B)^{-1}(R + \beta B^\top W_i A),$$

$$W_{i+1} = \frac{\frac{1}{2}Q + \frac{1}{2}U_{i+1}^\top S U_{i+1} + U_{i+1}^\top R}{1 - \beta},$$

which continues until $\| W_{i+1} - W_i \|$ is a small for some norm $\| \cdot \|$.

12.7   Continuous Methods for Continuous-State Problems

Most of the methods examined so far either assume that there were only a finite number of states, or approximate a continuous state with a finite set of values. These methods are reliable in that they will solve the problem, or will approach the solution as the discretization is made finer. However, discretization becomes impractical as one moves to larger problems. In this section we introduce a parametric approach due to Bellman et al. (1963).

We don't use discretization to solve linear-quadratic problems because we know the functional form of the solution. This allows us to focus on finding the appropriate coefficients. Linear-quadratic problems do not suffer a curse of dimensionality since the number of unknown coefficients do not grow exponentially in the dimension. Even though most dynamic programming problems do not have a useful functional form, we can still use the functional form approach by exploiting approximation ideas from chapter 6.

Recall the basic Bellman equation:

$$V(x) = \max_{u \in D(x)} \pi(u, x) + \beta E\{V(x^+)|x, u\} \equiv (TV)(x). \tag{12.7.1}$$

The unknown here is the function V. Discretization methods essentially approximate V with a step function, since it implicitly treats any state between x_i and x_{i+1} as either x_i or x_{i+1}. Chapter 6 presented better methods to approximate continuous functions. We apply those ideas here.

We assume that the payoff, motion, and value functions are all continuous functions of their arguments. The basic idea is that it should be better to approximate the continuous-value function with continuous functions and put no restrictions on the states and controls other than those mandated by the problem. Since the computer cannot model the entire space of continuous functions, we focus on a finitely parameterizable collection of functions,

$$V(x) \doteq \hat{V}(x; a). \tag{12.7.2}$$

The functional form $\hat{V}$ may be a linear combination of polynomials, or it may represent a rational function or neural network representation with parameters $a \in R^m$, or it may be some other parameterization specially designed for the problem.

Once we fix the functional form, we focus on finding coefficients $a \in R^m$ such that $\hat{V}(x; a)$ "approximately" satisfies the Bellman equation. Solving the Bellman equation, (12.7.1), means finding the fixed point of T, but that is the pure mathematical problem. The basic task for a numerical procedure is to replace T, an operator mapping continuous functions to continuous functions, with a finite-dimensional approximation, $\hat{T}$, which maps the set of functions of the form $\hat{V}$ into itself. If done properly, the fixed point of $\hat{T}$ should be close to the fixed point of T.

The construction of $\hat{T}$ relies on three critical steps. First, we choose some parameterization scheme $\hat{V}(x; a)$ with $a \in R^m$, and n points in the state space,

$$X = \{x_1, x_2, \ldots, x_n\}, \tag{12.7.3}$$

where $n \geq m$. Second, we then evaluate $v_i = (T\hat{V})(x_i)$ at each $x_i \in X$; we refer to this as the *maximization step*. The maximization step gives us values v_i which are points on the function $T\hat{V}$. We next use the information about $T\hat{V}$ contained in the $v_i, i = 1, \ldots, m$, to find an $a \in R^m$ such that $\hat{V}(x; a)$ best fits the $(v_i, x_i), i = 1, \ldots, n$, data; we call this the *fitting step*. The fitting step can be an unweighted nonlinear least squares procedure as in

$$\min_{a \in R^m} \sum_{i=1}^{n} (\hat{V}(x_i; a) - v_i)^2$$

or any other appropriate approximation scheme. This fitting step produces a new value function defined on all states x. The *parameteric dynamic programming algorithm* is outlined in algorithm 12.5.

Algorithm 12.5   Parametric Dynamic Programming with Value Function Iteration

Objective: Solve the Bellman equation, (12.7.1).

Initialization. Choose functional form for $\hat{V}(x; a)$, and choose the approximation grid, $X = \{x_1, \ldots, x_n\}$. Make initial guess $\hat{V}(x; a^0)$, and choose stopping criterion $\varepsilon > 0$.

Step 1. Maximization step: Compute $v_j = (T\hat{V}(\cdot; a^i))(x_j)$ for $x_j \in X$.

Step 2. Fitting step: Using the appropriate approximation method, compute the $a^{i+1} \in R^m$ such that $\hat{V}(x; a^{i+1})$ approximates the (v_i, x_i) data.

Step 3. If $\| \hat{V}(x; a^i) - \hat{V}(x; a^{i+1}) \| < \varepsilon$, STOP; else go to step 1.

Steps 1 and 2 in algorithm 12.5 constitute a mapping $\hat{T}$ taking $\hat{V}$, corresponding to a parameter vector a, to another function $\hat{T}\hat{V}$ corresponding to another coefficient vector, a'. $\hat{T}$ is therefore a mapping in the space of coefficients, a subspace of R^m.

Algorithm 12.5 presents the general idea; we now examine the numerical details. Rewrite (12.7.1) as

$$V(x) = \max_{u \in D(x)} \pi(u, x) + \beta \int V(x^+) \, dF(x^+ \mid x, u), \qquad (12.7.4)$$

where $F(x^+ \mid x, u)$ is the distribution of the future state x^+ conditional on the current state and control. The maximization steps compute

$$v_j = \max_{u \in D(x_j)} \pi(u, x_j) + \beta \int \hat{V}(x^+; a) \, dF(x^+ \mid x_j, u), \qquad x_j \in X. \qquad (12.7.5)$$

With the v_j values for the grid X, we next compute a new value function approximation $\hat{V}(x; a)$ which fits the new v_j values at the $x_j \in X$.

These expressions make clear the three kinds of problems we need to handle. The first type of numerical problem is evaluating the integral $\int \hat{V}(x^+) \, dF(x^+ \mid x, u)$. This would usually require numerical quadrature. If the integrand is smooth in x^+ for fixed x and u, a Gaussian approach is suggested. Less well-behaved integrals would require low-order Newton-Cotes formulas. High-dimensional integrands would require a monomial, Monte Carlo, or quasi–Monte Carlo method.

The second type of numerical problem appearing in (12.7.4) is the optimization problem, (12.7.5). If the objective in (12.7.5) is smooth in u, we could use faster methods such as Newton's method. It is important to choose an approximation scheme $\hat{V}$ which preserves any smoothness properties of the problem.

Third, given the v_i estimates of the $(T\hat{V})(x_i)$ values, we need to compute the new coefficients in $\hat{V}(x; a)$. The appropriate approximation procedure depends on the nature of V. If we expect V to be a smooth function, then orthogonal polynomial procedures may be appropriate. Otherwise, splines may be advisable. We will see below that these considerations are particularly important here.

There is substantial interaction across the three problems. Smooth interpolation schemes allow us to use Newton's method in the maximization step. They also make it easier to evaluate the integral in (12.7.5). Since the integral in (12.7.5) is costly to evaluate, we may want to use different rules when computing the gradients and Hessian, using the observation that low-quality gradient and Hessian approximations often suffice.

While algorithm 12.5 looks sensible, there are several questions concerning its value. First, convergence is not assured since $\hat{T}$ may not be a contraction map; in fact, we will see that it may be quite ill-behaved. The key detail is the choice of the approximation scheme incorporated in $\hat{V}(x;a)$ and the grid X. The discussion below will focus on the behavior of this algorithm for various choices of these elements.

We should emphasize that we can still use some of the techniques developed for the finite-state case. Algorithm 12.5 presents only value iteration, but we could also implement policy iteration. Many other procedures are not so easily adapted for this approach. The Gauss-Seidel ideas, particularly the upwind methods, do not have obvious counterparts consistent with the parametric approach in general. This leaves open the possibility that the finite-state approach may dominate the functional approximation approach for some problems because of the applicability of Gauss-Seidel acceleration ideas.

12.8   Parametric Approximations and Simulation Methods

The main idea of parametric dynamic programming methods is to parameterize the critical functions and find some parameter choice which generates a good approximation. One direct and simple implementation of that idea is to parameterize the control law, $\hat{U}(x;a)$, and through simulation find that coefficient choice, a, which generates the greatest value. In this section we will discuss a simple application of that approach.

Consider again the stochastic growth problem:

$$V(k) = \max_c u(c) + \beta E\{V(k - c + \theta f(k - c))|k, c\}, \tag{12.8.1}$$

where the θ are i.i.d. productivity shocks affecting the net output function f; this is a special case of (12.1.20). For smooth concave problems we know that the true policy and value functions, $C(k)$ and $V(k)$, are smooth functions, increasing in k. In this section we will use a simple simulation approach to solve the stochastic growth problem (12.8.1).

Instead of parameterizing $C(k)$, we parameterize the savings function, $S(k) \equiv k - C(k)$. We know that S is increasing but that $S(k_1) - S(k_2) \leq k_1 - k_2$ for $k_1 \geq k_2$; these properties allow us to examine a simple class of rules. We will examine linear rules; hence $\hat{S}(k) = a + bk$ for coefficients a and b where $b \in (0, 1)$. We will use simulation to approximate the value of a savings rule. Suppose that $\theta_t, t = 1, \ldots, T$ is a sequence of productivity shocks. Then, for a given initial value of k_0, the resulting paths for c_t and k_t are given by $c_t = k_t - \hat{S}(k_t)$ and $k_{t+1} = \hat{S}(k_t) + \theta_t f(\hat{S}(k_t))$, and the realized discounted utility is

$$W(\theta; \hat{S}) = \sum_{t=0}^{T} \beta^t u(c_t). \tag{12.8.2}$$

We can do this for several θ_t sequences. Let θ^i be the ith sequence drawn and let c_t^i be the resulting consumption when we compute (12.8.2). The value of a rule $\hat{S}(k)$ beginning at k_0 is $V(k_0; \hat{S}) = E\{W(\theta; \hat{S})\}$, which can be approximated by the sum

$$\frac{1}{N} \sum_{j=1}^{N} W(\theta^j; \hat{S}) = \frac{1}{N} \sum_{j=1}^{N} \sum_{t=0}^{T} \beta^t u(c_t^j). \tag{12.8.3}$$

Note that (12.8.3) is essentially an integral over the space of θ series. A literal "simulation" approach would construct each θ by a sequence of i.i.d. draws.

This value of $W(\theta; S)$ depends on the initial capital stock k_0, the particular realization of $\theta_t, t = 1, \ldots, T$, and the choices for a and b. The use of several θ realizations makes the average in (12.8.3) less sensitive to the particular realizations used.

Once we have a way to approximate $V(k_0; \hat{S})$ for a linear rule $\hat{S}$ parameterized by a and b, we optimize over a and b to approximate the optimal linear $\hat{S}(k)$ rule. Since k_0 is the initial capital stock in our definition of $V(k_0; \hat{S})$, this approximation depends on k_0, whereas the optimal rule does not. To reduce the sensitivity of the chosen S rule to k_0, we should choose k_0 to be close to the "average" capital stock.

This sounds easy but one can run into problems. Our procedure does not impose any restriction on $\hat{S}(k)$. In particular, $\hat{S}(k)$ could be negative at some k, or consumption $k - \hat{S}(k)$ could be negative, with either possibility causing problems because f and u are usually defined only for positive arguments. To deal with this problem, one should constrain the linear approximation, implying that $\hat{S}(k) = \min[\max[0, a + bk], k]$, or choose some transformation that avoids this possibility. The true rule may not be linear; in that case we could use a more flexible specification for $\hat{S}$.

The simulation approach is not efficient for smooth problems like (12.8.1) where we can exploit the continuity and concavity properties of the solution. However, more complex dynamic programming problems involving constraints, several dimensions, and/or integer variables may be approximately solved by simulation strategies. The key idea is to parameterize a family of control laws, use simulation to evaluate them, and choose the best. See Smith (1990) for an application of these ideas.

12.9 Shape-Preserving Methods

The parametric approach to dynamic programming is promising but can fail if we are not careful. To illustrate this, consider the problem (12.5.1) with a very concave

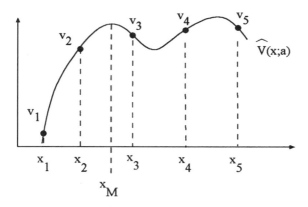

Figure 12.2
Dynamic programming and shape of value function interpolant

utility function. In figure 12.2, we display the results of a typical value function iteration. Suppose that we have chosen $x_i, i = 1, \ldots, 5$, for the nodes of the approximation
and that we computed v_1, v_2, v_3, v_4, and v_5 as in figure 12.2. These five points appear
to be consistent with an increasing and concave and value function. However,
applying interpolation to these data to fit $\hat{V}(x; a)$ may produce a curve, neither concave nor monotone increasing, such as $\hat{V}(x; a)$ in figure 12.2. Even worse is that the
maximum of $\hat{V}(x; a)$ is a point between x_2 and x_3, and even exceeds the maximum v_i
values.

While these internodal fluctuations are consistent with the approximation theory of
chapter 6, they can wreck havoc with dynamic programming. For example, suppose
that the true V is increasing and concave but that at some iteration $\hat{V}$ looks like $\hat{V}$ in
figure 12.2. In the next iteration, x_M will be considered a very desirable state, and
controls will be chosen to push the state towards x_M. The artificially high value of
$\hat{V}(x_M)$ will lead to artificially high values for $\hat{V}(x_2)$ and $\hat{V}(x_3)$ in the next maximization step. The errors at x_2 and x_3 could interact with the values computed elsewhere to produce even worse internodal oscillations at the next fitting stage. Once
this process begins, it can feed on itself and destabilize the value iteration procedure.

The problem here is the absence of shape-preservation in the algorithm. Shape-
preservation is valuable property, particularly in concave problems. If $\hat{V}$ and $\pi(x, u)$
are concave in x and u, the maximization step is a concave problem; hence the global
maximum is the unique local maximum and easy to find. Furthermore T is a shape-
preserving operator; that is, if $\pi(x, u)$ and the conditional expectation is concave in
(x, u) for concave V, then TV is concave if V is concave. Therefore, if $\hat{V}$ is concave

in x, then the $(T\hat{V})(x_i)$ points will be concave, and a shape-preserving scheme will cause $(\hat{T}\hat{V})(x)$ to be a concave function of x. Approximation methods should match the shape properties of the approximated objects.

This does not mean that we can't use the polynomial methods. In some instances these problems do not arise. For example, if $V(x)$ is C^∞ with well-behaved high-order derivatives, then orthogonal polynomial approximation is a good approximation choice, and there is less chance of these problems arising.

However, we still want to find more reliable procedures. Following is a discussion of methods that avoid these problems by design. The key idea is the use of shape-preserving approximation methods. Discretization methods will preserve shape and avoid these problems. More promising are the shape-preserving methods discussed in chapter 6.

Linear Interpolation

For one-dimensional problems disruptive internodal oscillations can be avoided by the simplest of all interpolation schemes—linear interpolation. Furthermore, as discussed in chapter 6, linear interpolation is shape-preserving. Therefore, if the v_i points are increasing and concave, so will be the interpolating function.

The problem with linear interpolation is that it makes the maximization step less efficient. The kinks in a linear interpolant will generally produce kinks in the objective of the maximization step, forcing us to use slower optimization algorithms. Kinks in the value function may cause the approximate policy function to be discontinuous, an unappealing property if the true policy function is continuous. Using linear interpolation is a costly way of preserving shape.

Multilinear Interpolation Methods

In multidimensional problems there are a couple of easy well-behaved approximation schemes which one can use. First, one could use the multilinear or simplicial interpolation methods discussed in chapter 6. The DYGAM package discussed in Dantzig et al. (1974) used multilinear interpolation. These methods eliminates problematic internodal oscillations since $\hat{V}$ at each point in the interior of a box is a convex combination of the values at the vertices. The fact that the interpolation scheme is monotone in the interpolation data means that $\hat{T}$ is monotone. Furthermore $\hat{T}$ inherits the contraction properties of T. Multilinear interpolation is costly to compute; a less costly alternative is multidimensional simplicial interpolation, as discussed in chapter 6.

Unfortunately, multilinear and simplicial interpolation have the same problems of one-dimensional linear interpolation and more. First, they preserve positivity and monotonicity but not concavity. Second, they also produce kinks in the value function and discontinuities in the policy function. These problems can be ameliorated by cutting the state space into small boxes, but only at substantial cost.

Schumaker Shape-Preserving Splines

For one-dimensional dynamic programming problems with smooth concave payoff and transition functions and concave C^1 solutions, the Schumaker quadratic shape-preserving spline procedure will produce C^1 approximations of the value function and continuous policy functions. The objective in the maximization step will always be concave and C^1, allowing us to use a rapid scheme such as Newton's method. We can also use a small number of approximation nodes since we do not need to worry about disruptive internodal fluctuations.

Judd and Solnick (1994) apply Shumaker's quadratic splines to the single good, deterministic optimal growth problem, (12.5.1). They found that the resulting approximations were very good, substantially dominating other methods. For example, the shape-preserving method using 12 nodes did as well as linear interpolation using 120 nodes and the discrete-state approximation using 1,200 points.

Shape-preserving Hermite interpolation is particularly valuable. In this approach, after one computes the value function at a node, one also uses the envelope theorem to compute the slope of the value function at essentially zero computational cost. This slope information can be used along with the level information in the Schumaker shape preserving scheme to arrive at an even better, but still stable, approximation of value function iteration. Examples in Judd and Solnick indicate that shape-preserving Hermite interpolation will produce highly accurate solutions using few approximation nodes.

12.10   Continuous-Time Problems

Value function iteration is an important method for solving discrete-time dynamic programming problems. Unfortunately, the structure of value function iteration is itself tied to the discrete nature of time in those models, and cannot be used for continuous-time problems, since there is no today-tomorrow distinction in continuous time.

One approach is to replace the continuous-time structure with a discrete-time structure with short periods and then use discrete-time methods. Using short periods will make the discount factor, β, close to unity, and imply very slow convergence.

Policy iteration can be implemented in autonomous infinite horizon problems. Suppose that $T = \infty$ in (12.2.1) and the payoff depends only on x and u. The Bellman equation for this problem is

$$\rho V(x) = \max_u \pi(x, u) + \sum_{i=1}^n V_{x_i}(x) f^i(x, u). \tag{12.10.1}$$

Suppose that the current guess for the value function is $V^i(x)$. The RHS of (12.10.1) produces the control law, $U^{i+1}(x)$ implied by the value function V^i. Substituting $U^{i+1}(x)$ into (12.2.4) produces the equation

$$\rho V^{i+1}(x) = \pi(x, U^{i+1}(x)) + \sum_{i=1}^n V_{x_i}^{i+1}(x) f^i(x, U^{i+1}(x)) \tag{12.10.2}$$

for the value V^{i+1} of the policy U^{i+1}. Equation (12.10.2) is a linear differential equation in the unknown V^{i+1}. If there is a steady state x^*, then $V(x^*)$ is known, and its value can serve as a boundary condition. The solution of (12.10.2) provides a new guess for the value function. This process produces a sequence of value and policy functions, and would continue until convergence has been reached.

Projection methods are natural for continuous-time problems and could be used to solve (12.10.2). Instead of implementing a policy function iteration, we will proceed in a more direct fashion working simultaneously with the Bellman equation and first-order conditions. We illustrate the idea with the problem stated in (12.2.5). Suppose that $u(c) = -c^{-1}$, $f(k) = 0.2k^{0.25}$, and $\rho = 0.05$, the example studied in table 12.2. The general idea is to parameterize both the value function $V(k)$ and the policy function $C(k)$, and use projection methods to solve the functional equations

$$0 = -\rho V(k) + u(C(k)) + V'(k)(f(k) - C(k)), \tag{12.10.3}$$

$$0 = u'(C(k)) - V'(k). \tag{12.10.4}$$

We approximate V and C with polynomials $\hat{V}(k) = \sum_{l=0}^6 a_l k^l$ and $\hat{C}(k) = \sum_{l=0}^6 b_l k^l$. The steady state is $k^* = 1$; we aim for a solution for $k \in [0.9, 1.1]$. We have fourteen unknown coefficients and two functional equations that we want to solve. We choose seven points, the Chebyshev zeros of T_7 adapted to the interval [0.9, 1.1]; these are $X = \{0.9025, 0.9218, 0.9566, 1.0000, 1.0434, 1.0782, 1.0975\}$. We then choose a and b so that both (12.10.1) and (12.10.2) are zero at $k \in X$. We use Newton's method to solve for a and b, which finds a candidate solution. We next need to check if these degree six polynomials are acceptable solutions to the system (12.10.3) and (12.10.4). To do this, we evaluate (12.10.3) and (12.10.4) over the interval [0.9, 1.1]. To eliminate units, we divide (12.10.3) by $\rho V(k^*)$, and we divide (12.10.4) by $u'(f(k^*))$. The result had normalized residuals all less than 10^{-8}. Also the policy function computed here differs by less than one part in 10^{-6} from that computed by reverse shooting applied to the optimal control formulation of this problem. Again we see that projection methods provide a powerful tool for solving a dynamic problem.

12.11   Further Reading and Summary

This chapter presented several approaches to solving finite- and infinite-horizon dynamic programming problems. Finite-horizon problems must use value function iteration. There are many methods available for infinite-horizon autonomous problems. The contraction nature of the basic dynamic programming operator leads us to reliable algorithms. We have seen how this idea can be carried out in value function iteration with both finite- and continuous-state spaces once we adopt appropriate approximation schemes. Christopeit (1983) and Kushner and Dupuis (1992) presents methods for solving stochastic control problems using discretization ideas.

Unfortunately, contraction-based value function iteration schemes are slow. Other methods rely on other properties of dynamic programming. First, policy function iteration results in substantial acceleration. Second, when we focused only on the nonlinear equation structure of the problem, we found that Gauss-Seidel acceleration methods from the nonlinear equation literature could be applied here. Upwind Gauss-Seidel combines the Gauss-Seidel acceleration method with dynamic properties of the dynamic programming problem.

Finite-state problems are easy to understand but time-consuming to solve. Since many problems have continuous states, we presented parametric methods that combine value and policy iteration ideas with approximation ideas. Parametric ideas can greatly improve convergence on simple problems. Johnson et al. (1993) examines the parametric approach for three- and four-dimensional problems. They can also make it possible to attack very large problems. The literature on neurodynamic programming (see Bertsekas 1996) solves very large problems using ideas similar to a combination of the parametric approach and downwind Gauss-Seidel iteration.

Some approaches to solving the linear-quadratic problem ignore the dynamic programming origins of the problem and deal with the Riccati equation as an algebraic problem. As such, the unknown elements of W in (12.6.5) could be fixed using nonlinear equation methods applied to the algebraic Riccati equation. The difficulty with this approach is the existence of extraneous solutions. This makes the choice of initial guess important. However, if one has a good initial guess, then a rapidly convergent nonlinear equation scheme may do better than the value or policy iteration schemes. Amman (1996) explores this idea. Other methods have been developed that exploit the specific algebraic structure of the Riccati equation. Anderson et al. (1996) is a recent review of this literature.

The recent Bertsekas books on dynamic programming contains a good introduction to numerical methods. The Rust (1996) survey focuses on numerical issues and presents the state of the art. Dynamic programming is a key step in some econometric procedures; see Keane and Wolpin (1994), Rust (1996), and Pakes (1996) for reviews of this literature.

Exercises

1. Consider (12.1.17) for $\beta = 0.8$, $u(c, l) = \log c + \log(1 - l)$, and $F(k, l) = k + \beta^{-1}(1 - \beta)k^{0.25}l^{0.75}$. Compute the steady state, k^*. Compute the value and optimal policy functions for $k \in [0.1k^*, 2k^*]$ using discretization methods, piecewise-linear interpolation, Chebyshev polynomial parameterizations (using both Chebyshev regression and Chebyshev interpolation), and Schumaker shape-preserving interpolation. Use both value and policy function methods, and develop Gauss-Seidel approaches. Compare the time and accuracy performance of the various methods. Repeat for $\beta = 0.96$. Then repeat for $\beta = 0.99$.

2. Suppose that a worker earns $w_t = 2 + t/20 - (t/20 - 1)^2$ in period t for $1 \leq t \leq 40$ and is retired for $41 \leq t \leq 55$. Suppose also that there is a safe asset paying interest at rate $r = 0.02$ and a risky asset with price equal to one and dividend equal to $Z \sim U[-0.1, 0.2]$ i.i.d. in each period. Assume a dynamic utility function $E\{\sum_{t=0}^{55} \beta^t u(c)\}$. Write a program to solve this life-cycle asset allocation problem for the cases $\beta = 0.96$ and $u(c) = \log c$, $(c + 0.5)^{0.5}$, and $-e^{-c}$. First, solve for the case where borrowing is not allowed. Second, solve for the case where the borrowing interest rate is $r = 0.1$.

3. Suppose that a monopolist faces a demand curve $D(p)$ and has a cost function of $C(q, Q)$ where q is current output and Q is an exponential lagged sum of past output, $Q_{t+1} = \lambda q_t + (1 - \lambda)Q_t$. Formulate the dynamic programming problem, and compute the value and policy functions for various values of $0 < \lambda < 1$, linear demand curves, and cost curves of the form $C(q, Q) = a + (b - c(Q + 1)^{-0.2})q$ where a, b, and c are positive. Use value iteration, policy iteration, and various gaussian acceleration methods.

4. Solve (12.1.12) with $\beta = 0.95$, $u(c) = \log c$, and $F(k) = k + 0.5(2 + \sin 2\pi k)k^{0.25}$. Discretize k, and use value function iteration, policy function iteration, and upwind Gauss-Seidel approaches to solve for $V(k)$, $k \in [0.1, 2]$.

5. Consider the following multidimensional growth problem. Assume there are two sectors where total output of the single good is

$$y = \sum_{i=1}^{2} f^i(k_i, l_i),$$

where k_i, l_i is the capital and labor used in sector i, and $f^i(k_i, l_i)$ is output in sector i of the single good. In each period output is allocated between consumption, c, and net investment in stock i, I_i, where consumption is

$$c = y - \sum_{i=1}^{2} I_i - \sum_{i=1}^{2} \gamma_i I_i^2$$

and where the γ_i are adjustment cost parameters. The problem reduces to

$$\max \sum_{t=0}^{\infty} \beta^t u\left(c_t, \sum_{i=1}^{2} l_{i,t}\right)$$

s.t. $k_{i,t+1} = k_{i,t} + I_{i,t}$,

$$c_t = \sum_{i=1}^{2} f^i(k_{i,t}, l_{i,t}) - \sum_{i=1}^{2} I_{i,t} - \sum_{i=1}^{2} \gamma_i I_{i,t}^2.$$

Solve this problem for capital stocks within 50 percent of the steady state for various choices of tastes and technology. First, take a discrete-state approach, using value function iteration, policy function iteration, upwind Gauss-Seidel, and alternative sweep methods. Second, take a parametric approach using regression on the grid consisting of Chebyshev zeros in each dimension. Third, use regression with a grid consisting of a low-discrepancy set of points. Compare the effectiveness of these methods.

6.   Suppose that a worker earns a wage w_t that follows a Markov process on a finite set of wages, can earn a safe interest rate of r on savings, cannot borrow, and has the dynamic utility function $\sum_{t=0}^{\infty} \beta^t u(c_t)$ where $\beta(1 + r) < 1$ and u is concave. Write a program that will solve the corresponding dynamic programming problem for the case of two wages, $w_t \in \{1, 5\}$, where the chance of a change in wage is 0.1 each period. Compare value function iteration, policy function iteration, and various Gauss-Seidel schemes for discretization schemes. Next try polynomial and spline approximation methods. Compute the ergodic distribution of savings. Next compute the impact of a 25 percent income tax on utility, the present value of tax revenues, and the ergodic distribution of savings.

7.   The simplest stochastic growth model with adjustment costs is

$$\max_c E\left\{ \int_0^{\infty} e^{-\rho t} u(c)\, dt \right\}$$

s.t. $dk = \varphi(f(k) - c)\, dt + \sigma(k)\, dz$,

where φ is a concave function, $\varphi'(0) = 1$. Derive its HJB equation and a computational scheme to compute the optimal consumption policy function.

8.   Solve (12.5.7) with values as follow:

a $u(c) = 5c - c^2/2, L(y) = 1, g(I) = \sqrt{I}, \beta = 0.9$, and $\theta \sim U[0, 2]$.

b. $u(c) = 5c - c^2/2, L(y) = 1, g(I) = 0, \beta = 0.9$, and $\theta \sim U[0, 2]$.

c. $u(c) = 5c - c^2/2, L(y) = y^2, g(I) = 0, \beta = 0.9$, and $\theta \sim U[0, 2]$.

Use both discretization and parameteric approaches.

IV PERTURBATION METHODS

13 Regular Perturbations of Simple Systems

In this chapter and the next two we examine *perturbation*, or *asymptotic*, methods of approximation. The basic idea of asymptotic methods is to formulate a general problem, find a particular case that has a known solution, and then use that particular case and its solution as a starting point for computing approximate solutions to nearby problems. This approach relies on implicit function theorems, Taylor series expansions, and techniques from bifurcation and singularity theory. These methods are widely used in mathematical physics, particularly in quantum mechanics and general relativity theory, with much success.

Economists have often used special versions of perturbation techniques, such as asymptotic methods in statistics and linearizing around a steady state. Unfortunately, many have eschewed rigorous perturbation methods based on mathematics, using instead intuitive, ad hoc procedures. While these ad hoc procedures are sometimes valid, little care is taken to state or check the implicit assumptions, and the ability to apply these ad hoc methods beyond simple problems is limited by the lack of a precise mathematical foundation.

More generally, the economics literature has not exploited the full range and power of asymptotic techniques. The advantage of proceeding formally is that problems that cannot be handled by intuitive informal approaches can be addressed easily within the formal framework. In this and the two following chapters we follow the mathematics literature, discussing when useful the connections to the procedures used in the economics literature.

This chapter presents the elementary structure of regular perturbation methods. We first state the implicit function theorem, which together with Taylor's theorem forms the foundation for regular perturbation methods in Euclidean spaces. We discuss comparative statics problems, the envelope theorem, and comparative dynamics problems, showing that they are all examples of the same regular perturbation ideas.

We then focus on dynamic recursive models, developing notation and methods that produce useful local approximations. We use these techniques to approximate the policy functions of dynamically stable stochastic control models near the steady state of their deterministic counterparts. We use local information to calculate linear and higher-order approximations of the solution to the deterministic problem near the steady state. We then show how to use such local information to approximate the solutions of stochastic problems. In this chapter we focus on systems with a single state variable and a single control variable; the next chapter discusses general systems.

The result of regular perturbation methods is a polynomial or similar function which approximates the true solution in a neighborhood of a special point. There are two reasons why these approximations may be valuable. First, if the expansions are asymptotically valid, they provide us with proofs of a function's local properties; that is the domain of comparative statics. That is not the main objective of this chapter. Instead, we aim to use these methods instead to construct good *numerical* approximations of *nonlocal* features. Even if the resulting series is not good by itself, the computed approximation may be a valuable input into more standard numerical procedures.

A *warning* to the reader should be made at this point. Many of the perturbation computations below are strictly formal. We do not always discuss the conditions under which these expansions are valid, since such problems are beyond the scope of this book. Instead, we describe diagnostics which check whether a formal expansion does well as an approximate solution, using the compute and verify approach to numerical error discussed in chapter 2. Even if we had all the asymptotic theory we would like, we would still need to use these diagnostics in any application to check if an expansion is reasonably accurate. These diagnostics show that the perturbation-based approximations do far better than one would expect of purely local methods.

13.1 Mathematics of Regular Perturbation Methods

Asymptotic methods depend on a few basic theorems. The critical theorems for regular perturbation theory are Taylor's theorem and the implicit function theorem for R^n. Taylor's theorems were theorems 2.6.1 and 2.6.2. We now state the implicit function theorem.

THEOREM 13.1.1 (Implicit function theorem)   If $H(x, y): R^n \times R^m \to R^m$ is C^k, $H(x_0, y_0) = 0$, and $H_y(x_0, y_0)$ is not singular, then there is a unique C^0 function $h: R^n \to R^m$ such that $y_0 = h(x_0)$ and for x near x_0, $H(x, h(x)) = 0$. Furthermore, if H is C^k, then h is C^k, and its derivatives can be computed by implicit differentiation of the identity $H(x, h(x)) = 0$.

Our techniques below will use Taylor's theorem and the implicit function theorem to examine functions implicitly defined by nonlinear equations in R^n. Together they allow us to implicitly compute the derivatives of h with respect to x at x_0. We will also use similar ideas to examine functions defined implicitly by differential and other functional equations. The formal foundation for those applications relies on generalizing Taylor's theorem and the implicit function theorem to Banach spaces. We will proceed intuitively, since these generalizations are beyond the scope of this text.

Meaning of "Approximation"

We often use the phrase "$f(x)$ approximates $g(x)$ for x near x_0," but the meaning of this phrase is seldom made clear. One trivial sense of the term is that

$$f(x_0) = g(x_0). \tag{13.1.1}$$

While this is certainly a necessary condition for an approximation, it is generally not by itself a useful concept because it says nothing about f at any x other than x_0. Approximating one function with another at a point x_0 usually means at least that

$$f'(x_0) = g'(x_0) \tag{13.1.2}$$

holds as well as (13.1.1). In this case we say that "f is a first-order approximation to g at $x = x_0$," or that "f is a linear approximation of g at $x = x_0$." Note the details: a *linear* approximation *at* x_0. The less specific nonlocal statement "f is a linear approximation of g" has no meaning here; instead, it is more appropriate when referring to the global types of approximation, such as least squares, studied in chapter 6. In general, we say that "f is an *nth order approximation* of g at $x = x_0$" if

$$\lim_{x \to x_0} \frac{\|f(x) - g(x)\|}{\|x - x_0\|^n} = 0, \tag{13.1.3}$$

which, for C^n f and g, is true iff $f^{(k)}(x_0) = g^{(k)}(x_0)$ for $k = 0, \cdots, n$.

While this seems rather obvious, these definitions are not always used in the economics literature. Some so-called linear approximations don't even satisfy (13.1.2). In these chapters, we use the mathematical meaning of approximation, and use other terms as needed when discussing ad hoc procedures.

Regular Perturbation: The Basic Idea

The basic idea behind regular perturbations is quite simple. Suppose that a problem reduces to solving

$$f(x, \varepsilon) = 0 \tag{13.1.4}$$

for x where ε is a parameter. We assume that for each value of ε the equation in (13.1.4) has a (possibly not unique) solution for x; in this way (13.1.4) is a collection of equations in x parameterized by ε. Let $x = x(\varepsilon)$ denote a smooth function such that $f(x(\varepsilon), \varepsilon) = 0$. In general, we cannot solve (13.1.4) for arbitrary ε, but there may be special values of ε for which (13.1.4) can be solved; these will serve as benchmarks.

To see how to proceed, consider the special case of differentiable f, scalar x and ε, $x(\varepsilon)$ unique, and $x(0)$ known. We can apply implicit differentiation to (13.1.4) to find

$$f_x(x(\varepsilon), \varepsilon)x'(\varepsilon) + f_\varepsilon(x(\varepsilon), \varepsilon) = 0, \tag{13.1.5}$$

which implicitly defines the derivative $x'(\varepsilon)$. Equation (13.1.5) is generally useless since it depends on the unknown function $x(\varepsilon)$. However, at $\varepsilon = 0$ (13.1.5) becomes linear equation in $x'(0)$ with solution $x'(0) = -f_\varepsilon(x(0),0)/f_x(x(0),0)$ which is known if $x(0)$ is known. This is well-defined only if $f_x \neq 0$, a condition which can be checked at $x = x(0)$. The linear approximation of $x(\varepsilon)$ for ε near zero is

$$x(\varepsilon) \doteq x^L(\varepsilon) \equiv x(0) - \frac{f_\varepsilon(x(0),0)}{f_x(x(0),0)} \varepsilon. \tag{13.1.6}$$

We can continue to differentiate to find higher-order derivatives of $x(\varepsilon)$. We differentiate (13.1.5) to find

$$f_x x'' + f_{xx}(x')^2 + 2f_{x\varepsilon}x' + f_{\varepsilon\varepsilon} = 0. \tag{13.1.7}$$

At $\varepsilon = 0$, (13.1.7) implies that

$$x''(0) = -\frac{f_{xx}(x(0),0)\,(x'(0))^2 + 2f_{x\varepsilon}(x(0),0)\,x'(0) + f_{\varepsilon\varepsilon}(x(0),0)}{f_x(x(0),0)}.$$

With this we can compute the quadratic approximation

$$x(\varepsilon) \doteq x^Q(\varepsilon) \equiv x(0) + \varepsilon x'(0) + \tfrac{1}{2}\varepsilon^2 x''(0). \tag{13.1.8}$$

We see some patterns developing from these computations of $x'(0)$ and $x''(0)$. The critical equation defining $x''(0)$ is a linear equation, as was the case when we computed $x'(0)$. Also the solution for $x''(0)$ is well-defined as long as $f_x(x(0),0) \neq 0$, just as was the case for $x'(0)$. Each time we differentiate (13.1.4) we get a new unknown derivative, but its value at $\varepsilon = 0$ is the unique solution to some linear equation. Since the solvability of each such linear problem depends solely on $f_x(x(0),0)$, if $f_x(x(0),0) \neq 0$, we can continue this process of constructing a Taylor expansion for $x(\varepsilon)$ as long as $f(x,\varepsilon)$ has the necessary derivatives.

Checking a Perturbation Approximation

Once we have a partial expansion for some function $x(\varepsilon)$ in terms of powers of ε, we would like to know if it is good for any interesting value of ε. Suppose that we are really interested in the case $\varepsilon = 1$. One way to check if the linear approximation $x^L(1)$ is a good approximation for $x(1)$ is to compute the residual $r \equiv f(x^L(1),1)$; if r is small, then we may decide that $x^L(1)$ is a good approximation to $x(1)$. Of course we must make f and r unit free if this test is to be substantive. We could also do this to evaluate the quality of the quadratic approximation $x^Q(1)$. Even if we could construct a convergent sequence z_k of successively higher-order approximations that converge to $x(1)$, we would still need to check the residual, and stop only when

$f(z_k, 1)$ and/or some other diagnostic test is small. Essentially we should apply the same diagnostic tests to $x^L(1)$ and $x^Q(1)$ as we would to determine when to stop a convergent sequence.

This is all rather obvious for differentiable functions of real variables, but this same idea applies for x's in general Banach spaces. We will not go into the formalism behind the methods we use below, but the idea is robust. First, express your problem as a continuum of problems parameterized by ε with the $\varepsilon = 0$ case known. Second, "differentiate" the continuum of problems with respect to ε. Third, "solve" the resulting equation for the implicitly defined derivatives at $\varepsilon = 0$. While the differentiation and solution steps are nontrivial problems in general, we will confine our analyses to cases where intuition and basic calculus produces the correct answers.

13.2 Comparative Statics

Although the terms "perturbation" and "asymptotic" may not be familiar, the ideas are common in economics. One form of perturbation analysis familiar to economists is comparative statics. To illustrate the connection between regular perturbation methods and comparative statics, we consider a familiar tax exercise.

Suppose that the demand for apples is $D(p)$ and the supply is $S(p - \tau)$ where p is the price of an apple paid by consumers and τ is the tax per apple paid by producers. The equilibrium equation for p given the tax rate τ is $0 = D(p) - S(p - \tau)$; denote this relation as $p = P(\tau)$. Therefore $P(\tau)$ is defined by the implicit relation

$$0 = D(P(\tau)) - S(P(\tau) - \tau). \tag{13.2.1}$$

We often want to know how a change in the tax rate will affect equilibrium price. To do this, we compute $P'(\tau)$ by differentiating (13.2.1) with respect to τ, yielding

$$0 = D'P' - S'(P' - 1) \Rightarrow P' = \frac{S'}{S' - D'} = \frac{\eta_S}{\eta_S - \eta_D}, \tag{13.2.2}$$

where η_S is the elasticity of supply, pS'/S, and η_D is the elasticity of demand, pD'/D, both of which depend on $p = P(\tau)$. In (13.2.2) we wrote the final answer in terms of elasticities at the equilibrium price given τ; one should generally write the results of perturbation methods in unit-free terms such as elasticities and shares.

Equation (13.2.2) expresses the local change in price relative to a small change in τ at any τ. In economic applications it is natural to expand $P(\tau)$ around $\tau = 0$, the competitive, tax-free case. This yields the local approximation

$$P(\tau) \doteq P(0) + \frac{\eta_S}{\eta_S - \eta_D} \tau. \tag{13.2.3}$$

We can use this approximation to compute other quantities of interest. Suppose that we want to compute the welfare consequences of the tax. To do so, we first define social surplus

$$SS(\tau) \equiv \int_0^{D(P(\tau))} (D^{-1}(p) - S^{-1}(p))dp + \tau D(P(\tau)). \tag{13.2.4}$$

We next compute the linear approximation of $SS(\tau)$. Differentiating (13.2.4) implies that $SS'(0) = 0$. Does this imply that there is no welfare loss from a small tax? That would be misleading. To avoid such misleading conclusions, we next compute $SS''(\tau)$ and computing the second-order expansion

$$SS(\tau) \doteq SS(0) + 0 \cdot \tau + \frac{1}{2} D(P(0)) \frac{\eta_D \eta_S}{\eta_S - \eta_D} \tau^2. \tag{13.2.5}$$

This is the common rule-of-thumb that the welfare cost of a tax is proportional to τ^2. The approximation in (13.2.5) is careful to use prices, quantities, and elasticities instead of derivatives; this is desirable because economic intuition is better expressed in terms of elasticities, which are unit-free, than in terms of derivatives.

Note that the linear term in the expansion of SS is zero and the first nontrivial term, also called the *dominant term*, is τ^2. While the dominant term is second-order, it is not true that it is negligible. Of course we could define a new variable $\psi = \tau^2$ and then the expansion of SS in terms of ψ begins with a term linear in ψ. On the other hand, we could define $\psi = \sqrt{\tau}$ and find that the first nontrivial term is fourth-order in ψ. Since the notion of nth order is not invariant to these nonlinear changes in variables, we focus instead on the dominant term of an expansion instead of the first-order term. Therefore one should continue the Taylor expansion of a function until a nonzero term is reached. We will use the common language of first-order, second-order, and so on, but it should be understood that any expansion should continue until a nonzero term appears.

Proceeding with successive differentiation of (13.2.1), we can compute several terms of a series expansion of P for τ near 0. It is common to stop at the first nontrivial term, since we generally use these methods to compute qualitative expressions. For numerical purposes it may be useful to compute higher-order terms. In this tax case we could compute arbitrarily high-order terms for $P(\tau)$ as long as $D(p)$ and $S(p)$ have sufficiently many derivatives.

Envelope Theorem

One of the more useful and familiar perturbation results is the *envelope theorem*. We discuss it here because we will frequently invoke it when doing perturbations.

THEOREM 13.2.1 (Envelope theorem):   Let

$$F(\varepsilon) = \max_{x} \ f(x, \varepsilon)$$

$$\text{s.t.} \quad g(x, \varepsilon) = 0 \tag{13.2.6}$$

define a parameterized collection of problems. Suppose that the parameterized Lagrangian is $\mathscr{L}(x, \lambda, \varepsilon) = f(x, \varepsilon) + \lambda^T g(x, \varepsilon)$, that $x^*(\varepsilon)$ is the solution function for (13.2.6), and that the corresponding shadow price vector is $\lambda^*(\varepsilon)$. Then

$$\frac{dF}{d\varepsilon} = \frac{d}{d\varepsilon}(\mathscr{L}(x^*(\varepsilon), \lambda^*(\varepsilon), \varepsilon)) = \frac{\partial f}{\partial \varepsilon}(x^*(\varepsilon), \varepsilon) + \lambda^*(\varepsilon)^\top \frac{\partial g}{\partial \varepsilon}(x^*(\varepsilon), \varepsilon).$$

The basic point of the envelope theorem is that the $\partial x^*/\partial \varepsilon$ term need not be computed to compute $dF/d\varepsilon$.

These simple examples in familiar contexts help us get an idea of how to think about perturbations. While the tax example is simple, it displays exactly how to compute a regular perturbation of a problem. Below we apply these ideas to more complex problems. However, the basic idea remains the same: A regular perturbation is nothing more than computing a derivative of an implicitly defined function.

13.3   Perturbing an IVP

We will often want to perturb dynamic systems. In this section we consider initial value problems; in the next section we consider boundary value problems.

Consider the continuum of IVP's indexed by the parameter ε:

$$\dot{x} \equiv \frac{\partial x(t, \varepsilon)}{\partial t} = g(x, t; \varepsilon),$$

$$x(0, \varepsilon) = x_0(\varepsilon). \tag{13.3.1}$$

For each value of ε (13.3.1) is an ordinary differential equation; in particular, it is an IVP. All terms are assumed to be C^∞ in the parameter ε and we presume that the function $x(t, \varepsilon)$ is smooth in both t and ε; see Hartman (1964) for a discussion of these issues. Suppose that we can easily solve the $\varepsilon = 0$ problem but not problems where

$\varepsilon \neq 0$. For example, consider the problem

$$\dot{x} = x + \varepsilon h(x), \quad x(0; \varepsilon) = 1. \tag{13.3.2}$$

At $\varepsilon = 0$, (13.3.2) is a linear IVP, and the solution is, $x = e^t$. However, for $\varepsilon \neq 0$ the system is nonlinear, and generally difficult if not impossible to solve analytically.

Perturbation methods study problems of the form in (13.3.1) where $\varepsilon \neq 0$ but is "close enough" to the $\varepsilon = 0$ case, and construct an approximation of the form

$$x(t, \varepsilon) \doteq \sum_{k=0}^{n} a_k(t) \frac{\varepsilon^k}{k!}, \tag{13.3.3}$$

where $a_k(t) = \partial^k x(t, 0)/\partial \varepsilon^k$. Notice that (13.3.3) is a power series in ε where the coefficients are functions of time.

The perturbation approach constructs conditions on the $a_i(t)$ functions that allow us to solve for them. The first step in constructing (13.3.3) is to compute $a_0(t)$, which is just the solution to (13.3.1) with $\varepsilon = 0$. We assume that this is available. For the example, (13.3.2), the coefficient of ε^0 in (13.3.3) is $a_0(t) = e^t$, since $x(t, 0) = e^t$. The next step is to compute $a_1(t) = (\partial x/\partial \varepsilon)(t, 0)$, which represents the impact on $x(t, \varepsilon)$ as ε increases from $\varepsilon = 0$. To find $(\partial x/\partial \varepsilon)(t, 0)$, we differentiate (13.3.1) with respect to ε and evaluate the result at $\varepsilon = 0$; the result is

$$\dot{a}_1(t) = g_x(a_0(t), t; 0) a_1(t) + g_\varepsilon(a_0(t), t; 0), \qquad a_1(0) = x_0'(0). \tag{13.3.4}$$

The key fact is that (13.3.4) is a linear IVP in the unknown function $a_1(t)$ with the initial condition $a_1(0) = x_0'(0)$. The existence theory for linear IVP's applies; in particular, if $|g_x(a(t), t, 0)|$ and $|g_\varepsilon(a_0(t), t, 0)|$ are bounded for $t \in [0, T]$ then a solution exists. Furthermore (13.3.4) has the closed-form solution

$$a_1(t) = a_1(0) e^{\int_0^t g_x(a_0(s), s; 0) ds} + \int_0^t e^{\int_s^t g_x(a_0(z), z; 0) dz} g_\varepsilon(a_0(s), s; 0) \, ds.$$

Just as the perturbation of a nonlinear equation in R^n produces a linear equation which we can solve, (13.3.4) shows that the perturbation of a nonlinear IVP produces a solvable linear IVP. For the example in (13.3.2), (13.3.4) implies $a_1(0) = x_0'(0)$, $a_0(t) = e^t$, $g_x(x, t; 0) = 1$, $g_\varepsilon(x, t; 0) = h(e^t)$, and the first-order approximation

$$x(t; \varepsilon) \doteq e^t + \varepsilon \left(x_0'(0) e^t + \int_0^t e^{\int_s^t e^z \, dz} h(e^s) \, ds \right)$$

which can be evaluated by quadrature for any t.

Taking the second derivative of (13.3.1) with respect to ε and evaluating the result at $\varepsilon = 0$ yields the first-order IVP

$$\dot{a}_2 = g_x a_2 + g_{xx} a_1^2 + g_{\varepsilon x} a_1 + g_{\varepsilon\varepsilon}, \qquad a_2(0) = x_0''(0), \tag{13.3.5}$$

where the arguments here of g and its derivatives are the same as in (13.3.4). Since we have solutions for a_0 and a_1, the only unknown function in (13.3.5) is $a_2(t)$; hence (13.3.5) is again a linear IVP, but now $a_2(t)$ is the unknown function. The initial condition for (13.3.1), $x(0, \varepsilon) = x_0(\varepsilon)$, implies that $a_2(0) = x_0''(0)$, the initial condition in (13.3.5). This IVP then fixes $a_2(t)$. The only assumptions we have used is that g and $x_0(\varepsilon)$ have the derivatives necessary for (13.3.4) and (13.3.5) to be well-defined.

We can apply this to the Solow growth model with taxes. Suppose that the capital stock grows according to $\dot{k} = sR(k)k - \delta k$, where $R(k)$ is the aftertax return on savings, $s > 0$ is the savings rate, and $\delta > 0$ is the depreciation rate. If capital income is taxed at the rate τ, then $R(k) = (1 - \tau)f'(k)$ if $f(k)$ is the aggregate production function. The steady state is defined by $s(1 - \tau)f'(k)k = \delta k$, and is stable and unique if $f(k)$ is concave. The steady state depends on τ; let $k^*(\tau)$ be the steady state capital stock for tax rate τ.

We examine the effect of a change in τ. To do this, we construct the continuum of problems where τ is now a smooth function, $\tau(\varepsilon)$, of ε

$$\dot{k}(t, \varepsilon) = s(1 - \tau(\varepsilon))kf'(k(t, \varepsilon)) - \delta k(t, \varepsilon),$$
$$k(0, \varepsilon) = k^*(\tau(0)). \tag{13.3.6}$$

If $\varepsilon = 0$, $k(t, 0) = k^*(\tau(0))$ for all t; that is, k begins and remains at the steady state corresponding to the tax when $\varepsilon = 0$. A change in ε will cause τ to change. Differentation of (13.3.6) shows

$$\dot{k}_\varepsilon(t, \varepsilon) = -s\tau'(\varepsilon)f'k + s(1 - \tau)f''k_\varepsilon k + (s(1 - \tau)f' - \delta)k_\varepsilon. \tag{13.3.7}$$

At $\varepsilon = 0$, $s(1 - \tau)f' = \delta$ and (13.3.7) can be written as

$$\frac{d}{dt}(k_\varepsilon(t, 0) - k_\varepsilon^\infty) = -\lambda(k_\varepsilon(t, 0) - k_\varepsilon^\infty),$$

where

$$k_\varepsilon^\infty = \frac{\tau'(0)\delta}{s(1 - \tau)^2 f''(k^*)},$$

$$\lambda = -s(1 - \tau)k^* f''(k^*) > 0.$$

This is a stock adjustment form, telling us that $k_\varepsilon(t, 0)$ converges to k_ε^∞, the change in the steady state k as ε increases, and does so at rate λ. The solution is $k_\varepsilon(t, 0) = (1 - e^{-\lambda t})k_\varepsilon^\infty$.

The use of continuous time here is inessential. The same procedures can be used to perturb discrete-time initial value problems. For example, the discrete-time version of the tax example is $k(t + 1) = k(t) + sR(k(t))k(t) - \delta k(t)$, and the steady state is defined by $s(1 - \tau)f'(k)k = \delta k$. We again let $\tau(\varepsilon)$ be a parameterization of the tax rate. The discrete-time version of (13.3.6) is the continuum of difference equations

$$k(t + 1, \varepsilon) = k(t, \varepsilon) + s(1 - \tau(\varepsilon))k(t, \varepsilon)f'(k(t, \varepsilon)) - \delta k(t, \varepsilon),$$

$$k(0, \varepsilon) = k^*(\tau(0)).$$

$$(13.3.8)$$

If $\varepsilon = 0$, $k(t, 0) = k^*(\tau(0))$ for all t; that is, k remains at the steady state. If we differentiate (13.3.8) with respect to ε and set $\varepsilon = 0$, we obtain a linear difference equation for $k_\varepsilon(t, 0)$, which in turn can be solved by standard means.

13.4   Perturbing a BVP: Comparative Perfect Foresight Dynamics

We next apply these methods to autonomous perturbations of boundary value problems. Suppose that we have a continuum of BVP's

$$\dot{x} = f(x, y, \varepsilon),$$

$$\dot{y} = g(x, y, \varepsilon),$$

$$(13.4.1)$$

$$x(0) = x_0(\varepsilon), \quad y(T) = y_T(\varepsilon).$$

All of the problems in (13.4.1) indexed by ε are autonomous since t never enters explicitly into (13.4.1). We generally construct (13.4.1) so that we know the solution to (13.4.1) for $\varepsilon = 0$, and we want to know the nature of the solution for positive ε. Let $x(t, \varepsilon), y(t, \varepsilon)$ be the solutions for (13.4.1) for $t \in [0, T]$ and small ε. Therefore we assume that the system (13.4.1) has a solution for all ε in some neighborhood of zero and that the solutions are arbitrarily differentiable in ε for small ε.

Since they are smooth functions of t and ε, the dependence of $x(t, \cdot)$ and $y(t, \cdot)$ on ε is linearly approximated at $\varepsilon = 0$ by their derivatives:

$$x(t, \varepsilon) = x(t, 0) + \varepsilon x_\varepsilon(t, 0) + \mathcal{O}(\varepsilon^2),$$

$$y(t, \varepsilon) = y(t, 0) + \varepsilon y_\varepsilon(t, 0) + \mathcal{O}(\varepsilon^2).$$

Therefore we are interested in computing the functions $x_\varepsilon(t, 0)$ and $y_\varepsilon(t, 0)$.

Given the critical role played by $x_\varepsilon(t, 0)$ and $y_\varepsilon(t, 0)$, we need to be clear as to their nature. First, for each t, they are the derivatives of $x(t, \varepsilon)$ $(y(t, \varepsilon))$ with respect to ε when $\varepsilon = 0$. Second, with $\varepsilon = 0$ fixed, we view both $x_\varepsilon(t, 0)$ and $y_\varepsilon(t, 0)$ as functions of t. It is this functional nature that we often exploit when we actually solve for the derivative functions $x_\varepsilon(t, 0)$ and $y_\varepsilon(t, 0)$. In the computations below, we will switch frequently between these two views.

Our smoothness assumptions allow us to differentiate (13.4.1) with respect to ε, which shows us that $x_\varepsilon(t, 0)$ and $y_\varepsilon(t, 0)$ are solutions to the perturbed system

$$\dot{x}_\varepsilon = f_x x_\varepsilon + f_y y_\varepsilon + f_\varepsilon,$$

$$\dot{y}_\varepsilon = g_x x_\varepsilon + g_y y_\varepsilon + g_\varepsilon, \tag{13.4.2}$$

$$x_\varepsilon(0, 0) = \frac{dx_0}{d\varepsilon}(0), \quad y_\varepsilon(T, 0) = \frac{dy_T}{d\varepsilon}(0),$$

where $f_x, f_y, f_\varepsilon, g_x$, and g_y are all evaluated at $(x(t, 0), y(t, 0), 0)$. When we rearrange terms, (13.4.2) becomes the linear BVP

$$\frac{d}{dt}\begin{pmatrix} x_\varepsilon(t, 0) \\ y_\varepsilon(t, 0) \end{pmatrix} = \begin{pmatrix} f_x & f_y \\ g_x & g_y \end{pmatrix}\begin{pmatrix} x_\varepsilon(t, 0) \\ y_\varepsilon(t, 0) \end{pmatrix} + \begin{pmatrix} f_\varepsilon \\ g_\varepsilon \end{pmatrix},$$

$$\tag{13.4.3}$$

$$x_\varepsilon(0, 0) = \frac{dx_0}{d\varepsilon}(0), \quad y_\varepsilon(T, 0) = \frac{dy_T}{d\varepsilon}(0).$$

Being a linear BVP (with possibly time-varying coefficients) we know that there is a solution to (13.4.3); see chapter 10 for methods to solve (13.4.3) for $x_\varepsilon(t, 0)$ and $y_\varepsilon(t, 0)$. We see that the perturbation of (13.4.1), a nonlinear BVP, produces (13.4.3), a linear BVP, which is a more tractable problem. To compute higher-order approximations of x and y, we compute higher-order derivatives with respect to ε, producing at each stage a linear BVP. In the next section we will solve a broad class of problems encountered in economics.

Nonautonomous Perturbations of a Perfect Foresight Model

The most common use of perturbation analysis arises in the study of perfect foresight economic models, and in the equilibrium response to "shocks" near a steady state. We will now consider nonautonomous perturbations of an autonomous equation. Many infinite-horizon, perfect foresight economic models reduce to the differential equations,

$$\dot{\lambda} = g^1(\lambda, k, \varepsilon h(t)), \tag{13.4.4a}$$

$$\dot{k} = g^2(\lambda, k, \varepsilon h(t)), \tag{13.4.4b}$$

with the boundary conditions,

$$\lim_{t \to \infty} |k(t)| < \infty, \quad k(0) = k_0(\varepsilon), \tag{13.4.5}$$

where λ, k are economic variables (both taken to be scalars in this example), ε is a scalar parameter, and $h(t)$ is bounded and eventually constant. The boundary conditions in (13.4.5) tell us that k is a predetermined variable and λ is an endogenous variable. Since the perturbation $h(t)$ is assumed to be eventually constant, the system (13.4.4) is autonomous after some point; we assume that the solution converges to the new steady state, telling us how the system behaves asymptotically. We assume that there is a unique solution to (13.4.4) for each ε. For each value of ε we have a different solution; denote the solutions $\lambda(t, \varepsilon)$ and $k(t, \varepsilon)$, making explicit the dependence on t and ε.

We are often interested in the induced change in a dynamic evaluation function

$$W(\varepsilon) = \int_0^\infty e^{-\rho t} v(\lambda(t, \varepsilon), k(t, \varepsilon)) \, dt,$$

where $v(\lambda, k)$ is the utility or profit flow expressed as a function of λ and k. Therefore we want to know $dW/d\varepsilon$ in the neighborhood of the $\varepsilon = 0$ paths. $W(\varepsilon)$ may represent the present value of profits, utility, or tax revenue, for example, associated with different ε changes. The change in W due to an infinitesimal change in ε is

$$\frac{dW}{d\varepsilon} = \int_0^\infty e^{-\rho t}(v_\lambda \lambda_\varepsilon(t; 0) + v_k k_\varepsilon(t; 0)) \, dt,$$

$$= \begin{pmatrix} v_\lambda(\lambda_0, k_0) \\ v_k(\lambda_0, k_0) \end{pmatrix}^\top \int_0^\infty e^{-\rho t} \begin{pmatrix} \lambda_\varepsilon(t, 0) \\ k_\varepsilon(t, 0) \end{pmatrix} dt, \tag{13.4.6}$$

where $\lambda_\varepsilon(t, \varepsilon), k_\varepsilon(t, \varepsilon)$ are the partial derivatives of $\lambda(t, \varepsilon)$ and $k(t, \varepsilon)$ with respect to ε. Since we are differentiating the functions at $\varepsilon = 0$, these derivatives are evaluated at $\varepsilon = 0$ in (13.4.6). Note that the final integral in (13.4.6) is actually the Laplace transform of $(\lambda_\varepsilon, k_\varepsilon)^\top$, which we denote by $(\Lambda_\varepsilon(s), K_\varepsilon(s))^\top$, evaluated at $s = \rho$.

Differentiation of the system (13.4.4) with respect to ε yields

$$\frac{d}{dt} \begin{pmatrix} \lambda_\varepsilon \\ k_\varepsilon \end{pmatrix} = J \begin{pmatrix} \lambda_\varepsilon \\ k_\varepsilon \end{pmatrix} + \begin{pmatrix} g_3^1(\lambda_0, k_0, 0)h(t) \\ g_3^2(\lambda_0, k_0, 0)h(t) \end{pmatrix}, \tag{13.4.7}$$

where J is the Jacobian of the vector function $G: R^2 \to R^2$ evaluated at (λ_0, k_0) where $G(\lambda, k) = (g^1(\lambda, k, 0), g^2(\lambda, k, 0))^\top$. The Laplace transform of (13.4.7) yields an algebraic equation in the transforms Λ_ε and K_ε; specifically, at each s we have

$$s\begin{pmatrix} \Lambda_\varepsilon(s) \\ K_\varepsilon(s) \end{pmatrix} = J\begin{pmatrix} \Lambda_\varepsilon(s) \\ K_\varepsilon(s) \end{pmatrix} + \begin{pmatrix} \lambda_\varepsilon(0,0) + g_3^1(\lambda_0, k_0, 0)H(s) \\ k_\varepsilon(0,0) + g_3^2(\lambda_0, k_0, 0))H(s) \end{pmatrix}, \tag{13.4.8}$$

where $\lambda_\varepsilon(0,0)$ is the change in λ at $t = 0$ induced by ε and $H(s)$ is the Laplace transform of $h(t)$. $\lambda_\varepsilon(0,0)$ is an unknown at this point, but the initial value of k is fixed, and fixed at $k_0(\varepsilon)$. This fact yields an initial condition for (13.4.7), $k_\varepsilon(0,0) = k_0'(0)$. The basic equation in the transform variables solves easily since for each s it is linear in the unknown $\lambda_\varepsilon(0,0)$, $\Lambda_\varepsilon(s)$, $K_\varepsilon(s)$. Hence

$$\begin{pmatrix} \Lambda_\varepsilon(s) \\ K_\varepsilon(s) \end{pmatrix} = (sI - J)^{-1}\begin{pmatrix} \lambda_\varepsilon(0,0) + g_3^1 H(s) \\ k_0'(0) + g_3^2 H(s) \end{pmatrix} \tag{13.4.9}$$

gives the solution for $\Lambda_\varepsilon(s)$ and $K_\varepsilon(s)$ in terms of $\lambda_\varepsilon(0,0)$.

To pin down $\lambda_\varepsilon(0,0)$, we need another boundary condition for (13.4.7). In order for this problem to be well-defined, we may need some information on the nature of the linearized system; in particular, to ensure the uniqueness of $\lambda_\varepsilon(0,0)$, we will assume that the eigenvalues of the linearized system, J, are distinct, real, and of opposite signs. This is the case in the anticipated economic applications, such as the optimal growth example cited above.[1] Let μ be the positive eigenvalue and ξ the negative eigenvalue.

In many applications, it can be proven that $k_\varepsilon(t,0)$ is bounded; we proceed under this assumption. In this case $K_\varepsilon(s)$ must be finite for all $s > 0$, since $K_\varepsilon(s)$ is $\int_0^\infty e^{-st}k_\varepsilon(t,0)dt$. In particular, $K_\varepsilon(\mu)$ must be finite for any positive eigenvalue, μ. However, if we try to evaluate (4.9) at $s = \mu$, we have a singularity problem. By the definition of μ being an eigenvalue $\mu I - J$ is a singular matrix. The matrix $(sI - J)^{-1}$ is

$$\frac{\begin{pmatrix} s - J_{22} & J_{12} \\ J_{21} & s - J_{11} \end{pmatrix}}{(s - \mu)(s - \xi)}.$$

In particular, the denominator is zero when $s = \mu$. Therefore the only way for $K_\varepsilon(\mu)$ in (13.4.9) to be finite is for

---

1. If the eigenvalues do not split in this fashion, we have either too many solution paths or too few, and perturbation methods are inapplicable because the equilibrium either fails to exist or is indeterminate.

$$\begin{pmatrix} \mu - J_{22} & J_{12} \\ J_{21} & \mu - J_{11} \end{pmatrix} \begin{pmatrix} \lambda_\varepsilon(0,0) + g_3^1 H(\mu) \\ k_0'(0) + g_3^2 H(\mu) \end{pmatrix} = \begin{pmatrix} 0 \\ 0 \end{pmatrix}$$

which implies two conditions for $\lambda_\varepsilon(0,0)$; however, since μ is an eigenvalue, these conditions are not independent so we have a unique $\lambda_\varepsilon(0,0)$. Therefore

$$\lambda_\varepsilon(0,0) = -\frac{(\mu - J_{11})(k_0'(0) + g_3^2 H(\mu))}{J_{21}} - g_3^1 H(\mu)$$

$$= -\frac{J_{12}(k_0'(0) + g_3^2 H(\mu))}{\mu - J_{22}} - g_3^1 H(\mu). \tag{13.4.10}$$

Once we have $\lambda_\varepsilon(0,0)$, (13.4.7) becomes a nonautonomous linear IVP which can be solved by standard methods, yielding a solution for both $k_\varepsilon(t,0)$ and $\lambda_\varepsilon(t,0)$. Substituting (13.4.10) into (13.4.9), and substituting the results into (13.4.6) yields

$$\frac{dW}{d\varepsilon} = \begin{pmatrix} v_\lambda \\ v_k \end{pmatrix}^\top (\rho I - J)^{-1} \begin{pmatrix} g_3^1 (H(\rho) - H(\mu)) - \dfrac{\mu - J_{11}}{J_{21}}(g_3^2 H(\mu) + k_0'(0)) \\ k_0'(0) + g_3^2 H(\rho) \end{pmatrix}.$$

$$\tag{13.4.11}$$

Application to the Simple Growth Model

We saw in chapter 10 that the simple optimal growth problem, (10.7.2), reduces to solving the BVP

$$\dot{c} = \frac{u'(c)}{u''(c)}(\rho - f'(k)),$$

$$\dot{k} = f(k) - c, \tag{13.4.12}$$

$$k(0) = k_0, \qquad 0 < \lim_{t \to \infty} |k(t)| < \infty.$$

We also saw that the steady-state capital stock, k^*, satisfied $f'(k^*) = \rho$, and the steady state consumption, c^*, satisfied $c^* = f(k^*)$. We can express consumption by a policy function, $c(t) = C(k(t))$. Hence $c^* = C(k^*)$. Moreover, since $c(0) = C(k(0))$, we can trace out $C(k)$ by resolving (13.4.12) with different values for $k(0)$.

Suppose that we want to know $C'(k^*)$. $C'(k^*)$ is an important quantity because it tells us how consumption changes as we change the capital stock in the neighborhood of the steady state. We already used a special method to compute $C'(k^*)$ in section 10.7 which led to the solution in (10.7.7). We repeat this problem here to illustrate a more general approach to determining such derivatives. Consider the continuum of problems,

$$\dot{c} = (\rho - f'(k))u'(c)/u''(c),$$

$$\dot{k} = f(k) - c,$$

$$(13.4.13)$$

$$k_0 = k^* + \varepsilon, \qquad 0 < \lim_{t \to \infty} |k(t)| < \infty.$$

Let $c(t, \varepsilon)$ and $k(t, \varepsilon)$ denote the consumption and capital stocks at time t in problem ε. Since $c(0, \varepsilon) = C(k^* + \varepsilon)$, $C'(k^*) = c_\varepsilon(0, 0)$. Applying the linearization (13.4.2) to (13.4.13) at $k = k^*$ and $c = c^*$ produces the linear system

$$\begin{pmatrix} \dot{c}_\varepsilon \\ \dot{k}_\varepsilon \end{pmatrix} = \begin{pmatrix} 0 & -f''u'(c)/u''(c) \\ -1 & \rho \end{pmatrix} \begin{pmatrix} c_\varepsilon, \\ k_\varepsilon \end{pmatrix},$$

$$k_\varepsilon(0, 0) = k_0'(0) = 1.$$

When we apply (13.4.10), we find that $c_\varepsilon(0, 0) = \mu$. Therefore $C'(k^*) = \mu$, the positive eigenvalue which is expressed in (10.7.7). This is a particularly useful application of the perturbation approach, one to which we will return below.

There are many deviations we can examine. For example, we could parameterize the production function as $(1 + \varepsilon h(t))f(k)$. The function $h(t) = 1$ represents an immediate and permanent productivity shock. When $h(t) = 1$, $g^1(c, k, \varepsilon) = (u'(c)/u''(c))(\rho - f'(k)(1 + \varepsilon))$ and $g^2(c, k, \varepsilon) = (1 + \varepsilon)f(k) - c$. Suppose that we are initially in a steady state $\varepsilon = 0$ of the system, namely $k_0 = k^*$ and $c_0 = c^*$ where $g^1(c^*, k^*, 0) = g^2(c^*, k^*, 0) = 0$ define the steady state values, c^* and k^*. Then the solutions are $c(t, 0) = c^*$ and $k(t, 0) = k^*$. Next consider a problem with a small ε. A change in ε away from zero would represent the perturbation of the economy away from the steady state due to an unanticipated immediate output-augmenting change in the production function. The new paths are $c(t, \varepsilon)$ and $k(t, \varepsilon)$. If $h(t)$ were non-constant, then a change in ε represents the introduction of a time-varying change in productivity; if $h(t) = \sin 2\pi t$, we would be modeling predictable, seasonal changes in productivity. In general, the appropriate choice of $h(t)$ and its place in g can represent a large variety of phenomena.

Perturbing Discrete-Time BVP's

As with IVP's, there is no essential difference between continous and discrete time. The discrete-time optimal growth problem, (12.1.12), leads to the discrete-time BVP implicitly defined by

$$u'(c(t)) = \beta u'(c(t+1))F'(k(t+1)),$$

$$k(t+1) = F(k(t)) - c(t), \tag{13.4.14}$$

$$k_0 = k^*, \qquad 0 < \lim_{t\to\infty} |k(t)| < \infty.$$

This is the discrete-time analogue to (13.4.12). Again we set up a continuum of problems parameterized by ε:

$$u'(c(t,\varepsilon)) = \beta u'(c(t+1,\varepsilon))F'(k(t+1,\varepsilon)),$$

$$k(t+1,\varepsilon) = F(k(t,\varepsilon)) - c(t,\varepsilon) \tag{13.4.15}$$

$$k_0 = k(0,\varepsilon) = k^* + \varepsilon, \qquad 0 < \lim_{t\to\infty} |k(t,\varepsilon)| < \infty.$$

At $\varepsilon = 0$ we have the steady state solution $k(t,0) = k^*$ and $c(t,0) = F(k^*) - k^*$. Differentiation of (13.4.15) with respect to ε and evaluating the result at $\varepsilon = 0$ produces a linear discrete-time BVP for the unknown discrete-time derivative functions $k_\varepsilon(t,0)$ and $c_\varepsilon(t,0)$, which can be solved using methods in section 10.2 or, more generally, methods discussed in the linear rational expectations literature; for a review of such methods, see Anderson et al. (1996).

13.5   Continuous-Time Deterministic Control

Many dynamic economic problems are expressed in dynamic programming terms. We first use basic perturbation ideas to compute a Taylor series approximation for the solution to the canonical single-state single-control continuous-time dynamic programming problem. We then illustrate some perturbation ideas by applying them to a simple growth problem.

The general single-state, single-control continuous-time dynamic programming problem is

$$V(x_0) = \max_u \int_0^\infty e^{-rt}\pi(x,u)\,dt$$

$$\text{s.t.} \quad \dot{x} = f(x,u), \tag{13.5.1}$$

$$x(0) = x_0.$$

In chapter 12 we saw that this dynamic programming problem implies the Bellman system for $U(x)$, the optimal control, and $V(x)$:

$$rV(x) = \pi(x, U(x)) + V'(x)f(x, U(x)), \tag{13.5.2a}$$

$$0 = \pi_u(x, U(x)) + V'(x)f_u(x, U(x)). \tag{13.5.2b}$$

Differentiation of (13.5.2a) with respect to x and application of (13.5.2b) yields

$$rV'(x) = \pi_x(x, U(x)) + V''(x)f(x, U(x)) + V'(x)f_x(x, U(x)). \tag{13.5.3}$$

Suppose that there is a steady state to the problem, that is, a value x^* such that $\dot{x} = f(x^*, U(x^*)) = 0$. A steady state is a solution to the nonlinear system

$$0 = f(x^*, u^*),$$

$$0 = \pi_u(x^*, u^*) + V'(x^*)f_u(x^*, u^*), \tag{13.5.4}$$

$$rV'(x^*) = \pi_x(x^*, u^*) + V'(x^*)f_x(x^*, u^*),$$

where the three unknowns are u^*, x^*, and $V'(x^*)$. We assume that (13.5.4) has a solution.

To proceed with the perturbation analysis below, we need to assume differentiability and stability of the problem its solution. We further assume that $V(x)$ and $U(x)$ are C^∞ in some neighborhood of x^* and that the solution $U(x)$ causes $\dot{x} = f(x, U(x))$ to be locally stable near the steady state x^*. These differentiability assumptions are clearly excessive but not unrealistic, since many applications assume that π and f are C^∞. Also we are assuming only local smoothness and stability. If these assumptions are significantly violated, our computations will likely be able to detect that. For example, local stability can be verified by examining the eigenvalues of the linearized system. We want the result to be a good solution over a nontrivial neighborhood of the steady state; if that is not true, the approximation will likely fail the diagnostics we discuss in section 13.9. We now proceed with the formal expansion.

With a steady state in hand, we aim to construct a local approximation to $V(x)$ and $U(x)$ near x^*. That is, we aim to compute the Taylor series expansions

$$V(x) = V(x^*) + V'(x^*)(x - x^*) + \tfrac{1}{2}V''(x^*)(x - x^*)^2 + \cdots,$$

$$U(x) = U(x^*) + U'(x^*)(x - x^*) + \tfrac{1}{2}U''(x^*)(x - x^*)^2 + \cdots. \tag{13.5.5}$$

We have x^*, $u^* = U(x^*)$, and $V'(x^*)$ from (13.5.4). We next move to calculate $U'(x^*)$ and $V''(x^*)$. This will give us a linear approximation to the policy function,

$U(x)$, near x^*. To do this we differentiate (13.5.3) and (13.5.2b) with respect to x to form

$$rV'' = \pi_{xx} + \pi_{ux}U' + V'''f + V''(2f_x + f_uU') + V'(f_{xx} + f_{ux}U'), \tag{13.5.6a}$$

$$0 = \pi_{ux} + \pi_{uu}U' + V''f_u + V(f_{ux} + f_{uu}U'). \tag{13.5.6b}$$

The system (13.5.6) holds at all x; since we don't know $V(x)$ nor $U(x)$ for $x \neq x^*$, (13.5.6) cannot tell us anything about their derivatives. However, we need only $U'(x^*)$ and $V'(x^*)$ to construct (13.5.5). To determine these values, we next let $x = x^*$ and impose the steady state conditions on (13.5.6). The result is a quadratic system of two equations,

$$rV'' = \pi_{xx} + \pi_{ux}U' + V''(2f_x + f_uU') + V'(f_{xx} + f_{ux}U'),$$
$$0 = \pi_{ux} + \pi_{uu}U' + V''f_u + V'(f_{ux} + f_{uu}U'). \tag{13.5.7}$$

where now the arguments of all functions in (13.5.7) are the steady state values of u and x, (u^*, x^*).

The key fact is that in the steady state system (13.5.7), we know x^*, $U(x^*)$, $V'(x^*)$, π and its derivatives, and f and its derivatives. This leaves only two unknowns, $U'(x^*)$ and $V''(x^*)$. The system (13.5.7) will have two solution pairs, but only one will make economic sense. In particular, the maximum principle implies not only the first-order condition (13.5.2b), but it also implies that V is concave at x^*. Hence $V''(x^*) < 0$. This concavity condition will often determine the desired solution to (13.5.7). If both solutions to (13.5.7) are consistent with $V''(x^*) < 0$, we cannot continue because that indicates indeterminacy in the underlying problem. We proceed from here under the assumption that there is a unique solution to (13.5.7) with $V''(x^*) < 0$.

At this point we should note that we have another way to compute $U'(x^*)$. In example (13.4.13) we showed how to compute the change in the control as we move the state away from its steady state value; that change is $U'(x^*)$. We could use the result of this BVP approach to compute $U'(x^*)$ and then use (13.5.6a) to compute $V''(x^*)$. This is in fact a little easier because we get $U'(x^*)$ directly when we linearize the corresponding optimal control problem and solve linear differential equations. In contrast, there are multiple solutions in (13.5.7), a quadratic system. In general, it is easier to compute $U'(x^*)$ as in (13.4.13) instead of analyzing the quadratic equation in (13.5.7). The gain here is slight but will be much more important in the multi-dimensional case.

Even though the dynamic programming formulation is not the best way to proceed for the linearization problem, it is advantageous for producing higher-order terms. We now turn to the necessary computations for those higher-order terms. With $U'(x^*)$ and $V''(x^*)$ in hand, we continue this process to get higher-order terms of the Taylor expansion, (13.5.5). Differentiating (13.5.6) with respect to x produces

$$0 = V''''f + V'''(f_x - r + 3(f_x + f_u U')) + U''(\pi_{ux} + 2V''f_u + f_{ux})$$

$$+ \pi_{xxx} + 2\pi_{xxx}U' + V''(3f_{xx} + 3f_{xu}U' + f_{uu}U'U')$$

$$+ V'(f_{xxx} + f_{xu}U' + r_{xux}U' + f_{xuu}U'U'), \tag{13.5.8}$$

$$0 = V'''f_u + U''(\pi_{uu} + V'f_{uu}) + \pi_{uxx} + 2\pi_{uux}U' + V''(2f_{uu}U' + 2f_{ux})$$

$$+ V'(f_{uxx} + 2f_{uxu}U' + f_{uuu}U'U').$$

Again, (13.5.8) is true everywhere. Since we don't know U and V everywhere, (13.5.8) is not useful for $x \neq x^*$. However, at the steady state (13.5.8) implies the linear system

$$\begin{pmatrix} f_x - r + 3(f_x + f_u U') & \pi_{ux} + 2V''f_u + V'f_{ux} \\ f_u & \pi_{uu} + V'f_{uu} \end{pmatrix} \begin{pmatrix} V''' \\ U'' \end{pmatrix} = \begin{pmatrix} A \\ B \end{pmatrix}, \tag{13.5.9}$$

where A and B involve neither $U''(x^*)$ nor $V'''(x^*)$. The matrix in (13.5.9) is a known real matrix at the steady state since $U'(x^*)$ and $V''(x^*)$ are known at this point as is the RHS of (13.5.9). Therefore (13.5.9) implies a unique solution for $U''(x^*)$ and $V'''(x^*)$ as long as the matrix is nonsingular, a condition that can be checked directly in any application.

Note what we have computed. Since we now have the first two derivatives of U at the steady state $x = x^*$, we can use them to compute a quadratic approximation of $U(x)$ based at x^*, which consists of the terms expressed in the second line of (13.5.5). Since we have the first three derivatives of V at $x = x^*$, we can use them to compute a cubic approximation of $V(x)$ based at x^*. We have therefore gone one degree beyond the result of linearizing the system near the steady state.

These manipulations can be continued to get even higher-order terms and poses several questions. Can we replicate this for multidimensional problems to construct multivariate Taylor expansions of policy and value functions? Can this procedure be completely mechanized? How valuable are the further expansions? Is this power series approximation approach an alternative to the numerical techniques explored before? We will address some of these issues below, but first we consider a simple problem where we can see clearly how to compute an arbitrarily long expansion.

Application to the Single Sector Growth Model

To demonstrate these perturbation methods, we will again look at the single-sector, single-good, continuous-time optimal growth problem

$$\max_c \int_0^\infty e^{-\rho t} u(c)\, dt$$

$$\text{s.t.} \quad \dot{k} = f(k) - c, \tag{13.5.10}$$

$$k(0) = k_0.$$

We now take a dynamic programming view instead of the optimal control perspective of (13.4.12). In (13.4.12), we focused on perturbations to the time path of captial and consumption. We will here compute approximations for the policy function.

To simplify the presentation, we will assume that $u(c) = c^{\gamma+1}/(\gamma + 1)$. Equation (10.7.5) shows that $C(k)$, the optimal policy function for the solution to (13.5.10), satisfies the differential equation

$$\gamma C'(k)(f(k) - C(k)) - C(k)(\rho - f'(k)) = 0. \tag{13.5.11}$$

We will use (13.5.11) to compute a Taylor series expansion for $C(k)$. Differentiation of (13.5.11) with respect to k yields

$$\gamma C''(f - C) + \gamma C'(f' - C') - C'(\rho - f') + Cf'' = 0 \tag{13.5.12}$$

Equation (13.5.12) holds at all k; at $k = k^*$ we have $\gamma C'(f' - C') + Cf'' = 0$, which is a quadratic equation in the only unknown, $C'(k^*)$, and which implies that

$$C'(k^*) = \frac{\rho}{2}\left(1 \pm \sqrt{1 + \frac{4f''f}{\gamma f'f'}}\right), \tag{13.5.13}$$

where we use the fact that $\rho = f'(k^*)$ and $f(k^*) = C(k^*)$. Since $\gamma < 0$, (13.5.13) has two solutions, but one is negative. Since we know $C' > 0$, we choose the positive root.

We can do this for an arbitrary number of derivatives. If we take (13.5.11) and differentiate it m times with respect to k we have for all k the identity

$$0 = \gamma \frac{d^m}{dk^m}(C'(f - C)) - \frac{d^m}{dk^m}(C(\rho - f'))$$

$$= \gamma \left(C'(f^{(m)} - C^{(m)}) + \sum_{j=1}^{m-2} \frac{m!}{j!(m-j)!} C^{(j+1)}(f^{(m-j)} - C^{(m-j)}) \right.$$

$$+ mC^{(m)}(f' - C') + C^{(m+1)}(f - C) \right)$$

$$- \left(\sum_{j=0}^{m-1} \frac{m!}{j!(m-j)!} C^{(j)}(-f^{(m-j+1)}) + C^{(m)}(\rho - f') \right). \tag{13.5.14}$$

At the steady state k^*, $f(k^*) = C(k^*)$ and $\rho = f'(k^*)$; therefore at the steady state (13.5.14) reduces to the equality

$$0 = \gamma \left(C'(f^{(m)} - C^{(m)}) + \sum_{j=1}^{m-2} \frac{m!}{j!(m-j)!} C^{(j+1)}(f^{(m-j)} - C^{(m-j)}) \right.$$

$$+ mC^{(m)}(f' - C') \right) - \left(\sum_{j=0}^{m-1} \frac{m!}{j!(m-j)!} C^{(j)}(-f^{(m-j+1)}) \right), \tag{13.5.15}$$

where now f and C are evaluated at $k = k^*$. Equation (13.5.15) implies that $C^{(m)}(k^*)$ is

$$C^{(m)}(k^*) = \left(\gamma \left(C'(k^*)f^{(m)}(k^*) + \sum_{j=1}^{m-2} \frac{m!}{j!(m-j)!} C^{(j+1)}(k^*)(f^{(m-j)}(k^*) - C^{(m-j)}(k^*)) \right) \right.$$

$$- \sum_{j=0}^{m-1} \frac{m!}{j!(m-j)!} C^{(j)}(k^*)(-f^{(m-j+1)}(k^*)) \right)$$

$$\times (\gamma(C'(k^*) - m(f'(k^*) - C'(k^*))))^{-1}. \tag{13.5.6}$$

If $C(k) = \sum_{n=0}^{\infty}(c_n/n!)(k - k^*)^n$, and $f(k) = \sum_{n=0}^{\infty}(f_n/n!)(k - k^*)^n$, are Taylor series expansions, then (13.5.16) implies the iterative scheme

$$c_m = \left(\gamma \left(c_1 f_m + \sum_{j=1}^{m-2} \frac{m!}{j!(m-j)!} c_{j+1}(f_{m-j} - c_{m-j}) \right) \right.$$

$$- \sum_{j=0}^{m-1} \frac{m!}{j!(m-j)!} c_j(-f_{m-j+1}) \right) (\gamma(c_1 - m(\rho - c_1)))^{-1}. \tag{13.5.17}$$

Table 13.1
Errors of the (13.5.17) solution to (13.5.10)

k	c	E_{10}	E_{120}
0.01	0.03782	2.0(−2)	2.2(−3)
0.05	0.06288	6.7(−3)	1.3(−3)
0.20	0.10272	3.0(−4)	2.2(−4)
0.50	0.14780	1.1(−5)	1.2(−5)
0.80	0.18092	1.7(−6)	1.7(−7)
0.90	0.19069	8.8(−9)	8.8(−9)
0.98	0.19817	1.2(−11)	1.2(−11)
1.00	0.20000	0	0
1.02	0.20182	1.2(−11)	1.8(−11)
1.10	0.20893	6.5(−9)	6.5(−9)
1.20	0.21754	9.1(−8)	9.1(−8)
1.40	0.23394	1.2(−6)	1.1(−6)
2.00	0.27840	9.1(−4)	6.3(−4)
2.09	0.28461	2.2(−3)	1.2(0)

These calculations compute the Taylor series for $C(k)$. The series defined in (13.5.17) may have poor convergence properties. In particular, it may have a singularity at $k = 0$ because $f(k)$ has infinite derivatives at $k = 0$. Since $C(k)$ is related to $f(k)$, it would not be surprising if the Taylor series for $C(k)$ were similarly behaved.

We illustrate the accuracy of the Taylor series defined in (13.5.7) by comparing them to the approximation from reverse shooting. Table 13.1 considers the case of $f(k) = 0.2k^{0.25}$, $u(c) = c^{-1}$, and $\rho = 0.05$. The columns labeled E_{10} and E_{120} display the magnitude of the errors of the degree 10 and degree 120 Taylor series approximations of $C(k)$. The "truth" is taken to be the result of a reverse shooting computation of $C(k)$ using RK4 and a step size of 10^{-5}. Both do very well for a large range of k, but the degree 120 expansion does about ten times better for k near 0. For $k > 2$ both expansions break down rapidly. This is expected, since the singularity in f at $k = 0$ makes it unlikely that any meaningful expansion around $k = 1$ has a radius of convergence greater than 1.

The ability to compute such high-order expansions is unusual, and one would seldom compute them even when possible. While it is an exaggeration, this example does illustrate the general structure of perturbation approaches. It also highlights the fact that the high-order terms can be computed, and that they can substantially improve the accuracy of the approximation. The results in table 13.1 also show that the approximation is far from being just locally good.

General Perturbations

So far we have based our approximation on already knowing the solution at a particular point, the steady state. Not all problems have such points. The perturbation idea may still be valuable if we have some examples where we know the entire solution and use these to approximate solutions to "nearby" problems where we initially have no information.

The general idea really is the same when we think in terms of general spaces. Suppose that we are trying to solve a functional equation, $\mathscr{F}(f) = 0$, for f in a function space. Suppose that we know of a similar functional equation $\mathscr{G}$, where we know the solution g^* such that $\mathscr{G}(g^*) = 0$. We then create a parameterized system, $\mathscr{H}(h, \varepsilon) = \varepsilon \mathscr{F}(h) + (1 - \varepsilon)\mathscr{G}(h)$. Let $h(\varepsilon)$ be implicitly defined by $\mathscr{H}(h(\varepsilon), \varepsilon) = 0$. In this form, forming the parameterized continuum of problems, is similar to the homotopy method discussed in chapter 5. To approximate a solution to $\mathscr{G}$, we use the known solution g^* to the equation $\mathscr{H}(\cdot, 0) = 0$ and then perturb $\mathscr{H}(h(\varepsilon), \varepsilon) = 0$ around $h(0) = g^*$ to compute $h_\varepsilon(0)$, $h_{\varepsilon\varepsilon}(0), \ldots$ and form an approximation of $h(1) \doteq h(0) + h_\varepsilon(0) + h_{\varepsilon\varepsilon}(0) + \cdots$ which approximately solves $\mathscr{F}(f) = 0$. This all sounds very abstract but can be illustrated by some simple perturbations of (13.5.11).

Again suppose we are trying to solve (13.5.11). To pin down the equation, we impose the "boundary condition" $C(k^*) = f(k^*)$; that is, we assume that for any choice of utility and production functions, $C(k^*) = f(k^*)$ where k^* is defined by $\rho = f'(k^*)$. Let ε parameterize tastes and/or technology so that we can examine the continuum of problems $\gamma(\varepsilon)$; for example, we assume that the utility function is $u(c) = c^{1+\gamma(\varepsilon)}/(1 + \gamma(\varepsilon))$ and that output is $y = f(k; \varepsilon)$. Equation (13.5.11) then implies the continuum of problems

$$C_k(k, \varepsilon)(f(k, \varepsilon) - C(k, \varepsilon)) + \gamma(\varepsilon)^{-1} C(k, \varepsilon)(f_k(k, \varepsilon) - \rho) = 0 \qquad (13.5.18)$$

with the boundary conditions $C(k^*(\varepsilon), \varepsilon) = f(k^*(\varepsilon), \varepsilon)$. The steady state condition $\rho = f_k(k^*(\varepsilon), \varepsilon)$ defines the function $k^*(\varepsilon)$ which expresses the steady state for each ε. As long as we know the solution to the $\varepsilon = 0$ case, we can attempt to construct an approximation of $C(k, \varepsilon)$ of the form

$$\sum_{i=0}^{n} \frac{\varepsilon^i}{i!} \frac{\partial^i C}{\partial \varepsilon^i}(k, 0).$$

There are several instances where we know the solution to (13.5.18). Suppose that we choose $\varepsilon \equiv -\gamma^{-1}$ to be the perturbation parameter, the differential equation, (13.5.18), for the consumption policy function, $C(k, \varepsilon)$, reduces to

$$C_k(k, \varepsilon)(f(k) - C(k, \varepsilon)) - \varepsilon C(k, \varepsilon)(f'(k) - \rho) = 0. \qquad (13.5.19)$$

When $\varepsilon = 0$, the utility function displays "infinite" curvature and the solution is $C(k, 0) = f(k)$. If we differentiate (13.5.19) with respect to ε, we can compute $C_\varepsilon(k, 0)$, which expresses how $C(k, \varepsilon)$ deviates from $f(k)$ as curvature retreats from infinity. Differentiation of (13.5.19) with respect to ε implies that

$$C_{k\varepsilon}(f - C) + C_k(-C_\varepsilon) - C(f' - \rho) - \varepsilon C_\varepsilon(f' - \rho) = 0. \tag{13.5.20}$$

At $\varepsilon = 0$, $C(k, 0) = f(k)$ and $C_k(k, 0) = f'(k)$. Therefore at all k,

$$C_\varepsilon(k, 0) = f\left(\frac{\rho}{f'} - 1\right) \tag{13.5.21}$$

Further differentiation will yield $C_{\varepsilon\varepsilon}(k, 0)$, $C_{\varepsilon\varepsilon\varepsilon}(k, 0)$, and so on.

For $f(k) = \rho k^\alpha / \alpha$, we have

$$C_{\varepsilon\varepsilon}(k) = \alpha^{-2} 2(\alpha - 1)\rho k^{1-\alpha}(k - k^\alpha),$$

$$C_{\varepsilon\varepsilon\varepsilon}(k) = \alpha^{-3} 6(\alpha - 1)\rho k^{1-2\alpha}(k - k^\alpha)(3k - 2\alpha k - k^\alpha). \tag{13.5.22}$$

We should emphasize the fact that all of these manipulations are formal. We have not presented the mathematical foundation necessary to prove that we are construcing asymptotically valid approximations. This is particularly apparent in the last case where any $\varepsilon < 0$ case implies a convex utility function.

Another example of (13.5.18) begins by noting that if $f(k) = \rho k$, then $C(k) = f(k) = \rho k$. This is the degenerate case where the marginal product of capital is constant and equals the constant pure rate of time preference. Suppose that $f(k)$ is instead a concave production function and $u'(c) = c^\gamma$. Consider the continuum of problems indexed by $\varepsilon \in [0, 1]$:

$$C_k(k, \varepsilon)[(1 - \varepsilon)\rho k + \varepsilon f(k) - C(k, \varepsilon)] + \gamma^{-1}C(k, \varepsilon)(\rho(1 - \varepsilon) + \varepsilon f' - \rho) = 0. \tag{13.5.23}$$

At $\varepsilon = 0$ we have the linear production function ρk and $C(k, 0) = \rho k$. At $\varepsilon = 1$ we have the general production function $f(k)$. By computing $C(k, 0)$, $C_\varepsilon(k, 0)$, $C_{\varepsilon\varepsilon}(k, 0)$, etc., we are computing the change in the consumption function as the production function evolves from the special case of ρk to $f(k)$. Straightforward calculations show that for this perturbation problem

$$C_\varepsilon(k, 0) = \gamma^{-1}(f' - \rho)k + f - \rho k \tag{13.5.24}$$

Further differentiation will yield higher-order derivatives.

A third example of (13.5.18) can be based on Chang's (1988) result that when $f(k) = \rho k^\alpha / \alpha$, $u(c) = c^{1+\gamma}/(1 + \gamma)$, and $\gamma = -\alpha$, equation (13.5.11) has the solution

$C(k) = \theta k$, where $\theta = -\rho/\gamma = \rho/\alpha$. This is another kind of special case around which we can perturb the problem. Suppose that we have $\gamma(\varepsilon) = \varepsilon - \alpha$ and want to find an approximate solution for γ near $-\alpha$. The system (13.5.18) becomes

$$(-\alpha + \varepsilon)C_k(k,\varepsilon)(f(k) - C(k,\varepsilon)) + C(k,\varepsilon)(f'(k) - \rho) = 0. \tag{13.5.25}$$

Perturbing (13.5.25) at $\varepsilon = 0$ yields

$$C_k(f - C) - \alpha(C_{k\varepsilon}(f - C) - C_kC_\varepsilon) + C_\varepsilon(f' - \rho) = 0, \tag{13.5.26}$$

which is the linear ordinary differential equation

$$\alpha C_{\varepsilon k}(f - C) - C_\varepsilon(\alpha C_k + (f' - \rho)) = C_k(f - C) \tag{13.5.27}$$

in the unknown function $C_\varepsilon(k,0)$. Furthermore we know that $C(k,0) = \theta k$ and $f(k) = \rho k^\alpha/\alpha$; this reduces (13.5.27) to

$$\psi'(x)(\rho k^\alpha - \rho k) - \psi(k)\rho k^{\alpha-1} = \rho^2\alpha^{-2}(k^\alpha - k), \tag{13.5.28}$$

where $\psi(k) = C_\varepsilon(k,0)$. We also know that the steady state is unaffected by such changes; hence we have the boundary condition $\psi(k^*) = C_\varepsilon(k^*,\varepsilon) = 0$ for all ε. This boundary condition guarantees a bounded solution for the linear differential equation in (13.5.28).

This perturbation is much more complex than the previous two but more typical of the outcome of perturbing a dynamic system. It corresponds with common sense: Differentiating a nonlinear system of real equations generally produces a linear set of real equations, and differentiating a system of nonlinear differential equations generally produces a system of linear differential equations. The first examples in this section were unusual in that perturbing nonlinear differential equations produced algebraic equations that can be viewed as degenerate linear differential equations. The linear differential equation (13.5.28) may itself be difficult to solve. However, it is a linear problem, and reliable numerical methods are available even if there is no closed-form solution. There is no guarantee that the problems which must be solved as part of a regular perturbation procedure are analytically soluble; they just happen to be in our simple examples. However, these problems will be more tractable than the original nonlinear problem being approximated, since the perturbation equations are generally linear.

13.6   Stochastic Control

We next add uncertainty to the infinite-horizon, single-state, single-control problem. The canonical problem is

$$V(x_0) = \max_u E\left\{ \int_0^\infty e^{-pt}\pi(x,u)\,dt \mid x(0) = x_0 \right\}$$

$$\text{s.t.} \quad dx = f(x,u)\,dt + \sqrt{2\varepsilon\sigma(x,u)}\,dz,$$

$$x(0) = x_0.$$

(13.6.1)

While dependence of (13.6.1) on ε is normally surppressed in the notation, we will add ε as a parameter and express the value function as $V(x,\varepsilon)$, emphasizing the fact that we are using the $\varepsilon = 0$ case as the basis of our approximation. If $V(x,\varepsilon)$ is C^2 in x, then stochastic optimal control theory (see equation 12.2.13) implies that for each ε, the value function $V(x,\varepsilon)$ solves the Bellman equation:

$$pV(x,\varepsilon) = \max_u \pi(x,u) + V_x(x,\varepsilon)f(x,u) + \varepsilon\sigma(x,u)V_{xx}(x,\varepsilon).$$

(13.6.2)

Proceeding as in the deterministic case, we let $u = U(x,\varepsilon)$ denote the control rule and find that (13.6.2) implies the system

$$pV = \pi + V_x f + \varepsilon\sigma V_{xx},$$

(13.6.3)

$$0 = \pi_u + V_x f_u + \varepsilon\sigma_u V_{xx}.$$

(13.6.4)

Of course we drop arguments of functions whenever they can be understood from context.

Formally we are again looking for the terms of the Taylor expansions of C and V, which are here expressed as

$$U(x,\varepsilon) \doteq U(x^*,0) + U_x(x^*,0)(x - x^*) + U_\varepsilon(x^*,0)\varepsilon$$

$$+ \frac{U_{xx}(x^*,0)(x - x^*)^2}{2} + U_{\varepsilon x}(x^*,0)\varepsilon(x - x^*) + \frac{U_{\varepsilon\varepsilon}(x^*,0)\varepsilon^2}{2} + \cdots, \quad (13.6.5)$$

$$V(x,\varepsilon) \doteq V(x^*,0) + V_x(x^*,0)(x - x^*) + V_\varepsilon(x^*,0)\varepsilon$$

$$+ \frac{V_{xx}(x^*,0)(x - x^*)^2}{2} + V_{\varepsilon x}(x^*,0)\varepsilon(x - x^*) + \frac{V_{\varepsilon\varepsilon}(x^*,0)\varepsilon^2}{2} + \cdots. \quad (13.6.6)$$

The validity of these simple methods in this case is surprising. Equations (13.6.3)–(13.6.3)–(13.6.4) are second-order differential equations when $\varepsilon \neq 0$, but they degenerate to first-order differential equations when $\varepsilon = 0$. Changing ε from zero to a nonzero value is said to induce a *singular perturbation* in the problem because of this change of order. Normally much more subtle and sophisticated techniques are required to use the $\varepsilon = 0$ case as a basis of approximation for nonzero ε. The remarkable feature of stochastic control problems, proved by Fleming (1971), is that perturbations of ε can be analyzed as a regular perturbation in ε. Furthermore we must emphasize the fact that $\varepsilon\sigma$ is the instantaneous variance, not the standard deviation. While it may appear that the perturbation is really second order, recall that risk premia are locally linear in variance. A simple regular perturbation analysis may have tried to derive a series in terms of the standard deviation. The important result of Fleming is that for this problem we can proceed in a regular perturbation fashion, but in the variance parameter.

At $\varepsilon = 0$ we have the deterministic solution. Our task now is to determine what happens as ε increases. To do this we differentiate (13.6.3)–(13.6.4) with respect to ε, and apply (13.6.4). This produces

$$rV_\varepsilon = V_{x\varepsilon}f + \sigma V_{xx} + \varepsilon\sigma V_{xx\varepsilon}, \tag{13.6.7}$$

$$0 = \pi_{uu}U_\varepsilon + V_{x\varepsilon}f_u + V_x f_{uu}U_\varepsilon + \sigma_u V_{xx} + \varepsilon\sigma_{uu}U_\varepsilon V_{xx} + \varepsilon\sigma_u V_{xx\varepsilon}. \tag{13.6.8}$$

When we impose $\varepsilon = 0$ and the steady state conditions for the deterministic problem, (13.6.7)–(13.6.8) reduce to

$$rV_\varepsilon = \sigma V_{xx}, \tag{13.6.9}$$

$$0 = \pi_{uu}U_\varepsilon + V_{x\varepsilon}f_u + V_x f_{uu}U_\varepsilon + \sigma_u V_{xx}, \tag{13.6.10}$$

at $\varepsilon = 0$ and $x = x^*$. This is a linear system in the unknowns V_ε and U_ε. Equation (13.6.9) implies that

$$V_\varepsilon = \frac{\sigma}{r} V_{xx}. \tag{13.6.11}$$

This is an intuitive result because it shows that the utility loss due to uncertainty is proportional to the variance and to the curvature of the value function.

To solve for U_ε and $V_{x\varepsilon}$, we differentiate (13.6.7) with respect to x, yielding

$$rV_{x\varepsilon} = V_{xx\varepsilon}f + V_{x\varepsilon}(f_x + f_u U_x) + (\sigma_x + \sigma_u U_x)V_{xx} + \sigma V_{xxx}$$

$$+ \varepsilon(\sigma_x + \sigma_u U_x)V_{xxx} + \varepsilon\sigma V_{xxx\varepsilon} \tag{13.6.12}$$

which at $\varepsilon = 0$ and $x = x^*$ reduces to

$$0 = -rV_{x\varepsilon} + V_{x\varepsilon}(f_x + f_u U_x) + (\sigma_x + \sigma_u U_x)V_{xx} + \sigma V_{xxx}. \tag{13.6.13}$$

Combining (13.6.10) and (13.6.13), we find that $V_{x\varepsilon}(x^*, 0)$ and $U_\varepsilon(x^*, 0)$ are determined by the linear system

$$\begin{pmatrix} \pi_{uu} + V_x f_{uu} & f_u \\ 0 & f_x + f_u U_x - r \end{pmatrix} \begin{pmatrix} U_\varepsilon \\ V_{x\varepsilon} \end{pmatrix} = \begin{pmatrix} -\sigma_u V_{xx} \\ -(\sigma_x + \sigma_u U_x) V_{xx} - \sigma V_{xxx} \end{pmatrix}, \quad (13.6.14)$$

where all functions are evaluated at the steady state value of x and $\varepsilon = 0$.

The results in (13.6.14) are interesting because of the information they require. Note that in order to compute the certainty nonequivalence correction term U_ε, we need to compute first the value of V_{xxx} at the deterministic steady state. Here we see an important application of the higher-order perturbation terms we computed for the deterministic model.

This can be continued to compute even higher-order approximations. Judd and Guu (1993) and Gaspar and Judd (1997) discuss this. These methods are not easy if they are done by hand. However, they can be automated; in fact Judd and Guu provides Mathematica programs and Gaspar and Judd provide Fortran programs to compute these expansions.

13.7 Perturbing Discrete-Time Systems

Since perturbation ideas are often used in discrete-time economic models, we will next show how to apply these ideas to discrete-time problems. Given the differences between continuous- and discrete-time, this attention to discrete-time models is not redundant. In particular, we see that we need to be careful in specifying the perturbation in the stochastic version of this analysis.

Deterministic Discrete-Time Control

We next show how to apply regular perturbation procedures to discrete-time control problems. Consider the problem

$$\max_{u_t} \sum_{t=0}^{\infty} \beta^t \pi(x_t, u_t)$$

$$\text{s.t.} \quad x_{t+1} = f(x_t, u_t), \tag{13.7.1}$$

where x and u are scalars. The Bellman equation is

$$V(x) = \max_u \pi(x, u) + \beta V(f(x, u)) \tag{13.7.2}$$

with the first-order condition

$$0 = \pi_u(x, u) + \beta V'(f(x, u)) f_u(x, u). \tag{13.7.3}$$

The solution is a value function, $V(x)$, and a control law, $U(x)$. The defining pair of equations is

$$V(x) = \pi(x, U(x)) + \beta V(f(x, U(x))), \tag{13.7.4}$$

$$0 = \pi_u(x, U(x)) + \beta V'(f(x, U(x)))f_u(x, U(x)). \tag{13.7.5}$$

To derive a Taylor expansion of $V(x)$ and $U(x)$ near x^*, the steady state, we examine the system

$$0 = \pi_u(x, U(x)) + \beta V'(f(x, U(x)))f_u(x, U(x)), \tag{13.7.6}$$

$$V'(x) = \pi_x(x, U(x)) + \beta V'(f(x, U(x)))f_x(x, U(x)). \tag{13.7.7}$$

The first equation, (13.7.6), is a repetition of (13.7.5). The second condition, (13.7.7), is derived from differentiating (13.7.2) with respect to x and using (13.7.3).

A steady state is a pair (x^*, u^*) such that

$$
\begin{aligned}
x^* &= f(x^*, u^*), \\
0 &= \pi_u(x^*, u^*) + \beta V'(x^*)f_u(x^*, u^*), \\
V(x^*) &= \pi(x^*, u^*) + \beta V(x^*), \\
V'(x^*) &= \pi_x(x^*, u^*) + \beta V'(x^*)f_x(x^*, u^*).
\end{aligned} \tag{13.7.8}
$$

We will assume that these four equations have solutions for the four steady state quantities x^*, u^*, $V(x^*)$, and $V'(x^*)$. As in the continuous-time case we need only assume local uniqueness and stability.

Differentiating (13.7.6)–(13.6.7) with respect to x yields

$$0 = \pi_{ux} + \pi_{uu} U' + \beta V''(f)[f_x + f_u U']f_u + \beta V'(f)[f_{ux} + f_{uu} U'], \tag{13.7.9}$$

$$V'' = \pi_{xx} + \pi_{xu} U' + \beta V''(f)[f_x + f_u U']f_x + \beta V'(f)[f_{xx} + f_{xu} U']. \tag{13.7.10}$$

At the steady state, $x^* = f(x^*, u^*)$. Therefore the steady state version of the system (13.7.9)–(13.7.10) is

$$
\begin{aligned}
0 = {}& \pi_{ux}(x^*, u^*) + \pi_{uu}(x^*, u^*)U'(x^*) \\
&+ \beta V''(x^*)[f_x(x^*, u^*) + f_u(x^*, u^*)U'(x^*)]f_u(x^*, u^*) \\
&+ \beta V'(x^*)[f_{ux}(x^*, u^*) + f_{uu}(x^*, u^*)U'(x^*)],
\end{aligned} \tag{13.7.11}
$$

$$V''(x^*) = \pi_{xx}(x^*, u^*) + \pi_{xu}(x^*, u^*)U'(x^*)$$
$$+ \beta V''(x^*)[f_x(x^*, u^*) + f_u(x^*, u^*)U'(x^*)]f_x(x^*, u^*)$$
$$+ \beta V'(x^*)[f_{xx}(x^*, u^*) + f_{xu}(x^*, u^*)U'(x^*)]. \tag{13.7.12}$$

These equations define a quadratic system for the unknowns $V''(x^*)$ and $U'(x^*)$. Again we use concavity to pick the correct solution, or we could compute these quantities by solving the corresponding discrete-time BVP.

Deterministic Growth

Let us take once more the simple optimal growth problem

$$\max_{c_t} \sum_{t=0}^{\infty} \beta^t u(c_t) \tag{13.7.13}$$

s.t. $k_{t+1} = F(k_t) - c_t.$

We could proceed as in the previous section. Instead, we will take a different approach, similar to that taken in Christiano (1990). The solution can be expressed as a policy function, $C(k)$, satisfying the Euler equation

$$u'(C(k)) = \beta u'(C(F(k) - C(k)))F'(F(k) - C(k)). \tag{13.7.14}$$

At the steady state, k^*, we have $F(k^*) - C(k^*) = k^*$, where (13.7.14) implies that $u'(C(k^*)) = \beta u'(C(k^*))F'(k^*)$, which in turn implies the steady state condition $1 = \beta F'(k^*)$ which uniquely determines k^*. Furthermore $k^* = F(k^*) - C(k^*)$ determines $C(k^*)$.

Taking the derivative of (13.7.14) with respect to k implies that

$$u''(C)C' = \beta u''(C(F - C))C'(F - C)[F' - C']F'(F - C)$$
$$+ \beta u'(C(F(k - C)))F''(F - C)[F' - C']. \tag{13.7.15}$$

At $k = k^*$, (13.7.15) reduces to (we will now drop all arguments)

$$u''C' = u''C'[F' - C'] + \beta u'F''[F' - C']. \tag{13.7.16}$$

In (13.7.16) we know the value of all the terms at $k = k^*$ except $C'(k^*)$. Equation (13.7.16) is a quadratic equation in $C'(k^*)$ with the solution

$$C' = \frac{1}{2}\left(1 - F' + \beta \frac{u'}{u''}F'' + \sqrt{\left(-1 + F' - \beta \frac{u'}{u''}F''\right)^2 + 4\frac{u'}{u''}F''}\right). \tag{13.7.17}$$

Most applications end with the computation of $C'(k^*)$, but we next compute higher-order terms of the Taylor expansion of $C(k)$ at $k = k^*$. If we take another derivative of (13.7.15) and set $k = k^*$, we find that $C''(k^*)$ must satisfy

$$u''C'' + u'''C'C'$$

$$= \beta u'''(C'F'(1 - C'))^2 F' + \beta u''C''(F'(1 - C'))^2 F'$$

$$+ 2\beta u''C'F'(1 - C')^2 F'' + \beta u'F'''(1 - C')^2 + \beta u'F''(-C''). \tag{13.7.18}$$

The key fact is that (13.7.18) is a linear equation in the unknown $C''(k^*)$. This analysis can continue to compute higher-order terms. While it is clear that the discrete-time case has greater algebraic complexity than the continuous-time case, symbolic software can easily handle the problems; see Judd and Guu (1993) for Mathematica programs to solve this problem.

Stochastic Growth

We can also apply perturbation ideas to approximate solutions to discrete-time stochastic growth problem, albeit with somewhat greater difficulty to illustrate the ideas, we examine the problem

$$\max_{c_t} E\left\{ \sum_{t=0}^{\infty} \beta^t u(c_t) \right\} \tag{13.7.19}$$

s.t. $k_{t+1} = (1 + \varepsilon z)F(k_t - c_t)$.

In this formulation we are assuming the k_t is the capital stock in hand at the beginning of period t and that out of it must come today's consumption, c_t, with the remaining capital, $k_t - c_t$, used in production and with the resulting output, $(1 + \varepsilon z)F(k_t - c_t)$, serving as the beginning-of-period capital stock in period $t + 1$. This formulation may seem awkward, but it keeps the analysis one-dimensional. If we assume, as is implicit in (13.7.13), that consumption choices are made after output is realized, then consumption depends on $(1 + \varepsilon z)F(k_t)$ which is a function of both z and k_t. We instead want to define the state k so that consumption depends only on k; this is example of how changing the state variable may affect the computational complexity of a problem. Therefore we assume that consumption is chosen and consumed at the beginning of the period, before output has been realized, effectively reducing the available capital stock. So we let ε be a scalar parameter, and assume that the random output in period t is $(1 + \varepsilon z)F(k_t - c_t)$ where z is a mean-zero random variable with unit variance. This analysis will also be different from the continuous-time case because here the perturbation parameter is ε, the standard deviation, not the variance.

Since we have a new state variable, we must redo the deterministic perturbation analysis. The solution of the deterministic case, $\varepsilon = 0$, can be expressed as a policy function, $C(k)$, satisfying the Euler equation

$$u'(C(k)) = \beta u'(C(F(k - C(k))))F'(k - C(k)). \tag{13.7.20}$$

At the steady state, k^*, $F(k^* - C(k^*)) = k^*$, and $1 = \beta F'(k^* - C(k^*))$, conditions which uniquely determine k^* and $C(k^*)$. Taking the derivative of (13.7.20) with respect to k implies that

$$u''(C(k))C'(k) = \beta u''(C(F(k - C(k))))C'(F(k - C(k)))$$
$$\times F'(k - C(k))[1 - C'(k)]F'(k - C(k))$$
$$+ \beta u'(C(F(k - C(k))))F'''(k - C(k))[1 - C'(k)]. \tag{13.7.21}$$

At $k = k^*$, (13.7.21) reduces to (we now drop all arguments of all functions)

$$u''C' = \beta u''C'F'[1 - C']F' + \beta u'F''[1 - C']. \tag{13.7.22}$$

Equation (13.7.22) is a quadratic equation with the solution

$$C' = \frac{1}{2}\left(1 - \beta - \beta^2 \frac{u'}{u''}F'' + \sqrt{\left(1 - \beta - \beta^2 \frac{u'}{u''}F''\right)^2 + 4\frac{u'}{u''}\beta^2 F''}\right).$$

If we take another derivative of (13.7.21) and set $k = k^*$, we find that

$$u''C'' + u'''C'C' = \beta u'''(C'F'(1 - C'))^2 F' + \beta u''C''(F'(1 - C'))^2 F'$$
$$+ 2\beta u''C'F'(1 - C')^2 F'' + \beta u'F'''(1 - C')^2$$
$$+ \beta u'F''(-C''),$$

which is a linear equation in the unknown $C''(k^*)$.

We now examine the fully stochastic problem (13.7.20). Again we express the consumption function in terms of the beginning-of-period capital stock. Note that the current productivity shock does not enter into the consumption function because it is not known at the time consumption is chosen, and the previous period's productivity shock does not affect current consumption beyond its impact on the current capital stock because productivity shocks are assumed to be i.i.d. With uncertainty, the Euler equation is

$$u'(C(k)) = \beta E\{u'(g(\varepsilon, k, z)) R(\varepsilon, k, z)\},\qquad(13.7.23)$$

where

$$g(\varepsilon, k, z) \equiv C((1 + \varepsilon z) F(k - C(k))),$$

$$R(\varepsilon, k, z) = (1 + \varepsilon z) F'(k - C(k)).\qquad(13.7.24)$$

Differentiating (13.7.24) with respect to ε yields (we drop arguments of F and C)

$$g_\varepsilon = C_\varepsilon + C'(zF - (1 + \varepsilon z) F' C_\varepsilon),$$

$$g_{\varepsilon\varepsilon} = C_{\varepsilon\varepsilon} + 2C_\varepsilon'(zF - (1 + \varepsilon z) F' C_\varepsilon) + C''(zF - (1 + \varepsilon z) F' C_\varepsilon)^2,\qquad(13.7.25)$$

$$+ C'(-zF' C_\varepsilon 2 + (1 + \varepsilon z) F''(C_\varepsilon^2 - (1 + \varepsilon z) F'(C_{\varepsilon\varepsilon}).$$

At $\varepsilon = 0$, (13.7.25) implies that

$$g_\varepsilon = C_\varepsilon + C'(zF - F' C_\varepsilon),$$

$$g_{\varepsilon\varepsilon} = C_{\varepsilon\varepsilon} + 2C_\varepsilon'(zF - F' C_\varepsilon) + C''(zF - F' C_\varepsilon)^2\qquad(13.7.26)$$

$$+ C'(-2zF' C_\varepsilon + F'' C_\varepsilon^2 - F' C_{\varepsilon\varepsilon}).$$

Differentiating (13.7.23) with respect to ε shows that

$$u'' C_\varepsilon = \beta E\{u'' g_\varepsilon (1 + \varepsilon z) F' + u' F' z - u'(1 + \varepsilon z) F'' C_\varepsilon\},\qquad(13.7.27)$$

$$u''' C_\varepsilon^2 + u'' C_{\varepsilon\varepsilon} = \beta E\{u''' g_\varepsilon^2 (1 + \varepsilon z) F' + 2u'' g_\varepsilon F' z$$

$$- 2u'' g_\varepsilon (1 + \varepsilon z) F'' C_\varepsilon + u'' g_{\varepsilon\varepsilon}(1 + \varepsilon z) F'$$

$$- 2u' zF'' C_\varepsilon + u'(1 + \varepsilon z) F''' C_\varepsilon^2 - u'(1 + \varepsilon z) F'' C_{\varepsilon\varepsilon}\}.\qquad(13.7.28)$$

Since $E\{z\} = 0$, we conclude from (13.7.27) that $C_\varepsilon = 0$, which in turn implies that

$$g_\varepsilon = C' zF,$$

$$g_{\varepsilon\varepsilon} = C_{\varepsilon\varepsilon} + 2C_\varepsilon' zF + C''(zF)^2 - C' F' C_{\varepsilon\varepsilon}.$$

Using the second-order terms in (13.7.28), we find that at $\varepsilon = 0$,

$$u''' C_\varepsilon^2 + u'' C_{\varepsilon\varepsilon} = \beta E\{u''' g_\varepsilon^2 F' + 2u'' g_\varepsilon F' z - 2u'' g_\varepsilon F'' C_\varepsilon + u'' g_{\varepsilon\varepsilon} F'$$

$$- 2u' zF'' C_\varepsilon + u' F''' C_\varepsilon^2 - u' F'' C_{\varepsilon\varepsilon}\}.$$

Using the normalization $E\{z^2\} = 1$, we find that

$$u'' C_{\varepsilon\varepsilon} = \beta[u''' C' C' F^2 F' + 2u'' C' F F' + u''(C_{\varepsilon\varepsilon} + C'' F^2 - C' F' C_{\varepsilon\varepsilon})F' - u' F'' C_{\varepsilon\varepsilon}].$$

Solving for $C_{\varepsilon\varepsilon}$ yields

$$C_{\varepsilon\varepsilon} = \frac{u''' C' C' F^2 + 2u'' C' F + u'' C'' F^2}{u'' C' F' + \beta u' F''}.$$

This exercise demonstrates that perturbation methods can also be applied to the discrete-time stochastic growth model, albeit at somewhat greater cost.

13.8 Perturbing Jump Process Control Problems

Our examples have concentrated on economic growth problems. In this section we use perturbation methods to examine a "patent race" problem, which is a simple jump process control problem. We do this because such problems have a structure very different from those studied above.

In this problem the controller is trying to reach some state at which he stops and receives a payment; we call it a patent race because it is similar to the problem a research and development program faces. The example below assumes a monopolist; Judd (1985) discusses the duopoly case. In this problem, the state is x, the distance from the objective; specifically, $x \leq 0$ and the prize is P and won when $x = 0$. The control is u, which is the instantaneous probability that progress will be made, and its cost is $\alpha u^2/2$. If the current state is x when a jump occurs and $s > x$ is the point it lands on, the probability density of where it lands is $f(s; x)$; we let $F(x)$ denote the probability that a jump from x will send the state to $x = 0$. If ρ is the rate of utility discount, the Bellman equation for the profit-maximizing control problem is

$$M(x) = \max_u \left\{ -\frac{\alpha u^2}{2} dt + M(x)(1 - \rho dt)(1 - u dt) \right.$$

$$\left. + (1 - \rho dt)\left(\int_x^0 M(s) f(s, x)\, ds \right) u\, dt + P F(x) u\, dt \right\}. \qquad (13.8.1)$$

The implied control law is

$$\alpha u = \int_x^0 M(s) f(s, x)\, ds + P F(x) - M(x). \qquad (13.8.2)$$

When we substitute the control law into (13.8.1), we arrive at

$$0 = \frac{\left(\int_x^0 M(s)f(s,x)\,ds + PF(x) - M(x)\right)^2}{2\alpha} - \rho M(x). \tag{13.8.3}$$

We will compute an approximation of the value function, $M(x)$, valid for an open set of parameter choices. We will take advantage of this example to show how we need to construct a parameter which is small in a meaningful sense. We will solve problems for which the prize, P, is small, since, if $P = 0$, then we know that the solution is $M(x) = 0$. But what does small P mean? If we express P in dollars instead of, say, Japanese yen, we automatically reduce P by two orders of magnitude. But such a change in units has no economic substance. The rule in perturbation methods is that the perturbation parameter should be dimensionless; only then will the concept of "small" not depend on the choice of units. To proceed in this fashion, one should examine dimensionless versions of a problem.

Define $m \equiv M/P$ to be the value of problem (13.8.1) relative to the prize. m is a dimensionless quantity representing the value of the game which will yield a substantive concept of small. Rewritten in terms of m, (13.8.3) becomes

$$m(x) = p\left(\int_x^0 m(s)f(s,x)\,ds + F(x) - m(x)\right)^2, \tag{13.8.4}$$

where $p \equiv P/2\alpha\rho$ is the size of the prize relative to the marginal cost of innovation and the cost of capital. Since the dimension of ρ is $(\text{time})^{-1}$ and that of α is $(\text{dollars}) \times (\text{time})$, p is dimensionless and will be our measure of the prize. Since m, p, f, and F are all dimensionless, (13.8.4) is a dimensionless representation of (13.8.3). When p is zero, (13.8.4) yields the obvious solution, $m(x) = 0$. When expressed in this fashion, we see that p may be zero either because P is zero or because $\alpha\rho$, the "costs," are infinite. The case of $\rho = \infty$ is the case where the controller discounts the future at an infinite rate.

We see that the trivial case of $p = 0$ corresponds to several situations. We are really assuming the the prize is small compared to the slope of the marginal cost curve and the value of the future to the controller. This will imply that the prize is to the first order equal to the costs and that the net profits of an innovator are small relative to the prize. The interpretation that the prize just covers the opportunity costs of innovative activity makes our focus on small p more plausible.

Once we transform (13.8.3) into a dimensionless equation, we also must transform other variables of interest; in particular, the control variable, u. However, u is not dimensionless because it measures effort per unit of time, has dimension time^{-1}, and depends on the time unit. We can rewrite (13.8.2) into the dimensionless form:

$$\tilde{u} \equiv \frac{u}{\rho} = 2p\left(\int_x^0 m(s)f(s,x)\,ds + F(x) - m(x)\right), \tag{13.8.5}$$

where $\tilde{u}$ is the dimensionless rate of effort per normalized unit of time.

We now illustrate computing a local solution to (13.8.4). If $p = 0$, then $m = 0$. We approximate $m(x;p)$ for small p up to $\mathcal{O}(p^n)$:

$$m(x;p) \approx pm_p(x;0) + p^2 m_{pp}(x;0)/2 + \cdots + p^n \frac{1}{n!}\frac{\partial^n m}{\partial p^n}(x,0). \tag{13.8.6}$$

Differentiating (13.8.4) with respect to p and evaluating at $p = 0$ shows that

$$m_p(x;0) = F(x)^2. \tag{13.8.7}$$

Taking a second derivative of (13.8.4) with respect to p, evaluating it at $p = 0$, and using the fact that $\partial m/\partial p\ (x;0) = F(x)^2$, we find that

$$m_{pp}(x;0) = 2F(x)\left(\int_x^0 F(s)^2 f(s,x)\,ds - F(x)^2\right) \tag{13.8.8}$$

Continuing in this fashion, we can recursively compute each derivative of $m(x;0)$ with respect to p justified by the known smoothness of m in terms of p. Note that *no* smoothness of m in x need be assumed.

From these expressions we may infer several obvious properties of the optimal control for small p. For example, if p is small, effort increases as one is closer to the finish. This follows from the observation that the $pF(x)$ term dominates in (13.8.6), implying that u rises as $F(x)$ and x rise. Also u falls as α and ρ rise, an intuitive result, since both represent costs.

13.9 Global Quality Test for Asymptotic Approximations

The ideas underlying the foregoing asymptotic methods validate only a local concept of approximation. In our growth examples, we can be confident about the asymptotic expansion of $C(k)$ around the steady state only for a sufficiently small neighborhood of the steady state. We saw in table 13.1 that the perturbation approximations do quite well even far from the steady state for a simple growth problem, but to do so, we had to find another way to compute the true solution. This approach to accuracy checking is desirable but generally not feasible; if we had the true answer from another method, why would we do a perturbation analysis?

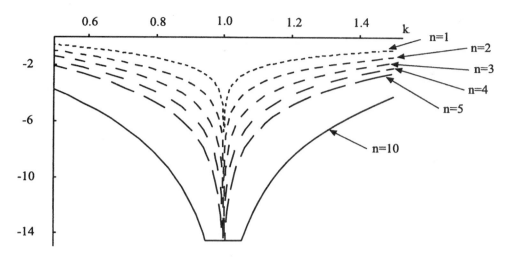

Figure 13.1
Euler equation residuals for Taylor series solutions of (13.5.10)

We next evaluate a simple Euler equation test of the global quality of the asymptotic approximations given in (13.5.17) by computing how well approximations for $C(k)$ do in solving the defining differential equation (13.5.11). More precisely, if $\hat{C}(k)$ is the asymptotic expansion of the consumption policy for (13.5.10), we compute

$$E(k) = \frac{\gamma C'(k)(f(k) - C(k)) - C(k)(\rho - f'(k))}{\rho C(k^*)}. \tag{13.9.1}$$

The definition of $E(k)$ includes a division to create a unit-free expression of the continuous-time Euler equation.

We consider the case of Cobb-Douglas production function with capital share 0.25, $\rho = 0.05$, and utility function c^{-1}. Figure 13.1 plots $\max[\log_{10} E(k), -15]$ for the degree $n = 1, 2, 3, 4, 5$, and 10 expansions; we put a floor at -15, since the computation of $E(k)$ has at most a precision of 10^{-15}. For degree 1 expansions, the log error quickly rises to -1. As we increase n, the log error falls uniformly over the interval [0.5, 1.5]. At $n = 5$, the log error is -2 over the region, and much better on [0.8, 1.2]. At $n = 10$, the log error even better, being -5 over [0.6, 1.4] and displaying essentially zero Euler equation error over [0.9, 1.1]. The quality of the $n = 10$ approximation indicated by our $E(k)$ measure is quite similar to the actual errors indicated in table 13.1 for the same problem.

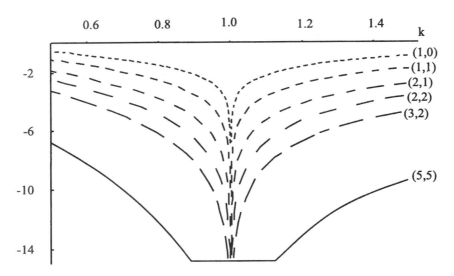

Figure 13.2
Euler equation residuals for Padé solutions of (13.5.10)

The perturbation procedure produces derivatives of $C(k)$ at $k = k^*$. We have so far used them to compute a Taylor expansion for $C(k)$. We could also use the derivative information to produce a Padé expansion. Figure 13.2 displays both the Euler equation errors for the degree 1 Taylor expansion and the $(1, 1)$, $(2, 1)$, $(2, 2)$, $(3, 2)$, and $(5, 5)$ Padé expansions; these choices use the same information as the degree 1, 2, 3, 4, 5, and 10 Taylor expansions. The Padé expansion does better than the Taylor expansion using the same information, particularly for capital stocks far from the steady state.

This example shows that high-order asymptotic expansions can be very accurate away from the central point of the expansion, particularly when Padé expansions are computed. We have also presented a diagnostic test that can be applied to any perturbation approximation and appears to indicate its quality. These expansions and the diagnostic tests can be computed quickly once we know the steady state.

Exercises

1. Consider the optimal growth problem in equation (13.5.10) with $u(c) = c^{0.2}$, $\rho = 0.05$, and Cobb-Douglas $f(k)$ with capital share 0.25 and steady state capital stock equal to 1. Compute the degree 5 Taylor expansion of the optimal consumption rule around the steady state. Compare it to the reverse shooting result.

2.   Compute the Taylor expansion around the steady state of degree 4 in k and degree 2 in ε for
      (13.7.19) with $\beta = 0.9$, $u(c) = \log c$, $\log z \sim N(0, 1)$, and $F(k) = k + 0.2k^{0.25}$. Can you do lengthen
      this to degree 4 in ε.

3.   Compute the degree 1, 2, 3, and 4 approximations of solutions to exercise 10.5 around the steady
      state. Compare the accuracy of the Taylor series approximations to the answers computed there.
      Suppose that we change the laws of motion to $dk_i = I_i dt + \sigma dz_i$ where the dz_i are i.i.d. white noises
      and formulate the problem as in (13.6.1). Compute the Taylor series approximation that is degree
      4 in k and degree 2 in σ. Compare the result to a projection method solution with small Euler
      equation methods.

4.   Compute the degree 1, 2, 3, and 4 approximations of the solution to exercise 10.6 around the steady
      state. Compare the accuracy of the Taylor series approximations to the answer computed there.
      Suppose that we change the laws of motion to $dQ = (q - Q/100)\, dt + \sigma\, dz$ where the dz is white
      noise. Compute the initial terms in the Taylor series expansion of the policy function with respect to
      (Q, σ) based at the deterministic steady state.

5.   Suppose that the production and utility functions in the continuous-time optimal growth problem
      (10.7.2) depends on time as in $f(k, t) = (1 + Ah(t))k^{\alpha}$ and $u(c, t) = (1 + Bg(t))c^{1+\gamma}/(1 + \gamma)$, where
      h and g are periodic with period one; that is, $h(t + 1) = h(t)$ for all t, and similarly for g. Linearize
      the resulting dynamic system to determine how the seasonal factors $h(t)$ and $g(t)$ affect the season-
      ality of output, savings, and interest rates.

6.   Consider the stochastic growth model with adjustment costs in exercise 12.7. Derive its HJB equa-
      tion, and compute some low-order Taylor expansions for the optimal consumption policy function
      around the deterministic steady state in terms of k and σ.

14 Regular Perturbations in Multidimensional Systems

We continue our study of perturbation methods, generalizing the methods of the previous chapter to the case of several dimensions. This extension is necessary to handle important questions with multiple capital stocks, multiple states, and heterogeneous agents. This results in a substantial increase in complexity, but the basic ideas remain unchanged.

We first review the multivariate version of the implicit function theorem. When we attempt to move beyond the simple linear term, we run into substantial notational problems since the objects being calculated are *tensors*, which are generalizations of matrices and vectors. We introduce Einstein summation notation which allows us to compactly express the nonlinear terms in a multivariate Taylor series expansion. This tensor notation approach also helps us write computer procedures to do these calculations, since tensor manipulations are easily implemented by symbolic manipulation programming languages such as MACSYMA, Maple, and Mathematica.

We then illustrate how to perturb multidimensional boundary value problems similar to those that arise in dynamic control problems. We first extend the Einstein summation notation to make it appropriate for optimal control problems, and then compute multivariate, nonlinear Taylor series expansions of solutions to both continuous- and discrete-time deterministic multidimensional control problems, and for stochastic continuous-time multidimensional control problems.

14.1 Multidimensional Comparative Statics and Tensor Notation

We first review the simple mechanics of comparative statics and the implicit function theorem. We then develop the tensor notation which is necessary to efficiently express the critical formulas for multidimensional analysis.

Multivariate Linear Approximation

Theorem 13.1.1 stated the general implicit function theorem for R^n. Comparative statics for multidimensional systems are constructed using this theorem and implicit differentiation. Let

$$H(x, h(x)) = 0 \tag{14.1.1}$$

implicitly define $h: R^n \to R^m$, where $H: R^n \times R^m \to R^m$. Suppose that we know $H(x_0, y_0) = 0$; then $h(x_0) = y_0$. Implicit differentiation of (14.1.1) with respect to x and evaluating the result at $x = x_0$ shows that the Jacobian h_x at $x = x_0$ is

$$h_x(x_0) = -H_y(x_0, y_0)^{-1} H_x(x_0, y_0), \tag{14.1.2}$$

which is well-defined as long as $H_y(x_0, y_0)$ is nonsingular. Equation (14.1.2) is the comparative static vector which expresses how $h(x)$ changes as we move x away from x_0.

The linear approximation of $h(x)$ based at $x = x_0$ is

$$h(x) \doteq h(x_0) + h_x(x_0)(x - x_0). \tag{14.1.3}$$

Equation (14.1.3) is just the beginning of the multivariate Taylor series approximation of $h(x)$ based at x_0. One may wonder why we would want to go beyond the first-order expression of (14.1.3) and construct higher-order terms of the Taylor series expansion, equation (1.6.2). While such higher-order terms may not be useful in *the qualitative* comparative static expressions we often see in economic analysis, they may be useful as a *numerical* approximation of $h(x)$ for x not too far from x_0. To do this in a clean and compact fashion, we need tensor notation.

Tensor Notation

In multidimensional perturbation problems, we use the multidimensional chain rule. Unfortunately, when applying the chain rule in R^n, we will have many summations, and conventional notation becomes unwieldy. To see this, look back on theorem 6.11.3; the central expression is one cluttered with several $\sum$ and ∂ signs. The *Einstein summation notation* for tensors and its adaptations will give us a natural way to address the notational problems.[1]

Tensor notation is just a way of dealing with multidimensional collections of numbers and operations involving them. First, suppose that a_i is a collection of numbers indexed by $i = 1, \ldots, n$, and that x^i is a singly indexed collection of real numbers. Then

$$a_i x^i \equiv \sum_i a_i x^i. \tag{14.1.4}$$

In this way we eliminate the $\sum$ symbol in sums. Of course one has to remember that the summation is over n dimensions, since n is not explicitly expressed; the value of n is understood in actual applications. Similarly suppose that a_{ij} is a collection of numbers indexed by $i, j = 1, \ldots, n$, and that x^i and y^j are singly indexed collections of real numbers. Then

1. The dubious reader should try to read the formulas in Bensoussan (1988) where conventional notation is used. We should also note that we use here only the notation of tensors, not the machinery of differential geometry which often accompanies the use of tensors.

$$a_{ij} x^i y^j \equiv \sum_i \sum_j a_{ij} x^i y^j. \tag{14.1.5}$$

In this way we again eliminate the summation symbols. The second item to note is the location of the index. We will often pair a superscript indexed collection x^i with a subscript indexed collection y_i and write $x^i y_i$ as shorthand for the sum $\sum_i x^i y_i$. On the other hand, $a_i^j x^i y_j$ means that $\sum_i \sum_j a_i^j x^i y_j$. The general rule is that if, in a multiplicative term, an index appears as both a subscript and a superscript, then we understand that we sum over that index and eliminate the $\sum$ symbols that would otherwise appear.

So far all of this looks familiar, since it is just a way of rewriting standard matrix and vector operations. If we think of a_j^i as a matrix, x_i as a row vector, and y^j as a column vector, then the product $x_i y^i$ represents the inner product of the vectors x and y, and $a_j^i x_i y^j$ is the quadratic form of the matrix a with the vectors x and y. We can also form new indexed collections of numbers from products. For example, the product $a_j^i x_i$ can be thought of as a singly indexed collection of numbers, z_j, which can also be thought of as a row vector. Therefore a_j^i acts as a linear map on x, just as a matrix. Unlike the case with vectors and matrices, the order in which we write the terms has no importance. Therefore $x_i y^j = y^j x_i$, and $a_j^i x_i y^j$, $x_i a_j^i y^j$, and $y^j a_j^i x_i$ express the same quadratic form. This is expected, for all we have done is dropped the $\sum$ symbol and multiplication is commutative. While the analogies with matrices and vectors are useful, we should not focus on them because we will be constructing complex collections of real numbers that are neither vectors nor matrices.

As long as indexes are not the same, arbitrary products are allowed. For example, $x_i y_j$ is the doubly indexed set of numbers, b_{ij}, where the (i, j) term equals the product of x_i and y_j; $x_i y_j$ is the *outer product* of x_i and y_j. In general, $a_{j_1,j_2,\dots,j_m}^{i_1,i_2,\dots,i_l}$ is a $l - m$ tensor, a set of numbers indexed by l superscripts and m subscripts. It can be thought of as a scalar-valued multilinear map on $(R^n)^l \times (R^n)^m$. This generalizes the idea that matrices are bilinear maps on $(R^n)^2$. The summation convention becomes particularly useful for higher-order tensors. For example, in R^n,

$$c_{j_3,i_4}^{i_3,j_4} = a_{j_1,j_2,j_3}^{i_1,i_2,i_3} b_{i_1,i_2,i_4}^{j_1,j_2,j_4} \equiv \sum_{i_1=1}^n \sum_{i_2=1}^n \sum_{j_1=1}^n \sum_{j_2=1}^n a_{j_1,j_2,j_3}^{i_1,i_2,i_3} b_{i_1,i_2,i_4}^{j_1,j_2,j_4}.$$

In our use the distinction between superscript and subscripts will not be exploited. Therefore the summation rule applies even if an index appears only as a subscript or only as a superscript. For example, $a^i x^i \equiv \sum_i a^i x^i$ and $a_{ij} x_i y_j \equiv \sum_{i,j} a_{ij} x_i y_j$. Also the "sum over repeated indexes" rule even applies within a single term. For example,

$a_i^i \equiv \sum_i a_i^i$; if we think of a as a matrix, then a_i^i is the trace of a. Also, if a_{ij} is a tensor, then a_{ii} is defined to be $\sum_i a_{ii}$, and is the trace of a.

Tensor-Style Multivariate Calculus

In our applications if $f: R \to R^m$, then f_j will be the derivative of f with respect to x_j. The following equation expresses the multivariate Taylor expansion in tensor notation:

$$f = f(x_0) + f_i(x^i - x_0^i) + \tfrac{1}{2} f_{ij}(x - x^0)^i(x - x^0)^j$$

$$+ \frac{1}{3!} f_{ijl}(x - x^0)^i(x - x^0)^j(x - x^0)^l + \cdots,$$

where $f_i \equiv (\partial f/\partial x_i)(x_0)$, $f_{ij} \equiv (\partial^2 f/\partial x_i \partial x_j)(x_0)$, and so on. This expression is much more compact than the conventional expression displayed in theorem 1.6.2 but conveys the same information. More generally, if $f: R^n \to R^m$, then f_j^i will be the derivative of the ith component of f with respect to x_j. Note that we are deviating from our previous conventions stated in chapter 1 concerning sub- and superscripts. Here x^i refers to the i component of the vector x, but f_i is still the ith component of the gradient of f. Since sub- and superscripts both refer to separate components of a single vector, we cannot distinguish different vectors by this distinction. Therefore different vectors and tensors must use different letters.

We will make extensive use of the multivariate chain rule. If $f: R^n \to R^m$, $g: R^m \to R^l$ and $h(x) = g(f(x))$, then $h: R^n \to R^l$, and the Jacobian of h is

$$h_j^i \equiv \frac{\partial h^i}{\partial x_j} = g_l^i f_j^l.$$

Furthermore the 1–2 tensor of second-order derivatives is

$$h_{jk}^i \equiv \frac{\partial^2 h^i}{\partial x_j \partial x_k} = g_{lm}^i f_k^m f_j^l + g_l^i f_{jk}^l.$$

This can be continued to express arbitrary derivatives.

14.2 Linearization of Multidimensional Dynamic Systems

A frequent technique in studying a dynamical system is to first compute its stationary points, namely its steady states, and then examine the response of the system to small deviations from the steady state; this is expressed in impulse response functions. In the last chapter we showed how to do this for optimal control problems with one state and one control variable. We next develop this technique for problems with several state variables. We begin our discussion of multidimensional systems by reviewing the standard linearization method. In succeeding sections we develop the necessary mathematics for computing higher-order approximations of such systems.

In dynamic economics, multidimensional systems are generally of the form

$$\dot{x} = f(x, \lambda, u),$$

$$\dot{\lambda} = g(x, \lambda, u),$$

$$0 = h(x, \lambda, u, \mu), \tag{14.2.1}$$

$$x(0) = x_0, \quad \lim_{t \to \infty} |x(t)|, |\lambda(t)|, |\mu(t)| < \infty.$$

In optimal control problems, $x \in R^n$ is the state vector, $u \in R^m$ are the controls, $\lambda \in R^n$ is the costate vector, $f: R^n \times R^n \times R^m \to R^n$, $g: R^n \times R^n \times R^m \to R^n$, and $h: R^n \times R^n \times R^m \times R^l \to R^{m+l}$. In other contexts x is the set of predetermined variables the λ are the free dynamic variables; that is, the value of λ at $t = 0$ is not fixed exogenously but rather limited by asymptotic conditions on the system (14.2.1). In general, $\mu \in R^l$ is a collection of nondynamic variables which may arise, say, due to nonlinear constraints on the states and controls. In general dynamic models there is no restriction that x and λ be of equal length; we will stay with the equal length assumption here, but the generalization is direct.

Generally, the vectors u and μ are fixed once x and λ are determined. We therefore assume that the relation $0 = h(x, \lambda, u, \mu)$ can be inverted, yielding functions $\mathscr{U}(x, \lambda)$ and $\mathscr{M}(x, \lambda)$ that satisfy $0 = h(x, \lambda, \mathscr{U}(x, \lambda), \mathscr{M}(x, \lambda))$, and that these expressions can be implicitly differentiated to find the Jacobians $\mathscr{U}_x$ and $\mathscr{U}_\lambda$. In this case we can rewrite (14.2.1) as

$$\dot{x} = f(x, \lambda, \mathscr{U}(x, \lambda)),$$

$$\dot{\lambda} = g(x, \lambda, \mathscr{U}(x, \lambda)). \tag{14.2.2}$$

A steady state of (14.2.1) is a triple $(x^*, \lambda^*) \equiv Z^*$, u^*, and μ^* such that $0 = f(Z^*, u^*) = g(Z^*, u^*) = h(Z^*, u^*, \mu^*)$. We will make a crucial existence and uniqueness assumption about (14.2.1). We assume that for each value of $x(0)$ near the steady state, there is a unique value of $\lambda(0)$ near λ^* such that the system (14.2.1) is bounded. This property of local uniqueness and stability needs to be established by theory. Fortunately failures that are local in nature will be revealed in perturbation analysis.

We next consider what happens to the solution as we slightly change the initial value of x away from the steady state, assuming that the solution to (14.2.1) leads back to the steady state. We proceed in the manner described in section 13.1. We define a continuum of problems all with the dynamic structure of (14.2.2) but with the parameterized initial conditions $x(0, \varepsilon) = x^* + \varepsilon \xi_x(0)$. These initial conditions together with stability will imply the parameterized solutions $x(t, \varepsilon)$ for x and $\lambda(t, \varepsilon)$ for λ. We want to compute both $\xi_\lambda(t) \equiv \lambda_\varepsilon(t, 0)$ and $\xi_x(t) \equiv x_\varepsilon(t, 0)$, the initial deviations of λ and x from their steady state values as we change ε. Our objective is to compute the relation between the exogenous perturbation vector $\xi_x(0)$ and the endogenous $\xi_\lambda(t)$ and $\xi_x(t)$ paths.

To accomplish this, we differentiate (14.2.2) and the parameterized initial conditions $x(0, \varepsilon) = x^* + \varepsilon \xi_x(0)$ with respect to ε. The result is a system of linear differential equations and boundary conditions for $\xi_x(t)$ and $\xi_\lambda(t)$:

$$\dot{\xi} = \begin{pmatrix} \dot{\xi}_x \\ \dot{\xi}_\lambda \end{pmatrix} = \begin{pmatrix} f_x + f_u \mathcal{U}_x & f_\lambda + f_u \mathcal{U}_\lambda \\ g_x + g_u \mathcal{U}_x & g_\lambda + g_u \mathcal{U}_\lambda \end{pmatrix} \begin{pmatrix} \xi_x \\ \xi_\lambda \end{pmatrix}, \tag{14.2.3}$$

where the matrix in (14.2.3), denoted A, is evaluated at Z^*, and where $\xi \equiv (\xi_x^\mathsf{T}, \xi_\lambda^\mathsf{T})^\mathsf{T}$. The solution to (14.2.3) is $\xi = \xi(0) e^{At}$, where $\xi(0)$ is the initial value of ξ. Given a value for $\xi_x(0)$, we fix the value of $\xi_\lambda(0)$ by imposing asymptotic stability on the linear system (14.2.3),

$$\lim_{t \to \infty} |\xi(0) e^{At}| < \infty. \tag{14.2.4}$$

The combination of the initial condition $\xi_x(0)$ and the asymptotic stability condition (14.2.4) on (14.2.3) creates a boundary value problem. We saw in chapter 10 that we solve this problem by writing A in its Jordan canonical form, $N^{-1}DN$, and rearrange and decompose D and N^{-1},

$$D = \begin{pmatrix} D_1 & 0 \\ 0 & D_2 \end{pmatrix}, \quad N^{-1} = \begin{pmatrix} N_{11} & N_{12} \\ N_{21} & N_{22} \end{pmatrix},$$

so that D_1 is stable and D_2 unstable. In this form the solution is

$$\xi_\lambda(0) = -N_{22}^{-1} N_{21} \xi_x(0). \tag{14.2.5}$$

This assumes that N is nonsingular. This is not always satisfied in practice. Even if N is nonsingular, it may be ill-conditioned. If N is singular or ill-conditioned, then one must use another method to solve the linear problem (14.2.3)–(14.2.4). The key goal here is to compute $\xi_\lambda(0)$; how one accomplishes this is not important to the next steps.

In general, the predetermined variables' initial value, $x(0)$, determines the initial value of λ through the stability condition in (14.2.1). Let $\lambda = \Lambda(x)$ be that map for general value of x. Equation (14.2.5) expresses how a small change in x near x^* equal to $\varepsilon\xi_x(0)$ leads to a small change in the predetermined variables equal to $\varepsilon\xi_\lambda(0)$ near the steady state. Equation (14.2.5) tells us that $\Lambda_x(x^*) = -N_{22}^{-1}N_{21}$.

A recursive formulation aims to determine $U(x)$, the functional relation between the control and the state. Our specification (14.2.1) just defines a relation between u and (x, λ) which was denoted $\mathscr{U}(x, \lambda)$. The function $U(x)$ is defined in $U(x) = \mathscr{U}(x, \Lambda(x))$; that is, to find u given x, we first compute $\Lambda(x)$ and then use $\mathscr{U}$. Since $\Lambda_x(x^*) = -N_{22}^{-1}N_{21}$ this implies that

$$\frac{\partial U}{\partial x}(x^*) = \frac{\partial \mathscr{U}}{\partial x}(x^*, \lambda^*) - \frac{\partial \mathscr{U}}{\partial \lambda}(x^*, \lambda^*)\, N_{22}^{-1}N_{21}. \tag{14.2.6}$$

Since $\mathscr{U}_x$ and $\mathscr{U}_\lambda$ can be determined at the steady state, (14.2.6) expresses all the derivatives in $U_x(x^*)$ in terms of the steady state x^* and the derivatives of f, g, and h at the steady state. Equation (14.2.6) expresses the linear approximation of $U(x)$ at $x = x^*$ in terms of the primitives in (14.2.1).

These calculations have produced the relation between the equilibrium value of u and the state x. With this we can determine the dynamic behavior over time of u and x. Substituting $\lambda = \Lambda(x)$ into (14.2.1) produces the equilibrium dynamic law of motion

$$\dot{x} = f(x, \Lambda(x), U(x)), \tag{14.2.7}$$

which is now the equilibrium system expressed solely in terms of x. For x near x^*, (14.2.7) has the linear approximation $\dot{x} = B(x - x^*)$, where

$$B = f_x(x^*, \lambda^*, u^*) + f_\lambda(x^*, \lambda^*, u^*)\Lambda_x(x^*) + f_u(x^*, \lambda^*, u^*)U_x(x^*).$$

Since the linear approximation has the solution e^{Bt}, the *impulse response function* with respect to the state x_i is the ith component of the vector function e^{At} and expresses the impact over time of a "shock" to x at $t = 0$.

Example: Time to Build

We will next linearize a time-to-build model that represents the idea that it takes time for investment expenditures to augment the productive capital stock. We assume two stocks of capital: k_1, the maturing capital, and k_2, the productive capital. Production of the one final good is $f(k_2)$ and is split between consumption c and investment. Investment expenditures consist of two types: additions to k_1 and the costs of the capital maturation process, $\beta_1 k_1$. Productive capital depreciates at the rate δ_2, and maturing capital becomes productive capital at the rate δ_1. Let c be consumption. The resulting optimal control problem is

$$\max_c \int_0^\infty e^{-\rho t} u(c)\, dt$$

(14.2.8)

$$\text{s.t. } \dot{k}_1 = f(k_2) - c - \delta_1 k_1 - \beta_1 k_1,$$

$$\dot{k}_2 = \delta_1 k_1 - \delta_2 k_2.$$

The Hamiltonian is

$$H = u(c) + \lambda_1 (f(k_2) - c - \delta_1 k_1 - \beta_1 k_1) + \lambda_2 (\delta_1 k_1 - \delta_2 k_2),$$

and the costate equations are

$$\dot{\lambda}_1 = \rho \lambda_1 - \lambda_1(-\delta_1 - \beta_1) - \lambda_2 \delta_1,$$

$$\dot{\lambda}_2 = \rho \lambda_2 - \lambda_1 f'(k_2) - \lambda_2(-\delta_2).$$

The maximum principle implies that $0 = u'(c) - \lambda_1$, which can be inverted to define consumption as a function of λ_1, which we will express as $c = C(\lambda_1)$.

The steady state costate conditions are

$$0 = (\rho + \delta_1 + \beta_1)\, \lambda_1 - \lambda_2 \delta_1,$$

$$0 = -\lambda_1 f'(k_2) + \lambda_2 (\rho + \delta_2),$$

which implies that the steady-state stock of productive capital, k_2^*, is the solution to

$$f'(k_2^*) = \frac{(\rho + \delta_1 + \beta_1)\,(\rho + \delta_2)}{\delta_1}.$$

The linearization matrix in (14.2.3) for (14.2.7) around its steady state is

$$A = \begin{pmatrix} -\delta_1 - \beta_1 & f' & -C' & 0 \\ \delta_1 & -\delta_2 & 0 & 0 \\ 0 & 0 & \rho + \delta_1 + \beta_1 & -\delta_1 \\ 0 & -\lambda_1 f'' & -f' & \rho + \delta_2 \end{pmatrix}.$$

The matrix A has four distinct eigenvalues, two stable and two unstable. To continue the example, we make the specific assumptions $u(c) = \log c$, $f(k_2) = k_2^\alpha$,

$\alpha = 0.25$, $\rho = 0.05$, $\delta_1 = 1.0$, $\delta_2 = 0.15$, and $\beta_1 = 0.2$ The steady state is $k_2^* = 1.0$, $k_1^* = 0.15$, $c^* = 0.82$, $\lambda_1^* = 1.2195$, $\lambda_2^* = 1.5244$, and the linearized system matrix is

$$A = \begin{pmatrix} -1.2 & 0.25 & 0.67 & 0 \\ 1.0 & -0.15 & 0 & 0 \\ 0 & 0 & 1.25 & -1.0 \\ 0 & 0.23 & -0.25 & 0.2 \end{pmatrix}.$$

The two stable eigenvectors and eigenvalues are

$$\mu_1 = -1.3721, \quad v_{\mu_1} = \begin{pmatrix} -0.77 \\ 0.63 \\ -0.04 \\ -0.01 \end{pmatrix}, \quad \mu_2 = -0.2568, \quad v_{\mu_2} = \begin{pmatrix} -0.07 \\ 0.73 \\ -0.38 \\ -0.57 \end{pmatrix},$$

and the unstable components are

$$\xi_1 = 0.3068, \quad v_{\xi_1} = \begin{pmatrix} 0.32 \\ 0.71 \\ 0.46 \\ 0.43 \end{pmatrix}, \quad \xi_2 = 1.4221, \quad v_{\xi_2} = \begin{pmatrix} -0.26 \\ -0.16 \\ -0.94 \\ 0.16 \end{pmatrix},$$

A choice for the matrix N is

$$N = \begin{pmatrix} -1.18 & 0.20 & 0.32 & 0.20 \\ 0.57 & 0.54 & -0.40 & -0.88 \\ 0.47 & 0.71 & -0.01 & 0.90 \\ 0.05 & 0.12 & -0.96 & 0.79 \end{pmatrix}.$$

This implies that

$$\Lambda^* \equiv \Lambda_k(k^*) = -N_{22}^{-1} N_{21} = \begin{pmatrix} -0.41 & -0.57 \\ -0.57 & -0.85 \end{pmatrix}.$$

Since $u'(c) = \lambda_1$, we know that $c = \mathcal{U}(k, \lambda) = \lambda_1^{-1}$, and $C(k) = \mathcal{U}(k, \Lambda(k))$, which implies that

$$\begin{pmatrix} C_{k_1} \\ C_{k_2} \end{pmatrix} = \begin{pmatrix} \mathcal{U}_{k_1} + \mathcal{U}_{\lambda_1}\Lambda_{11}^* + \mathcal{U}_{\lambda_2}\Lambda_{12}^* \\ \mathcal{U}_{k_2} + \mathcal{U}_{\lambda_1}\Lambda_{21}^* + \mathcal{U}_{\lambda_2}\Lambda_{22}^* \end{pmatrix} = \begin{pmatrix} 0.28 \\ 0.38 \end{pmatrix}.$$

Since $k_2^* = 1.0$, $k_1^* = 0.15$, and $c^* = 0.82$. The final conclusion is that a one dollar increase in k_2, the productive capital stock, will result in a 38-cent increase in consumption and that a one-dollar increase in k_1, the maturing capital stock, will result in a 28-cent increase in consumption.

Discrete-Time Systems

We can perform the same operations on discrete-time systems. Suppose that $z \in R^m$, $f: R^{2m} \rightarrow R^m$, and we want to solve

$$f(z_t, z_{t+1}) = 0. \tag{14.2.9}$$

In the case of a discrete-time control problem, we should think of z as a stack of state, costate, and control variables. We again begin by computing the steady state equation

$$f(z^*, z^*) = 0 \tag{14.2.10}$$

for, z^*, the steady state value of z. We then linearize (14.2.9) at z^* to arrive at the linear system

$$f_{z_t}(z^*, z^*)(z_t - z^*) + f_{z_{t+1}}(z^*, z^*)(z_{t+1} - z^*) = 0.$$

At this point we have arrived at a linear dynamic model, the kind examined in the linear rational expectations literature. If $f_{z_{t+1}}(z^*, z^*)$ is invertible, we can write

$$z_{t+1} - z^* = -(f_{z_{t+1}}(z^*, z^*))^{-1} f_{z_t}(z^*, z^*)(z_t - z^*)$$

and apply eigenvalue decomposition methods to the discrete-time system. As with the continuous-time case, asymptotic boundedness conditions may tie down the values of the components of z not predetermined. If $f_{z_{t+1}}(z^*, z^*)$ is singular, then special methods are required. The reader is referred to the linear rational expectations literature (e.g., Anderson et al. 1996 for a review) for a discussion of solution methods.

14.3   Locally Asymptotically Stable Multidimensional Control

In section 14.2 we saw how to compute linear and higher-order approximations of near–steady state dynamics. If we were to stay with problems that can be expressed solely in terms of ordinary differential equations, that would suffice. However, many economic problems, particularly those involving uncertainty and strategic behavior, cannot be so simply expressed. We will next develop a multidimensional version of high-order asymptotic techniques for problems in recursive equilibrium form.

The general n-dimensional deterministic control problem with m controls is

$$\max_{u} \int_0^\infty e^{-\rho t} \pi(x, u)\, dt$$

$$\text{s.t.} \quad \dot{x} = f(x, u),$$

(14.3.1)

where $x \in R^n$ is the state, $u \in R^m$ is the control, and π is a concave return function. By the second welfare theorem, the solution to the general problem is also an equilibrium solution to the complete market dynamic equilibrium problem. Since our general problem includes the possibility of multiple consumption goods (represented by components of u), multiple capital stocks (represented by components of x), and multiple agents whose aggregate utility function maximized by equilibrium represented by $\pi(x, u)$, the computed solutions also describe dynamic competitive general equilibrium in such models.

Extended Tensor Notation Conventions

We will use the conventional tensor notation introduced in section 14.1, but we need to adapt it for optimal control problems. Specifically we adopt additional conventions so that we can distinguish between states and controls in an efficient fashion.

In our augmented tensor notation, superscripts will still refer to different components of a tensor, whereas subscripts will refer to derivatives of those component functions. Furthermore, in order to distinguish between states and controls, we will let $i, j, k, l \ldots$, index states and $\alpha, \beta, \gamma, \ldots$, index controls. Therefore, if $f(x, u)$ is a vector-valued function of the state variables x and the controls u, then

$$f \equiv \begin{pmatrix} f^1(x, u) \\ f^2(x, u) \\ \vdots \\ f^n(x, u) \end{pmatrix},$$

where f^i is the ith component function. The matrix of derivatives with respect to the state variables is denoted by the tensor

$$f_i^j(x, u) \equiv \frac{\partial f^j}{\partial x_i}(x, u).$$

Note that at any point (x, u), $f_i^j(x, u)$ is a 1–1 tensor. The derivatives with respect to controls are denoted by the tensor

$$f_\alpha^j(x, u) \equiv \frac{\partial f^j}{\partial u_\alpha}(x, u).$$

and also form a 1–1 tensor. Furthermore the cross derivatives with respect to controls and states are denoted by the tensor

$$f_{\alpha i}^j(x, u) \equiv \frac{\partial^2 f^j}{\partial u_\alpha \partial x_i}(x, u).$$

Continuing in this fashion, we can express any order of derivative of f.

We will frequently run into expressions of the form $f(x, U(x, \varepsilon), \varepsilon)$. In these cases we will need to use the chain rule. For example, if $g(x, \varepsilon) \equiv f(x, U(x, \varepsilon), \varepsilon)$, then

$$\frac{\partial g}{\partial x_i} \equiv g_i = f_i + f_\alpha U_i^\alpha, \quad \frac{\partial g}{\partial \varepsilon} \equiv g_\varepsilon = f_\alpha U_\varepsilon^\alpha + f_\varepsilon.$$

With this extended Einstein notation in hand, we continue our discussion of perturbation methods applied to multidimensional models.

Computing Taylor Series Expansions for General Optimal Control Problems

The general deterministic problem includes an arbitrary complete market dynamic equilibrium with multiple consumption goods (represented by components of u), multiple capital stocks (represented by components of x), and multiple agents whose aggregate utility function maximized by equilibrium represented by $\pi(x, u)$. We will now proceed with a dynamic programming approach to this analysis. The Bellman equation for the value function, $V(x)$, is

$$\rho V(x) = \max_u \, \pi(x, u) + V_i(x) f^i(x, u).$$

The first-order conditions with respect to the u_α, $\alpha = 1, \ldots, m$, are

$$0 = \pi_\alpha(x, u) + V_i(x) f_\alpha^i(x, u). \tag{14.3.2}$$

Equation (14.3.2) looks like one equation, but it is really m equations, one for each α. Since α is not bound by an implicit summation, as i is, it is understood to be free in (14.3.2). The reader must keep this in mind to understand the equations below.

Equations (14.3.2) implicitly define the optimal control, $u = U(x)$, where the policies $u_\alpha = U^\alpha(x)$ must satisfy

$$0 = \pi_\alpha(x, U(x)) + V_i(x) f_\alpha^i(x, U(x)). \tag{14.3.3}$$

In combination, the Bellman equation and (14.3.2) imply the system

$$0 = \pi(x, U(x)) + V_i(x)f^i(x, U(x)) - \rho V(x), \tag{14.3.4}$$

$$0 = \pi_\alpha(x, U(x)) + V_i(x)f_\alpha^i(x, U(x)), \tag{14.3.5}$$

which defines the value function, $V(x)$, and the policy function, $U(x)$.

Our objective here is to solve for both the value function and the policy function. In fact we are going to compute Taylor series expansions

$$V(x) = V(x^0) + V_i(x - x^0)^i + \tfrac{1}{2}V_{ij}(x - x^0)^i(x - x^0)^j$$

$$+ \frac{1}{3!}V_{ijl}(x - x^0)^i(x - x^0)^j(x - x^0)^l + \cdots,$$

$$U^\alpha(x) = U(x^0) + U_i^\alpha(x - x^0)^i + \tfrac{1}{2}U_{ij}^\alpha(x - x^0)^i(x - x^0)^j$$

$$+ \frac{1}{3!}U_{ijl}^\alpha(x - x^0)^i(x - x^0)^j(x - x^0)^l + \cdots. \tag{14.3.6}$$

To compute these U_i^α, U_{ij}^α, U_{ijl}^α, V_i, V_{ij}, and V_{ijl} coefficients, we just differentiate the underlying system, (14.3.4)–(14.3.5), with respect to the x_i, and solve for the undetermined coefficients. If we differentiate (14.3.4) with respect to x_j and use the envelope theorem, we find that

$$\rho V_j = \pi_j + V_{ij}f^i + V_i f_j^i. \tag{14.3.7}$$

In order to keep down the clutter, we will not write the arguments of π, V, and U, and their derivatives, since they will be the same as they are in the basic system, (14.3.4)–(14.3.5), and clear from context.

The steady state is determined by the conditions

$$0 = f^i(u, x),$$

$$\rho V(x) = \pi(x, u) + V_i(x)f^i(x, u),$$

$$0 = \pi_\alpha(u, x) + V_i(x)f_\alpha^i(u, x),$$

$$\rho V_j(x) = \pi_j(u, x) + V_{ij}(x)f^i(u, x) + V_i(x)f_j^i(u, x),$$

which yield the steady state quantities u^*, x^*, $V(x^*)$, and $V_j(x^*)$. Note that the $V_j(x^*)$ values are the linear coefficients in the expansion of V in (14.3.6), and knowing the steady state will also yield $V(x^*)$ and $U(x^*)$, two more terms in (14.3.6).

We next compute the V_{ij} and U_j^β terms. If we differentiate (14.3.5) with respect to the x_j, we find that

$$0 = \pi_{\alpha j} + \pi_{\alpha \beta} U_j^\beta + V_{ij} f_\alpha^i + V_i (f_{\alpha j}^i + f_{\alpha \beta}^i U_j^\beta). \tag{14.3.8}$$

Note that (14.3.8) is a system of conditions, one for each αj pair. In this case we can express U_j^β in terms of V and its derivatives

$$U_j^\beta = -Q^{\alpha \beta} (\pi_{\alpha j} + V_{ij} f_\alpha^i + V_i f_{\alpha j}^i),$$

where $Q^{\alpha \beta}$ is the tensor function defined by $(\pi_{\alpha \beta} + V_i f_{\alpha \beta}^i) Q^{\alpha \beta} = \delta_\beta^\alpha$ where $\delta_\beta^\alpha = 1$ if $\alpha = \beta$ and 0 otherwise. Therefore $Q^{\alpha \beta}$ is the tensor (matrix) inverse of $\pi_{\alpha \beta} + V_i f_{\alpha \beta}^i$. Differentiating (14.3.7) with respect to x_l implies that

$$\rho V_{jl} = \pi_{jl} + \pi_{j\gamma} U_l^\gamma + V_{ijl} f^i + V_{ij} (f_l^i + f_\gamma^i U_l^\gamma)$$
$$+ V_{il} f_j^i + V_i (f_{jl}^i + f_{j\gamma}^i U_l^\gamma). \tag{14.3.9}$$

Substituting our solution for the U_j^β tensor (matrix) into (14.3.9) yields (remember that the U_j^β tensor is the same as the U_l^γ tensor, since the indexes are just dummy variables)

$$\rho V_{jl} = \pi_{jl} + V_{ijl} f^i + V_{ij} f_l^i + V_{il} f_j^i + V_i f_{jl}^i$$
$$- (\pi_{j\gamma} + V_{ij} f_\gamma^i + V_i f_{j\gamma}^i) Q^{\alpha \gamma} (\pi_{\alpha l} + V_{il} f_\alpha^i + V_i f_{\alpha l}^i). \tag{14.3.10}$$

The system of equations in (14.3.10) hold at each state x. If we evaluate (14.3.10) at the steady state, then $f^i = 0$ and (14.3.10) becomes the Riccati-like equation

$$\rho V_{jl} = \pi_{jl} + V_{ij} f_l^i + V_{il} f_j^i + V_i f_{jl}^i$$
$$- (\pi_{j\gamma} + V_{ij} f_\gamma^i + V_i f_{j\gamma}^i) Q^{\alpha \gamma} (\pi_{\alpha l} + V_{il} f_\alpha^i + V_i f_{\alpha l}^i). \tag{14.3.11}$$

Solving the Riccati equation at the steady state yields the steady state values of V_{jl} and, through (14.3.8), the steady state values of U_l^γ. But we already have the solutions for the steady state values of U_l^γ because the U_l^γ tensor is nothing but the linear approximation, $U_x(x^*)$ computed in section 14.2 by applying the eigenvalue decomposition method to linearizing the system (14.2.1). Furthermore that approach is a good one to use to compute U_l^γ. While we have not accomplished anything new at this point, the expressions in (14.3.8) and (14.3.9) lay the foundation for the higher-order terms.

We now find out how easy it is to compute the higher–order terms. Differentiating (14.3.9) with respect to x_m implies that

$$\rho V_{jlm} = \pi_{jlm} + \pi_{jl\gamma} U_m^\gamma + \pi_{jym} U_l^\gamma + \pi_{jy\delta} U_m^\delta U_l^\gamma + \pi_{jy} U_{lm}^\gamma$$

$$+ V_{ijlm} f^i + V_{ijm}(f_l^i + f_\gamma^i U_l^\gamma) + V_{ij}(f_{lm}^i + f_{\gamma m}^i U_l^\gamma + f_\gamma^i U_{lm}^\gamma)$$

$$+ V_{ilm} f_j^i + V_{il}(f_{j\gamma}^i U_m^\gamma + f_{jm}^i) + V_{im}(f_{jl}^i + f_{j\gamma}^i U_l^\gamma)$$

$$+ V_i(f_{jlm}^i + f_{jl\gamma}^i U_m^\gamma + f_{j\gamma m}^i U_l^\gamma + f_{j\gamma}^i U_{lm}^\gamma). \tag{14.3.12}$$

When we rewrite (14.3.8) as

$$0 = (\pi_{\alpha\beta} + V_i f_{\alpha\beta}^i) U_l^\beta + \pi_{\alpha l} + V_{il} f_\alpha^i + V_i f_{\alpha l}^i$$

and differentiate this expression with respect to x_m, we find that

$$0 = (\pi_{\alpha\beta} + V_i f_{\alpha\beta}^i) U_{lm}^\beta$$

$$+ (\pi_{\alpha\beta\gamma} U_m^\gamma + \pi_{\alpha\beta m} + V_{im} f_{\alpha\beta}^i + V_i f_{\alpha\beta m}^i + V_i f_{\alpha\beta\gamma}^i U_m^\gamma) U_l^\beta$$

$$+ \pi_{\alpha lm} + \pi_{\alpha l\gamma} U_m^\gamma + V_{ilm} f_\alpha^i + V_{il}(f_{\alpha m}^i + f_{\alpha\gamma}^i U_m^\gamma)$$

$$+ V_{im} f_{\alpha l}^i + V_i(f_{\alpha lm}^i + f_{\alpha l\gamma}^i U_m^\gamma). \tag{14.3.13}$$

An efficient way to compute the steady state solutions for V_{ilm} and U_{lm}^β in (14.3.13) is immediately apparent. Consider (14.3.13) for a fixed lm pair. The $\pi_{\alpha\beta} + V_i f_{\alpha\beta}^i$ tensor appears repeatedly for each lm pair. Hence we can use the steady state value of the $Q^{\alpha\beta}$ tensor (an inversion which is done just once) to express U_{lm}^β linearly in terms of the known steady state values of various steady state derivatives and V_{ilm}. After we gather terms, it takes just two matrix multiplications for each lm pair to determine the coefficients of the affine representation

$$U_{lm}^\beta = Q^{\alpha\beta}[(\pi_{\alpha\beta\gamma} U_m^\gamma + \pi_{\alpha\beta m} + V_{im} f_{\alpha\beta}^i + V_i f_{\alpha\beta m}^i + V_i f_{\alpha\beta\gamma}^i U_m^\gamma) U_l^\beta$$

$$+ (\pi_{\alpha lm} + \pi_{\alpha l\gamma} U_m^\gamma + V_{il}(f_{\alpha m}^i + f_{\alpha\gamma}^i U_m^\gamma) + V_{im} f_{\alpha l}^i + V_i(f_{\alpha lm}^i + f_{\alpha l\gamma}^i U_m^\gamma)]$$

$$+ (\pi_{\alpha\beta} + V_i f_{\alpha\beta}^i)^{-1} f_\alpha^i V_{ilm}.$$

These representations of the U_{lm}^β can then be substituted into the steady state value of (14.3.12), the critical fact being that $f^i = 0$ in the steady state version of (14.3.12) which kill off the one instance of V_{ijlm} to produce a system of equations linear in the V_{jlm}.

The final important fact is that we can repeat this to compute the third-order terms of U in a similar sequentially linear fashion. We may ask how big can we go in this fashion. Clearly the greater the dimension, the fewer higher-order terms we can add to the expansion. Gaspar and Judd (1997) discuss some of these feasibility issues.

14.4   Perturbations of Discrete-Time Problems

We will now repeat this perturbation analysis for the discrete-time canonical control
problem

$$
V(x) = \max_u \sum_{t=0}^{\infty} \beta^t \pi(x_t, u_t)
$$

$$
\text{s.t.} \quad x_{t+1} = F(x_t, u_t),
$$

$$
x_0 = x,
$$

(14.4.1)

where $x \in R^n$ is the vector of states, $u \in R^m$ the vector of controls, and $F(x, u)$ the law
of motion. Again we begin with the Bellman dynamic programming equation:

$$
V(x) = \max_u \pi(x, u) + \beta V(F(x, u)).
$$

(14.4.2)

If the optimal control law is $u = U(x)$, the first-order condition implies that

$$
0 = \pi_\alpha(x, U(x)) + \beta V_i(F(x, U(x))) F_\alpha^i(x, U(x)),
$$

(14.4.3)

and the envelope theorem applied to the Bellman equation implies that

$$
V_j(x) = \pi_j(x, U(x)) + \beta V_i(F(x, U(x))) F_j^i(x, U(x)).
$$

(14.4.4)

The steady state is defined by values for x, u, and $V_i(x)$, which satisfy

$$
\pi_\alpha(x, u) + \beta V_i(F(x, u)) F_\alpha^i(x, u) = 0,
$$

$$
\pi_j(x, u) + \beta V_i(F(x, u)) F_j^i(x, u) = V_j(x),
$$

(14.4.5)

$$
x - F(x, u) = 0.
$$

We assume that we have found a locally unique and stable steady state, with steady
state solutions to 14.4.6 equal to (x^*, u^*, V_i^*).

We next move to computing U_l^α and V_{jl}. To do this, we differentiate both (14.4.3)
and (14.4.4) with respect to each x_l, yielding the systems

$$
V_{jl}(x) = \pi_{jl} + \pi_{j\alpha} U_l^\alpha + \beta V_{im}(F)[F_l^m + F_\alpha^m U_l^\alpha] F_j^i + \beta V_i(F)[F_{j\alpha}^i U_l^\alpha + F_{jl}^i],
$$

$$
0 = \pi_{\alpha l} + \pi_{\alpha\phi} U_l^\phi + \beta V_{im}(F)[F_\gamma^m U_l^\gamma + F_l^m] F_\alpha^i + \beta V_i(F)[F_{\gamma\alpha}^i U_l^\alpha + F_{\alpha l}^i],
$$

(14.4.6)

where each instance of F, π, and their derivatives is evaluated at $(x, U(x))$, and each
instance of U and its derivatives is evaluated at x. The steady state version of (14.4.6)

$$V_{jl}(x^*) = \pi_{jl} + \pi_{j\alpha}U_l^\alpha + \beta V_{im}(x^*)[F_l^m + F_\alpha^m U_l^\alpha]F_j^i + \beta V_i(x^*)[F_{j\alpha}^i U_l^\alpha + F_{jl}^i],$$

$$0 = \pi_{\alpha l} + \pi_{\alpha\phi}U_l^\phi + \beta V_{im}(x^*)[F_\gamma^m U_l^\gamma + F_l^m]F_\alpha^i + \beta V_i(x^*)[F_{\gamma\alpha}^i U_l^\alpha + F_{\alpha l}^i], \tag{14.4.7}$$

where now each instance of F, π, and their derivatives is evaluated at the steady state values (x^*, u^*), and each instance of U and its derivatives is evaluated at x^*. Note that because $x^* = F(x^*, u^*)$, all instances of V and its derivatives in (14.4.7) are evaluated at x^*. This is the Riccati system of equations for the unknown matrices $U_l^\alpha(x^*, u^*)$ and $V_{jl}(x^*, u^*)$, and it can be solved using the standard methods for solving Riccati systems. However, we can also compute the values of U_l^α via the discrete-time analogue of (14.2.6), and with these values in hand use (14.4.7) to solve for the values of V_{jl}, an easy task since (14.4.7) is linear in the V_{jl} values.

The next step is to compute the quadratic-cubic terms V_{jlm} and U_m^α. To do this, we let $V^+ \equiv V(F(x, U(x)))$, $V_i^+ \equiv V_i(F(x, U(x)))$, etc., and differentiate the system (14.4.6) with respect to x_m, yielding

$$V_{jlm} = \pi_{jlm} + \pi_{jl\alpha}U_m^\alpha + [\pi_{jm\phi} + \pi_{j\alpha\phi}U_m^\alpha]U_l^\phi + \pi_{j\phi}U_{lm}^\phi$$

$$+ \beta V_i^+[F_{jlm}^i + F_{jl\alpha}^i U_m^\alpha + F_{j\phi m}^i U_l^\phi + F_{j\alpha\phi}^i U_m^\alpha U_l^\phi + F_{j\phi}^i U_{lm}^\phi]$$

$$+ \beta V_{in}^+[F_m^n + F_\alpha^n U_m^\alpha][F_{jl}^i + F_{j\phi}^i U_l^\phi]$$

$$+ \beta V_{in}^+[F_l^n + F_\phi^n U_l^\phi][F_{jm}^i + F_{jm}^i U_m^\alpha]$$

$$+ \beta V_{in}^+[F_{lm}^n + F_{l\alpha}^n U_m^\alpha + F_{\phi m}^n U_l^\phi + F_{\alpha\phi}^n U_m^\alpha U_l^\phi + F_\phi^n U_{lm}^\phi]F_j^i$$

$$+ \beta V_{inp}^+[F_m^p + F_\alpha^p U_m^\alpha][F_l^n + F_\phi^n U_l^\phi]F_j^i, \tag{14.4.8}$$

$$0 = \pi_{\alpha lm} + \pi_{\alpha\phi l}U_m^\phi + \pi_{\alpha\phi m}U_l^\phi + \pi_{\alpha\phi\gamma}U_m^\phi U_m^\gamma + \pi_{\alpha\phi}U_{lm}^\phi$$

$$+ \beta V_i^+[F_{\alpha lm}^i + F_{\alpha\gamma l}^i U_m^\gamma + F_{\alpha\phi m}^i U_l^\phi + F_{\alpha\phi\gamma}^i U_l^\phi U_m^\gamma + F_{\alpha\phi}^i U_{lm}^\phi]$$

$$+ \beta V_{in}^+[F_m^n + F_\alpha^n U_m^\alpha][F_{\alpha l}^i + F_{\alpha\phi}^i U_l^\phi]$$

$$+ \beta V_{in}^+[F_l^n + F_\phi^n U_l^\phi][F_{\alpha m}^i + F_{\alpha\phi}^i U_m^\phi]$$

$$+ \beta V_{in}^+[F_{lm}^m + F_{l\gamma}^m U_m^\gamma + F_{\phi m}^m U_l^\phi + F_{\phi\gamma}^m U_m^\gamma U_l^\phi + F_\phi^m U_{lm}^\phi]F_\alpha^i$$

$$+ \beta V_{inp}^+[F_m^p + F_\gamma^p U_m^\gamma][F_l^n + F_\phi^m U_l^\phi]F_\alpha^i. \tag{14.4.9}$$

Equations (14.4.8) and (14.4.9) hold for all x. At x^* we have $F(x^*, U(x^*)) = F(x^*, u^*) = x^*$, and all the V^+ terms and their derivatives become $V(x^*)$ terms. The result is a linear set of equations in the unknown values of $V_{inp}(x^*)$ and $U_{in}^\gamma(x^*)$.

We again see that the higher-order terms can be computed by linear operations. While the discrete-time case is notationally denser, this is not of much concern because it all can be automated. However, the computational burden is substantially greater due to the presence of the composition of functions. Continuous-time formulations are clearly more convenient.

14.5 Multisector Stochastic Growth

For the multidimensional case, the stochastic problem is

$$\max_{u} E\left\{\int_0^\infty e^{-\rho t}\,\pi(x,u)\,dt\,\big|\,x_0\right\}$$

$$\text{s.t.} \quad dx = f(x,u)\,dt + \sqrt{2\varepsilon}\,I\,dz,$$

where dz is a vector of i.i.d. white noises of unit variance; to keep the notation simple, we will assume that the variance-covariance matrix is I. The Bellman equation is

$$0 = \max_{u}\,\pi(x,u) + V_i f^i + \varepsilon V_{ii} - \rho V, \tag{14.5.1}$$

and the Euler equation (the first-order condition) is

$$0 = \pi_\alpha + V_i f_\alpha^i. \tag{14.5.2}$$

Differentiating (14.5.1) with respect to ε and using the envelope theorem yields

$$0 = V_{i\varepsilon} f^i + V_{ii} + \varepsilon V_{ii\varepsilon} - \rho V_\varepsilon. \tag{14.5.3}$$

At the steady state of the deterministic case studied in the previous section, (14.5.3) reduces to $0 = V_{ii} - \rho V_\varepsilon$, which implies that

$$V_\varepsilon = \rho^{-1} V_{ii}. \tag{14.5.4}$$

Equation (14.5.4) tells us, to a first order, how an increase in variance affects the value. The term V_{ii} is the trace of the Hessian of V and is a measure of the curvature of the deterministic value function, so it is known or at least is calculable by the methods used above. Equation (14.5.4) has a natural interpretation. It says that the change in value from adding a unit of variance equals the discounted value of the curvature of the deterministic problem.

We next determine how ε affects U. Differentiating (14.5.3) with respect to x_j implies that

$$0 = V_{ij\varepsilon}f^i + V_{i\varepsilon}(f_\alpha^i U_j^\alpha + f_j^i) + V_{iij} + \varepsilon V_{iij\varepsilon} - \rho V_{j\varepsilon}. \tag{14.5.5}$$

When we impose the steady state requirements, we get

$$0 = V_{i\varepsilon}(f_\alpha^i U_j^\alpha + f_j^i) + V_{iij} - \rho V_{j\varepsilon}. \tag{14.5.6}$$

The derivative of (14.5.2) with respect to ε is

$$0 = \pi_{\alpha\beta}U_\varepsilon^\beta + V_{i\varepsilon}f_\alpha^i + V_i f_{\alpha\beta}^i U_\varepsilon^\beta. \tag{14.5.7}$$

Equations (14.5.6) and (14.5.7) produce U_ε^β and $V_{j\varepsilon}$ at $x = x^*$ and $\varepsilon = 0$.

We next want to see how ε affects the slopes of U which is expressed by the tensor $U_{j\varepsilon}^\beta$. The derivative of (14.5.5) with respect to x_k is

$$0 = V_{ijk\varepsilon}f^i + V_{ij\varepsilon}(f_k^i + f_\alpha^i U_k^\alpha) + V_{ik\varepsilon}(f_\alpha^i U_j^\alpha + f_j^i) + V_{i\varepsilon}(f_{jk}^i + f_{j\alpha}^i U_k^\alpha)$$

$$+ V_{i\varepsilon}(f_{\alpha k}^1 U_j^\alpha + f_{\alpha\beta}^1 U_j^\alpha U_k^\beta + f_\alpha^i U_{jk}^\alpha) + V_{iijk} + \varepsilon V_{iijk\varepsilon} - \rho V_{jk\varepsilon}, \tag{14.5.8}$$

which has the steady state equation

$$0 = V_{ij\varepsilon}(f_k^i + f_\alpha^i U_k^\alpha) + V_{ik\varepsilon}(f_j^i + f_\alpha^i U_j^\alpha) + V_{i\varepsilon}(f_{jk}^i + f_{j\alpha}^i U_k^\alpha$$

$$+ f_{\alpha k}^i U_j^\alpha + f_{\alpha\beta}^i U_j^\alpha U_k^\beta + f_\alpha^i U_{jk}^\alpha) + V_{iijk} - \rho V_{jk\varepsilon}. \tag{14.5.9}$$

The derivative of (14.5.7) with respect to x_k is

$$0 = \pi_{\alpha\beta k}U_\varepsilon^\beta + \pi_{\alpha\beta\gamma}U_\varepsilon^\beta U_k^\gamma + V_{ik\varepsilon}f_\alpha^i + V_{i\varepsilon}(f_{\alpha k}^i + f_{\alpha\beta}^i U_k^\beta)$$

$$+ V_{ik}f_{\alpha\beta}^i U_\varepsilon^\beta + V_i(f_{\alpha\beta k}^i + f_{\alpha\beta\gamma}^i U_k^\gamma)U_\varepsilon^\beta + V_i f_{\alpha\beta}^i U_{\varepsilon k}^\beta. \tag{14.5.10}$$

Equations (14.5.9) and (14.5.10) produce $U_{k\varepsilon}^\beta$ and $V_{jk\varepsilon}$, which tell us how the slopes of the policy function are affected by a change in uncertainty.

This approach can be taken to compute any derivative of U and V with respect to ε; however, we do not continue this here because of the obvious algebraic costs. Again we find that we can compute a formal power series for V in multidimensional problems in a sequentially linear fashion.

Alternative Approaches

Regular perturbation takes an implicit differentiation approach to compute a Taylor series approximation of the nonlinear functions U and V. We showed that this approach can be used to compute both linear and nonlinear approximations to U based at the deterministic steady state. In some areas of economics, this is not the usual approach to finding linear functions that "approximate" optimal and equilibrium policy functions U.

One alternative approach is to find the deterministic steady state but then replace the original nonlinear optimal control problem with a linear-quadratic problem that is similar to the original problem. The linear-quadratic problem can then be solved using standard methods. The resulting linear control law is then used instead of the nonlinear U to analyze the original problem. The strategy of finding a linear-quadratic problem similar to the nonlinear model is an intuitively appealing approach, since we know how to solve linear-quadratic problems.

Magill (1977) applies this approach to the general multivariate problem

$$\max_u \int_0^\infty e^{-\rho t} \pi(x, u)\, dt$$

$$\text{s.t.} \quad dx = f(x, u)dt + \sigma(x)\, dz.$$

(14.5.11)

He first computes the deterministic steady state values of x, u, and λ, the shadow price of x; call them x^*, u^*, and λ^*. He constructs the matrices

$$Q = \begin{pmatrix} \pi_{xx} & \pi_{xu} \\ \pi_{ux} & \pi_{uu} \end{pmatrix} + \sum \lambda_i^* \begin{pmatrix} f_{xx}^i & f_{xu}^i \\ f_{ux}^i & f_{uu}^i \end{pmatrix},$$

$$C = f_x, \, D = f_u,$$

where all functions are evaluated at the steady state. He showed that the solution to

$$\max_{\delta_x, \delta_u} E \left\{ \int_0^\infty e^{-\rho t} \begin{pmatrix} x^* + \delta_x \\ u^* + \delta_u \end{pmatrix}^\top Q \begin{pmatrix} x^* + \delta_x \\ u^* + \delta_u \end{pmatrix} dt \right\}$$

$$\text{s.t.} \quad dx = (C\delta_x + D\delta_u)\, dt + \sigma(x^*)\, dz,$$

locally approximates the solution[2] to (14.5.11) if $\sigma(x) = 0$. Kydland and Prescott (1982) later describes the same procedure but only for the case where f is linear; this linearity restriction implies that the Hessian of $f(x, u)$ is zero, reducing Q to just a linear-quadratic approximation of π near the steady state. In general, however, the quadratic approximation of π is not adequate.

---

2. Magill further describes how to take this linear approximation, form a linear stochastic model, and compute the implied spectral properties of the linear approximation. He proposed taking these spectral results and comparing them to the spectral properties of actual data. Versions of this proposal, usually limited to variance-covariance comparisons, have been used frequently in business cycle analysis. Kydland and Prescott (1982) is an early example of this strategy.

Magill's method differs from the perturbation method in that the idea here is to replace the nonlinear problem with a linear-quadratic problem, whereas the perturbation approach focuses on computing derivatives of the nonlinear problem. In fact Kydland and Prescott, in their implementation of this approach, do not claim to be computing those derivatives. However, Magill's procedure does produce the same linear approximation as we did in section 14.3. Many "linearization" procedures have been offered for dynamic economic models, with the literature making little effort to sort out the differences. Some are probably equivalent with the perturbation approach of mathematical literature, but some are not. In particular, McGrattan (1990) proposed an alternative approach that differs substantially from perturbation.[3] First, she also computes the steady state, (x^*, u^*) of the optimal path. Second, she replaces $\pi(x, u)$ with its quadratic expansion around $x = x^*$ and $u = u^*$, and replaces $f(x, u)$ with its linear expansion around $x = x^*$ and $u = u^*$. She then examines the linear-quadratic problem

$$\max_c \int_0^\infty e^{-\rho t}(\pi(z^*) + \pi_z(z^*)(z - z^*) + \tfrac{1}{2}(z - z^*)^\top \pi_{zz}(z^*)(z - z^*)) \, dt$$

(14.5.12)

s.t. $\dot{x} = f(z^*) + f_z(z^* - z),$

where $z \equiv (x, u)$. This approach is one interpretation of the idea to approximate a nonlinear problem by "linearizing the law of motion and using a quadratic approximation of the objective function near the steady state."

Despite the similarity, the answers from (14.5.12) are substantially different from the answers computed by perturbation methods and Magill's method. To see this, apply (14.5.12) to the simple growth problem

$$\max_c \int_0^\infty e^{-\rho t} u(c) \, dt$$

s.t. $\dot{k} = f(k) - c.$

The resulting approximate policy function is $C(k) = f(k^*) + \rho(k - k^*)$, which is not the true linear approximation of C at k^* and implies behavior very different from that implied by the true solution; in particular, the approximation implies that the rate of convergence to the steady state is zero. The problem is that (14.5.12) leaves

---

3. We discuss the continuous-time version of McGrattan, but there is no mathematically substantive difference between the continuous- and discrete-time versions as far as these issues are concerned.

out the terms in Magill's Q that arise from the curvature of f at the steady state. While this does replace the nonlinear problem with a "similar" linear-quadratic one, it may produce a policy function substantially different from the policy function of the initial nonlinear problem. Also the results are sensitive to changes in the formulation. If, instead of letting c be the control, we choose $I = k$ to be the control and define $c = f(k) - I$, then the results of (14.5.12) will agree with Magill's approach.

This example illustrates the hazards of following an ad hoc approach. The advantage of regular perturbation methods based on an implicit function formulation is that one directly computes the Taylor expansions in terms of whatever variables one wants to use, and that expansion is the best possible asymptotically.

Another important distinction between Magill, McGrattan, and Kydland and Prescott, on the one hand, and the regular perturbation approach, is the way uncertainty is handled. These linear-quadratic approximations ignore the $C_\sigma(k)$ terms computed in section 14.5 and hence are at best only "half-linear" approximations. That is fine for computing the spectrum of consumption, income, and other controls and states (e.g., as is done in Magill), since the C_σ correction disappears in the differencing. However, if one were to use this method to match spectra of, say, asset prices, then there may be problems, for higher-order derivatives of u and f and the value of C_σ may affect the linear behavior of the variables being studied.

Furthermore the motivation behind the quadratic approximation approach is a conceptual dead end if one wants to go beyond this level of approximation. This way of approaching the problem may lead one to think that the way to do a third-order approximation would be to take a third-order polynomial approximation around the deterministic steady state and solving that control problem. Of course there is no exact solution for third-order problems, possibly leading one to think that a third-order approximation is not possible. The approach in this chapter does not lead to any such conceptual blocks because it motivates all calculations from a Taylor series expansion point of view and in fact demonstrates that they are *easier*.

The only assumption made by regular perturbation methods is that the problems are sufficiently differentiable[4] so that the implicit function theorem (or its Banach space generalization) applies. While it is advisable to check for the applicability of the implicit function theorem, we do not do that here; the reader is, however, assured that the examples in this chapter can be so justified. In the next chapter we will see some cases where the implicit function theorem does not hold.

---

4. Differentiability is also implicitly assumed in the ad hoc approaches.

14.6 Further Reading and Summary

This and the previous chapter have presented the general approach of regular perturbation methods for approximating implicitly defined functions. These methods are often used in economics for qualitative analysis, but we show that they also have substantial numerical potential. The mathematical foundations for perturbation methods tell us that they produce good approximations locally. Furthermore we can test any resulting expansion to determine the range over which it is reliable, using our basic "compute but verify" approach.

Regular perturbation methods are based on implicit function theorems. See Zeidler (1986), Krasnosel'skii and Zabreiko (1984), and Aubin and Ekeland (1984) for Banach space versions of implicit function theorems.

The applications to optimal control problems is based on the results in Fleming (1971), Fleming and Souganides (1986), and Bensoussan (1988). Specific applications in the economics literature include Albrecht et al. (1991) and Caputo (1990a, 1990b); Anderson (1993) contains several Mathematica programs for perturbation methods. Dotsey and Mao (1992) evaluates some linearization methods. Judd (1996) reviews economic applications of perturbation methods. The local, certainty equivalent, approximation approach developed in Magill (1977) has been used extensively in real business cycle analyses, but the higher-order procedures have not been used much in economics.

Exercises

1. Assume an exchange economy with two agents with CES utility over two goods. Compute the degree 4 Taylor series for equilibrium based at points where the agents have the same utility and endowment. Repeat for three-agent economies. Compare with nonlinear equation solutions.

2. Compute the degree 1, 2, 3, and 4 approximations of solutions to exercise 10.8 around the steady state. Compare the accuracy of the Taylor series approximations to the answers computed there. Suppose that we change the laws of motion to

    $$dk_c = I_c dt + \varepsilon \sigma_c dz_c,$$

    $$dk_I = I_I dt + \varepsilon \sigma_I dz_I,$$

    where dz_c and dz_I are uncorrelated white noise processes. Compute the first certainty non-equivalence term for the investment policy functions.

3. Compute the quadratic expansion of (14.4.1) around the steady state for $\pi(x, u) = u^{1/2} + 0.01 x^{1/2}$, $\beta = 0.9$, and $F(x, u) = x^{0.25} - u$

15 Advanced Asymptotic Methods

In this chapter we continue our examination of asymptotic methods of approximation. Regular perturbation methods for constructing a function $y = f(x)$ such that $H(x, f(x)) = 0$ near $y_0 = f(x_0)$ are successful when Taylor series computations and simple versions of the implicit function theorem (IFT) are applicable. These methods are not always successful; in particular, the implicit function theorem fails when the Jacobian matrix $H_y(x_0, y_0)$ is singular, and some functions do not possess simple power series expansions. In some cases special techniques can handle these problems and be used to produce approximations similar to Taylor expansions. This chapter presents elementary examples using some of these methods.

Sometimes the IFT fails because there are multiple solutions to $H(x, f(x))$ at (x_0, y_0). Section 15.1 presents bifurcation methods that can often handle such conditions. Section 15.2 applies these methods to portfolio problems. Sometimes implicit solutions are unique, but there does not exist a simple power series expansion. However, power series are special in that they use only integral powers. Section 15.3 introduces the general concepts of a *gauge system* and an *asymptotic approximation*, and section 15.4 introduces the method of undetermined gauges and shows how to use it to solve a simple adverse selection problem.

Economic analyses often find it convenient to assume that uncertainty is small, and therefore would naturally like to compute Taylor expansions around the deterministic case; unfortunately, Taylor expansions often do not exist for such integrals. In section 15.5 we introduce an approach that can approximate such "small noise" integrals.

The final portion of this chapter shows how we can combine the projection and perturbation methods to arrive at hybrid procedures. Both projection and perturbation methods produce a series to approximate a function of interest, but they arrive at this similar condition in very different ways. In hybrid methods, one combines the complementary strengths of perturbation and projection methods to arrive at a hybrid series that does better than either projection or perturbation methods do alone. We outline the general idea and discuss a simple example.

15.1 Bifurcation Methods

Suppose that we want to approximate the function $h(\varepsilon)$ implicitly by $H(h(\varepsilon), \varepsilon) = 0$ at $x_0 = h(0)$ but that the conditions of the IFT, theorem 13.1.1, do not hold; in particular, $H_x(x_0, 0)$ may be singular. Such points may be bifurcation points and can be handled by bifurcation methods, to which we now turn.

The key step comes from l'Hospital's rule. If the assumptions in theorem 13.1.1 hold, then differentiation of the implicit expression $H(h(\varepsilon), \varepsilon) = 0$ with respect to ε

produces the equation

$$h'(0) = -\frac{H_\varepsilon(x_0, 0)}{H_x(x_0, 0)}.$$

But, if $H_x(x_0, 0) = 0$, $h'(0)$ has the form $0/0$ at $x = x_0$. l'Hospital's rule then implies

$$h'(0) = -\frac{H_{\varepsilon\varepsilon}(x_0, 0)}{H_{\varepsilon x}(x_0, 0)}.$$

One way to view the process below is that we first find an x_0 such that $H_x(x_0, 0) = 0$, and then apply l'Hospital's rule to compute $h'(0)$.

The formal approach to these calculations uses ideas from bifurcation theory. We first saw the idea of bifurcations in our discussion of branch points in homotopy methods in chapter 5. Here we will define the notion formally.

DEFINITION   Suppose that $H: X \times R \to X$ and $H(x^0, \varepsilon_0) = 0$. Then (x^0, ε_0) is a *bifurcation point* if there exist two sequences (y^n, ε_n) and (z^n, ε_n) such that $H(y^n, \varepsilon_n) = H(z^n, \varepsilon_n) = 0$, $\lim_{n\to\infty} y^n = \lim_{n\to\infty} z^n = x^0$ and $\lim_{n\to\infty} \varepsilon_n = \varepsilon_0$, but $y^n \neq z^n$ for all n.

DEFINITION   A function $f: R^n \to R^m$ is *diffeomorphic* to $g: R^n \to R^m$ at $z = z_0$ iff there exists a differentiable function $h: R^n \to R^n$ which is invertible at $z = z_0$ and $f(h(z)) = g(z)$ in some open neighborhood of $z = z_0$.

Theorem 15.1.1 shows how we can extend the implicit function theorem near bifurcation points.

THEOREM 15.1.1 (Bifurcation theorem on R)   Suppose that $H: R \times R \to R$ and $H(x, \varepsilon) = 0$ for all x if $\varepsilon = 0$. Furthermore suppose that

$$H_x(x_0, 0) = 0 = H_\varepsilon(x_0, 0), \qquad H_{x\varepsilon}(x_0, 0) \neq 0, \tag{15.1.1}$$

for some $(x_0, 0)$. Then

i. If $H_{\varepsilon\varepsilon}(x_0, 0) \neq 0$, there is an open neighborhood $\mathcal{N}$ of $(x_0, 0)$ and a function $h(\varepsilon), h(\varepsilon) \neq 0$ for $\varepsilon \neq 0$, such that $H(h(\varepsilon), \varepsilon) = 0$ and locally $H(x, \varepsilon)$ is diffeomorphic to $\varepsilon(\varepsilon - x)$ or $\varepsilon(\varepsilon + x)$ on $\mathcal{N}$.

ii. If $H_{\varepsilon\varepsilon}(x_0, 0) = 0 \neq H_{\varepsilon\varepsilon\varepsilon}(x_0, 0)$, then there is an open neighborhood $\mathcal{N}$ of $(x_0, 0)$ and a function $h(\varepsilon), h(\varepsilon) \neq 0$ for $\varepsilon \neq 0$, such that $H(h(\varepsilon), \varepsilon) = 0$ and $H(x, \varepsilon)$ is diffeomorphic to $\varepsilon^3 - x\varepsilon$ or $\varepsilon^3 + x\varepsilon$ on $\mathcal{N}$.

iii. In both cases, $(x_0, 0)$ is a bifurcation point.

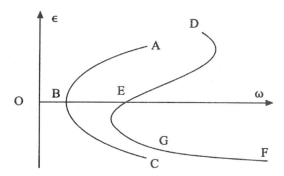

Figure 15.1
Bifurcation points

Figure 15.1 shows both kinds of bifurcations. Suppose that the curve *ABC* together with the ω axis is the zero set of $H(\omega, \varepsilon)$; then *B* is a bifurcation point of the $\varepsilon^3 - \omega\varepsilon$ type of bifurcation, called a *pitchfork bifurcation*. Similarly, if the curve *DEGF* together with the ω axis is a zero set, then *E* is a bifurcation point of $\varepsilon^2 - \omega\varepsilon$ type of bifurcation, called a *transcritical bifurcation*.

We also have a multidimensional version of theorem 15.1.1. In this case we are searching for a one-dimensional path in (x, y) space that satisfies the implicit relation $H(y, x, \varepsilon) = 0$.

THEOREM 15.1.2 (Bifurcation theorem on R^n)   Suppose that $H: R^m \times R^n \times R \to R^n$ and $H(y^0, x, \varepsilon) = 0$ for all x if $\varepsilon = 0$. Furthermore suppose that for some $(y^0, x^0, 0)$, H is analytic in a neighborhood of $(y^0, x^0, 0)$, $H_x(y^0, x^0, 0) = 0_{n \times n}$, $H_\varepsilon(y^0, x^0, 0) = 0_n$, and $\det(H_{x\varepsilon}(y^0, x^0, 0)) \neq 0$. Then there is an open neighborhood $\mathcal{N}$ of $(y^0, x^0, 0)$ and a locally analytic function $h(\varepsilon) \equiv (h^y(\varepsilon), h^x(\varepsilon))$, $h(\varepsilon) \neq 0$ for $\varepsilon \neq 0$, such that $H(h^y(\varepsilon), h^x(\varepsilon), \varepsilon) = 0$ on $\mathcal{N}$.

The proofs of these theorems rely on results in analytic bifurcation theory; see Zeidler (1986). Generalizations of these results for x, y, and ε in Banach spaces exist, and they will surely be useful in future developments but are beyond the scope of this text.

15.2   Portfolio Choices for Small Risks

The basic portfolio problem is a good example where bifurcation methods can be used. Suppose that an investor has W in wealth to invest in two assets. The safe asset yields R per dollar invested and the risky asset yields Z per dollar invested. If a proportion ω of his wealth is invested in the risky asset, final wealth is $Y = W((1 - \omega)R + \omega Z)$. We assume that he chooses ω to maximize $E\{u(Y)\}$ for some concave, von Neumann-Morgenstern utility function $u(\,\cdot\,)$.

We want to "linearize" around the deterministic case of $\varepsilon = 0$. The first problem we encounter is that if we eliminate risk by replacing Z with its mean, $\bar{Z}$, the resulting problem is unbounded if $R \neq \bar{Z}$ and indeterminate if $R = \bar{Z}$. Since the former case is untenable, we opt for the latter. We create a continuum of portfolio problems by assuming

$$Z = R + \varepsilon z + \varepsilon^2 \pi, \tag{15.2.1}$$

where $E\{z\} = 0$. At $\varepsilon = 0$, Z is degenerate and equal to R. If $\pi > 0$, we model the intuitive case of risky assets paying a premium. Note that we multiply z by ε and π by ε^2. Since $\text{var}\{\varepsilon z\} = \varepsilon^2 \sigma_z^2$, this models the standard result in finance that risk premia are roughly proportional to variance.

We now investigate the collection of portfolio problems indexed by ε in (15.2.1). The first-order condition for ω, after dividing by εW, is, for all ε, equivalent to

$$0 = E\{u'(WR + \omega W(\varepsilon z + \varepsilon^2 \pi))(z + \varepsilon \pi)\} \equiv G(\omega, \varepsilon). \tag{15.2.2}$$

We can divide by εW to arrive at (15.2.2), since this condition defines the solution to the decision problem even when $\varepsilon = 0$. We know from concavity of $u(c)$ that there is a unique solution to (15.2.2) for ω if $\varepsilon \neq 0$. However, at $\varepsilon = 0$, ω can be anything since the two assets are perfect substitutes. The indeterminacy of ω at $\varepsilon = 0$ follows from the fact that

$$0 = G(\omega, 0), \qquad \forall \omega. \tag{15.2.3}$$

We want to solve for $\omega(\varepsilon)$ as a Taylor series in ε. We don't know if we can, but suppose that we can. Implicit differentiation implies that

$$0 = G_\omega \omega' + G_\varepsilon. \tag{15.2.4}$$

In (15.2.4) we differentiate G, an integral. We would like to pass the derivative operator through the integral. To do this, we need to recall the following result from integration theory:

LEMMA 15.2.1   Let $f(x, y): R \times R \to R$ be differentiable in y, and define $F(y) = \int_a^b f(x, y)\, dx$. If $f_y(x, y)$ is bounded in an open neighborhood of $[a, b] \times y_0$, then $F(y)$ is differentiable at y_0 and

$$\frac{dF}{dy}(y_0) = \int_a^b \frac{df}{dy}(x, y_0)\, dx.$$

For now, we will assume that lemma 15.2.1 applies. In that case we find

$$G_\varepsilon = E\{u''(Y)\, W(\omega z + 2\omega\varepsilon\pi)(z + \varepsilon\pi) + u'(Y)\pi\}, \tag{15.2.5}$$

$$G_\omega = E\{u''(Y) W(z + \varepsilon\pi)^2 \varepsilon\}. \tag{15.2.6}$$

At $\varepsilon = 0$, $G_\omega = 0$ for all ω. This implies that at no point $(\omega, 0)$ can we apply the implicit function theorem to (15.2.3) to solve for $\omega'(0)$. Moreover we do not know $\lim_{\varepsilon \to 0} \omega(\varepsilon)$. Therefore, following theorem 15.1.1, we look for a bifurcation point, ω_0, satisfying

$$0 = G_\varepsilon(\omega_0, 0) \tag{15.2.7}$$

which is one of the conditions in (15.1.1) for theorem 15.1.1. At $\varepsilon = 0$, (15.2.5) reduces to $0 = u''(RW)\, \omega_0 \sigma_z^2 W + u'(RW)\pi$ which implies that

$$\omega_0 = -\frac{\pi}{\sigma_z^2} \frac{u'(WR)}{Wu''(WR)}. \tag{15.2.8}$$

Now that we have our candidate for a bifurcation point, we need to check the boundedness condition in lemma 15.2.1 for the derivatives in (15.2.5)–(15.2.6). This depends on the nature of u and the density of z. For example, if z were log normal, as long as u' and u'' do not have exponential growth that offsets the normal density's tail behavior, lemma 15.2.1 applies. This is not an innocent assumption, however. For example, suppose that the solution (15.2.8) implies that consumption is negative in some states (as may occur if one shorts the safe asset to increase his position in the risky asset), and that $u'(0) = \infty$. Then the integrands in (15.2.5)–(15.2.6) will not be bounded, and the solution (15.2.8) is not valid. The approach we are using is to proceed as if lemma 15.2.1 holds, and then check its validity in a neighborhood of the candidate point (15.2.8).

An alternative is to assume that z has support $[-\varepsilon, \varepsilon]$ and $u''(RW) \neq \infty$; this is the approach Samuelson (1970) took. However, we will sometimes want to allow z with infinite support. Then we will need to assume that Y avoids singularities of u and its derivatives; it may be necessary to assume that $u''(c)$ is defined for all c, even $c < 0$. We will face the same problem below when we take higher-order derivatives of G, where again, we will have to check that lemma 15.2.1 applies. The basic fact is that we will be assuming that the dominant considerations are the properties of the utility function near RW and the moments of z, and that we can pass differentiation through the integral sign. This is strictly more general than the Samuelson approach.

Now that we have found a candidate bifurcation point, we can continue to derive the Taylor series. The formula (15.2.8) is the simple portfolio rule from linear-quadratic analysis, indicating that ω is the product of risk tolerance and the risk premium per unit variance. However, ω_0 is not an approximation to the portfolio choice at any particular variance. Instead, ω_0 is the limiting portfolio share as the variance vanishes. If we want the linear and quadratic approximations of $\omega(\varepsilon)$ at $\varepsilon = 0$, we must go further, since the quadratic approximation to $\omega(\varepsilon)$ is $\omega(\varepsilon) \doteq \omega(0) + \varepsilon\omega'(0) + (\varepsilon^2/2)\,\omega''(0)$.

To calculate $\omega'(0)$ and $\omega''(0)$, we need to do two more rounds of implicit differentiation. If we differentiate (15.2.4) with respect to ε, we find that

$$0 = G_{\omega\omega}\,\omega'\omega' + 2G_{\omega\varepsilon}\,\omega' + G_\omega\omega'' + G_{\varepsilon\varepsilon},$$

where (without loss of generality, we assume that $W = 1$)

$$G_{\varepsilon\varepsilon} = E\{u'''(Y)(\omega z + 2\omega\varepsilon\pi)^2\,(z + \varepsilon\pi) + u''(Y)\,2\omega\pi(z + \varepsilon\pi) + 2u''(Y)(\omega z + 2\omega\varepsilon\pi)\pi\},$$

$$G_{\omega\omega} = E\{u'''(Y)(z + \varepsilon\pi)^3\varepsilon\},$$

$$G_{\omega\varepsilon} = E\{u'''(Y)(\omega z + 2\omega\varepsilon\pi)(z + \varepsilon\pi)^2\varepsilon + u''(Y)(z + \varepsilon\pi)\,2\pi\varepsilon + u''(Y)(z + \varepsilon\pi)^2\}.$$

At $\varepsilon = 0$, $G_{\varepsilon\varepsilon} = u'''(R)\omega_0^2\,E\{z^3\}$, $G_{\omega\omega} = 0$, and $G_{\omega\varepsilon} = u''(R)\,E\{z^2\} \neq 0$. Therefore theorem 15.1.1 applies and

$$\omega' = -\frac{1}{2}\frac{u'''(R)}{u''(R)}\frac{E\{z^3\}}{E\{z^2\}}\,\omega_0^2. \tag{15.2.9}$$

Equation (15.2.9) is a simple formula. It shows that as riskiness increases, the change in ω depends on u'''/u'' and the ratio of skewness to variance. If u is quadratic or z is symmetric, ω does not change to a first order. We could continue this and compute more derivatives of $\omega(\varepsilon)$ as long as u is sufficiently differentiable.

We end the development of this example here. However, it is clear we could do much with this. We computed the asset demand function in terms of ε. We could similarly expand supply functions as well as equilibrium prices and trades. Our asset demand example is just one simple application.

15.3   Gauge Functions and Asymptotic Expansions

In the previous chapter we computed asymptotic expansions of the form $\sum_{i=1}^{n} a_i\varepsilon^i$. In this chapter we will examine cases where this may not be valid. To deal with these cases, we use a more general formulation of expansions. A system of *gauge functions* is a sequence of functions, $\{\delta_n(\varepsilon)\}_{n=1}^{\infty}$, such that

$$\lim_{\varepsilon \to 0} \frac{\delta_{n+1}(\varepsilon)}{\delta_n(\varepsilon)} = 0. \tag{15.3.1}$$

The terminology is appropriate because we will "gauge" the asymptotic behavior of $f(x)$ against the asymptotic behavior of the gauge functions. An *asymptotic expansion* of $f(x)$ near $x = 0$ is any expansion $f(0) + \sum_{i=1}^{n} a_i \delta_i(x)$ where, for each $k < n$,

$$\lim_{x \to 0} \frac{f(x) - (f(0) + \sum_{i=1}^{k} a_i \delta_i(x))}{\delta_k(x)} = 0. \tag{15.3.2}$$

The notation

$$f(x) \sim f(0) + \sum_{i=1}^{n} a_i \delta_i(x) \tag{15.3.3}$$

expresses the asymptotic relations in (15.3.2).

In regular perturbations and Taylor series expansions using the parameter ε, the sequence of gauge functions is $\delta_k(\varepsilon) = \varepsilon^k$. This is not the only possible set of gauge functions. For example, $\delta_k(x) = x^{k/2}$ is also a gauge system. Some functions have asymptotic expansions which are not Taylor expansions. For example, $e^{x^{1/3}}$ does not have a Taylor expansion around $x = 0$ because its derivative, $x^{-2/3} e^{x^{1/3}}/3$, is not finite at $x = 0$. However, the series

$$e^{x^{1/3}} \sim 1 + x^{1/3} + \frac{1}{2}(x^{1/3})^2 + \frac{1}{6}(x^{1/3})^3 + \cdots \tag{15.3.4}$$

is an asymptotic expansion around $x = 0$. The crucial limitation of Taylor series is that they necessarily use the gauge functions x^k for positive integers k. There is no expansion of $e^{x^{1/3}}$ in that gauge, but (15.3.4) is asymptotic in the gauge $\delta_k(x) = x^{k/3}$. The methods behind asymptotic expansions are substantively important generalizations of the basic idea behind Taylor series expansions

15.4 Method of Undetermined Gauges

In our portfolio problem we assumed that the risky return depended on ε according to the form $R + \varepsilon z + \varepsilon^2 \pi$. This is only one way to parameterize a continuous collection of portfolio problems. We could have written $R + \varepsilon z + \varepsilon \pi$ to represent a continuum of portfolio problems. The difference is economically substantive: The choice we made implies a risk premium, $\varepsilon^2 \pi$, that is quadratic in ε and hence proportional to the variance, whereas the $R + \varepsilon z + \varepsilon \pi$ alternative implies a risk premium proportional to ε and the standard deviation. The reason we chose $R + \varepsilon z + \varepsilon^2 \pi$ was the basic portfolio theory result that the risk premium should be proportional to variance, not standard deviation.

In general, any asymptotic problem involves a choice of gauge functions. We chose the parameterization (15.2.1) and used the gauge family ε^k to find a Taylor series for $\omega(\varepsilon)$. We could use the parameterization $Z = R + \sqrt{\varepsilon} z + \varepsilon \pi$ and use the gauge family $\varepsilon^{k/2}$ for an expansion of $\omega(\varepsilon)$ near $\varepsilon = 0$, since those two combinations are equivalent. We will see below that we cannot use the parameterization $R + \varepsilon z + \varepsilon \pi$ and the gauge family ε^k. We must choose a gauge family that is appropriate for the parameterization.

The portfolio problem was a special case where we had good intuition. In some analyses we may not have such strong guidance in choosing a combination of parameterization and gauge family. We then must determine the appropriate gauge as well as the coefficients. We will first discuss how bad combinations of parameterizations and gauge families would be detected in the portfolio problem. Then we analyze an adverse selection problem, endogenously determining the appropriate gauge as we construct an asymptotic expansion. These examples will show that we can often determine the correct gauge for a parameterization even if we don't begin the analysis with a good idea.

Alternative Gauges in the Portfolio Problem

Say we did not know that risk premia were proportional to variance. Given this lack of information, we might (wisely) assume the more general functional form

$$Z = R + \varepsilon z + \varepsilon^v \pi, \tag{15.4.1}$$

where v is left free and attempt to compute an asymptotic expansion similar to (15.4.1). The general idea is to allow v to be free until we need to fix it to compute an asymptotic expression. With the parameterization in (15.4.1), the first-order condition becomes (after dividing by ε)

$$0 = E\{u'(R + (\varepsilon z + \varepsilon^v \pi)\omega)(z + \varepsilon^{v-1}\pi)\} \equiv G(\omega, \varepsilon; v) \tag{15.4.2}$$

for all ε. Again $0 = G(\omega, 0; v)$ for all ω and $v > 0$. Implicit differentiation of (15.4.2) again implies that

$$0 = G_\omega \omega' + G_\varepsilon, \tag{15.4.3}$$

but now (with $Y \equiv R + (\varepsilon z + \varepsilon^v \pi)\omega$)

$$G_\varepsilon = E\{u''(Y)(\omega z + v\omega\varepsilon^{v-1}\pi)(z + \varepsilon^{v-1}\pi) + u'(Y)\,\varepsilon^{v-2}\,(v-1)\pi\},\tag{15.4.4}$$

$$G_\omega = E\{u''(Y)(z + \varepsilon^{v-1}\pi)^2\varepsilon^{v-1}\}.\tag{15.4.5}$$

At a bifurcation point where $\omega = \omega_0$, we must have

$$0 = \lim_{\varepsilon \to 0} G_\varepsilon\,(\omega_0, \varepsilon; v).\tag{15.4.6}$$

We saw that if $v = 2$, we can use the bifurcation theorem to construct an asymptotic expansion for $\omega(\varepsilon)$. We now show what would go wrong if we choose some other v.

If we choose $v = 1$, the implicit function condition (15.4.3) reduces to $0 = (\omega' + \omega)\,E\{u''(Y)z^2\}$ for all ε. Since $E\{u''(Y)z^2\} < 0$, this implies the differential equation $0 = \omega' + \omega$ for all ε. If $v = 1$, (15.4.6) reduces to $0 = \omega_0(\sigma_z^2 + \pi^2)u''(R)$ which implies that $\omega_0 = 0$, which in turn serves as an initial condition to the differential equation $0 = \omega' + \omega$. Hence $\omega(\varepsilon) = 0$ for all ε, a result we know to be false since $\omega = 0$ satisfies the first-order condition (15.4.2) for $\varepsilon > 0$ only if $\pi = 0$. If $1 \neq v < 2$, the dominant term in G_ε in (15.4.4) as $\varepsilon \to 0$ is $\varepsilon^{v-2}\,(v-1)\pi\,E\{u'(Y)\}$ which diverges as $\varepsilon \to 0$, and this is inconsistent with (15.4.6). Any $v > 2$ will not work because

$$\lim_{\varepsilon \to 0} G_\varepsilon = E\{u''(Y)\omega z^2\} = 0$$

implies that $\omega_0 = 0$, which, after further differentiation of (15.4.2), will imply an infinite leading coefficient of the expansion.

These calculations show that the only way for the condition $G_\varepsilon\,(\omega_0, 0; v) = 0$ to tie down ω_0 is for $v = 2$. These calculations show us that a bad choice for a gauge will often make its inappropriateness apparent. Through this kind of analysis, we can determine the gauges to be used in an asymptotic expansion. The next section pursues this idea in a well-known model of asymmetric information.

An Adverse Selection Example

The portfolio problem is a bit too simple, since we intuitively knew the correct gauge. We next apply the method of undetermined gauges to analyze a simple adverse selection problem, a problem where the correct gauge is not obvious.

Recall the RSW model of adverse selection described in chapter 4. Assume that the high (low) risk type receives observable income of 1 with probability q (p), $q < p$, and zero otherwise. In the Nash equilibrium (if it exists) the high-risk type consumes q in each state, and the low-risk type consumes x in the good state, and y otherwise. The state-contingent consumptions x and y are fixed by the incentive compatibility condition $u(q) = p\,u(x) + (1-p)\,u(y)$, and the zero-profit condition, $y = p(1-x)/(1-p)$. Substitution yields the single equation for x:

$$u(q) = pu(x) + (1-p)\,u\left(\frac{p(1-x)}{1-p}\right). \tag{15.4.7}$$

If $q = p$, then $x = y = p = q$ is the unique solution. We seek solutions to (15.4.7) for $q = p - \varepsilon$ where $\varepsilon > 0$ is small, modeling situations where the risk differences are small. The solution, x, will depend on ε, and it is implicitly defined by

$$u(p - \varepsilon) = pu(x(\varepsilon)) + (1-p)u\left(\frac{p(1-x(\varepsilon))}{1-p}\right). \tag{15.4.8}$$

We first attempt a standard regular perturbation approach. Suppose that $x(\varepsilon) \sim p + \sum_{i=1}^{\infty} \alpha_i \varepsilon^i$. A Taylor series expansion of (15.4.8) around $\varepsilon = 0$ implies that

$$u(p) - u'(p)\varepsilon + \frac{1}{2}u''(p)\varepsilon^2 + \cdots$$

$$= p\left(u(p) + u'(p)(\alpha_1\varepsilon + \alpha_2\varepsilon^2 + \cdots) + \frac{1}{2}u''(p)(\alpha_1\varepsilon + \alpha_2\varepsilon^2 + \cdots)^2 + \cdots\right)$$

$$+ (1-p)\left(u(p) + u'(p)\left(\frac{-p}{1-p}\right)(\alpha_1\varepsilon + \alpha_2\varepsilon^2 + \cdots)\right.$$

$$\left. + \frac{1}{2}\left(\frac{p}{1-p}\right)^2 u''(p)(\alpha_1\varepsilon + \alpha_2\varepsilon^2 + \cdots)^2 + \cdots\right).$$

Combining like terms, we find that

$$u(p) - u'(p)\varepsilon + \frac{1}{2}u''(p)\varepsilon^2 + \cdots$$

$$= u(p)(p + (1-p)) + \varepsilon(p\alpha_1 u'(p) - p\alpha_1 u'(p))$$

$$+ \varepsilon^2\left(p\alpha_2 u'(p) + \frac{1}{2}p\alpha_1 u''(p) - p\alpha_2 u'(p) + \cdots\right) + \cdots,$$

which implies that $-u'(p)\varepsilon + \frac{1}{2}u''(p)\varepsilon^2 = 0 + \mathcal{O}(\varepsilon^2)$, but this cannot be true as $\varepsilon \to 0$, since $u'(p) \neq 0$.

The problem is that regular perturbation *assumes* that there is an asymptotic expansion of x of the form $\sum_{i=1}^{\infty} \alpha_i \varepsilon^i$. Suppose instead that

$$x(\varepsilon) \sim p + \sum_{i=1}^{\infty} \alpha_i \varepsilon^{v_i} \tag{15.4.9}$$

for some increasing sequence of reals, v_i. We will now determine this sequence as part of the asymptotic expansion. We call this the *method of undetermined gauges*. In regular perturbation we know the gauge functions and need to determine only the coefficients. Here we must determine both.

When we substitute (15.4.9) into the Taylor expansion of (15.4.8), we get

$$u(p) - u'(p)\varepsilon + \frac{1}{2}u''(p)\varepsilon^2$$

$$= p\left(u(p) + u'(p)(\alpha_1\varepsilon^{v_1} + \alpha_2\varepsilon^{v_2} + \cdots) + \frac{1}{2}u''(p)(\alpha_1\varepsilon^{v_1} + \alpha_2\varepsilon^{v_2} + \cdots)^2 + \cdots\right)$$

$$+ (1-p)\left(u(p) + u'(p)\left(-\frac{p}{1-p}\right)(\alpha_1\varepsilon^{v_1} + \alpha_2\varepsilon^{v_2} + \cdots)\right.$$

$$\left. + \frac{1}{2}u''(p)\left(\frac{p}{1-p}\right)^2(\alpha_1\varepsilon^{v_1} + \alpha_2\varepsilon^{v_2} + \cdots)^2 + \cdots\right) \qquad (15.4.10)$$

Combining like terms yields

$$-u'(p)\varepsilon + \frac{1}{2}u''(p)\varepsilon^2 + \cdots$$

$$= \frac{1}{2}u''(p)p(\alpha_1^2\varepsilon^{2v_1} + 2\alpha_1\alpha_2\varepsilon^{v_1+v_2} + \alpha_2^2\varepsilon^{2v_2} + \cdots)$$

$$+ \frac{1}{2}u''(p)\frac{p^2}{1-p}(\alpha_1^2\varepsilon^{2v_1} + 2\alpha_1\alpha_2\varepsilon^{v_1+v_2} + \alpha_2^2\varepsilon^{2v_2} + \cdots) \qquad (15.4.11)$$

Since $0 < v_1 < v_2 < v_3 < \cdots$, we know that $2v_1 < v_1 + v_2 < 2v_2$ and that $2v_2$ is less than the power of any ε term which is not in (15.4.11). Therefore the dominant term as $\varepsilon \to 0$ on the RHS is ε^{2v_1}, the next dominant is $\varepsilon^{v_1+v_2}$, and so on. If the two sides of (15.4.11) are to match, $\varepsilon = \varepsilon^{2v_1}$ and $2v_1 < v_1 + v_2$; but $\varepsilon = \varepsilon^{2v_1}$ only if $v_1 = \frac{1}{2}$ and $2v_1 < v_1 + v_2$ is guaranteed, since $v_2 > v_1$. Hence

$$0 = \varepsilon\left(u'(p) + \frac{1}{2}p\alpha_1^2 u''(p) + \frac{1}{2}\frac{p^2}{1-p}\alpha_1^2 u''(p)\right),$$

which implies that

$$\alpha_1 = \sqrt{-2\frac{u'(p)}{u''(p)}\frac{(1-p)}{p}}. \qquad (15.4.12)$$

The next terms are

$$\frac{1}{2} u''(p)\varepsilon^2 = u''(p)p\,\alpha_1\alpha_2\varepsilon^{\nu_1+\nu_2} + u''(p)\,\frac{p^2}{1-p}\alpha_1\alpha_2\varepsilon^{\nu_1+\nu_2}. \tag{15.4.13}$$

Since $\nu_1 = \frac{1}{2}$ and comparability of these terms requires that $2 = \nu_1 + \nu_2$, we conclude that $\nu_2 = 1\frac{1}{2}$ and that solving for α_2 is a linear problem. We could continue this indefinitely. By flexibly specifying all the parameters of an asymptotic expansion, including the ν_i exponents, we can compute asymptotic expressions for a greater variety of problems.

An alternative procedure would be to compute asymptotic expansions of each term in (15.4.8), which here would just be the Taylor expansions. This results in

$$u(p) - \varepsilon u'(p) + \frac{\varepsilon^2}{2} u''(\rho) + \cdots$$

$$= p\left(u(p) + u'(p)(x-p) + \frac{u''(p)(x-p)^2}{2} + \cdots \right)$$

$$+ (1-p)\left(u(p) - u'(p)\frac{p}{1-p}(x-p) + u''(p)\left(\frac{p}{1-p}\right)^2\frac{(x-p)^2}{2} + \cdots \right),$$

which in turn implies that

$$-\varepsilon u'(p) + \cdots = \frac{(x-p)^2}{2}u''(p)\frac{p}{1-p} + \cdots. \tag{15.4.14}$$

If we view the displayed terms in (15.4.14) as a quadratic equation and solve for x in terms of ε, we get $x \sim p + \sqrt{-2(u'(p)/u''(p))((1-p)/p)}\varepsilon^{1/2}$ which is the same as (15.4.12). While this second procedure seems simpler, it is not as clean. Notice that it forces one to solve a nonlinear equation, whereas the perturbation approach involves only linear equations. That is not a problem here, but with more variables it will be. In general, the earlier approach is more robust.

15.5   Asymptotic Expansions of Integrals

Integrals frequently take the form

$$\int_D f(x)\,e^{-\lambda g(x)}dx, \tag{15.5.1}$$

where λ is a large parameter and $g(x)$ is a positive function. In such cases it is useful to compute asymptotic expansions in λ which approximate (15.5.1) asymptotically as λ goes to infinity. Before considering the proper way to do this, we consider the Taylor series approach. If $\lambda = \infty$, then (15.5.1) is zero for "nice" $g(x)$, such as x^2. Also, if we define $\varepsilon = \lambda^{-1}$, then $\varepsilon \to 0$ as $\lambda \to \infty$. This suggests defining $I(\varepsilon) \equiv \int_D f(x)e^{-g(x)/\varepsilon}\, dx$, noting that $I(0) = 0$, and applying Taylor's theorem to $I(\varepsilon)$. The difficulty becomes apparent immediately. Assuming that we can pass differentiation through the integral, $I'(\varepsilon) = \int_0 f(x)(g(x)/\varepsilon^2)e^{-g(x)/\varepsilon}\, dx$. Taking the limit of $I'(\varepsilon)$ as $\varepsilon \to 0$ will be difficult because the $e^{-g(x)/\varepsilon}$ term goes to zero, but the $g(x)/\varepsilon^2$ goes to infinity if $g(x) \neq 0$. Therefore the standard regular perturbation approach fails.

The basic idea we pursue here is that when λ is large the major contribution of the integrand in (15.5.1) is in the neighborhood of the point that maximizes $e^{-\lambda g(x)}$, which is the minimum of $g(x)$. Suppose that we can assume that $g(0) = 0$ and $g(x)$ is uniquely minimized at $x = 0$. For large λ, if $x \neq 0$, then $e^{-\lambda g(x)} \ll e^{-\lambda g(0)} = 1$. As long as $f(x)$ does not offset this for values of x away from 0, the integral (15.5.1) is determined largely by $e^{-\lambda g(x)}f(x)$ for x near 0.

Hermite Integrals

We begin our discussion of the asymptotic expansions of integrals by recalling special properties of integrals of the form

$$\int_{-\infty}^{\infty} f(x)\, e^{-\lambda x^2}\, dx. \tag{15.5.2}$$

These facts will help us understand why the asymptotic expansions which we examine below do as well as they do.

First, integrals of the form (15.5.2) integrate exactly when $f(x)$ is a polynomial. The general formulas for $\lambda > 0$ are

$$\int_{-\infty}^{\infty} x^{2n}e^{-\lambda x^2}\, dx = \frac{1 \cdot 3 \cdot 5 \cdots (2n-1)}{2^n \lambda^n} \sqrt{\frac{\pi}{\lambda}}. \tag{15.5.3}$$

Of course $\int_{-\infty}^{\infty} x^{2n+1}e^{-\lambda x^2}\, dx = 0$ for all integers $n \geq 0$.

Second, even if $f(x)$ is not a polynomial, we may be able to replace it with a Taylor series expansion around $x = 0$; this is the beginning of the Laplace approach. This results in the identity

$$\int_{-\infty}^{\infty} e^{-\lambda x^2}f(x)\, dx = \int_{-\infty}^{\infty} e^{-\lambda x^2}\left(f(0) + xf'(0) + \frac{x^2}{2}f''(0) + \cdots + R_n(x)\right) dx, \quad (15.5.4)$$

where $R_n(x)$ is the remainder term in the Taylor expansion of f. The polynomial terms in the Taylor series will integrate exactly. The remainder term, $R_n(x)$, will not generally integrate, but $R_n(x)$ is negligible for small x by construction, and for large x the $e^{-\lambda x^2}$ factor will crush $R_n(x)$ as long as $R_n(x)$ does not grow more rapidly than $e^{\lambda x^2}$. Since many reasonable functions satisfy this growth condition, a good approximation is formed from (15.5.4) by dropping $R_n(x)$. This approximation is the basic idea behind Laplace's approximation.

Portfolio Applications

We next discuss a portfolio application of the Laplacian approximation. Suppose that we want to evaluate the value of

$$\frac{1}{\sigma\sqrt{2\pi}} \int_{-\infty}^{\infty} (B + Se^{z+\mu})^\gamma e^{-z^2/2\sigma^2} \, dz, \tag{15.5.5}$$

which is the expected utility from holding B units of the numéraire and S units of an asset having a lognormal distribution with log mean μ and log variance σ. The integral (15.5.5) is, modulo a linear change of variables, the same kind as (15.5.1). The case of small σ here corresponds to a large λ in (15.5.1). If σ is small then the expectation in (15.5.5) is well-approximated by $(B + S)^\gamma$. In many cases it is reasonable to assume that σ is small and consider using an asymptotic method to compute expected utility. If we define $\lambda = (\sigma^2)^{-1}$, then (15.5.5) takes the form (15.5.1).

Table 15.1 shows that the approximation in (15.5.4) does very well when applied to (15.5.5). We choose $\gamma = -3$ and, for the sake of simplicity, set $B = S = 1$ and $\mu = 0$. We examine degree 1, 3, and 5 Taylor series approximations for $u(1 + e^z)$ and let $\sigma \in \{0.01, 0.1, 0.2, 0.4, 1.0\}$. For $\sigma = 0.01$ even the linear approximation of $u(1 + e^z)$ results in an excellent approximation of the integral. For larger σ the extra terms help. For $\sigma = 1$, even the fifth-order approximation does not produce a good approximation of the integral; of course $\sigma^{-1} = 1$ is a long way from $\sigma^{-1} = \infty$ which is the case where the approximation is exact.

Table 15.1
Errors in the Laplacian approximation of (15.5.5)

	σ				
n	0.01	0.1	0.2	0.4	1.0
1	2.5(−5)	2.5(−3)	9.8(−3)	3.7(−2)	1.7(−1)
3	−1.1(−9)	−1.2(−5)	−1.9(−4)	−2.9(−3)	−7.6(−2)
5	1.3(−10)	8.8(−8)	5.5(−6)	3.2(−4)	4.9(−2)

An Intuitive Derivation of Laplace's Formula

We will next apply these ideas to examine a more general problem. The following procedure illustrates the basic ideas and also generates the coefficients for Laplace's formula. The techniques used here may be useful to compute expansions that don't fit Laplace's method exactly. Also an ambitious reader could use the following procedure to derive multidimensional expansions.

Suppose that we want to approximate

$$I(\lambda) \equiv \int_{-\infty}^{\infty} e^{-\lambda g(x)} f(x)\, dx, \tag{15.5.6}$$

where $g(x)$ is nonnegative and minimized at $x = 0$, with $g''(0) > 0$. Using Taylor expansions around $x = 0$ for both $g(x)$ and $f(x)$ (we let f_n and g_n denote the nth derivatives of f and g), we approximate the integrand with

$$e^{-\lambda(g_0 + g_2 x^2/2 + g_3 x^3/6 + \cdots)} \left(f_0 + f_1 x + \frac{f_2 x^2}{2} + \cdots \right),$$

which we factor into three pieces:

$$(e^{-\lambda g_0})(e^{-\lambda g_2 x^2/2}) \left(e^{-\lambda(g_3 x^3/6 + \cdots)} \left(f_0 + f_1 x + \frac{f_2 x^2}{2} + \cdots \right) \right). \tag{15.5.7}$$

The first piece, $e^{-\lambda g_0}$, is a constant factor. The second is the normal density function with variance $(\lambda g_2)^{-1}$. The third piece, for large λ and small x, can be further approximated and replaced by a low-order Taylor series. We are then left with an integral of the form

$$e^{-\lambda g_0} \int_{-\infty}^{\infty} e^{-\lambda g_2 x^2/2} P(x, \lambda x^3)\, dx, \tag{15.5.8}$$

where $P(x, \lambda x^3)$ is a low-order polynomial representing the Taylor expansion of the third piece in (15.5.7) in terms of λx^3 and x. At this point we do not specify the order of the polynomial approximation in P; we will see below how to determine that. The integral in (15.5.8) will be an asymptotically valid approximation of (15.5.6) as $\lambda \to \infty$ for two reasons. First, for large λ and $|x|$ not small, $e^{-\lambda g_2 x^2/2}$ is trivial and will crush the neglected terms of f. Second, when $|x|$ is small, the integrands in (15.5.8) and (15.5.6) are similar. The formal analysis of Laplace's method makes rigorous these approximation arguments. We will proceed formally.

Having replaced (15.5.6) with (15.5.8), we can just compute (15.5.8), an integral with an analytic solution. After integrating out the x variable we then combine like powers of λ to compute the coefficients of like powers of λ in the final expansion. However, we should point out a complication due to the presence of λ in the exponential term $e^{-\lambda g_2 x^2/2}$. When we compute (15.5.8), we need to use the change of variables $y = \sqrt{\lambda}\, x$ to replace (15.5.8) with

$$\frac{e^{-\lambda g_0}}{\sqrt{\lambda}} \int_{-\infty}^{\infty} e^{-g_2 y^2/2}\, P\left(\frac{y}{\sqrt{\lambda}}, \frac{y^3}{\sqrt{\lambda}}\right) dy. \tag{15.5.9}$$

This shows that each power of λ will arise from two sources: First, each will arise directly in the second component in P, and second, they will less directly appear in the other components of P through the change of variables. Furthermore both the first and second components of P contains powers of $y/\sqrt{\lambda}$. This tells us that if we are to have an accurate expansion in terms of λ and its powers, we will need to include high-order terms in the original construction of P if we are going to get all the appropriate λ terms. Hence, for a two-term expansion, we need all terms which yield either $\lambda^{-1/2}$ or λ^{-1} terms after the change of variables in (15.5.9).

For the case of a two-term expansion, we let

$$P = \left(1 - \frac{\lambda g_3 x^3}{6} - \frac{\lambda g_4 x^4}{24} + \frac{\lambda^2 g_3^2 x^6}{72}\right)\left(f_0 + f_1 x + \frac{f_2 x^2}{2}\right).$$

With the change in variable in (15.5.9), P becomes

$$P = \left(1 - \frac{y^3 \lambda^{-1/2} g_3}{6} - \frac{\lambda^{-1} g_4 y^4}{24} + \frac{\lambda^{-1} g_3^2 y^6}{72}\right)\left(f_0 + f_1 y \lambda^{-1/2} + \frac{f_2 y^2 \lambda^{-1}}{2} + \cdots\right),$$

which, when we multiply and keep only constant, $\lambda^{-1/2}$, and λ^{-1} terms, becomes

$$P = f_0 + \left(f_1 y - \frac{g_3 f_0 y^3}{6}\right)\lambda^{-1/2}$$

$$+ \left(\frac{f_2 y^2}{2} - \frac{f_0 g_4 y^4}{24} - f_1 y^4 g_3 + \frac{f_0 g_3^2 y^6}{72}\right)\lambda^{-1} + \cdots.$$

We then integrate with respect to y using (15.5.3) and arrive at the two-term Laplace's formula

$$I(\lambda) \sim \sqrt{\frac{2\pi}{\lambda g_2}}\, e^{-\lambda g_0}\left(f_0 + \frac{1}{\lambda}\left[\frac{f_2}{2 g_2} - \frac{f_0 g_4}{8 g_2^2} - \frac{f_1 g_3}{2 g_2^2} + \frac{5 f_0 g_3^2}{24 g_2^3}\right]\right). \tag{15.5.10}$$

Most readers will rationally conclude that this is a lot of algebra and be deterred. It is not surprising that these formulas, particularly the higher-order terms, are seldom used in economics. No one wants to spend time keeping track of the Taylor expansions and changes of variables involved. However, all of this can be automated with symbolic software. The Taylor expansions, the change of variables, the Gaussian integration, and the extraction of coefficients are all examples of what symbolic software is built for. The wide availability of symbolic languages now makes these techniques much more accessible.

Stirling's Formula

One important and nonobvious application of Laplace's method is Stirling's formula for $n!$. The factorial function arises in many contexts in economics. Being a function of integers, we generally do not use continuous function tools in such analyses. For example, comparative statics would be difficult, since the derivative of $n!$ is a problematic idea.

Fortunately there is a smooth, monotonic approximation to $n!$, called *Stirling's formula*. It is well known that $n! = \Gamma(n+1)$ where $\Gamma(\lambda) \equiv \int_0^\infty e^{-x} x^{\lambda-1}\, dx$. If we were to directly apply Laplace's method to $\Gamma(n)$, we would take $g(x) = -\ln x$ and $f(x) = e^{-x} x^{-1}$ in (15.5.1). However, since $\ln x$ has no minimum on $[0,\infty)$, we cannot do this. Fortunately a change of variables will help. If we let $x = y\lambda$, then

$$\Gamma(\lambda) = \lambda^\lambda \int_0^\infty e^{-\lambda(y-\ln y)} y^{-1} dy.$$

Now $g(y) = y - \ln y$, and $f(y) = y^{-1}$. The minimum of $y - \ln y$ occurs at $y = 1$. At $y = 1$,

$$g(y) = y - \ln y \sim 1 + \tfrac{1}{2}(y-1)^2 - \tfrac{1}{3}(y-1)^3 + \tfrac{1}{4}(y-1)^4 + \cdots.$$

Application of (15.5.10) implies the two-term approximation

$$\Gamma(\lambda) \sim \sqrt{2\pi} \lambda^{\lambda-(1/2)} e^{-\lambda} \left(1 + \frac{1}{12\lambda}\right). \tag{15.5.11}$$

Stirling's formula is just the one-term expansion,

$$n! = \Gamma(n+1) \sim \sqrt{2\pi}(n+1)^{n+(1/2)} e^{-(n+1)}. \tag{15.5.12}$$

The two-term extension is

$$n! \sim \sqrt{2\pi}(n+1)^{n+(1/2)} e^{-(n+1)} \left(1 + \frac{1}{12(n+1)}\right), \tag{15.5.13}$$

Table 15.2
Relative error of Laplace approximations of $n!$

n	1	5	10	20
Stirling's formula	0.04	0.01	0.008	0.004
Two-term Laplace	5(−4)	8(−5)	3(−5)	8(−6)
Three-term Laplace	3(−4)	1(−5)	2(−6)	3(−7)

and the three-term extension is

$$n! \sim \sqrt{2\pi}(n+1)^{n+(1/2)}e^{-(n+1)}\left(1 + \frac{1}{12(n+1)} + \frac{1}{288(n+1)^2}\right). \tag{15.5.14}$$

Table 15.2 displays the quality of Stirling's formula and higher-order Laplace expansions.

Note how well Laplace's method does. The theory says only that Stirling's formula does well when n is large. Table 15.2 shows that Stirling's formula does surprisingly well when n is actually small, and that the second and third terms of the Laplace expansion both improve the approximation substantially.

15.6 Hybrid Perturbation-Projection Methods

We saw in chapter 11 that a key step in projection methods of solving operator equations was the choice of a basis. Our earlier discussion focused on general purpose bases such as Chebyshev polynomials. While these bases may be adequate, we use very little information about the solution, primarily differentiability properties, in selecting among them. In this section we use perturbation methods to generate special purpose bases tailored to the problem at hand, adapting the papers of Geer and Andersen (1989, 1990) to a simple economics problem.

The general idea springs from the following observation. Suppose that we want to solve $\mathcal{N}f = 0$ for some operator $\mathcal{N}$, a type of problem we discussed in chapter 12. The key insight is that both projection and perturbation methods create approximations of the form

$$\hat{f} = \sum a_i\varphi_i(x) \tag{15.6.1}$$

to solve such problems. First, consider perturbation methods. In regular perturbation methods the coefficients are fixed to be $a_i = \varepsilon^i$, and the functions $\varphi_i(x)$ are computed via perturbation methods. The $\varphi_i(x)$ functions produced by perturbation methods are very good functions for the problem at hand and are the best possible asymptotically. The problem is that fixing $a_i = \varepsilon^i$ may not be optimal when ε is not small.

Second, consider projection methods. In projection methods the basis functions $\varphi_i(x)$ are fixed a priori and the coefficients a_i are computed via projection methods. The coefficients are chosen to be the best possible choices relative to the $\varphi_i(x)$ and relative to some criterion. However, the bases are seldom the best possible for the problem. We usually choose general bases that satisfy some general criteria, such as smoothness and orthogonality conditions. Such bases may be adequate, but not the best. In particular, when we examine multidimensional problems, we often use tensor or complete bases that are quite large. It would be better if we had bases that were tailored for the problem.

The critical difference between perturbation and projection methods lies in what is fixed a priori and what is computed. Furthermore the strengths and weaknesses are complementary. The perturbation method does a good job at producing $\varphi_i(x)$ functions but is limited in its choices of the a_i coefficients, whereas the projection method chooses the a_i coefficients optimally but is limited in its $\varphi_i(x)$ choices. The *hybrid perturbation–projection* method combines the two methods in a way that takes advantage of their complementary strengths by choosing well both the basis functions and their coefficients. Algorithm 15.1 summarizes the procedure. First one formulates a continuum of problems which includes the specific problem we are trying to solve. This continuum should be parameterized by some ε which can be used as a perturbation parameter. Second, we use perturbation methods to construct a finite set of basis functions. Third, one uses projection methods to find a linear combination of the basis functions which approximately solves the problem of interest.

Algorithm 15.1   Hybrid Projection-Perturbation Method

Objective: Solve an equation $\mathcal{N}f = 0$.

Initialization. Construct a continuum of problems $\mathcal{H}(\varepsilon)f = 0$, where $\mathcal{H}(0)f = 0$ has the known solution f_0, and $\mathcal{H}(1) = \mathcal{N}$.

Step 1. Solve a perturbation problem, arriving at an approximation

$$f(x) \sim \sum_{i=1}^{n} \delta_i(\varepsilon)\varphi_i(x)$$

for some gauge sequence δ_i.

Step 2. Apply a projection method, using the basis $\varphi_i(x)$, to choose the a_i coefficients that produce a good solution of the form

$$\hat{f}(x) = \sum_{i=1}^{n} a_i\varphi_i(x).$$

To illustrate the hybrid perturbation–projection method, consider the continuous-time one-sector deterministic growth problem and the perturbations we examined in section 13.5; specifically, we consider the parameterized family

$$C_k(k, \varepsilon)(f(k) - C(k, \varepsilon)) - \varepsilon C(k, \varepsilon)(f'(k) - \rho) = 0, \qquad (15.6.2)$$

where $\varepsilon \equiv -\gamma^{-1}$ is the perturbation parameter. When $\varepsilon = 0$, the utility function displays "infinite" curvature and the solution is $C(k, 0) = f(k)$. We found that the first perturbation showed that

$$C_\varepsilon(k, 0) = f\left(\frac{\rho}{f'} - 1\right). \qquad (15.6.3)$$

Further differentiation of (15.6.2) yields

$$C_{\varepsilon\varepsilon}(k, 0) = \frac{2\rho(f' - \rho)f''}{(f')^4}. \qquad (15.6.4)$$

This is a process that can continue indefinitely. Note the differences between the collection $\{C, C_\varepsilon, C_{\varepsilon\varepsilon}\}$ and the polynomial bases we used in chapter 11. The functions used in C_ε and $C_{\varepsilon\varepsilon}$ involve k^α and other fractional powers of k, functions that are not spanned by finite sets of ordinary polynomials.

We next compare the quality of the perturbation approximation and the hybrid result using the example $\gamma = -2$, $\alpha = 0.25$, $\rho = 0.05$, and $f(k) = 0.2k^{0.25}$. In this case the collection $\{C, C_\varepsilon, C_{\varepsilon\varepsilon}\}$ spans the same functions as does $\{k^{0.25}, k, k^{1.75}\}$. The regular perturbation approach forms the approximation

$$C(k, \varepsilon) \doteq \sum_{i=0}^{n} \frac{\varepsilon^i}{i!} \frac{d^i C}{d\varepsilon^i}(k, 0).$$

The choice $\gamma = -2$ corresponds to $\varepsilon = 0.5$. In this case the three-term perturbation approximation is

$$\hat{C}_p(k) = 0.1k^{0.25} + 0.25k - 0.15k^{1.75}.$$

$\hat{C}_p$ does a very poor job because it has a maximum error of 30 percent on the interval $k \in [0.5, 1.5]$. In fact it is foolish to expect this perturbation will do well, since we are expanding around $\varepsilon = 0$ and negative values of ε are economically nonsensical.

Regular perturbation imposes $a_i = \varepsilon^i/i!$, which are the correct choices for ε very close to zero. However, as ε moves away from zero, alternative choices may be better. The hybrid perturbation–projection method is to use the functions $C(k, 0)$, $C_\varepsilon(k, 0)$,

$C_{\varepsilon\varepsilon}(k,0)$, $C_{\varepsilon\varepsilon\varepsilon}(k,0)$, etc., as basis functions, and let projection conditions determine the $a_i(\varepsilon)$ coefficients in the series

$$\sum_{i=0}^{n} a_i(\varepsilon) \frac{d^i C}{d\varepsilon^i}(k,0).$$

If we use the C, C_ε, and $C_{\varepsilon\varepsilon}$ functions as basis elements, and collocate at the three zeros of the cubic Chebyshev polynomial adapted to $[0.5, 1.5]$, we arrive at the approximation

$$\hat{C}_{h,1}(k) = 0.1341\, k^{0.25} + 0.0761\, k^{1.0} - 0.0101\, k^{1.75}.$$

$\hat{C}_{h,1}$ has a maximum relative error of 0.1 percent, much better than that for $\hat{C}_p$. This should not come as too much of a surprise, since choosing the optimal coefficients should do better than just taking the integral powers of ε. It is somewhat surprising that it does two orders of magnitude better based on so few points. This example also shows that even if the perturbation result does poorly, we can still use the functions to construct a good approximation.

While $\hat{C}_{h,1}$ does well, there may be a natural element to add to the basis. In particular, $\hat{C}_{h,1}$ does not include a constant term. We next add 1 to our hybrid basis, collocate at the degree four Chebyshev zeros, and arrive at the approximation

$$\hat{C}_{h,2}(k) = -0.0266 + 0.1772\, k^{0.25} + 0.0527\, k^{1.0} - 0.0033\, k^{1.75}.$$

$C_{h,2}$ has a maximum relative error of 0.03 percent, even better than $\hat{C}_p$. Figure 15.2 displays the graphs of the Euler equation errors, (15.6.2), normalized by ρC, for $\hat{C}_p(k)$, $\hat{C}_{h,1}(k)$, and $\hat{C}_{h,2}(k)$. We see that the Euler equation errors are rather uniform over the range $k \in [0.5, 1.5]$ and that the Euler equation errors are good indicators for the error of each approximation.

This example illustrates the potential of the hybrid perturbation–projection method. The perturbation phase constructs a basis that is tailored for the problem at hand. With such a tailored basis the projection step should do well with a small number of basis elements. General bases will likely incorporate basis elements that are of little value and unlikely to incorporate individual elements that efficiently capture the true shape of the solution. Furthermore all the advantages which arise with general bases can be achieved with the bases constructed by perturbation methods. For example, many general bases are orthogonal, a fact that assists the projection method in computing the coefficients. The bases constructed by perturbation methods are unlikely to be orthogonal, but one can construct an equivalent orthogonal basis using the Gram-Schmidt process. The resulting orthogonal

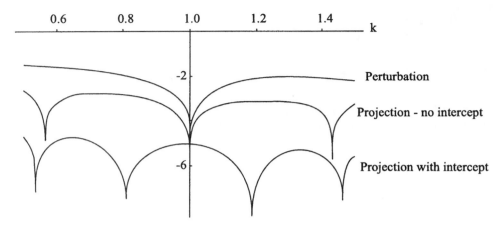

Figure 15.2
Euler equation errors for hybrid methods

basis retains the information from the perturbation process but will help to avoid ill-conditioning problems.

The hybrid method is potentially very useful in problems with several dimensions where general bases, even complete polynomial bases, are large. All that is necessary is a single parameter that can smoothly move the problem from a case with a known solution to the case of interest. The number of perturbation functions needed for the projection step depends on how much the problem changes as the parameter changes, not on the number of dimensions of the problem. Better bases may be possible by using more than one perturbation parameter and perturbing around more than one degenerate case. The key point is that the size of the resulting basis is under the control of the analyst, not dictated by the dimensionality of the problem.

15.7   Further Reading and Summary

The asymptotic methods discussed in this chapter have not been used much in economics. Judd and Guu (1996) follow up on Samuelson (1970) and compute asymptotic expansions for equilibrium asset prices. Dixit (1991) derives asymptotic rules for stochastic control problems with adjustment costs. Laplace's method is used in the statistical literature; for example, see Tierney and Kadane (1986) and Tierney et al. (1986). Similar asymptotic methods were used in Holly and Phillips (1979) and Ghysels and Lieberman (1983).

The asymptotic methods presented in this chapter go beyond simple applications of the Taylor series and implicit function theorems. The basic bifurcation ideas presented here are based on the Lyaponuv-Schmidt procedure; see Zeidler (1986) and Aubin and Ekeland (1984) for extended presentations. The unknown gauge procedures are based on the Newton polygon method; see Zeidler (1986) for a discussion. Bleistein and Handelsman (1976) and Estrada and Kanwal (1994) present the foundations behind Laplace's method. Economists are somewhat more familiar with the Hopf bifurcation and other methods from dynamical systems theory; see Chow and Hale (1982), Benhabib and Nishimura (1979), and Zhang (1988). The bifurcation methods from dynamical theory are related to the bifurcation methods we presented and can also be used for computational purposes. Bender and Orszag (1978) give a good general introduction to many applied mathematics techniques.

Symbolic software, such as Macsyma, Maple, and Mathematica, is useful in deriving all the critical formulas in this chapter and possible extensions. For example, it would be very difficult to derive high-order terms in a multidimensional application of Laplace's method, but symbolic software following Laplace's approach could sort out the critical elements.

This and the previous chapters have just touched on asymptotic methods. Bensoussan (1986) presents a much greater variety of procedures, including much more difficult singular perturbation problems. Budd et al. (1993) applies singular perturbation methods to a dynamic game. Judd (1996) reviews perturbation methods.

Exercises

1. Suppose that there are three risk types in the RSW model, an agent has an endowment of w_1 or w_2 with $w_1 > w_2$, and with the probability of a type i agent having the higher-value endowment being p_i, i, $i = 1, 2, 3$, $p_1 \geq p_2 \geq p_3$. Express the Rothschild-Stiglitz Nash equilibrium allocations. At $p_1 = p_2 = p_3 = p$ the equilibrium degenerates to perfect insurance. Consider the perturbation $p_1 = p$, $p_2 = p - \alpha\varepsilon$, $p_3 = p - \varepsilon$, where $0 \leq \alpha \leq 1$. Compute first- and second-order asymptotic expansions for equilibrium allocations in terms of ε. If $\alpha = 0$ or $\alpha = 1$, this problem reduces to a two-type model. For small ε, what is the worst α from the type 1 agents' perspective? Compare the answers from perturbation methods to those obtained using nonlinear equation methods.

2. Assume that there are two investors of different tastes over final wealth and different initial wealth investing in two risky assets. Compute the equilibrium asset prices for risky assets using theorem 15.1.2, assuming exponential utility and log normal returns. Compare results to nonlinear equation methods of solution.

3. Assume that $u(c) = c^{1+\gamma}/(1 + \gamma)$. Write programs to compute

$$\frac{1}{\sqrt{2\pi}\sigma} \int_{-\infty}^{\infty} u(R + e^{z+\mu})e^{-z^2/2\sigma^2} dz$$

in two ways. First, use Gauss-Hermite quadrature rules of varying precision. Second, replace $u(c)$ with an nth-order Taylor expansion based at $c = c_0$. Compute and compare the two ways for $R = 1.01$, $\mu = 0.06$, 0.12, $\sigma = 0.2, 0.4, 1.0$, $c_0 = R + e^\mu, R + e^{\mu-\sigma}, R + e^{\mu+\sigma}$, and $n = 1, 2, 3, 4, 5$. Report on the time versus accuracy trade-offs across the methods. Which are efficient?

4.   Repeat exercise 3 for the multidimensional case. That is, use the two methods to compute approximations to

$$\int_{-\infty}^{\infty} \cdots \int_{-\infty}^{\infty} u(c) e^{-z_1^2/2\sigma_1^2} \cdots e^{-z_n^2/2\sigma_n^2} \, dz_1 \cdots dz_n,$$

where

$$c = R + e^{z_1 + \mu_1} + \cdots + e^{z_n + \mu_n}.$$

Use the range of μ's and σ's listed in exercise 3. How do the methods compare as n goes from 1 up to 6?

5.   Consider the first-order condition for portfolio allocation

$$0 = \int_{-\infty}^{\infty} u'(\omega R + (1 - \omega) e^{z+\mu})(R - e^{z+\mu}) e^{-z^2/2\sigma^2} \, dz$$

for various CRRA functions u. The optimal ω can be computed by solving this first-order condition. How are the solutions for ω affected by the choice of technique used to compute the integral? (Use the techniques described in exercise 3 and the parameter values specified there.)

6.   Solve (15.6.2) using the hybrid perturbation–projection method for various CRRA utility functions and various CES production functions. Compare to other alternative bases such as bases in $\log k$.

V APPLICATIONS TO DYNAMIC EQUILIBRIUM ANALYSIS

16 Solution Methods for Perfect Foresight Models

Dynamic models of equilibrium are increasingly used in economic analysis, but they present computational challenges. Sometimes dynamic models have equilibria that are solutions to some social planner's problem. In those cases we can apply the numerical dynamic programming and optimal control methods presented in chapters 10–12. However, many interesting problems have neither a closed-form solution nor any optimality characterization; this is particularly the case for problems in public finance, macroeconomics, and industrial organization where distortions of some sort preclude a social planner characterization. In those cases we must develop more general methods.

In this and the next chapter, we focus on methods for solving dynamic equilibrium models. In this chapter we discuss methods for solving nonlinear perfect foresight competitive models. There are two approaches to computing equilibrium in such models. First, we can focus on computing the equilibrium path of endogenous variables, such as prices and quantities. This is essentially the same approach as that of computable general equilibrium: Treat goods consumed at different times as different commodities, and compute the price of each time-differentiated good; we call this the *time domain* approach. Time domain methods produce large systems of nonlinear equations. Some methods exploit the dynamic structure to reduce equilibrium to the solution of a system of difference or differential equations. In general, the challenge is to find some structure that replaces large systems of nonlinear equations with more manageable problems.

The second approach is a recursive one, similar to dynamic programming methods of chapter 12. This approach first identifies state variables and expresses the equilibrium decision and pricing feedback rules as functions of the state variables. Recursive approaches are particularly useful in autonomous problems. Even though the recursive approach is not necessary for most of the deterministic models of this chapter, we introduce recursive equilibrium methods here because it is easy to highlight their key features. In the next chapter we take up stochastic rational expectations models where the recursive approach is the only practical approach. In this chapter we also apply the recursive approach to a simple time consistency problem, indicating the usefulness of the recursive approach in dynamic strategic contexts.

In all cases methods for solving perfect foresight models combine many tools of numerical analysis. Computing demand and supply in dynamic models require us to combine optimization and optimal control methods. Computing equilibrium requires us to apply nonlinear equation methods. We will often use approximation and projection methods to construct approximate solutions. We can create efficient algorithms by appropriately combining these various techniques.

16.1 A Simple Autonomous Overlapping Generations Model

We first examine computational methods for a simple, real, two-period overlapping generations (OLG) model. Assume that each individual lives for two periods, working in the first, and consuming in both the first and second periods. We assume that the common concave utility function is $u(c^y) - v(l) + \beta u(c^o)$, where c^y (c^o) is consumption in youth (old age) and l is labor supply in youth. We assume that a single good is used for both consumption and investment, and produced according to a concave gross production function $F(k, l)$, where k is the beginning-of-period capital stock; hence $k_{t+1} = F(k_t, l_t) - c_t$. Capital is owned solely by the old.

Let c_t^a be consumption in period t by age group $a \in \{y, o\}$ agents. The wage in period t is $w_t = F_l(k_t, l_t)$, and the gross return on capital is $R_t \equiv F_k(k_t, l_t)$. The old consume their wealth implying $c_t^o = R_t k_t$. The first-order condition for the young leisure-consumption decision is $w_t u'(c_t^y) = v'(l_t)$, and the intertemporal savings-consumption choice implies that $u'(c_t^y) = R_{t+1} u'(c_{t+1}^o)$. The budget constraint for the young born in period t is $(w_t l_t - c_t^y) R_{t+1} - c_{t+1}^o = 0$. The capital stock obeys the law of motion $k_{t+1} = w_t l_t - c_t^y$.

Dynamic Representation

In some cases we may be able to form a simple dynamic representation of equilibrium; this example is one such case. We attempt to represent equilibrium in the form

$$x_{t+1} = G(x_t) \tag{16.1.1}$$

for some list of variables x. In forming this system, it generally takes some introspection to choose x. In this model the beginning-of-period capital stock, k_t, is a predetermined state variable. We could include many other variables (and their lags) in the predetermined state vector, but we prefer to use a state of minimal size. We need to include endogenous variables in the state variable, enough so as to fix all other current endogenous variables. In our problem the current labor supply, l_t, is such a variable. The predetermined plus endogenous variables should be chosen so that they fix all future variables. We choose $x_t \equiv (k_t, l_t)^\top$.

Second, we express G efficiently. In this case, given $x_t = (k_t, l_t)^\top$, we compute

$$\begin{pmatrix} k_{t+1} \\ l_{t+1} \end{pmatrix} = x_{t+1} = G(x_t) \equiv \begin{pmatrix} G^1(k_t, l_t) \\ G^2(k_t, l_t) \end{pmatrix} \tag{16.1.2}$$

as follows:

1. Compute $R_t = F_k(k_t, l_t)$, $w_t = F_l(k_t, l_t)$, and $c_t^o = R_t k_t$.
2. Solve for c_t^y in $w_t u'(c_t^y) = v'(l_t)$.

3. Compute $k_{t+1} = w_t l_t - c_t^y$.

4. Solve for R_{t+1} in $u'(c_t^y) = R_{t+1} u'(R_{t+1} k_{t+1})$.

5. Solve for l_{t+1} in $R_{t+1} = F_k(k_{t+1}, l_{t+1})$.

There may be multiple solutions in some steps. In particular, step 4 may have multiple solutions if $u(c) = \log c$. In our examples we presume step 4 has a unique solution.

More generally, $x_t \in R^n$ is a list of variables, the equilibrium path is expressed implicitly as $H(x_t, x_{t+1}) = 0$ for some system of equations $H: R^{2n} \to R^n$, and the corresponding dynamic evolution law $x_{t+1} = G(x_t)$ is implicitly defined by $H(x, G(x)) = 0$. In such cases one must use nonlinear equation methods to compute x_{t+1} from x_t. Now that we have formulated our model as a dynamic system, we can begin computing the solution.

Steady States of Overlapping Generations Models

The next step is computing the steady-state. A steady state is characterized in our example by the equations

$$wu'(c^y) = v'(l), \quad u'(c^y) = Ru'(c^o), \quad R = F_k(k, l),$$

$$c^o = (wl - c^y)R, \quad k = wl - c^y, \quad w = F_l(k, l). \tag{16.1.3}$$

Let R^*, w^*, k^*, and l^* denote the steady state values for R, w, k, and l.

Local Analysis: Determinacy of the Steady State and Perturbations

Once we have computed a steady state, we must check that it is locally determinate. That is, we must show that for capital stocks near the steady state capital stock, k^*, there is a unique path consistent with the dynamical system $x_{t+1} = G(x_t)$ which converges to (k^*, l^*). If the system is not locally determinate, then either there is no such path or there is a continuum of such equilibrium paths. It is reasonable to assume that there is a steady state, but there is no presumption that it is locally determinate.

We check determinacy by applying the linearization methods discussed in chapters 13 and 14 to the dynamical system (16.1.2). In this case we need to compute the matrix $\begin{pmatrix} G_k^1 & G_l^1 \\ G_k^2 & G_l^2 \end{pmatrix}$ at the steady state values for k and l, and to compute its eigenvalues. Since we have one predetermined variable and one endogenous variable, determinacy requires one eigenvalue with modulus less than one and one eigenvalue with modulus greater than one. If these eigenvalue conditions do not hold, then the system is not locally determinate, and we must stop. We proceed under the assumption that the system is locally determinate.

Global Analysis of Autonomous Systems

Once we have computed a steady state and checked that it is locally determinate, we can compute a convergent path. We first compute convergent paths for k_0 close to k^*. Let $L(k)$ be the unique choice of l for each k that guarantees convergence. We want to know its slope near the steady state. The identity $l_{t+1} = L(k_{t+1})$, implies the functional relation

$$L(G^1(k, L(k))) = G^2(k, L(k)) \tag{16.1.4}$$

for all k. Differentiation of (16.1.4) at $k = k^*$ implies that

$$L'(k^*)(G_k^1(k^*, l^*) + G_l^1(k^*, l^*)L'(k^*)) = G_k^2(k^*, l^*) + G_l^2(k^*, l^*)L'(k^*),$$

which is a quadratic equation in $L'(k^*)$. We pick that solution that implies convergence.

Local determinacy implies that we can use the shooting methods of chapter 10 to solve for convergent paths. Forward shooting is probably a poor choice, so we discuss reverse shooting for our example. Once we have the steady state values k^* and l^*, we pick an $\varepsilon > 0$, define $l^- \equiv l^* - \varepsilon L'(k^*)$, $k^- \equiv k^* - \varepsilon$, and execute the implicitly defined iteration

$$(k_s, l_s) = G(k_{s+1}, l_{s+1}) \tag{16.1.5}$$

with the initial condition $(k_0, l_0) = (k^-, l^-)$. Here s is the number of periods until (k, l) hits (k^-, l^-), a point on the stable manifold near the steady state if we start at (k_s, l_s). Symmetrically we also execute (16.1.5) with $(k_0, l_0) = (k^+, l^+)$ where $l^+ \equiv l^* + \varepsilon L'(k^*)$, $k^+ \equiv k^* + \varepsilon$. The two reverse shootings trace out two (k, l) paths, whose union approximates the stable manifold in (k, l) space.

Both of these methods can be applied to compute convergent paths for general OLG models. The key fact is that autonomous OLG models are dynamic systems, and their dynamics can be computed using perturbation and shooting methods if the equilibrium is locally determinate.

16.2   Equilibrium in OLG Models: Time Domain Methods

We next discuss methods to compute equilibria for a wider variety of OLG models, including ones with long finite lives and temporary time-varying factors. The logic here differs from the previous section in that it relies on simple supply and demand aspects of the problem, and less on the formal dynamics. In this section we maintain the assumptions of a single good used for investment and consumption, and produced according to a CRTS production function $F(k, l)$. We assume each agent lives for D periods and has a general utility function $U(c_1, l_1, \ldots, c_D, l_D)$.

Computing Dynamic Supply and Demand

The first step in solving general equilibrium model in chapter 5 was to compute the demand of each agent. We can similarly compute supply and demand for each agent in OLG models in terms of the dynamic sequence of prices. The key organizing idea in solving the general OLG model is that each agent in an OLG model cares about only a few prices, and equilibrium is a path of prices along which supply and demand are in balance. We first choose some combination of variables whose paths characterize equilibrium. This could be a sequence of factor supply variables, a sequence of price variables, or some combination. We analyze the simple example of section 16.1 and focus on the gross interest rate, R_t, and wage, w_t, paths. The idea is to search for interest rate and wage paths that imply that supply equals demand in the factor markets at every time t. If we had several commodities or several factors, we would have to compute a price path for each such good; otherwise, all the details are unchanged.

The factor supply implications of a (R_t, w_t) sequence in the two-period OLG model of the previous section can also be easily computed. The (k_{t+1}^s, l_t^s) factor supply path is fixed by the life-cycle first-order conditions and budget constraint

$$u'(c_t^y) = R_{t+1} \beta u'(R_{t+1} k_{t+1}^s),$$

$$w_t u'(c_t^y) = v'(l_t^s), \tag{16.2.1}$$

$$k_{t+1}^s = w_t l_t^s - c_t^y.$$

Equation (16.2.1) has a unique solution for (k_{t+1}^s, l_t^s) and c_t^y, since utility is concave.

Since $F(k, l)$ is CRTS, for each (R_t, w_t) pair there is a unique capital stock demand k_t^d determined by the marginal productivity condition $R_t = F_k(k_t^d, l_t^s)$ and labor demand l_t^d determined by $w_t = F_l(k_t^s, l_t^d)$. This (k_t^d, l_t^d) path describes the demand implications of the (R_t, w_t) path.

In more general OLG models, the factor supplies and demands of each generation depend on several realizations of R and w, and factor supply in each period depends on the decisions of agents from several cohorts. Suppose that agents live for D periods and that each agent in each cohort has the same tastes and endowment. The factor supply problem for each agent is the solution to a life-cycle problem; let $K_t^{s,a}((R_t, w_t)_{t=1}^\infty)$ be the supply of capital at time t by agents born in period $t - a + 1$. Then

$$K_t^s((R_t, w_t)_{t=1}^\infty) = \sum_{a=1}^{D} K_t^{s,a}((R_t, w_t)_{t=1}^\infty)$$

expresses the total supply of capital at time t as a function of the factor price sequence $(R_t, w_t)_{t=1}^\infty$; similarly $L_t^s((R_t, w_t)_{t=1}^\infty)$, $K_t^d((R_t, w_t)_{t=1}^\infty)$, and $L_t^d((R_t, w_t)_{t=1}^\infty)$ represent labor supply, and capital and labor demand at time t. Equilibrium is then expressed as a sequence $(R_t, w_t)_{t=1}^\infty$ such that

$$K_t^s((R_t, w_t)_{t=1}^\infty) = K_t^d((R_t, w_t)_{t=0}^\infty), \qquad t = 1, 2, \ldots,$$

$$L_t^s((R_t, w_t)_{t=1}^\infty) = L_t^d((R_t, w_t)_{t=1}^\infty), \qquad t = 1, 2, \ldots. \tag{16.2.2}$$

Initially capital is owned by the agents alive at time $t = 1$, and it is an endowment that enters the budget constraint of the agents alive at $t = 1$. The aggregate capital stock specifies the capital supply at $t = 1$.

The simple OLG model we described above is just one such example of (16.1.2). All intertemporal perfect foresight models boil down to systems such as (16.2.2) for appropriate definitions of k and l. We are not assuming that the model is autonomous; policy variables can change with time, and we could have time-varying technology and tastes. Below we present methods for solving general perfect foresight models expressed in the form (16.2.2).

A Tatonnement Method

The system (16.2.2) states the problem in terms of basic supply and demand concepts, but since it is a problem with an infinite number of unknowns, it is not possible to solve numerically. We need to reduce this problem to a finite-dimensional problem, but we also want to exploit special features of OLG models that can help.

The first step we take is to assume that equilibrium converges to the steady state, that $(R_t, w_t) = (R^*, w^*)$, their steady state values, for $t > T$ for some large T, and find the subsequence $(R_t, w_t)_{t=1}^T$ at which factor markets clear in periods 1 through T. This truncates the system and generates little error if T is large enough. The desire to make T large means that we still have a large number of unknowns.

There are two ways commonly used to solve the resulting finite-dimensional system. The first approach uses a price-adjustment method motivated by the supply-demand intuition. Given a $(R_t, w_t)_{t=1}^T$ sequence, one calculates the resulting excess demand sequence and adjusts the factor price sequence guess so as to reduce (hopefully) the excess demand. A Gauss-Jacobi tatonnement procedure is outlined in algorithm 16.1.

Algorithm 16.1   OLG Tatonnement Algorithm

Objective: Solve (16.2.2) given the initial capital stock k_0^s.

Initialization. Choose target horizon T, adjustment factor $\lambda > 0$, and convergence criterion $\varepsilon > 0$. Choose an initial guess $(R_t^0, w_t^0)_{t=0}^T$ for the initial factor price path; set R_t and w_t equal to their steady state values for $t > T$.

Step 1. Given the guess $(R_t^i, w_t^i)_{t=0}^T$, compute the demand and supply paths, $(k_t^d, l_t^d)_{t=1}^T$ and $(k_t^s, l_t^s)_{t=0}^T$, assuming that $(R_t, w_t) = (R^*, w^*)$ for $t > T$.

Step 2. If each component of $(k_t^d - k_t^s, l_t^d - l_t^s)_{t=0}^T$ has magnitude less than ε, STOP; else, go to step 3.

Step 3. Compute a new guess for $(R_t, w_t)_{t=0}^T$ from the excess demand vector. That is, for each $t = 0, 1, \ldots, T$,

$$R_t^{i+1} = R_t^i + \lambda(k_t^d - k_t^s), \quad w_t^{i+1} = w_t^i + \lambda(l_t^d - l_t^s);$$

then go to step 1.

This problem uses basic supply-demand intuition, raising (lowering) the factor price in periods when the factor is in excess demand (supply). At best this method converges linearly, but it often has problems converging. It is a Gauss-Jacobi approach. A Gauss-Seidel approach would be impractical because it is too costly to recompute the excess demands $k_t^d - k_t^s$ and $l_t^d - l_t^s$ whenever some R_t or w_t is changed. A block Gauss-Seidel adaptation may be sensible if large blocks are used.

Algorithm 16.1 computes equilibrium for periods 1 through T. We would also like the factor supplies at $t > T$ to equal their steady state values. We cannot also impose that condition. Instead, we check the excess demand for labor and capital at some times $t > T$ implied by our computed prices for $t \leq T$ and steady state prices for $t > T$. If they are all "small," we then accept the solution. If the excess demands are unacceptably large, we then try again using a larger T. Even if a choice of T is deemed to small, its "solution" could be used in constructing the initial guess for a larger T.

This procedure *assumes* convergence to a steady state. It also works best if the convergence is monotonic. If convergence involves cycles, a condition which is likely if there are any complex eigenvalues in the linearized system, then the results can be very sensitive to the choice of T.

It is natural to truncate the horizon when solving an infinite-horizon problem, and this is inherent in any time domain procedure where we compute the sequence of prices. However, these methods must be used carefully. In general, the solution of the time T truncated problem should be accepted only if the candidate solution is not sensitive to T and only if the deviations from equilibrium at times $t > T$ are not economically significant. These comments apply to any method that truncates the horizon, including the ones we explore next.

A Fixed-Point Iteration Method

A second procedure is a fixed-point iteration approach. Here we take a factor price sequence, use supply conditions to compute factor supplies, and then apply the factor demand equations to that factor supply sequence to arrive at the factor demand prices. This continues until the factor price sequence nearly repeats itself. Algorithm 16.2 makes this explicit.

Algorithm 16.2   OLG Fixed-Point Iteration Algorithm

Objective: Solve (16.2.2) given the initial capital stock k_0^s.

Initialization. Choose target horizon T, adjustment factor $\lambda > 0$, and convergence criterion $\varepsilon > 0$. Choose initial guess $(R_t^0, w_t^0)_{t=0}^T$ for the initial factor price path; set R_t and w_t equal to their steady state values for $t > T$.

Step 1. Given the guess $(R_t^i, w_t^i)_{t=0}^T$, compute the factor supply paths, $(k_t^s, l_t^s)_{t=0}^T$, assuming that $(R_t, w_t) = (R^*, w^*)$ for $t > T$.

Step 2. Given factor supply sequence $(k_t^i, l_t^i)_{t=0}^T$, compute the factor return sequence $(R_t^+, w_t^+)_{t=0}^T$ implied by the marginal product seqence $(F_k(k_t^i, l_t^i), F_l(k_t^i, l_t^i))_{t=0}^T$.

Step 3. If each component of $(R_t^+ - R_t^i, w_t^+ - w_t^i)_{t=0}^T$ has magnitude less than ε, STOP. Else, go to step 4.

Step 4. Compute a new guess $(R_t^{i+1}, w_t^{i+1})_{t=0}^T$: For each $t = 0, 1, \ldots, T$,

$$R_t^{i+1} = R_t^i + \lambda(R_t^+ - R_t^i), \quad w_t^{i+1} = w_t^i + \lambda(w_t^+ - w_t^i),$$

and go to step 1.

This is a conventional fixed-point iteration, "hog-cycle" approach with the extrapolation parameter λ. If $\lambda = 1$ leads to unstable iterations, one should try $\lambda < 1$ to stabilize the sequence. If the iterates appear to converge but slowly, then one should try values for λ that exceed unity to accelerate convergence. As with the tatonnement algorithm, we check if T is large enough by evaluating excess demands at some times $t > T + 1$.

There is no reason to be confident that either the tatonnement or fixed-point iteration methods will work. If the system of equations were diagonally dominant, we would expect convergence. However, in many models the supply of capital at time t depends significantly on the several interest rates, not just on R_t, and diagonal dominance is unlikely to hold. Generally, we cannot expect good perfomance from either of these methods.

Newton's Method and Nonlinear Equation Methods

A third approach is to use Newton's method or any of the other standard nonlinear equation solution methods without taking any advantage of the dynamic structure of the problem. A potentially important advantage of Newton's method is its local quadratic convergence. The strategy is fairly simple. We use step 1 in the tatonnement algorithm to compute the excess demand vector,

$$E \equiv (k_t^d - k_t^s, l_t^d - l_t^s)_{t=1}^T$$

as a function of

$$P \equiv (R_1, w_1, R_2, w_2, ..., R_T, w_T, R^*, w^*, ...).$$

The variable P has $2T$ unknowns, and the E vector has $2T$ components. Once we have written a routine that computes E as a function of P, we then use a Newton routine to compute a zero of $E(P)$.

Parametric Path Method

We saw in section 11.3 how to solve dynamic control problems by parameterizing the solution and choosing coefficients for the parametrization which result in the best solution. We can again use that idea to solve discrete-time perfect foresight models. In the previous section we proposed solving the system

$$E(P) = 0,$$

where $E(P)$ is the excess demand vector for a price vector P. There we allowed P to vary freely for periods 1 to T but imposed steady state values for $t > T$.

Let $\Psi(t; a)$ be some parameterization of functions of time. The *parametric path* method parameterizes the R_t sequence with $\Psi(t; a^R)$, parameterizes w_t with $\Psi(t; a^w)$ where $a^R, a^w \in R^m$, $m < T$, where hopefully m is much less than T. Let $P(a^R, a^w)$ represent the price vector P, which is implied by the parameter choices a^R and a^w. The task is to find coefficients a^R and a^w such that $E(P(a^R, a^w)) = 0$. This is generally impossible, since a^R and a^w have dimension less than T. Instead, we use some projection method to find a^R and a^w coefficients such that $E(P(a^R, a^w))$ is close to being the zero vector. The least squares approach solves

$$\min_{a^R, a^w} \sum_{i=1}^{2T} E_i(P(a^R, a^w))^2,$$

and alternative methods would fix some system of projection functions Π: $R^{2T} \to R^{2m}$ and solve the system

$$\Pi(E(P(a^R, a^w))) = 0.$$

Price path parameterizations should utilize basic features of factor price paths. The basic assumption in our methods is that factor prices converge to a steady state after some time T. If this is true, then it is also likely that such convergence takes place smoothly. One parameterization that models such paths is $a + (\sum_i b_i t^i)e^{-\lambda t}$ where a, b, and $\lambda > 0$ are free parameters. The polynomial piece allows for substantial flexibility at early times t, but this parameterization forces the path to converge to a through the dampening powers of the negative exponential.

In many applications the solution will not be smooth in the first few periods. This can arise, for example, if one is modeling anticipated changes in taxation or monetary policy. The parametric path can still be used in many cases. As long as these discrete changes are confined to early times $t < T_1$, then the solution for $t > T_1$ will likely be smooth. One could compute each factor price for each $t < T_1$ but approximate prices for $t > T_1$ parametrically.

An advantage of the parametric path method is that one can choose T to be large without having to solve a system of $2T$ equations in $2T$ unknowns. In any case the parametric path method can exploit smoothness properties of the price path and substantially reduce the dimensionality of the problem.

Application: Evaluation of Empirical Methods

Solutions to dynamic models can be used to address many questions. One important application is using them to evaluate empirical analyses. In this section we discuss one such exercise.

One of the great debates in empirical public finance is the effect of Social Security on savings. Feldstein (1974) argued that Social Security has reduced national saving, whereas Barro (1974) argued that Social Security has had no effect on savings. The empirical approaches to this question typically regress consumption on a variety of variables, but focus on a Social Security wealth (SSW) variable, that is, some variable that measures the privately perceived value of Social Security promises. Under Feldstein's arguments, the coefficient on SSW should be positive due to a wealth effect, but Barro invokes Ricardian neutrality to argue for a zero coefficient.

Since these empirical studies were not based on a structural model, the implications of the regression coefficients are unclear. Auerbach and Kotlikoff (1983) uses an OLG model to address the reliability of the methods used in this literature. We know the true answer in the Auerbach-Kotlikoff model: People live finite lives and regard SSW as wealth because it will be financed by taxes on people not yet born. Using their model, Auerbach and Kotlikoff (1983) simulate the response to the introduction of Social Security, assuming that the economy is initially in the no–Social Security steady state. This generates consumption, output, wage, interest rate, and SSW data. They then use this data in regression methods to "estimate" the response of consumption to SSW. They find that the regression results have little informative value in predicting the actual long-run response of consumption and savings to Social Security in their model. This is not surprising, for the regressions are not structural in any way nor based on even a reduced form for the critical behavioral functions.

While the Auerbach-Kotlikoff (1983) exercise is limited to a particular issue, the strategy is clear. The idea is to numerically solve a structural model, use it to generate data, and then apply an empirical method to the data. Since we know the true structure of the model generating the data, we can determine whether the empirical procedure can be used to infer properties of the structural model. Full structural empirical analysis is preferable but often infeasible. This approach allows one to use structural ideas to evaluate reduced-form empirical methods.

16.3 Fair-Taylor Method

The methods discussed in the previous section focused on supply-demand ideas, often ignoring dynamic elements. The Fair-Taylor method uses dynamic structure to solve perfect foresight models that have a relatively simple dynamic structure. We illustrate it here by applying it to the linear perfect foresight problem

$$y_t = \alpha y_{t+1} + x_t \tag{16.3.1}$$

with the side condition

$$-\infty < \lim_{t \to \infty} y_t < \infty. \tag{16.3.2}$$

In (16.3.1), y is the endogenous variable and x is a bounded exogenous variable. We focus on the problem of finding y_0 such that (16.3.1) and (16.3.2) hold. The true solution is

$$y_0 = \sum_{t=0}^{\infty} \alpha^t x_t.$$

The simple dynamic structure of (16.3.1) allows us to exploit dynamic ideas. The Fair-Taylor method first fixes a horizon T. Given a value for y_{T+1} (for the sake of simplicity we set $y_{T+1} = 0$), the collection

$$y_t = \alpha y_{t+1} + x_t, \qquad t = 0, 1, \ldots, T, \tag{16.3.3}$$

is a system of $T + 1$ equations in the $T + 1$ unknowns y_t. To solve (16.3.3), Fair-Taylor first makes a guess $Y_{T,t}^0$ for each y_t, $t = 1, \ldots, T$; again, assume that each initial guess is 0. Next the Fair-Taylor method creates a sequence of approximations. Let $Y_{T,t}^j$ denote the approximation for y_t in iteration j when we fix the horizon at T. Given the guess $Y_{T,t}^j$, the next iterate $Y_{T,t}^{j+1}$ is defined by the type I iteration (over t)

$$Y_{T,t}^{j+1} = \alpha Y_{T,t+1}^j + x_t, \qquad t = 0, 1, \ldots, T. \tag{16.3.4}$$

The iteration in (16.3.4) is called a *Type I iteration*. In (16.3.4) the new guess for y_t, $Y_{T,t}^{j+1}$, is computed by applying the RHS of (16.3.1) to the old guess of y_{t+1}, $Y_{T,t+1}^j$. For each j, $j = 1, \ldots, T$, we repeat (16.3.4); iterations over j are called *Type II iterations*. The combination of Type I and II iterations constitute a Gauss-Jacobi approach to solving (16.3.3), since the $j + 1$ guesses $Y_{T,t}^{j+1}$ are based only on the $Y_{T,t}^j$. $Y_{T,t}^{j+1}$ does not change if we set $j > T$, so we stop at $j = T$. More generally, the Fair-Taylor method stops at some earlier j if, for all t, $|Y_{T,t}^{j+1} - Y_{T,t}^j|$ is less than some convergence criterion.

Type I and II iterations solve the problem for a given terminal time T and terminal guess y_{T+1}. We next adjust the horizon. To do so, we now take the $Y_{T,t}^T$ solution and use it as the initial guess to compute the next problem where we let $T + 1$ be the terminal period; that is

$$Y_{T+1,t}^0 = Y_{T,t}^T, \qquad t = 0, 1, \ldots, T.$$

We now need a value for $Y_{T+1,T+1}^0$; again we choose zero. We continue to increase the terminal time until the successive paths change little; the iterations over successively larger T are called *Type III iterations*. As long as $\alpha < 1$, $Y_{T,0}^T$ converges to the correct value of y_0 as $T \to \infty$. In this example we set $Y_{T,T+1}^j = 0$ for each Type II iteration j and terminal date T; this choice should not affect the solution and has no impact on the final solution for this problem since $\alpha < 1$.

More generally, we try to find some bounded sequence y_t which solves the equation

$$g(y_t, y_{t+1}, x_t) = 0. \tag{16.3.5}$$

The Type I and II iterations in Fair-Taylor algorithm are implicitly defined by

$$g(Y_{T,t}^{j+1}, Y_{T,t+1}^j, x_t) = 0, \qquad t = 0, \ldots, T, \ j = 0, 1, \ldots. \tag{16.3.6}$$

In (16.3.6) each $Y_{T,t}^{j+1}$ is solved by a nonlinear equation solver if a direct solution is not available. Type III iterations then increase T until such changes produce little effect.

We next compare the Fair-Taylor method to reverse shooting. The reverse shooting method also fixes a horizon T, makes a guess for y_{T+1}, and solves (16.3.1). However, it implements the Gauss-Seidel iteration

$$Y_{T,t} = \alpha Y_{T,t+1} + x_t, \qquad t = T, T-1, \ldots, 0, \tag{16.3.7}$$

in one pass and with operation cost proportional to T. By computing the $Y_{T,t}$ sequence beginning with $t = T$ instead of $t = 0$, we bring the information at T immediately down to all earlier values of $Y_{T,t}$; in this example reverse shooting exploits the same idea as that used in the upwind Gauss-Seidel method of dynamic programming. The reverse shooting idea here is also equivalent to back-substitution in linear systems, since the linear system in (16.3.3) is triangular. Since reverse shooting solves the problem in one pass for a given T, we might as well take a large T and solve (16.3.7) once as opposed to trying out several different smaller T. In the more general problem (16.3.5), reverse shooting is the iteration

$$g(Y_{T,t}, Y_{T,t+1}, x_t) = 0, \qquad t = T, T-1, \ldots, 0.$$

Here we eliminate the need for Type I and II iterations.

This discussion has examined only problems with purely expectational variables since none of the components of y were predetermined. The Fair-Taylor method can be adapted to include predetermined variables; see Fair and Taylor (1983) for details.

16.4   Recursive Models and Dynamic Iteration Methods

The previous sections examined dynamic models and computed the time path of equilibrium prices. When a model depends on calendar time, those methods are the most natural to use.

For many perfect foresight models, equilibrium prices depend on some time-independent "state" of the economy at the time, where by state we mean a vector of variables that describes the economic condition of the economy. Such state variables may include capital stock, consumption habit, lagged prices, stock of government bonds, and so forth. In the equilibria of these deterministic models, the equilibrium at time t is determined solely by the state at time t, and it is independent of calendar time conditional on knowing the state. The transition from time t to time $t+1$ is determined by the state at time t. In time-autonomous models we may compute the time-autonomous transition rules instead of paths.

To illustrate recursive methods, we return to the simple deterministic, representative agent growth problem

$$\max_{c_t} \sum_{t=0}^{\infty} \beta^t u(c_t) \tag{16.4.1}$$

s.t. $\quad k_{t+1} = F(k_t) - c_t$.

We focus not on the equilibrium time path for c_t but rather on the rule, $c_t = C(k_t)$, relating the current capital stock to the equilibrium consumption choice. The equilibrium rule contains all the information we need to compute the equilibrium price path for any intial condition; therefore, by solving for $C(k)$, we are solving *all* perfect foresight problems of this model. Also, since we are looking for a function that is used at all time t, we have no need to truncate the horizon; therefore the problems that arise from truncation in time domain approaches, such as the sensitivity to the choice of the truncation time T, will not arise here.

In this section we will focus on the abstract iteration procedures in function spaces as well as the ways in which we implement the ideal iterations on real computers. While there will be some differences between the ideal and numerical processes, we will prescribe methods that minimize the differences.

Operator Representation of Equilibrium

The equilibrium consumption rule $C(k)$ satisfies

$$u'(C(k)) = \beta u'(C(F(k) - C(k)))F'(F(k) - C(k)) \tag{16.4.2}$$

This Euler equation can be represented as a zero of an operator as in

$$0 = u'(C(k)) - \beta u'(C(F(k) - C(k)))F'(F(k) - C(k))$$

$$\equiv (\mathcal{N}(C))(k). \tag{16.4.3}$$

$\mathcal{N}$ is an operator from continuous functions to continuous functions. From this perspective we are looking for a function C that $\mathcal{N}$ maps to the zero function.

Even though the Euler equation defines (16.4.3) in terms of one function $C(k)$, it is useful to think about the Euler equation more abstractly in ways not related to the economics. Note that the unknown function, C, occurs in four spots in (16.4.2). Let us consider the four occurrences of C independently and define the operator $\mathcal{F}$:

$$0 = u'(C_1) - \beta u'(C_2(F - C_3))F'(F - C_4)$$

$$\equiv \mathcal{F}(C_1, C_2, C_3, C_4). \tag{16.4.4}$$

When we rewrite the Euler equation in terms of the operator $\mathcal{F}$, we find that we are looking for a function C that solves the equation

$$0 = \mathcal{F}(C, C, C, C) \equiv \mathcal{N}(C). \tag{16.4.5}$$

The more general representation of (16.4.4) suggests a wide variety of iteration schemes. Before plunging ahead with a problem, it is best to examine various formulations, since different formulations will suggest different numerical approaches.

Sufficiency Problems and Boundary Conditions

Euler equations are necessary conditions for equilibrium and are the focus of our analysis. However, they are not sufficient conditions, for there often are solutions to the Euler conditions corresponding to excessive savings paths that violate the transversality condition at infinity. In this particular problem, all of those bad paths have the property that the capital stock does not converge to the steady state; therefore, if we find a solution with this property, we can reject it. In this model Amir et al. (1991) have shown that a sufficient condition for a policy function to be a local interior solution to the dynamic optimization problem is that $(C(x) - C(y))/(x - y) < 1$ for all x, y in the interval of permissible states. Therefore, if we have a solution C to the Euler equation, we can check this condition. In many optimal growth problems, we know that there is a bounded capture region (see Brock and Mirman 1972) under the optimal policy and, hence, in equilibrium; this is another condition that can be checked. The approach we use is to first find a $C(k)$ that solves (16.4.5) and check that it satisfies sufficient conditons.

Most solution methods for recursive models focus only on the Euler equations and ignore these global considerations. However, we must check that any candidate solution satisfies these critical global conditions. If a candidate does not, we then try again to find an acceptable solution. From a mathematical perspective this is bad practice. It would be far better to incorporate these global considerations as boundary conditions imposed on (16.4.5) that eliminate the extraneous solutions. Fortunately the models that economists have studied so far have enough inherent stability that the Euler equation methods are generally successful, but possibly only because of luck. This issue is not unique to this particular model, but generic in rational expectations modeling. We will not deal formally with this problem, since ex post checking and good initial guesses appear to suffice for the problems we discuss in this book; also such a discussion would take us far too deeply into functional analysis and beyond the scope of this text. However, this does not diminish the fact that analysts must be aware of the dangers involved when one does not incorporate stability conditions from dynamic theory into their numerical algorithms.

Since all of the methods to compute policy functions are examples of the projection approach, we will use the general projection method outline of chapter 11 as an outline of our discussion of them. We will first review various ways in which the problem may be formulated, and then discuss ways to find the solution.

Policy Function Representation

The discussion after (16.4.1) focused on the mathematically pure versions of the problem. The function $C(k)$ which solves (16.4.2) is not likely to be a simple function. All methods that do not discretize the state space parameterize the policy function $C(k)$ in some way. That is, they choose some functional form $\hat{C}(k; a)$ where each vector of coefficients a represents an approximation of $C(k)$ and then find a such that

$$0 \doteq \mathcal{N}(\hat{C}(\cdot\,; a)). \tag{16.4.6}$$

This representation limits our search for an approximate solution to the collection of functions spanned by various choices of a.

The literature has used various approximation schemes discussed in chapter 5 as well as some others. Obvious choices are piecewise linear functions, ordinary polynomials, splines, and Chebyshev polynomials. As long as we expect $C(k)$ to be smooth and lacking regions of high curvature, polynomial forms for $\hat{C}(k; a)$ are likely to work well. We know $C(k)$ is increasing; this indicates that we may want to use a shape-preserving method.

We also know that $C(k)$ is always positive; we can guarantee this by using a shape-preserving spline, or approximating $\log C(k)$. Positivity of $C(k)$ can be important since many common specifications of tastes imply that $u'(c)$ is not defined if $c < 0$. Approximation schemes that keep $\hat{C}(k; a)$ positive will guarantee that $u'(\hat{C}(k; a))$ is defined at all k for all choices of the a parameters.

Recursive methods do not truncate the horizon as did time domain methods. Since any numerical method must discretize the problem somewhere, we see here that we are replacing time truncation with discretization in the space of permissible policy functions, a discretization in the spectral domain. Which is better will depend on the problem. Time domain problems produces prices that satisfy equilibrium conditions for some initial period but may do poorly at later times. Recursive methods aim to produce approximations that have small errors at all times.

Time Iteration

We have seen that there are various ways to parameterize the policy function. The common factor is that they all reduce the problem to finding a finite number of parameters, a. We next discuss three iterative methods for computing the solution. This leads to choose the kind of iteration scheme used to determine a, the second key difference among methods. We first examine one problem-specific, iteration scheme that has been used in several economic contexts.

Time iteration is a natural iterative scheme for solving Euler equations. Time iteration implements the iterative scheme

$$0 = u'(C_{i+1}) - \beta u'(C_i(F - C_{i+1})) F'(F - C_{i+1}), \tag{16.4.7}$$

where i indexes the successive iterates. In terms of the notation defined in (16.4.4), time iteration implements the nonlinear functional iteration implicitly defined by

$$0 = \mathscr{F}(C_{i+1}, C_i, C_{i+1}, C_{i+1}). \tag{16.4.8}$$

The unique feature of time iteration is that it has some economic intuition. The basic idea is that if $C_i(k)$ is tomorrow's consumption policy function, then today's policy, denoted by $C_{i+1}(k)$, must satisfy

$$u'(C_{i+1}(k)) = \beta u'(C_i(F(k) - C_{i+1}(k)))F'(F(k) - C_{i+1}(k)). \tag{16.4.9}$$

As we let i increase, $C_i(k)$ hopefully converges to the infinite horizon solution. The critical fact is the monotonicity property of (16.4.9); that is, if $C_i'(k) > 0$ and $C_i(k) < C_{i-1}(k)$, then $C_{i+1}(k) < C_i(k)$ and C_{i+1} is an increasing function. Because of the monotonicity properties of the Euler equation, time iteration is reliable and convergent even though it uses only the Euler equation. Since we are solving the problem backward from a finite initial condition, time iteration will not converge to paths that violate global conditions such as the TVC_∞. This is one case where we are imposing a boundary condition.

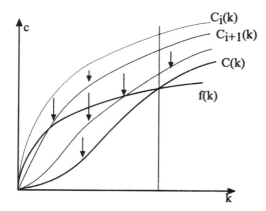

Figure 16.1
Time iteration method

The convergence result for the theoretical time iteration[1] scheme suggests that we use it for computational purposes. Algorithm 16.3 presents a computational implementation of time iteration.

Algorithm 16.3   Time Iteration for (16.4.2)

Initialization.   Pick a set of points k_j, $j = 1, \ldots, n$. Choose an approximation scheme $\hat{C}(k; a)$, $a \in R^m$, $m \le n$, and choose a^0 so that $\hat{C}(k; a^0) \doteq F(k)$. Choose a stopping criterion $\varepsilon > 0$.

Step 1. Given $\hat{C}(\cdot; a^i)$, compute $C_{i+1}(k_j)$ from (16.4.9) for k_j, $j = 1, \ldots, n$.

Step 2. Find an $a^{i+1} \in R^n$ so that the function $\hat{C}(\cdot; a^{i+1})$ approximates the data $(k_j, C_{i+1}(k_j))$.

Step 3. If $\|\hat{C}(\cdot; a^{i+1}) - \hat{C}(\cdot; a^i)\| < \varepsilon$, STOP; else go to step 1.

Figure 16.1 shows successive iterates of $C_i(k)$ where the initial guess has consumption exceeding output at all k. The iterates converge monotonically downward to the solution. We define $f(k) = F(k) - k$.

Unfortunately, time iteration is slow. Various acceleration schemes can speed up convergence, but it will remain slow. The reasons for its slow speed is that (16.4.9) involves a separate nonlinear equation for each k_j. Furthermore convergence for time iteration, as with value function iteration, is linear at best. Therefore we need many

---

1. Since $C(k)$ is related one to one to the marginal value of k, it is clear that this scheme for computing $C(k)$ is equivalent to using value iteration to compute the value function but is not the same as applying policy iteration to the dynamic programming version of this problem.

iterations to find a good approximation to the infinite-horizon problem, and each iteration is slow.

Unfortunately, it is the pure mathematical process described in (16.4.9) that is reliable and convergent, not necessarily the numerical procedure. In algorithm 16.3 we need to specify a particular approximation scheme $\hat{C}(k; a)$, and each iteration computes the solution to the Euler equation at only a finite number of k values. Convergence of the pure mathematical scheme in (16.4.8) does not imply convergence of algorithm 16.3 in general.

It is nontrivial to find a numerical process that inherits the reliability properties of the pure mathematical process, (16.4.8). One must choose the points and approximation scheme carefully. One reliable procedure is to choose a shape-preserving approximation scheme. It is obvious that the $\hat{C}(k; a)$ iterates in algorithm 16.3 will be monotone in k if the approximation procedure in step 2 is shape-preserving, but not otherwise in general. Many applications choose a piecewise linear approximation scheme, which is shape-preserving, when choosing the functional form for $\hat{C}(k; a)$. However, piecewise linear schemes will create kinks in the nonlinear equation problems in step 1 of algorithm 16.3. Better would be smoother shape-preserving schemes, such as the Schumaker shape-preserving quadratic spline scheme. Shape nonpreservation can generate convergence problems here as discussed in chapter 12. Other approximation schemes, such as polynomials and splines, may work, but they may also produce convergence problems.

Fixed-Point Iteration

We next develop a fixed-point iteration scheme for solving (16.4.3). Fixed-point iteration schemes were discussed in both chapters 3 and 5 to solve equations in R^n. The time iteration scheme discussed in the preceding section is an important special case of an iterative process since monotonicity properties of the iteration procedure lead to global convergence. In general, iteration schemes do not possess such properties. We now turn to a simple fixed-point iteration method.

Fixed-point iteration applied to (16.4.3) implements the iterative scheme defined implicitly by

$$0 = \mathscr{F}(C_{i+1}, C_i, C_i, C_i). \tag{16.4.10}$$

This has an advantage in that C_{i+1} is easy to compute since at any k,

$$C_{i+1}(k) = (u')^{-1}(\beta u'(C_i(F(k) - C_i(k))) F'(F(k) - C_i(k)))$$

$$\equiv (T_{fp}(C_i))(k). \tag{16.4.11}$$

Algorithm 16.4 implements fixed-point iteration.

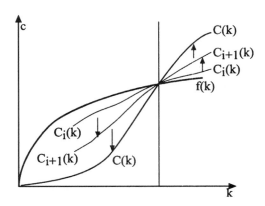

Figure 16.2
Fixed-point iteration method

Algorithm 16.4   Fixed-Point Iteration for (16.4.2)

Initialization. Pick a set of points $k_j, j = 1, \ldots, n$. Choose an approximation scheme $\hat{C}(k; a)$, $a \in R^m$, $m \le n$, and choose a^0 so that $\hat{C}(k; a^0) \doteq F(k) - k$. Choose a stopping criterion $\varepsilon > 0$.

Step 1. Compute $C_{i+1}(k_j)$ using (16.4.11) for k_j, $j = 1, \ldots, n$.

Step 2. Find an $a^{i+1} \in R^n$ so that the function $\hat{C}(\cdot; a^{i+1})$ approximates the data $(k_j, C_{i+1}(k_j))$.

Step 3. If $\|\hat{C}(\cdot; a^{i+1}) - \hat{C}(\cdot; a^i)\| < \varepsilon$, STOP; else go to step 1.

Algorithm 16.4 is the same as algorithm 16.3 except that we replace a nonlinear equation problem in step 1 of algorithm 16.3 with simply computing $C_{i+1}(k_j)$ by just plugging k_j into the expression for $(T_{fp}(C_i))(k)$ in (16.4.11).

Figure 16.2 shows successive iterates of $C_i(k)$ where the initial guess has consumption equal to output. We define $f(k) = F(k) - k$. Since the initial guess goes through the steady state, the iterates rotate counterclockwise to the solution.

We have seen that both fixed-point iteration and time iteration are cases of different indexing schemes in (16.4.8) and (16.4.10). We could define many other schemes by using different combinations of i and $i + 1$ indexing. We could even define schemes which include $i - 1$ indexes. Once we have expressed the problem in the form (16.4.4) and (16.4.5), many schemes suggest themselves. We have just presented two common schemes. Since they both arise from economic intuition, it is not clear that they are the best from a numerical approach.

Fixed-Point Iteration and Stability

Unlike time iteration, fixed-point iteration may be unstable. It is not surprising that stability is a problem for fixed-point iteration, since it is essentially executing a hog-cycle iteration. We now consider the stability of fixed-point iteration. This exercise will introduce us to a way that will help us choose among iteration schemes and convert unstable ones into stable ones. Fixed-point iteration is defined by $C_{i+1} = \Psi$, where Ψ is implicitly defined by

$$u'(\Psi(k)) = \beta u'(C(F(k) - C(k)))F'(F(k) - C(k)). \tag{16.4.12}$$

Let k^* denote the steady state capital stock. Suppose that $C(k, \varepsilon) = \bar{C}(k) + \varepsilon\xi(k)$, for some fixed consumption function $\bar{C}(k)$ and some deviation function $\xi(k)$. We want to study how Ψ changes as C changes in the direction of $\xi(k)$. As we change ε away from $\varepsilon = 0$, Ψ will change, with the (Gateaux) derivative in the ξ direction at $\varepsilon = 0$ being defined by

$$u''(\Psi(k))\Psi_\varepsilon(k)$$

$$= \beta u''(\bar{C}(F(k) - \bar{C}(k)))\xi(F(k) - \bar{C}(k))F'(F(k) - \bar{C}(k))$$

$$+ \beta u''(\bar{C}(F(k) - \bar{C}(k)))\bar{C}'(F(k) - \bar{C}(k))\,[-\xi(k)]F'(F(k) - \bar{C}(k))$$

$$+ \beta u'(\bar{C}(F(k) - \bar{C}(k)))F''(F(k) - \bar{C}(k))\,[-\xi(k)]. \tag{16.4.13}$$

At the fixed point C, $C = \Psi$, and at the steady state k^*, $\beta F'(k^*) = 1$. Therefore at k^* we conclude that

$$u''(C(k^*))\Psi_\varepsilon(k^*) = \xi(k^*)[u''(C(k^*))[1 - C'(k^*)] - \beta u'(C(k^*))F''(k^*)]. \tag{16.4.14}$$

If fixed-point iteration is to be stable, we must have $|\Psi_\varepsilon(k^*)| < |\xi(k^*)|$, which, since $C' > 0$ and $u'F''/u'' > 0$, is equivalent to

$$1 - \bar{C}'(k^*) - \beta\frac{u'}{u''}F''(k^*) > -1, \tag{16.4.15}$$

where the value of $C'(k^*)$ was computed in (13.7.17).

The LHS of (16.4.15) is always less than one, implying that any failure of convergence is due to exploding oscillations. Since C' is greater as u is more linear, the LHS will exceed 2 if absolute risk aversion, u'/u'', is sufficiently small. Therefore instability is a possibility. In particular, it is straightforward to show that if $f(k) = 0.2k^{0.25}$, $\beta = 0.9$, and $u = c^{0.01}$, then (16.4.15) is not satisfied and fixed-point iteration is unstable. For this example, fixed-point iteration is stable for empirically relevant choices of tastes and technology.

This stability analysis focused on the pure mathematical problem (16.4.12), not on any particular computational implementation. However, convergence problems in (16.4.12) will probably cause convergence problems in algorithm 16.4. A natural way to address convergence problems of the kind in (16.4.12) is to dampen the iteration, as in the scheme

$$0 = \mathscr{F}(C_{i+1/2}, C_i, C_i, C_i),$$

$$C_{i+1} = (1 - \lambda)C_{i+1/2} + \lambda C_i, \tag{16.4.16}$$

with $\lambda < 1$.

Initial Guesses and Boundary Conditions

We have focused on the iterative steps of time iteration and fixed-point iteration. We need to emphasize two details that may greatly affect an algorithm's efficiency. First, the initial guess in any iterative scheme is important. Second, many functional equations are not properly specified until one imposes some side-conditions, called boundary conditions. In perfect foresight models we have good answers to these problems.

First, knowledge of the steady state gives us a boundary condition. If the steady state capital stock is k^* and the steady state consumption is c^*, then we know $C(k^*) = c^*$. We can impose this on each iterate of time iteration or fixed-point iteration, or parameterize our solution family so as to make this true for each element.

Second, linearizing the problem around the steady state often provides us with a good initial guess. Here the tangent hyperplane of the stable manifold will be useful, since it is the linear approximation of the equilibrium decision rule in the neighborhood of the steady state.

16.5 Recursive Models with Nonlinear Equation Methods

The previous sections used solution methods that are closely related to the theoretical treatment of the pure mathematical problem, (16.4.5). However, our parametric approximation schemes reduce the problem to a finite-dimensional nonlinear equation in the unknown coefficients. In this section we basically ignore the dynamic nature of the true problem and treat the approximate Euler equation (16.4.6) as a nonlinear equation in the unknown parameters and apply standard methods for nonlinear equations to solve it.

This has the advantage that it actually formulates the problem in the most flexible fashion; that is, after making the approximation decisions implicit in (16.4.6), the problem is just a nonlinear equation in R^n, nothing more and nothing less. For example, we could use Newton's method; if Newton's method works, it has quadratic convergence asymptotically. Other methods, such as a homotopy method, could also be used. The choice will depend on the size of the problem and its curvature properties. It may be that some special structure of a problem will make time iteration or fixed-point iteration useful. However, by focusing on the nonlinear equation nature of (16.4.6), we now begin to consider a variety of methods that do not immediately come to mind when we view the functional problem (16.4.6) from an economic perspective. While economics ideas may be useful in devising numerical solutions, it is often useful to stop thinking economics and start thinking mathematics once one has a characterization of equilibrium.

We will now describe more fully the details of a Chebyshev-Newton projection method approach to the problem. First of all, we approximate C with the linear representation

$$\hat{C}(k;a) = \sum_{i=1}^{n} a_i \psi_i(k), \tag{16.5.1}$$

where $\psi_i(k) \equiv T_{i-1}(2(k-k_m)/(k_M-k_m)-1)$ and n is the number of terms used. The domain D of our approximation will be some interval $[k_m, k_M]$. Since the special properties of Chebyshev polynomials apply to their restriction to $[-1, 1]$, we need to apply the linear transformation $2(k-k_m)/(k_M-k_m)-1$ to k to permit us to form Chebyshev polynomials on D. k_m and k_M are chosen so that the solution will have k confined to $[k_m, k_M]$. In particular, $[k_m, k_M]$ must contain the steady state, a point that we can determine before calculations begin. The Euler equation implies the residual function

$$R(k;a) = u'(\hat{C}(k;a)) - \beta u'(\hat{C}(F(k) - \hat{C}(k;a);a))F'(F(k) - \hat{C}(k;a)). \tag{16.5.2}$$

We have several ways to compute a. First, we consider collocation. We choose n values of k, denoted by k_j, $j = 1, \ldots, n$. Orthogonal collocation chooses the k_j to be the n zeros of ψ_{n+1}, which are themselves linear transforms of the Chebyshev zeros. We then form the collection of equations

$$R(k_j;a) = 0, \qquad j = 1, \ldots, n. \tag{16.5.3}$$

This is now a nonlinear system of equations in the unknown $a \in R^n$. To find a, we can use any nonlinear equation method. We choose to use Newton's method.

Table 16.1
Chebyshev coefficients for consumption function

i	$n = 2$	$n = 5$	$n = 9$	$n = 15$
1	0.0589755899	0.0600095844	0.0600137797	0.0600137922
2	0.0281934398	0.0284278730	0.0284329464	0.0284329804
3		−0.0114191783	−0.0113529374	−0.0113529464
4		0.0007725731	0.0006990930	0.0006988353
5		−0.0001616767	−0.0001633928	−0.0001634209
6			0.0000427201	0.0000430853
7			−0.0000123570	−0.0000122160
8			0.0000042498	0.0000036367
9			−0.0000011464	−0.0000011212
10				0.0000003557
11				−0.0000001147
12				0.0000000370
13				−0.0000000129
14				0.0000000052
15				−0.0000000015

Note: Each entry is the coefficient of the ith Chebyshev polynomial (over the interval $[0.333, 1.667]$) in the n-term approximation of the consumption policy function in (16.5.3) for the case discussed in section 16.5.

Table 16.1 displays an instance of this procedure where capital share is 0.25, $\gamma = -0.9$, and $[k_m, k_M] = [0.333, 0.667]$. The different columns display the solutions for a for various choices of n. The key fact to note is that the coefficients are stable as n increases. This is due to the orthogonality properties of the Chebyshev basis. This property is useful because one can first solve the $n = 2$ case, an easy problem solved rapidly, and then use that solution as an initial guess for higher choices of n. Note also how the coefficients drop rapidly in the $n = 5$, 9, and 15 cases. In light of theorem 6.4.2, this indicates that we are approximating a smooth function. Since the high-order Chebyshev coefficients are so small and stable as we increase n, we feel comfortable in accepting the solution to (16.5.3) with $n = 15$ as our solution to (16.4.2).

The Galerkin method is another alternative. We need to define a norm. Since we use Chebyshev polynomials as a basis, we will use the inner product

$$\langle f(k), g(k) \rangle \equiv \int_{k_m}^{k_M} f(k) g(k) w(k) dk,$$

where

$$w(k) \equiv \left(1 - \left(2\frac{k - k_m}{k_M - k_m} - 1\right)^2\right)^{-1/2}.$$

With this choice of inner product, the basis is orthogonal. The Galerkin method computes the n projections

$$P_i(a) \equiv \int_{k_m}^{k_M} R(k; a)\, \psi_i(k)\, w(k)\, dk, \qquad i = 1, \ldots, n, \tag{16.5.4}$$

and chooses a so that $P(a) = 0$. Here the difficulty is that each $P_i(a)$ needs to be computed numerically. We use Gauss-Chebyshev quadrature because the basis elements are Chebyshev polynomials. That is, we approximate $P_i(a)$ with

$$\hat{P}_i(a) \equiv \sum_{j=1}^{m} R(k_j; a)\, \psi_i(k_j) \tag{16.5.5}$$

for some $m > n$, with the k_j being the m zeros of ψ_{m+1}. We then solve the nonlinear system

$$\hat{P}_i(a) = 0, \qquad i = 0, \ldots, n. \tag{16.5.6}$$

The system (16.5.6) can also be solved using any nonlinear equation solving algorithm. The differences between collocation and Galerkin turn out to be trivial for the problem in table 16.1, a fact that indicates the power of collocation even for nonlinear problems.

Alternative Bases

We approximated $C(k)$ with polynomials in k in our example, but this is only one possibility. We next consider the alternative of approximating the log of consumption with polynomials in $\log k$, that is,

$$\hat{C}(k; a) = e^{\sum_{i=0}^{n} a_i(\log k)^i}. \tag{16.5.7}$$

This functional form spans a different space of functions compared to the Chebyshev polynomial approximation scheme. By the Stone-Weierstrass theorem, both approximation schemes will do well as n goes to infinity, but the practical objective is to find an approximation to C involving a small number of free parameters.

   After some adjustments we can combine the approximation scheme (16.5.7) with projection methods. Consider, for example, the collocation method. We first choose the collocation points. The functional form is no longer a polynomial in k; instead, it is a polynomial in $\log k$. This suggests using points x_i such that $\log x_i$ are zeros of Chebyshev polynomials in the interval $[\log k_m, \log k_M]$. With this set of collocation points we then solve the collocation equations just as we (16.5.3). The only difference is the functional form used for $\hat{C}$ and the collocation points.

There is no general rule for which basis is better. For the example presented in table 16.1, the log basis does better. There are cases where polynomials in k will do better. For example, suppose that one wants to solve a linear-quadratic problem using projection methods. We know that the solution is linear in k, implying that a basis in k would do better than a basis on $\log k$. These observations indicate that it is valuable to be flexible in the choice of bases. One way to improve an approximation is to add terms from an existing basis, but another way is to try an alternative basis.

16.6   Accuracy Measures

An important question is how good is the resulting approximation and how many polynomial terms do we need to get a good approximation. There are two ways to do this. First, find another, more "reliable" way to solve the problem and compare the answer. Second, compute a measure of inaccuracy.

For this deterministic problem, we can do both. First, we compute a conservative, reliable benchmark using discretization procedures described in chapter 10. We get some idea of the accuracy of these projection method techniques by comparing it with the presumably very accurate solution from the discretized problem. The results are shown in table 16.2. We assumed a CRRA utility function, $u(c) = c^{\gamma+1}/(\gamma+1)$ and a Cobb-Douglas production function $f(k) = Ak^{\alpha}$, $\alpha = 0.25$, where A is chosen so

Table 16.2
Policy function errors

k	y	c	$n = 20$	$n = 10$	$n = 7$	$n = 4$	$n = 2$
0.5	0.1253211	0.1010611	1(−7)	5(−7)	5(−7)	2(−7)	5(−5)
0.6	0.1331736	0.1132936	2(−6)	1(−7)	1(−7)	2(−6)	8(−5)
0.7	0.1401954	0.1250054	2(−6)	3(−7)	3(−7)	1(−6)	2(−4)
0.8	0.1465765	0.1362965	1(−6)	4(−7)	4(−7)	4(−6)	2(−4)
0.9	0.1524457	0.1472357	1(−6)	3(−7)	3(−7)	5(−6)	2(−4)
1.0	0.1578947	0.1578947	4(−6)	0(−7)	1(−7)	2(−6)	1(−4)
1.1	0.1629916	0.1683016	4(−6)	2(−7)	2(−7)	1(−6)	9(−5)
1.2	0.1677882	0.1784982	3(−6)	2(−7)	2(−7)	4(−6)	7(−6)
1.3	0.1723252	0.1884952	7(−7)	4(−7)	4(−7)	3(−6)	9(−5)

that the deterministic steady state is $k = 1$. We choose $\gamma = -0.9$. The third column gives the consumption choice as a function of capital indicated by the discrete state space method where we used 800,001 uniformly distributed capital stock levels in the interval $[0.5, 1.3]$. The fourth through eighth columns give the difference between the discrete solution and the projection method (collocation at Chebyshev zeros) solution for $n = 20$, 10, 7, 4, and 2, where n is the maximum degree Chebyshev polynomial included in the approximation. Note that the approximation of the aggregate consumption function for $n = 10$ disagrees with the discrete state space result by no more than one part in 10,000, an acceptable error for most purposes. Note that the $n = 10$ approximation appears to be better than $n = 20$. It is unclear which is better, since there is error in the discrete state space algorithm and the differences between the $n = 10$ and $n = 20$ solutions are within the error bounds for the discrete state space algorithm. This numerical experiment shows that the projection method works well for the discrete-time optimal growth model, demonstrating its usefulness even for the nonstandard functional equations that arise often in discrete-time economic models.

16.7   Tax and Monetary Policy in Dynamic Economies

We have primarily examined equilibria that are solutions to optimization problems. However, these methods can also be used to analyze models with distortions. We demonstrate this by applying them to simple dynamic models of equilibrium with money and taxes. Considerations of space limit our discussions below; the reader should turn to the cited papers for the details.

Taxation

Brock and Turnovsky (1980) show that equilibrium with taxation in the simple growth model described in section 11.5 solves the system

$$\dot{c} = \gamma c(\rho - f'(k)(1 - \tau)),$$
$$\dot{k} = f(k) - c - g, \tag{16.7.1}$$

where $\tau(t)$ is the tax on capital income at time t, and $g(t)$ is government expenditure at t. The boundary conditions are

$$k(0) = k_0,$$
$$0 < \lim_{t \to \infty} | c(t) | < \infty.$$

The fact that equilibrium reduces to the differential equation (16.7.1) implies that we can depend on any of the methods we have used to solve differential equations. Following Judd (1985), we can proceed by a perturbation method analysis of (16.7.1) to examine various policy "shocks" using linearization and Laplace transform methods. The conceptual experiment is as follows: Let us assume that the "old" tax policy was constant, $\tau(t) = \bar{\tau}$, and that it has been in place so long that, at $t = 0$, the economy is at the steady state corresponding to $\bar{\tau}$. Note that this also assumes that for $t < 0$, agents expect that $\tau(t) = \bar{\tau}$ for all t, even $t > 0$. Hence, at $t = 0$, $k(0) = k^{ss}(\bar{\tau})$.

However, at $t = 0$, agents are told that future tax policy will be different. Say that they find out that $\tau(t) = \bar{\tau} + h(t)$, $t \geq 0$; that is, $h(t)$ will be the change in the tax rate at time t. Similarly spending is $\bar{g} + g(t)$. The new system is

$$\dot{c} = \gamma c(\rho - f'(k)(1 - \bar{\tau} - h)),$$
$$\dot{k} = f(k) - c - \bar{g} - g, \tag{16.7.2}$$

together with the boundary conditions of (16.7.1). We could just solve the new nonlinear BVP. Instead we will use perturbation methods to approximate the effects.

We need to parameterize the new policy so that it fits the setup in section 13.4 for perturbing boundary value problems. We do this by defining

$$\tau(t, \varepsilon) = \bar{\tau} + \varepsilon h(t), \quad g(t, \varepsilon) = \bar{g} + \varepsilon g(t) \tag{16.7.3}$$

and the corresponding continuum of BVPs

$$c_t(t, \varepsilon) = \gamma c(t, \varepsilon)(\rho - f'(k(t, \varepsilon))(1 - \tau(t, \varepsilon))),$$
$$k_t(t, \varepsilon) = f(k(t, \varepsilon)) - c(t, \varepsilon) - g(t, \varepsilon), \tag{16.7.4}$$

where we explicitly indicate the dependence of c and k on both ε and t.

We differentiate (16.7.4) with respect to ε and solve for $c_\varepsilon(t, 0)$ and $k_\varepsilon(t, 0)$ after imposing the asymptotic boundedness, all a direct application of (13.4.9). In particular, Judd (1985) shows that if $I = \dot{k}$ is net investment, the impact of ε on I is

$$I_\varepsilon(0) = \frac{\gamma c \rho}{1 - \bar{\tau}} H(\mu) + \mu G(\mu) - g(0), \tag{16.7.5}$$

where

$$G(s) = \int_0^\infty g(t)e^{-st}\,dt, \quad H(s) = \int_0^\infty h(t)e^{-st}\,dt,$$

$$\mu = \frac{\rho}{2(1-\bar{\tau})}\left(1 + \sqrt{1 - \frac{4\gamma(1-\bar{\tau})\theta_L\theta_c}{\sigma\theta_K}}\right),$$

$$\theta_K = \frac{k^*f'(k^*)}{f(k^*)}, \quad \theta_L = 1 - \theta_K, \quad \theta_c = \frac{f(k^*) - \bar{g}}{f(k^*)},$$

and σ is the elasticity of substitution between k and l in production. In this problem, μ is the positive eigenvalue of the linearized system, and θ_K, θ_L, and θ_c are the steady state shares of capital income, labor income, and consumption. $G(s)$ and $H(s)$ are the Laplace transforms of the policy innovation functions $g(t)$ and $h(t)$; note that (16.7.5) depends on sums of $g(t)$ and $h(t)$ discounted at the rate μ. This implies that if the tax policy change is h, the $\varepsilon = 1$ case in (16.7.4), then the first-order approximation to the new level of investment at $t = 0$ is $I_\varepsilon(0)$.

The formula (16.7.5) is an example of the kind of qualitative information revealed by perturbation exercises. First, future tax increases reduce investment. Second, government spending has an ambiguous impact on investment, with current spending crowding out investment but future spending "crowding in" investment. Third, since investment and output are related, we know that any initial increase in investment will immediately lead to an increase in output.

Local Analysis of Monetary Models

Monetary economic problems differ from other problems because of the special properties of money. One of the simplest models of money is the Sidrauski model. It assumes that each infinitely lived representative agent maximizes $\int_0^\infty e^{-\rho t}u(c,m)\,dt$ where c is consumption and m is real balances, subject to his budget constraint. Fischer (1979) shows that if θ is the constant rate of money creation, then equilibrium paths for c, m, the inflation rate π, and the capital stock k solve the system

$$0 = -[\rho + \pi]u_c(c,m) + u_m(c,m) + u_{cc}(c,m)\dot{c} + u_{cm}(c,m)\dot{m},$$

$$0 = [f'(k) + \pi]u_c(c,m) - u_m(c,m), \tag{16.7.6}$$

$$0 = \dot{k} - [f(k) - c],$$

where $\pi \equiv \theta - (\dot{m}/m)$.

Fischer looked for a Tobin effect in this model; that is, he examined the effect of inflation on capital accumulation. To do this, he computed the steady state, which is characterized by $f'(k^*) = \rho$, $\pi = \theta$, and $c = f(k^*)$. The real side of the steady state is unaffected by inflation. He then asked how investment is affected by inflation when the capital stock is close to but not equal to the steady state. To do this, he linearized the system (16.7.6) around its steady state. The linear approximation implies a net investment process equal to $\dot{k} \doteq -\lambda(k - k^*)$, where λ is the stable eigenvalue of the linearized system. Assuming reasonable utility functions, Fischer showed that if $k < k^*$, savings is higher in economies with higher rates of money creation, θ.

The two previous examples show how the perturbation methods we discussed in chapters 14 and 15 can be applied to local analysis of perfect foresight models. Local analysis of such models is a powerful technique that can be applied to both continuous-time models and discrete-time models.[2] Since we only need to compute the Jacobian of a dynamic system and its eigenvector-eigenvalue decomposition, we can apply these noniterative methods to many large systems.

Solving the Grossman-Weiss Model of Money

A recent paper by Li (1998) is a good example of how to rigorously approach the numerical analysis of a dynamic economic problem. She takes the Grossman-Weiss (1983) model of money demand. If θ is the constant growth rate of money supply and p_t is the price level, then define $q_1 \equiv (p_1 + \theta)/(1 + \theta)$ and $q_t \equiv p_t/(1 + \theta)$ for $t \geq 2$. Equilibrium in the model is a solution to the nonlinear second-order difference system

$$q_t + \phi\left(\frac{q_t}{q_{t+1}}\right) q_{t-1} = 1, \tag{16.7.7}$$

where ϕ is a known function depending on tastes and technology; in Li's example,

$$\phi(x) = \frac{\beta^{-1/\gamma}}{\beta^{-1/\gamma} + x^{(1+\gamma)/\gamma}},$$

where $u(c) = c^{1+\gamma}/(1 + \gamma)$ and β is the discount factor. The initial value q_1 is fixed by the stability condition $\lim_{t\to\infty} q_t < \infty$. It can be shown that the equilibrium satisfies $q_{t+1} = g(q_t)$ for some function g which we will compute. Applying (16.7.7) implies that g satisfies the fixed-point expression

---

2. Cooley and Hansen (1989) advocate an iterative approach similar to time iteration to solve discrete-time versions of these problems but do not present any evidence that their iterative approach has any advantages over the direct noniterative approach presented here and in previous papers.

$$g(x) = 1 - x\phi\left(\frac{g(x)}{g(g(x))}\right) \equiv \mathcal{F}(g).\tag{16.7.8}$$

The steady state price is $p^* \equiv (1+\theta)/(1+\phi(1))$.

Li first shows that if $3\phi'(1) \leq 1 - \phi(1)$, then the operator $\mathcal{F}$ is a contraction mapping on a problem-specific space[3] of functions X. Therefore the iteration

$$g^{j+1} = \mathcal{F}(g^j)\tag{16.7.9}$$

converges to the unique fixed point.

So far this is just standard existence theory. We want to develop a numerical approach and analyze its properties. It is important to realize that the properties of the abstract operator $\mathcal{F}$ do not necessarily carry over to its computable approximations. Li recognizes this and proceeds to analyze a particular numerical approximation of the iteration in (16.7.9). Let X^h be the set of piecewise linear splines in X with nodes in $\{0, h, 2h, \ldots, 1\}$, and let $\mathcal{F}^h(g)$ be the spline approximation of $\mathcal{F}(g)$. Since $\mathcal{F}^h(g)$ is defined by (16.7.8), it can be directly computed. Li shows that $\mathcal{F}^h(g)$ is a contraction on X^h and that the iteration $g^{j+1} = \mathcal{F}^h(g^j)$ converges linearly to a unique spline function. She then implements the fixed-point iteration for $h = 1/29$ and finds a spline which satisfies (16.7.7) with error less than 10^{-10}.

Li's careful and complete analysis is common in the mathematical literature but is unusual in the economics literature. Her approach is promising for many other fixed-point problems: Define the relevant space of computable functions, define a numerical operator on that space, demonstrate a contraction property for the *computable* approximation of the original operator, compute a fixed point of the computable operator, and show it to be close to the fixed point of the original operator. We should also note that her analysis of (16.7.7) applies to any problem of the form (16.7.8) not just the initial motivating example from monetary economics.

16.8 Recursive Solution of an OLG Model

The methods we used to produce recursive solutions of infinite-horizon models can also be used to solve the OLG model we first examined in section 16.1. More generally, these recursive methods can be used to compute equilibria of OLG models.[4]

---

3. We refer the reader to Li (1998) for the specific details.

4. Given the large literature on indeterminacy in OLG models, we must emphasize that any recursive equilibrium that we compute may represent just one out of many equilibria. Also there are sunspot equilibria that are being ignored by these methods. The goal here is to find one equilibrium, not all.

Recall the model from section 16.1. The natural state variable is the beginning-of-period capital stock k which is owned by the old. Let $S(k)$ be the savings of the young, $R(k)$ the marginal product of capital, $W(k)$ the marginal product of labor, and $L(k)$ the labor supply if k is the capital stock. These functions must satisfy the Euler equations:

$$0 = u'(L(k)W(k) - S(k)) - \beta u'(S(k)R(S(k)))R(S(k)),$$

$$0 = W(k)u'(L(k)W(k) - S(k)) - v'(L(k)),$$

$$R(k) \equiv F_k(k, L(k)),$$ (16.8.1)

$$W(k) \equiv F_l(k, L(k)).$$

In (16.8.1), we view $S(k)$ and $L(k)$ as the unknown functions, substituting the definitions for $R(k)$ and $W(k)$ into the first two equations. We then parameterize S and L and solve for their unknown coefficients using any of the methods discussed above. The easiest to implement would be Newton's method, since that could be applied directly to (16.8.1). Both time and fixed-point iteration could also be implemented once we properly index the occurences of $S(k)$ and $L(k)$. In all these methods, if we knew that the steady state was locally determinate and stable, it would be natural to impose steady state conditions requiring that S and L equal their steady state values when k is the steady state value of capital. This approach can be easily extended to the case of OLG models where agents live three, four, or more periods. As always, the key step is characterizing equilibrium in terms of some functional equation.

16.9 "Consistent" Capital Income Taxation

Optimal taxation of factor income is a typical example of dynamic inconsistency of optimal plans. Formulation and computation of "consistent" taxation policies is a difficult problem since closed-form solutions are generally unavailable (see Turnovsky and Brock 1980). In this section we will characterize dynamically consistent taxation of capital income to finance a public good, and we will use a projection technique to solve the resulting nonlinear equations.

We assume the continuous-time, inelastic labor supply, single-good continuous-time growth model with the addition of a public good. We assume that the intertemporal utility function is

$$\max \int_0^\infty e^{-\rho t} \left(u(c + g) + v(g) \right) dt,$$ (16.9.1)

where g is a public good. We assume capital evolves according to

$$\dot{k} = f(k) - c - g. \tag{16.9.2}$$

This may appear to be a strange utility function, since it says that all consumption should be through the public good; we choose it because it is simple. If taxes were lump-sum, then all income would be taxed away to finance g; hence lower tax rates indicate the degree to which the distortionary costs of taxation are recognized. We assume that public good is financed by a tax on capital income, $kf'(k)$, at a rate of τ. We will allow no bonds; hence $g = \tau kf'(k)$.

We focus on consistent equilibria in which all decisions depend only the real state variables, which in this model is only aggregate capital. Therefore we are looking for an aggregate consumption function, $C(k)$, and the equilibrium tax function, $T(k)$. We will also compute the planner's value function, $V(k)$, which is defined to be the present value of social utility given that the current capital stock is k and that future governments will follow the consistent equilibrium in making tax policy. We will let $\Psi(k)$ denote total consumption, $C(k) + T(k)$.

Dynamic programming ideas impose several conditions for these functions. The dynamic programming problem of the representative agent shows that the aggregate consumption function will obey

$$0 = \Psi'(k)(f(k) - \Psi(k)) - \frac{u'(\Psi(k))}{u''(\Psi(k))}(\rho - f'(k)(1 - T(k))). \tag{16.9.3}$$

The policymaker wants to maximize the present value of utility, including the utility of public good consumption. Let $V(k)$ be the equilibrium value function for a policymaker when the current capital stock is k. Since the policymaker can determine the tax rate for only a moment, he will have no influence on contemporaneous consumption. Therefore, at the margin, any decision to increase taxation and public good consumption crowds out investment one for one. Given a private consumption function, $C(k)$, the policymaker solves the problem

$$\rho V(k) = \max_{\tau}[u(C(k) + \tau kf'(k)) + v(\tau kf'(k))$$

$$+ V'(k)(f(k) - C(k) - \tau kf'(k))]. \tag{16.9.4}$$

The first-order condition for the government is

$$u'(\Psi(k)) + v'(T(k)kf'(k)) = V'(k). \tag{16.9.5}$$

The three equations (16.9.3) and (16.9.4), and (16.9.5) characterize the three functions $V(k)$, $C(k)$, and $T(k)$, which describe the consistent equilibrium. Each unknown

Table 16.3
Dynamically consistent tax policy

	$\lambda_g = 10^{-4}$					$\lambda_g = 10^{-3}$			
k	c	g	τ	s	k	c	g	τ	s
0.5	0.1360	0.0058	0.14	0.0322	0.5	0.1557	0.0125	0.30	0.0125
0.6	0.1547	0.0064	0.15	0.0213	0.6	0.1764	0.0142	0.32	−0.0004
0.7	0.1727	0.0071	0.15	0.0102	0.7	0.1983	0.0161	0.35	−0.0153
0.8	0.1903	0.0077	0.16	−0.0011	0.8	0.2192	0.0175	0.37	−0.0300
0.9	0.2073	0.0083	0.17	−0.0125	0.9	0.2382	0.0187	0.38	−0.0434
1.0	0.2241	0.0089	0.18	−0.0241	1.0	0.2563	0.0200	0.40	−0.0563
1.1	0.2406	0.0096	0.19	−0.0358	1.1	0.2744	0.0215	0.42	−0.0696
1.2	0.2568	0.0102	0.20	−0.0475	1.2	0.2925	0.0230	0.44	−0.0832
1.3	0.2729	0.0109	0.20	−0.0593	1.3	0.3104	0.0245	0.46	−0.0968
1.4	0.2887	0.0116	0.21	−0.0712	1.4	0.3281	0.0261	0.48	−0.1106

function will be approximated by a high-order polynomial. For the case of a value-less public good, the solution is known—set $T(k) = 0$, and $C(k)$ and $V(k)$ equal to their first-best values. This provides us with a test case.

Table 16.3 gives some results for two particular cases. It assumes that $u(c) = (c + g)^{\gamma_c+1}/(\gamma_c + 1)$ and $v(g) = \lambda_g g^{\gamma_g+1}/(\gamma_g + 1)$, with $\gamma_c = \gamma_g = -2$. We assume that $\rho = 0.05$ and $f(k) = 0.2k^{0.25}$. The entries give consumption (c), savings (s), government expenditure (g), and the tax rate (τ) at various values of the capital stock (k). We use Chebyshev polynomials and Chebyshev collocation. We first solved the model for $\lambda_g = 0$ and found that the result was accurate to several digits, giving us some confidence in the approach. The two panels in table 16.3 correspond to two positive values for λ_g. The results are interesting. As the value of the public good increases, the consumption function rises at all capital stocks, since the higher value of g causes higher taxation of investment income which in turn discourages savings. Also note that the tax rate rises as the economy grows through capital accumulation. This reflects the fact that the efficient ratio between public and private consumption should be roughly constant, and as the economy grows, the share of output that goes into consumption rises.

The other interesting feature is how the steady state of the economy is affected by the fiscal policy. When $\lambda_g = 0$, taxes are always zero and the capital stock converges to 1. However, when $\lambda_g = 10^{-4}$, the steady state tax rate is 0.16 and capital converges to 0.8, which is 20 percent below the no-tax case. As λ_g increases, the steady state tax rate increases and the steady state capital stock falls. Note, however, that government expenditures are always a small fraction of output and that the tax rates are moderate, despite the fact that first-best for this problem would have all consumption be in the form of g. Therefore even the time-consistent solution involves a substantial amount of foresight and intertemporal forebearance on the part of successive governments.

This was obviously a stripped down analysis of an important problem. However, it shows that basic numerical methods can be used to model strategic decision-making by a foresightful policymaker with limited commitment powers.

16.10   Further Reading and Summary

This chapter has shown how to solve some simple perfect foresight dynamic economic models. While we have focused on competitive equilibrium models, that was not necessary. To solve for a time path of prices and allocations, we compute the dynamic demand and supply paths implied by a truncated path of prices and apply some nonlinear equation procedure to find the truncated price sequence that implies zero excess demand. This approach combines two kinds of problems we studied before. First, computing the dynamic supply and demand often involves solving optimal control problems at the level of the consumers and firms. Second, computing equilibrium prices is a problem in nonlinear equations.

To solve for the laws of motion and price laws in a recursive model, we construct an operator which characterizes the equilibrium laws and use projection methods to approximate them. These projection methods use approximation methods, integration techniques, plus nonlinear equations. In either case, solving perfect foresight models is made feasible by appropriately combining basic numerical methods.

Newton's method is increasingly used in this literature; for example, see Burdick (1994) and Gilli and Pauletto (1998). Even if the horizon is too long for Newton's method, we could still feed $E(P)$ to conventional equation solvers. Hughes Hallett and Piscitelli (1998) advocates reordering the equations and then using Gaussian substitution schemes. Juillard et al. (1998) compares Newton's method with Gaussian substitution methods. The tatonnement and fixed-point methods are just two possible approaches but, as with standard Gauss-Jacobi and fixed-point methods, are unlikely to be the best choices.

Exercises

1.   Assume an OLG model where agents live for four periods with utility function over consumption c_a at age a and labor supply l_a at age a equal to $\sum_{a=1}^{4} c_a^{1+\gamma}/(1+\gamma) - \sum_{a=1}^{3} l_a^{\nu}$. Also assume that the production function is $f(k,l) = k^\alpha l^{1-\alpha}$. Assume that $\alpha \in [0.2, 0.5]$, $\nu \in [1.1, 5]$, and $\gamma \in [-0.5, -5]$. Write a routine to compute steady states and their local determinacy. For the determinate cases, use

and compare the tatonnement, fixed-point iteration, Newton's method, Fair-Taylor, and the parametric path methods to compute the time path of interest rates and wages starting at a point where each cohort has half the steady state wealth for that cohort.

2.   Reconsider exercise 1. For the determinate cases, compute the linear equilibrium decision rules in the neighborhood of the steady state.

3.   Consider (16.4.2) for $u(c) = c^{1+\gamma}/(1 + \gamma)$ and $F(k) = k + Ak^{\alpha}$. Let $\gamma \in [-0.5, -5]$, $\alpha \in [0.2, 0.5]$, and $\beta \in [0.6, 0.99]$; choose A so that the steady state capital stock is 1. Use and compare the time iteration, fixed-point iteration, and Newton iteration methods with various bases. Which method with which bases does best in general? Which projection methods—collocation, Galerkin, least squares, or subdomain—do best?

4.   Compute and compare solutions to the model in Auerbach, Kotlikoff, and Skinner (1983) using their Gauss-Jacobi scheme, Newton's method, and parameterized paths.

17 Solving Rational Expectations Models

The previous chapter presented solution methods for perfect foresight models of dynamic economic equilibrium. We next extend these models to include stochastic elements. As in the deterministic case, there are a few special models with explicit solutions. While these special cases are sufficient in some interesting contexts, they cannot be applied to most economic problems.[1]

In this chapter we apply present basic methods to solve rational expectations models of stochastic dynamic competitive equilibrium. We begin with solving three models with exogenous state variables. The Lucas (1978) asset pricing model is particularly easy to solve numerically, since it reduces to a linear Fredholm integral equation. We will discuss both simulation and integral equation methods to solve the Lucas asset pricing model. Second, we examine monetary models; they lead to non-linear Fredholm integral equations which we solve by adapting the linear Fredholm equation methods presented in chapter 10. Third, we solve for a rational expectations equilibrium of an asset market with asymmetric information. This requires the full use of the projection method technology, since discretization methods cannot succeed.

We then examine models with endogenous state variables. We begin with the commodity storage problem examined by of Gustafson (1958), Wright and Williams (1982, 1984), and Miranda and Helmburger (1988). We use the commodity model to illustrate the time iteration and fixed-point iteration solution methods in a stochastic context. An important aspect of the commodity market problem is that commodity stocks cannot be negative, a fact that causes equilibrium price and storage functions to have a kink. The kinks make simple polynomial approximations of the price function inappropriate, forcing us to use less efficient approximation methods. Wright and Williams instead solve the commodity model by parameterizing a critical conditional expectation that is a smooth function of the conditioning information and can be well-approximated by a low-order polynomial. Wright and Williams's idea to parameterize a smooth conditional expectations function results in a substantially better method.

We next discuss the solution of a simple stochastic growth model with both an endogenous and an exogenous state variable. We use this model to illustrate three kinds of procedures. We first present a standard projection method combining a Chebyshev polynomial approximation of the unknown function, a Gaussian quadrature method to compute the conditional expectation, and the Powell hybrid

---

1. See Hansen and Sargent (1990) for an excellent and wide-ranging discussion of linear-quadratic rational expectations models and their computational methods.

method to fix the unknown coefficients. Second, we develop fixed-point iteration methods, one using deterministic quadrature ideas and the other a simulation method used in den Haan-Marcet (1990). Third, we present a time iteration procedure.

The problems we tackle in this chapter show how to combine standard numerical techniques for approximation, integration, and nonlinear equations to solve rational expectations models. We finish the chapter by indicating the robustness of these methods. Section 17.9 indicates how they could be applied to more general models, with several states, agents, and goods, and with distortions. Also the matching of computational method with economic examples in this chapter (and in the literature) has little substantive content, since each method discussed below could be applied to each of the problems. In summary, this chapter presents several methods for solving rational expectations models.

17.1 Lucas Asset-Pricing Model

One of the simplest rational expectations problems is asset pricing with homogeneous investors. In this section we present the Lucas (1978) asset pricing model and use various procedures to compute the equilibrium asset pricing rule.

The Model

Assume that there is a single asset that pays dividends, y_{t+1}, according to the AR (1) stochastic process,

$$y_{t+1} = \rho y_t + \varepsilon_{t+1}, \tag{17.1.1}$$

where ε_t is an i.i.d. innovation process. Suppose that there is no other source of income in this economy and that all investors have a common concave von Neumann-Morgenstern utility function over the consumption process c_t equal to $E\{\sum_{t=0}^{\infty} \beta^t u(c_t)\}$. If we let p_t denote the asset price at time t, then the equilibrium price process must satisfy

$$u'(y_t)p_t = \beta E\{u'(y_{t+1})(y_{t+1} + p_{t+1})|y_t\}. \tag{17.1.2}$$

Equation (17.1.2) is an expression for the time series p_t and as such something that is difficult to compute directly. If instead we define $p(y)$ to be the ex-dividend price of a share in any period when the dividend is y, then Lucas (1978) shows that $p(y)$ solves

$$u'(y_t)p(y_t) = \beta E\{u'(y_{t+1})(y_{t+1} + p(y_{t+1}))|y_t\}. \tag{17.1.3}$$

We can rewrite (17.1.3) as

$$p(y_t) = \beta E\left\{\frac{u'(y_{t+1})}{u'(y_t)} y_{t+1} | y_t\right\} + \beta E\left\{\frac{u'(y_{t+1})}{u'(y_t)} p(y_{t+1}) | y_t\right\}. \tag{17.1.4}$$

Equation (17.1.4) has the form of the linear Fredholm integral equation

$$p(y) = g(y) + \beta \int K(y, z) p(z) \, dz, \tag{17.1.5}$$

where

$$g(y) = \beta \int \frac{u'(z)}{u'(y)} z \, q(z|y) \, dz,$$

$$K(y, z) = \frac{u'(z)}{u'(y)} q(z|y),$$

and $q(z|y)$ is the density of the time $t+1$ dividend conditional on the time t dividend.

Solution by Simulation

We first use a simple simulation strategy to solve (17.1.3). Simple recursion arguments show that $p(y)$ can be expressed as

$$p(y_0) = (u'(y_0))^{-1} E\left\{\sum_{t=1}^{\infty} \beta^t u'(y_t) | y_0\right\}. \tag{17.1.6}$$

Therefore we need only to approximate the infinite sum in (17.1.6). More precisely, we first draw a sequence of T i.i.d. innovations, ε_t, and form the dividend sequence $y_t, t = 1, \ldots T$, implied by the process (17.1.1) with y_0 given. Since the sum in (17.1.6) is infinite, T needs to be large enough so that the truncation error of using (17.1.6) is acceptably small. We next define the sum

$$P(y_0; \varepsilon) = (u'(y_0))^{-1} \sum_{t=1}^{T} \beta^t u'(y_t). \tag{17.1.7}$$

$P(y_0; \varepsilon)$ is the price of the asset if the time zero dividend is y_0, the ε sequence is perfectly foreseen, and the world ends at time T. However, the ε_t shocks are not known at $t = 0$. We then repeat this for several draws of $\varepsilon \in R^T$; denote the j'th sequence as $\varepsilon^j, j = 1, \ldots, m$. Each ε^j sequence implies a different dividend sequence and a different value for $P(y_0; \varepsilon^j)$. Our estimate of $p(y_0)$, denoted $\hat{p}(y_0)$, is the average of the $P(y_0; \varepsilon)$:

$$\hat{p}(y_0) = \frac{1}{m} \sum_{j=1}^{m} P(y_0; \varepsilon^j). \tag{17.1.8}$$

If we want to approximate the price function $p(y)$, we need to repeat this for a variety of y_0 values. We implement (17.1.8) for N such initial values, denoted y_0^i, $i = 1, \ldots, N$, to generate the $\hat{p}(y_0^i)$ estimate of $p(y_0^i)$. We then use these data to construct an approximation for the pricing function. Since the procedure behind (17.1.7) is a Monte Carlo method, the errors in the $\hat{p}(y_0^i)$ estimates will be nontrivial. Therefore, to compute an approximation to the $p(y)$ function, it is best to use several y_0^i values, use different ε draws for each y_0^i, and then approximate $p(y)$ by regressing the $\hat{p}(y_0^i)$ values on the y_0^i values.

Simulation methods are most appropriate when the desired accuracy is moderate and the dividend process is complicated. For example, if dividends follow

$$y_t = a_0 + a_1 y_{t-1} + a_2 y_{t-2} + \cdots + a_l y_{t-l} + \varepsilon_t,$$

then the l lags create an l-dimensional structure which would challenge other methods. However, simulation methods would be applied just as above.

Discrete-State Approximation

Tauchen (1991) recognized that (17.1.3) is a linear Fredholm integral equation of the second kind, and applied the procedures similar to those described in section 10.8. The key step replaces the continuous-space Markov process over y with a finite-state Markov process. We apply (10.8.7) directly to (17.1.5), using the Gauss-Hermite quadrature nodes y_i and weights ω_i. This results in the linear system of equations for the unknown values $p(y_i)$,

$$p(y_i) = g(y_i) + \beta \sum_{j=1}^{n} p(y_j) \frac{u'(y_j)}{u'(y_i)} \omega_j \frac{q(y_j|y_i)}{w(y_j)}. \tag{17.1.9}$$

We solve (17.1.9) to compute approximations to $p(y)$ for $y_i \in Y$; call the solutions $\hat{p}_i$. The procedure so far just approximates $p(y)$ on Y. To approximate p elsewhere, we use the Nystrom extension as defined in equation (10.8.10). The final approximation is

$$\hat{p}(y) = g(y) + \beta \sum_{j=1}^{n} \hat{p}_j \frac{u'(y_j)}{u'(y)} \omega_j \frac{q(y_j|y)}{w(y_j)}, \tag{17.1.10}$$

which is defined for all y.

17.2 Monetary Equilibrium

We next develop methods to compute equilbrium in a stochastic monetary model. More precisely, assume an infinite-life representative agent model with utility function $u(c, m)$ over consumption c and real balances m, and discount factor β. We assume that the (real) endowment process, w_t, is stochastic with w_t known before consumption is chosen in period t. Let p_t be the price level. The consumption choice and level of real balances are functions of the current wage. However, in equilibrium, consumption must equal the endowment. Assume that θ_t is the ratio of money stock at time t to that at time $t - 1$; hence $\theta - 1$ is the money growth rate in period t. We assume lump-sum subsidies (or lump-sum taxes) are used to finance the monetary policy. The equilibrium price and real balances path then satisfy

$$u_c(w_t, m_t)m_t = \beta E\left\{ (u_c(w_{t+1}, m_{t+1}) + u_m(w_{t+1}, m_{t+1})) \frac{m_{t+1}}{\theta_{t+1}} | w_t, \theta_t \right\}. \tag{17.2.1}$$

We will first assume that money growth is constant, equal to θ, and that w_t are i.i.d. random variables with density $f(w)$. In this case the current (exogenous) wage is a sufficient statistic for the system, and real balances are a function of the current wage. The equilibrium function for real balances can be written $m(w)$ and must satisfy

$$u_c(w_t, m(w_t))m(w_t) = \beta E\left\{ (u_c(w_{t+1}, m(w_{t+1})) + u_m(w_{t+1}, m(w_{t+1}))) \frac{m(w_{t+1})}{\theta} | w_t \right\}. \tag{17.2.2}$$

We immediately recognize that (17.2.2) is a nonlinear Fredholm integral equation. We solve it by generalizing the methods we used for linear Fredholm equations. We first choose some integration formula with n nodes $\{w_1, \ldots, w_n\}$ and n weights $\{\omega_1, \ldots, \omega_n\}$ for the integral in (17.2.2), arriving at the finite set of equations

$$u_c(w, m(w_i))\, m(w_i) = \beta \frac{1}{n} \sum_{j=1}^{n} (u_c(w_j, m(w_j)) + u_m(w_j, m(w_j)))\omega_j\, m(w_j)\, \theta^{-1} f(w_j), \tag{17.2.3}$$

where $i = 1, \ldots, n$. We fix the n values of $m(w_i)$ by solving the n nonlinear algebraic equations in (17.2.3).

We can also take a projection approach. We begin by approximating m with a polynomial, $\hat{m}$,

$$\hat{m}(w; a) = \sum_{j=1}^{n} a_j w^{j-1},$$

and then rewrite the equilibrium condition (17.2.2) as an integral equation for the approximation m:

$$u_c(w, \hat{m}(w; a))\, \hat{m}(w; a) = \beta \int (u_c(z, \hat{m}(z; a))$$
$$+\, u_m(z, \hat{m}(z; a)))\hat{m}(z; a)\, \theta^{-1}\, f(z)\, dz. \qquad (17.2.4)$$

Our task is to find a set of coefficients, a, which approximately solves (17.2.4). To do this, we construct the finite set of equations

$$u_c(w, \hat{m}(w_i; a))\hat{m}(w_i; a) = \frac{1}{n}\beta \sum_{j=1}^{n}(u_c(w_j, \hat{m}(w_j; a))$$
$$+\, u_m(w_j, \hat{m}(w_j; a)))\hat{m}(w_j; a)\, \theta^{-1}\, f(w_j), \qquad (17.2.5)$$

where $i = 1, \ldots, n$. We fix the n undetermined coefficients in a by solving the n nonlinear algebraic equations in (17.2.5). The discretization approach in (17.2.5) is equivalent to a collocation strategy. One could also use least squares, Galerkin, or subdomain conditions.

This is a simple model of monetary equilibrium, but we must make some cautionary remarks. We have ignored important features of monetary theory, such as indeterminacy and sunspot equilibria. Our recursive formulation implicitly assumes uniqueness and excludes dependence on sunspotlike variables.

17.3   Information and Asset Markets

We next develop numerical methods for a model of asymmetric information in asset markets. This is an area of economic research that has relied almost exclusively on models with very special functional forms—exponential utility and Gaussian returns. They often critically rely on the presence of "noise traders" whose behavior is insensitive to price and information. We see that projection methods can handle these problems with ease and apparent accuracy, and do so without making any ad hoc deviations from agent rationality.

We assume three groups of identical investors, each individual having W dollars per person to invest in two assets. The safe asset pays out R dollars in the second period per dollar invested, and the risky asset pays out Z dollars per share. Therefore, if an investor buys ω shares of the risky asset at price p dollars per share, his second period consumption will be $c = (W - \omega p) R + \omega Z$, and the first-order condition for ω will be

$$0 = E\{u'(c) (Z - pR)|I\}, \tag{17.3.1}$$

where I is the investor's information set. We will assume that there is only one share of the risky asset available; hence, the price p must be set so that the total demand for the risky asset is one.

We examine a generalization of Grossman's (1976) model. We assume that three types of investors have different information. As in Grossman, Z is normally distributed, $Z \sim N(\mu, \sigma^2)$, and an agent of type i receives a signal $y_i = Z + \varepsilon_i$, where $\varepsilon_i \sim N(\mu, \sigma_\varepsilon^2)$ and are independently distributed. We will assume that each agent initially has W dollars in cash.

We deviate from Grossman by permitting general utility functions. The equilibrium price of the risky asset is a function of the distribution information $p = p(y)$, since each agent can condition only on the price and his own information, which implies that his equilibrium trading strategy can be expressed as $\omega_i = \omega_i(p, y_i)$. Equilibrium is then any price function $p(y)$ and trading function triple $(\omega_1(p, y_1), \omega_2(p, y_2), \omega_3(p, y_3))$ that satisfies two sets of conditions. First, each agent must be on his demand curve, implying that

$$E_{y,z} \{u_i'(C_i(y, Z))(Z - p(y)R)|p, y_i\} = 0, \qquad i = 1, 2, 3, \tag{17.3.2}$$

where $C_i(y, Z) \equiv (W - \omega_i(p(y), y_i)p(y)) R + \omega_i(p(y), y_i)Z$. Second, the market clears for each possible information distribution; that is, for all ω, total demand equals one, the supply, implying that

$$\sum_1^3 \omega_i(p(y), y_i) - 1 = 0. \tag{17.3.3}$$

We have four unknown functions: $p(y)$, $\omega_1(p, y_1)$, $\omega_2(p, y_2)$, and $\omega_3(p, y_3)$. They are hopefully identified by the four conditions in (17.3.2) and (17.3.3). Do there exist such functions? That is an existence question that we do not address. In fact we will proceed without any assurance that there does exist any equilibrium. This may make some uncomfortable. We proceed anyway for three reasons. First, if we did have an existence proof, or if we used the approximate equilibrium notions presented in Allen (1985a, b, 1992) and Anderson and Sonnenschein (1982) we would proceed as below. Second, if equilibrium does not exist, then it would be surprising if the method below would work. Third, any candidate solution produced by the method below that passes our diagnostics is an ε-equilibria for small ε; if there are no pure equilibria, then they provide natural alternative solutions wherein the agents make small optimization errors. None of this is to say that existence theory is unimportant, just that it is not an absolute prerequisite to doing computational work.

We return to computing an equilibrium. It is impossible to solve for (17.3.2) and (17.3.3) exactly; we attempt to find good polynomial approximations to the critical functions. We approximate the ω_i, $i = 1, 2, 3$, with the finite-order polynomials

$$\hat{\omega}_i(p, y_i) = \sum_{j,k=0}^{n} a_{jk}^i p^j y_i^k, \qquad i = 1, 2, 3, \tag{17.3.4}$$

and we approximate $p(y)$ with a finite-order polynomial

$$\hat{p}(y) = \sum_{j,k,l=0}^{n} a_{jkl} y_1^j y_2^k y_3^l. \tag{17.3.5}$$

We use polynomials[2] in (17.3.4)–(17.3.5) to approximate the price and trading functions; this choice is motivated by the belief (or, more precisely, the guess) that the true equilibrium price and trading functions are smooth in y.

To identify the unknown coefficients in p and ω_i, we replace the conditional expectations conditions in (17.3.2) with a finite number of projections of its unconditional expectation, that is, we form the system of equations

$$0 = E_{y,z} \left\{ u_i'(\hat{C}_i(y, Z))(Z - \hat{p}R) p^l y_i^j \right\}, \qquad j, l = 0, 1, \ldots, n, \ i = 1, 2, 3, \tag{17.3.6}$$

where $\hat{C}_i(y, Z) \equiv (W - \omega_i(\hat{p}(y), y_i)\hat{p}(y)) R + \hat{\omega}_i(\hat{p}(y), y_i)Z$. We also impose a finite number of projection conditions on the market-clearing condition, (17.3.3):

$$0 = E_{y,z} \left\{ \left(\sum_{1}^{3} \hat{\omega}_i(p, y_i) - 1 \right) y_1^j y_2^k y_3^l \right\}, \qquad j, k, l = 0, 1, \ldots, n. \tag{17.3.7}$$

We have reduced an infinite-dimensional problem, (17.3.2)–(17.3.3), to (17.3.6)–(17.3.7) which has a finite number of unknowns. We next need to replace the integrals in (17.3.6)–(17.3.7) with numerical quadrature formulas; Bernardo and Judd (1994) use product Gaussian quadrature. This step transforms (17.3.6)–(17.3.7) into a computable system of equations. At this point we can now solve the nonlinear system for the unknown coefficients; Bernardo and Judd use the Powell hybrid method because they were able to find satisfactory initial guesses. Otherwise, one could use a homotopy approach to guarantee convergence to a solution.

---

2. In practice, one should use orthogonal polynomial representations; we use polynomials here to reduce the notational burden.

Note that we don't know if there is a solution to the finite-dimensional system (17.3.6)–(17.3.7), with or without quadrature approximations of the integrals. Even if there is an equilibrium to the underlying infinite-dimensional model in (17.3.2)–(17.3.3), there may not be a solution to the finite-dimensional approximate system (17.3.6)–(17.3.7). Bernardo and Judd find solutions that satisfy the nonlinear equation solver's stopping rule, but that only indicates the existence of approximate solutions. Even if we have a solution of (17.3.6)–(17.3.7), we need to ask if it is satisfactory. To do so, Bernardo and Judd evaluate versions of (17.3.6) with some $j, l > n$ to see if there were economically significant errors in the first-order conditions. If significant errors are detected, then one should begin again with higher-order polynomials. The market-clearing condition (17.3.7) is only a weighted average condition; to see if it is an acceptable approximation, Bernardo and Judd compute the excess demand at values of y not used in the procedure; if the excess demand is excessive at too many values of y, we should also begin again. Bernardo and Judd find examples where solutions using cubic polynomials do very well when tested by these diagnostics. That may not always be the case, which is why these diagnostics must be evaluated.

This asset market example is a particularly interesting application of the projection method. Many dynamic economic models, such as the Lucas asset pricing model, can be solved by using a finite-state approximation, and the collocation method often implicitly reduces to such an approach. Theory tells us that this problem cannot be solved in an accurate and robust fashion with a finite-state approximation. If there were only a finite number of information states, then equilibrium will generically be fully revealing; see Radner (1979). Not only are discrete-state approximations probably inefficient for asymmetric information models but would inappropriately prejudge the nature of the final outcome. Therefore, if we are interested in a robust analysis of partially revealing rational expectations equilibria, we cannot use discrete approximations.

17.4. Commodity Storage Models

Euler equation methods for rational expectation models were first developed in studying commodity markets, beginning with Gustafson (1958) and continued with papers by Wright and Williams (1982a, 1984), and Miranda and Helmburger (1988). Numerical methods are almost the only way to analyze this model.[3] We discussed the

---

3. Aiyagari et al. (1989) examined a special case with a closed-form solution.

dynamic programming solution to this problem in chapter 12. We study this problem because it is an important class of models and clearly highlights many of the problems involved in solving rational expectations models generally.

Let p_t be the price in period t, x_t the cumulative postharvest stock in period t, I_t the inventory on hand at the beginning of period t, and r the constant interest rate. We assume that $D(p)$ is the demand function and that the current price equals $P(c)$ if current consumption is c; hence $c = D(P(c))$. Let θ_t be the period-t harvest; hence the period-t postharvest stock is $x_t = I_t + \theta_t$, and inventories follow the law $I_{t+1} = x_t - D(p_t)$. Let $g(I)$ be the marginal convenience value of inventories, which is also the rental return to holding inventories.

Prices are assumed set by a competitive market with risk-neutral speculators. If stocks are low, then the current price may be so high relative to the expected future price that the speculators hold nothing; otherwise, speculators will increase their holdings until the current price equals the discounted expected future price plus convenience value. Therefore competitive equilibrium is characterized by the conditions:

$$I_{t+1} = x_t - D(p_t) \geq 0,$$

$$p_t \geq g(0) + \beta E\{p_{t+1}|p_t\}, \tag{17.4.1}$$

$$0 = (p_t - g(I_{t+1}) - \beta E\{p_{t+1}|p_t\})I_{t+1}.$$

These conditions constitute a simultaneous and dynamic set of relations among price, inventories, and demand.

Equilibrium without Stockouts

If we assume that $g(0) = \infty$, the nonnegativity condition $I_t \geq 0$ will never bind, and we can ignore it. In this "no-stockout" case, the equilibrium condition reduces to the simple equations

$$x_{t+1} = x_t - D(p_t) + \theta_{t+1}, \tag{17.4.2}$$

$$p_t = g(x_t - D(p_t)) + \beta E_t\{p_{t+1}|p_t\}. \tag{17.4.3}$$

While g has the economic interpretation of convenience return, it can also be viewed as a barrier function approach to solving the nonnegativity constraints in (17.4.1), since it makes it infinitely costly to hit the nonnegativity constraint. Equation (17.4.3) is based only on the first-order condition, and it is simpler than the complementary slackness expressions of (17.4.1). In many cases one can introduce a barrier term like g, possibly giving it economic interpretation, and proceed using only first-order conditions.

A natural state variable for this problem is x_t. In a stationary equilibrium, all other equilibrium variables, in particular, the price and carryover, will depend solely on x_t. In our first solution method, we characterize the equilibrium in terms of the carryover rule. Let $I(x)$ be the carryover rule, equal to $x - D(p)$ if the current postharvest stock is x. Then consumption equals $x - I(x)$, and price equals $P(x - I(x))$. If $I(x)$ is carried over today, the next period's total postharvest stock equals $I(x) + \theta$. The Euler equation (17.4.2) and equation (17.4.3) can be combined to imply that

$$P(x - I(x)) = g(I(x)) + \beta E\{P(I(x) + \theta - I(I(x) + \theta))\}. \tag{17.4.4}$$

Equation (17.4.4) characterizes $I(x)$. We now turn to methods for solving (17.4.4).

We first approach (17.4.4) in the same way we approached dynamic models in chapter 16. If we define an operator $\mathscr{F}: (C^0)^5 \to C^0$,

$$\mathscr{F}(I_1, I_2, I_3, I_4, I_5)(x) = P(x - I_1(x)) - g(I_2(x))$$
$$- \beta E\{P(I_3(x) + \theta - I_4(I_5(x) + \theta))\}, \tag{17.4.5}$$

then finding a solution to (17.4.4) is equivalent to finding a function $I(x)$ such that $0 = \mathscr{F}(I, I, I, I, I) \equiv \mathscr{N}(I)$. We have the same range of methods available to use here as in chapter 16, since the only added wrinkle here is the presence of an expectation. We will examine both the time iteration and fixed-point iteration methods presented in chapter 16.

Time Iteration

Time iteration is implicitly defined in

$$P(x - I^{k+1}(x)) - g(I^{k+1}(x)) = \beta E\{P(I^{k+1}(x) + \theta - I^k(I^{k+1}(x) + \theta))\}. \tag{17.4.6}$$

Specifically, given the function I^k and some x, we can solve for the value of $I^{k+1}(x)$ that solves (17.4.6); since this can be done for each x, we have defined the function I^{k+1}. The advantage of this procedure is that convergence is likely (often easily proved), for it follows a simple dynamic economic logic. However, convergence will be slow.

The iteration in (17.4.6) is an abstract, ideal mathematical process that is useful for economic theory but cannot be exactly represented on the computer. There are two basic numerical issues to implementing (17.4.6). First, we need to choose how to approximate the $I^k(x)$ functions. Let $\hat{I}(x; a)$ denote the functional form we use where a is the vector of parameters in the approximation.

Second, we need to approximate the expectation in (17.4.6); we use the integration formula

$$E\{P(\hat{I}(x;a) + \theta - \hat{I}(\hat{I}(x;a) + \theta;a))\} \doteq \sum_{i=1}^{m} \omega_i P(\hat{I}(x;a) + \theta_i - \hat{I}(\hat{I}(x;a) + \theta_i;a))$$

$$(17.4.7)$$

for some set of θ_i nodes and ω_i weights. The choice of quadrature formulas in (17.4.7) depends on the nature of the problem. If $P(c)$ is smooth, we expect $I(x)$ to also be smooth and smooth $\hat{I}$ approximation schemes are appropriate. If $P(c)$ and the $\hat{I}(x;a)$ are both smooth, then Gaussian quadrature rules are likely to be efficient if θ has a smooth density. Note how the form of $\hat{I}$ is important. If $\hat{I}(x;a)$ is not smooth in x, such as would be the case if $\hat{I}$ were piecewise linear interpolation, then it may not be wise to use a quadrature formula designed for smooth integrands; it is the form of, $\hat{I}$, not $I(x)$, which is critical since we are integrating $\hat{I}$, not I, in (17.4.6). Algorithm 17.1 implements time iteration to determine the coefficients of $\hat{I}$.

Algorithm 17.1   Time Iteration in (17.4.6)

Initialization. Choose a finite set of points $x_i \in X$, and an approximation scheme $\hat{I}(x;a)$. Choose stopping criterion $\varepsilon > 0$.

Step 1. For each $x_i \in X$, solve for I_i in

$$P(x_i - I_i) = g(I_i) + \beta\left(\sum_{j=1}^{m} \omega_i P(I_i + \theta_j - \hat{I}(I_i + \theta_j; a^k))\right).$$

Step 2. Determine a^{k+1} such that $\hat{I}(x; a^{k+1})$ approximates the (I_i, x_i) data generated in step 1.

Step 3. STOP if $\|a^k - a^{k+1}\| < \varepsilon$; otherwise go to step 1.

We should note a significant but subtle difference between what we do here and what was done in (17.1.8) in the asset pricing model. One interpretation of the (17.1.8) approach is that the continuous-state dividend process is approximated by a finite grid consisting of the x_i points and that (17.1.8) solves a finite-state problem. In this problem, solving the Euler equation for only the finite collection of x_i is not equivalent to assuming that the commodity inventory process is confined to a discrete grid. This is clear because $x_i + \theta_j$, a value for the future stock level that appears in the algorithm, may not be a member of X. If we forced the state x to lie on the grid in each period then the Euler equation would generally not have a solution. Euler equation methods are basically inconsistent with discrete endogenous state problems.

These points also make clear the difference between Euler equation methods and Bellman equation methods from dynamic programming. One can use finite-state approximations for dynamic programming problems, since a finite-state dynamic programming problems does have a Bellman equation, whereas there is no Euler equation for a problem with a discrete choice set.

Fixed-Point Iteration

A simple fixed-point iteration scheme rewrites (17.4.6) as

$$I^{k+1}(x) = x - P^{-1}\left(\beta E\{P(I^k(x) + \theta - I^k(I^k(x) + \theta))\} + g(I^k(x))\right)$$

$$\equiv \mathcal{G}(I)(x).$$

(17.4.8)

We also choose some integration formula for the integrals in (17.4.8) to arrive at an approximation of $\mathcal{G}$:

$$\hat{\mathcal{G}}(I)(x) = x - P^{-1}\left(\beta \sum_{i=1}^{m} \omega_i P(I(x) + \theta_i - I(I(x) + \theta_i)) + g(I(x))\right),$$

(17.4.9)

where ω_i and θ_i are the integration weights and nodes. A computer implementation of fixed-point iteration combines the $\hat{I}$ approximation scheme and $\hat{\mathcal{G}}$ to arrive at algorithm 17.2.

Algorithm 17.2 Fixed-Point Iteration in (17.4.8)

Initialization. Choose a finite set of points $x_i \in X$, and an approximation method $\hat{I}(x; a)$.

Step 1. Evaluate $I_i = \hat{\mathcal{G}}(I)(x_i)$ for each $x_i \in X$.

Step 2. Determine a^{k+1} such that $\hat{I}(x; a^{k+1})$ approximates the (I_i, x_i) data generated in step 1.

Step 3. STOP if $\|a^k - a^{k+1}\|$ is small; otherwise, go to step 1.

Equilibrium with Stockouts

In some cases we will not want to include convenience value in our analysis. Then $g \equiv 0$, and it becomes possible that the nonnegativity constraint will bind in equilibrium with nontrivial probability. In this case the equilibrium conditions (17.4.1) imply the complementary slackness conditions on $I(x)$:

$$P(x - I(x)) = \begin{cases} \beta E\{P(I(x) + \theta - I(I(x) + \theta))\}, & \text{if } I(x) > 0, \\ P(x), & \text{if } I(x) = 0. \end{cases}$$

In this case we will focus on the equilibrium prices instead of the equilibrium inventory holdings.[4] Either all current supply is consumed, in which case the price is the demand price for that quantity, or some is stored, in which case the current price must equal the expected future value. In equilibrium the current price is the greater of those two prices, implying the dynamic relation

$$p_t = \max[\beta E_t\{p_{t+1}\}, P(x_t)].$$

We solve for the equilibrium price function, denoted $h(x)$. Since $h(x)$ is the current price in a stationary equilibrium, (17.4.1) implies the functional equation

$$h(x) = \max[\beta E\{h(\theta + (x - D(h(x))))\}, P(x)]. \tag{17.4.10}$$

Theory (see Gustafson 1958) tells us that there does exist a solution to this equation, that it is nonnegative, continuous, nonincreasing, and that there is a p^* such that $h(x) = P(x)$ whenever $P(x) \geq p^*$ and $h(x) > P(x)$ whenever $P(x) < p^*$. Equation (17.4.10) can be solved in two ways. Gustafson parameterized $h(x)$ in a piecewise-linear fashion and computed equilibrium using the time iteration scheme

$$h_{j+1}(x) = \max\left[\beta E\{h_j(\theta + (x - P^{-1}(h_{j+1}(x))))\}, P(x)\right].$$

Deaton (1992) also parameterized h in a piecewise-linear fashion (with 100 nodes) and executed the iteration

$$h_{j+1}(x) = \max\left[\beta E\{h_j(\theta + (x - P^{-1}(h_j(x))))\}, P(x)\right],$$

which is an application of the fixed-point iteration scheme.

This shows that we can use the same methods for the constrained case as for the unconstrained case, but we must be careful due to the kink. Piecewise-linear functions can handle the kink but at some cost, since the presence of kinks makes it more difficult to solve the nonlinear equations implicit in time iteration. This fact makes fixed-point iteration attractive. However, one needs a large set of nodes in either case to get a good approximation. While these problems are not important for this small problem, they will be far more complex problems. This leads us to ask if there is a better way to handle problems with constraints.

Wright-Williams Smoothing

The procedures above focused on finding an approximation to either the inventory holding rule, $I(x)$, or the equilibrium price rule, $h(x)$. These functions will have kinks

---

4. We could have taken this approach to the no-stockout case also. We are switching approaches to demonstrate the variety of possible methods.

if a nonnegativity constraint binds, a feature that complicates the approximation problem. In particular, we cannot take advantage of the strong approximation methods available for smooth functions.

Wright and Williams (1984) proposed that one instead focus on approximating the conditional expectation $E\{p_{t+1}|I_{t+1}\}$. This conditional expectation is also a sufficient description of equilibrium, since I_{t+1} completely describes the situation at the end of period t. The advantage is that $E\{p_{t+1}|I_{t+1}\}$ is likely to be smooth in I_{t+1}, making it easier to approximate and permitting the use of more powerful approximation methods. This insight has turned out to be of substantial value in solving rational expectations problems.

We first define $\psi(I_{t+1}) = E\{p_{t+1}|I_{t+1}\}$ to be today's expectation of tomorrow's price conditional on the end-of-period-t grain inventory being I_{t+1}. With this function we can compute the current price and inventory decisions. If the postharvest stock is x, the current price and end-of-period inventory must satisfy the pair of equations

$$p = \max[P(x), \beta\psi(I)],$$
$$I = x - D(p).$$
(17.4.11)

The system (17.4.11) has a unique solution for any x as long as ψ is nondecreasing function. Let $h(x; \psi)$ and $I(x; \psi)$ denote the solutions for price and carryover given x. We are not parameterizing these functions; h and I here are just used to express the current equilibrium relation between x and the resulting price and carryover if ψ is the conditional expectation function; note that the function ψ is the argument, not $\psi(x)$ or any other instance of ψ. Whenever we need to know $h(x; \psi)$ or $I(x; \psi)$ at some particular x, we solve the system (17.4.11). The presence of a maximum does not make (17.4.11) difficult to solve. The trick is to first check if $I = 0$ and $p = P(x)$ is an equilibrium; if not, the problem has an interior solution that can be computed quickly if ψ and D are smooth.

Using these facts, we arrive at the equation

$$\psi(y) = \beta E\{h(y + \theta; \psi))]\}.$$
(17.4.12)

Equation (17.4.12) expresses the stationary equilibrium condition for the conditional expectation function ψ. Time iteration is the sequence defined by

$$\psi^{j+1}(y) = E\{h(y + \theta; \psi^j))]\}.$$
(17.4.13)

The Wright-Williams procedure is now clear. One first picks a collection of values for I and θ, a polynomial parameterization scheme for ψ, and an initial (increasing) guess ψ^0. Suppose that we have the j guess, ψ^j. For each (I, θ) pair, we compute $h(I + \theta; \psi^j)$. This generates data that are used in a fitting step to compute the new approximation $\psi^{j+1}(I)$, which is the expectation of $h(I + \theta; \psi^j)$ given I. This continues until the difference between the ψ^j and ψ^{j+1} functions is small.

We mentioned that ψ should be a nondecreasing function. One could ensure this by using shape-preserving approximation schemes for ψ. More commonly, ψ is parameterized using a low-order polynomial, and the number of θ values used exceeds the polynomial degree so that the fitting step is a regression. This will often avoid shape problems.

17.5   A Simple Stochastic Dynamic Growth Model

The commodity storage model has a single, endogenous state variable. We next examine a simple model with one exogenous and one endogenous state variable. We use a simple stochastic growth model to present several computational methods for solving these more general rational expectations problems. This stochastic growth model is also one that has been studied in the computational literature.

We consider the stochastic optimization problem

$$\max_{c_t} E \left\{ \sum_{t=0}^{\infty} \beta^t u(c_t) \right\}$$

$$\text{s.t.} \quad k_{t+1} = F(k_t, \theta_t) - c_t, \tag{17.5.1}$$

$$\ln \theta_{t+1} = \rho \ln \theta_t + \varepsilon_{t+1},$$

where θ_t is a productivity parameter and $\varepsilon_t \sim N(0, \sigma^2)$ is a series of i.i.d. innovations. The solution is characterized by

$$u'(c_t) = \beta E\{u'(c_{t+1})F_k(k_{t+1}, \theta_{t+1})|k_t, \theta_t\}. \tag{17.5.2}$$

In this problem both the beginning-of-period capital stock and the current value of θ are needed for a sufficient description of the state. Hence $c_t = C(k_t, \theta_t)$ for some policy function C, and the Euler equation implies that

$$0 = u'\left(C(k, \theta)\right) - \beta E \left\{u'(C(F(k, \theta) - C(k, \theta), \theta^+))\right.$$

$$\left. \times F_k(F(k, \theta) - C(k, \theta), \theta^+)|\theta\right\}, \tag{17.5.3}$$

where θ is the current productivity level and θ^+ is the random variable denoting the next period's productivity level. Even though we begin with an optimization problem, the solution is also the unique competitive equilibrium where (17.5.3) characterizes the equilibrium decision rules. Our presentation is of general interest because many equilibrium analyses, with and without distortions, often reduce to equations similar to (17.5.3).

There are a variety of ways to express equilibrium. One way is to focus on the time series (c_t, k_t) of consumption and capital. This approach attempts to find a time series that satisfies

$$u'(c_t) = \beta E\{u'(c_{t+1})F_k(k_{t+1}, \theta_{t+1})\},$$

$$k_{t+1} = F(k_t, \theta_t) - c_t.$$

This is the stochastic version of the Arrow-Debreu approach, wherein we compute a sequence of state-contingent factor prices and capital stock levels that satisfies the equilibrium conditions. While this approach can be used it quickly becomes intractable as we add both time and uncertainty, since the number of state-contingent commodities grows rapidly.

We instead must take a recursive approach focusing on (17.5.3). The functional equation (17.5.3) can be written in several ways. Note that the consumption policy function C appears in four places. If we define

$$\mathscr{F}(C_1, C_2, C_3, C_4) = u'(C_1(k, \theta)) - \beta E\{u'(C_2(F(k, \theta) - C_3(k, \theta)), \theta^+)$$
$$\times F_k(F(k, \theta) - C_4(k, \theta), \theta^+)|\theta\},$$

then equilibrium is defined by the functional equation $0 = \mathscr{F}(C, C, C, C) \equiv \mathscr{N}(C)$. In this way, we can deal with several methods in a unified fashion.

17.6 Projection Methods with Newton Iteration

In this section we review the details of applying alternative versions of the projection method to (17.5.3); this is largely taken from Judd (1992). In this section we will use the Powell hybrid method to find the unknown coefficients. This approach to finding the unknown coefficients is totally lacking in economic motivation but takes advantage of the quadratic (or, at least, superlinear) local convergence properties of Newton-type methods. We examine a variety of choices for the other pieces of the projection method.

We could use (17.5.3) as our residual function. However, it could be too nonlinear, particular for highly concave utility functions. Our algorithm might do better if we make it more like a linear problem. To that end we rewrite (17.5.3) it as

$$0 = C(k, \theta) - (u')^{-1}(\beta E \{u'(C(k^+, \theta^+)) F_k(k^+, \theta^+)|\theta\})$$

$$\equiv \mathcal{N}(C), \qquad\qquad\qquad\qquad\qquad\qquad (17.6.1)$$

where

$$k^+ \equiv F(k, \theta) - C(k, \theta),$$

$$\ln \theta^+ \sim N(\rho \ln \theta, \sigma^2).$$

Note that the RHS of (17.6.1) has two terms, one linear in $C(k, \theta)$ and the other is similar to a CRTS function of next period's potential consumption values. Note also that the $(u')^{-1}(\cdot)$ operation in (17.6.1) will unwrap some of the nonlinearity arising from the u' operation inside the expectation, hopefully leaving us with a more linear problem.

Galerkin and Orthogonal Collocation Methods

The procedure is similar to the deterministic case, but there are some extra twists due to the stochastic shocks. First of all our approximation of the policy function is now given by the double sum

$$\hat{C}(k, \theta; a) = \sum_{i=1}^{n_k} \sum_{j=1}^{n_\theta} a_{ij} \psi_{ij}(k, \theta), \qquad\qquad\qquad (17.6.2)$$

where $\psi_{ij}(k, \theta) \equiv T_{i-1}(2(k - k_m)/(k_M - k_m) - 1) T_{j-1}(2(\theta - \theta_m)/(\theta_M - \theta_m) - 1)$. The form in (17.6.2) is a tensor-product approach to two-dimensional approximation. It is reasonable here because the dimension is low, and it is a straightforward extension of the one-dimensional techniques to higher dimensions.

Projection methods generally assume that the problem lives on a compact domain. The stochastic growth problem we specified in (17.5.1) often has an unbounded ergodic set. In practice, we specify a compact set of (k, θ) pairs over which we try to solve (17.6.1). Our choice for this compact set is represented by four parameters in (17.6.2): k_M, k_m, θ_M, and θ_m. The capital stock bounds k_m and k_M are chosen so that k is usually confined to $[k_m, k_M]$, and similarly for θ_M and θ_m. Since θ is exogenous, this can be easily accomplished for θ. If we truncate the innovation ε so that $\varepsilon \in [\varepsilon_m, \varepsilon_M]$, then θ is confined to $[\theta_m, \theta_M]$ where $\ln \theta_m = \varepsilon_m(1 - \rho)^{-1}$ and $\ln \theta_M = \varepsilon_M(1 - \rho)^{-1}$. Appropriate choices for k_m and k_M are more problematic and generally cannot be made until after some experimentation finds a capture region. In this problem we do know the steady state for the deterministic case of $\theta = 1$ and $\varepsilon \equiv 0$; one suspects that this deterministic steady state is roughly in the middle of the range of frequently visited capital stocks, implying that k_m should be less than the deterministic steady state and k_M greater. We initially aim to find a $\hat{C}(k, \theta; a)$ which nearly satisfies (17.6.2) on the rectangle $[k_m, k_M] \times [\theta_m, \theta_M]$.

Since tomorrow's log productivity level, $\ln \theta^+$, conditional on today's log productivity level, $\ln \theta$, is distributed as $\rho \ln \theta + \sigma Z$ for $Z \sim N(0, 1)$, combining (17.6.1) and (17.6.2) implies that

$$
0 = \hat{C}(k, \theta; a) - (u')^{-1} \left(\beta \int_{-\infty}^{\infty} I(k, \theta, z; a) \frac{e^{-z^2/2}}{\sqrt{2}} \, dz \right)
$$

$$
= \mathcal{N}(\hat{C}(\cdot; a))(k, \theta), \tag{17.6.3}
$$

where

$$
I(k, \theta, z; a) \equiv u'(\hat{C}(F(k, \theta) - \hat{C}(k, \theta; a), e^{\sigma z} \theta^\rho; a))
$$

$$
\times F_k(F(k, \theta) - \hat{C}(k, \theta; a), e^{\sigma z} \theta^\rho) \pi^{-1/2}.
$$

In (17.6.3), $\mathcal{N}$ involves an integral that cannot generally be evaluated explicitly. In forming the residual function, we need to use an approximation $\hat{\mathcal{N}}$ of $\mathcal{N}$, formed here by replacing the integral in (17.6.3), with a finite sum

$$
\int_{-\infty}^{\infty} I(k, \theta, z; a) \frac{e^{-z^2/2}}{\sqrt{2}} \, dz \doteq \sum_{j=1}^{m_z} I(k, \theta, \sqrt{2} z_j; a) \, \omega_j,
$$

where ω_j, z_j are Gauss-Hermite quadrature weights and nodes.

We can now define the residual function

$$
R(k, \theta; a) = \hat{C}(k, \theta; a) - (u')^{-1} \left(\beta \sum_{j=1}^{m_z} I(k, \theta, \sqrt{2} z_j; a) \, w_j \right)
$$

$$
\equiv \hat{\mathcal{N}}(\hat{C})(k, \theta). \tag{17.6.4}
$$

With this residual function, we can proceed with standard projection methods. A collocation method starts by choosing m_k capital stocks, $\{k_i\}_{i=1}^{m_k}$, and m_θ productivity levels, $\{\theta_i\}_{j=1}^{m_\theta}$, and then finds some a so that $R(k_i, \theta_j; a) = 0$ for all $i = 1, \ldots, m_k$ and $j = 1, \ldots, m_\theta$.

A Galerkin approach first forms the $n_k n_\theta$ projections

$$
P_{ij}(a) \equiv \int_{k_m}^{k_M} \int_{\theta_m}^{\theta_M} R(k, \theta; a) \, \psi_{ij}(k, \theta) W(k, \theta) \, d\theta \, dk, \qquad i = 1, \ldots, n_k, j = 1, \ldots, n_\theta,
$$

$$
\tag{17.6.5}
$$

where $W(k, \theta)$ is the product Chebyshev weight adapted for the rectangle $[k_m, k_M] \times [\theta_m, \theta_M]$, and then chooses a so that $P_{ij}(a) = 0$ for all i and j. Note that at this point each $P_{ij}(a)$ is a function only of a, since (17.6.5) integrates the integrands over the k and θ dimensions. Again $P_{ij}(a)$ needs to be computed numerically. Since the ψ_{ij} are Chebyshev polynomials, we use Gauss-Chebyshev quadrature points. Specifically, if we use m_k values of k and m_θ values of θ to compute the projections in (17.6.5), we solve the system

$$\hat{P}_{ij}(a) \equiv \sum_{l_k=1}^{m_k} \sum_{l_\theta=1}^{m_\theta} R(k_{l_k}, \theta_{l_\theta}; a) \psi_{ij}(k_{l_k}, \theta_{l_\theta}) = 0, \qquad i = 1, \ldots, n_k, j = 1, \ldots, n_\theta,$$

$$(17.6.6)$$

where

$$k_{l_k} = k_m + \tfrac{1}{2}(k_M - k_m)\,(z_{l_k}^{m_k} + 1), \qquad l_k = 1, \ldots, m_k,$$

$$\theta_{l_\theta} = \theta_m + \tfrac{1}{2}(\theta_M - \theta_m)\,(z_{l_\theta}^{m_\theta} + 1), \qquad l_\theta = 1, \ldots, m_\theta,$$

$$z_l^n \equiv \cos\left(\frac{(2l-1)\pi}{2n}\right), \qquad l = 1, \ldots, n.$$

The nonlinear system of equations (17.6.6) imposes $n_k\, n_\theta$ conditions that hopefully determine the $n_k\, n_\theta$ unknown coefficients in a, which then fixes our approximation $\hat{C}(k, \theta)$.

Accuracy Checks—A Bounded Rationality Measure

Once we have a candidate solution, we want to check its quality. A direct procedure is to check how much, if at all, $\hat{\mathcal{N}}(\hat{C})$ differs from the zero function. First we should understand what a deviation from zero means in economic terms. Consider (17.6.4). It is the difference between consumption at a capital stock k and productivity level θ, and what that consumption would be if an optimizing agent knew that tomorrow he will use the consumption rule $\hat{C}$, and that personal and aggregate wealth will both be $F(k, \theta) - C(k, \theta)$. Therefore our residual function (17.6.4) applied to the approximate solution is the one-period optimization error in consumption terms. The function

$$E(k, \theta; a) \equiv \frac{R(k, \theta; a)}{\hat{C}(k, \theta; a)} \tag{17.6.7}$$

yields a dimension-free quantity expressing that optimization error as a fraction of current consumption. We use $E(k, \theta; a)$ for our accuracy index.

This approach to accuracy checking expresses the resulting errors in economic terms, essentially in terms of how irrational agents would be in using the approximate rule. If this relative optimization error were found to be about 0.1, then we would know that the approximation implies that agents make 10 percent errors in their period-to-period consumption decisions, a magnitude that few economists would find acceptable. However, if this index were found to be 10^{-6}, then the approximation implies that agents made only a $1.00 mistake for every $1,000,000 they spent. While such an approximation, $\hat{C}$, may not be the mathematically exact equilibrium decision rule, it is hard to argue that real world agents would actually do better. Therefore $\hat{C}$ is as plausible a description of human behavior as the mathematically exact zero of the operator $\mathcal{N}$.

The philosophy behind this accuracy check is that we should find an ε such that our approximation is an ε-equilibrium. The advantage of this approach is that our attempt to approximate an exact equibrium becomes reinterpreted as a search for an approximate equilibrium. The disadvantage of focusing on ε-equilibrium is the likely existence of an open set of such equilibria. However, as long as the problem is well-conditioned, something that can be numerically checked, that set is likely to be small, and even negligible for many purposes.

Initial Guess

The initial guess is always important in any nonlinear equation procedure, particularly for methods that may not converge. Our initial guess is the value for a such that $\hat{C}(k, \theta; a) = k(F(1, 1) - 1)$. This initial guess is the linear consumption function going between the origin and the deterministic steady state and does not depend on θ. Since $\hat{C}$ is a polynomial, there is such an a, but the exact value of a will depend on k_m and k_M. Its advantage is that it is a simple one; we do not do any problem-specific manipulations to construct a good initial guess. One important property is that it is a rule that is consistent with global stability and the transversality condition at infinity for the deterministic problem.

Finding an initial guess is often the most difficult part of solving nonlinear systems when one is not using a homotopy method. It is good to have a variety of strategies for generating initial guesses. In solving (17.6.1), an alternative procedure would be to use the perturbation methods discussed in chapter 14 to construct the locally valid linear approximation to $C(k, \theta)$ near the deterministic steady state. Another possibility is to first use the least squares approach to find a low-order solution and use it as the initial guess for the projection system (17.6.6). The global convergence properties of least squares algorithms would keep this step from diverging, and the result would hopefully be a good initial guess for (17.6.6). Some generate an initial guess by using the simple continuation method of section 5.8 beginning with a version of (17.6.1) with a known closed-form solution. This will probably work, but it will be slow, and at that point one might as well use a full homotopy approach. Fortunately the simple linear guess worked fine for solving (17.6.6), and the Powell hybrid solver always converged for the examples below.

Results for Galerkin and Orthogonal Collocation Methods

With our approximation method and accuracy checks determined, we can now see how good our approximate solutions are and how fast we can compute them. To do so, we make taste and technology specifications that bracket a wide range of empirically plausible values. Table 17.1 summarizes typical cases. We again have assumed that $u(c) = c^{\gamma+1}/(\gamma+1)$, and $F(k) = k + Ak^\alpha$ where A is chosen so that the deter-

Table 17.1
Log$_{10}$ Euler equation errors

γ	ρ	σ	$\|E\|_\infty$	$\|E\|_1$	$\|E_I\|_\infty$	$\|E\|_\infty$	$\|E\|_1$	$\|E_I\|_\infty$
			$(2, 2, 2, 2)^a$			$(4, 3, 4, 3)^a$		
−15.00	0.80	0.01	−2.13	−2.80	−2.58	−3.00	−3.83	−3.70
−15.00	0.80	0.04	−1.89	−2.54	−2.28	−2.44	−2.87	−2.59
−15.00	0.30	0.04	−2.13	−2.80	−2.58	−2.97	−3.83	−3.70
−0.10	0.80	0.01	−0.01	−1.22	−1.34	−1.68	−2.65	−2.70
−0.10	0.80	0.04	−0.01	−1.19	−1.20	−1.48	−2.22	−1.89
−0.10	0.30	0.04	0.18	−1.22	−1.35	−1.63	−2.65	−2.74
			$(7, 5, 7, 5)^a$			$(7, 5, 20, 12)^a$		
−15.00	0.80	0.01	−4.28	−5.19	−5.00	−4.43	−5.18	−4.91
−15.00	0.80	0.04	−3.36	−4.00	−3.70	−3.30	−3.95	−3.67
−15.00	0.30	0.04	−4.24	−5.19	−4.96	−4.38	−5.18	−4.87
−0.10	0.80	0.01	−3.40	−4.37	−4.35	−3.47	−4.39	−4.32
−0.10	0.80	0.04	−2.50	−3.22	−2.93	−2.60	−3.17	−2.91
−0.10	0.30	0.04	−3.43	−4.37	−4.36	−3.49	−4.39	−4.33
			$(10, 6, 10, 6)^a$			$(10, 6, 25, 15)^a$		
−15.00	0.80	0.01	−5.48	−6.43	−6.19	−5.61	−6.42	−6.11
−15.00	0.80	0.04	−3.81	−4.38	−4.11	−3.88	−4.37	−4.11
−15.00	0.30	0.04	−5.45	−6.43	−6.15	−5.57	−6.42	−6.08
−0.10	0.80	0.01	−5.09	−6.12	−5.94	−5.17	−6.15	−5.94
−0.10	0.80	0.04	−2.99	−3.68	−3.37	−3.09	−3.64	−3.38
−0.10	0.30	0.04	−5.17	−6.12	−6.01	−5.23	−6.14	−5.99

a. This four-tuple denotes the values of $(n_k, n_\theta, m_k, m_\theta)$ for the block below.

ministic steady state is $k = 1$. Throughout table 17.1, $\alpha = 0.25$, $k_m = 0.3$, and $k_M = 2.0$. We also chose $m_z = 8$, the eight-point, fifteenth-order accurate Gauss-Hermite quadrature rule to compute the conditional expectation. Table 17.1 lets σ and ρ vary; for each choice, θ_M is set equal to the long-run value of θ which would occur if $\varepsilon_t = 3\sigma$ for all t (in the notation above, this implies that $\varepsilon_m = 3\sigma$), and $\theta_m = 1/\theta_M$. It is extremely unlikely for θ to spend much if any time outside of $[\theta_m, \theta_M]$.

Table 17.1 is composed of six blocks of error entries, each block corresponding to a particular choice of the 4-tuple $(n_k, n_\theta, m_k, m_\theta)$. For example, the block headed by the 4-tuple $(2, 2, 2, 2)$ is the case where the $\hat{C}(k, \theta) = a_1 + a_2 k + a_3 \theta + a_4 k\theta$. The label $(2, 2, 2, 2)$ also indicates that we choose an orthogonal collocation procedure which fixes a so that the Euler equation fits exactly at the four zeros of $\psi_{3,3}$. The 4-tuple $(10, 6, m_k, m_\theta)$ corresponds to allowing k terms up to k^9, θ terms up to θ^5, and all possible pairwise products of those k and θ terms.

To test for the quality of the candidate solution, we evaluate $E(k, \theta; a)$ defined in (17.6.7) at a large number of (k, θ) combinations that themselves were not used in finding a solution. We defined the relative error at (k, θ) to be $E(k, \theta; a)$. The entries are the base 10 logarithm of various norms of $E(\cdot)$. Columns 4, 5, 7, and 8 report $\log_{10}\|E\|_\infty$ and $\log_{10}\|E\|_1$. All of these norms were calculated by using 8000-grid points in $[k_m, k_M] \times [\theta_m, \theta_M]$, 100 in $[k_m, k_M]$ and 80 in $[\theta_m, \theta_M]$. Base 10 logs of these norms are natural measures for our exercise. $\log_{10}\|E\|_\infty$ is the maximum error we found, and $\log_{10}\|E\|_1$ represents the average error. For example, an entry of -3 under the $\log_{10}\|E\|_\infty$ column says that a person with \$1,000 of consumption makes at *most* a one dollar error in current consumption in each period relative to the next period's consumption. Since solution paths concentrate near the center of the state space, we are particularly concerned about accuracy there. We define E_I to be E restricted to the inner rectangle $[k'_m, k'_M] \times [\theta'_m, \theta'_M]$ where $[k'_m, k'_M] \subset [k_m, k_M]$ and $[\theta'_m, \theta'_M] \subset [\theta_m, \theta_M]$; we take the smaller k (θ) interval to be the middle half of the larger interval. Columns 6 and 9 reports $\log_{10}\|E_I\|_\infty$.

There are several points to note. First, note that the errors are rather small. Even for the $(2, 2, 2, 2)$ case, the errors are roughly one dollar per hundred, as long as the utility function is as concave as $\log c$. Second, as we allow the approximation to use more terms the errors fall until in the $(10, 6, 10, 6)$ case, we often find optimization errors of less than one dollar per million. Third, the various norms of the residual function have very similar values, indicating that the errors are uniformly small. In particular, the similarity in values for the norms of E and E_I indicates that the solution is almost as good at the edges of the state space as in the middle.

Fourth, these methods are fast. We report times on a Compaq 386/20, a dinosaur by today's standards; the content of the times we report lies in the relative speeds.

The solutions in the $(2,2,2,2)$ case were solved in 0.2 to 0.4 seconds and in the $(4,3,4,3)$ case in 1.1 to 2 seconds. The slow parameterization throughout table 17.1 was $\gamma = -15.0$, $\rho = 0.8$, and $\sigma = 0.04$, which took 3 seconds for the $(4,3,4,3)$ case. The speed advantage of orthogonal collocation is demonstrated by the fact that the $(7,5,7,5)$ cases generally took 8 to 18 seconds, whereas the $(7,5,20,12)$ Galerkin cases took three times as long, which is expected since the projections were integrals using 240 points instead of 35. An intriguing exception was the slow parameterization which took nearly two minutes for collocation but only a minute and a half for Galerkin. Apparently the extra information used by the Galerkin procedure helped the nonlinear equation solver avoid bad directions. The $(10,6,10,6)$ cases generally took 27 to 72 seconds with the bad parameterization taking 100 seconds. The corresponding $(10,6,20,15)$ cases took roughly four times as long.

Fifth, note that the orthogonal collocation method does remarkably well given the small amount of computation. This is indicated by the small optimization errors and that the Galerkin procedures which use many more points achieved only slightly greater accuracy. In general, the collocation schemes yielded the most accuracy per unit of time.

Another way to check for accuracy is to see how the computed solution changes when we use higher-order and different quadrature schemes. Again we find trivial sensitivity to these changes. For example, using $m_z = 4$ instead of 8 resulted in very few differences (table 17.1 was unchanged) and cut the running time by almost half.

As with the deterministic case we have ignored transversality considerations in our solution method. Again we should check that the solutions are stable, as they always were. In the stochastic case we have no clear alternative that will ensure convergence to a stable solution, since we do not know a priori any point on the policy function. While solving operator equations without imposing boundary conditions is not proper procedure, it appears to be possible for these problems.

Alternative Bases and Projections

Tables 17.2 and 17.3 discuss the results when we attempt alternative implementations of the projection ideas. Each choice was motivated by some optimality or conditioning consideration. We will now see how important they were. Table 17.2 re-examines some of the cases in table 17.1 using theoretically inferior methods.

The pair of columns under G gives the $\log_{10}\|E\|_\infty$ error measure and running times when we used the projection procedures with Chebyshev polynomials and Chebyshev zeros. The pair of columns under P refers to $\log_{10}\|E\|_\infty$ and running times when we used ordinary polynomials instead of Chebyshev polynomials, but still fit the residual conditions at the Chebyshev zeros. The results under G and P should be identical

Table 17.2
Alternative implementations

γ	ρ	σ	G^a		P^b		U^c		UP^d	

γ	ρ	σ	G^a		P^b		U^c		UP^d	
			\multicolumn{8}{c}{$n_k = 7$ $\quad n_\theta = 5$ $\quad m_k = 7$ $\quad m_\theta = 5$}						
−15.0	0.8	0.04	−3.18	1:15	−2.13	:40	−3.06	1:05	−2.19	:44
	0.3	0.01	−4.35	:11	−4.35	:52	−4.07	:08	−4.07	1:47
−0.9	0.8	0.04	−3.43	:05	−3.43	:19	−3.42	:08	−3.42	:39
	0.3	0.01	−4.03	:07	−4.03	:30	−3.76	:07	−3.76	1:10
−0.1	0.8	0.04	−2.50	:07	−2.50	:41	−2.52	:06	−2.52	:42
	0.3	0.01	−3.42	:08	−3.42	1:30	−3.18	:07	−3.18	:24
			\multicolumn{8}{c}{$n_k = 10$ $\quad n_\theta = 6$ $\quad m_k = 25$ $\quad m_\theta = 15$}						
−15.0	0.8	0.04	−3.87	4:20	−3.90	24:44	−3.90	3:41	−3.36	42:15
	0.3	0.01	−5.68	2:19	−5.14	11:31	−5.49	2:14	−5.30	8:06
−0.9	0.8	0.04	−4.00	1:31	−4.00	5:17	−4.01	1:31	−4.01	5:02
	0.3	0.01	−5.40	1:23	−4.63	7:13	−5.25	1:20	−5.13	6:01
−0.1	0.8	0.04	−3.09	1:31	−3.09	9:16	−3.10	1:32	−3.07	12:01
	0.3	0.01	−5.27	1:32	−4.02	7:25	−5.09	1:27	−3.27	8:32

a. Chebyshev polynomial basis, Chebyshev zeros used in evaluating fit.
b. Ordinary polynomial basis, Chebyshev zeros used in evaluating fit.
c. Chebyshev polynomial basis, uniform grid points.
d. Ordinary polynomial basis, uniform grid points.

Table 17.3
Tensor product versus complete polynomials

γ	ρ	σ	Tensor product			Complete polynomials		
			$n = 3$	$n = 6$	$n = 10$	$n = 3$	$n = 6$	$n = 10$
−15.0	0.8	0.04	−2.34[a]	−3.26	−3.48	−1.89	−3.10	−4.06
			:01[b]	:13	14:21	:03	:07	1:09
−0.9	0.3	0.10	−2.19	−3.60	−5.27	−2.14	−3.55	−5.22
			:01	:08	1:21	:01	:05	:32
−0.1	0.3	0.01	−1.00	−2.84	−5.21	−0.99	−2.83	−5.17
			:01	:08	1:24	:01	:05	:35

Note: The tensor product cases in this table used orthogonal collocation with $n_k = n_\theta = m_k = m_\theta = n$ to identify the n^2 free parameters. The complete polynomial cases used Galerkin projections to identify the $1 + n + n(n + 1)/2$ free parameters.
a. $\text{Log}_{10}\|E\|_\infty$.
b. Computation time expressed in minutes : seconds.

if we had infinite precision arithmetic and Newton's method always converged. In several cases the results were the same, but the P times were far slower. P was faster in one case but yielded an approximation with substantially larger error: The solver could not make good progress so it stopped early. The slower time and premature stopping are both reflections of the conditioning problems associated with ordinary polynomials.

The columns under U give the accuracy and running time when we used Chebyshev polynomials but used a uniform grid to compute the projections. Here G should do better, since interpolation at a uniform grid is generally inferior to interpolation at Chebyshev zeros. Running times should not be affected much, since the Chebyshev approximation approach helps keep the nonlinear system well-conditioned. We see that accuracy is generally the same or worse, and running times are the same or slower.

The final column, labeled UP, refers to the straightforward approach of using ordinary polynomials and uniform grid points. Here we have a substantial loss of speed to attain the same or lower-quality approximations. The loss of speed by a factor of two to ten demonstrates clearly the value of orthogonal polynomial approximations and Gaussian quadrature. Since this is a rather simple problem, one suspects that the difference will be far greater in more complex problems.

As predicted by theory, the condition numbers of the Jacobian were strongly related to these performance indices. The cases in table 17.1 always had Jacobians with condition numbers under 10^3 and usually of the order 10. The P cases in table 17.2 had condition numbers several orders of magnitude greater, sometimes as great as 10^7. The U cases had condition numbers between 10^2 and 10^4, and the UP cases had condition numbers as large as those in the P cases. Our experiments also indicated that the condition number of the jacobian at our initial guess was of the same order of magnitude as the condition number at the solution. This suggests a useful procedure. If the Jacobian's condition number is large at the initial guess, then one should change the basis, fitting conditions, or something to reduce the initial conditioning of the problem, whereas a low initial condition number is evidence that the problem will be well-behaved.

Table 17.3 demonstrates the advantages of a complete polynomial basis. We report $\log_{10}\|E\|_\infty$ and, below it, the running time for a few cases. The parameter n is one more than the maximum exponent. For example, the $n = 3$ case under "tensor product" refers to using the tensor product of quadratic polynomials in k and θ, where under "complete polynomials" it refers to using the basis $\{1, k, \theta, k^2, k\theta, \theta^2\}$. The complete polynomial basis generally yields a lower-quality fit; the exception occurs because the Newton solver had difficulty converging for the tensor product basis but not for the complete polynomial basis. However, the slightly lower accuracy for fixed n was achieved in much less time. Since the real objective is to find a method that achieves maximal accuracy for fixed time, table 17.3 shows that the complete polynomial basis generally gives most accuracy per unit time. Since this is clear for a two-dimensional problem, we can expect that there will be even larger gains from using complete bases in higher dimensions.

Value of Nonlinear Transformations

All of these examples of solutions to (17.5.3) used (17.6.1) instead of Euler equation (17.5.3). When (17.5.3) is used instead, the results are substantially inferior in terms of speed and accuracy, particularly when γ is large in magnitude. This is not surprising since we used a Newton-style method for solving (17.6.2), and the Jacobian of (17.6.5) was better conditioned when R is taken from (17.6.1) than when it is taken from (17.5.3). While this may appear lucky, the key fact is that (17.6.1) has two pieces, one linear in the unknown Chebyshev coefficients and the other "more linear" than (17.5.3). Again the initial condition number was very good at predicting performance.

17.7   Fixed-Point Iteration

We next examine a fixed-point iteration procedure similar to the fixed-point iteration examined in chapter 16. We first discuss a direct implementation of the fixed-point iteration idea and then present a simulation alternative.

Gaussian Quadrature Implementation

In fixed-point iteration we execute the iteration

$$C_{i+1}(k, \theta) = (u')^{-1}(\beta E\{u'(C_i(k^+, \theta^+)) F_k(k^+, \theta^+)|\theta\}),$$

$$k^+ \equiv F(k, \theta) - C_i(k, \theta), \tag{17.7.1}$$

$$\theta^+ \sim N(\rho \ln \theta, \sigma^2).$$

Note that this is a simple rewriting of (17.6.1). The key computational task is to compute the right hand side for several (k, θ) choices and interpolate to get successive iterates of C. Essentially the RHS of (17.7.1) is tomorrow's return on saving one more dollar today conditional on today's (k, θ) and assuming that one follows the rule $c = C(k, \theta)$ at all times.

In this model the RHS of (17.7.1) is just a simple integral over θ^+, tomorrow's productivity level conditional on the current k and θ. Since all the elements are smooth and the disturbances Gaussian, the four- or five-point Gauss-Hermite rule is adequate. Therefore, to compute the, say, quadratic, solution to this problem, one need only examine a handful of k and θ values. This results in a very rapid way to compute an iterate. This method may converge slowly if at all, just as was the case with fixed-point iteration in the perfect foresight case in chapter 16. However, convergence problems may be solved by the extrapolation or dampening adjustments.

Simulation Implementation

A natural approach to solving (17.7.1) is to use numerical quadrature methods to evaluate the conditional expectation on the RHS of (17.7.1); that is, for each θ, use quadrature methods to compute the integral which corresponds to the conditional expectation. In this model it is easy to compute the conditional expectation, but this direct approach may not be available in general.

den Haan and Marcet (1990) use the fixed-point iteration method in (17.7.1), but they use simulation and regression methods instead of deterministic integration methods to approximate the key conditional expectation in (17.7.1). They first define the conditional expectation function

$$\psi(k_t, \theta_t) = E\{u'(c_{t+1})F_k(k_{t+1}, \theta_{t+1})|\theta_t, k_t\}$$

and parameterize ψ with a functional form $\hat{\psi}(k, \theta; a)$.[5] They next simulate a θ_t path to use in each subsequent iteration.

Their iteration procedure begins with a guess for the a coefficients in $\hat{\psi}(k, \theta; a)$. From this guess, they compute the implied consumption rule $c = \hat{C}(k, \theta; a) = (u')^{-1}(\beta\hat{\psi}(k, \theta; a))$. They then simulate the stochastic system

$$k_{t+1} = F(k_t, \theta_t) - \hat{C}(k_t, \theta_t; a)$$

for T periods to generate a time series $(c_t, k_t)_{t=1}^{T}$. They then choose the next value of a to solve

$$\min_a \sum_{t=1}^{T} (u'(c_{t+1})F_k(k_{t+1}, \theta_{t+1}) - \hat{\psi}(k_t, \theta_t; a))^2,$$

5. den Haan and Marcet express log consumption as a polynomial in $\log k$ and $\log \theta$ to keep consumption positive, but that is not critical for the basic idea.

a nonlinear regression of $u'(c_{t+1})F_k(k_{t+1}, \theta_{t+1})$ on the $(\theta_t, k_t)_{t=1}^T$ data. The den Haan-Marcet (dHM) procedure continues until the a iterates converge.[6]

The dHM procedure is a fixed-point iteration using simulation and regression to compute the critical conditional expectation. Since it is a fixed-point iteration, extrapolation and dampening can be used to address convergence problems. The use of simulation is intuitively natural and related to rational expectations learning ideas. However, the dHM method suffers from sensitivity to random simulation error. Since the critical integrals in this problem are of low-dimension, it is doubtful that there is any advantage to using simulation methods over deterministic quadrature methods. Comparisons of the running times reported in den Haan and Marcet with the times reported in tables 17.2 and 17.3 show that conventional projection methods are far faster then the dHM procedure for the stochastic growth problem 17.5.1.

17.8   Time Iteration

The time iteration method revolves around a dynamic interpretation of the Euler equation (17.5.2). Suppose that $C_T(k, \theta)$ is the time T policy function. To compute $C_{T-1}(k, \theta)$, we solve (17.5.1) for each (k, θ) pair. More precisely, for each (k, θ) we find the c that solves

$$0 = u'(c) - \beta E\{u'(C_T(F(k, \theta) - c, \theta^+))F_k(F(k, \theta) - c, \theta^+)|\theta\}. \qquad (17.8.1)$$

The solution to (17.8.1) is the consumption that equates current marginal utility of consumption with the expected marginal utility of consumption in the next period where the consumption rule is C_T. With C_{T-1} so determined at each (k, θ), we then iterate and compute C_{T-2}, C_{T-3}, and so on. When the iterates are close, we quit.

Pure time iteration is not possible for a computer since we cannot solve (17.8.1) at each (k, θ). We must therefore use some approximation scheme for C. Coleman (1990) used bilinear finite elements to approximate C. Specifically, he divided (log k, log θ) space into equi-sized rectangles and on each rectangle approximated the policy

---

6. Den Haan and Marcet refer to their method as "parameterized expectations." This is a misleadingly broad term, since parameterizing expectations goes back to parametric methods in dynamic programming (Bellman 1962 and Daniel 1978), and the use of polynomial parameterizations of conditional expectations functions in Euler equations was introduced previously by Wright and Williams (1984). Also the parameterization aspects of the dHM algorithm are independent of the simulation aspects. Therefore the term "parameterized expectations" does not focus on the key novel and distinguishing feature of the method in den Haan and Marcet (1990), that being the use of a simulated time series to compute the key integrals instead of the conventional quadrature methods used by earlier writers. To avoid confusion, we refer to their method as the dHM method.

function with a linear combination of 1, $\log k$, $\log \theta$, and $(\log k)(\log \theta)$. The basis is the tensor product of tent functions in $(\log k, \log \theta)$ space.

Suppose that we have an approximation $\hat{C}_T(k, \theta)$. To compute $\hat{C}_{T-1}(k, \theta)$, we first solve (17.5.1) for each $(\log k, \log \theta)$ pair in the grid. That is, for each $(\log k, \log \theta)$ in the grid, we find the c which solves (17.8.1) and set $\hat{C}_{T-1}(k, \theta) = c$. With $\hat{C}_{T-1}$ so determined at each $(\log k, \log \theta)$ on the grid, Coleman defines $\hat{C}_{T-1}$ to be the bilinear interpolant of the data on the grid.

A drawback of the Coleman procedure is the slow convergence of the integration method. Coleman used Gauss-Hermite quadrature that is appropriate given the log normal density for θ. However, because $\hat{C}_T$ is only C^0, the rate of convergence is not greater than a Newton-Cotes rule. Therefore Coleman used a large number of points in the quadrature rule.

Such low-order approximations necessitate many grid points; Coleman used a grid of 50 capital stocks and 20 productivity levels for a total of 1000 free parameters. Such a large number of free parameters results in a time-consuming computation, much slower than the the projection procedures using orthogonal polynomial approximations. One can use smooth approximation schemes for $\hat{C}$ instead of the piecewise linear log procedure used by Coleman. However, Coleman's finite-element procedure is less likely to have shape problems than more aggressive schemes such as collocation with orthogonal polynomials.

17.9   Generalizations

Our examples have been relatively simple, involving only single goods and single agents, and were cases where equilibrium was equivalent to a known social planning problem. The techniques presented above are not limited to such simple models. In this section we present some examples that indicate how to apply these methods to more substantive problems.

Growth with Tax Distortions

We first show how to add a tax distortion to the simple stochastic growth model presented in section 17.5. First, since the rate of return on capital net of depreciation is $f_k \equiv F_k - 1$, if it is taxed at a state-contingent rate $\tau(k, \theta)$, then equilibrium is the solution to the Euler equation

$$u'(C(k, \theta)) = \beta E\{u'(C(k^+, \theta^+))\left(1 + (1 - \tau(k^+, \theta^+))f_k(k^+, \theta^+)\right)|\theta\},$$

$$k^+ \equiv F(k, \theta) - C(k, \theta). \tag{17.9.1}$$

Note that (17.9.1) is a simple modification of (17.5.3). This is not the solution to any social planner's problem, but the key mathematical structure of this problem is similar to the first-order conditions in (17.5.3).

In tax problems we often need to compute a revenue function. Let $R(k,\theta)$ be the discounted value of current and future government tax revenue if the current state is (k,θ) and all revenues are lump-sum rebated. $R(k,\theta)$ is the solution to the integral equation

$$u'(C(k,\theta))(R(k,\theta) - \tau(k,\theta)kf_k(k,\theta)) = \beta E\left\{u'(C(k^+,\theta^+))\,R(k^+,\theta^+)|\theta\right\}. \quad (17.9.2)$$

Note that (17.9.2) is linear in $R(k,\theta)$ once we have the solution to $C(k,\theta)$. Therefore we can apply linear integral methods to solve (17.9.2) for $R(k,\theta)$.

We also will want to compute the equilibrium value function. Let $W(k,\theta)$ be the discounted value of current and future utility if the current state is (k,θ). $W(k,\theta)$ is the solution to the integral equation

$$W(k,\theta) = u(C(k,\theta)) + \beta E\{W(k^+,\theta^+)|\theta\}. \quad (17.9.3)$$

As with (17.9.2), (17.9.3) is linear in $W(k,\theta)$ once we have the solution to $C(k,\theta)$, and we can apply linear integral equation methods to solve (17.9.3) for $W(k,\theta)$.

Heterogeneous Agent Models

We next present an example with heterogeneous agents taken from Gaspar and Judd (1997). Suppose we take the model of section 17.5 but assume two infinitely lived types of agents with different utility functions; let $u_i(c_i)$ be the utility function of type i agents. Suppose that the only available asset is the risky capital stock. Then the state variable is $(k,\theta) \equiv (k_1, k_2, \theta)$ where k_i is the capital stock held by type i agents, $i = 1, 2$. The equilibrium consumption rule for type i agents is $C_i(k,\theta)$ and the consumption policy functions are characterized by the pair of Euler equations

$$0 = u_i'\left(C_i(k,\theta)\right) - \beta E\{u_i'(C_i(k^+,\theta^+))F_1(k_1^+ + k_2^+,\theta^+)|\theta\}, \qquad i = 1, 2,$$

$$k_i^+ \equiv k_i F_1(k_1 + k_2, \theta) + \tfrac{1}{2}(F(k_1 + k_2, \theta) - (k_1 + k_2)F_1(k_1 + k_2, \theta)) - C_i(k,\theta),$$

$$(17.9.4)$$

where $k_i F_1$ is type i's asset income and $\tfrac{1}{2}(F - (k_1 + k_2)F_1)$ is a type i's share of labor income.

The system (17.9.4) consists of two Euler equations with two unknown two-dimensional functions. We can use the methods used to solve (17.5.3). In (17.9.4) each C_i appears on the LHS alone, just as in (17.5.3); therefore we can use time iteration or function iteration just as easily here as before. For example, function iteration would implement the iteration

$$C_i^{j+1}(k,\theta) = (u_i')^{-1}(\beta E\{u_i'(C_i^j(k^+,\theta^+))F_k(k_1^+ + k_2^+, \theta^+)|\theta\}), \quad i = 1,2. \qquad (17.9.5)$$

One could also construct a system of projection conditions equal in number to the number of unknown coefficients and use Newton's method to solve for the unknown coefficients. Judd, Kubler, and Schmedders (1997a, b) examine some two-agent models. Gaspar and Judd (1997) evaluates alternative methods for two-, three-, four-, and five-agent problems. Furthermore Gaspar and Judd (1997) present a model where different agents have stochastic lifetimes and where different agents face different tax rates on asset income. The addition of multiple agents to the analysis creates larger systems but do not present fundamentally different challenges. However, as the number of unknown functions increases, the relative rankings of various methods change; Gaspar and Judd provide some examples of this.

Elastic Labor Supply

Many models have multiple choice variables, leading to multiple Euler equations. We next illustrate how to use our Euler equation methods to where we have both consumption and labor supply decisions. The representative agent model with elastic labor supply solves the problem

$$\max_{c_t, l_t} E\left\{\sum \beta^t u(c_t, l_t)\right\}$$

$$\text{s.t.} \quad k_{t+1} = k_t + \theta_t f(k_t, l_t) - c_t, \qquad\qquad (17.9.6)$$

$$\ln \theta_{t+1} = \rho \ln \theta_t + \varepsilon_{t+1}.$$

In this model we assume that θ_t is known when c_t and l_t are chosen. This implies that a stationary solution for c and l choices will depend on k and θ, and they can be denoted $c = C(k,\theta)$ and $l = L(k,\theta)$. There are two Euler equations, one for each choice variable; they are

$$u_c(c,l) = \beta E\{u_c(c^+, l^+)(1 + \theta^+ f_k(k^+, l^+))\},$$

$$u_c(c,l)\,\theta f_l(k,l) = -u_l(c,l), \qquad\qquad (17.9.7)$$

where

$$c \equiv C(k,\theta), \quad l \equiv L(k,\theta),$$

$$k^+ \equiv k + \theta f(k,l) - c, \quad c^+ \equiv C(k^+,\theta^+), \quad l^+ \equiv L(k^+,\theta^+).$$

To solve (17.9.6), we just apply our methods to the Euler equation pair in (17.9.7) to compute the policy functions $C(k, \theta)$ and $L(k, \theta)$. In general, problems with several choice variables are solved by specifying policy functions and a system of Euler equations for these variables, parameterizing the policy functions, and applying some iterative scheme to construct a sequence of policy function approximations that appear to converge to policy functions. After convergence, one should examine the apparent solutions fit with the Euler equation system at states not used in the computation.

17.10   Further Reading and Summary

This chapter has presented an overview of the problems in solving rational expectations models of various types. The examples presented illustrate how one can combine basic numerical analysis tools from approximation theory, nonlinear equations, and numerical quadrature to solve rational expectations problems. The Lucas asset pricing model reduces to a linear Fredholm equation and simple monetary models reduce to nonlinear Fredholm equations. The commodity market model is a simple example of rational expectations modeling with an endogenous state, as is the stochastic growth model. We again see the use of various iteration schemes, time iteration and other fixed-point iteration approximation schemes being the most common but with a Newton approach often dominating. Better examples of the value of these methods is the analysis in Wright and Williams (1984) which adds endogenous supply considerations to the model described in (17.4.1), and the several applications in Williams and Wright (1991). The stochastic growth model has been used to evaluate various methods; Danthine et al. (1989) and the Taylor and Uhlig (1990) symposium reviews the issues in rational expectations computations.

Bernardo and Judd (1994, 1997a, b) contain several applications of the approach to asset market equilibrium presented in section 17.3. Ausubel (1990a, b) presents a numerical analysis of markets with asymmetric information. His approach is somewhat more problem specific but reduces to a system of differential equations, a more conventional numerical problem. Corb used projection methods to solve a nonlinear multidimensional extension of the Kyle model. Ashcroft (1995) uses special bases and projection methods to solve option pricing problems.

We gave in this chapter only the barest introduction to heterogeneous agent analysis. Gaspar and Judd (1997) present some simple examples. den Haan (1995) analyzes models with a nontrivial income distribution. We have ignored dynamic games; Judd (1990) and Rui and Miranda (1996) discuss projection solution methods for solving dynamic games.

Table 17.4
Projection method menu

Approximation	Integration	Projections	Equation solver
Piecewise linear	Newton-Cotes	Galerkin	Newton
Polynomials	Gaussian rules	Collocation	Powell
Splines	Monte Carlo	Method of moments	Fixed-point iteration
Neural networks	Quasi–Monte Carlo	Subdomain	Time iteration
Rational functions	Monomial rules	Least squares	Homotopy
Hybrid constructions	Interpolatory rules		
	Asymptotics		

This chapter has also presented just a small sampling of rational expectations models we can solve. The key idea is that there are four basic decisions to make: how to parameterize the unknown functions, how to compute integrals, what projection criterion to use in fixing the unknown parameters, and how to solve the projection conditions. Table 17.4 lists several possibilities for each choice. Since these decisions are mostly independent, it is clear that there are many possible combinations. While some combinations are unlikely to be useful, many combinations are competitive with the best depending on the problem. Only a few combinations of have been explored in the literature. The important lesson is that an analyst should be flexible, and be able to try several alternatives.

Exercises

1. Use both the simulation method and the linear Fredholm integral equation methods to solve the Lucas asset pricing model (17.1.1)–(17.1.2). Specifically, assume $u(c) = c^{1+\gamma}/(1+\gamma)$ and $\varepsilon_t \sim N(0, \sigma^2)$ with $\gamma \in [-0.5, -5]$ and $\rho \in [0.01, 0.99]$.

2. Solve (17.2.1) with $u(c, m) = -c^{-2} + m - m^2/2$, $\theta_t = 1.0$, $\beta = 0.95$, and w_t i.i.d. distributed $U[1, 2]$. Recompute for the cases of $\theta = 1.1$ and $\theta = 0.9$. Which value of θ produced the greatest expected utility at the mean wage level?

3. Solve (17.4.1) with $\theta \sim U[0, 3]$, $P(q) = 5 - q$, and $g(I) = \sqrt{I}$ using fixed-point iteration and time iteration.

4. Resolve (17.4.1) with $\log \theta_{t+1} = \rho \log \theta_t + \varepsilon_t$, $\varepsilon_t \sim N[0, 1]$, and $\rho = 0.5$.

5. Solve (17.9.6) with $u(c, l) = c^{1+\gamma}/(1+\gamma) - l^\nu$, $\gamma \in \{-.5, -1.1, -3\}$, $\nu \in \{1.1, 2, 5\}$ and Cobb-Douglas $f(k, l)$ with capital share equal to 0.33.

6. Redo exercise 5 except add a labor income tax rate τ_L with lump-sum rebate of revenues. Compute the revenue function and the function relating expected utility to the state of the economy.

7.   Redo exercise 6 with an autoregressive labor income tax rate.

8.   Solve (17.5.3) using time iteration, fixed-point iteration with quadrature, the dHM procedure, and Newton iteration methods. Use ordinary and Chebyshev polynomials and in both levels and logs. Use the initial guess $C(k, \theta; a) = k(F(1, 1) - 1)$. Use the specifications for utility, production, and β used in table 17.1. Which bases produce the approximations with the smallest Euler equation errors? Which coefficient solution method does best per unit time?

9.   Repeat exercise 8 for a variety of cases with attention to initial guesses. First take your solution from exercise 8, randomly perturb each coefficient by 1 percent, and use that for the initial guess for each method. Which methods do better for this initial condition? Repeat this several times. Do this again with random 5 percent and 10 percent errors.

10. Repeat exercise 8 but now first use the Newton iteration method with collocation, a Chebyshev polynomial basis in logs, and initial guess $C(k, \theta; a) = k(F(1, 1) - 1)$. Then take that answer and use it as the initial guess for the fixed-point iteration methods, both the quadrature method and the dHM method. Compare the running time of the Newton method with initial guess $C(k, \theta; a) = k(F(1, 1) - 1)$ and the running times of the fixed-point iteration methods using the Newton solution as the initial guess. In the case of the dHM method, repeat several times using different simulated innovation samples, and compute the variance of the predicted consumption at $k = 0.8$ and $\theta = 1$.

References

Aarts, E., and J. Korst. 1990. *Simulated Annealing and Boltzmann Machines*. New York Wiley.

Acton, F. 1996. *Real Computing Made Real: Preventing Errors in Scientiric and Engineering Calculations*. Princeton: Princeton University Press.

Adomian, G. 1986. *Nonlinear Stochastic Operator Equations*. Orlando: Academic Press.

Aiyagari, S. R., Z. Eckstein, and M. Eichenbaum. 1989. Inventories and price fluctuations under perfect competition and monopoly. In T. Kollintzas, ed., *The Rational Expectations Equilibrium Inventory Model: Theory and Applications*. Lecture Notes in Economics and Mathematical Systems 322. New York: Springer, pp. 34–68.

Akin, J. E. 1982. *Application and Implementation of Finte Element Methods*. Orlando: Academic Press.

Albrecht, J. W., B. Holmlund, and H. Lang. 1991. Comparative statics in dynamic programming models with an application to job search. *Journal of Economic Dynamics and Control* 15: 755–69.

Allen, B. 1992. Approximate equilibria in microeconomic rational expectations models. *Journal of Economic Theory* 26: 244–60.

Allen, B. 1985. The existence of fully rational expectations approximate equilibria with noisy price observations. *Journal of Economic Theory* 37: 213–53.

Allen, B. 1985b. The existence of rational expectations equilibria in a large economy with noisy price observations. *Journal of Mathematical Economics* 14: 67–103.

Allgower, E. L., and K. Georg. 1990. *Numerical Continuation Methods: An Introduction*. New York: Springer.

Aluffi-Pentini, F., V. Parisi, and F. Zirlli. 1984. A differential-equations algorithm for nonlinear equations. *ACM Transactions on Mathematical Software* 10: 299–316.

Aluffi-Pentini, F., V. Parisi, and F. Zirilli. 1984. Algorithm 617. DAFNE—A differential equations algorithm for nonlinear equations. *ACM Transactions on Mathematical Software* 10: 317–24.

Ames, W. F. 1977. *Numerical Methods for Partial Differential Equations*. Orlando: Academic Press.

Amir, R., L. J. Mirman, and W. R. Perkins. 1991. One-sector nonclassical optimal growth: Optimality conditions and comparative dynamics. *International Economic Review* 32: 625–44.

Amman, H., D. Kendrick, and J. Rust, eds. 1996. *Handbook of Computational Economics*, vol. 1. Amsterdam: Elsevier.

Amman, H. 1996. Numerical methods for linear-quadratic models. In H. Amman et al., eds., *Handbook of Computational Economics*, vol. 1. Elsevier: Amsterdam.

Anderson, E., et al. 1992. *LAPACK User's Guide*. Philadelphia: SIAM, 1992.

Anderson, E. W., L. P. Hansen, E. R. McGrattan, and T. J. Sargent. 1996. Mechanics of forming and estimating dynamic linear economies. In H. Amman et al., eds., *Handbook of Computational Economics*, vol. 1, Amsterdam: Elsevier.

Anderson, R. M., and H. Sonnenschein. 1982. On the existence of rational expectations equilibrium. *Journal of Economic Theory* 26: 261–78.

Anderson, G. S. 1993. Symbolic algebra programming for analyzing the long-run dynamics of economic models. In H. Varian, ed., *Economic and Financial Modeling with Mathematica*. New York: Springer.

Araujo, A., and J. A. Scheinkman. 1977. Smoothness, comparative dynamics, and the turnpike property. *Econometrica* 45: 601–20.

Arifovic, J. 1994. Genetic algorithm learning and the cobweb model. *Journal of Economic Dynamics and Control* 18: 3–28.

Arrow, K. J., and F. H. Hahn. 1971. *General Competitive Analysis*. San Francisco: Holden-Day.

Ascher, U. M., R. M. M. Matthiej, and R. D. Russell. 1988. *Numerical Solution of Boundary Value Problems for Ordinary Differential Equations*. Englewood Cliffs, NJ: Prentice-Hall.

Ashcroft, R. N. 1995. Asset pricing with spectral methods. Ph. D. dissertation. Stanford University.

Atkinson, K. 1989. *An Introduction to Numerical Analysis*. New York: Wiley.

Aubin, J.-P., and I. Ekeland. 1984. *Applied Nonlinear Analysis*. New York: Wiley.

Auerbach, A. J., and Laurence J. Kotlikoff. 1987. *Dynamic Fiscal Policy*. Cambridge: Cambridge University Press.

Auerbach, A. J., and Laurence J. Kotlikoff. 1983. An examination of empirical tests of social security and savings. In E. Helpman, A. Razin, and E. Sadka, eds., *Social Policy Evaluation: An Economic Perspective*. New York: Academic Press.

Auerbach, A., L. Kotlikoff, and J. Skinner. 1983. The Efficiency Gains from Dynamic Tax Reform. *International Economic Review* 24: 81–100.

Ausubel, L. M. 1990a. Partially-revealing rational expectations equilibrium in a competitive economy. *Journal of Economic Theory* 50: 93–126.

Ausubel, L. M. 1990b. Insider trading in a rational expectations economy. *American Economic Review* 80: 1022–41.

Balcer, Y., and K. L. Judd. 1985. Dynamic effects of tax policy. Mimeo. Northwestern University.

Barro, R. 1974. Are government bonds net wealth? *Journal of Political Economy* 82: 1095–1117.

Barron, A. R. 1993. Universal approximation bounds for superpositions of a sigmoidal function. *IEEE Transactions on Information Theory* 39: 930–45.

Bazaraa, M., and C. M. Shetty. 1979. *Nonlinear Programming: Theory and Algorithms*. New York: Wiley.

Bellman, R. E. 1957. *Dynamic Programming*. Princeton: Princeton University Press.

Bellman, R., R. Kalaba, and B. Kotkin. 1963. Polynomial approximation—A new computational technique in dynamic programming: Allocation processes. *Mathematics of Computation* 17: 155–61.

Bender, C. M., and S. A. Orszag. 1978. *Advanced Mathematical Methods for Scientists and Engineers*. New York: McGraw-Hill.

Benhabib, J., and K. Nishimura. 1979. The Hopf bifurcation and the existence and stability of closed orbits in multisector models of optimal economic growth. *Journal of Economic Theory* 21: 421–44.

Bennett, C. H., and R. Landauer. 1985. The fundamental physical limits of computation. *Scientific American* 253-1: 48–71.

Bensoussan, A. *Perturbation Methods in Optimal Control*. New York: Wiley, 1988.

Beneveniste, A., M. Métivier, and P. Priouret. 1990. *Adaptive Algorithms and Stochastic Approximations*. Berlin: Springer.

Bernardo, A., and K. L. Judd. 1994. Asset market equilibrium with general securities, tastes, returns, and information asymmetries. Mimeo. Hoover Institution. 1994.

Bernardo, A. 1996. The choice between regulatory and contractual restrictions on insider trading: A welfare analysis. Mimeo. University of California-Los Angeles.

Bernardo, A., and K. L. Judd. 1997a. Efficiency of asset markets with asymmetric information. Mimeo. Hoover Institution.

Bernardo, A., and K. L. Judd. 1997b. Volume and price formation in an asset trading model with asymmetric information. UCLA Working Paper.

Bertsekas, D. 1982. *Constrained Optimization and LaGrange Multiplier Methods*. New York: Academic Press.

Bertsekas, D. 1976. *Dynamic Programming and Stochastic Control*. New York: Academic Press.

Bertsekas, D. P. 1995. *Dynamic Programming and Optimal Control*, vol. 1. Belmont, MA: Athena Scientific.

Bertsekas, D. P. 1995. *Dynamic Programming and Optimal Control*, vol. 2. Belmont, MA: Athena Scientific.

Bertsekas, D. P., and J. N. Tsitsiklis. 1996. *Neuro-dynamic Programming*. Belmont, MA: Athena Scientific.

Bertsekas, D. P., and S. E. Shreve. 1978. *Stochastic Control: The Discrete Time Case*. New York: Academic Press.

Bertsekas, D. P., and J. N. Tsitsiklis. 1989. *Parallel and Distributed Computation: Numerical Methods*. Englewood Cliffs, NJ: Prentice Hall.

Berz, M., C. Bischof, G. Corliss, and A. Griewank. 1996. *Computational Differentiation: Techniques, Applications, and Tools*. Philadelphia: SIAM.

Bizer, D., and K. L. Judd. 1989. Taxation and uncertainty. *American Economic Review* 79: 331–36.

Blackwell, D. 1965. Discounted dynamic programming. *Annals of Mathematical Statistics* 36: 226–35.

Bleistein, N., and R. A. Handelsman. 1976. *Asymptotic Expansions of Integrals*. New York: Holt, Rinehart and Winston.

de Boor, C. 1978. A *Practical Guide to Splines*. New York: Springer.

de Boor, C., and B. Swartz. 1977. Piecewise monotone interpolation. *Journal of Approximation Theory* 21: 411–16.

Border, K. C. 1985. *Fixed Point Theorems with Applications to Economics and Game Theory*. Cambridge: Cambridge University Press.

Botha, J. F., and G. F. Pinder. 1983. *Fundamental Concepts in the Numerical Solution of Differential Equations*. New York: Wiley.

Boucekkine, R. 1995. An alternative methodology for solving nonlinear forward-looking models. *Journal of Economic Dynamics and Control* 19: 711–34.

Bovenberg, A. L., and L. H. Goulder. 1991. Introducing intertemporal and open economy features in applied general equilibrium models. In H. Don, T. van de Klundert, and J. van Sinderen, eds, *Applied General Equilibrium Modelling*. Dordrecht: Kluwer Academic, pp. 47–64.

Boyd, J. P. 1989. *Chebyshev and Fourier Spectral Methods*. Berlin: Springer.

Braess, D. 1986. *Nonlinear Approximation Theory*. Berlin: Springer.

Bratley, P., and B. L. Fox. 1988. Algorithm 659 implementing Sobol's quasirandom sequence generator. *ACM Transactions on Mathematical Software* 14: 88–100.

Bratley, P., B. L. Fox, and L. E. Schrage. 1987. *A Guide to Simulation*. 2d ed. New York: Springer.

Brent, R. P. 1973. Some efficient algorithms for solving systems of nonlinear equations. *SIAM Journal on Numerical Analysis* 10: 327–44.

Brock, W. A. 1975. A simple perfect foresight monetary model. *Journal of Monetary Economics* 1: 133–50.

Brock, W. A., and W. D. Dechert. 1988. Theorems on distinguishing deterministic from random systems. In W. A. Barnett, E. R. Berndt, and H. White, eds., *Dynamic Econometric Modeling: Proceedings of the Third International Symposium in Economic Theory and Econometrics*. International Symposia in Economic theory and Econometrics series. New York: Cambridge University Press, pp. 247–65.

Brock, W. A., D. Hsieh, and B. LeBaron. 1991. *Nonlinear Dynamics, Chaos, and Instability*. Cambridge: MIT Press.

Brock, W. A., and L. J. Mirman. 1972. Optimal economic growth and uncertainty: The discounted case. *Journal of Economic Theory* 4: 479–513.

Brock, W. A. 1986. Distinguishing random and deterministic systems: Abridged version. *Journal of Economic Theory* 40: 168–95.

Brock, W. A., and S. J. Turnovsky. 1981. The analysis of macroeconomic policies in perfect foresight equilibrium. *International Economic Review* 22: 179–209.

Brown, D. J., P. M. DeMarzo, and B. C. Eaves. 1996. Computing equilibria when asset markets are incomplete. *Econometrica* 64: 1–27.

Brock, W. A., and A. G. Malliaris. 1989. *Differential Equations, Stability and Chaos in Dynamic Economies*. Amsterdam: North Holland.

Budd, C., C. Harris, and J. Vickers. 1993. A model of the evolution of duopoly: Does the asymmetry between firms tend to increase or decrease? *Review of Economic Studies* 60: 543–73.

Burnett, D. S. 1987. *Finite Element Analysis*. Reading, MA: Addison-Wesley.

Canzoneri, M. B., and D. W. Henderson. 1991. *Monetary Policy in Interdependent Economies: A Game-Theoretic Approach*. Cambridge: MIT Press.

Caputo, M. R. 1990. How to do comparative dynamics on the back of an envelope in optimal control theory. *Journal of Economic Dynamics and Control* 14: 655–83.

Caputo, M. R. 1990. Comparative Dynamics via envelope methods in variational calculus. *Review of Economic Studies* 57: 689–97.

Burdick, C. A. 1994. Transitional dynamics in a monetary economy. Ph.D. dissertation. Stanford University.

Burnett, D. S. 1987. *Finite Element Analysis*. Reading, MA: Addison-Wesley.

Canuto, C., M. W. Hussaini, A. Quarteroni, and T. A. Zang. 1988. *Spectral Methods in Fluid Dynamics*. New York: Springer.

Carter, R. G. 1993. Numerical experience with a class of algorithms for nonlinear optimization using inexact function and gradient information. *SIAM Journal of Scientific Computing* 14: 368–88.

Chaitin-Chatelin, F., and V. Frayssé. 1996. *Lectures on Finite Precision Computations*. Philadelphia: SIAM.

Chang, F.-W. 1988. The inverse optimal problem: A dynamic programming approach. *Econometrica* 56: 147–72.

Cheney, E. W. 1966. *Introduction to Approximation Theory*. New York: McGraw-Hill.

Cho, I.-K., and T. J. Sargent. 1996. Neural networks for encoding and adapting in dynamic economics. In Amman et al., eds., *Handbook of Computational Economics*, vol. 1. Amsterdam: Elsevier.

Chow, S.-N., J. Mallet-Pamet, and J. A. Yorke. 1978. Finding zeroes of maps: Homotopy methods that are constructive with probability one. *Mathematics of Computation* 32: 887–99.

Chow, S.-N., and J. K. Hale. 1982. *Methods of Bifurcation Theory*. New York: Springer.

Christiano, L. J. 1990. Solving the stochastic growth model by linear-quadratic approximation and by value-function iteration. *Journal of Business and Economic Statistics* 8: 23–26.

Christopeit, N. 1983. Discrete approximation of continuous time stochastic control systems. *SIAM Journal on Control and Optimization* 21: 17–40.

Chung, K. L. 1974. *A Course in Probability Theory*, 2d ed. New York: Academic Press.

Chung, K. L. 1949. An estimate concerning the Kolmogoroff limit distribution. *Transactions of the American Mathematical Society* 67: 36–50.

Cohen, A. M., and D. A. Gismalla. 1985. The construction of quadrature rules by parameter optimization. *International Journal of Computational Mathematics* 17: 203–14.

Cohen, A. M., and D. A. Gismalla. 1986. Some integration for symmetric functions of two variables. *International Journal of Computational Mathematics* 19: 57–68.

Coleman, W. J., II. 1990. Solving the stochastic growth model by policy function iteration. *Journal of Business and Economic Statistics* 8: 27–29.

Cooley, T., and G. Hansen. 1989. The inflation tax in a real business cycle model. *American Economic Review* 79: 733–48.

Costantini, P., and F. Fontanella. 1990. Shape-preserving bivariate interpolation. *SIAM Journal of Numerical Analysis* 27: 488–506.

Cranley, R., and T. N. L. Patterson. 1976. Randomization of number theoretic methods for multiple integration. *SIAM Journal of Numerical Analysis* 13: 904–14.

Cronshaw, M. B., and D. G. Luenberger. 1994. Strongly symmetric subgame perfect equilibria in infinitely repeated games with perfect monitoring and discounting. *Games and Economic Behavior* 6: 220–37.

Cuyt, A., and L. Wuytack. 1986. *Nonlinear Numerical Methods: Theory and Practice*. Amsterdam: North-Holland.

Daniel, J. W. 1976. Splines and efficiency in dynamic programming. *Journal of Mathematical Analysis and Applications* 54: 402–407.

Danthine, J.-P., J. B. Donaldson, and R. Mehra. 1989. On some computational aspects of equilibrium business cycle theory. *Journal of Economic Dynamics and Control* 13: 449–70.

Dantzig, G. B., R. P. Harvey, Z. F. Lansdowne, and R. D. McKnight. 1974. DYGAM—A computer system for the solutions of dynamic programs. Control Analysis Corporation, Palo Alto, CA, August.

Davis, P. J., and P. Rabinowitz. 1984. *Methods of Numerical Integration*, 2d ed. New York: Academic Press.

Deaton, A., and G. Laroque. 1992. On the behavior of commodity prices. *Review of Economic Studies* 59: 1–23.

den Haan, W. 1995. Aggregate shocks and cross-sectional dispersion. Discussion Paper. Department of Economics, UCSD.

Dixit, A. 1991. Analytical approximations in models of hysteresis. *Review of Economic Studies* 58: 141–51.

Dotsey, M., and C. S. Mao. 1992. How well do linear approximation methods work? *Journal of Monetary Economics* 29: 25–58.

Denardo, E. V. 1967. Contraction mappings in the theory underlying dynamic programming. *SIAM Review* 9: 165–77.

Dennis, J. E., Jr., and R. B. Schnabel. 1983. *Numerical Methods for Unconstrained Optimization and Nonlinear Equations*. Prentice Hall Series in Computational Mathematics. Englewood Cliffs, NJ: Prentice Hall.

Dennis, J. E., Jr., and R. B. Schnabel. 1989. A view of unconstrained optimization. In G. L. Nemhauser, A. H. G. Rinnooy Kan, and M. J. Todd, eds., *Optimization*. Amsterdam: North-Holland.

Devroye, L. 1986. *Non-uniform Random Variate Generation*. New York: Springer.

Dixon, P., and B. Parmenter. 1996. Computable general equilibrium modelling for policy analysis and forecasting. In H. Amman et al., eds., *Handbook of Computational Economics*, vol. 1. Amsterdam: Elsevier.

Donovan, G. C., A. R. Miller, and T. J. Moreland. 1993. Pathological functions for Newton's method. *American Mathematical Monthly*, 100: 53–58.

Doren, C. C. Y. 1986. Limiting distribution for random optimization methods. *SIAM Journal on Control and Optimization* 24: 76–82.

Dorsey, R. E., and W. J. Mayer. 1992. Genetic algorithms for estimation problems with multiple optima, non-differentiability and other irregular features. Mimeo. University of Mississippi.

Dwyer, G. P., Jr. 1997. Random number generators. Mimeo.

Eaves, B. C. 1971. Computing kakutani fixed points. *SIAM Journal of Applied Mathematics* 21: 236–44.

Eaves, B. C. 1972. Homotopies for computation of fixed points. *Mathematical Programming* 3: 1–22.

Elhay, S., and J. Kautsky. 1987. Algorithm 655 IQPACK: FORTRAN subroutines for the weights of interpolatory quadratures. *ACM Transactions on Mathematical Software* 13: 399–416.

Ermoliev, Y., and R J.-B. Wets, eds. 1988. *Numerical Techniques for Stochastic Optimization*. Berlin: Springer.

Estrada, R., and R. P. Kanwal. 1994. *Asymptotic Analysis: A Distributional Approach*. Boston: Birkhauser Press.

Evans, G. 1993. *Practical Numerical Integration*. New York: Wiley.

Fair, R., and J. Taylor. 1983. Solution and maximum likelihood estimation of dynamic nonlinear rational expectation models. *Econometrica* 51: 1169–85.

Feldstein, M. 1974. Social security, induced retirement, and aggregate capital accumulation. *Journal of Political Economy* 82: 905–26.

Fershtman, C., and M. Kamien. Dynamic duopolistic competition with sticky prices. *Econometrica* 55: 1151–64.

Fischer, S. 1979. Capital accumulation on the transition path in a monetary optimizing model. *Econometrica* 47: 1433–39.

Fleming, W. H. 1971. Stochastic control for small noise intensities. *SIAM Journal of Control* 9: 473–517.

Fleming, W., and P. E. Souganides. 1986. Asymptotic series and the method of vanishing viscosity. *Indiana University Mathematics Journal* 35: 425–47.

Fletcher, C. A. J. 1984. *Computational Galerkin Techniques*, New York: Springer.

Fletcher, C. A. J. 1988. *Computational Techniques for Fluid Dynamics, 2 vols.* Berlin: Springer.

Fox, B. L. 1986. Algorithm 647: Implementation and relative efficiency of quasirandom sequence generators. *ACM Transactions on Mathematical Software* 12: 362–76.

Fritsch, F. N., and R. E. Carlson. 1980. Monotone piecewise cubic interpolation. *SIAM*, 17: 238–46.

Fudenberg, D., and J. Tirole. 1991. *Game Theory*. Cambridge: MIT Press.

Garcia, C. B., and W. I. Zangwill. 1981. *Pathways to Solutions, Fixed Points, and Equilibria*. Englewood Cliffs, NJ: Prentice Hall.

Gaspar, J., and K. L. Judd. 1997. Solving large-scale rational expectations models. *Macroeconomic Dynamics* 1: 45–75.

Geer, J. F., and C. M. Andersen. 1990. A hybrid perturbation-Galerkin technique that combines multiple expansions. *SIAM Journal of Applied Mathematics* 50: 1474–95.

Geweke, J. 1996. Monte Carlo simulation and numerical integration. In H. Amman et al., eds., *Handbook of Computational Economics*, vol. 1. Amsterdam: Elsevier.

Ghysels, E., and O. Lieberman. 1993. Dynamic regression and filtered data series: A Laplace approximation to the effects of filtering in small samples. Mimeo. University of Montreal.

Gill, P. E., W. Murray, and M. H. Wright. 1981. *Practical Optimization*. London: Academic Press, 1981.

Gill, P. E., W. Murray, M. A. Saunders, and M. White. 1989. Constrained nonlinear programming. In G. L. Nemhauser, A. H. G. Rinnooy Kan, and M. J. Todd eds., *Optimization*. Amsterdam: North-Holland.

Gill, P., W. Murray, M. A. Saunders, J. Tomlin, and M. H. Wright. 1982. A note on interior point methods for linear programming. *COAL Newsletter* 13: 13–19.

Gilli, M., and G. Pauletto. 1998. Nonstationary iterative methods for solving models with forward looking variables. *Journal of Economic Dynamics and Control* (forthcoming).

Goffe, W. L., G. C. Ferrier, and J. Rogers. 1992. Simulated annealing: An initial application in econometrics. *Computational Economics* 5: 133–46.

Goffe, W. L., G. C. Ferrier, and J. Rogers. 1994. Global optimization of statistical functions with simulated annealing. *Journal of Econometrics*, 60: 65–99.

Goldberg, D. E. 1989. *Genetic Algorithms in Search, Optimization, and Machine Learning*. Reading, MA: Addison-Wesley.

Goldfarb, D., and M. J. Todd. 1989. Linear Programming. In G. L. Nemhauser, A. H. G. Rinnooy Kan, and M. J. Todd, eds., *Optimization*. Amsterdam: North-Holland.

Golomb, M. 1959. Approximation by Functions of Fewer Variables. In R. E. Langer, *On Numerical Approximation*. Madison: University of Wisconsin Press, pp. 275–327.

Golub, G. H., and C. F. van Loan. 1983. *Matrix Calculations*. Baltimore: Johns Hopkins University Press.

Gottlieb, D., and S. A. Orszag. 1977. *Numerical Analysis of Spectral Methods: Theory and Applications*, Philadelphia: SIAM-CBMS.

Greenblatt, S. A. 1994. Tensor methods for full-information maximum likelihood estimation: Unconstrained estimation. *Journal of Computational Economics* 7: 89–108.

Griewank, A., and G. F. Corliss, ed. 1991. *Automatic Differentiation of Algorithms: Theory, Implementation, and Application.* Philadelphia: SIAM.

Grossman, S. J., and O. D. Hart. 1983. An analysis of the principal–agent problem. *Econometrica* 51: 7–45.

Grossman, S. 1976. On the efficiency of competitive stock markets where agents have diverse information. *Journal of Finance* 18: 81–101.

Grossman, S. J., and J. E. Stiglitz. 1980. On the impossibility of informationally efficient markets. *American Economic Review* 70: 393–408.

Gustafson, R. L. 1958. Carryover levels for grains. Technical Bulletin No. 1178. U.S. Department of Agriculture.

den Haan, W., and A. Marcet. 1990. Solving the stochastic growth model by parameterizing expedtations. *Journal of Business and Economic Statistics* 8: 31–34.

Haas, A. 1987. The multiple prime random number generator. *ACM Transactions on Mathematical Software* 13: 368–81.

Hageman, L. A., and D. M. Young. 1981. *Applied Iterative Methods.* Orlando: Academic Press.

Halton, J. M. On the efficiency of evaluating certain quasi-random sequences of points in evaluating multi-dimensional integrals. *Numerische Mathematik* 3: 84–90.

Halton, J. H., and D. C. Handscomb. 1957. A method for increasing the efficiency of Monte Carlo integration. *Journal of the ACM* 4: 329–40.

Hammersley, J. M., and D. C. Handscomb. 1964. *Monte Carlo Methods.* London: Chapman and Hall.

Hansen, L. P., and T. J. Sargent. 1996. Recursive linear models of dynamic economies. Unpublished manuscript.

Hart, O. D. 1975. On the optimality of equilibrium when the market structure is incomplete. *Journal of Economic Theory* 11: 418–43.

Haselgrove, C. B. 1961. A method for numerical integration. *Mathematical Computation* 15: 323–37.

Hartman, P. 1964. *Ordinary Differential Equations.* New York: Wiley.

Haubrich, J. G. 1994. Risk aversion, performance pay, and the principal-agent problem. *Journal of Political Economy* 102: 258–76.

Hlawka, E. 1961. Funktionen von beschrankter Variation in der Theorie den Gleichverteilung. *Annali de Matematica Puraed Applicata* (Bologna) 54: 325–33.

Holland, J. H. 1975. *Adaptation in Natural and Artificial Systems.* Ann Arbor: University of Michigan Press.

Holly, A., and P. C. B. Phillips. 1979. A saddlepoint approximation to the distribution of the k-class estimator in a coefficient in a simultaneous system. *Econometrica* 47: 1527–48.

Hornik, K., M. Stinchcombe, and H. White. 1989. Multi-layer feedforward networks are universal approximators. *Neural Networks* 2: 359–66.

Hornik, K., M. Stinchcombe, and H. White. 1990. Universal approximation of an unknown mapping and its derivatives using multilayer feedforward networks. *Neural Networks* 3: 551–60.

Horst, R., and P. M. Pardalos, eds. 1995. *Handbook of Global Optimization.* Dordrecht: Kluwer.

Hua, L. K., and Y. Wang. 1981. *Applications of Number Theory to Numerical Analysis.* Berlin: Springer.

Hughes Hallett, A. J., and L. Piscitelli. 1998. Simple reordering techniques for expanding the convergence radius of first-order iterative techniques. *Journal of Economic Dynamics and Control* (forthcoming).

Hull, J. 1989. *Options, Futures, and Other Derivative Securities.* Englewood Cliffs, NJ: Prentice Hall.

Jensen, M. C., and K. J. Murphy. 1990. Performance pay and top-management incentives. *Journal of Political Economy* 98: 225–64.

Johnson, S., J. R. Stedinger, C. A. Shoemaker, Y. Li, and J. A. Tehada-Guibert. 1993. Numerical solution of continuous-state dynamic programs using linear and spline interpolation. *Operations Research* 41: 484–500.

Juillard, M., D. Laxton, P. McAdam, and H. Pioro. 1998. An algorithm competition: First-order iterations versus Newton-based techniques. *Journal of Economic Dynamics and Control* (forthcoming).

Judd, K. L. 1982. An alternative to steady-state comparisons in perfect foresight models. *Economics Letters* 10: 55–59.

Judd, K. L. 1985. Credible Spatial Preemption, *Rand Journal of Economics*, 16: 153–66.

Judd, K. L. 1985. Short-run analysis of fiscal policy in a simple perfect foresight model. *Journal of Political Economy* 93: 298–319.

Judd, K. L. 1985. Closed-loop equilibrium in a multistage innovation race. Unpublished manuscript.

Judd, K. L. 1987. Debt and distortionary taxation in a simple perfect foresight model. *Journal of Monetary Economics* 20: 51–72.

Judd, K. L. 1987. Welfare cost of factor taxation in a perfect foresight model. *Journal of Political Economy* 95: 675–709.

Judd, K. L. 1990. Asymptotic methods in dynamic economic models. Mimeo. Hoover Institution, Stanford University.

Judd, K. L. 1992. Projection methods for solving aggregate growth models. *Journal of Economic Theory* 58: 410–52.

Judd, K. L. 1997. Computational economics and economic theory: Substitutes or complements? *Journal of Economic Dynamics and Control* 21: 907–42.

Judd, K. L., and S.-M. Guu. 1993. Perturbation solution methods for economic growth models. In H. Varian, eds., *Economic and Financial Modeling with Mathematica*. New York: Springer.

Judd, K. L. 1996. Approximation, perturbation, and projection methods in economic analysis. In H. Amman, D. Kendrick, and J. Rust, eds., *Handbook of Computational Economics*. Amsterdam: Elsevier.

Judd, K. L., and J. Conklin. 1995. Computing supergame equilibrium. Mimeo.

Judd, K. L., and S.-M Guu. 1996. Bifurcation approximation methods applied to asset market equilibrium. Mimeo. Hoover Instiution.

Judd, K. L., and S.-M. Guu. 1997. Asymptotic methods for aggregate growth models. *Journal of Economic Dynamics and Control* 21: 1025–42.

Judd, K. L., F. Kubler, and K. Schmedders. 1997. Computing equilibria in infinite horizon finance economies: The case of one asset. Mimeo. Hoover Institution.

Judd, K. L., F. Kubler, and K. Schmedders. 1997. Incomplete asset markets with heterogeneous tastes and idiosyncratic income. Mimeo.

Judd, K. L., and A. Solnick. 1994. Numerical dynamic programming with shape-preserving splines. Mimeo.

Kalaba, R., L. Tesfatsion, and J.-L. Wang. 1983. A finite algorithm for the exact evaluation of higher order partial derivatives of functions of many variables. *Journal of Mathematical Analysis and Applications* 92: 552–63.

Kalaba, R., and L. Tesfatsion. 1991. Solving nonlinear equations by adaptive homotopy continuation. *Applied Mathematics and Computation* 41: 99–115.

Kamien, M. I., and N. L. Schwartz. 1981. *Dynamic Optimization: The Calculus of Variations and Optimal Control in Economics and Management*. New York: North Holland.

Kan, A., H. G. Rinnooy, and G. T. Timmer. 1989. Global optimization. In G. L. Nemhauser, A. H. G. Rinnooy Kan, and M. J. Todd, eds., *Optimization*. Amsterdam: North-Holland.

Karmarkar, N. 1984. A new polynomial-time algorithm for linear programming. In *Pr ̲ ̲ings of the 16th Annual ACM Symposium on the Theory of Computing*, pp. 302–11.

Kaufmann, W. J., III, and L. L. Smarr. 1993. *Supercomputing and the Transformation of Science*. New York: Scientific American Library.

Kehoe, T. J. 1991. Computation and multiplicity of equilibria. In W. Hildenbrand and H. Sonnenschein, eds., *Handbook of Mathematical Economics*, vol. 4. Amsterdam: North-Holland.

Kendrick, D. Research opportunities in computational economics. *Computational Economics* 6: 257–314.

Kendrick, D. 1995. Ten Wishes. *Computational Economics* 8: 67–80.

Kendrick, D. A. 1996. Sectoral economics. In H. Amman et al., eds., *Handbook of Computational Economics*, vol. 1. Amsterdam: Elsevier.

Keane, M., and K. Wolpin. 1994. The solution and estimation of discrete choice dynamic programming models by simulation: Monte Carlo evidences. *Review of Economics and Statistics* 76: 648–72.

Kollerstrom, N. 1992. Thomas Simpson and "Newton's method of approximation": An enduring myth. *British Journal of History of Science* 25: 347–54.

Lemarechal, C. Nondifferentiable Optimization. 1989. In G. L. Nemhauser, A. H. G. Rinnooy Kan, and M. J. Todd, eds., *Optimization*. Amsterdam: North-Holland.

Kautsky, J., and S. Elhay. 1982. Calculation of the weights of interpolatory quadratures. *Numerical Mathematics* 40: 407–22.

Keast, P. 1973. Optimal parameters for multidimensional integration. *SIAM Journal of Numerical Analysis* 10: 831–38.

Kiefer, J. 1962. On large deviations of the empiric d.f. of vector chance variables and a law of the iterated logarithm. *Pacific Journal of Mathematics* 11: 649–60.

Kirkpatrick, S., C. D. Gelatt, Jr., and M. P. Vecchi. 1983. Optimization by simulated annealing. *Science* 220: 671–75.

Kloek, T., and H. K. van Dijk. 1978. Bayesian estimates of equation system parameters: An application of integration by Monte Carlo. *Econometrica* 46: 1–20.

Koksma, J. F. 1942. Een algemeene stelling uit de theorie der gelijkmatige verdeeling modulo 1. *Mathematica B (Zut phen)* 7–11.

Kolmogorov, A. N. 1957. On the representation of continuous functions of many variables by superposition of continuous functions of one variable and addition. *Doklady Akademii Nauk SSSR* 114: 953–56.

Korobov, N. M. 1959. On approximate calculations of multiple integrals. Doklady Akademii Nauk SSSR 124: 1207–10 (in Russian).

Korobov, N. M. 1960. Properties and calculation of optimal coefficients. Soviet Mathematics, Doklady 1: 696–700.

Krasnosel'skii, M. A., and P. Zabreiko. 1984. *Geometrical Methods of Nonlinear Analysis*. Berlin: Springer.

Kubicek, M., and V. Hlavacek. 1983. *Numerical Solution of Nonlinear Boundary Value Problems with Applications*. Englewood Cliff, NJ: Prentice Hall.

Kuipers, L., and H. Niederreiter. 1974. *Uniform Distribution of Sequences*. New York: John Wiley.

Kulisch, U. W., and W. L. Miranker. 1986. The arithmetic of the digital computer: A new approach. *SIAM Review* 28: 1–40.

Kushner, H. J., and D. S. Clark. 1978. *Stochastic Approximation Methods for Constrained and Unconstrained Systems*. New York: Springer.

Kushner, H. J., and P. G. Dupuis. 1992. *Numerical Methods for Stochastic Control Problems in Continuous Time*. New York: Springer.

Kushner, H. J., and H. Huang. 1979. Rates of Convergence for Stochastic Approximation Type Algorithms. *SIAM Journal of Control and Optimization* 17: 607–17.

Kushner, H. J., and H. Huang. 1981. Asymptotic Properties on Stochastic Approximations with Constant Coefficients. *SIAM Journal of Control and Optimization* 19: 87–105.

Kydland, F. E., and E. C. Prescott. 1982. Time to build and aggregate fluctuations. *Econometrica* 50: 1345–70.

Kyle, A. S. 1985. Continuous auctions and insider trading. *Econometrica* 53: 1315–35.

Laitner, J. 1990. Tax changes and phase diagrams for an overlapping-generations model. *Journal of Political Economy* 98: 193–220.

Laitner, J. 1987. The dynamic analysis of continuous-time life cycle saving growth models. *Journal of Economic Dynamics and Control* 11: 331–57.

Laitner, J. 1989. Transition time paths for overlapping-generations models. *Journal of Economic Dynamics and Control* 7: 111–29.

Lapidus, L., and G. F. Pinder. 1982. *Numerical Solution of Partial Differential Equations in Science and Engineering*. New York: Wiley.

Lemke, C. E., and J. T. Howson. 1964. Equilibrium points of bimatrix games. *SIAM Journal of Applied Mathematics* 12: 413–23.

Li, J. 1998. Numerical analysis of a nonlinear operator equation arising from a monetary model. *Journal of Economic Dynamics and Control* (forthcoming).

Lick, W. J. 1989. Difference equations from differential equations. Lecture Notes in Engineering 41. Berlin: Springer.

Lipton, D., J. Poterba, J. Sachs, and L. Summers. 1982. Multiple shooting in rational expectations models. *Econometrica* 50: 1329–34.

Ljung, L., and T. Soderstrom. 1983. *Theory and Practice of Recursive Identification*. Cambridge: MIT Press.

Lucas, R. E., Jr. 1978. Asset prices in an exchange economy. *Econometrica* 46: 1429–45.

Luenberger, D. 1984. *Linear and Nonlinear Programming*. Reading, MA: Addison-Wesley.

Magill, M. 1977. A Local Analysis of N-Sector Capital Accumulation under Uncertainty. *Journal of Economic Theory* 15: 211–18.

Malliaris, A G., and W. A. Brock. 1982. *Stochastic Methods in Economics and Finance*. Amsterdam: North-Holland.

Marimon, Ramon, E. McGrattan, and T. J. Sargent. 1990. Money as a medium of exchange in an economy with artificially intelligent agents. *Journal of Economic Dynamics and Control* 14: 329–73.

Marks, R. E. 1992. Breeding hybrid strategies: Optimal behaviour for oligopolists. *Journal of Evolutionary Economics* 2: 17–38.

Marsaglia, G. 1968. Random numbers fall mainly in the planes. *Proceedings of the National Academy of Sciences* 60: 25–28.

Mas-Colell, A. 1974. A note on a theorem of F. Browder. *Mathematical Programming* 6: 229–33.

McGrattan, E. R. 1990. Solving the stochastic growth model by linear-quadratic approximation. *Journal of Business and Economic Statistics* 8: 41–43.

McKelvery, R. D. 1996. A Lyapunov function for Nash equilibria. Social Science Working Paper 953. California Institute of Technology.

McKelvey, R. D. 1998. Computation of equilibria in finite games. *Handbook of Computational Economics*, forthcoming.

Miranda, M. J., and P. G. Helmburger. 1988. The effects of commodity price stabilization programs. *American Economic Review* (March): 46–58.

Miranda, M. J., and J. W. Glauber. 1993. Estimation of dynamic nonlinear rational expectations models of primary commodity markets with private and government stockholding. *Review of Economics and Statistics* 75: 463–70.

Miranda, M., and X. Rui. 1997. Maximum likelihood estimation of the nonlinear rational expectations asset pricing model. *Journal of Economic Dynamics and Control* 21: 1493–510.

More, J. J., and S. J. Wright. 1993. *Optimization Software Guide*. Philadelphia: SIAM.

Murdock, J. A. 1991. *Perturbations: Theory and Methods*, New York: Wiley-Interscience.

Mysovskikh, I. P. 1975. On Chakalov's theorem. *USSR Comput. Math. Math. Phys.* 15: 221–27.

Nagurney, A. 1993. *Network Economics: A Variational Inequality Approach*. Dordrecht: Kluwer.

Nagurney, A. 1996. Parallel computation. In H. Amman et al., eds., *Handbook of Computational Economics*. Amsterdam: Elsevier.

Niederreiter, H. 1972. On a number-theoretical integration method. *Aequationes Mathematicae* 8: 304–311.

Niederreiter, H. 1978. Quasi–Monte Carlo methods and pseudo-random numbers. *Bulletin of the American Mathematical Society* 84: 957–1041.

Niederreiter, H. 1992. *Random Number Generation and Quasi–Monte Carlo Methods*. Philadelphia: SIAM.

Niederreiter, H., and K. McCurley. 1979. Optimization of functions by quasi-random search methods. *Computing* 22: 119–23.

Nurnberger, G. 1989. *Approximation by Spline Functions*. Berlin: Springer.

Ortega, J. M., and W. C. Rheinboldt. 1970. *Iterative Solution of Nonlinear Equations in Several Variables*. New York: Academic Press.

Paskov, S. H. 1993. Average case complexity of multivariate integration for smooth functions. *Journal of Complexity* 9: 291–312.

Paskov, S. H., and J. F. Traub. 1995. Faster evaluation of financial derivatives. *Journal of Portfolio Management* 22: 113–20.

Paskov, S. H. 1994. New methodologies for valuing devrivatives. Technical Report. Computer Sciences Department, Columbia University.

Paskov, S. H. 1995. Termination criteria for linear problems. *Journal of Complexity* 11: 105–37.

Papageorgiou, A., and J. F. Traub. 1997. Faster evaluation of multidimensional integrals. Mimeo. Columbia University.

Papageorgiou, A., and J. F. Traub. 1996. Beating Monte Carlo. *RISK* 9: 63–65.

Phelan, C. J., and R. M. Townsend. 1991. Formulating and computing solutions to the infinite period principal-agent problem. *Review of Economic Studies* 58: 853–81.

Piessens, R., E. de Doncker-Kapenga, C. W. Uberhuber, and D. K. Kahaner. 1983. *QUADPACK: A Subroutine Package for Automatic Integration*. Berlin: Springer.

Pissanetzky, S. 1984. *Sparse Matrix Technology*. London: Academic Press.

Powell, M. J. D. 1981. *Approximation Theory and Methods*. Cambridge: Cambridge University Press.

Powell, M. J. D. 1970. A hybrid method for nonlinear equations. In P. Rabinowitz, ed., *Numerical Methods for Nonlinear Algebraic Equations*. London: Gordon and Breach.

Prenter, P. M. 1989. *Splines and Variational Methods*. New York: Wiley.

Press, W. H., B. P. Flannery, S. A. Teukolsky, and W. T. Vetterling. 1986. *Numerical Recipes: The Art of Scientific Computing*. New York: Cambridge University Press.

Puterman, M. L. 1994. *Markov Decision Processes*. New York: Wiley.

Puterman, M. L., and S. L. Brumelle. 1979. On the convergence of policy iteration in stationary dynamic programming. *Mathematics of Operations Research* 4: 60–69.

Puterman, M. L., and M. C. Shin. 1978. Modified policy iteration algorithms for discounted Markov decision problems. *Management Science* 24: 1127–37.

Quirmbach, H. 1993. R&D: Competition, risk, and performance. *Rand Journal of Economics* 24: 157–97.

Radner, R. 1979. Rational expectations equilibrium: Generic existence and the information revealed by prices. *Econometrica* 47: 655–78.

Rall, L. B. 1981. *Automatic Differentiation: Techniques and Applications.* Lecture Notes in Computer Science 120. Berlin: Springer.

Rasch, and Williamson. 1990. On shape-preserving interpolation and semi-Lagrangian transport. *SIAM Journal of Scientific Statistical Computation* 11: 656–87.

Rheinboldt, W. C. 1986. *Numerical Analysis of Parameterized Nonlinear Equations.* New York: Wiley.

Rice, J. R. 1983. *Numerical Methods, Software, and Analysis.* New York: McGraw-Hill.

Richtmeyer, R. D. 1952. On the evaluation of definite integrals and a quasi–Monte Carlo method based on properties of algebraic numbers. Report LA-1342. Los Alamos: Los Alamos Scientific Laboratories.

Ripley, B. D. 1987. *Stochastic Simulation.* New York: Wiley.

Rivlin, T. J. 1969. *An Introduction to the Approximation of Functions.* Waltham, MA: Blaisdell.

Rivlin, T. J. 1990. *Chebyshev Polynomials: From Approximation Theory to Algebra and Number Theory.* New York: Wiley-Interscience.

Robbins, H., and S. Monro. 1951. A stochastic approximation method. *Annals of Mathematical Statistics* 22: 400–407.

Roberts, S. M., and J. S. Shipman. 1971. *Two Point Boundary Value Problems: Shooting Methods.* New York: Elsevier.

Ross, S. M. 1990. A *Course in Simulation.* New York: Macmillan.

Ross, S. M. 1983. *Introduction to Stochastic Dynamic Programming.* New York: Academic Press.

Roth, K. F. 1954. On the irregularities of distribution. *Mathematika* 1: 73–79.

Rothschild, M., and J. Stiglitz. 1976. Equilibrium in competitive insurance markets: An essay on the economics of imperfect information. *Quarterly Journal of Economics* 90: 629–49.

Rubinstein, R. V. 1981. *Simulation and the Monte Carlo Method.* New York: Wiley.

Rui, X., and M. Miranda. 1996. Solving nonlinear dynamic games via orthogonal collocation: An application to international commodity markets. *Annals of Operations Research* 68: 89–108.

Rust, J. 1996. Numerical Dynamic Programming in Economics. In H. Amman et al., eds., *Handbook of Computational Economics.* Amsterdam: Elsevier.

Saad, Y. 1984. Practical use of some Krylov subspace methods for solving indefinite and nonsymmetric linear systems. *SIAM Journal on Scientific and Statistical Computing* 51: 203–28.

Saad, Y., and M. H. Schulz. 1986. GMRES: A generalized minimum residual algorithm for solving nonsymmetric linear systems. *SIAM Journal on Scientific and Statistical Computing* 7: 856–69.

Samuelson, P. A. 1970. The fundamental approximation theorem of portfolio analysis in terms of means, variances and higher moments. *Review of Economic Studies* 37: 537–42.

Santos, M. S. 1994. Smooth dynamics and Computation in models of economic growth. *Journal of Economic Dynamics and Control* 18: 879–95.

Santos, M. S., and J.-L. Vila. 1991. Smoothness of the policy function in continuous times economic models: The one-dimensional case. *Journal of Economic Dynamics and Control* 15: 741–53.

Sargent, T. J. 1987. *Macroeconomic Theory.* Orlando: Academic Press.

Sargent, T. J. 1987. *Dynamic Macroeconomic Theory.* Cambridge: Harvard University Press.

Scarf, H. E. 1967. The approximation of fixed points of a continuous mapping. *SIAM Journal of Applied Mathematics* 15: 328–43.

Scarf, H. 1982. The computation of equilibrium prices: An exposition. In K. Arrow and M. Intriligator, eds., *Handbook of Mathematical Economics.* Amsterdam: North-Holland.

Scarf, H., with T. Hansen. 1973. *Computation of Economic Equilibria.* New Haven: Yale University Press.

Schmedders, K. 1996. Damped asset trading in the general equilibrium model with incomplete asset markets. Technical Report 96-11. Department of Operations Research, Stanford University.

Schmedders, K. 1998. Computing equilibria in the general equilibrium model with incomplete asset markets. *Journal of Economic Dynamics and Control* (forthcoming).

Schnabel, R. B., and T.-T. Chow. 1985. Tensor methods for unconstrained optimization using second derivatives. *SIAM Journal on Optimization* 1: 293–315.

Schumaker, L. L. 1983. On shape-preserving quadratic spline interpolation. *SIAM Journal of Numerical Analysis* 20: 854–64.

Shoven, J. B., and J. Whalley. 1992. *Applying General Equilibrium*. New York: Cambridge University Press.

Smith, A., Jr. 1990. *Three Essays on the Solution and Estimation of Dynamic Macroeconomic Models*. Ph.D. dissertation. Duke University.

Sobol, I. M. 1979. On the systematic search in a hypercube. *SIAM Journal of Numerical Analysis*, 16: 790–93.

Solis, F. J., and R. J. B. Wets. 1981. Minimization by random search techniques. *Mathematics of Operations Research* 1: 19–30.

Spear, S., and S. Srivastava. On repeated moral hazard with discounting. *Review of Economic Studies* 54: 599–617.

Spence, A. M. 1974. Competitive and optimal responses to signals: An analysis of efficiency and distribution. *Journal of Economic Theory* 7: 296–332.

Stewart, G. W. 1984. *Introduction to Matrix Computations*. New York: Academic Press.

Stoer, J., and R. Burlisch. 1980. *Introduction to Numerical Analysis*. New York: Springer.

Stokey, N., and R. Lucas. 1989. *Recursive Methods in Economic Dynamics*, Cambridge: Harvard University Press.

Stroud, A. H. 1971. *Approximate Calculation of Multiple Integrals*. Englewood Cliffs, NJ: Prentice Hall.

Stroud, A., and D. Secrest. 1966. *Gaussian Quadrature Formulas*. Englewood Cliffs, NJ: Prentice Hall.

Sugihara, M., and Murota, K. 1982. A note on Haselgrove's method for numerical integration. *Mathematics of Computation* 39: 549–54.

Tauchen, G., and R. Hussey. 1991. Quadrature-based methods for obtaining approximate solutions to the integral equations of nonlinear rational expectations models. *Econometrica* 59: 371–96.

Tauchen, G. 1986. Statistical properties of generalized method-of-moments estimates of structural parameters obtained from financial market data. *Journal of Business and Economic Statistics* 4: 397–416.

Taylor, J. B., and H. Uhlig. 1990. Solving nonlinear stochastic growth models: A comparison of alternative solution methods. *Journal of Business and Economic Statistics* 8: 1–18.

Tesfatsion, L. 1992. Nonlocal automated comparative static analysis. *Computer Science in Economics and Management* 5: 313–31.

Tierney, L., and Kadane, J. B. 1986. Accurate approximations of posterior moments and marginal densities. *Journal of the American Statistical Association* 18: 82–86.

Tierney, L., R. E. Kass, and J. B. Kadane. 1986. Fully exponential Laplace approximations to expectations and variances of nonpositive functions. *Journal of the American Statistical Association* 81: 82–86.

Traub, J. F., and H. Wozniakowski. 1980. *A General Theory of Optimal Algorithms*. New York: Academic Press.

Traub, J. F., and H. Wozniakowski. 1980. Convergence and complexity of interpolatory-Newton iteration in a Banach space. *Computational Mathematics with Applications* 6: 385–400.

Traub, J. F., and H. Wozniakowski. 1992. The Monte Carlo algorithm with a pseudorandom generator. *Mathematics of Computation* 58: 323–39.

Traub, J. F., G. W. Wasilkowski, and H. Wozniakowski. 1988. *Information-based complexity*. New York: Academic Press.

Trick M., and S. Zin. 1997. Spline approximations to value functions: A linear programming approach. *Macroeconomic Dynamics* 1: 255–77.

Turnovsky, S. J., and W. A. Brock. 1980. Time consistency and optimal government policies in perfect foresight equilibrium. *Journal of Public Economics* 13: 183–212.

Varian, H. 1978. *Microeconomic Theory*. New York: Norton, 1978.

Vose, M. D. 1991. Generalizing the notion of schema in genetic algorithms. *Artificial Intelligence* 50: 385–96.

Weiser, A., and S. Zarantonello. 1988. A note on piecewise linear and multilinear table interpolation in many dimensions. *Mathematics of Computation* 50: 189–96.

White, H. 1992. *Artificial Neural Networks: Approximation and Learning Theory*. Oxford: Blackwell.

White, R. E. 1985. *An Introduction to the Finite Element Method with Applications to Nonlinear Problems*. New York: Wiley.

Wright, B., and J. Williams. 1984. The welfare effects of the introduction of storage. *Quarterly Journal of Economics* 99: 169–92.

Wright, B., and J. Williams. 1982. The economic role of commodity storage. *Economic Journal* 92: 596–614.

Wright, B., and J. Williams. 1982. The roles of public and private storage in managing oil import disruptions. *Bell Journal of Economics* 13: 341–53.

Williams, J., and B. Wright. 1991. *Storage and Commodity Markets*. Cambridge: Cambridge University Press.

Wilson, C. 1977. A model of insurance markets with incomplete information. *Journal of Economic Theory* 16: 167–207.

Wilson, R. 1971. Computing equilibria of *N*-person games. *SIAM Journal of Applied Mathematics* 21: 80–87.

Wilson, R. 1996. Nonlinear pricing and mechanism design. In H. Amman et al., eds., *Handbook of Computational Economics*, vol. 1. Amsterdam: Elsevier.

Wilson, R. 1992. Computing simply stable equilibria. *Econometrica* 60: 1039–70.

Wozniakowski, H. 1991. Average case complexity of multivariate integration. *Bulletin of the American Mathematical Society* 24: 185–94.

Young, D. M. 1971. *Iterative Solution of Large Linear Systems*. New York: Academic Press.

Young, D. M., and R. T. Gregory. 1988. *A Survey of Numerical Mathematics*, 2 vols. New York: Dover.

Young, S. W. 1967. Piecewise monotone polynomial interpolation. *Bulletin of the American Mathematical Society* 73: 642–43.

Ypma, T. J. 1995. Historical development of the Newton-Raphson method. *SIAM Review* 37: 531–51.

Zeidler, E. 1986. *Nonlinear Functional Analysis and Its Applications*, vol 1. New York: Springer.

Zhang, W.-B. 1988. Hopf bifurcations in multisector models of optimal economic growth. *Economic Letter* 26: 329–34.

Zwillinger, D. 1992. *Handbook of Integration*. Boston: Jones and Bartlett.

Index